COLLECTED WORKS OF JOHN STUART MILL

VOLUME X

The Collected Edition of the works of John Stuart Mill has been planned and is being directed by an editorial committee appointed from the Faculty of Arts and Science of the University of Toronto, and from the University of Toronto Press. The primary aim of the edition is to present fully collated texts of those works which exist in a number of versions, both printed and manuscript, and to provide accurate texts of works previously unpublished or which have become relatively inaccessible.

Essays on Ethics, Religion and Society

by JOHN STUART MILL

Editor of the Text

J. M. ROBSON

Professor of English
Victoria College, University of Toronto

Introduction

F. E. L. PRIESTLEY

Professor of English
University College, University of Toronto

Essay on Mill's Utilitarianism

D. P. DRYER

Professor of Philosophy
University of Toronto

UNIVERSITY OF TORONTO PRESS
ROUTLEDGE & KEGAN PAUL

© *University of Toronto Press 1969*
Printed in Canada
SBN 8020 1521 2

London: Routledge & Kegan Paul
SBN 7100 6233 8

This volume has been published
with the assistance of a grant
from the Canada Council

Contents

APPENDICES

Introduction

THE ESSAYS collected in this volume are the main documents for the illustration and exposition of John Stuart Mill's thoughts on ethics and religion and their function in society. Since his system of ethics is avowedly Utilitarian, these documents, arranged chronologically, present the development of Mill's Utilitarianism as given in published utterance. Questions about the precise nature of his doctrine are capable of being approached in various ways, of which we have, in this edition, chosen two. It is possible to take the essay *Utilitarianism* as Mill's definitive statement of his doctrine and subject it to a rigorous analysis, seeking precise shades of meaning, testing the logical consistency and coherence of the argument, by means of the techniques and criteria of the modern philosopher. This task and this approach have been undertaken here by Professor D. P. Dryer, whose thorough and careful study follows this general introduction. It is also possible to follow the patterns of thought, and the patterns of exposition, in the successive works included here, and to treat them in terms of the history of ideas—in this case the development of Mill's ideas—and in terms of rhetoric, or what might be called the strategy or tactics of presentation and argument. This is to remember that Mill is not purely a philosopher, but a man of letters and a controversialist. It is this second task, and this second approach, that I undertake in this general introduction.

MILL, BENTHAM, AND UTILITARIANISM

It is natural for discussions of Mill's variations from Benthamism to start with evidence of his discontent or restiveness under Bentham's rule, and the main documents called in to supply that evidence are the *Autobiography* and the essays on Bentham and on Coleridge. As one reads Mill's retrospective account of what he himself was like before the mental crisis of 1826, that is, during the period of complete committal to Benthamism, one is struck by how closely the portrait of the young Mill resembles the portrait the more mature Mill draws of Bentham. Bentham's "principle of utility" was "the keystone" which "gave unity" to his conceptions of things, and formulated for him "a creed, a doctrine, a philosophy, . . . a religion."[1] The "description so often given of a Benthamite, as a mere reasoning machine," he says, "was during two or three years of my life not altogether untrue of me." Zeal "for what I thought the good of mankind was my strongest sentiment. . . . But my zeal was as yet little else, at that period of my life, than zeal for speculative opinions. It had not its root in genuine benevolence, or sympathy with mankind; though these qualities held their due place in my ethical standard. Nor was it connected with any high enthusiasm for ideal nobleness." "[My] father's teachings tended to the undervaluing of feeling"—as also did Bentham's. (76–7.)

As he looks back on what he was, Mill recognizes of course in himself the suppressed potentialities that differentiate him from Bentham: "no youth of the age I then was, can be expected to be more than one thing, and this was the thing I happened to be," but of the absent "high enthusiasm for ideal nobleness," he comments: "Yet of this feeling I was imaginatively very susceptible; but there was at that time an intermission of its natural aliment, poetical culture, while there was a superabundance of the discipline antagonistic to it, that of mere logic and analysis" (76–7). He also recognizes from this later perspective the power of his father's feelings, but the fact remains that the feelings are given little place in James Mill's system. The whole Benthamite system of the regeneration of mankind, to which the young Mill fully subscribed, was to be the "effect of educated intellect, enlightening the selfish feelings" (78). The inevitable egoism of man was to be modified into an enlightened egoism.

The first movement of emancipation from the narrow mould of Benthamism was a very slight one: the rejection of Bentham's contempt for poetry. This came first through "looking into" Pope's *Essay on Man*, and realizing how powerfully it acted on his imagination, despite the repugnance to him of its opinions. It is significant that in retrospect Mill connects this momentary stirring of the imagination by poetry, quite apart from the appeal of its opinions, with the "inspiring effect," "the best sort of enthusiasm," roused by biographies of wise and noble men. These stirrings are, as he points out, of greater meaning from the vantage-point of maturity than they were at the time. They did not affect the "real inward sectarianism" of his youth; they were evidence merely of a suppressed potentiality (79–80). It is, nevertheless, this suppressed potentiality which distinguishes the young Mill from Bentham himself.

The actual process of cracking the shell of his "inward sectarianism" begins with his mental crisis in the autumn of 1826. The great end of Ben-

---

[1]The preceding quotations are from Mill's *Autobiography* (New York: Columbia University Press, 1924), 47. Subsequent references to this edition are given in parentheses.

thamism was the production of pleasure (or, to accept Bentham's extension, happiness). Now Mill found his life devoid of happiness. To the vital question, "Suppose that all your objects in life were realized; that all the changes in institutions and opinions which you are looking forward to, could be completely effected at this very instant: would this be a great joy and happiness to you?" his "irrepressible self-consciousness distinctly answered, 'No!'" And, as he puts it, "the whole foundation on which my life was constructed fell down." (94.)

What is strongly suggested by Mill's account, and by the criticism of the doctrine of association taught him by his father and Bentham which immediately follows in the *Autobiography*, is that the crisis of apathy, of loss of incentive, had brought home to him with full force the objection commonly made to Utilitarianism as a system of ethics, that it provided no source of obligation. "I was," he says, ". . . left stranded . . . with a well-equipped ship and a rudder, but no sail; without any real desire for the ends which I had been so carefully fitted out to work for: no delight in virtue, or the general good. . . . [N]either selfish nor unselfish pleasures were pleasures to me." To "know that a feeling would make me happy if I had it, did not give me the feeling." ". . . I became persuaded, that my love of mankind, and of excellence for its own sake, had worn itself out. . . ." (97–8, 95.) The cause of his state he finds in the education to which he had been subjected, which was, as he recognizes, the kind of education through which Bentham and James Mill looked for the progressive improvement of mankind. His teachers, he says, "seemed to have trusted altogether to the old familiar instruments, praise and blame, reward and punishment," linked to behaviour in the educational pattern of association derived from Helvetius (96). These associations Mill now saw as artificial and mechanical, not natural. They are, in fact, deliberately created or cultivated prejudices (or, to use a more modern terminology, states of conditioning). There is thus a conflict between this whole area of Bentham's thought and that area which concerns itself with critical analysis. Bentham's constructive thought, his plan for progress through enlightenment, reveals a fatal dichotomy. In so far as it is conceived in terms of rewards and punishments to induce the desired behaviour by mechanical association, that is, in so far as it derives from Helvetius and Beccaria, it is at odds with the kind of enlightenment represented by Bentham's critical attacks on received notions and stereotyped habits of thought, conducted through rational analysis. As Mill points out, "we owe to analysis our clearest knowledge of the permanent sequences in nature; the real connexions between Things, not dependent on our will and feelings; natural laws. . . ." "The very excellence of analysis . . . is that it tends to weaken and undermine whatever is the result of prejudice. . . ." (97, 96.)

A consideration of these passages in the *Autobiography* indicates first of all that Mill is separating the two aspects of Bentham's system, the constructive and the critical, and showing why he largely rejects the former, while still generally approving of the latter. This whole procedure suggests a detached and rational weighing of Benthamism difficult to reconcile with the obvious agitation of Mill's mind at this time. But to a large extent the agitation is in fact connected with the detached rational estimate. There can be no doubt that the maturing Mill became intellectually dissatisfied with the narrow and rigorous schematization which both Bentham and his father delighted in. Nor is there much doubt that any wavering or back-sliding, any questioning of the orthodox doctrine of what was to James Mill, as to John Stuart, a "religion," smacked to both of heresy and betrayal. It is significant that as late as 1833, Mill is still anxious to keep his heretical views from his father. Some of the anguish, then, is undoubtedly that of a pillar of the faith, beset by intellectual doubts, and in constant communion with the founder of the church.

But much in the *Autobiography* also suggests a less rational and perhaps even more powerful influence at work. This is an enormous sense of the impoverishment of his own nature, of the denial of a vital part of it, of a suppression of its full potentialities, through the narrowness of the system in which he had been educated. It would be hard to find in any autobiography a passage with more dreadful implications than the one in which Mill records that he read through the whole of Byron, "to try whether a poet, whose peculiar department was supposed to be that of the intenser feelings, could rouse any feeling in me" (103). The nightmarish sense of a paralyzed sensibility, to be tested by the most violent provocation at hand, as if one were applying a powerful current to a nerve one feared to be dead, conveys a profound sense of despair, more profound than that in Arnold's "buried life."

As is well known, it was from Wordsworth's poems that Mill derived "a medicine for [his] state of mind," "a source of inward joy, of sympathetic and imaginative pleasure, which could be shared in by all human beings. . . ." "From them," he says, "I seemed to learn what would be the perennial sources of happiness, when all the greater evils of life shall have been removed. . . . I needed to be made to feel that there was real, permanent happiness in tranquil contemplation. . . . And the delight which these poems gave me, proved that with culture of this sort, there was nothing to dread from the most confirmed habit of analysis." (104.) One is again reminded of Arnold, and his tribute to Wordsworth as the poet who, "when the age had bound Our souls in its benumbing round, . . . spoke, and loosed our heart in tears," and who "shed On spirits that had long been dead, Spirits dried up and closely furl'd, The freshness of the early world."[2]

In his depression, Mill had been brought to the belief that "the habit of

[2]Matthew Arnold, "Memorial Verses," ll.45–7, 54–7.

analysis has a tendency to wear away the feelings . . . " (96). Since he had been taught by his education not only that the proper exercise of the mind was this habit of analysis, but also that "the pleasure of sympathy with human beings, and the feelings which made the good of others . . . the object of existence, were the greatest and surest source of happiness" (97), he had seemed to be faced with a dilemma. It is from this dilemma that Wordsworth delivered him, as the last sentence quoted above shows.

In his rebellion, emotional and intellectual, against Bentham, Mill sees himself, in retrospect, as if in violent reaction. He notes of a later stage that he had "now completely turned back from what there had been of excess in my reaction against Benthamism" (169). He describes himself, during the reaction, as influenced by the Coleridgeans, and moving towards their position. But he also speaks of the truths "which lay in my early opinions, and in no essential part of which I at any time wavered" (118).

The central question of the nature of Mill's Utilitarianism clearly involves his attitude towards Bentham and Bentham's system. But the implications of his reaction against Bentham are neither clear-cut nor simple. An analogy is suggested by his own description of his early enthusiasm for Benthamism as a religion. Heretics are not all of one sort: some reject the old religion totally and subscribe to another set of beliefs, some wish to abandon parts of the orthodox doctrine as excrescences or debasements or perversions, some question the definitions and doctrines and seek a re-definition. Mill had obviously been brought up to accept Benthamism as the full and orthodox doctrine of the utilitarian creed. As a heretic, he could either see himself as rejecting Utilitarianism or as rejecting Bentham's definition of it. It is clear that he saw himself as doing the latter.

"REMARKS ON BENTHAM'S PHILOSOPHY"

That Mill's heresy is of the "revisionist" sort is made evident not only by the very obvious fact of his defence of Utilitarianism in the essay on that subject, but by an examination of the essays on Bentham and on Coleridge. The "Remarks on Bentham's Philosophy" which Mill wrote anonymously in 1833 as an appendix to Lytton Bulwer's *England and the English* is notable for its direct challenge of Bentham's interpretation of the doctrine of Utility: "he has practically, to a very great extent, confounded the principle of Utility with the principle of specific consequences. . . . He has largely exemplified, and contributed very widely to diffuse, a tone of thinking, according to which any kind of action or any habit, which in its own specific consequences cannot be proved to be necessarily or probably productive of unhappiness . . . is supposed to be fully justified. . . ."[3] This confusion has been

[3]"Remarks on Bentham's Philosophy," 8 below. Subsequent references are to the present edition, and are given in parentheses.

the "source of the chief part of the temporary mischief" Bentham as a moral philosopher "must be allowed to have produced" (7–8). He has ignored the question whether acts or habits not in themselves necessarily pernicious, may not form part of a pernicious character. In ignoring states of mind as motive and cause of actions, Bentham is in fact ignoring some of the consequences, for "any act . . . has a tendency to fix and perpetuate the state or character of mind in which itself has originated" (8). And by thus limiting consideration of the morality of an act to "consequences" narrowly conceived, Bentham has, Mill implies, given some sanction to those who see Utilitarianism as merely a doctrine of expediency; "a more enlarged understanding of the 'greatest-happiness principle,' " which took far more into account than Bentham's "consequences," would not be open to this interpretation (7).

Although Bentham entitles his work *Introduction to the Principles of Morals and Legislation*, it is perhaps fortunate, says Mill, that he concerns himself mainly with legislation rather than morals, "for the mode in which he understood and applied the principle of Utility" was more conducive to valuable results in relation to legislation (7). But even here, the narrowness of his definition of the principle leads him to fail in "the consideration of the greater social questions—the theory of organic institutions and general forms of polity; for those . . . must be viewed as the great instruments of forming the national character . . . " (9). The deficiency in Bentham's understanding of the principle of Utility is further aggravated, in his speculations on politics, by the deficiency of his method of "beginning at the beginning": he starts with a view of man in society without a government, and then considers sorts of government as alternative constructions to be hypothetically applied and evaluated. This method, says Mill, "assumes that mankind are alike in all times and all places, that they have the same wants and are exposed to the same evils, and that if the same institutions do not suit them, it is only because in the more backward stages of improvement they have not wisdom to see what institutions are most for their good" (16). This is vastly to over-simplify the real problem of politics. It is to ignore the function of political institutions as "the principal means of the social education of a people," to be fitted specifically to the particular needs of the circumstances and national character at a particular stage of civilization. Since different stages demand the production of different effects, no one social organization can be fitted to all circumstances and characters.

The reductive simplicity of this aspect of Bentham's thought proceeds ultimately from the similar simplicity of his view of human nature. He "supposes mankind," writes Mill, "to be swayed by only a part of the inducements which really actuate them; but of that part he imagines them to be much cooler and more thoughtful calculators than they really are" (17).

He ignores the profound effect of habit and imagination in securing political acquiescence, and the effect upon habit and imagination of continuity of political structure and especially its outward forms. He ignores, in short, what Burke calls "prejudice," and which Burke rightly recognizes as to some extent indicating an adaptation of institutions, "associated with all the historical recollections of a people," to their national character (17). It is this historical continuity "which alone renders possible those innumerable compromises between adverse interests and expectation, without which no government could be carried on for a year, and with difficulty even for a week."

If the narrowness of Bentham's view of human nature introduces such serious deficiencies into his political thought, in the area of moral thought Mill sees its effect as positively vicious. In asserting that "men's actions are always obedient to their interests," Bentham by no means intended "to impute universal selfishness to mankind, for he reckoned the motive of sympathy as an *interest*. . . . He distinguished two kinds of interests, the self-regarding and the social. . . ." But the term *interest* in vulgar usage gets restricted to the self-regarding, and indeed the "tendency of Mr. Bentham's own opinions" was to consider the self-regarding interest "as exercising, by the very constitution of human nature, a far more exclusive and paramount control over human actions than it really does exercise." As soon as Bentham has shown the direction in which a man's selfish interest would move him, he habitually "lays it down without further parley that the man's interest lies that way" (14). This assertion Mill goes on to support with quotations from Bentham's *Book of Fallacies*. "By the promulgation of such views of human nature, and by a general tone of thought and expression perfectly in harmony with them," he flatly charges, "I conceive Mr. Bentham's writings to have done and to be doing very serious evil. . . . It is difficult to form the conception of a tendency more inconsistent with all rational hope of good for the human species, than that which must be impressed by such doctrines, upon any mind in which they find acceptance." "I regard any considerable increase of human happiness, through mere changes in outward circumstances, unaccompanied by changes in the state of the desires, as hopeless. . . . No man's individual share of any public good which he can hope to realize by his efforts, is an equivalent for the sacrifice of his ease, and of the personal objects which he might attain by another course of conduct. The balance can be turned in favour of virtuous exertion, only by the interest of *feeling* or by that of *conscience*—those 'social interests,' the necessary subordination of which to 'self-regarding' is so lightly assumed." (15.)

Mill reinforces his case by further criticism of Bentham's psychology—the inadequacy of his list of motives, or "springs of action," the inferiority of his doctrine to Hartley's in omitting "the moral sense," the falseness of his notion that "all our acts are determined by pains and pleasures *in prospect*," as implied in the calculus of *consequences* (12). Mill also introduces something like Godwin's distinction between the morality of an act and the virtue of the actor. The virtuous man is deterred, not by a view of consequences, or of future pain, but from the painful "thought of committing the act," a pain which precedes the act. "Not only *may* this be so," Mill adds, "but unless it be so, the man is not really virtuous." Again, consequences depend on deliberation, but he who deliberates "is in imminent danger of being lost" (12). Mill might seem here to be arguing a doctrine of "moral sense," an immediate, not deliberative apprehension of the moral quality of an act. He is certainly defining virtue in terms of moral disposition, or motive, like the intuitionists. But in view of his rejection in *Utilitarianism* of any cognitive element in "moral sense," we must conclude that here the deterrent "painful thought" performs only a psychological, not an epistemic function. What Mill is doing, then, is substituting an account of moral sense in terms of his empirical psychology for that offered by the intuitionists. His reference to Hartley serves to remind us that Hartley also attempts to reconcile in this fashion, at least to some degree, the opposed empirical and intuitionist schools of moral philosophy.

Where Bentham is successful, Mill argues, is in those areas which do not involve moral philosophy. Penal law, for example, "enjoins or prohibits an action, with very little regard to the general moral excellence or turpitude which it implies. . . ." The legislator's object "is not to render people incapable of *desiring* a crime, but to deter them from actually *committing* it" (9). Again, in his efforts to reduce law to a science, in his deductions of principles, and the separating of historical, technical, and rational elements, in his exploding of "fantastic and illogical maxims on which the various technical systems are founded" (10), in his concepts of codification of the law, Bentham, operating purely critically, is brilliantly successful, and Mill pays him full tribute.

How far Mill's estimate of Bentham, in this essay of 1833, is accurate or just to Bentham need not concern us here. What we are solely concerned with is to determine the exact state of Mill's own thought, and particularly of its relation at this point to Utilitarianism.

What we first note is the sharp separation of Bentham as moral philosopher from Bentham as analyst and proponent of the philosophy of law, the first being attacked as not only inadequate but positively pernicious, the second being praised almost without qualification. We note secondly that Bentham the moral philosopher is described almost totally in terms of what he derives from Helvetius and Beccaria: the egoistic psychology, the reduction of motive to simple, undifferentiated pleasure and pain, the defining of virtue and vice simply by means of consequences, the restriction of consideration to the action and not including the virtue of the actor or his motives, the mechanical theory of association which, by linking pain or pleasure to certain actions, will "educate" the egoistic individual into socially useful behaviour. The extent to which Bentham in fact modifies the rigorous pattern of Helvetius and Beccaria is minimized. Mill suggests, indeed, that the modifications weigh very lightly in Bentham's own habits of thought.

What we have in this essay is, then, a point-by-point rejection of practically all the main elements in the structure of the system of Utilitarianism as conceived by Helvetius and Beccaria. It is clear that if their system is taken to be the pure and orthodox doctrine, Mill is at this moment an anti-Utilitarian. But it is also clear from the essay that this is not how the matter appeared to Mill. He insists rather that the structure he is attacking is not the true doctrine, but a false one raised entirely upon the foundations of a false psychology, a false view of human nature. He is, in short, not the type of heretic who rejects the whole religion, but the type who sees himself, not as a heretic, but as the exponent of the true faith, warped in its transmission by the narrowness of vision of the prophets before him.

"SEDGWICK"

The essay on Bentham, written in 1838 as a review of Bentham's collected *Works*,[4] and the essay on Coleridge, published in 1840, continue the pattern established by the essay of 1833. But in the meantime Mill had been provoked by Sedgwick's *Discourse* into a defence of Utilitarianism. This, being a public and avowed performance, and not, like the earlier essay, anonymous, gave Mill a limited opportunity, as he says, to insert into his defence of "Hartleianism and Utilitarianism a number of the opinions which constituted my view of those subjects, as distinguished from that of my old associates." "My relation to my father would have made it . . . impossible . . . to speak out my whole mind . . . at this time." He was obliged "to omit two or three pages of comment on what I thought the mistakes of utilitarian moralists, which my father considered as an attack on Bentham and on him."[5]

The modern reader, with the less-guarded essay of 1833 to place beside the defence of 1835, can savour the ironies of the situation. As he reads Mill's scornful rejection of Sedgwick's argument that "waiting for the calculations of utility" is immoral, since "to hesitate is to rebel,"[6] he is likely to recall the passage Mill wrote in 1833: "The fear of pain *consequent* upon

---

[4]Though generally taken to be a review of the whole of Bowring's edition of Bentham's *Works*, the article reviews only Parts I to IV of that edition (all that had appeared to that point); for a description of these parts and their place in the edition, see Bibliographic Appendix, 512 below.

[5]*Autobiography*, 140–1. Cf. Professor Robson's comments, cxviii below.

[6]"Sedgwick," 66 below. Subsequent references are to the present edition, and are given in parentheses.

the act, cannot arise, unless there be *deliberation*; and the man as well as 'the woman who deliberates,' is in imminent danger of being lost.[7] And as he reads the attack on Sedgwick's contention that the principle of utility has a "debasing" and "degrading" effect (66), he remembers, from the text of 1833, that "the effect of such writings as Mr. Bentham's, if they be read and believed and their spirit imbibed, must either be hopeless despondency and gloom, or a reckless giving themselves up to a life of that miserable self-seeking, which they are there taught to regard as inherent in their original and unalterable nature" (16).

Mill's relation to his father has not only made it impossible, as he says, to speak out his whole mind; it has undoubtedly forced him into a degree of disingenuousness. As he begins his defence of the theory of utility against Sedgwick's attack, he lays down a *caveat*: "No one is entitled to found an argument against a principle, upon the faults or blunders of a particular writer who professed to build his system upon it, without taking notice that the principle may be understood differently, and has in fact been understood differently by other writers. What would be thought of an assailant of Christianity, who should judge of its truth or beneficial tendency from the view taken of it by the Jesuits, or by the Shakers?" (52.) In the context, the implication is that the wrong understanding of the principle of utility is Paley's; in the context of the essay of 1833 the wrong view can also be Bentham's. "A doctrine is not judged at all until it is judged in its best form" (52). This *caveat* is repeatedly, but often unobtrusively, inserted into the attack on Sedgwick. Mill speaks of the doctrine of utility "when properly understood." He insists that "clear and *comprehensive* views of education and human culture" must form the basis of a philosophy of morals; that "all our affections . . . towards human beings . . . are held, *by the best teachers of the theory of utility*" to originate in the natural human constitution; he accuses Sedgwick of "lumping up" the theory of utility with "the theory, *if there be such a theory*, of the universal selfishness of mankind" (71; italics added).

It is clear to those who know the essay of 1833 that the *caveat* is directed against Bentham, that Bentham is the counterpart of the Jesuits and Shakers, but no explicit sign of this intention appears. The only mention of Bentham in the whole essay is indeed, when set against the context of 1833, highly misleading: Paley, says Mill, would doubtless admit that men are acted upon by other than selfish motives, "or, in the language of Bentham and Helvetius, that they have other interests, than merely self-regarding ones" (54). This remark does not, it will be noted, actually make any statement about the doctrines of Bentham and Helvetius, but only about their language—specifically the term "interest"—but it permits the reader to interpret it as a statement about doctrine.

[7]"Remarks on Bentham's Philosophy," 12.

Mill does, however, in spite of these ambiguities, insert some of those ideas that he sees as modifications or correctives of Benthamism. When, for example, he attributes the "lax morality taught by Paley" to Paley's confusion of utilitarianism with expediency, and objects at length to the narrow definition of "consequences" (56), he directs nominally against Paley the same arguments he directed in 1833 against Bentham. His insistence on the importance of poetry, along with autobiographies and novels, in broadening views of human nature, in supplying knowledge of "true human feeling" (56), and in the formation of character, again parallels passages in the *Autobiography* and in the essay of 1833. So does his list of feelings—the chivalrous point of honour, envy and jealousy, ambition, covetousness; although his immediate point is to analyze them all into products of association, he is nevertheless suggesting an enlargement of Bentham's "springs of action." And his comment upon the effects of the "excessive cultivation" of "habits of analysis and abstraction upon the character" records precisely the same rebellion as that recorded in the *Autobiography*. The steady emphasis upon character and motive, the inclusion of effects on character among "consequences" of an act, and the tendency to turn attention away from Bentham's sort of "consequences" to these, insert into the essay, at least by implication, many of the fundamental criticisms of Bentham made in 1833.

"BENTHAM"

By 1838 James Mill, as well as Bentham, was dead, and John Stuart Mill was free to write without wounding his father by his heresy or disloyalty. The essay on Bentham is his first public exercise of this freedom. His emancipation is proclaimed in the opening paragraph, where he praises in perfectly equal terms Bentham and Coleridge, "the two great seminal minds of England in their age," the proponents of the philosophy in which Mill had been reared, and of the philosophy which he in general thinks of as its antithesis. In the context of the relatively long essay on Bentham, this first paragraph and the one following it create a peculiar effect. We are told that both men effected a revolution in the "general modes of thought and investigation" of their time, that both were closet-students, never read by the multitude, that their influences have "but begun to diffuse themselves" over society at large, Bentham's over the "Progressive class," Coleridge's over the "Conservative," and that to Bentham it was given "to discern more particularly those truths with which existing doctrines and institutions were at variance; to Coleridge, the neglected truths which lay *in* them"—talents which suggest in broad and relatively conventional terms Progressive and Conservative attitudes.[8] The reader of 1838 might well have wondered why this very general preamble

[8]"Bentham," 77 below. Subsequent references are to the present edition, and are given in parentheses.

and this laudatory but unspecific tribute to Coleridge should preface a long and detailed essay concerned exclusively with Bentham. As we are now able to recognize, and as probably the reader of 1840 could recognize with the essay on Coleridge before him, the introductory paragraphs are not an introduction to the essay on Bentham. They are an introduction to Mill's thoughts about Bentham, which is a somewhat different and more complex subject. We can now see, with the *Autobiography* available to us, why Mill thinks of Coleridge as well as Bentham at this point. The reader of "Coleridge" would understand the force of the final introductory sentence about each philosopher's approach to doctrines and institutions.

Any reader, however, is likely to feel that the treatment of Bentham in the essay contrasts in its severity with the praise in the introduction, and indeed Mill himself at a later date had misgivings.[9] The contrast is perhaps more apparent than real. As in the essay of 1833, Mill does not underestimate what he takes to be Bentham's real achievement: "to refuse an admiring recognition of what he was, on account of what he was not" is an error, he says, "no longer permitted to any cultivated and instructed mind" (82). The praise he now gives Bentham goes a good deal further than Mill was willing to go in 1833. At that time it was difficult for him to value any but the critical side of Bentham's philosophy. Now he discriminates and elaborates. Bentham is still the great "*subversive*, or, in the language of continental philosophers, the great *critical*, thinker of his age and country" (79). But his importance is to be estimated fully neither by the quality of his critical analysis—which shows no subtlety or power of recondite analysis—nor by his achievement in the area in which he really excelled, the correction of practical abuses. His importance lies in his widespread and lasting influence. "It was not Bentham by his own writings; it was Bentham through the minds and pens which those writings fed—through the men . . . into whom his spirit passed" (79). And this spirit was not purely negative and critical; it included a positive and constructive element. He "made it a point of conscience" not to assail error "until he thought he could plant instead the corresponding truth" (82). But again, his real value lies not in those conclusions he took for truth, but in the method, combining critical analysis with positive synthesis. He reformed philosophy, but it "was not his doctrines which did this, it was his mode of arriving at them." "It was not his opinions, in short, but his method, that constituted the novelty and the value of what he did; a value beyond all price, even though we should reject the whole, as we unquestionably must a large part, of the opinions themselves." (83.)

[9]See John M. Robson, "John Stuart Mill and Jeremy Bentham, with some Observations on James Mill," in M. MacLure and F. W. Watt, eds., *Essays in English Literature from the Renaissance to the Victorian Age* (Toronto: University of Toronto Press, 1964), 259–62.

Freed of the necessity of accepting and praising Bentham's opinions, and free to make this radical disjunction of his method from its doctrinal product, Mill can praise whole-heartedly. It was the doctrines that had been the stumbling-block. As soon, however, as he begins to examine the method to which he has ascribed a revolutionary novelty, he is seized by fresh doubts. The novelty and originality are perhaps not in the method after all, but in "the subjects he applied it to, and in the rigidity with which he adhered to it" (83). The method, considered as a logical conception, has certain affinities "with the methods of physical science, or with the previous labours of Bacon, Hobbes, or Locke. . ." (83). The novelty now becomes "not an essential consideration" of the method, but of its application. And here the novelty appears in "interminable classifications," "elaborate demonstrations of the most acknowledged truths." "That murder, incendiarism, robbery, are mischievous actions, he will not take for granted without proof. . . ." (83.)

Up to this point, one gets a sense of deliberate anticlimax, starting with a great seminal mind, dismissing the doctrines and opinions produced by it, praising the method it developed, only to cast suspicion on the originality involved, and ending with a reduction to the phrases above, with the slighting "interminable," "elaborate," "most acknowledged." Having thus invited the reader virtually to dismiss Bentham, doctrines, method, and all, Mill proceeds to a patient and detailed demonstration of the value, despite its and its begetter's shortcomings, of Bentham's method, the "method of detail." In it Mill sees an "application of a real inductive philosophy to the problems of ethics." And so, after an anticlimactic nadir, we come back to praise.

The peculiarity of this pattern is open to more than one explanation. It could be a purely rhetorical device, in which Bentham's opponents are thrown off balance and disarmed by concession after concession, until, just as all seems conceded and their victory complete, Bentham's greatness is re-asserted on grounds they had overlooked. But one gets the sense here rather of following the windings of Mill's own mind, as he sorts out what he himself has acquired from Bentham: not doctrine, for much of that he had rejected in 1833; not method, for he himself had argued for an imitation of the inductive sciences rather than of geometry in moral and political philosophy. It could then only be the way in which Bentham had developed and applied the method, the precise nature of the "habit of analysis" he and James Mill had taught their pupil. From his father Mill had learned, he believed, subtlety of analysis; from Bentham the "exhaustive method."[10]

And this of course brings Mill back again, after giving Bentham due credit, to the limitations of the "habit of analysis" in general, and to Bentham's

[10]Cf. *ibid.*, 267–8, where Professor Robson suggests that Mill was praising not the detail of Bentham's method, but his very adoption of a method in ethics, politics, and sociology.

limitations in particular. In what seems to be a general anxiety in this work to be fair to his subject, he first explains the sort of breadth Bentham's mind possessed: "he sees every subject in connexion with all the other subjects with which in his view it is related. . ." (88–9). He thus preserves himself against one kind of narrow and partial views—but "Nobody's synthesis can be more complete than his analysis" (89), and a system based upon an imperfect analysis will be exceedingly limited in its applicability. Bentham's analysis is limited in various ways: first of all by his contemptuous dismissal of all other thinkers and schools of thought, whose speculations he dismissed as "vague generalities." The "nature of his mind," says Mill, "prevented it from occurring to him, that these generalities contained the whole unanalysed experience of the human race" (90). One catches here, particularly in the last phrase, a hint of Mill's own discovery, recorded in the *Autobiography*, of the vast areas of human experience, and especially of the unanalyzed and unanalyzable experience embodied in imaginative writing, which Bentham so glibly dismissed.

Furthermore, in ignoring thinkers of the past, Bentham is ignoring "the collective mind of the human race." "The collective mind does not penetrate below the surface, but it sees all the surface." And by refusing to consider views opposed to his own, Bentham limits his own vision, for "none are more likely to have seen what he does not see, than those who do not see what he sees" (91).

It is at this point that Mill develops his theory of the half-truth, conceived generally in terms of polarity. "The hardiest assertor . . . of the freedom of private judgment—the keenest detector of the errors of his predecessors, and of the inaccuracies of current modes of thought—is the very person who most needs to fortify the weak side of his own intellect, by study of the opinions of mankind in all ages and nations, and of the speculations of philosophers of the modes of thought most opposite to his own." "A man of clear ideas errs grievously if he imagines that whatever is seen confusedly does not exist. . . ." (91.)

Bentham's most serious limitation, however, was "the incompleteness of his own mind as a representative of universal human nature. In many of the most natural and strongest feelings of human nature he had no sympathy; from many of its graver experiences he was altogether cut off; and the faculty by which one mind understands a mind different from itself, and throws itself into the feelings of that other mind, was denied him by his deficiency of Imagination." (91.) Behind these sentences lie not only the explanation of the incompleteness of Bentham's analysis of human nature, of the reductive simplicity of his "springs of action," but also a strong suggestion of Mill's own experience in the early years recorded in the *Autobiography*— of the sensitivities of an imaginative child and youth dismissed as nonsense.

This suggestion is reinforced by the description Mill gives, immediately after this passage, of the sort of Imagination Bentham lacked—a description in words taken from Wordsworth's *Preface* to the *Lyrical Ballads* of 1800. Without this imagination, Mill continues, "nobody knows even his own nature, further than circumstances have actually tried it and called it out" (92). There can be no doubt that at this point he is recalling his own emotional crisis, and the release of self-knowledge he owed to Wordsworth.

Bentham's knowledge of human nature is "wholly empirical," that is, based on his own experience, and "he had neither internal experience nor external. . . ." "He was a boy to the last. Self-consciousness . . . never was awakened in him." "Knowing so little of human feelings, he knew still less of the influences by which those feelings are formed. . . ." (92, 93.) Mill's sentences flow on, one after the other, evenly, balanced, poised, and almost totally damning.

From Bentham's denial of "all truths but those which he recognizes" flows the bad influence he has had upon his age: "he has, not created a school of deniers, for this is an ignorant prejudice, but put himself at the head of the school which exists always. . . : thrown the mantle of intellect over the natural tendency of men in all ages to deny or disparage all feelings and mental states of which they have no consciousness in themselves" (93).

It will be noted that this is a very different accusation, in its description of the source and nature of Bentham's bad influence, from that of 1833. Then the influence was ascribed to his positive doctrines; now it arises from his failure to recognize that his own truths are merely "fractional truths." And after praise of "one-eyed men," Mill sets out to assert the value of Bentham's limited visions of these fractional truths. The assessment suggests why he has substituted "fractional" for "half"; as he details Bentham's conception of human nature, and then the elements ignored by it, the fraction representing Bentham's share of the whole truth becomes evidently small. "Man is never recognised by him as a being capable of pursuing spiritual perfection as an end; of desiring, for its own sake, the conformity of his own character to his standard of excellence, without hope of good or fear of evil from other source than his own inward consciousness." This "great fact in human nature escapes him." (95.) If he occasionally speaks of "love of justice" as inherent in almost all mankind, it is impossible to tell "what sense is to be put upon casual expressions so inconsistent with the general tenor of his philosophy" (95n). Neither the word "self-respect" nor the idea it indicates occurs even once in his writings. The sense of honour, of personal dignity, the love of beauty, of order, of congruity, the love of abstract power, of action,—none of these "powerful constituents of human nature" finds a place among his "Springs of Action." Even his doctrine of sympathy does not include "the love of *loving*, the need of a sympathising support, or of objects of admiration and reverence." These omissions arise, not from the absence of these elements in Bentham's own nature, but from his having "confounded all disinterested feelings which he found in himself, with the desire of general happiness" (96)—that is, although Mill does not explicitly say so, from a deficiency of analysis.

In 1833, it was the reduction of motives in Bentham's view of human nature that led to his bad influence; now the influence is minimized: "he has not been followed in this grand oversight by any of the able men who, from the extent of their intellectual obligations to him, have been regarded as his disciples." "If any part of the influence of this cardinal error has extended itself to them, it is circuitously, and through the effect on their minds of other parts of Bentham's doctrines." (97.)

But having thus, after a fashion, absolved Bentham from the serious charges made in 1833, Mill now goes on to examine, "in a spirit neither of apology nor of censure, but of calm appreciation," how much Bentham's view of human nature will accomplish in morals, and how much in political and social philosophy. In morals, it will do nothing "beyond prescribing some of the more obvious dictates of worldly prudence, and outward probity and beneficence" (97–8). For Mill, full emphasis is on the word "outward." In short, Benthamite ethics will be merely prudential and external. Self-education, "the training, by the human being himself, of his affections and will," is "a blank" in his system, and without it, the regulation of outward actions "must be altogether halting and imperfect" (98). The system is not, then, valid even as a system of prudential and external ethics.

Moreover, the system is totally useless for regulating "the nicer shades of human behaviour, or for laying down even the greater moralities . . . which tend to influence the depths of the character quite independently of any influence on worldly circumstances" (98). In Bentham's *Deontology*, one finds that the *petite morale* almost alone is treated, "and that with the most pedantic minuteness, and on the quid pro quo principles which regulate trade" (99). The fraction of truth in Bentham's ethics has by now become an infinitesimal.

What of his social doctrine? Again, "it will do nothing . . . for the spiritual interests of society; nor does it suffice of itself even for the material interests" (99). It offers, in effect, an exact parallel with the ethics. It ignores national character as the ethics ignore individual character. "A philosophy of laws and institutions, not founded on a philosophy of national character, is an absurdity" (99). But Bentham's opinions on national character would be even more worthless than his totally inadequate opinions on individual character. "All he can do is but to indicate means by which, in any given state of the national mind, the material interests of society can be protected," leaving to others the important question whether the use of those means would injure the national character (99). His philosophy can, then, "teach the means of organizing and regulating the merely *business* part of the social arrangements"—and that is all (99). It cannot deal with anything involving reference to moral influences. Bentham mistakenly thought the business part of human affairs was the whole of them, or at least all that the legislator and moralist are concerned with. Since for Mill the "business part" cannot be dealt with without reference to moral influences, and a philosophy of morals not founded on a philosophy of character is as absurd as a philosophy of laws and institutions not founded on a philosophy of national character, Bentham's social philosophy and moral philosophy are alike absurd.

Yet he goes on to speak of the "business part" as the field of Bentham's greatness, "and there he is indeed great" (100). The greatness is entirely as a critical philosopher, except in the philosophy of law. As in 1833, here he can praise Bentham unreservedly. But as he turns, with obvious relief, to this area, he tries to temper his judgment on Bentham's performance in moral and social philosophy, using a mathematical image more admirable for its neatness than for its cogency. He has, after all, reduced the "fractional truths" in Bentham virtually to vanishing point. Now he praises Bentham for having "originated more new truths" than the world "ever received, except in a few glorious instances, from any other individual. . . . Nor let that which he did be deemed of small account because its province was limited. . . . The field of Bentham's labours was like the space between two parallel lines; narrow to excess in one direction, in another it reached to infinity." (100.) As Mill well knows, in the mathematical juggling implied in his image, the area enclosed by his parallel lines will remain an infinite area however closely the distance between the lines approaches zero without reaching it. He has brought Bentham's lines very close together indeed; the precise nature of their infinite extension would perhaps be hard for Mill to define.

Even his praise of Bentham's philosophy of law is rather more tempered than in 1833 or, to put it perhaps more accurately, Bentham's status as legal philosopher is more sharply separated from his status as political philosopher. The same accomplishments are praised, and the same large reservation is made about Bentham's ignoring of national character in his thoughts on government. But new criticisms are introduced. "The Benthamic theory of government has made so much noise in the world of late years; it has held such a conspicuous place among Radical philosophies, . . . that many worthy persons imagine there is no other Radical philosophy extant" (105–106). Of the "three great questions in government," the first two, "to what authority is it for the good of the people that they should be subject," and "how are they to be induced to obey that authority," must have varied answers according to the "degree and kind of civilization" already attained by a people, and their "peculiar aptitudes for receiving more" (106). These questions Bentham does not seriously concern himself with. The third question, "how are abuses of this authority to be checked," has a less variable answer, and is Bentham's main concern. His answer is, by responsibility of the authority to "the numerical majority," whose interest he takes to coincide with the interest of the whole community. This assumption, the "fundamental doctrine of Bentham's political philosophy," Mill challenges. "Is it, at all times and places, good for mankind to be under the absolute authority of the majority of themselves?" Since this absolute authority will control, not only actions, but minds, opinions, and feelings, he goes on to demand, "Is it . . . the proper condition of man, in all ages and nations, to be under the despotism of Public Opinion?" (106–107.) Of the three great questions in government, then, Bentham virtually ignores two, and supplies a questionable answer for the third. The Radical philosophy which has become so dominant through his influence places all its faith in the rule of a numerical majority, a faith Mill was increasingly inclined to question.

Mill challenges, in fact, that whole concept of government which Halévy has described as "the artificial identification of interests," and which he sees as the Benthamite doctrine. To achieve an identity of interests, Mill says, would be to achieve identity of "partialities, passions, and prejudices," "to make one narrow, mean type of human nature universal and perpetual, and to crush every influence which tends to the further improvement of man's intellectual and moral nature" (107). The doctrine, in short, by which Benthamism aims at producing a just yet stable society, will end by producing a static one, and the static society becomes an unjust society. There must be provision, then, for "a perpetual and standing Opposition to the will of the majority," and not, as in Bentham's scheme, for every ingenious means of "riveting the yoke of public opinion" round the necks of all public functionaries. "Wherever all the forces of society act in one single direction, the just claims of the individual human being are in extreme peril." The exercise of the power of the majority must be "tempered by respect for the personality of the individual, and deference to superiority of cultivated intelligence" (108–109).

Having thus again, on the subject of government, reduced Bentham's "fractional truth" to virtual insignificance, Mill again starts to redress the balance by asserting the value of Bentham's "political speculations." What he has just been suggesting as a misuse of Bentham's "great powers," the exhausting of "all the resources of ingenuity in devising means for riveting the yoke of public opinion closer and closer," he now describes as pointing out "with admirable skill the best means of promoting, one of the ideal qualities of a perfect government—identity of interest between the trustees and the community for whom they hold their power in trust" (109). The shift from blame to praise of Bentham is accompanied, one notes, by a shift in interpretation of the doctrine of identity of interests: it is no longer the identity (and identification) of the interests of the individual and of the community, but of the interests of the rulers and of the community. Since Bentham relies on responsibility of the rulers to the numerical majority as the "best means of promoting" this end, a principle Mill has just attacked, it is difficult to see how the variation can salvage Bentham's value.[11] Mill also praises Bentham for his attention to "interest-begotten prejudice," particularly as displayed in "class-interest, and the class morality founded thereon," although noting at the same time that in the psychology of self-deception religious writers, with their superior knowledge of the "profundities and windings of the human heart," had penetrated much deeper than he (109).

Then finally, Mill turns to the subject in which we are most interested, and which he gives every evidence of having deliberately avoided. "It may surprise the reader," he says, and indeed it may, "that we have said so little about the first principle . . . with which his name is more identified than with anything else; the 'principle of utility,' or, as he afterwards named it, 'the greatest-happiness principle.' " A great deal could be said on the subject, "on an occasion more suitable for a discussion of the metaphysics of morality, or on which the elucidations necessary to make an opinion on so abstract a subject intelligible could be conveniently given." But a discussion of the principle of utility is not "in reality necessary for the just estimation of Bentham" (110). On the face of it, to say that the discussion of a philosopher's "first principle," the principle with which his name is identified, is not necessary for a just estimation of him is a surprising *dictum*. It is here also of very great importance. Obviously, if the principle of utility is irrelevant to an estimate of Bentham, Bentham is irrelevant to an estimate of the principle of utility. The process of separation of Bentham from the doctrine is complete.

But the fact of Bentham's Utilitarianism remains to be explained, or even explained away. It is there in Bentham's system, Mill says in effect, from a special kind of psychological compulsion. To Bentham, "systematic unity was an indispensable condition of his confidence in his own intellect," and the principle of utility serves to create that systematic unity: "it was necessary to him to find a first principle which he could receive as self-evident, and to which he could attach all his other doctrines as logical consequences" (111). This was, then, a psychological necessity for Bentham; he had to have a system. But the value of his thought clearly does not lie in the

[11]Mill struggled with this general problem, of course, for the next twenty years, resolving it (to his satisfaction and in theory) only in his *Considerations on Representative Government*.

system or in the achievement of its construction. The implication is strong that another principle might easily have given him another system, that this would have given him equal confidence, and produced equally valuable results. This is why, presumably, an estimate of his achievement does not depend on the validity of his principle or of his system.

Thus, by another route, Mill brings us back to the conclusion that Bentham's greatness does not lie in his body of doctrines, but in his method. Yet the method itself, which for Bentham is clearly inseparable from system-building, has been opened further to criticism. As to the "greatest-happiness principle," Mill records his entire agreement with the principle "under proper explanations"—a significant qualification. These explanations he obviously has no intention of going into in detail at this time, but he drops a few hints. "We think utility, or happiness, much too complex and indefinite an end to be sought except through the medium of various secondary ends. . . ." Mankind, being "much more nearly of one nature, than of one opinion about their own nature," can agree more readily about these intermediate ends than about the first principles; and "the attempt to make the bearings of actions upon the ultimate end more evident than they can be made by referring them to the intermediate ends, and to estimate their value by a direct reference to human happiness, generally terminates in attaching most importance, not to those effects which are really the greatest, but to those which can most easily be pointed to and individually identified" (110–11). So much for the "felicific calculus."

Then Mill repeats the charge of 1833: that Bentham ignores, among his "consequences," the effect of actions upon the agent's own mind and character. He further expands this theme. "The cold, mechanical, and ungenial air which characterizes the popular idea of a Benthamite" is a result of Bentham's one-sided treatment of actions and characters solely in terms of the *moral* view. And again, this error belongs to him, "not as a utilitarian, but as a moralist by profession" (112). Mill's correction is to distinguish three aspects of every human action: the moral (of its *right* and *wrong*), the aesthetic (of its *beauty*), the sympathetic (of its *loveableness*). "The first addresses itself to our reason and conscience; the second to our imagination; the third to our human fellow-feeling" (112). In effect, Mill is rejecting the tendency of strict Utilitarianism to ignore the morality of the agent, as he has done in insisting on effects on character as consequences. He does not here, like William Godwin, distinguish and separate the morality of an action (judged by consequences) and the morality of an agent (judged by motive or intention), since he clearly sees these as only artificially separable. His introduction of the aesthetic is also notable—it clearly reflects the response recorded in the *Autobiography* to narratives of great lives, and it brings Mill at this point curiously close to the school of Shaftesbury.

It seems certain that thoughts of his own childhood and youth are in Mill's mind at this point, since he moves directly from these considerations of the qualities of an action to Bentham's peculiar dislike of discussions of taste ("as if a person's tastes did not show him to be wise or a fool, cultivated or ignorant, gentle or rough, sensitive or callous, generous or sordid, benevolent or selfish, conscientious or depraved," Mill observes (113) in a tone of rebuke), and to his equally peculiar opinions on poetry. The famous "push-pin is as good as poetry" is shown to be less anti-cultural than its quoters usually suppose, but "All poetry is misrepresentation" is allowed to be Bentham's characteristic view (114). This view proceeds, as does Bentham's intricate and involved style, from a fallacious view of the nature and possibility of precision in language. The view carries with it the paradox that in trying to write with absolute precision, Bentham "could stop nowhere short of utter unreadableness, and after all attained no more accuracy than is compatible with opinions as imperfect and one-sided as those of any poet or sentimentalist breathing" (115).

So closes the "impartial estimate" of Bentham's "character as a philosopher, and of the results of his labours to the world." And again, the paradoxical statement, that after "every abatement . . . there remains to Bentham an indisputable place among the great intellectual benefactors of mankind" (115). What is one to make of the paradox? Is the praise merely the tribute of personal loyalty to an early guide, philosopher, and friend, all of whose ideas have been outgrown? This is perhaps the dominant impression given by the footnote Mill added to refute Brougham's view of Bentham's character, but here the concern is with defence of character. In the essay itself, there is no separation of Bentham the man from Bentham the philosopher, which would have been an obvious way of paying personal tribute. It is, on the contrary, clear that Mill, while undercutting and dismissing virtually all Bentham's claims to serious consideration as a thinker, nevertheless retains in some peculiar way a great respect for him as an intellectual influence and force. And although his specific praise is directed almost entirely to the critical side of Bentham's work, to his demolishing of legal fictions, and so on, it is apparent that Mill, as in 1833, sees him as more than a preparatory destroyer, more than a Voltaire, for example. He is not merely the wrecker clearing old houses from the site to prepare for new building; he is in some sense an architect of the new, even if his plans seem all wrong. I spoke earlier about different kinds of heretic, and perhaps Mill would not object to the suggestion of an analogy drawn from the history of Buddhism. The two great branches of Buddhist thought were named (by the later branch) the Hīnayāna, or Inferior Vehicle, and the Mahāyāna, or Great Vehicle. Ānanda, the first reciter of the Scriptures (Sūtra), was held by the Mahāyāna to have had an imperfect grasp of their meaning, and to have taught them to disciples with an equally imperfect grasp. He nevertheless made the Great Vehicle, the more enlightened interpretation, possible; and also, through his own teachings and those of his disciples, established the Buddhism which the Mahāyāna would re-interpret and reform. If one grants that Utilitarianism has no Buddha, and consequently no inspired Scriptures, it is still possible to see Bentham as the Ānanda of Utilitarianism, the Benthamites as Hīnayāna Utilitarians, and Mill as seeking to establish Mahāyāna Utilitarianism. This would make Bentham, like Ānanda, a "great seminal mind," one who has opened up "rich veins of original and striking speculation," one who has been "the teacher of the teachers," whose modes of thought have "inoculated a considerable number of thinking men." He has established a whole school of Utilitarians and Radicals, based on his Inferior Vehicle; this is the great preliminary accomplishment to prepare for the Great Vehicle. Consequently, although Bentham's statement of the doctrines is now to Mill erroneous and therefore unimportant as a statement of the true religion, Bentham himself is to be honoured.

"COLERIDGE"

When we turn to the essay on Coleridge, first published in 1840, we have been led by the Bentham essay into certain expectations. We are now to see examined the other "seminal mind," and perhaps to inspect other half or fractional truths. A reader with a clear memory of the earlier essay might also wonder whether Coleridge's truths are to be subjected to the same rather devastating scrutiny as Bentham's. The opening of the essay is so close in its pattern to the earlier one as to arouse this suspicion. For here again, Bentham and Coleridge are praised equally as "the great questioners of things established"; Bentham, "beyond all others," has led men to ask of a received opinion, Is it true?; Coleridge, What is the meaning of it? Both have exerted influence far beyond their immediate followers. Coleridge is praised for his Burkean sense of the collective wisdom enshrined in long-established beliefs, whose duration is "at least proof of an adaptation in it to some portion or other of the human mind, . . . some natural want or requirement of human nature which the doctrine in question is fitted to satisfy. . . ."[12] Each of them thus sees what the other does not.

In all this expansive tolerance and appreciation, the harsh comments on Bentham seem forgotten, and the reader who recalls phrases from the essay on Bentham is likely to read with some surprise the pronouncements, "If a book were to be compiled containing all the best things ever said on the

[12]"Coleridge," 119 below. Subsequent references are to the present edition, and are given in parentheses.

rule-of-thumb school of political craftsmanship, and on the insufficiency for practical purposes of what the mere practical man calls experience, it is difficult to say whether the collection would be more indebted to the writings of Bentham or of Coleridge," and "Of their methods of philosophizing, the same thing may be said: they were different, yet both were legitimate logical processes." (121.) And those who remember the whittling away of Bentham's claims to originality here discover that his originality is greater than Coleridge's: "Bentham so improved and added to the system of philosophy he adopted, that for his successors he may almost be accounted its founder; while Coleridge . . . was anticipated in all the essentials of his doctrine by the great Germans of the latter half of the last century. . ."; "he is the creator rather of the shape in which it has appeared among us, than of the doctrine itself." (121.)

After this opening, very close in its tone of relaxed generosity to the introduction in the companion essay, Mill turns to an elaboration of his theory of half-truths, which he now gives not merely a supplementary rôle, as in the first essay, but a function of active dialectic. He emphasizes the importance, "in the present imperfect state of mental and social science, of antagonist modes of thought," illustrating by examples of the controversy between primitivists and progressivists, and between supporters and opponents of aristocracy (122). But just when his reference to "Continental philosophers" has led the reader to expect a further development of the dialectic pattern, he virtually rejects it for a theory of alternative extremes between which opinion oscillates. All that is positive in opposed opinions is often true, and it would be easy to choose a path "if either half of the truth were the whole of it," but it is very difficult to frame, "as it is necessary to do, a set of practical maxims which combine both" (123).

He finds at this point, in other words, no evidence in the history of opinion to support a belief either in the dialectic process, by which thesis and antithesis produce a synthesis, or in half-truths which become supplementary and form a whole. Even if a just balance between extremes exists in the mind of the wiser teacher, "it will not exist in his disciples, still less in the general mind" (124). Improvement consists only in a lessening of the amplitude of swings of the pendulum. The image suggests a remote hope of an eventual dead centre, but the passage is, for Mill, curiously pessimistic.[13] In this context he treats the "Germano-Coleridgian doctrine" in terms of reaction against eighteenth-century empiricism. What the change here in the exposition of half-truths as oscillations rather than as supplementary discoveries

[13]Going beyond this immediate context, one should note Mill's qualified approval of the Saint-Simonian and Comtean notion of the alternation of "critical" and "organic" periods, an alternation that does not preclude a final period in which freedom would unite with order (without, for Mill, any suggestion of an Hegelian synthesis).

implies, is that Mill is prepared to grant only limited validity to the "Germano-Coleridgian doctrine," viewing it as an excessive swing of the pendulum rather than as a valuable corrective and completion of its opposite half-truth.

And this indeed is what his treatment suggests. As he describes the opposed philosophies, the versions he offers indicate, if not a bias, at least a very uneven grasp of the two. When he ascribes to Kant, for example, a claim that the human mind has "a capacity, within certain limits, of perceiving the nature and properties of 'Things in themselves,' " and when he describes what he takes to be Coleridge's (and Kant's) theory of perception and of *a priori* truths (125), one feels that his comprehension is so faulty as to suggest that he has not taken the metaphysical and epistemological parts of their philosophy very seriously. In similar fashion, he seems to accept unquestioningly the vulgar misinterpretation of the "common sense" of the Scottish school. There is no reason to suspect Mill in this of deliberate distortion or bias. As he says, "Disputants are rarely sufficient masters of each other's doctrines, to be good judges what is fairly deducible from them," or, he might have said, to be good judges of the doctrines. And, he continues, "To combine the different parts of a doctrine with one another, and with all admitted truths, is not indeed a small trouble, nor one which a person is often inclined to take for other people's opinions. Enough if each does it for his own. . . ." (128.) Mill recognizes indeed that each philosophy, the empirical and the rational, "has been able to urge in its own favour numerous and striking facts" which have taxed the metaphysical resources of the other philosophy to explain. His own opinion, which he presents, he says, as a "bare statement," is that the truth lies with empiricism, with "the school of Locke and of Bentham" (128).

Taken as a declaration of adherence, not to these two philosophers and their doctrines in detail, but to the general philosophy which they represent, this "bare statement" makes it clear that whatever half-truths he is going to find in Coleridge will not be found in his metaphysical positions, in his theory of knowledge, or of the imagination. The philosophical Coleridge who today attracts so much attention, particularly from literary critics, forms no part of Mill's concern. And if the reader has been led by the openings of this and the companion essay on Bentham to expect the Coleridge half to be fitted neatly to the Bentham half, as indeed he might well be, he will be surprised by the relative scarcity of specific references to Bentham and his ideas. He will find, after a description of the state to which English institutions were brought in the eighteenth century, an expansion of the comparison made in the first essay: "This was . . . a state of things which . . . was sure in no great length of time to call forth two sorts of men—the one demanding the extinction of the institutions and creeds which had hitherto existed; the other that they be made a reality: the one pressing the new doctrines to their utmost consequences; the other reasserting the best meaning and purposes of the old. The first type attained its greatest height in Bentham; the last in Coleridge." (145–6.)

The one extensive and important reference to Bentham is in relation to first principles of government. Coleridge's theory of government, although "but a mere commencement, not amounting to the first lines of a political philosophy," is still asserted to be superior to any other the age has produced, including the Benthamic (153). "The authors and propounders" of the Benthamic theory (presumably Bentham and James Mill) "were men of extraordinary intellectual powers, and the greater part of what they meant by it is true and important. But when considered as the foundations of a science, it would be difficult to find among theories proceeding from philosophers one less like a philosophical theory, or, in the works of analytical minds, anything more entirely unanalytical." And Mill then proceeds to apply to the "complex notions" of "interest" and "general interest" the sort of critical analysis Bentham liked to apply to traditional phrases, "breaking them down into the elements of which they are composed" (153). The analysis reveals and challenges many of Bentham's assumptions.

It first challenges Bentham's assumption that the interests of the middle class are most likely to be identical with the general interest, interpreting "interest" in Benthamic terms: "If by men's interest be meant what would appear such to a calculating bystander, judging what would be good for a man during his whole life, and making no account, or but little, of the gratification of his present passions, his pride, his envy, his vanity, his cupidity, his love of pleasure, his love of ease"—one notes how Mill here implies that Bentham unconsciously substitutes an "ideal spectator" for the actual man, and also how once again he calls attention to the limitations of Bentham's "springs of action"—"it may be questioned whether, in this sense, the interest of an aristocracy, and still more that of a monarch, would not be as accordant with the general interest as that of either the middle or the poorer classes. . ." (154). The point here is that interests in this idealized form would in fact be identical. Every man, no matter what his class, would take the same detached, unimpassioned, and unbiased view of the consequences of each action. "And if men's interest, in this understanding of it, usually governed their conduct," Mill adds, "absolute monarchy would probably be the best form of government" (154). He thus suggests a complete hiatus between the psychological premises on which Bentham's political system is founded, and its conclusions, which favour a democracy with power in the hands of the middle class.

But men in fact, he goes on, "usually do what they like, often being perfectly aware that it is not for their ultimate interest, still more often that it is not for the interest of their posterity. . ." (154). Nor, when they do believe an object is permanently good for them, do they assess its value accurately. The problem of politics is not whose *permanent* interests are likely "to be most in accordance with the end we seek to obtain," but "who are they whose immediate interests and habitual feelings" are. And the end itself, the "general good," is "a very complex state of things, comprising . . . many requisites which are neither of one and the same nature, nor attainable by one and the same means." "A government must be composed out of the elements already existing in society, and the distribution of power in the constitution cannot vary much or long from the distribution of it in society itself." (154.)

Mill makes no explicit connection between these criticisms of Bentham and the ideas of Coleridge, but an implicit connection is established by the tenor of the whole essay, which constantly sets up the views of Coleridge, or of the "Germano-Coleridgian school," against the *esprit simpliste* of the eighteenth-century thinkers. Where the Lockean school, for example, had in thinkers like Condillac "affected to resolve all the phenomena of the human mind into sensation, by a process which essentially consisted in merely *calling* all states of mind, however heterogeneous, by that name," a philosophy consisting "solely of a set of verbal generalizations, explaining nothing, distinguishing nothing, leading to nothing" (129), Coleridge not only takes up the more complex analysis of Hartley, but tries to solve difficulties remaining in Hartley's system.[14] Again, the Continental *philosophes*, in their simple optimism, assume that the destruction of institutions will itself establish the ideal society. Coleridge, on the other hand, is aware of the problems of establishing and maintaining a society, of the difficulty of obtaining the habit of obedience and acquiescence on which a society depends. He defines the three requisites: a system of education in discipline, a feeling of allegiance or loyalty, and a principle of social cohesion (a national sense or sense of community). The recognition of these requisites by the Germano-Coleridgian school provides the first inquiry into the "inductive laws of the existence and growth of human society." This school is the first to have produced a philosophy of society, "in the only form in which it is yet possible, that of a philosophy of history, . . . a contribution, the largest yet made by any class of thinkers, towards the philosophy of human culture" (139). Mill sees this contribution as springing particularly from their recognition of national character, and its formation by national education, which is at once the source of permanence and of progress in a society, the first as a system of

---

[14]This is not to argue that Mill deserted the empirical and associationist school; his allegiance is perfectly clear, whatever the modifications, in his *Logic*, his edition of James Mill's *Analysis of the Phenomena of the Human Mind*, and in his *Examination of Sir William Hamilton's Philosophy*, to mention only the most obvious examples.

discipline, the second as a stimulant to the faculties. The Germano-Coleridgian school, in their views on "the various elements of human culture and the causes influencing the formation of national character, . . . throw into the shade everything which had been effected before. . ." (141).[15]

Coleridge's views on the Established Church and on the English Constitution are also set against the context of the eighteenth-century thinkers, the simple views both of those who clung to them because they were there, and of those who hoped great things from their abolition. Coleridge's clear separation[16] of the function of the Church as the *clerisy* from the functions of a church as a religious body, his objection to identifying the Church with its clergy, constitute in Mill's view a fruitful analysis of a complex relationship of an institution to its society. Similarly, his views on the opposite interests of the State in permanence and progression, and his relating of these interests to the five classes of citizens, strike Mill as a valid analysis of the English political scene.

Even in political economy, where he finds Coleridge generally "an arrant driveller" he praises his opposition to "the *let alone* doctrine," and his insistence on "the idea of a *trust* inherent in landed property." The first opposes the dominant eighteenth-century purely negative view of government, in favour of a view of the State as "a great benefit society, or mutual insurance company, for helping . . . that large proportion of its members who cannot help themselves," and Mill quotes with approval Coleridge's three "positive ends" for government to pursue. The second rejects the Lockean view of *property*, as absolute proprietorship, in respect to land, as distinguished from the produce of labour. Mill here develops his own argument, that "when the State allows any one to exercise ownership over more land than suffices to raise by his own labour his subsistence and that of his family, it confers on him power over other human beings" (156–8). This power the State ought to control.

There are clearly a number of leading ideas which Mill shares with Coleridge, and which no doubt he acquired from the Coleridgians. But any Coleridgian must be struck by the limitations, rather than the extent, of the influence. It is significant that the greatest bulk of quotation is from *Church and State* and *Literary Remains*. The emphasis throughout is on political and social thought, and particularly on modes of analysis, not unlike Bentham's, but yielding very different results. One gets the impression that Mill has been most struck by seeing the "habit of analysis" at work in a mind

[15]While Mill remained interested in this area, he never fully worked out the problems of reconciliation here indicated; his "Ethology" was not written.

[16]A separation made clearer and more complete by Mill than by Coleridge, and so carrying rather different implications.

operating from very different assumptions than Bentham, and capable of
more subtle analysis. More important still, it is a mind alive to the complexity of human nature, of human society, of human institutions, and a
healthy corrective to the arid and formalist reduction of eighteenth-century
thought. Contact with this mind has brought Mill out of the eighteenth
century—but it has not destroyed totally his allegiance to his upbringing.

"WHEWELL"

If Mill's residual allegiance is evident in the essay on Coleridge, it is vastly
more so in that on Whewell. As we have seen in the review of Sedgwick, if
an outsider attacked Bentham, Mill sprang to the defence, even if the attack
made charges he himself had made. In part he responds, one senses, as to a
family affair: it is one thing to criticize one's relatives; for a stranger to make
the same criticisms is a different matter. But there is more to it than this. At
an earlier stage, it seems clear, Mill had hoped to establish a distinction
between Benthamism and Utilitarianism. If, as seemed evident, Utilitarianism
was becoming fixed in the popular mind as a system of egoistic hedonism, as
what Carlyle called a "pig philosophy," the fault was Bentham's, and it was
necessary, for the defence of Utilitarianism, to disavow a great part of his
doctrines. The public must be taught that Benthamism is not true Utilitarianism. This is a conviction which Mill holds unwaveringly, however much his
emotional attitude towards Bentham shifts and changes. The Benthamite
doctrines he attacked in 1833 he continues to reject. But he does come to a
questioning of his early tactics. If these failed to break the popular identification of Benthamism and Utilitarianism, then attacks on Bentham's doctrines
merely provided support for the opponents of Utilitarianism. The comparison with religious reformers again springs to mind. Worshippers who are
firmly held within the general faith, but discontented with the formulation of
its doctrines, can be led into a reformed church; but attacks on the established
orthodoxy will not necessarily convert the pagan—they may simply provide
aid and comfort to the enemies of religion.

So Mill felt by the 1850s. The reaction again Utilitarianism, powerfully
voiced by Carlyle, had been gaining in strength. It was soon to be reinforced
by the eloquence of Ruskin and the savage comedy of Dickens. Utilitarianism
itself was in danger. As Mill later recorded in the *Autobiography* (153), he
continued to think his criticism of Bentham's doctrines in 1838 (and presumably also in 1833) was just, but he came to doubt "whether it was right
to publish it at that time." The doubt is clearly as to tactics: "Bentham's
philosophy, as an instrument of progress, has been to some extent discredited
before it had done its work, and . . . to lend a hand towards lowering its
reputation was doing more harm than service to improvement." This doubt

as to tactics is expressed more strongly in 1854–5 than in 1861, as Professor Robson has noted.[17] Later, as Mill comments in the *Autobiography*, when he sensed a "counter-action . . . towards what is good in Benthamism," he felt justified in reprinting the "Bentham" and "Coleridge" essays, especially as he had "balanced" his criticisms of Bentham by "vindications of the fundamental principles of Bentham's philosophy" (153)—which earlier he would have called fundamental principles of Utilitarianism. Where he has toned down the explicit distinction between and separation of "Benthamism" and "Utilitarianism rightly understood," this is a change, not of his own doctrine, but of tactics. The new tactics are to include defence of Bentham, supplemented by a restatement of the fundamental principles. The new testament of Utilitarianism is to enlarge and correct the old, but not explicitly reject it.

The way in which the new tactics operate is first illustrated in the essay on Whewell's moral philosophy. The separation of Benthamism from the "principle of utility" is included, but not emphasized. "It would be quite open to a defender of the principle of utility, to refuse encumbering himself" with a defence of either Paley or Bentham. "The principle is not bound up with what they have said in its behalf, nor with the degree of felicity which they may have shown in applying it."[18] Whewell is wrong in imagining that Bentham either thought himself, or was thought by others, to be the discoverer of the principle. He was instead the first to erect on the principle, as a foundation, "secondary or middle principles, capable of serving as premises for a body of ethical doctrine not derived from existing opinions, but fitted to be their test." This "great service," which for the first time makes possible "a scientific doctrine of ethics on the foundation of utility," Bentham performed "in a manner, as far as it goes, eminently meritorious, and so as to indicate clearly the way to complete the scheme" (173). His eye was focussed rather on the exigencies of legislation than on those of morals.

This judgment of Bentham is in substance the same as that of 1838, but the difference in tone, and the lessening of emphasis on the negative interpretation, and increase on the positive, reveal the new approach. Bentham's deficiencies are not denied, nor left unmentioned—his practical conclusions in morals were "mostly right," "as far as they went," but "there were large deficiencies and hiatuses in his scheme of human nature and life, and a consequent want of breadth and comprehension in his secondary principles, which led him often to deduce just conclusions from premises so narrow as to provoke many minds to a rejection of what was nevertheless truth" (173–4). He is the Bacon of moral science, not only in having, like Bacon, established a *method*, but also, like Bacon, in having worked many problems on insuffi-

[17]See the Textual Introduction, cxxn and cxxin below.
[18]"Whewell," 167 below. Subsequent references are to the present edition, and are given in parentheses.

cient data. Again, these are the same judgments as in 1838, shorn of the condemnatory tone and the rhetorical expansion. No suggestion is now made that Bentham's shortcomings have led him into dangerous error, or that he has rendered any real disservice to the cause of Utilitarianism. All the emphasis is on his positive, though limited, service to morals. There is a further important positive defence of Bentham in this essay. Mill charges Whewell with a "serious injustice" to Bentham, in citing the *Deontology* as "the authentic exposition of Bentham's philosophy of morals," for making that book representative of all Utilitarianism, and for creating an "imaginary sect, of which the *Deontology* is to be considered the gospel." The work "was not, and does not profess to be written by Bentham" (174–5). Yet Mill himself had, in 1838, deplored the *Deontology*, without denying Bentham's authorship.

In conformity with the new tactics, most of the essay is a defence of the principle of utility, in the broader sense Mill would accept. In this sense, Whewell himself becomes a Utilitarian, since he speaks of moral rules as means to an end, and "of the peace and comfort of society; of making man's life tolerable; of the satisfaction and gratification of human beings; of preventing a disturbed and painful state of society." "When real reasons are wanted, the repudiated happiness-principle is always the resource." In asserting that "when general rules are established, the feelings which gather round these 'are sources not of opposition, but of agreement;' that they 'tend to make men unanimous; and that such rules with regard to the affections and desires as tend to control the repulsive and confirm the attractive forces which operate in human society . . . agree with that which is the character of moral rules,' " Whewell is actually expressing Benthamism (192–3).

Much also of the essay is defence by attack on Whewell's own intuitionist moral theory. Here Mill can apply the actual analytic method of Bentham to the concept of "right" and of "Rights." With a debator's ruthlessness, he pushes Whewell's Voluntarism into a conclusion he can charge with Hobbism, and with a combination of logic and fierce wit he exposes Whewell's three "vicious circles." He reduces Whewell's doctrine to farce by comparing Whewell and Bentham in "a parallel case," the "principles of the art of navigation" (191).

But at two points he finds himself dealing with charges against Bentham very like charges he has himself made. The first is that Bentham does not sufficiently recognize "what Dr. Whewell calls the historical element of legislation." Bentham imagines, says Whewell, "that to a certain extent his schemes of law might be made independent of local conditions," although he recognizes "that different countries must to a certain extent have different laws" (195). Mill, too, had complained of Bentham's ignoring "national character." He had seemed, in fact, in the essay on Coleridge, to be in sympathy with the view that the "long duration of a belief . . . is at least proof of an adaptation in it to some portion or other of the human mind. . ." (120). Now he writes: "The fact that . . . a people prefer some particular mode of legislation, on historical grounds—that is, because they have been long used to it,—is no proof of any original adaptation in it to their nature or circumstances, and goes a very little way in recommendation of it as for their benefit now" (196). What Whewell calls "an historical element," which looks very much like what Mill called "national character," is now reduced to "the existing opinions and feelings of the people," which are indeed "partly the product of their previous history" (196). These opinions and feelings, Mill now says, limit what the legislator can do, not what is desirable to be done. Bentham is to be defended, then, by separating in him the ideal legislator and the practical.[19] This would seem to be a topic on which Mill has either modified or suppressed his earlier views. He appears here to be giving a sanction to *a priori* schemes of legislation, schemes which in Bentham's case he has found to be based on too narrow a view of human nature to be tenable. He seems also to be lessening the importance of that *inductive* science of politics he had praised in the Coleridgians. But this is not the only possible conclusion. Given Mill's doctrine of progress, and his tendency to see national character in terms of stages of progress in political maturity, changes in national character are clearly an essential process towards a conceivable ideal political society. His real quarrel with Bentham, which is suppressed here, is that his views on national character, like his views on human character, are so narrowly based as to be virtually worthless.

Similarly, when he defends Bentham against Whewell's charge that he "does not fully recognise 'the moral object of law' " (196), we recall Mill's own complaint, that man is "never recognised by him as a being capable of pursuing spiritual perfection as an end; of desiring, for its own sake, the conformity of his own character to his standard of excellence, without hope of good or fear of evil from other source than his own inward consciousness" ("Bentham," 95). We recall that for "self-education; the training, by the human being himself, of his affections and will," Bentham's system provides a complete blank (*ibid.*, 98). This complaint is so identical in essence to Whewell's charge that Mill's reply here provides an extreme example of the new tactics. Since Whewell is primarily concerned with moral philosophy, Mill has to defend Bentham as a moral philosopher, and the charge he now has to deal with is a highly central and important one. He is obviously in a difficult position. "It is fortunate for the world," he had written in 1838, "that Bentham's taste lay rather in the direction of jurisprudential than of properly

[19]This defence is also offered in the Introduction to Bentham's *Works*. In general, it may be said, Mill uses it to explain the position of the Philosophic Radicals, and especially of James Mill, on the Reform Bill of 1832 and related measures.

ethical inquiry" (*ibid.*, 98). Now he is faced with defending incompetence. It is significant that he delays this vital issue until the end of his essay, that he gives it very brief treatment, and that he seizes gladly upon the particular issue of the laws of marriage to escape from further dealing with the general charge. His specific general defence of Bentham, that no one more than he "recognises that most important, but most neglected, function of the legislator, the office of an instructor, both moral and intellectual" (197), neatly side-steps the whole issue of what sort of moral instruction Bentham's legislator conceived of giving, or was capable of giving.

Throughout the essay, one can sense that Mill is happiest in attacking Whewell, happy in defending Utilitarianism in his own terms, and not happy but skilful in defending Bentham at carefully chosen points and by carefully chosen stratagems. It must have been with a feeling of relief that he turned to the other half of the new tactics, the definition of Utilitarianism in terms of his own doctrine. Here he could be much more master of the field of battle, choosing his ground and the directions of attack to suit his own purposes. For *Utilitarianism* is rather a campaign than a philosophical treatise. The essay on Whewell had in several ways prepared for the main battle: in its devastating attack on the intuitionist school, in its rejection of the notion that Utilitarianism was incompatible with religious orthodoxy, and in its suggestion of a universal, if often unconscious, acceptance of the principle of utility. The reduction of possible moral theories to only two possibles, the breaking of the link between the attacked theory (the intuitionist) and orthodoxy, and the argument that even those who thought they were intuitionists (like Whewell) were really Utilitarians, prepared the way for asserting Utilitarianism as the only possible universal ethical doctrine.

UTILITARIANISM

In the "General Remarks" which constitute the opening chapter of *Utilitarianism*, Mill lays the foundation for the arguments to follow. As in the Whewell essay, he reduces the choice of schools of moral philosophy to two, the *a priori* and the *a posteriori*, rejecting the first, and asserting that whatever consistency any moral beliefs have attained is mainly due to the "tacit influence of a standard not recognized" by the *a priori* moralists, but indispensable to them.[20] He points to the endless controversies and disagreements over the criterion of right and wrong, over the *summum bonum*, over the foundation of morality, to suggest that the whole *a priori* effort to derive a moral system from a first principle has been a mistaken one, and that the

---

[20]*Utilitarianism*, 205 below. Subsequent references are to the present edition, and are given in parentheses.

demand for proof of first principles is futile. He repeats, by implication, his old charge that those who attempt to create a system of moral or political science on the analogy of mathematics, instead of the inductive sciences, are doomed to failure. But now his argument is reinforced by the contention that the confusion about the status and function of first principles extends to the sciences, including mathematics: "the detailed doctrines of a science are not usually deduced from, nor depend for their evidence upon, what are called its first principles." Algebra, for example, "derives none of its certainty from what are commonly taught to learners as its elements, since these . . . are as full of fictions as English law, and of mysteries as theology" (205). This attack on the *a priori* and deductive in its traditional home and birth-place is a powerful preparation for his argument for the *a posteriori* moral philosophy.

Again, questions of ultimate ends are not amenable to direct proof. There is a "larger meaning of the word proof," a kind of proof which is "within the cognisance of the rational faculty," and which that faculty deals with otherwise than "solely in the way of intuition." This is the mode by which "considerations may be presented capable of determining the intellect either to give or withhold its assent to the doctrine; and this is equivalent to proof" (208). The description of the mode, and the explicit rejection of the purely intuitive, again suggest the method of the inductive sciences. Mill intends, he says, to give such "rational grounds" for accepting or rejecting "the utilitarian formula" (208).

But first it is necessary that the formula should be correctly understood, not dealt with in "the very imperfect notion ordinarily formed of its meaning," but cleared of grosser misconceptions and mistaken interpretations (208). These may, of course, include, although Mill does not say so, the misconceptions and misinterpretations, not only of the enemies of Utilitarianism, but also of its advocates. Of all the tasks before him in the essay, the restatement of what the doctrine is, the freeing of it from the adverse limitations imposed on it by Bentham, is obviously of the utmost importance. And here he can at last present his own interpretation, free of the necessity of either attacking or defending Bentham, at least explicitly. The second chapter, "What Utilitarianism Is," becomes a defence and exposition of the doctrine according to Mill.

Before offering the formal definition from which he intends to develop his exposition, Mill deals with what he calls the "ignorant blunder" of supposing that the Utilitarians, "those who stand up for utility as the test of right and wrong," use the term utility in the colloquial sense of the useful as opposed to the pleasurable (209). Since the doctrine as developed by Helvetius, Beccaria, and Bentham defines utility in terms of pleasure and avoidance of pain, the modern reader might find this apparent reversion to the classical separation of *utile* and *dulce* surprising and irrelevant. But partly through Bentham's own insensitivity to the aesthetic, and partly through the narrow concept of education characteristic of the founders of the doctrine and many of their followers, Utilitarianism had indeed come to be associated with an ignoring of the aesthetic, and with an arid and doctrinaire approach to education and life. This view of the philosophy is immortally enshrined in Dickens' Gradgrind and M'Choakumchild in *Hard Times*, and in his address to "Utilitarian economists, . . . Commissioners of Fact," urging them to cultivate in the poor "the utmost graces of the fancies and affections, to adorn their lives, so much in need of ornament," and not to drive romance utterly out of their souls. Mill himself had experienced the sort of starvation of the imagination and feelings Dickens is talking of, and had, like Dickens, recognized it as an unfortunate aspect of Benthamism. The new tactics I have spoken of lead him here to no admission of the source of this view of Utilitarianism, but merely to a dismissal of it as an ignorant blunder.

In accordance with the same tactics, he defines "the creed" in strict Benthamite terms: "Utility, or the Greatest Happiness Principle, holds that actions are right in proportion as they tend to promote happiness, wrong as they tend to produce the reverse of happiness. By happiness is intended pleasure, and the absence of pain; by unhappiness, pain, and the privation of pleasure." Again, "pleasure, and freedom from pain, are the only things desirable as ends. . . ." (210.) The creed, as a confession of faith, is to be totally orthodox. He and Bentham are of the same faith. The difference is to lie in exegesis.

The first point to clarify concerns the nature of pleasure. To see in the pursuit of pleasure "a doctrine worthy only of swine" (here Mill undoubtedly recalls Carlyle's phrase, "pig-philosophy"), to identify Utilitarianism with Epicureanism, and hold both in contempt, has been the practice of its "German, French, and English assailants." But the Epicureans themselves recognize that "a beast's pleasures do not satisfy a human being's conceptions of happiness." Every known Epicurean theory assigns "a much higher value as pleasures" to the pleasures of the intellect, of the feelings and imagination, and of moral sentiments (the hierarchy suggests that of Hartley) than to those of "mere sensation." It is true that Utilitarian writers in general have "placed the superiority of mental over bodily pleasures chiefly in the greater permanency, safety, uncostliness, &c., of the former"—(an obvious allusion to Bentham's use of the "felicific calculus" to give qualitative hierarchy a quantitative basis)—but it is "quite compatible with the principle of utility" to recognize that, as a matter of fact, "some *kinds* of pleasure are more desirable and valuable than others," and it would be absurd, since quality enters into our estimation of all other things, that the "estimation of pleasures should be supposed to depend on quantity alone" (210–11).

The insistence on qualitative assessment means more than a mere rejection of Bentham's famous remark about push-pin and poetry. It involves primarily a rejection of the reductionist Helvetian psychology, which tended to analyse *all* pleasure ultimately down to simple sensual pleasure, in favour of the Hartleian, which recognizes that the process of association actually gives rise to a qualitative hierarchy of pleasures, ending with those of theopathy and the moral sense. Hartley thus offers an escape from the genetic reductionism which says, in effect, since all feelings, including the loftiest, originate in simple pleasure-pain reactions of sensation, they are ultimately nothing but these simple reactions. It is the reductionist psychology implicit in the calculus which lays Utilitarianism open to the charge of being simple hedonism. Moreover, it is the Hartleian, rather than the Helvetian psychology, which allows the possibility of Mill's doctrine of progress, which allows him to assert that "it is better to be a human being dissatisfied than a pig satisfied; better to be Socrates dissatisfied than a fool satisfied."

Since the term "pleasure" is so strongly associated with simple hedonism, Mill not only follows Bentham in substituting for it the broader term "happiness," but moves from it to the still broader one, "satisfaction." He thus broadens the whole base of the theory. In escaping from the narrow circle of the reductionist psychology, he may seem to be building his own circular argument. When he says, for example, that it is an "unquestionable fact" that "those who are equally acquainted with, and equally capable of appreciating and enjoying, both, do give a most marked preference to the manner of existence which employs their higher faculties" (211), the "fact" is unquestionable because those who do not so choose are *ipso facto* judged not "equally acquainted" or "equally capable." And when he asserts that "no person of feeling and conscience would be selfish and base" (211), it is clear that selfishness and baseness denote a person of no feeling and conscience. But what Mill is actually doing is calling attention to a range of motives qualitatively different from simple pleasure, and confirmed by observation as operative in human nature. The establishing of an ideal of higher conduct, of pursuits suitable to a "being of higher faculties," and the refusal to sink into a low category, may be motivated by pride, by the love of liberty and personal independence, by the love of power, the love of excitement, but it is most properly described as proceeding from "a sense of dignity." And this in fact, says Mill, leads to the greatest happiness. It is a necessary part of his doctrine of progress that men, unless rendered incapable "not only by hostile influences, but by mere want of sustenance," will voluntarily choose the higher pleasures (213).

Beccaria and Bentham had avoided qualitative assessments in the belief that the quantitative is more certain and more readily determined. Mill rapidly dismisses the calculus of pleasure and pain. Quantity of pleasure and pain is no more readily measured than quality. In either case, the only test is in "the feelings and judgment of the experienced" (213).

And finally, the Utilitarian standard is not "the agent's own greatest happiness, but the greatest amount of happiness altogether." Utilitarianism could, therefore, only attain its end "by the general cultivation of nobleness of character" (213–14). By this line of argument, Mill has brought the doctrine round to an apparent total conformity with orthodoxy, to the view that virtue is the sole source of happiness. The doctrine of utility becomes "the rules and precepts for human conduct, by the observance of which an existence such as has been described might be, to the greatest extent possible, secured to all mankind; and . . . to the whole sentient creation." The two great obstacles are selfishness and want of mental cultivation, which both make life "unsatisfactory." The "highest virtue which can be found in man," as long as the world is in its present imperfect state, is the readiness to make an absolute sacrifice of one's own happiness. "The utilitarian morality does recognise in human beings the power of sacrificing their own greatest good for the good of others." And, paradoxically, "the conscious ability to do without happiness gives the best prospect of realizing such happiness as is attainable" (214–18). By this point, the simple original statement of doctrine, "that pleasure, and freedom from pain, are the only things desirable as ends," might seem to have been transformed out of existence. The transformation is no doubt partly tactical, at least in its mode of presentation, to show the compatibility of the doctrine with orthodox morality, but for the most part it is an elaboration of Mill's genuine view of the doctrine, as more briefly suggested in his earlier attacks on Bentham. If there is a special tactical intention in his assertion that "in the golden rule of Jesus of Nazareth, we read the complete spirit of the ethics of utility," it is still a profound part of Mill's interpretation of the doctrine, that "as between his own happiness and that of others, utilitarianism requires" the agent to be "as strictly impartial as a disinterested and benevolent spectator," and that the doctrine of utility is as connected as any other ethical system with "beautiful or more exalted developments of human nature" and with varied "springs of action" (218–19).

This is the major re-statement of the essay. Mill easily disposes of some of the common charges against the doctrine, once he has established his own definition. Like William Godwin, he distinguishes between the morality of an action and the moral worth of an agent, and acknowledges that most actions will have a view to the good of a small circle of immediate family and friends, rather than the whole of society. Like Godwin, too, he dismisses the notion that every act must proceed from a detailed and deliberate calculation of consequences. Many of these points, like the defence against the charge that the doctrine is one of mere expediency, had been dealt with in the "Whewell" essay.

In the third chapter, on the ultimate sanction of the principle of utility, he turns to the accusation that Utilitarianism provides no basis for obligation. In what might be termed the prototype of the doctrine, as presented by Helvetius, this accusation is well grounded. The psychology of Helvetius is so firmly fixed in egoistic hedonism that the impartial and disinterested spectator Mill posits is an impossibility, as is any motive which could lead to a preference for the general pleasure over the personal. But as we have seen, Mill's radically different view of human nature, including a relatively orthodox view of moral character, creates for him no such problem. The aim of the Utilitarian philosophy is, as he defines it, to create through the improvement of education a "feeling of unity with our fellow-creatures" and to root it deeply in our character (227). When he links this aim with Christ's intention, he is again asserting the compatibility of his doctrine with Christian ethical orthodoxy, and at the same time intimating that the source of obligation, in Christian and Utilitarian alike, must lie in moral disposition. Both ethics must rely on the formation of moral character, on the sentiments of the "ordinarily well brought up young person" (227).

The external sanctions of reward and punishment, whether physical or moral, whether from God or from our fellow men, along with disinterested devotion to God or to one's fellow men, can be just as operative for any ethical system. So too with the internal sanction of the sense of duty. The pain attendant on the violation of duty is the essence of Conscience. Granted, says Mill, that Conscience is a highly complex feeling, "encrusted over with collateral associations," but its binding force is constituted by it *qua* feeling —"a mass of feeling which must be broken through in order to do what violates our standard of right." The ultimate internal sanction of all morality, then, is "a subjective feeling in our own minds." Where the feeling does not exist, nor does the sanction. The belief in God, as an internal sanction, apart from expectation of reward or punishment (the external sanction), "only operates on conduct through, and in proportion to, the subjective religious feeling." It will be noted that Mill by-passes the hotly argued question of the nature of Conscience: "Whatever theory we have of the nature or origin of conscience," he says, "this is what essentially constitutes it"—a feeling (228–9). He thus sweeps aside the whole tradition, represented by the Cambridge Platonists and their successors, of Conscience as rational and cognitive in essence. This is again a reflection of his own views and at the same time a tactical move. It is not unorthodox to define Conscience as a feeling, and he has already argued that Utilitarianism is directed towards, and is capable of, producing such a feeling. The true Utilitarian will develop a Christian Conscience.

If the Christian objects that the Utilitarian Conscience is "implanted," whereas the Christian is innate, Mill has an answer. Those who prefer the innate may consider the "regard to the pleasures and pains of others" as the innate feeling which is the essence of Conscience. And this indeed would be orthodox Utilitarianism as well. But acquired moral feelings are just as natural as innate ones. Echoing Burke's "Art is man's nature" (and behind Burke, Aristotle) Mill asserts, "It is natural to man to speak, to reason, to build cities, to cultivate the ground, though these are acquired faculties"; the "moral faculty, if not a part of our nature, is a natural outgrowth from it. . ." (230). Indeed, the Utilitarian philosophy is based upon the naturalness of the social feelings of mankind. If social sentiments were artificial associations, they "might be analysed away" (231). Ultimately, then, the source of the feeling of the obligation is in the Conscience, which is itself a development and cultivation of the natural social feelings. And once again, apart from the elimination of the supernatural, Mill has suggested the compatibility of Utilitarianism and orthodox Christianity. He has also, of course, developed in detail an area of human behaviour and an area of Utilitarian theory neglected by Bentham.

The fourth chapter, "Of what sort of proof the principle of utility is susceptible," has been prepared for in the first chapter. The logic of the argument of this chapter, like that of the previous chapters, is rigorously examined in Professor Dryer's essay (lxxiiiff below). What is important in the context of my argument is the discussion of virtue, which again has the effect of radically modifying the original doctrine, despite Mill's assertion to the contrary. The doctrine, says Mill, maintains "not only that virtue is to be desired, but that it is to be desired disinterestedly, for itself." The Utilitarians "not only place virtue at the very head of the things which are good as means to the ultimate end, but they also recognise as a psychological fact the possibility of its being, to the individual, a good in itself. . . ; and hold, that the mind is not in a right state, . . . not in the state most conducive to the general happiness, unless it does love virtue in this manner..." (235).

This is a very clever, and very carefully composed statement. It gives the appearance of putting Utilitarianism even more on the side of orthodoxy, of recognizing virtue as an end in itself, along with happiness. It would be easy for the orthodox to miss the qualifications. "Actions and dispositions are only virtuous because they promote another end than virtue"—that is, happiness. Once Utilitarians have decided "what *is* virtuous," they then "place virtue at the very head" (235). Would their decisions concerning what is virtuous coincide with the decisions of the orthodox? Is the "virtue" to be desired by the Utilitarians identical with the "virtue" to be pursued by the orthodox Christian? And is there not a difference between accepting virtue as an end in itself, and accepting "as a psychological fact" that it may become "to individuals" an end in itself? In fact, the modifications of Utilitarian doctrine are here more apparent than real. The associationist explanation of how minds come to think of what were originally means to an end as part of the end itself does not affect the real category of virtue. It does, however, by implication, perhaps remind the orthodox that in their own ethical system, virtue was originally a means to salvation, not an end in itself.

The psychological emphasis in this statement about utility and virtue might at first sight seem a digression from the subject of the chapter. It is instead a necessary preparation, for the only "proof" of which the principle of utility is susceptible is psychological. It can be determined only by "practised self-consciousness and self-observation, assisted by observation of others" (237). Examination of the psychological evidence leads Mill to an account, in terms of Hartleian associationism, of the relations of will, desire, and habit. The will to virtue must start by desire and become habitual through education. "Will is the child of desire, and passes out of the dominion of its parent only to come under that of habit" (239). Habit alone imparts certainty in establishing a stable state of the will. The state of the will is a means to good, not intrinsically a good. Hence nothing is a good that is not pleasurable or a means to pleasure or to avoiding pain, and "the principle of utility is proved." Whether the proof induces assent or not, Mill leaves to "the consideration of the thoughtful reader" (239). The kind of thoughtful reader he hoped for is undoubtedly someone like Professor Dryer, whose patient and careful analysis below ought to be read with care. The ordinary reader, less patient and less expert, might well be brought up short by Mill's last paragraphs. After so much movement away from the original pleasure-pain formula, after pleasure had given way to happiness, then to satisfaction, then apparently to the pursuit of virtue, he has suddenly, in the space of one long paragraph, been whirled rapidly through a lecture on the psychology of volition to a Q.E.D. of the original premises. The performance is a *tour de force* that must have had for many readers the baffling fascination of a magician's trick. What is significant for the argument I have been conducting, however, is that in thus coming back full circle Mill is completing his tactical manoeuvre. He is not discarding Bentham and the original statement of the creed; he is giving the old creed its proper interpretation. He began with the formal (and narrow) statement, he elucidated, elaborated, corrected, and defended—now he brings the whole *corpus* of his exposition back to its starting point in the formal enunciation of the doctrine.

The fifth chapter of the essay is, in a sense, an appendix. In choosing "Justice and Utility" as its subject, Mill is able once again to argue that the principle of utility is not a principle of mere expediency. And since the concept of justice is associated with ideas of natural law, of absolute standards, and of the general ethical position implied in the title of Cudworth's treatise, *The Eternal and Immutable Morality*, its discussion permits Mill to argue in detail, as he has argued generally elsewhere, that it is possible to derive from the principle of utility moral standards and rules as satisfactory as those of the intuitionist school. He consequently starts by attacking first the philosophy of innate ideas, and then that of moral sense. First he insists that "intellectual instincts" are no more infallible in judgment than animal instincts are in action (240). Then, turning to the second school, he inquires whether we have a sense of justice, peculiar and immediate like our senses of colour or taste. This inquiry he disposes of by an inductive appeal to the evidence, listing six varied notions of what is just or unjust.

He then proceeds to an analysis of the *feeling* which accompanies the idea of justice, examining on the way concepts of duty, rights, doctrines of punishment, doctrines of just wage, just taxation. The only sure criterion in all these matters is social utility. And justice is "a name for certain classes of moral rules, which concern the essentials of human well-being more nearly, and are therefore of more absolute obligation, than any other rules for the guidance of life. . ."; it is "a name for certain moral requirements, which, regarded collectively, stand higher in the scale of social utility, and are therefore of more paramount obligation, than any others. . ." (255, 259). Justice "is involved in the very meaning of Utility, or the Greatest-Happiness Principle." "Bentham's dictum, 'everybody to count for one, nobody for more than one,' might be written under the principle of utility as an explanatory commentary." (257.)

Two things are significant about the conclusion. One is that Mill repeats the definition of justice three times, with little substantial variation, as if to drive home again and again the two claims, that justice is not only *not* explained away and reduced to expediency by the principle of utility, but that it retains something like absolute status, and that the traditional concept of justice as fair play for all stands at the very heart of the doctrine. The other significant thing is the introduction of Bentham's name and his dictum, so that the pattern of affirming the unity of old creed and new exegesis noted at the end of chapter four is repeated at the end of the whole essay. Bentham is gathered in by name into the fold of the new church.

AUGUSTE COMTE AND POSITIVISM

It is perhaps not too fanciful to see an analogy between Mill's attitude towards Comte and his later attitude towards Bentham, and to see this essay as a further practice of what I have called Mill's new tactics. Indeed the parallel is suggested by his comment at the opening of the essay, that the time has come to express a judgment on Positivism, now that Comte has "displayed a quantity and quality of mental power, and achieved an amount of success, which have not only won but retained the high admiration of thinkers as radically and strenuously opposed as it is possible to be, to nearly the whole of his later tendencies, and to many of his earlier opinions."[21] That Mill himself is one of the thinkers so described the rest of the essay makes evident. "It would have been a mistake," he continues, "had such thinkers busied themselves in the first instance with drawing attention to what they regarded as errors in his great work. Until it had taken the place in the world of thought which belonged to it, the important matter was not to criticise it, but to help in making it known." (264.) These sentences parallel exactly the terms in which he had defined his reasons for adopting the new tactics in dealing with Bentham. And the parallel suggests further that Mill, in seeing the need for the same tactics, sees at least something of the same relationship between Comte and Positivism as he had seen between Bentham and Utilitarianism: namely, a valid and important doctrine harmed in its definition and interpretation by the limitations of its proponent. And since Mill is not likely to extend these protective tactics to doctrines opposed to Utilitarianism, it also appears that he sees in Utilitarianism and Positivism a common cause.

This he soon makes fully explicit. He defines the "fundamental doctrine" of Positivism in very broad terms: "We have no knowledge of anything but Phaenomena; and our knowledge of phaenomena is relative, not absolute. We know not the essence, nor the real mode of production, of any fact, but only its relations to other facts in the way of succession or of similitude. These relations are constant. . . . The constant resemblances . . . and the constant sequences . . . are termed their laws. The laws of phaenomena are all we know respecting them." (265.) Only through these laws can we predict, and in some cases, control effects. This general statement of empiricism Mill easily identifies with the scientific mode of philosophy, imperfectly but partly grasped by Bacon and Descartes, fully by Newton, Hume, and Thomas Brown; and "the same great truth formed the groundwork of all the speculative philosophy of Bentham, and pre-eminently of James Mill. . . ." "The philosophy called Positive is not a recent invention of M. Comte, but a simple adherence to the traditions of all the great scientific minds whose discoveries have made the human race what it is." (267.)

Comte thus joins Bentham (and James Mill) as an apostle of the true philosophy, and an opponent of the Theological and Metaphysical—or, as Mill prefers to put it, a supporter of the Phaenomenal and Experiential philosophy against the "Personal, or Volitional explanation of facts" and the "Abstractional or Ontological" (267). Comte "has taken his place in a fight long since engaged, and on the side already in the main victorious." He is on the side of the Nominalists against the Realists, of the Rationalists against the Voluntarists, the latter conflict being here defined in secular

[21]*Auguste Comte and Positivism*, 263 below. Subsequent references are to the present edition, and are given in parentheses.

terms. Like Montesquieu, "even Macchiavelli," Adam Smith "and the political economists universally," Bentham "and all thinkers initiated by him," Comte believes that "social phaenomena conform to invariable laws," as do the phaenomena of Nature. He rejects "the whole system of ideas connected with supernatural agency," and like Mill, sees the doctrine of Voluntarism as stemming from ignorance. "No one, probably," Mill scoffingly remarks, "ever believed that the will of a god kept parallel lines from meeting, or made two and two equal to four; or ever prayed to the gods to make the square of the hypothenuse equal to more or less than the sum of the squares of the sides." "In the case of phaenomena which science has not yet taught us either to foresee or to control, the theological mode of thought [that is, the Voluntarist] has not ceased to operate: men still pray for rain, or for success in war, or to avert a shipwreck or a pestilence, but not to put back the stars in their courses, . . . or to arrest the tides." (288.) Like Bentham, Comte rejects the whole philosophy of law based on "the imaginary law of the imaginary being Nature," along with divine rights and Natural Rights (299). In brief, Comte is, insofar as he expresses the fundamental principle of Positivism, a good Utilitarian, and conversely, Utilitarians are good Positivists. "All theories in which the ultimate standard of institutions and rules of action was the happiness of mankind, and observation and experience the guides . . . are entitled to the name Positive, whatever, in other respects, their imperfections may be" (299). As we have seen, they are also entitled, with the same qualification, to the name Utilitarian.

Granted this move towards identifying the two doctrines in their fundamental principles, it is with no surprise that we discover that "M. Comte has got hold of half the truth. . ." (313). But by this time, the other half is not in the possession of Coleridgians or Kantians. Whatever weight Mill may have given in 1838 and 1840 to the notion of a synthesis of doctrinal thesis and antithesis, that notion has now been superseded by the progressive hierarchy of Comte.[22] Theological thought yields to Metaphysical, Metaphysical to Positive. The whole tradition of Germano-Coleridgian thought is now relegated to the Metaphysical. The half of truth M. Comte has not got is to be found, not there, but in "the so-called liberal or revolutionary school." As in the earlier case of Bentham and Coleridge, and of the two traditions they represent, "each sees what the other does not see, and seeing it exclusively, draws consequences from it which to the other appear mischievously absurd" (313). The near-identity of phrasing makes more emphatic the radical change of reference. The two halves of truth now belong both within the same fundamental philosophic tradition.

To the extent to which Comte is an enemy of "the whole *a priori* philosophy, in morals, jurisprudence, psychology, logic," and on the side of "obser-

[22]Cf. xx–xxi, xxix above.

vation and experiment" (300), he is, if not thoroughly Utilitarian, at least a valuable ally. In some respects (but only some), he is a sounder ally than Herbert Spencer or G. H. Lewes, both of whom fall back on *a priori* logic for their "ultimate test of truth" in "the inconceivability of its negative" (301). It is the total and radical nature of Comte's rejection of "the metaphysical mode of thought" that seems to constitute his main claim to Mill's praise (301). When the rigorous principle is applied, for example, to Bentham's conception of social science, it leads Comte to the same conclusions as Mill had been led to earlier: that to start from "universal laws of human nature" and draw deductions from them is fallacious, because "as society proceeds in its development, its phaenomena are determined, more and more, not by the simple tendencies of universal human nature, but by the accumulated influence of past generations over the present. The human beings themselves, on the laws of whose nature the facts of history depend, are not abstract or universal but historical human beings, already shaped, and made what they are, by human society. This being the case, no powers of deduction could enable any one, starting from the mere conception of the Being Man, placed in a world such as the earth may have been before the commencement of human agency, to predict and calculate the phaenomena of his development. . . ." Facts of history must be "empirically considered" (307).[23]

Comte is, indeed, superior to Bentham in the greater rigour of his insistence on the empirical and inductive. "All political truth he deems strictly relative, implying as its correlative a given state or situation of society" (323). In thus emphasizing the importance of history as the body of social phaenomena from which the social scientist draws his conclusions by induction, Comte makes his greatest contribution. He is at his most striking in his long survey of universal history. This survey is concerned with "the main stream of human progress, looking only at the races and nations that led the van. . . . His object is to characterize truly, though generally, the successive states of society through which the advanced guard of our species has passed, and the filiation of these states on one another—how each grew out of the preceding and was the parent of the following state." (318.) As Mill's phrases, "led the van" and "advanced guard," indicate, his approval of Comte as historian attaches to his philosophy of history as a doctrine of progress, his rôle as a new and more thorough Condorcet, more than to any really scientific quality in his historiography. Since Mill's own Utilitarianism is strongly progressive, he welcomes the presentation of a mass of historical evidence, admittedly selective rather than truly "universal," which offers inductive and empirical support for the "fact" of progress.

There is no doubt that Mill finds Comte's analysis, in general terms,

[23]Probably Mill is here recalling not only Coleridge's influence on him, but also Macaulay's criticism of James Mill's *Essay on Government*.

sound. He also praises the nice balance Comte observes between treating history (as Carlyle does) in terms of the influence of individuals, and treating it in terms solely of general causes. He is not unjust to the past, seeing (as Condorcet and Godwin had before him, though Mill does not note this) "in all past modes of thought and forms of society . . . a useful, in many a necessary, office, in carrying mankind through one stage of improvement into a higher." He avoids the error of regarding the intellectual "as the only progressive element in man, and the moral as too much the same at all times to affect even the annual average of crime" (322–3). He links, in short, intellectual to moral progress. Nor does Comte think of moral progress as dependent solely on intellectual improvement. "He not only personally appreciates, but rates high in moral value, the creations of poets and artists in all departments, deeming them, by their mixed appeal to the sentiments and the understanding, admirably fitted to educate the feelings of abstract thinkers, and enlarge the intellectual horizon of people of the world" (324). Once again we hear unvoiced echoes of Mill's view of Bentham and his limitations, from some of which at least Comte is free.

But at the same time, the balance must not be allowed to tip too far in reaction. Comte is not so far from Bentham as to hand over progress to the poets and artists. He does indeed, like Bentham, insist that "the main agent in the progress of mankind is their intellectual development," and while it is true that the passions are "a more energetic power than a mere intellectual conviction," the passions "tend to divide, not to unite, mankind." "It is only by a common belief that passions are brought to work together, and become a collective force. . . ." The passions are the gale, but Reason must be the compass. "All human society," as Godwin had argued, "is grounded on a system of fundamental opinions, which only the speculative faculty can provide," and which only improvement of the speculative faculty can improve (316). Herbert Spencer is wrong in asserting that "ideas do not govern and overthrow the world; the world is governed or overthrown by feelings, to which ideas serve only as guides." That is, he is wrong if he thinks this a refutation of Comte. The sentiments "are only a social force at all, through the definite direction given to them by . . . some . . . intellectual conviction," and the sentiments do not of themselves "spontaneously throw up" convictions (317). "To say that men's intellectual beliefs do not determine their conduct, is like saying that the ship is moved by the steam and not by the steersman" (317).

In many respects, then, Comte can be praised as another apostle of the true faith, a true Utilitarian in his fundamental principles, and free of some of the limitations of personality and of intellectual equipment which so narrowed Bentham. But his own limitations are more disastrous than Bentham's.

Even in the earlier work with which the first part of Mill's essay deals, the *Cours de Philosophie Positive*, there is much that arouses Mill's strong disapproval. In the first place, Comte's psychology is inadequate. He gives psychology as a science no place in his classification, and "always speaks of it with contempt." He reduces it, in fact, to a branch of physiology, totally rejecting introspection, or "psychological observation properly so called . . . internal consciousness." As Mill dryly observes, "How we are to observe other people's mental operations, or how interpret the signs of them without having learnt what the signs mean by knowledge of ourselves, he does not state" (296). Comte relies, as "Organon for the study of 'the moral and intellectual functions' " on Phrenology, which, says Mill, is in process of becoming discredited as a science. Moreover, it tends to be entirely meaningless unless related to a psychology of association. Comte shows no knowledge, and makes no use, of the work of Hartley, Brown, and James Mill. The real scientific development of psychology has been made by Bain and Herbert Spencer. Comte's failure to take psychology seriously as a mental science is not a "mere hiatus" in his system, but "the parent of serious errors in his attempt to create a Social Science" (298).

Probably even more culpable, from Mill's point of view, are some of Comte's political attitudes, his reliance on authority, his eagerness to commit power to single persons or small groups, his rejection, not only of popular sovereignty, but of any principle of responsibility. It is not only that Comte runs foul of most of Mill's fundamental political principles, and those of the Utilitarians generally, but also of the ethical attitudes underlying them. "No one to count as more than one" is an axiom at the heart of the Utilitarian ethic. Further, Mill is clearly shocked to find that Comte relegates to the "metaphysical," and hence to oblivion, "the first of all the articles of the liberal creed, 'the absolute right of free examination, or the dogma of unlimited liberty of conscience.' " Comte accepts the *legal* right, but "resolutely denies" the *moral* right (301). On a strict Utilitarian basis, of course, Comte is quite correct, and Mill himself would found an absolute right not on natural rights but on permanent utility. But he is pushed here, as in *On Liberty*, away from Utilitarian relativism into something like "metaphysical" absolutism, for fear, as he says, of the use to be made of the contrary doctrine. And although Comte by no means wishes "intellectual dominion to be exercised over an ignorant people," and is as strong an advocate of popular education as any Utilitarian, viewing the possibilities of such education with a "startling" optimism, his scheme to have a "salutary ascendency over opinion" exercised by an *organized* body of "the most eminent thinkers" makes Mill decidedly nervous (314). So does Comte's dismissal of the whole revolutionary and liberal set of ideas as "metaphysical" and merely negative, and consequently as a serious impediment to the reorganization of society (301). Mill himself had insisted on the negative nature of eighteenth-century revolutionary thought, and the aberration of Rousseau in trying to found a positive philosophy of government on negation, but again he senses the presence of dangerous conclusions and applications. Though there is truth in what Comte says, Mill feels like the man "who being asked whether he admitted that six and five make eleven, refused to give an answer until he knew what use was to be made of it" (302).

Underlying his misgivings about the use Comte wishes to make of these ideas is his lively distrust of the whole programme for the future of society Comte seems to envisage. On the "statical" side of social phænomena, the laws of social existence "considered abstractedly from progress," Comte is relatively satisfactory. On the "dynamical" side, that of social progress, the laws of the evolution of the social state, he is at his weakest, trite and often invalid (309). For Mill, of course, the "statical" is important as a preliminary to the "dynamical"; his real concern is with the means of ensuring the progress of society and of man in society. Comte's means seem to him totally wrong.

Apart from the ideas we have been examining, there is much in the first part of the essay on Comte with which we need not concern ourselves here. The very interesting sections in which Mill discusses and criticizes Comte's classification of the sciences, his philosophy of science, the Organon of Discovery and the Organon of Proof, the difference between Laws and Causes, and so on, are important in other contexts. Our concern has been with the ethical, and with the political insofar as it touches the ethical.

In part two of the essay, as Mill turns to Comte's later writings, the balance of praise and blame shifts radically. None the less, the Religion of Humanity can be made to coincide in its essentials, as Mill sees them, with the essential ethical basis of Utilitarianism, and Comte can remain in some sense a high priest of the true creed. "The power which may be acquired over the mind by the idea of the general interest of the human race, both as a source of emotion and as a motive to conduct, many have perceived; but we know not if anyone, before M. Comte, realized so fully as he has done, all the majesty of which that idea is susceptible." "We, therefore, not only hold that M. Comte was justified in the attempt to develop his philosophy into a religion, and had realized the essential conditions of one, but that all other religions are made better in proportion as, in their practical result, they are brought to coincide with that which he aimed at constructing." (334–5.)

But if Comte is right in general principle, he is often wrong in interpretation and application. He falls into the error often charged against the Utilitarian moralists, in requiring "that the test of conduct should also be the exclusive motive to it" (335). And in his enthusiasm for loving one's neighbour, he insists on conscious suppression of all self-regarding actions. If he merely meant "that egoism is bound, and should be taught, always to give way to the well-understood interests of enlarged altruism," no one could object, least of all Mill. But his naïve phrenology, combined with a biological theory of organic growth or atrophy through use or disuse, leads him to something like the old ascetic mortification of the flesh (335).

Mill sees in this tendency a symptom of a general trend in Comte's thought which underlies many of his errors, a tendency to accept as axiomatic "that all perfection consists in unity." "Why is it necessary," asks Mill, "that all human life should point but to one object, and be cultivated into a system of means to a single end? May it not be the fact that mankind, who after all are made up of single human beings, obtain a greater sum of happiness when each pursues his own, under the rules and conditions required by the good of the rest, than when each makes the good of the rest his only subject. . . ?" (337.) Comte's passion for "unity" and "systematization" leads not only to a denial of the value Mill places upon variety, but to a system of compulsion towards uniformity. In Halévy's terms, Comte plans the "artificial identification of interests," while Mill believes in the "natural identification of interests," as his words above indicate.

The "mania for regulation" by which Comte seems obsessed appears in full development in the *cultus* of the Religion of Humanity. The elaborate provision of ceremony, ritual, and doctrine strikes Mill, of course, as an unseemly imitation of Roman Catholicism. Earlier in the essay, in discussing Comte's treatment of history, Mill had remarked that Comte had no understanding of Protestantism (321). It is equally evident that Mill has no understanding of Catholicism. It is interesting to recall how many writers, in the period from the French Revolution on into the nineteenth century, either from a conviction that Christianity ought to be destroyed, or from a belief that the Enlightenment had in fact virtually destroyed it, urge the creation of a new religion to supply the social need once filled by Christianity. And it is important to note how their conceptions differ as to what religion is, how it functions in society, and particularly how it serves as a social bond. The English Protestants define religion in terms of feeling, and of ethical attitudes. Arnold can thus express the hope that poetry can take over the task formerly performed by religion.[24] Their emphasis is wholly on the individual, and the inner sentiments; they do not think at all in terms of any need of a corporate church, of corporate worship, of external ritual or sacraments. The Continental Catholics, on the contrary, think mainly in these terms, of

---

[24]Cf. John M. Robson, *The Improvement of Mankind: The Social and Political Thought of John Stuart Mill* (Toronto: University of Toronto Press, 1968), 122n: "Bain reports, without noticeable sympathy, that Mill 'seemed to look upon Poetry as a Religion, or rather as Religion and Philosophy in one.' "

religion as a corporate public act, of communal participation in ritual, of public symbols and festivals. The whole contrast is pointed up by Mill's rather astonished comment that Comte proposes prayers and devotional practices, not because the individual's "feelings require them, but for the premeditated purpose of getting his feelings up" (343). If Mill understands, as he undoubtedly does, some aspects of human psychology much better than Comte, it is also true that Comte understands others better than Mill.

The contrast is not simply that of Protestant and Catholic views of religion, however. There is also a contrast in their views of the primary need religion must fulfil for society. Just as Mill and Arnold differ in their diagnoses of English society, Mill fearing an excessive unity and uniformity, Arnold fearing an excess of individuality leading to moral and social anarchy, so Mill and Comte differ. Comte observes that in the pre-Positivist stage of society "the free development of our forces of all kinds was the important matter." Now, "the principal need is to regulate them." From this doctrine, Mill expresses his "entire dissent." He sees in Comte's scheme "an elaborate system for the total suppression of all independent thought." It seems obvious that Comte is concerned about the instability of the French society, about what he sees as the continuing effects of the negative and destructive forces of the Revolution. He sees the intellectuals as "desiring only to prolong the existing scepticism and intellectual anarchy," and as "rootedly hostile to the construction of the new" religious and social order (351–2). He has no faith in popular rule: "Election of superiors by inferiors, except as a revolutionary expedient, is an abomination in his sight." He has only "detestation and contempt" for "parliamentary or representative institutions in any form," and for a system in which the executive is responsible to an elected body (344). But Mill turns no attention to the national and historical context of Comte's project. And for this he has a double justification. Comte himself is presenting his system not in historical and relativist, but in absolute terms, taking the French situation as universal for the Positive period of history.[25] Moreover, for Mill there is no historical situation in any country in the mid-nineteenth century for which Comte's system would be valid.

There is no need here, nor would it be appropriate, to discuss all the interesting ideas in the essay. Mill's comments on the rôle of women, on Comte's views of the family and of marriage, on proper wages for workmen, on the idle rich, on "useful" knowledge, on Comte's system of education, on his limitation of books, provide links to a wide range of his writings. One curious note is that where Comte puts forward ideas which are "Positivist" in a twentieth-century sense, Mill sometimes disagrees. When Comte says,

[25]Here one recalls Mill's criticism of Bentham's propensity to legislate for all mankind, regardless of the implications of the title of his *Influence of Time and Place in Matters of Legislation*.

for example, that the scientist's concern with "complete proof," and a "perfect rationalization of scientific processes" is mere pedantry, and it "ought to be enough that the doctrines afford an explanation of phaenomena, consistent with itself and with known facts, and that the processes are justified by their fruits" (356). Mill disapproves, although he praises the comment "that the infinitesimal calculus is a conception analogous to the corpuscular hypothesis in physics; which last M. Comte has always considered as a logical artifice; not an opinion respecting matters of fact" (365).

The essay closes, in conformity with Mill's tactics, after so much devastating criticism, with high praise. Comte, like Descartes and Leibniz, whom he most resembles, has an "extraordinary power of concatenation and co-ordination," and has "enriched human knowledge with great truths and great conceptions of method." He is, in fact, greater than his predecessors, "not intrinsically, yet by the exertion of equal intellectual power in a more advanced state of human preparation" (368). His absurdities appear more ridiculous than theirs because our age is less tolerant of palpable absurdities.

The "concatenation and co-ordination" clearly refer to the sweeping view of history as a record of human progress. The "great truths and great conceptions of method" must apply, not to the "systematization, systematization, systematization," but to the fundamental Positivist principles, so closely identified with the Utilitarian, and to the scientific method, the use of history in search of generalizations and "laws" of human behaviour which Mill himself advocates.[26] Comte emerges finally, then, as a high priest of Utilitarianism and of the Religion of Humanity, misled into becoming High Priest and Pontiff of his absurd *cultus*.

THREE ESSAYS ON RELIGION

The essays which Helen Taylor published after Mill's death as *Three Essays on Religion*, present, as she points out in her Introductory Notice, his "deliberate and exhaustive treatment of the topics under consideration." She also notes that although the first two, on Nature and on the Utility of Religion, were written between 1850 and 1858, while the third, on Theism, was not written until between 1868 and 1870, Mill certainly "considered the opinions expressed in these different Essays, as fundamentally consistent," and "his manner of thinking had undergone no substantial change."[27] Indeed, the various allusions to religious thought in his earliest ethical writings, the treatment of religious ideas in *On Liberty*, and in *Auguste Comte and Positivism*,

---

[26]See especially Mill's *Logic*, Book VI, Chap. x, "Of the Inverse Deductive, or Historical Method."

[27]*Three Essays on Religion*, 371–2 below. Subsequent references are to the present edition, and are given in parentheses.

all suggest that Mill's opinions on what his orthodox contemporaries meant by religion, both revealed and natural, stayed virtually constant throughout his mature career. All that changed was the openness and explicitness of his attack.

The fundamentals of his position have already been made clear. His thinking is firmly rooted in empiricism; his whole concept of truth is strongly defined by the "canons of induction"—truth is what can be proved by induction from empirical experience. His concept of a true religion is consequently of a religion of naturalism, as opposed to one of supernaturalism, a religion of the this-worldly as opposed to one of the other-worldly. The sort of religion he can approve of he finds in Comte's Religion of Humanity. The ethical system dependent on this religion is the Utilitarian. And finally, he sees this religion as an instrument of progress, of an emergent ethical evolution. These simple attitudes, which underlie all his comments on religion, provide the basic points of reference for the more elaborate treatment in the three essays.

The essay "The Utility of Religion" is directed towards persuading the reader that all the needs, both of society and of the individual, commonly thought of as satisfied by orthodox religion, can be fully satisfied without it, and that in fact the effects ascribed to religion have been due, not to religion itself, but to the force of opinion. Religious authority, by being in control of opinion and of education, has received credit for the support of the virtues, and for the instilling of them in the young, but Mill insists that the results of control by religious authority in no way differ from the results obtainable by essentially secular control: "early religious teaching has owed its power over mankind rather to its being early than to its being religious" (410). As to the sanctions religion lends to morality through its system of eternal rewards and punishments, morality needs no supernatural sanctions: moral truths are strong enough in their own evidence to retain the belief of mankind when once they have acquired it. Moreover, an application of Bentham's calculus reinforces the impressions gained by observation that even infinite rewards and punishments postponed to the after life and never witnessed have little effect on ordinary minds. The real sanctions come from public opinion and the passions affected by it: "the love of glory; the love of praise; the love of admiration; the love of respect and deference; even the love of sympathy. . . ." "The fear of shame, the dread of ill repute or of being disliked or hated, are the direct and simple forms of its deterring power." "Belief, then, in the supernatural . . . cannot be considered to be any longer required, either for enabling us to know what is right and wrong in social morality, or for supplying us with motives to do right and to abstain from wrong." (417.) Cannot an ethical system for both society and the individual, then, be purely secular? Cannot the public and private morality be imposed merely by the power of education and public opinion, in the tradition of Utilitarianism? What need is there of a substitute Religion of Humanity to replace the old supernatural religion?

Once again, as Mill proceeds to answer these questions (which he does not explicitly ask) our thoughts revert to the *Autobiography* and the description of the crisis of his youth. "Religion and poetry," he now writes, "address themselves, at least in one of their aspects, to the same part of the human constitution: they both supply the same want, that of ideal conceptions grander and more beautiful than we see realized in the prose of human life. Religion, as distinguished from poetry, is the product of the craving to know whether these imaginative conceptions have realities answering to them in some other world than ours." Religion adds to "the poetry of the supernatural" a positive belief which unpoetical minds can share with the poetical. It satisfies the craving for "the better which is suggested" by the good partially seen and known on earth, the craving for "higher things." The question for Mill is not whether this "poetry of the supernatural" is valuable: he readily acknowledges that it meets an important psychological need—but whether it has to be connected with the supernatural. Is it necessary, he asks, "to travel beyond the boundaries of the world which we inhabit" to obtain this good, or is "the idealization of our earthly life, the cultivation of a high conception of what *it* may be made . . . not capable of supplying a poetry, and, in the best sense of the word, a religion, equally fitted to exalt the feelings, and (with the same aid from education) still better calculated to ennoble the conduct, than any belief respecting the unseen powers" (420).

Such a religion can even offer, in terms of the human species, the aspirations appropriate to immortality and, in conjunction with a faith in progress, an earthly Paradise: "if individual life is short, the life of the human species is not short; its indefinite duration is practically equivalent to endlessness; and being combined with indefinite capability of improvement, it offers to the imagination and sympathies a large enough object to satisfy any reasonable demand for grandeur of aspiration" (420). Once man has abandoned the "baseless fancies" of supernatural immortality, his mind will expand into new dimensions at thoughts of the Grand Etre and its limitless future. When it has expanded from love of country to love of the world, as it can be made to expand by proper training, the universal morality will be the Utilitarian:

A morality grounded on large and wise views of the good of the whole, neither sacrificing the individual to the aggregate nor the aggregate to the individual, but giving to duty on the one hand and to freedom and spontaneity on the other their proper province, would derive its power in the superior natures from sympathy and benevolence and the passion for ideal excellence: in the inferior, from the same feelings cultivated up to the measure of their capacity, with the superadded force of shame. . . . A support in moments of weakness would not be a problematical future existence, but the approbation . . . of those whom we respect, and ideally of all those, dead or living, whom we admire or venerate. . . . To call these sentiments by the name morality . . . is claiming too little for them. They are a real religion. . . . (422.)

Here is undoubtedly Mill's lasting confession of faith. The Religion of Humanity fulfils all the conditions he demands: "The essence of religion is the strong and earnest direction of the emotions and desires towards an ideal object, recognized as of the highest excellence, and as rightfully paramount over all selfish objects of desire" (422). It fulfils them for him much more satisfactorily than orthodox (or unorthodox) Christianity.

Given an understanding of Mill's religious position, and of the principles on which it is based, the long essay on Theism offers the reader no surprises. There can in fact be few works of Mill's which show so little originality. Any reader familiar with nineteenth-century writings on religion will find himself constantly recalling other expressions of the same views. Much of the essay could as readily have been written by Huxley. The elaborate attack on *a priori* and *a posteriori* "proofs" of the Being and Attributes of God, carrying one's mind back to Samuel Clarke and the eighteenth century, seems quaintly old-fashioned, especially when the *a priori* is so easily dismissed as "unscientific" (434). The most entertaining passages are those which exhibit the full savagery of Mill's combative style, such as the one in Part II on man's God-given potentialities for development: "It is to suppose that God could not, in the first instance, create anything better than a Bosjeman or an Andaman islander, or something still lower; and yet was able to endow the Bosjeman or the Andaman islander with the power of raising himself into a Newton or a Fénelon. We certainly do not know the nature of the barriers which limit the divine omnipotence; but it is a very odd notion of them that they enable the Deity to confer on an almost bestial creature the power of producing by a succession of efforts what God himself had no other means of creating." (459.) Or again, in Part III, on God's being either unable or unwilling to grant our desires: "Many a man would like to be a Croesus or an Augustus Caesar, but has his wishes gratified only to the moderate extent of a pound a week or the Secretaryship of his Trades Union" (466). The writing is often as lively as Mill's best, even where the ideas are commonplace.

The criticism of Hume's essay on miracles in Part IV (471), the remarks on brain and mind and the warning against "giving *à priori* validity to the conclusions of an *à posteriori* philosophy" in Part III (461) are of interest as examples either of Mill's wish to be fair, or of his insistence on precise argument. But perhaps the most interesting part for its content is the final one, in which, like Tennyson and Browning, Mill asserts the value of imaginative aspirations, of hope, and of "cleaving to the sunnier side of doubt," as Tennyson puts it. One senses again here that other side of Mill, responding in something like poetic terms to the realities of the human situation and of human psychology. "To me it seems that human life, small and confined as it is, and as, considered merely in the present, it is likely to remain even when the progress of material and moral improvement may have freed it from the greater part of its present calamities, stands greatly in need of any wider range and greater height of aspiration for itself and its destination, which the exercise of imagination can yield to it without running counter to the evidence of fact . . ." (483). Or, as Arnold put it, "men have such need of joy! But joy whose grounds are true. . . ."[28]

Again, when Mill praises "the tendency, either from constitution or habit, to dwell chiefly on the brighter side both of the present and of the future," noting that "a hopeful disposition gives a spur to the faculties and keeps all the active energies in good working order," or when he observes that it is not necessary "for keeping up our conviction that we must die, that we should be always brooding over death," that we should not "think perpetually of death, but . . . of our duties, and of the rule of life" (484), we seem to be listening to Tennyson's Ancient Sage. When "the reason is strongly culti-vated, the imagination may safely follow its own end, and do its best to make life pleasant and lovely inside the castle, in reliance on the fortifications raised and maintained by Reason round the outward bounds." The "indulgence of hope with regard to the government of the universe and the destiny of man after death . . . is legitimate and philosophically defensible." Such a hope "makes life and human nature a far greater thing to the feelings, and gives greater strength as well as greater solemnity to all the sentiments which are awakened in us by our fellow-creatures and by mankind at large" (485). Throughout this last section, Mill emphasizes the importance of the imagina-tion, not to supplant reason, but to supplement it. Ultimately it is this addition of imagination to reason, of poetry to fact, which constitutes religion, espe-cially "that real, though purely human religion, which sometimes calls itself the Religion of Humanity and sometimes that of Duty" (488).

Although there are clear connections between the essay "Nature" and the other two essays on religion, it does not fit simply into the pattern I have been tracing, nor are the issues it discusses all related simply or exclusively to Mill's religious thought. For some classes of reader, it will be by far the most interesting of the three essays. For students of literature concerned with the development of Romanticism, for example, it will be an important document.

It is easy to recognize in the essay a number of distinct, though related, themes. The words "nature" and "natural" have become a source, says Mill, of "false taste, false philosophy, false morality, and even bad law" (373).

[28]Matthew Arnold, "Obermann Once More," ll.237–8.

The last term, recalling Bentham's attacks on the concept of Natural Law, points up the first theme: an attack on "the great *à priori* fallacies," which are to be exposed here, as the list suggests, in aesthetic theory, in philosophy, and in moral philosophy (383). The attack involves the rejection of Nature as an aesthetic norm, and of Nature as an ethical norm, and the repudiation generally of the injunction to "follow Nature." Since these "*à priori* fallacies," including the establishing of Nature as a norm, are based upon what Mill sees as a false metaphysical view of Nature, the first step is to correct this view. The "Nature" of a thing is simply "its entire capacity of exhibiting phenomena." "Nature in the abstract is the aggregate of the powers and pro- perties of all things. Nature means the sum of all phenomena, together with the causes which produce them. . . ." (374.) There is no justification for opposing Nature and Art, "Art is as much Nature as anything else . . . ; Art is but the employment of the powers of Nature for an end" (375). In this purely empirical sense, everything is Nature, and everything must conform to Nature, Nature being simply what *is*.

But there is another sense in which Nature means phaenomena not caused by man, and in this sense a distinction can be made between Nature and Art. In this case, says Mill, the artificial is an improvement; man controls Nature to improve it. "If the artificial is not better than the natural, to what end are all the arts of life?" "All praise of Civilization, or Art, or Contrivance, is so much dispraise of Nature. . . ." (381.) So also in the ethical sphere. Cruelty is as natural as benevolence, and "the most criminal actions are to a being like man, not more unnatural than most of the virtues." "There is hardly a bad action ever perpetrated which is not perfectly natural, and the motives to which are not perfectly natural feelings." (401.) The moral man is, like the carefully tilled garden, a work of Art, not of Nature. "This artificially created or at least artificially perfected nature of the best and noblest human beings, is the only nature which it is ever commendable to follow" (396–7).

The setting up of Civilization in opposition to Nature, and the allusion to the "artificially perfected nature" of the best human beings point up the exact object of Mill's attack. In the conflict between the competing Romantic doctrines of primitivism and progress, Mill is on the side of progress. He is particularly antagonistic towards the sentimental Romantic primitivism which exalts the natural instincts. "Savages are always liars," he remarks (395). The sentiment of justice is wholly artificial in origin. No virtues are natural to man, merely a capacity for acquiring them (and also for acquiring vices). It is the duty of man to amend nature, including his own.

The notion of Nature as a norm is not, however, solely associated with or derived from primitivism. It is also part of Deist optimism, of the natural theology Mill attacks in the essay "Theism." For the astro- and physicotheologians, Nature exhibited not merely a physical order, but an ethical one. But, asks Mill, "how stands the fact? That next to the greatness of these cosmic forces, the quality which most forcibly strikes every one who does not avert his eyes from it is their perfect and absolute recklessness." Nature is totally amoral. "All which people are accustomed to deprecate as 'disorder' and its consequences, is precisely a counterpart of Nature's ways." "If imitation of the Creator's will as revealed in nature, were applied as a rule of action . . . ; the most atrocious enormities of the worst men would be more than justified by the apparent intention of Providence that throughout all animated nature the strong should prey upon the weak." Since Nature has no right or wrong, "Conformity to nature, has no connection whatever with right and wrong" (400).

The attack on the natural theologians links this essay with the essay on Theism, and the doctrine put forward in that essay, that the state of the natural world is compatible with a theory of a wise and benevolent, but not an omnipotent Creator, is put forward here, with an interesting reference to Leibniz. Much of the argument on the evidence offered by Nature for *a posteriori* discovery of the divine attributes parallels the more formal argument of the later essay on Theism. But there is much more looking backward to the eighteenth century and its controversies here; the essay on Theism, although it glances back occasionally, is solidly fixed in the world of Darwin and of the Higher Criticism.

Finally, it is possible to see in the essay on Nature a further significance. From the time of Helvetius and the early French Utilitarians, the taint of "naturalism" had clung to the doctrine. In its most narrowly rigorous form, it insisted that the sole absolute good was pleasure, the sole absolute evil, pain. It reduced motivation to the natural instinct to seek pleasure and avoid pain. In referring everything in ethics and in politics to these irreducible natural elements, and explaining everything in terms of primary natural instincts, it was not indeed setting up the natural as a norm, as the pattern of what ought to be. But it was setting up the natural as the pattern of what has to be, of what is and is inescapable. Moreover, in finding the origins of normative ideas, of ideals of value, in the purely natural, it attacked the validity usually ascribed to them. Those opponents who saw in the Helvetian doctrine a system of hedonist, egoist naturalism had some good reasons for their judgment. And it is a short step from proclaiming the inevitability of the natural to accepting it as the norm. If it is inevitably natural for dogs to bark and bite, then let them delight to do so. The natural becomes the right.

The "naturalistic" fallacy can then, and historically does, become part not only of the metaphysical views of Nature associated with Shaftesburian deists, neo-classical literary critics and pre-Romantic primitivism, but also of narrowly empirical Utilitarians. And since the Utilitarians tend to be "naturalistic" in the other sense of rejecting the supernatural and the "metaphysical," the "naturalism" ascribed to them is seen as of the most opprobrious sort. As we have seen, Mill is constantly aware of the need to break the association of Utilitarianism with the tradition of Helvetius' pattern. The essay on Nature, in defining precisely his attitude towards Nature and the natural, and the relation of the natural to the ethical norms of Utilitarianism, is Mill's main reply to those who still think of Utilitarianism in the old terms of the "naturalistic" fallacy.

University of Toronto

F.E.L.P.

Mill's Utilitarianism

THE MAJORITY of serious students of ethics today are utilitarians, and those who are not see utilitarianism as the chief position in need of amendment. John Stuart Mill's writings on ethics, and especially on utilitarianism, are thus of vital contemporary interest and importance. More than any other thinker, Mill is responsible for laying down the principal directions ethics has taken since his day. He did not, however, embody his full views in any single volume or one set of writings, and the main lines in ethics which he sketched were worked out in detail only after his death by Henry Sidgwick. A generation later, G. E. Moore sought to refine upon Sidgwick's results, and subsequent ethical theory has taken Moore's work as its starting point.

The most complete guide to undertaking a detailed examination of Mill's ethical views is his *Utilitarianism,* and so I have used it as the basis of this introductory essay. His other essays on ethics are valuable as supplements to the opinions he puts forward in this work, and they are referred to where appropriate. Five main topics have been selected for detailed treatment in the discussion that follows. The first section sorts out some of Mill's more important principles. Section II examines his dictum that the sole evidence that anything is desirable is that people desire it. In the third, consideration is given to what Mill holds that this evidence discloses. Section IV deals with Mill's analysis of moral concepts. The discussion concludes with an examination of his views on the use of the principle of utility.

I. THE PRINCIPLE OF UTILITY

Mill writes, "happiness is the sole end of human action, and the promotion of it the test by which to judge of all human conduct. . . ."[1] He also makes it clear that the test is its promotion of happiness "to the greatest extent possible" (214). By such conduct Mill does not mean that which would promote happiness to the greatest extent conceivable, but that which would promote it to a greater extent than would any alternative. Mill also makes it

[1] *Utilitarianism,* 237. Subsequent references are to the present edition of *Utilitarianism,* and are given in parenthesis.

clear that when he speaks of the promotion of happiness as "the test by which to judge of all human conduct," the aspect of conduct of which he means that it is a test is whether it should be done.[2] He thus holds that the test of whether something should be done is whether it would promote more happiness than would any alternative to it. Mill implies that if an action would satisfy this test, it should be done, and that if it would not, it is not one that should be done. Accordingly, the main principle which Mill maintains is that something should be done if and only if it would cause more happiness than would any alternative, and that something should not be done if and only if it would fail to cause as much happiness as would some alternative.

The chief support Mill offers for this principle is that "happiness is desirable, and the only thing desirable, as an end. . ." (234). He distinguishes things desirable as a means and things desirable for their own sake. What is desirable for its own sake he speaks of as desirable as an end. He argues that it is because happiness is the only thing desirable for its own sake that the test of conduct generally is its promotion of happiness. The principle he employs in taking this step is that if there is one sort of thing which is alone desirable for its own sake, then the promotion of it is the test of all human conduct. By test of human conduct he means test of what should be done. An action is then one that should be done if and only if it satisfies this test. Mill thus takes it for granted that something should be done if and only if its consequences would be more desirable than would those of any alternative to it.

From his main principle in turn Mill draws a conclusion about what it would be right to do and what it would be wrong to do. The question of whether it would be right or wrong to do a certain action is a question about its morality. Mill writes, "the morality of an individual action is . . . a question . . . of the application of a law to an individual case" (206). He thus holds that it would be wrong to do a certain action only if it would be at variance with a certain rule. If we ask what sort of rule he is referring to, Mill makes it clear that he means a rule that should generally be observed. By his main principle Mill has already given a general answer as to what should be done. In accordance with it he holds that a certain rule is one that should generally be observed if and only if its general observance would cause more happiness than would any alternative to its general observance.[3]

[2]*A System of Logic*, 8th ed. (London: Longmans, Green, Reader, and Dyer, 1872), II, 552–4 (VI, xii, 6).

[3]"[H]appiness is the sole end of human action, and the promotion of it the test by which to judge of all human conduct; from whence it necessarily follows that it must be the criterion of morality, since a part is included in the whole." Morality consists of "the rules . . . by the observance of which . . . [happiness] might be, to the greatest extent possible, secured. . . ." (*Utilitarianism*, 237, 214.)

Mill thus maintains that it would be wrong to do a certain action only if it would be at variance with such a rule.[4]

Some prolixity is required to clarify what Mill understands by an action that would cause more happiness than any alternative to it.[5] The only respect in which an action is thereby compared to its alternatives is its consequences, and the only consequences by which it is compared are those consisting of happiness and unhappiness. Mill writes, "By happiness is intended pleasure, and the absence of pain; by unhappiness, pain, and the privation of pleasure" (210). He states: "Of . . . philosophers who have taught that happiness is the end of life . . . [the] happiness which they meant was not a life of rapture; but moments of such, in an existence made up of few and transitory pains, many and various pleasures. . ." (215). Hence the only consequences of an action that are relevant are pleasures and pains. All the pleasures and pains among the consequences of an action are relevant, whether remote or near, whether experienced by humans or by other sentient creatures.[6]

If Mill held that the only relevant difference among pleasures and pains was whether one was greater than another, there would be only six possibilities for the total effects of an action. They would contain (1) an excess of pleasure over pain, (2) an excess of pain over pleasure, (3) an excess of neither, (4) pleasure and no pain, (5) pain and no pleasure, (6) neither pleasure nor pain. Mill argues, however, that pleasures and pains differ in a further respect which is relevant—some are more desirable than others.[7] Accordingly, eight possibilities may be distinguished with regard to the total effects of an action:

(1) They contain some pleasures and no pains.

(2) They contain both pleasures and pains, and regardless of whether there is an excess of pleasure over pain, the pleasures are on the whole more desirable than the pains are undesirable.

(3) They contain both pleasures and pains; neither the pleasures nor pains are of sorts such that the pleasures on the whole are more desirable than the pains are undesirable or such that the pains on the whole are more undesirable than the pleasures are desirable; but there is an excess of pleasure over pain.

(4) They contain some pains and no pleasures.

(5) They contain both pleasures and pains, and regardless of whether

---

[4]"[A]ctions are right in proportion as they tend to promote happiness, wrong as they tend to produce the reverse of happiness" (*ibid.*, 210).

[5]Cf. G. E. Moore, *Ethics* (London: Oxford University Press, 1911), Chapter 1.

[6]See *Utilitarianism*, 214; "Sedgwick," 69.

[7]"According to the Greatest Happiness Principle . . . the ultimate end . . . is an existence exempt as far as possible from pain, and as rich as possible in enjoyments, both in point of quantity and quality . . ." (*Utilitarianism*, 214).

there is an excess of pain over pleasure, the pains are on the whole more undesirable than the pleasures are desirable.

(6) They contain both pleasures and pains; neither the pleasures nor pains are of sorts such that the pleasures on the whole are more desirable than the pains are undesirable or such that the pains on the whole are more undesirable than the pleasures are desirable; but there is an excess of pain over pleasure.

(7) They contain no pleasures or pains.

(8) They contain both pleasures and pains, and regardless of whether there is an excess of pleasure over pain, of pain over pleasure, or an excess of neither, the pleasures and pains they contain are of sorts such that the pleasures on the whole are not more desirable than the pains are undesirable and such that the pains on the whole are not more undesirable than the pleasures are desirable.

If (1) or (2) or (3) holds of a certain action, Mill would classify it as one that would cause an excess of happiness over unhappiness. If (4) or (5) or (6) holds, he would classify it as one that would cause an excess of unhappiness over happiness. If one of the other alternatives holds, he would classify an action as one that would cause an excess of neither.

Having distinguished the possibilities for any action, taken by itself, we may notice how any two actions taken at random may stand to one another in these respects. Since there are three possibilities for each, there are nine possible combinations. Call one action A and the other B. (1) Both A and B would cause an excess of happiness. (2) A would cause an excess of happiness but B would cause an excess of neither. (3) A would cause an excess of happiness but B would cause an excess of unhappiness. (4) A would cause an excess of neither but B would cause an excess of happiness. (5) Both would cause an excess of neither. (6) A would cause an excess of neither but B would cause an excess of unhappiness. (7) A would cause an excess of unhappiness but B would cause an excess of happiness. (8) A would cause an excess of unhappiness but B would cause an excess of neither. (9) Both would cause an excess of unhappiness. Within (9) three possibilities are to be distinguished: (9.1) B would cause a greater excess of unhappiness. (9.2) Neither would cause a greater excess of unhappiness. (9.3) A would cause a greater excess of unhappiness. Also, within (1), that is, where both A and B would cause an excess of happiness, three possibilities are to be distinguished: (1.1) A would cause a greater excess of happiness. (1.2) Neither would cause a greater excess of happiness. (1.3) B would cause a greater excess of happiness. There are thus thirteen ways in which any two actions may stand to one another. These thirteen ways may be grouped into three. If (1.1), (2), (3), (6) or (9.1) obtains, Mill would say that A would cause more happiness than B or that B would cause less than A. If (1.3), (4), (7), (8) or (9.3) obtains, he would say that B would cause more happiness than A or that A would cause less than B. If any of the three remaining combinations obtains, he would say that either would cause as much happiness as the other.

We have noticed three ways in which Mill would hold that any two actions taken at random could stand to one another. If any set of two or more actions is considered, we may notice three ways in which one of the actions of the set might stand to the others: (1) it would cause more happiness than any of the others, (2) it would cause less happiness than some of the others, (3) it would cause as much happiness as any of the others. The only sort of set of two or more actions to which Mill directs attention is that made up of a certain action and of the alternatives to it. This set includes whatever an agent would succeed in doing upon a given occasion if he tried hard enough, and excludes whatever he would not succeed in doing no matter how hard he tried. Accordingly, Mill would distinguish three ways in which an action may stand to the alternatives to it: (1) it would cause more happiness than any alternative, (2) it would cause less happiness than some alternative, (3) it would cause as much happiness as any alternative.

So far attention has been paid to one set of features of which Mill's main principle makes mention, apart from their role in it. There is a second set of features of actions which this principle mentions—whether it is one that should be done or one that should not. What Mill's main principle asserts is a relation between features of the first set and features of the second. It asserts that something should be done if and only if it would cause more happiness than any alternative; that something should not be done if and only if it would cause less happiness than some alternative; and that a certain action is not one that should not be done if and only if it would cause as much happiness as any alternative.

By his main principle Mill thus declares that a certain feature is a universal and peculiar feature of actions that should be done, and that a certain other feature is a universal and peculiar feature of actions that should not be done. It implies that whenever anyone judges that a certain action should be done, this is a condition that must be fulfilled for the judgment to be true. This is the case whether the judgment is about a past or future action, an actual or possible action, something done by oneself or another, or something done by an individual, a nation, or any group. Mill's principle does not, however, imply that the only way by which anyone can know whether a certain action should be done is by seeking to make out whether it would cause more happiness than any alternative. Although Mill speaks of it as the "sole criterion," his principle is quite compatible with using many other tests. It is compatible with using now one test and now another. Nor does Mill's principle imply that it affords the only universal test by which to judge what should be done. All that it does imply is that whatever other test be used, it must yield results compatible with this principle. Mill's principle does not supply the only test; it only lays down a condition to which any test must comply.

Although Mill's principle sets forth a universal and peculiar feature of actions that should be done, there is nothing about it which implies that this is the only universal and peculiar feature of such actions. It would be compatible with it to maintain, for instance, that something should be done if and only if it is commanded by God. Mill's principle provides nothing that rules this out. Indeed, it is conceivable that there are ten thousand other universal and peculiar features of actions that should be done. One consequence which Mill draws from his principle is that it would be wrong to do a certain action only if it would violate a rule the general observance of which would cause more happiness. Many would agree with Mill in this. They would agree that whenever anyone does what is wrong, he is violating a rule the general observance of which would in fact cause more happiness. But they would not hold that this is the reason it would be wrong to do it. They would hold that the reason it is wrong to do any action is that it violates God's law. They would urge that God wants his creatures to be happy and that because of this whoever disobeys God's laws violates a law the general observance of which would cause more happiness. They would agree with Mill that by doing what is wrong someone violates a rule the general observance of which would cause more happiness. But they would say that it is not because of this that someone is doing wrong; it is rather because he breaks a rule laid down by God.

There is nothing in this view incompatible with what we have so far seen of Mill's main principle. When we notice how Mill deals with such a view, we find that he takes a further step. He holds not merely that someone does what is wrong only if he breaks a rule the general observance of which would cause more happiness, but also that what he does is wrong because it violates such a rule. Mill maintains not merely that those rules which should generally be observed would in fact cause more happiness, but also that it is because their general observance would cause more happiness that they should be observed. He does not thereby deny that by violating rules that should generally be observed, someone is disobeying God's will. But he holds that the reason why a rule should be generally observed is not because it is prescribed by God but because its observance would cause more happiness.[8]

There is a further implication differentiating Mill from the view we have been considering. Those who maintain that the reason why a certain action is wrong is that it violates a rule laid down by God are committed to holding that if God should will something other than the happiness of his creatures, then an action would be wrong even though it would not violate a rule whose

[8]See "Sedgwick," 53; "Blakey," 27; *Utilitarianism*, 222.

general observance would cause more happiness. Anyone who holds that an action is wrong because it violates a rule laid down by God is committed to holding that if there is no god or if he lays down no rules for men, then there is nothing which it would be wrong to do or wrong not to do. Mill not only holds that an action is wrong if it violates a rule the general observance of which would cause more happiness, he also contends that it is because it violates such a rule that an action is wrong. He thereby implies that even if God should will something other than the happiness of his creatures, or even if there is no god, an action would be wrong if it were to violate a rule the general observance of which would cause more happiness.[9] In the first step, Mill asserts that a certain feature is a universal and peculiar feature of actions that should be done. In the second step, he states that it is because they have this feature that actions should be done.

There is nothing incompatible between Mill's principle and the view that something should be done if and only if it would bring about a greater realization of men's capacities than would any alternative. But his principle is incompatible with the view that something should be done because it would have this result. Similarly, Mill's principle is not incompatible with the view that something should be done if and only if it would bring about a greater fulfilment of human wants than would any alternative. But it is incompatible with the view that something should be done because it would have this result. One alternative to Mill's principle is the view that something should be done because it would maximize human happiness. Another alternative to it is that something should be done because it would maximize the agent's happiness. The former is the humanistic variant to Mill's principle; the latter the egoistic variant to it. In contrast to both, Mill's principle is the universalistic variant. Many other alternatives to Mill's principle are conceivable. One view already noted is that which maintains that something should be done because it would maximize fulfilment of human wants. The universalistic variant to this view is that something should be done because it would maximize fulfilment of wants generally. The egoistic variant is that something should be done because it would maximize fulfilment of the agent's wants. The theistic variant to this is that something should be done because it would maximize fulfilment of God's wants. Still another alternative is the view that something should be done because it would maximize the fulfilment of human capacities. Two further conceivable views are the egoistic and universalistic variants of this.

All such views differ from Mill's principle in but one respect. They all agree that there is some feature which not only holds of every action that should be done and only of such, but which also constitutes the reason why it should be done. They all agree that this feature consists in a respect in

9See "The Utility of Religion," 417.

which an action compares with its alternatives. They are also all agreed that this feature consists in how an action's consequences would compare with those of its alternatives. These several views differ from each other and from Mill's principle only in the sorts of consequences which they specify and the sorts of beings to whom they accrue.

The chief support that Mill offers for his main principle, to vindicate it against such other views, is that happiness is the only thing desirable for its own sake. From this contention it does indeed follow that an action would have more desirable consequences than any alternative if and only if it would cause more happiness. But this contention does not by itself support his main principle. It does so only if a further premise is added, namely, that something should be done if and only if it would have more desirable consequences than any alternative. Mill does not explicitly avow this further premise. Yet, since he holds that the contention which he offers in support of his main principle does in fact support it, he may be presumed to take this premise for granted as not requiring any attention or defence. It then looks as if Mill contends that something should be done because it would cause more happiness, but that it is not only because of this that it should be done; that the reason in turn why what would cause more happiness should be done is that happiness is the only thing desirable for its own sake.

One can at most speculate as to how Mill would meet this challenge. He might retort that the fact that an action would have more desirable consequences than any alternative could not be the ultimate reason why it should be done, since the ultimate reason why something should be done must consist in some other fact about it than the fact that it should be done, but in saying that an action would have more desirable consequences than any alternative, nothing more nor less is then said than that it should be done. Although it is not transparently evident that these are but two ways of saying the same thing, it is far from implausible to urge that by analysis they amount to the same. Two steps are involved in the analysis: (1) something should be done if and only if it would on the whole be more desirable for it to be done than any alternative; (2) it would on the whole be more desirable for something to be done than any alternative to it if and only if what would come of its being done would be more desirable than what would come of any alternative to it. If each of these is analytically true, nothing further is required.

In behalf of the first step, the following may be urged. Whenever it is said that something should be done it is implied that it is capable of being done. It is also implied that it is capable of not being done, that is, that some alternatives are capable of being done in its stead. When it is said that something should be done, it is not only implied that it is one of a number of alternatives; it is also implied that it stands in a certain relation to the others. When it is said that something should be done, it is not implied that it would be more desirable for some alternative to it to be done; nor is it implied that it would be as desirable for some alternative to be done in its stead. What is rather implied is the denial of both these implications. When it is said that something should be done, it is thus implied that it would on the whole be more desirable for it rather than any alternative to be done.[10] In behalf of the second step the following may be urged. It cannot be denied that an action may have consequences, and that whether it would be desirable for it to be done is affected by what would come of its being done. Nor can it be denied that the desirability of some alternative being done is affected by the desirability of what would come of it. It is then more desirable on the whole that one alternative rather than another be done if and only if what would come of the first would be more desirable than what would come of the other. Hence it would on the whole be more desirable for something to be done rather than any alternative if and only if what would come of it would be more desirable than what would come of any alternative.

The chief premise that Mill offers in support of his main principle is that happiness is the only thing desirable for its own sake. This premise affords support only in conjunction with the added premise, that something should be done if and only if it would have more desirable consequences than any alternative. Consequently, Mill's contention that happiness is the only thing desirable for its own sake cannot support his main principle against any sort of ethical theory which rejects the second premise. Against any such theory he seeks to vindicate his main principle by clearing up the relation of the conception of a wrong action and of an action which there is an obligation not to do to that of an action that should not be done.[11] On the other hand, any sort of ethical theory that rejects Mill's main principle but which holds that whether something should be done turns on how its consequences would compare with those of any alternative to it need not be incompatible with the second premise. To vindicate his main principle against any theory of that sort, it is sufficient for Mill to make good his contention that happiness is the only thing desirable for its own sake.[12]

Before we go on to examine how Mill seeks to make good this contention, certain implications of it may be noted. It implies that if A are the consequences of one action, X, and B the consequences of another action, Y, A would be more desirable for their own sake than B if and only if they would contain more happiness. It implies that if A should be the consequences of some other action than X, they would still be more desirable for

---

[10]Mill comes closest to this when he writes: "The hygienic and medical arts assume, the one that the preservation of health, the other that the cure of disease, are fitting and desirable ends. These . . . propositions . . . do not assert that anything is, but enjoin or recommend that something should be. They are . . . expressed by the words *ought* or *should be*. . . ." (*Logic*, II, 552–3; VI, xii, 6.)

[11]See §§ IV and V, xcv–cxiii below.   [12]See §§ II and III, lxxiii–xcv below.

their own sake than B. It thus implies that whether the consequences of an action are more desirable for their own sake than those of another does not depend on what action they are the consequences of. Mill's contention also implies that if A are the consequences of a natural occurrence and B the consequences of another natural occurrence, A would still be more desirable for their own sake than B. This thus means that whether one set of consequences is more desirable for its own sake than another does not depend on what caused them. It does not depend on A or B being a set of consequences. Mill's contention that happiness is the only thing desirable for its own sake has therefore a wider scope than his main principle. It implies that any state of affairs is more desirable for its own sake than another if and only if it contains more happiness than the other.

When Mill is described as speaking of one state of affairs as "containing more happiness" than another, it must be borne in mind that this expression is used in the same sense as that in which he understands the consequences of one action as related to those of another when he regards one action as "causing more happiness" than the other. Accordingly, Mill's contention that happiness is the only thing desirable for its own sake may be stated more fully as signifying that something is desirable for its own sake if and only if it is a state of affairs of one of three sorts: (1) a state containing some pleasure and no pain; (2) a state containing both pleasure and pain, but in which, whether or not there is an excess of pleasure over pain, the pleasures on the whole are more desirable than the pains are undesirable; (3) a state containing both pleasure and pain, and in which, although neither the pleasures nor pains are of sorts such that the pleasures on the whole are more desirable than the pains are undesirable or such that the pains on the whole are more undesirable than the pleasures are desirable, there is an excess of pleasure over pain. Mill likewise holds that something is undesirable for its own sake if and only if it is a state of affairs the opposite of one of these three.

Mill's contention implies that no inanimate thing or state of affairs made up only of inanimate things is desirable or undesirable for its own sake. It implies that no human being or human disposition is desirable or undesirable for its own sake. According to it, the only sort of matter that is desirable or undesirable for its own sake is a state of affairs comprising sentient beings. It implies that neither justice nor liberty nor peace is desirable for its own sake. It implies, moreover, that there is nothing desirable for its own sake save where there is life; and that there is nothing undesirable for its own sake save where there is life. Although Mill's contention affirms a certain universal and peculiar feature of whatever is desirable for its own sake, it does not also state any such feature of whatever is desirable. While it implies that an inanimate thing, a human being, or justice or liberty or peace or life is not desirable for its own sake, it does not imply that none of these can be desirable for what will come of it. Mill's contention implies that although a certain state of affairs is desirable for its own sake, it may still be undesirable; and even though a certain state of affairs is undesirable for its own sake, it may still be desirable, for what comes of it. Mill's main principle implies that even if it would be undesirable for a certain action to be done, it would not follow that it should not be done. It implies that even if a certain action would have desirable effects, it should not be done, if some alternative to it would have more desirable effects. Mill's principle implies that even though the consequences of a certain action would on the whole be undesirable for their own sake, it may still be the case that it should be done. This would be the case if the consequences of any alternative to it would be more undesirable for their own sake.

II. THE EVIDENCE OF WHAT IS DESIRABLE

MILL'S ARGUMENT to support his contention that happiness is the only thing desirable for its own sake contains two steps. In the first step he seeks to show that happiness is desirable; in the second, he seeks to show that it is the only thing desirable for its own sake. He writes, in the first step:

The only proof capable of being given that an object is visible, is that people actually see it. . . . In like manner . . . the sole evidence it is possible to produce that anything is desirable, is that people do actually desire it. . . . No reason can be given why the general happiness is desirable, except that each person, so far as he believes it to be attainable, desires his own happiness. This, however, being a fact, we have . . . all the proof . . . which it is possible to require, that happiness is a good: that each person's happiness is a good to that person, and the general happiness, therefore, a good to the aggregate of all persons. (234.)

In the second step Mill acknowledges that men actually "do desire things which, in common language, are decidedly distinguished from happiness" (235). But he endeavours to show that "Whatever is desired otherwise than as a means to some end beyond itself, and ultimately to happiness, is desired as itself a part of happiness. . ." (237). Central to both steps in his argument is Mill's contention that the sole evidence that anything is desirable is that it is desired.

G. E. Moore urges that by asserting that the fact that something is desired is evidence that it is desirable, Mill is holding that if anything is desired it is desirable; and that by affirming that this is the sole evidence, Mill is holding that nothing is desirable unless desired. Moore also interprets Mill as inferring from this that "desirable" means "desired." He points out, moreover, that Mill uses the words "good" and "desirable" interchangeably. Hence

Moore contends that Mill is claiming that "good" means "desired."[13] Moore urges two objections against Mill: first, that "desirable" does not mean "desired," and secondly, that even if something is desirable if and only if it is desired, it is fallacious to infer that "desirable" means "desired." Both objections fail to apply to Mill; Mill does not draw the inference Moore attributes to him, nor does he maintain that "desirable" means "desired." Mill also does not hold that "visible" means "seen." Instead he asserts that the proof that something is visible is that it is seen. Similarly, what he affirms is that the sole evidence that anything is desirable is that it is desired.

To this Moore urges two further objections, independent of the foregoing. The fact that something is desired would be evidence that it is desirable if and only if it is the case that from the mere fact that anything is desired it follows that it is also desirable. But from the mere fact that something is desired Moore objects that it does not follow that it is desirable. Moore does not question Mill's contention that the fact that something is seen is proof that it is visible, for by "visible" is meant "capable of being seen." He contends, however, that Mill is wholly unwarranted in arguing that "in like manner" the fact that a thing is desired is evidence that it is desirable, for he points out that by "desirable" is not meant "capable of being desired." Just as "detestable" means not "capable of being detested" but "worthy of being detested," so similarly, Moore urges, when something is said to be desirable, what is meant is that it ought to be desired, that it is worthy of being desired. From the fact that something is actually desired it does not follow that it ought to be desired.

Moore urges a second objection against anyone who would try to save Mill's dictum by holding that Mill uses "desirable" in it to mean "capable of being desired." He points out that Mill puts forth this dictum to establish the conclusion that the general happiness is the only thing desirable for its own sake. If Mill is construed as using "desirable" in the sense of "capable of being desired" in his premise, Moore contends that his argument then becomes fallacious, since Mill does not use "desirable" in this sense in the conclusion. If anyone should still try to save Mill's argument against this objection by urging that in the conclusion as well Mill means by "desirable," "capable of being desired," Moore contends that this will not do. He points out that in saying that happiness alone is desirable for its own sake, Mill makes it clear that he means that it alone is good for its own sake. Moore also points out that in saying that the general happiness alone is desirable for its own sake, Mill does not mean that it alone is capable of being desired for its own sake. Since Mill himself mentions that each person desires his own happiness, he acknowledges that men are capable of desiring something

[13]G. E. Moore, *Principia Ethica* (Cambridge: Cambridge University Press, 1903), §40.

other than the general happiness for its own sake. Moore calls attention to another connection in which Mill makes this point. Mill remarks that it is a mistake to "confound the rule of action with the motive of it," and continues, "ninety-nine hundredths of all our actions are done from other motives. . ." (219). Here too Mill makes it clear that, in saying that the general happiness is the only thing desirable for its own sake, he in no way holds that the only desire from which men can act or the only desire of which they are capable is desire for the general happiness.[14]

D. Raphael and E. W. Hall seek to defend Mill against these objections urged by Moore.[15] They contend that Moore's objections are beside the point, since they criticize Mill for doing something which he does not profess to do. They urge that Mill does not claim to prove that happiness is desirable because it is desired. They direct attention to what Mill has to say upon this matter. Mill writes, "The medical art is proved to be good, by its conducing to health. . . ." He generalizes, "Whatever can be proved to be good, must be so by being shown to be a means to something admitted to be good without proof" (207–208). Here Mill is saying two things: first, that whatever can be proved to be good can be so proved only by being shown conducive to something else that is good; second, that since something cannot be proved to be desirable for its own sake by being shown to be desirable as a means to something else, no proof can be given of what is desirable for its own sake. This conclusion Mill at once qualifies: "Questions of ultimate ends are not amenable to direct proof." Mill still concedes that such questions are not amenable to what is "commonly understood by proof," but he contends that they are amenable to a "larger meaning of the word proof. . . . Considerations may be presented capable of determining the intellect either to give or withhold assent." Moore recognizes that Mill does not claim to give a proof of what things are desirable for their own sake in terms of what is commonly understood by proof. He agrees with Mill that no such proof can be given of what things are desirable for their own sake. Moore also agrees with Mill that considerations may be presented in favour of thinking that certain things and not others are desirable for their own sake. Raphael and Hall err in accusing Moore of taking Mill to be offering a proof in the "commonly understood" sense. Moore's objection is rather that one consideration which Mill presents "to determine the intellect to give assent" to what is desirable is invalid. Because something is desired it does not follow that it is desirable. Hence the fact that something is desired does not constitute evidence that it is desirable.

[14]"Bentham," 96; "Remarks on Bentham's Philosophy," 112.
[15]D. D. Raphael, "Fallacies in and about Mill's *Utilitarianism*," *Philosophy*, 30 (1955), 344–57; E. W. Hall, "The 'Proof' of Utility in Bentham and Mill," *Ethics*, 60 (1949), 1–18.

To make good his defence of Mill, Raphael must show that this consideration which Mill presents is not open to Moore's objection. Raphael points
out that in his *Logic* Mill maintains that whoever says that something should
be done is recommending that it be done. Such a person, Mill writes, "speaks
in rules, or precepts."[16] Mill continues, such "propositions . . . enjoin or
recommend that something should be. They are . . . expressed by the words
ought or *should* be."[17] Second, Raphael contends that Mill holds that "all
rules or precepts are aimed at the promotion of ends." He is referring to
Mill's remark, "All action is for the sake of some end, and rules of action,
it seems natural to suppose, must take their whole character and colour from
the end to which they are subservient" (206). Third, Raphael takes Mill as
holding that "an ultimate end is that by reference to which we prove the
propriety of adopting subordinate ends or particular rules." He thereby
construes Mill as maintaining that whenever men recommend something as
desirable, their recommendations must ultimately have reference to an ultimate end. Finally, Raphael ascribes to Mill the view that "the ultimate end
or criterion of human action is what human beings desire."[18] Accordingly,
Raphael maintains that what Mill means by his dictum that "the sole evidence . . . that anything is desirable, is that people do actually desire it" is
that when "we recommend . . . as 'desirable' . . . our recommendations must
ultimately have reference to actual desires."[19]

Raphael's interpretation of Mill's dictum fails to free it of the objection
urged by Moore. For Moore urges that even if someone aims at a certain
thing as an ultimate end, that is, as an end for its own sake, it still makes
sense to ask whether that at which he aims is desirable for its own sake. From
the fact that it is aimed at for its own sake, it does not follow that it is desirable for its own sake. Raphael also misrepresents Mill's dictum, in construing it as maintaining that when anything is recommended as desirable,
the recommendation must ultimately have reference to men's desires. He
construes it in this way by ascribing to Mill the view that when anything is
recommended as desirable, it can be recommended only by reference to an
ultimate end. Mill, however, does not hold that something can be shown to
be desirable only by being shown to be a means to an ultimate end. He is
instead concerned with how it is possible to make out what is desirable for
its own sake. It is just in this connection that he puts forth his dictum.

Mill not only speaks of what is desired and what is desirable. Again and
again he speaks of ends. In doing so, he makes many statements reminiscent
of Aristotle. Aristotle writes, "Every action and pursuit is thought to aim
at some good; and for this reason the good has rightly been declared to be
that at which all things aim. . . . Will not the knowledge of it, then, have a

---

[16]*Logic*, II, 546 (VI, xii, 1).
[18]Raphael, 346.
[17]*Ibid.*, 553 (VI, xii, 6)
[19]Raphael, 348.

great influence on life?"[20] In a similar vein, as we have seen, Mill says, "All action is for the sake of some end, and rules of action, it seems natural to suppose, must take their whole character and colour from the end to which they are subservient. When we engage in a pursuit, a clear and precise conception of what we are pursuing would seem to be the first thing we need...." (206.) Mill also asserts, "Questions about ends are ... questions what things are desirable." The "sole evidence it is possible to produce that anything is desirable, is that people do actually desire it" (234). Aristotle writes, "If, then, there is some end of the things we do, which we desire for its own sake (everything else being desired for the sake of this) ... this must be the good and the chief good."[21] In virtue of such similarities, the objection Moore urges against Mill is equally applicable to Aristotle's arguments. Moore would contend that because there is that which is desired for its own sake, and all else that is desired is desired for the sake of it, it does not follow that it is desirable for its own sake, or that it alone is desirable for its own sake.

Mill also writes, "happiness is desirable, and the only thing desirable, as an end...." Each of virtue, pleasure, money, power, and fame, "once desired as an instrument for the attainment of happiness, has come to be desired for its own sake. In being desired for its own sake it is, however, desired as *part* of happiness. The person is made, or thinks he would be made, happy by its mere possession.... Whatever is desired otherwise than as a means ... to happiness, is desired as itself a part of happiness...." (236–7.) Aristotle similarly writes,

Not all ends are final ends.... Now we call that which is in itself worthy of pursuit more final than that which is worthy of pursuit for the sake of something else, and that which is never desirable for the sake of something else more final than the things that are desirable both in themselves and for the sake of that other thing, and therefore we call final without qualification that which is always desirable in itself and never for the sake of something else. Now such a thing happiness, above all else, is held to be; for this we choose always for itself and never for the sake of something else, but honour, pleasure, reason, and every virtue we choose indeed for themselves..., but we choose them also for the sake of happiness, judging that by means of them we shall be happy. Happiness, on the other hand, no one chooses for the sake of these, nor, in general, for anything other than itself.[22]

Here Aristotle distinguishes what is worthy of pursuit from what is pursued and what is desirable from what is desired. Yet in the third sentence he again exposes himself to Moore's objection: because something is chosen

[20]Aristotle, *Nicomachean Ethics*, trans. W. D. Ross (London: Oxford University Press, 1928), 1094a1.
[21]*Ibid.*, 1094a17.
[22]*Ibid.*, 1097a27.

for its own sake and never for the sake of something else, it does not follow that it is "worthy of pursuit," "desirable in itself," or "always desirable in itself." In his *Logic*, Mill asserts: "Every art . . . enunciates the object aimed at, and affirms it to be a desirable object. The builder's art assumes that it is desirable to have buildings. . . . The hygienic and medical arts assume, the one that the preservation of health, the other that the cure of disease, are fitting and desirable ends."[23] Aristotle similarly writes, "In different actions and arts . . . the good of each [is] that for whose sake everything else is done . . . the end."[24] To this Moore's objection again applies. Undeniably that for the sake of which everything that is done in a certain sphere of activity is often something good, something desirable. But because there is that in a certain art or sphere of activity for the sake of which everything within it is done, it does not follow that it is desirable. Here it is to be noted that Mill is in complete accord with Moore's objection. He follows up the last passage by writing, "To this art [the Art of Life] . . . all other arts are subordinate; since its principles are those which determine whether the special aim of any particular art is worthy and desirable." Here Mill clearly recognizes that the fact that something is the aim of a certain pursuit in no way implies that that aim is desirable. Elsewhere Mill makes it quite clear that he holds that whether a certain pursuit should be engaged in depends not on what its aim is but on whether the consequences of engaging in it would be more desirable.

The core of Moore's objection to Mill's dictum, on the evidence for what is desirable, is that from the fact that something is aimed at, it does not follow that it ought to be aimed at; and that from the fact that something is desired, it does not follow that it ought to be desired. Mill is in complete accord with Moore on the general point of which these are instances. He devotes his entire essay, "Nature," to refuting the notion that nature, that which is, determines that which ought to be.[25] Mill is also in full agreement with the specific point Moore urges in objection to him. Neither nature generally nor man's own nature can determine what ought to be. Many a propensity is to be extirpated.[26] Because men have a propensity or desire for something, it in no way follows that it ought to be desired. A further look may then be taken at Mill's argument to see if it is free of Moore's objection.

In support of the conclusion that only happiness is desirable for its own sake, Mill urges that only happiness is desired for its own sake. Moore contends that in speaking of what is desirable for its own sake, Mill is speaking of what ought to be desired for its own sake. Moore objects that from the fact that something is desired it does not follow that it ought to be desired. We may then inquire what can be inferred from the premise that only happi-

[23]*Logic*, II, 552 (VI, xii, 6).   [24]*Nicomachean Ethics*, 1097a16.
[25]See "Nature," 377.   [26]*Ibid.*, 398.

ness is desired for its own sake. If something is incapable of being done, it cannot be the case that it ought to be done. Accordingly,

(a) Only that which is capable of being desired for its own sake ought to be desired for its own sake.

Moore does not question that whatever is desired for its own sake is capable of being desired for its own sake. Similarly, it seems that

(b) Only that which is desired for its own sake is capable of being desired for its own sake.

Completing the argument,

(c) Only that which is desired for its own sake ought to be desired for its own sake.

(d) Only happiness is desired for its own sake.

(e) Hence, only happiness is desirable for its own sake.

The question at issue is not whether (d) is correct, but whether (c) is. Statement (c) follows from (a) and (b), so what calls for scrutiny is (b). If something is desired for its own sake it follows that it is capable of being desired for its own sake. It does not in like manner hold, nor can it be inferred from this, that if something is alone desired for its own sake it alone is capable of being desired for its own sake. Mill, however, does not include (b) in his argument. He does not hold that whatever is visible is seen; he contends rather that only that which is seen is that for which there is evidence that it is capable of being seen. Mill is similarly concerned to determine whether there is evidence that anything other than happiness is capable of being desired for its own sake. He urges that the only evidence that is offered is that virtue, money, power, and fame are desired for their own sake. Mill does not reject this evidence. Instead, he seeks to show that when any of these is desired for its own sake, it is desired only as a part of happiness. Instead of (b), Mill would aver

(b') Only that which is desired for its own sake is that for which there is evidence that it is capable of being desired for its own sake.

From (a) follows

(a') Only that for which there is evidence that it is capable of being desired for its own sake is that for which there is evidence that it ought to be desired for its own sake.

From (b') and (a') follows

(c') Only that which is desired for its own sake is that for which there is evidence that it ought to be desired for its own sake.

Moore objects to Mill's dictum, on the evidence for what is desirable, by construing it as affirming that from the fact that something is desired it follows that it ought to be desired. Mill, however, does not hold that from the fact that something is desired, it follows that it ought to be desired. He does not maintain that whatever is desired ought to be desired; he speaks rather of the only evidence that something is desirable. Moore says that by "desirable" Mill means "ought to be desired," and it is only on this interpretation that he raises his objection against Mill's dictum. If Moore is correct in this, then what Mill's dictum maintains is (c′). Moore's objection against Mill's dictum carries no weight against it; there is nothing incompatible in affirming (c′) and denying that whatever is desired ought to be desired.

Moore is correct in pointing out that when Mill argues that happiness is the only thing desirable for its own sake, he means by "desirable" not "capable of being desired" but "good," and that by "desirable for its own sake" he means "good in itself," "intrinsically good." Moore also contends that by "desirable" Mill, or anyone else, means "ought to be desired" or that which it would be good to desire. There is a fatal objection to this contention, at least in regard to Mill. Since Mill holds by his main principle that something ought to be done only if it would cause more happiness, he holds that something ought to be desired only if desiring it would cause more happiness. Hence if Mill is construed as meaning by "desirable," "ought to be desired," he would then be maintaining that the consequences of an action would be desirable only if desiring them would cause more happiness. But this is clearly not what Mill contends; for him the consequences of an action would be more desirable only if that action would cause more happiness.

There is a further objection to contending that "desirable" means "ought to be desired," which applies to Mill, or to anyone who agrees with him that something should be done only if its consequences would be more desirable. For he then holds that something ought to be desired only if the effects of desiring it would be more desirable. But if "desirable" is construed as "ought to be desired," Mill would then have to say that the consequences of an action would be desirable only if desiring these consequences would have more desirable consequences. He would similarly have to say that the consequences of desiring the consequences of a certain action would be desirable only if desiring them in turn would have more desirable effects. And so on. But Mill clearly does not think that the desirability of the consequences of an action is affected by what would be the consequences of desiring these consequences, or by what would be the consequences of desiring the consequences of desiring the consequences of the action. He maintains that the consequences of an action would be more desirable only if it would cause more happiness.

Moore overlooks certain differences between the conception of that which ought to be desired and the conception of that which is desirable. When it is said that something ought to be done, it is implied that there is some respect in which it stands in contrast to anything capable of being done instead of it. "Ought" is a superlative, as is also the conception of that which ought to be desired, but the adjective, "desirable," is a positive term, which takes the comparative "more desirable" and the superlative "most desirable." In accord with Mill's assumption that something ought to be done only if what would come of it would be more desirable for its own sake, something ought to be desired for its own sake only if what would come of so desiring it would be more desirable for its own sake. Hence if something ought to be desired for its own sake, it does not follow that it would be desirable for its own sake; and because something would be desirable for its own sake, it does not follow that it ought to be desired for its own sake. Since Mill's dictum on the evidence for what is desirable cannot be taken as a dictum on the evidence for what ought to be desired, it must be given some other interpretation than that set forth in the preceding paragraph.

It is doubtful whether anyone sincerely believes that a certain thing should be done without feeling on the whole in favour of its being done. It is similarly extremely doubtful that anyone believes that something would be undesirable without feeling some displeasure at the thought of it, or that anyone is genuinely convinced that something would be desirable without to some measure feeling pleased at the thought of it. Someone may, indeed, believe that something would be desirable in a certain respect, and yet on the whole not be in favour of it, through thinking it undesirable in other respects. Nonetheless, Mill points out that no one feels pleased to some measure at the thought of a certain state of affairs, without feeling some desire for its occurrence (237). Someone does not therefore manage to convince another that something would be desirable unless he induces him to feel some desire for it. This suggests that what Mill may be maintaining by his dictum is that no one has evidence for believing something desirable unless he has some desire for it. If it is interpreted in this way, it may be objected that people often believe that others desire something, and desire it for its own sake, without thinking that it would be desirable for its own sake. It may also be objected that on occasion a man is well aware that he desires something for its own sake, but still does not think that it would be desirable. These objections merely show that someone may believe that something is desired without believing that it would be desirable. They do not show that anyone is ever convinced that something would be desirable without having some desire for it. There is a further objection to Mill's dictum, if it is interpreted in this way. Someone has a desire for something whenever he believes it would be desirable. He has some desire for it, whether he is correct or mistaken in believing that it would be desirable. Consequently the fact that he has a desire for something cannot serve as evidence that what he believes would be desirable would really be such. What is rather the case is that the fact that someone believes that something would be desirable is evidence that he has some desire for it.

Although the fact of something's being desired cannot serve as evidence for the correctness of all judgments of what is desirable, it may still be the case that there are some such judgments for which it alone can serve as evidence. It is important to note the limitations which Mill himself places on the dictum that the only evidence that something is desirable is that it is desired. He does not hold that this is the evidence for all sorts of judgments of what is desirable. Nor does he claim that all desires are qualified to serve as evidence. Mill does not state that the only evidence that something is desirable as a means is that it is desired. He maintains that something is good as a means, desirable as a means, if and only if it would bring about something else that is desirable (207–8). He would contend that there is no evidence that it is desirable as a means unless there is evidence that it would have a certain effect. If something is desired in the belief that something desirable would come of it, Mill does not hold that such a desire is evidence that something desirable would come of it. He maintains that whether something is desired or not, it is desirable as a means just so long as it would have some desirable effects. He thus does not claim that the fact something is desired is either the sole evidence or even a part of the evidence to support a judgment that it is desirable as a means.

Mill also does not hold that the fact that something is desired is the sole evidence to support a judgment that it is intrinsically desirable, that is, desirable for its own sake. On this point he writes, "No reason can be given why the general happiness is desirable, except that each person, so far as he believes it to be attainable, desires his own happiness. This, however, being a fact, we have . . . all the proof . . . that each person's happiness is a good to that person, and the general happiness, therefore, a good to the aggregate of all persons." (234.) Countless critics have urged that it is fallacious for Mill to infer that since each desires his own happiness therefore everyone desires the general happiness. Mill, however, does not here infer that the general happiness is desired. What he argues, rather, is that it is desirable. In this passage he certainly claims that the fact that each desires his own happiness is evidence that the happiness of each is desirable. But he does not base his claim that the general happiness is desirable on the evidence that it is desired. In a letter he explains, "when I said that the general happiness is a good . . . I merely meant . . . to argue that since A's happiness is a good, B's a good, C's a good, &c., the sum of all these goods must be a good."[27] Mill is holding that if the happiness of A is intrinsically desirable and the happiness of B is intrinsically desirable and the happiness of C is intrinsically desirable, then the "sum" of the happiness of A and the happiness of B and the happiness of C is intrinsically desirable. Put generally, what Mill is arguing is that a whole is intrinsically desirable if it is made up of components which are

[27]*Letters of John Stuart Mill*, ed. Hugh S. R. Elliot (London: Longmans, Green, 1910), II, 116 (to Henry Jones, 13/6/68).

intrinsically desirable and which exceed intrinsically undesirable components. Mill does not hold that the fact that a whole is desired for its own
sake is either necessary or sufficient evidence that it is made up of an excess
of intrinsically desirable components. Thus a second sort of judgment to
which Mill does not apply his dictum is a judgment that something is intrinsically desirable because it is a whole containing an excess of intrinsically
desirable components.

Moore and C. I. Lewis distinguish two further sorts of judgments of what
is desirable to which Mill, for similar reasons, would not regard his dictum
as applicable.[28] It does not apply to a judgment that something is desirable
because it is a component of something intrinsically desirable. For example,
when he considers it by itself, a mountain climber may well regard the toil
he undergoes in reaching a mountain peak as undesirable in itself. Yet he
would regard it as desirable because it enhances the desirability of the
experience of reaching the mountain top, making the venture far more
desirable than it would have been had he reached the peak by helicopter. In
considering his toil as desirable for this reason, the climber is making a
judgment which in one respect resembles judging that something is desirable
as a means. He regards it as desirable because of its relation to something
else. In another respect it differs. When something is judged desirable as a
means, it is merely claimed that it would bring about something else desirable,
whereas the climber regards one component of an experience as desirable
because its experienced quality enhances the desirability of the whole
experience of which it is a part. Although Mill also distinguishes that which
is desirable because a part of happiness from that which is desirable because
a means to happiness, he fails to mention that the fact that someone desires
something because he "thinks he would be made" happy by its mere possession, supplies no evidence that it would actually enhance his happiness (236).
A fourth sort of judgment is exemplified by the lover of mountain scenery
who regards a certain mountain as desirable because of the delight to be had
in beholding it. He is not regarding the mere existence of the mountain as
desirable for its own sake. He regards the mountain as desirable because
the experience of beholding it is desirable.

We have noticed four distinct ways in which something may be judged to
be desirable: (1) as a means, (2) because it enhances the intrinsic desirability of something of which it is a part, (3) because it is an object of an
intrinsically desirable experience, (4) intrinsically, because made up of an
excess of intrinsically desirable components. By the fourth sort of judgment
something is judged intrinsically desirable; by the other three, extrinsically
desirable. All four sorts make the claim that something is desirable because it

[28]See More, *Ethics*, 167, 250, *Principia Ethica*, §121; C. I. Lewis, *An Analysis of Knowledge and Valuation* (La Salle, Illinois: Open Court, 1946), 486, 432.

stands in a certain relation to something else. The evidence required for each is evidence that the relation obtains. Consequently no judgment of one of these sorts is one in which a desire for what is judged desirable is evidence of the correctness of the judgment. A fifth sort of judgment, fundamentally distinct from these four, is that something is intrinsically desirable independent of its relation to something else. For brevity, we may refer to such a judgment as a judgment of what is "desirable of itself." Judgments of the other four sorts are logically dependent on judgments of this sort, for what they affirm to be desirable they imply is related in a certain way, directly or indirectly, to something desirable of itself. The fifth sort of judgment is logically independent of the other four.

For someone to be assured whether he is correct in judging that something is desirable of itself, one preliminary is that he avoid confusing this judgment with the other four. For a judgment of this sort, it would be out of place to adduce the kind of evidence distinctively relevant to one of the four other sorts of judgments. When Mill speaks of desires as evidence of what is desirable, he would regard this dictum as holding only for judgments of the fifth sort. The same is true when he speaks of a preference for one sort of matter over another as evidence that the one is more desirable than the other. Even for judgments of the fifth sort Mill does not claim that every sort of desire or preference can serve as evidence. He does not hold that a desire for something qualifies as evidence if it rests on the belief that it would have desirable effects, or upon the beliefs on which judgments of the other three sorts rest. He contends that someone's preference for one sort of matter over another does not qualify as evidence unless he has had experiences of matters of both sorts and his preference is based on such experiences (211). He would not hold that his preference is based on such experiences unless they led him to it. Mill would hold that a preference by someone who has had such experiences would not qualify as evidence unless he was gladder at the one than the other. He therefore maintains that a preference for one sort of matter over another qualifies as evidence so long as it rests on nothing but having had experiences of matters of both sorts and having been gladder at the one than the other.

It may be presumed that Mill likewise holds that someone's desire for something of a certain sort does not qualify as evidence unless it rests on experience of matters of that sort. When someone desires something, he prefers its existence to its non-existence. Since he argues that a preference for one matter over another does not qualify as evidence unless it rests on experience of matters of both sorts, Mill may be presumed to hold that someone's desire for a certain thing does not qualify as evidence unless he has had experience of something of its sort, as well as some experience from which such a thing was absent. Mill would also hold that a desire by someone who had had such an experience would not qualify as evidence unless he was glad at what he experienced. He then holds that someone's desire for something qualifies as evidence so long as it rests on nothing but having had experience of something of that sort and having been glad at it. It would serve as evidence for someone else, as well as for him who had the desire. Mill would certainly admit that if someone was glad at what he experienced because he expected that something desirable would come of it, or if his gladness was mediated by another of the four sorts of judgments distinguished above, such gladness would not count as evidence. For the same reason, if he was glad at it because of the kind of person he is, that is, because he desired things of that sort, his gladness would not count as evidence, if his desire in turn was mediated by any of the four other sorts of judgments. Someone's gladness at what he experienced counts as evidence only if he was glad at it on its own account, only, that is, if his gladness was unaffected by any beliefs he has about its relation to other things. If this is a correct interpretation of Mill's dictum, he then holds that someone's preference or desire for something qualifies only secondarily as evidence, and that the primary evidence anyone has of what is desirable of itself is having experienced it and being glad at it.

III. WHAT IS DESIRABLE FOR ITS OWN SAKE

HAVING FIXED on what Mill holds is the only ultimate evidence of what is desirable, we may now turn to what he maintains such evidence discloses. Mill urges that no one is ever glad on its own account at some state which his experience has disclosed to him unless some pleasure occurred in it, and therefore that no one is led by such experiences to desire like states to come about unless he expects that they will be pleasant. He also urges that no one is ever sorry on its own account about some state with which his experience has acquainted him unless there was something painful in it. Accordingly, the first thing which Mill argues that the relevant evidence discloses is that nothing is desirable of itself unless it is a state in which some pleasure is experienced and nothing is undesirable of itself unless it is a state in which some pain is felt.

Moore attacks Mill for maintaining that only pleasure is desired.[29] He concedes that in instances of many desires, pleasure is one feature of that of which someone is desirous. But he urges that on such occasions, what someone looks forward to and is desirous of is a pleasant walk or a pleasant conversation with a certain person, a pleasant party with certain companions or a pleasant smoke. To this some retort that while sometimes a walk, sometimes

[29]*Principia Ethica*, §42.

a smoke, sometimes a party is desired, each is desired only for the sake of the pleasure it will afford, so that it is pleasure alone which is desired for its own sake. Against this others urge that while the pleasure is one element of what someone looks forward to when he desires a walk, a smoke, or a party, the walk or the smoke or the party is also a component of what he is desirous of. Aristotle points out that when someone desires a certain walk but is denied it and is provided something else that affords him pleasure, his desire for the walk remains unfulfilled.[30] If pleasure alone were desired for its own sake, any pleasure would serve to fulfil a desire. Yet when someone desires a certain pleasant thing, his desire is fulfilled only by it, not by any pleasure at random. Secondly, Moore urges that on many occasions there is no expectation of pleasure characterizing that which someone is desirous of. Often someone desires to eat when hungry. While he feels pleasure at the prospect of eating, the prospect before his mind is simply that of eating certain things. A spectator watching a football game wants his team to score a goal. That of which he is thinking and of which he is desirous is its scoring. He has no thought of pleasure. When someone is struggling with a certain problem he desires a solution. No thought of pleasure is before his mind. Thirdly, Moore urges that although occasions are conceivable on which someone desires nothing but pleasure, if any occur, they are very rare; for what generally seems to be found is that someone is desirous of a pleasure of a certain sort, that is, a state characterized not only by pleasure but by other features as well.

There is nothing in these objections put by Moore which Mill does not agree with or which is incompatible with the evidence he adduces for what is desirable. Mill does not hold that only pleasure is desired. He agrees that there are many occasions on which that of which someone is desirous includes no thought of pleasure. Mill points out that many things are desired as a means to a certain end, and he notices that when something is desired as a means, there is very often no thought of it as pleasant. Mill also does not maintain that whenever something is desired without thought of what will come of it, it may be described as being desired for its own sake. He points out that men often desire something simply because they are in the habit of pursuing it, and have no thought of what it will lead to. He adds, "any . . . person whose purposes are fixed, carries out his purposes without any thought of the pleasure he has in contemplating them, or expects to derive from their fulfilment . . ." (238). He does indeed contend that nothing is desired for its own sake unless it is expected that it will be a state of affairs in which some pleasure will be experienced. But he does not claim that there are any occasions upon which pleasure alone characterizes what is desired. Although he contends that only what is desired for its own sake is evidence of

[30]*Nicomachean Ethics*, 1175b1.

what is desirable of itself, he does not think that whenever someone desires something for its own sake this counts as evidence; he holds that a man's desire of this sort counts as evidence only if it is based on experience of similar matters and he was glad on its own account at what he experienced.

According to Mill, the evidence whether one matter is more desirable of itself than another is of the same kind. He urges that no one who has ever actually had experience of two occasions in which only pleasure of the same sort was felt is gladder on its own account about one than the other unless it was more pleasant. Nor, he argues, is anyone, who has had experience of two occasions in which only pain of the same sort was felt, sorrier on its own account about one than the other unless more pain was felt in it; and no one is led by such experiences to prefer one to another of that sort unless he expects it would be less painful. No one with experience of toothaches prefers of itself a more severe to a less severe toothache. Accordingly, Mill argues, the relevant evidence further shows that as between two states in which only pleasure of the same sort is felt, one is more desirable of itself than the other only if it is more pleasant; and as between two states in which only pain of the same sort is felt, one is more undesirable of itself than the other only if it is more painful.

What evidence has someone in judging between states in which different sorts of pleasure or pain are felt? The same kind of evidence, Mill maintains. Someone has ultimate evidence for thinking the one more desirable of itself than the other only if he experienced both and was gladder at one than the other. Even though a toothache was more painful than a grief, someone has evidence for concluding that the grief was more undesirable of itself than the toothache if he experienced both and was sorrier at the grief. As between two painful states of different sorts Mill holds that the ultimate evidence that one was more undesirable of itself than the other is that someone who experienced both is sorrier at the one than the other. As between two pleasant states of different sorts he holds that regardless of whether one was more pleasant than the other, the ultimate evidence that it was more desirable of itself is that someone who experienced both was gladder at the one and is led by this to prefer, in the future, experiences like the one to experiences like the other. From this Mill ventures also to generalize what sorts of experiences are more desirable of themselves, independent of whether they are more pleasant: "the pleasures of the intellect, of the feelings and imagination, and of the moral sentiments [have] a much higher value as pleasures than . . . those of mere sensation," than "bodily pleasures" (211). For such a generalization that compares sorts of pleasures, the experiences of many are clearly relevant: "Of two pleasures, if there be one to which all or almost all who have experience of both give a decided preference, irrespective of any feeling of moral obligation to prefer it, that is the more desirable pleasure" (211).

In making the generalization that pleasant experiences of one sort are more desirable of themselves than those of another sort, Mill does not deny that a certain experience of a less desirable sort may be so much more pleasant than one of a more desirable sort as to be more desirable than it, or that certain painful experiences of a less undesirable sort may be so much more painful as to be more undesirable. He does not deny that a certain bodily agony may be more undesirable of itself than a certain grief. Here too Mill holds that the ultimate evidence someone has that the bodily agony was of such an intensity that it was more undesirable than the grief, is his having experienced both and being sorrier about the agony (213).

Moore charges that Mill's contention that some experiences are more desirable of themselves than others, even though not more pleasant, is inconsistent with his contention that nothing is desirable of itself unless it is a state in which some pleasure is experienced. Raphael seeks to free Mill of this charge of inconsistency by urging that Mill does not hold that it is possible "that a pleasure of higher quality may contain a lesser or no greater quantity of pleasure than a pleasure of lower quality."[31] Raphael continues, "Mill's criterion is preference, and I think he would say that to prefer one pleasure to another is to desire it the more strongly. And since he says later, in Chapter IV, that to desire a thing is the same as to think it pleasant, it follows, on this view, that to prefer a thing is to think it more pleasant." Mill certainly holds that whoever prefers one thing to another desires it more. He also writes, "desiring a thing and finding it pleasant . . . are . . . inseparable" (237). But he does not claim that no one desires one thing more than another unless he expects that it will be more pleasant. Instead he writes,

> If I am asked . . . what makes one pleasure more valuable than another, merely as a pleasure, except its being greater in amount, there is but one possible answer. . . . If one of the two is, by those who are competently acquainted with both, placed so far above the other that they prefer it, even though knowing it to be attended with a greater amount of discontent, . . . we are justified in ascribing to the preferred enjoyment a superiority in quality, so far outweighing quantity as to render it, in comparison, of small account. (211.)

In pursuing the point further, Raphael gives up his contention that "the distinction of quality is, at bottom, the same as the distinction of quantity." He no longer interprets Mill as holding that it is impossible for one experience to be more desirable of itself unless it is more pleasant. Instead, he takes Mill to mean that one experience is never *in fact* more desirable of itself unless it is more pleasant. In support of this, Raphael points out that when Mill remarks that it is "better to be Socrates dissatisfied than a fool satisfied," Mill also denies that "this preference takes place at a sacrifice of happiness" (212). Raphael urges that although Socrates is dissatisfied and the fool not, it

[31]Raphael, 352.

is consistent for Mill to maintain that Socrates is happier than the fool and his happiness more desirable, in so far as Socrates "enjoys a greater balance of pleasure over pain, than the fool." Raphael does indeed show that in maintaining that it is better to be Socrates dissatisfied than a fool satisfied, it would be consistent for Mill to hold that no experience is more desirable of itself than another unless it is more pleasant. In making this point, however, Raphael fails to show that Mill does in fact maintain that one experience is more desirable of itself than another only if it is more pleasant. Mill speaks, instead, of "what makes one pleasure more valuable than another . . . except its being greater in amount"; he writes of being "justified in ascribing . . . a superiority in quality, so far outweighing quantity . . ." (211). In a journal of 1854, Mill remarks, "Quality as well as quantity of happiness is to be considered; less of a higher kind is preferable to more of a lower."[32] Raphael himself acknowledges that Mill would "say that a superior pleasure may be less intense than an inferior."

Moore, however, charges that "Mill's judgment of preference, so far from establishing the principle that pleasure alone is good, is obviously inconsistent with it. . . . If one pleasure can differ from another in quality, that means, that a pleasure is something complex, something composed, in fact, of pleasure *in addition to* that which produces pleasure."[33] Mill is involved in no difficulty here. When he holds that only a pleasure is desirable of itself he is not holding that only the pleasantness of a pleasant experience is desirable. By a pleasure he understands a pleasant experience. He maintains that only a complex, that is, an experience having pleasantness as one of its features, is desirable of itself. The inconsistency with which Moore charges Mill is this:

Mill, therefore, in admitting that a sensual indulgence can be directly judged to be lower than another pleasure, in which the degree of pleasure involved may be the same, is admitting that other things may be good, or bad, quite independently of the pleasure which accompanies them. . . . [I]f you say, as Mill does, that quality of pleasure is to be taken into account, then you are no longer holding that pleasure *alone* is good as an end, since you imply that something else, something which is *not* present in all pleasures, is *also* good as an end.[34]

This charge is easily rebutted. In holding that some experiences are more desirable of themselves than others, although not more pleasant, Mill certainly admits that the intrinsic desirability of an experience may be enhanced by other components of it than the pleasure enjoyed in it. He would therefore agree with Moore that such components "may be good . . . independently of the pleasure which accompanies them." But Mill would hold that such components are desirable as contributing to the intrinsic desirability of the

---

[32]"Diary," in *Letters*, ed. Elliot, II, 381 (23/3/54).
[33]*Principia Ethica*, §48.   [34]*Ibid.*, §48.

experience. He does not maintain that any experience is desirable of itself if it has such other components but is not also pleasant. Consequently, when Mill argues that the relevant evidence shows that nothing is desirable in itself unless it is a state in which some pleasure is enjoyed, it is not inconsistent for him to argue that the relevant evidence also shows that some pleasant experiences are more desirable of themselves although not more pleasant.

One writer contends that Mill means by " 'pleasure,' whatever is made the object of desire."[35] Mill, however, does not hold that whenever anyone desires something as a means—say, having a tooth extracted—it is to be described as a pleasure. Mill also mentions that men often desire something simply because they are in the habit of pursuing it and that "any . . . person whose purposes are fixed, carries out his purposes without any thought of . . . pleasure." Another writer contends that Mill uses "pleasure" as "a technical term for whatever anyone desires for its own sake."[36] Mill, however, does not regard an enjoyable experience as any less a pleasure when it comes to a man without having been desired. He maintains that some experiences are desired for their own sake more than others although not more pleasant. Moreover, while he holds that there is no happiness without pleasure, he does not think that when someone desires happiness for its own sake, what he desires is to be described as a pleasure.

Mill does not hold that the only things that are desirable of themselves are transient experiences in which pleasure alone is felt or that the only things that are undesirable of themselves are transient experiences in which pain alone is felt. He does not question that even if it involves both pleasure and pain, the whole of a man's life, or some prolonged portion of it, may be desirable or undesirable of itself. We might expect Mill to hold that one portion of a man's life is more desirable than another if the pleasant experiences comprising it are more pleasant and more numerous and the painful less painful and less numerous, provided these component experiences are not of more desirable sorts than others; and that in so far as some of the component experiences are of more desirable sorts than others, one portion of a man's life is more desirable if its components are more desirable and its more desirable components are more numerous. In one passage Mill speaks as if one portion of a man's life is happier and more desirable so long as these conditions alone are fulfilled. He writes, ". . . Greatest Happiness . . . is an existence exempt as far as possible from pain, and as rich as possible in enjoyments, both in point of quantity and quality. . . ." He immediately adds, "the test of quality, and the rule for measuring it against quantity, being the preference felt by those who, in their opportunities of experience . . . are

[35]Anon., "Utilitarianism," in J. O. Urmson, ed., *The Concise Encyclopaedia of Western Philosophy and Philosophers* (London: Hutchinson, 1960), 384.
[36]Anon., "John Stuart Mill," *ibid.*, 268.

best furnished with the means of comparison" (214). In this passage Mill speaks as if he regards the intrinsic desirability of a portion of a man's life, taken on the whole, as dependent only on the intensity and intrinsic desirability of each of the several component pleasant and painful experiences and upon the proportion among them.

Elsewhere, however, Mill does not maintain that there is immediate evidence for the intrinsic desirability only of momentary experiences. For he urges that evidence that a man's happiness is desirable is furnished by the fact that he desires it (234). From what Mill says regarding preferences, it is clear that he would not hold that a man's desire for happiness supplied evidence unless he had experience of the matters comprising happiness and was glad at them. Mill also urges that the evidence that one sort of life is more desirable of itself than another is preference (211). But he does not hold that a man's preference is evidence that one "mode of existence" is on the whole more desirable of itself than another, unless his experience has acquainted him with both and he was gladder at one sort than the other. He then holds that the ultimate evidence that one portion of a man's life was intrinsically more desirable than another is that he who had experience of both was gladder on the whole at it. Mill would not hold that someone's being gladder at one portion of life is evidence that it was more desirable on the whole, unless he was acquainted with the many experiences comprising each. In what way would he take account of the component experiences? In looking back over a portion of his life, someone will look upon some experiences that were quite desirable of themselves as detracting from the desirability of the whole and will see others of little desirability in themselves as appreciably enhancing the desirability of the whole. In assessing the intrinsic desirability, on the whole, of a portion of a man's life, the desirability of each component experience to be reckoned with is not the desirability it has of itself but its desirability as contributing to the intrinsic desirability of that portion of life on the whole. In desiring his own happiness henceforth, moreover, it is then reasonable for a man to rate any experience that may befall him not in terms of its intrinsic desirability but in terms of its desirability as enhancing the desirability of his life on the whole.

When Mill speaks of the most desirable life for a man as an "existence exempt as far as possible from pain, and as rich as possible in enjoyments, both in quantity and quality," he holds that a man's life is intrinsically more desirable the greater the preponderance of intrinsically desirable experiences comprising it. It is indeed logically possible that the greater the preponderance of intrinsically desirable experiences comprising a man's life the more it would also be made up of component experiences which enhanced its desirability on the whole. Yet it seems doubtful that this often in fact would be the case. Mill hardly faces this issue. At all events, he would hold that the reason why any experience is desirable as a component of happiness is not that it is desirable of itself but that it enhances the desirability of the life of which it is a part. It is doubtless not because he regards active pleasures as more pleasant or as of an intrinsically more desirable sort, but because he regards them as enhancing the desirability of life, that Mill speaks of a man's happiness as greater if it includes "many and various pleasures, with a decided predominance of the active over the passive . . ." (215).

Although Mill neglects to distinguish the desirability of a pleasant experience as a part of happiness from its desirability of itself, he uses this distinction with regard to other matters. Mill acknowledges that men desire for their own sake "things which, in common language, are decidedly distinguished from happiness" (235). He cites virtue, money, power, fame. In order to show that desires for these do not supply evidence that other things than happiness are intrinsically desirable, Mill seeks to argue that when any of these comes to be desired no longer as a means, it is desired only as a part of happiness. Moore urges three objections against this.[37] He contends that "these admissions are . . . in . . . glaring contradiction with his argument that pleasure . . . is the only thing desired." He reproaches Mill for holding that " 'money,' these actual coins . . . are . . . a part of my pleasant feelings." He condemns Mill for holding that "what is only a means to an end, is the same thing as a part of that end." When Mill speaks of things desired as a part of happiness, he is not speaking of them as a part of pleasant feelings but as a part of "an existence made up of few and transitory pains, many and various pleasures. . ." (215). Mill's contention that nothing is desired for its own sake save that which involves some pleasant experience is not contradicted by his contention that objects of desire are characterized by other features as well. Mill also does not claim that whatever is desired as a means to happiness is desired as a part of happiness. He claims rather that certain things desired as a means to happiness come through that association to be desired no longer as a means, and that when this has occurred, they are desired as a part of happiness. C. D. Broad attacks Mill for contending that originally human beings desire things because they expect them to be pleasant and later come to desire other things as well by association. He urges that "it is unlikely that" humans in early infancy "have the experience of desiring . . . for a reason at all."[38] But Mill does not hold that infants originally desire things only because they expect them to be pleasant. He points out that it is not the case that whatever even adults desire "they have the experience of desiring . . . for a reason."[39]

[37]*Principia Ethica*, §43.
[38]*Five Types of Ethical Theory* (London: Kegan Paul, 1930), 190.
[39]*Utilitarianism*, 238; "Sedgwick," 59.

Mill seeks to show that only happiness is intrinsically desirable by arguing that when anything else—virtue, fame, power, money—once desired as a means to happiness, comes to be desired for its own sake, it is desired only as a part of happiness. Even if that which is desired is in fact a part of "an existence made up of few and transitory pains, many and various pleasures," this does not show that it is desired only as a part of happiness. Mill argues: "What was once desired as an instrument for the attainment of happiness, has come to be desired for its own sake. In being desired for its own sake it is, however, desired as *part* of happiness. The person is made, or thinks he would be made, happy by its mere possession. . . ." (236.) This argument is open to more serious objections. If Mill can succeed in showing that virtue, or fame, or power, or money comes to be desired only as a part of happiness, he can no longer hold that it is desired for its own sake. He then removes his ground for arguing that the "ingredients of happiness are very various, and each of them is desirable in itself. . ." (235). And even if he is successful in showing that each comes to be desired only as a part of happiness, this in no way establishes that each is desirable as a part of happiness. The fact that a certain individual desires money because "it has come to be itself a principal ingredient of the individual's conception of happiness" or because he "thinks he would be made happy by its mere possession" does not show that his happiness would in fact be enhanced thereby.

Mill is particularly concerned about virtue. He notices that a man is not virtuous unless he enjoys acting virtuously (239). Virtuous conduct is therefore not only desirable of itself; it is also a pleasant activity which is desirable because it enhances a man's happiness. Mill also notices that men cannot be virtuous without acting disinterestedly (235). He urges that it is desirable that they be virtuous, for they then have dispositions leading them to do what is desirable (235). Mill hereby acknowledges that in this respect virtue is desirable as instrumental to happiness, not desirable as a component of happiness which enhances it. Although it is desirable that men be virtuous as a means to happiness, Mill notices that a man cannot be virtuous if he desires to be virtuous or to do what is virtuous as a means to happiness. A man cannot be virtuous unless he desires to do what is virtuous for its own sake. What appears to trouble Mill is how to acknowledge the disinterestedness of virtue without acknowledging that it is something other than happiness desired for its own sake, and therefore desirable for its own sake. The solution Mill adopts is that when a man desires virtue for its own sake, he desires it only as a part of happiness, that is, in the belief that it will enhance his happiness. This solution will not do. If a man desires to be virtuous because it will enhance his happiness, he falls short of being genuinely virtuous just as when he desires to be virtuous as a means to happiness. When a man desires to be virtuous he also hopes for happiness, but he does not desire to be virtuous out of the hope that it will yield him happiness. Mill overlooks another solution which his own line of reasoning affords. No one who considers the matter dispassionately regards it as desirable of itself that the virtuous suffer and the evil be meted out happiness.

Mill maintains that only happiness or what includes happiness is intrinsically desirable. He also commonly speaks of only a life or an extended portion of a life as happy or unhappy. This raises a further issue. If Mill thinks that only a period of life comprising several component experiences can be happy or unhappy, he must then deny that any momentary pleasant experience is intrinsically desirable and that any transient painful experience is intrinsically undesirable. On the other hand, Mill holds that if someone who has had first-hand acquaintance with an experience is glad on its own account that it occurred, this is conclusive evidence that it was intrinsically desirable. He would hold that this evidence would not be upset if later someone would be gladder if that particular pleasant experience had not occurred because it detracted from the happiness of a period of life of which it was a part. Mill also seems to maintain that if, among its many consequences, the only effect that an action has on a certain man is to cause him some brief pleasure, it then causes him happiness. Even if the brief pleasure it caused him was such that it detracted from his happiness, Mill would have to admit that it was intrinsically desirable. He can then not continue to adhere to the contention that the relevant evidence shows that only happiness is intrinsically desirable. Mill would not be troubled by this qualification, for he can still maintain that happiness or what includes happiness is invariably intrinsically more desirable than that which does not.

If Mill held that happiness is the only thing intrinsically desirable, he could not claim that the effects of one action are intrinsically more desirable than those of another if and only if it causes more happiness. But he can maintain this because he contends that the effects of one action are intrinsically more desirable than those of another if the one set of effects contains more happiness than does the other. Mill does not support this contention by direct appeal to the ultimate evidence for what is desirable but by inference from what it discloses. His inference is that since it is intrinsically desirable for A to be happy and intrinsically desirable for B to be happy and intrinsically desirable for C to be happy, it is intrinsically desirable for A and B and C each to be happy.[40] While he would hold that the reason why any experience is desirable as a component of a certain man's happiness is not that it is intrinsically desirable but that it enhances the desirability of his life on the whole, a like consideration does not apply regarding the "general happiness." Mill contends that a state of affairs comprising the happiness

[40]See lxxxii above.

and unhappiness of many beings is intrinsically more desirable the more happiness it comprises and the greater the preponderance of happiness over unhappiness within it. Some critics charge him with introducing an extraneous consideration when he adds Bentham's dictum, "everybody to count for one, nobody for more than one." Mill, however, points out that when this dictum is understood as asserting that "equal amounts of happiness are equally desirable, whether felt by the same or by different persons," and that "one person's happiness, supposed equal in degree (with the proper allowance made for kind), is counted for exactly as much as another's," all that is spelled out by it is that the preponderance of happiness over unhappiness be "both in point of quantity and quality" and in nothing else (257, 214).

IV. ANALYSIS OF MORAL CONCEPTS

WE HAVE NOW to consider a further set of objections urged against Mill's utilitarianism. It is urged that if it is correct, whenever someone could more effectively promote the general happiness by taking another's automobile and continuing to use it without his consent, it would be quite right for him to do so. Whenever someone could make better use of another's house or clothing or other possession, there would be nothing wrong in his stealing it. The fact that it belonged to another would be irrelevant. It is contended that utilitarianism rides roughshod over all rights, not only rights of property. If a wife and children are burdened with a cantankerous husband and father, it would be right for her to drown him secretly and replace him with another husband, if everybody affected would be happier in consequence. Since utilitarianism reckons only with consequences, it is also urged that it can find no place for what is fair or just, or for men being rewarded as they deserve. Because it is unfair of a father to provide for some of his children while neglecting the others, or for some to cheat on their income tax while deriving the advantages from those who make full returns, or for many to toil long hours with little returns while the idle and lazy enjoy an abundance of good things, or for one to receive the credit for what another has accomplished—all this is irrelevant, so long as the resultant enjoyment is maximized. If the happiness of a country is best realized by slavery, it is claimed that any appeal to the injustice of slavery or to men's right to freedom are considerations of which utilitarianism can take no account.[41]

Utilitarianism is also criticized for holding that men have but one duty, to maximize enjoyment. This is not a duty to any specific persons. Humans and other animals are looked upon as only so many "dumping grounds" on

[41] J. Rawls, "Justice as Fairness," *Philosophical Review*, 67 (1958), 164–94.

which to bestow enjoyment. It is not denied that people have duties to promote the happiness of others, but what is urged is that they have duties to provide different sorts of happiness to different persons and other duties to certain persons than to promote their happiness.[42] A man has a duty to afford his wife certain enjoyments which he does not have a duty to furnish other women. He has duties to his children which he does not owe to other children. The happiness which he owes his children is different from that which he owes his wife. When someone has hired a man to paint his house, he thinks that it is right to pay him because he has promised to. He does not reckon whether some alternative use of his money would more effectively promote the general happiness. It is urged that utilitarianism takes account only of consequences but that duties such as these arise from an antecedent relationship in which someone stands to certain persons. It is pointed out that besides these duties, men have duties which they owe to all men—to tell the truth, for instance. Granted that this duty may be outweighed on occasion by a more stringent obligation, it is argued that it does not cease whenever the general happiness would be more effectively promoted by neglecting it. It is not denied that by doing what is right a man very often does what will in fact promote the general happiness, but it is urged that utilitarianism is guilty of gross oversimplification, disregarding the diversity of considerations determining what is the right thing to do. In virtue of these it is contended that it is very often morally incumbent on a man to do a certain thing whether or not it would maximize the general happiness.

Most of these objections are not to Mill's contention that happiness is the only thing intrinsically desirable; they rather criticize Mill for contending that questions of right and wrong are questions of what would have the most desirable consequences. Mill seeks to cope with objections such as these by elucidating what is implied when it is asserted that it would be right or wrong or unjust to do a certain thing, and by analyzing what is meant when someone is said to have a right to something or to have an obligation to do a certain thing.

Mill notices that very often when people say that a certain thing ought not to be done they would not also be prepared to say that it would be wrong to do it. He writes, "the morality of an individual action is not a question of direct perception, but of the application of a law to an individual case" (206). He maintains that whenever it is asserted that it would be wrong to do a certain action, it is claimed that there is some "rule of morality" against it. He also writes, "it would be unworthy of an intelligent agent not to be consciously aware that the action is of a class which, if practised generally, would be generally injurious. . ." (220). From this it might be thought that

[42]E. F. Carritt, *Theory of Morals* (London: Oxford University Press, 1928), 40.

Mill holds that all that is contained in the claim that there is a rule of morality against a certain action is that it is an action of a kind which generally ought not to be done. If this is Mill's view, there is a fatal objection to it. Glancing at his fuel gauge, a motorist thinks he ought to get more gasoline. He thinks that he ought to do so in the belief that a motorist in general ought to replenish his supply of fuel when it is almost exhausted. Yet he would not think that he would be doing something wrong if he were not to get more gasoline. Mill does not maintain that to claim that there is a rule of morality against a certain action is simply to claim that it is an action of a kind which generally ought not to be done.

In his essay, *On Liberty*, Mill distinguishes two sorts of rules of conduct. He holds that a rule of conduct is not part of the law of the land unless infractions of it incur punishment by the government. To laws he contrasts rules sanctioned by general condemnation.[43] Since he also speaks of these as sanctioned by "moral coercion,"[44] it might be thought that he holds that when anyone claims that there is a rule of morality against a certain action, all that he is claiming is that it is an action of a kind which incurs general condemnation. Mill, however, does not deny that men often believe that it would be wrong to do a certain action although well aware that it is not of a sort that is generally condemned.[45] He does not maintain that the fact that an action is of a kind that incurs general condemnation entails that there is some rule of morality against it.[46] Instead, he writes, "We do not call anything wrong, unless we mean to imply that a person ought to be punished in some way or other for doing it; if not by law, by the opinion of his fellow creatures. . ." (246). Mill thus urges that when it is said that it would be wrong to do a certain action it is implied not that it is an action of a kind which is in fact generally condemned but rather that it is of a kind which ought in general to be condemned by others. In the same passage, he continues, "This seems the real turning point of the distinction between morality and simple expediency." He contends that when it is said that it would be wrong to do a certain action, it is implied what others ought to do about it, by way of condemnation. For this, if for no other reason, the distinction between the notion of "wrong" and the notion of "ought not" cannot be erased.

Mill distinguishes something further implied in the claim that there is a rule of morality. He urges that no one claims that there is a rule of morality against a certain action without implying that it is a rule which ought in

---

[43]*On Liberty* (London: Parker, 1859), 14–15.
[44]*Ibid.*, 21.
[45]See "The Utility of Religion," 410.
[46]See "Whewell," 184.

general to be observed.[47] The claim that a certain action is contrary to a rule which ought in general to be observed implies that it is an action of a kind which in general ought not to be done. The former is a stronger claim than the latter. When someone has in mind actions of a certain description and believes that such actions in general ought not to be done, his belief implies that actions of that description are in general capable of being avoided. But his belief does not also imply that men in general are capable of understanding the description of action which he has in mind or that they are capable of avoiding such actions through having such a description in mind. On the other hand, whoever claims that a certain rule ought in general to be observed implies that men in general are capable of observing it. He therefore implies that actions of the kind covered by the rule are of a description which is intelligible to men generally, and that it is a description simple enough and precise enough so that men generally are capable of making out whether some action they are considering would accord with the rule. Consequently someone may be correct in claiming that actions of a certain sort ought not to be done, but not correct in claiming that a rule against them ought in general to be observed.

Mill maintains that two claims are made when it is asserted that it would be wrong to do a certain action: it is not only implied that it is an action of a kind which ought in general to be condemned; it is also implied that it would be contrary to a rule which ought in general to be observed. If such an assertion carried only these two implications, it would not be inconsistent for someone to hold that it would be wrong for him to do a certain thing but deny that he ought not to do it. Although Mill does not speak clearly on this matter, something he says in discussing the concept of justice is applicable. He points out that even though a man believed that a certain action was of a sort which in general would be unjust, he would not regard that particular action as unjust if he believed that it would not be wrong to do it (259). It may be presumed that Mill similarly holds that even if someone believed that a certain action was of a kind which in general would be wrong, he would still not think that it would be wrong to do it if he did not think that it ought not to be done. He then acknowledges that when it is asserted that it would be wrong to do a certain action it is implied that it ought not to be done.

Some thinkers hold that "ought" is ambiguous. They contend that when it is said that someone ought to do something, sometimes all that is asserted is that he has an obligation to do it, while at other times this is not implied.[48]

[47]Morality may be defined as "the rules and precepts for human conduct, by the observance of which an existence such as has been described might be, to the greatest extent possible, secured to all mankind..." (*Utilitarianism*, 214).

[48]H. A. Prichard, *Moral Obligation* (New York: Oxford University Press, 1950), 67.

Mill notices that an action is spoken of as one that ought to be done both in contexts in which it is said that there is an obligation to do it and in contexts in which this would not also be said.[49] But he does not accept the view that "ought" is ambiguous on this account. He maintains that what differentiates a context in which it is said that someone has an obligation is that something more is then asserted. Mill holds that when it is asserted that someone has an obligation to do a certain thing it is implied that this is so in virtue of the sort of action it is. He contends that this assertion also carries an implication as to adverse responses by others for failure to act: "We do not call anything wrong, unless we mean to imply that a person ought to be punished in some way or other for doing it. . . . It is a part of the notion of Duty in every one of its forms. . . ." (246.) From this passage it might seem that Mill regards the claim that there is an obligation to do a certain thing as equivalent to the claim that it would be wrong not to do it. Mill, however, mentions two respects in which these claims differ. He notices that one obligation may be overruled by another. When it is, it would not be wrong to fulfil it (259). Consequently the claim that someone has an obligation to do a certain thing implies rather that there is a presumption that it would be wrong for him not to do it. For the same reason, it implies not that he ought to do it but that there is a presumption that he ought to.

In the passage cited Mill continues: "It is a part of the notion of Duty in every one of its forms, that a person may rightfully be compelled to fulfil it. Duty is a thing which may be *exacted* from a person. . ." (246.) Exacted by whom? Mill distinguishes a perfect from an imperfect obligation according to whether there is some assignable person to whom a man is under an obligation (247). H. L. A. Hart contends that when it is asserted that one person, A, has an obligation to some assignable person, B, to do X, it is implied that it would be morally legitimate for B to compel A to do X, but not that it would be morally legitimate for others to compel A to do X.[50] Mill does not agree that when it is asserted, for example, that a wife has certain obligations to her husband, it is implied that it would not be wrong for him to force her to fulfil them. He holds rather that when it is asserted that A has an obligation to some assignable person, B, to do X, it is implied that it would in general not be wrong for others to compel A to do X, but he does not hold that it is implied that there are certain assignable persons for whom it would not be wrong to exercise such compulsion. As an example of an imperfect obligation Mill mentions the obligation to be generous. Although Mill writes, "It is a part of the notion of Duty in every one of its forms, that a person may rightfully be compelled to fulfil it," he later abandons this

[49]See *Logic*, II, 552–4 (VI, xii, 6). Cf. *Letters*, ed. Elliot, I, 229–31 (to W. G. Ward, 28/11/59).
[50]"Are There Any Natural Rights?" *Philosophical Review*, 54 (1955), 178, 183, 184.

contention, and takes it rather as a distinguishing mark of a perfect obliga-tion. For when it is said that someone has an obligation to be generous, Mill points out that it is not implied that it would not be wrong for others to force him to be generous. All that is implied is that there is a presumption that it would be wrong for him not to be generous.

Hand in hand with the question of what is claimed when someone is said to have an obligation is the question of what is claimed when someone is said to have a certain right. Some urge that sometimes when it is asserted that a man has a right to do something, all that is meant is that it would be right, that is, not wrong, for him to do it.[51] Mill does not acknowledge that this assertion ever bears this sense, for when it is asserted that a man has a certain right, it is implied that his right is capable of being violated by others. What more is implied? One suggestion is that to assert that a man has a right to something is equivalent to saying that others ought not to deprive him of it. Mill does not accept this view. Someone may hold that motorists who are running out of gasoline ought to stop at the nearest service station and yet deny that the operators of service stations have a right to their patronage. Mill would hold that by denying that they have a right to such patronage, one is denying that such motorists ought to be compelled to give the nearest service station their patronage. He maintains that when it is claimed that a man has a right to a certain thing, it is implied that in general others ought to prevent anyone from depriving him of it (250). Mill also contends that it is not claimed that a man has a right to a certain thing unless it is implied that others have an obligation not to deprive him of it. But he does not hold that this claim implies that it would invariably be wrong for anyone to deprive him of it, for the obligation not to deprive him of it may be overruled by another obligation. Mill therefore holds that the claim that a man has a right to a certain thing implies rather that there is a presumption, that is, that in general, it would be wrong for anyone to deprive him of it.

Mill rejects the view that no one can have an obligation without another person having a right. He points out that when it is said that someone has an obligation to be generous, it is not implied that others have a right to his generosity. Mill certainly holds that the claim that a man has a right to a cer-tain thing implies that others have an obligation not to deprive him of it. This he classifies as a perfect obligation: "duties of perfect obligation are those duties in virtue of which a correlative *right* resides in some person or per-sons. . ." (247). From this it may be thought that Mill holds that no one can have an obligation to an assignable person without the latter having a right. The ascription to Mill of such a view is not borne out by his own analysis, for he holds that the assertion that someone has an obligation not to deprive A of X implies that it would in general not be wrong for others to

[51]*Ibid.*, 179.

prevent him from depriving A of X. But Mill contends that the assertion that A has a right to X carries a stronger implication, namely, that others in general ought to prevent anyone from depriving A of X. If it would in general not be wrong for others to prevent anyone from depriving A of X, it does not follow that they also ought to.

Mill's analysis of the concept of justice can readily be shown in relation to his analyses of the concepts that have just been considered. Here as hitherto the question is not what actions or sorts of actions Mill maintains are unjust, but what he holds is being said about an action when it is asserted that it would be unjust to do it. Mill makes five main points. First, he writes, "Justice implies something which it is . . . wrong not to do. . ." (247). Here Mill is maintaining that when it is asserted that it would be unjust for some-one to do a certain thing, it is implied that it would be wrong for him to do it. It therefore implies whatever the latter implies. Accordingly, he states, "the idea of penal sanction . . . enters not only into the conception of injustice, but into that of any kind of wrong. We do not call anything wrong, unless we mean to imply that a person ought to be punished in some way or other for doing it; if not by law, by the opinion of his fellow creatures. . . ." (246.) Mill's second point is that "Justice implies something which it is not only . . . wrong not to do, but which some individual person can claim from us as his moral right" (247). He here notices that not all actions re-garded as wrong are also classified as unjust. Mill's third point is that when it is asserted that it would be unjust for someone to do a certain thing, it is implied that if he were to do it he would be violating an obligation that he has to some other assignable person (247). Mill's fourth point is that when it is asserted that it would be unjust for someone to do a certain thing, it is implied that he would thereby be depriving another person of something to which he has a right. Speaking of "this distinction . . . which exists between justice and the other obligations," he writes, "justice, the term, . . . involve[s] the idea of a personal right . . . injustice . . . implies two things—a wrong done, and some assignable person who is wronged" (247). Here Mill urges that someone is not described as having done anything unjust if the wrong that he did was to other animals or to himself. He is not described as having done something unjust unless he is regarded as having done something wrong to another human being. When we think that it would be unjust for someone to do a certain thing, we imply that it would not in general be wrong for others to compel him not to do it. This implication is contained in Mill's third point. He brings out a further implication of his fourth point when he writes: "When we think that a person is bound in justice to do a thing, it is an ordinary form of language to say, that he ought to be compelled to do it" (245).

Mill's fifth and last point is contained in the statement, "Wherever there is a right, the case is one of justice. . ." (247). If Mill means by this that whenever someone is said to have a right to something it is implied that it would be unjust to deprive him of it, then this fifth point is not compatible with what he says elsewhere. Mill holds that when it is claimed that a man has a right to a certain thing, it is implied that in general it would be wrong for anyone to deprive him of it. But he acknowledges that the obligation not to deprive him of it may be overruled by other considerations: "to save a life, it may not only be allowable, but a duty, to steal, or to take by force, the necessary food or medicine, or to kidnap, and compel to officiate, the only qualified medical practitioner. In such cases . . . we usually say, not that justice must give way to some other moral principle, but that what is just in ordinary cases is, by reason of that other principle, not just in the particular case." (259.) Mill hereby points out that the claim that a man has a right to a certain thing does not imply that it would invariably be wrong for anyone to deprive him of it. In this passage he also writes, "justice is a name for certain moral requirements . . . of more paramount obligation, than any others." Mill would certainly agree that the obligation to do what is just is absolutely paramount over all other considerations. But he also points out in this passage that the respect in which it is paramount is that when someone believes that a certain particular action would be of a sort which in general is unjust, but also believes that it would not be wrong to do it, he would not say that it would be unjust but not wrong to do it. He would instead say that since it would not be wrong to do it, it would not be unjust to do it. Mill points out that no one regards a certain action as unjust unless he also regards it as wrong.

Having focussed on Mill's analyses of four chief concepts—right and wrong, obligation, a right, justice—we have now to notice certain bearings of these analyses. Mill holds that when it is asserted that it would be wrong for a man to do a certain action, it is not only implied that he ought not to do it, it is also implied that it is contrary to a rule which ought in general to be observed and that it is an action of a kind which ought in general to be condemned. He contends that this is all that is implied. Asserting that it would be wrong to do a certain action is then a short-hand way of making three distinct ought statements in regard to it. The adjectives "right" and "wrong" could then be eliminated from language. It is useful to retain them as a short-hand way of making these three distinct ought statements at once. A similar point applies to the other three concepts. Mill maintains that when it is asserted that a man has an obligation to do a certain action, all that is implied is that it is an action of a kind which in general it would be wrong not to do; and that when it is also understood that he is under an obligation to some assignable person to do it, all that is implied in addition is that it would in general not be wrong for others to compel him to do it. Since these implications in turn are equivalent to a number of ought statements, the assertion that someone has an obligation to do a certain action is also a short-hand way of making several ought statements in regard to it. Mill also holds that when it is asserted that a man has a right to a certain thing, it is not only implied that others in general ought to prevent anyone from depriving him of it; it is also implied that it would in general be wrong for anyone to deprive him of it. The noun, "a right," could then be eliminated from language by replacing it with the several ought statements to which it is equivalent. Finally, Mill maintains that when it is asserted that it would be unjust for a certain man to do a certain action, it is not only implied that it would be wrong for him to do it; all that is implied in addition is that if he were to do it he would be violating someone's right. Since each of these implications in turn is equivalent to a number of ought statements, the adjectives "just" and "unjust" could be eliminated from language, but are useful to retain as short-hand devices for asserting a cluster of ought statements.

Mill errs in two respects in his analysis of the concept of justice. When it is claimed that a man has a right to worship in accord with the dictates of his own conscience, it is not implied that if someone were to prevent him from worshipping in this manner, he would be doing something unjust. Similarly, a man who tortures or murders another is not described as doing something unjust, even though it is held that he is doing another wrong and is doing something that others in general ought to prevent anyone from doing. Consequently, Mill is not correct in maintaining that a man is described as doing something unjust whenever he is regarded as doing something wrong and as violating another's right. Sidgwick points out that Mill is also not correct in maintaining that whenever it is asserted that it would be unjust for someone to do a certain thing it is implied that others ought to compel him not to do it.[52] When it is claimed that a father is unjust to one of his children, it is not implied that others ought to use compulsion to prevent him. Mill can hardly be blamed for falling short in analysis of the concept of justice where others generally have failed. Although he is mistaken as to the specific set of ought statements which he holds is implied by the claim that it would be unjust to do a certain thing, his mistake in this does not show that there is not some set of ought statements to which this claim is equivalent.

What emerges from Mill's analyses is that there is a common element to assertions using the terms right and wrong, obligation, a right, just and unjust. He does not maintain that all these are but different ways of saying that a certain action ought or ought not to be done, or that they are not different from each other. He holds that each implies nothing but a number of ought statements. The correctness of each cannot be made out without making out whether what it implies is correct. Hence each can be made out

[52]H. Sidgwick, The Methods of Ethics (London: Macmillan, 7th ed., 1907), 265.

to be correct if there is some answer in general as to what ought to be done and what ought not. To make out whether it would be wrong for a certain person to do a certain thing, it is not sufficient to make out that he ought not to do it. Mill holds that it also has to be made out that it would be contrary to a moral principle for him to do it. Mill contends that it would be contrary to a moral principle only if it would be contrary to a rule which ought in general to be observed. If there is a general answer as to what ought to be done, it can then be made out what rules ought generally to be observed and what sorts of actions ought in general to be condemned. Since the question whether it would be wrong for a certain action to be done is a question in part whether it would be contrary to a moral principle, the question whether it would be right or wrong for a certain action to be done is a question about the morality of it. Mill holds that since questions of whether it would be unjust for a man to do a certain thing, or of whether he has a certain obligation or a certain right, also carry implications about what it would be wrong to do, they also are moral questions. If there is a general answer as to what ought to be done, the answers to moral questions can be made out. Mill holds that if there is such a general answer, it will apply not only to moral questions, but also wherever the question of what ought to be done arises and where moral considerations do not.[53]

Mill seeks to bring out how it can be determined whether it would be wrong to do a certain action by analyzing what is implied when it is asserted that it would be wrong to do it. We might similarly expect him to grapple with the question of how the correctness of any ought statement can be determined by inquiring what is implied by any such statement. Instead of taking this course, he inquires if there is a test in general for what ought to be done. We have seen that Mill maintains that something ought to be done if and only if it would maximize happiness. In putting forth this principle, Mill does not claim that when it is asserted that something ought to be done, it is implied that it would maximize happiness; he claims rather that it provides a test. Mill's analyses of assertions employing the concepts of wrong, obligation, a right and justice are logically independent of his claim as to what is the supreme test of what ought to be done. He holds that it is the supreme test of the correctness of such assertions because they are equivalent to sets of ought statements and it is the supreme test of ought statements generally: "if . . . happiness is the sole end of human action, and the promotion of it the test by which to judge of all human conduct . . . it necessarily follows that it must be the criterion of morality, since a part is included in the whole."[54]

Two parts may be distinguished in Mill's contention as to what provides

[53]See *Logic*, II, 552–6 (VI, xii, 6–7).
[54]*Utilitarianism*, 237; cf. "Whewell," 189.

a supreme test. Although he does not say it, it may be presumed that he holds, in the first place, that when it is asserted that something ought to be done, it is implied that its consequences would be intrinsically more desirable than those of any alternative. The second step is his contention that the test of whether the consequences of something would be intrinsically more desirable than those of any alternative is afforded by whether it would cause more happiness. This he derives from the more general contention that the supreme test of whether one state of affairs is intrinsically more desirable than another is whether it contains more happiness. We may notice the bearing of each step in turn on moral judgments. In accord with the first step, Mill holds not only that a man ought not to do a certain action if and only if some alternative would have more desirable consequences, but also that a certain rule ought in general to be observed if and only if the observance of it would in general have more desirable consequences than would failure to observe it. The first step implies also that actions of a certain sort ought in general to be condemned if and only if the condemnation of such actions would in general have more desirable consequences than the absence of such general condemnation. Accordingly, Mill maintains that it would in fact be wrong for a man to do a certain action if and only if three conditions are fulfilled: (1) some alternative would have more desirable consequences, (2) it would be contrary to a rule the observance of which would in general have more desirable consequences than would failure to observe it, and (3) it is an action of a kind the condemnation of which would in general have more desirable consequences than the absence of such general condemnation.

By virtue of the second step, Mill contends that the supreme test of whether some alternative to a certain action would have more desirable consequences is whether it would cause more happiness; and that the supreme test of whether the observance of a certain rule would have more desirable consequences is whether the observance of it would cause more happiness.[55] He therefore maintains that it would be correct to claim that it would be wrong for a certain man to do a certain action if and only if three conditions are fulfilled: (1) some alternative to it would cause more happiness, (2) it would be contrary to a rule the observance of which would in general cause more happiness than would failure to observe it, and (3) it is an action of a kind the condemnation of which would in general cause more happiness than would the absence of such general condemnation. In like fashion the conditions can be spelled out which Mill implies must be fulfilled for anyone to be correct in claiming that a certain man has an obligation to do a certain thing, that he has a right to a certain thing, or that it would be unjust for him to do a certain thing.

[55]See *Utilitarianism*, 214; "Whewell," 172; "Remarks on Bentham's Philosophy," 8.

V. THE USE OF THE PRINCIPLE OF UTILITY

IN MAINTAINING that the supreme test of whether something ought to be done is whether it would maximize happiness, Mill does not hold that this is the only test which is used, or can be used, or ought to be used. He recognizes that many other tests are used and holds that others are often more suitable. He suggests, for example, that as a test of conduct, it is often helpful for a man to ask himself whether a morally perfect being would approve of it.[56] In speaking of other tests as often more suitable, Mill claims that other ways are available for making out whether something ought to be done than by considering directly all the happiness and unhappiness it would cause and comparing this with all the happiness and unhappiness that would be caused by each alternative to it. Mill speaks of a "subordinate," "intermediate," or "secondary" principle as being employed when it is determined that something ought to be done not by reckoning with these considerations but by reckoning with some other feature of it.[57] He contends that it is not even possible to make out the morality of a certain action without taking account of whether it accords with a rule of morality. But even when moral considerations do not arise, Mill recognizes that men usually make out what ought to be done, and he urges that it is usually suitable for them to make out what ought to be done not by means of the supreme principle but by some intermediate principle. He holds that some intermediate principle is also often more suitable for making out whether a certain rule ought in general to be observed and is such that infractions of it ought in general to be condemned. In what he maintains is the supreme test, Mill is making three claims: (1) that something ought to be done if and only if it would maximize happiness, (2) that the ultimate reason why something ought to be done is because it would maximize happiness, and (3) that other tests are sound or suitable only if they would yield results compatible with it. In speaking of intermediate principles as "corollaries" of the supreme principle, he means that they are sound only if they yield results compatible with it.

There are many theories of morality which Mill rejects. He rejects the theory that what is meant by calling an action wrong or that the reason why an action is wrong is that it is the breaking of a divine commandment. He rejects such a theory even when it is united with a form of utilitarianism, as in Paley and Austin. He rejects the doctrine that any information about nature suffices to tell men what is right or wrong.[58] He objects to Comte for contending that anything is wrong if done from some other motive than

---

[56]See "Theism," 486.
[57]See *Utilitarianism*, 224–5; "Whewell," 173; "Bentham," 110; "Blakey," 29 below.
[58]See "Nature," 378.

desire for the greatest happiness of humanity.[59] He criticizes Bentham for not allowing that some experiences are more desirable than others independently of how pleasant they are. A further theory which Mill is particularly concerned to reject is what he calls the intuitive theory of morality.[60] By it he understands the theory that it is intuitively self-evident what kinds of actions are wrong and what kinds are obligatory, and that all that is required to make out that some particular action would be wrong, or another obligatory, is to make out that it would be an action of some such kind. Mill does not deny that there is an intuitive character to the manner in which many moral judgments are made. Quite often someone thinks a particular action would be wrong because it is of a kind which he believes to be wrong. Not questioning the belief he is employing, a certain kind of action presents itself to his mind as wrong in itself (227). Mill would also agree with W. D. Ross's remark, "When a plain man fulfils a promise . . . what makes him think it right to act in a certain way is the fact that he has promised to do so—that and, usually, nothing more. That his act will produce the best possible consequences is not his reason for calling it right."[61] But Mill would object that because the only thing that makes a man think that it would be wrong to do a certain action is the kind of action it is, it does not follow that the only reason why it would be wrong for him to do it is that it is an action of that kind. Because men often act upon a belief that actions of a certain kind are wrong, without reasoning further about it, he holds that it is not correct to infer that no reasons are to be given in behalf of such a belief and that certain kinds of actions are simply wrong in themselves.

Mill agrees with the intuitive theory that no one can make out by the principle of utility alone whether a certain action would be wrong or another obligatory. He would also point out that the principle of utility does not entail that men have but one obligation to others—to do what will cause most happiness. Because a certain action would cause most happiness it does not follow that it would not be wrong for others to compel it to be done. Moreover, the principle of utility does not entail that there is but one rule determining what is right or wrong. It does not imply that it would be wrong to do something if and only if it would cause less happiness than some alternative. If someone does something that will cause less happiness than would some alternative, it does not follow that he ought to be condemned by others for having done it. Far from maintaining that there is but one kind of action that is wrong, Mill holds that there are as many different kinds of wrong actions as there are rules which ought to be observed and ought to be enforced by moral sanctions. For determining in particular what is right or wrong,

---

[59]See *Auguste Comte and Positivism*, 335.
[60]See *Utilitarianism*, 206; "Whewell," 170; "Sedgwick," 51.
[61]*The Right and the Good* (Oxford: The Clarendon Press, 1930), 17.

Mill contends that such rules are indispensable as subordinate principles. He also holds that such rules are often sufficient, no appeal to the principle of utility being called for.

When does Mill think that it is in place to appeal to the principle of utility to determine what it is right or wrong to do? He urges that someone is not warranted in believing that it would not be wrong to do a certain action simply because he is warranted in thinking that, considered by itself, it would cause more happiness. He writes, "though the consequences in the particular case might be beneficial—it would be unworthy of an intelligent agent not to be consciously aware that the action is of a class which, if practised generally, would be generally injurious. . . ."[62] Here Mill speaks of appeal to the principle of utility to determine whether it would be wrong to do a particular action. Yet the appeal that is made is not to determine whether the particular action would have undesirable consequences but whether performance of actions of its kind would in general have undesirable consequences. Mill also holds that to be assured that it would be wrong to do a particular action, it is often sufficient for someone to think that it would be contrary to some rule which he believes ought generally to be observed, without testing on each occasion the correctness of the rule on which he is relying.[63]

A second sort of occasion on which Mill speaks of appeal to the principle of utility being called for is one in which someone is subject to conflicting rules. He writes, "only in . . . cases of conflict between secondary principles is it requisite that first principles should be appealed to" (226). Here appeal to utility is made to determine what particular action it would not be wrong to do. But Mill does not hold that when someone is faced with conflicting obligations, he can determine what it would not be wrong for him to do by disregarding his conflicting obligations and using the principle of utility to ascertain which action would have more desirable consequences. For whenever there is a question of whether it would be wrong to do a certain thing, the question of whether it would violate some rule remains. He holds rather that appeal to the principle of utility is called for to determine which obligation takes precedence. Yet Mill does not maintain that whenever there is a conflict of obligations such appeal is called for. He does not deny that such occasions recur and that men encounter them with their minds made up as to what kinds of obligation take precedence over others. They believe, for instance, that the obligation not to lie takes precedence in general over the obligation not to injure another, that the obligation not to injure another is more stringent than the obligation to help another, and that the obligation to help another who has helped one is greater than the obligation to benefit another

---

[62]*Utilitarianism*, 220; cf. "Whewell," 180.
[63]See *Utilitarianism*, 225; "Bentham," 111.

who has not. Beliefs in rules of precedence such as these are second-order moral beliefs. Although he holds that it is often sufficient for men to resolve a conflict by means of such a belief, without appealing to the principle of utility, Mill urges that men cannot in the end be assured that they are correct in believing that one kind of obligation takes precedence in general over another without reckoning whether neglect of it would in general be more detrimental to human happiness than neglect of the other. Even where someone is correct in believing that one kind of obligation takes precedence in general over another, Mill urges that such a belief will not always suffice to enable him to resolve a conflict of obligations.

A third sort of occasion on which he speaks of appeal to the principle of utility being called for is one that presents an exception to a rule of precedence. He writes: "justice is a name for certain moral requirements . . . of more paramount obligation, than any others. . . . [P]articular cases may occur in which some other social duty is so important, as to overrule any one of the general maxims of justice. Thus, to save a life, it may not only be allowable, but a duty, to steal, or take by force, the necessary food or medicine, or to kidnap, and compel to officiate, the only qualified medical practitioner." (259.)

Mill urges that all moralists recognize that every rule of morality admits of exceptions, and that there are occasions on which it would not be wrong to do a certain action even though it would violate a rule of morality. They thereby acknowledge that for it to be wrong to do a particular action, it is not sufficient that it be contrary to a rule of morality. Some further condition must be met. Mill points out that all moralists recognize that it would not be wrong for someone to do a certain action unless he also ought not to do it. Consequently if a certain action would violate a rule of morality, but it is not the case that it ought not to be done, it would then not be wrong to do it. Mill urges that where other moralists are at a loss is to state when this further condition is met. He not only affirms the principle that a certain action ought not to be done only if it would cause less happiness; he also speaks of appeal to this principle as called for to determine when to make an exception to a primary rule of morality, to determine when, for instance, it would not be wrong to steal, to lie, or to betray a solemn trust.

As an example of when it would not be wrong for someone to tell a certain lie, Mill cites an occasion in which "the withholding of some fact (as of information from a malefactor, or of bad news from a person dangerously ill) would preserve some one (especially a person other than oneself) from great and unmerited evil, and when the withholding can only be effected by denial" (223). Mill also points out that to be assured that it would not be wrong for a man to tell a certain lie, it is not sufficient to reckon with the "great evil" it would spare some person; against this must be weighed counter considerations.[64] Account must be taken of the damage the lie may do in "weakening the trustworthiness of human assertion" and in undermining the benefits dependent upon it. Secondly, account must be taken of the damage the man's lie may do in "weakening reliance" others will place on his veracity on future occasions. Third, account must be taken of the degree to which his readiness to lie upon one occasion may "enfeeble" his "sensitive feeling on the subject of veracity," thereby making him less reluctant to lie on other occasions and further damaging his trustworthiness.

We have noticed four sorts of occasions which Mill speaks of as calling for appeal to the principle of utility on a moral question. In the first it is appealed to to determine whether a rule ought generally to be observed; in the second, to determine whether one kind of obligation takes precedence over another; in the third, to determine when to make an exception to such a rule of precedence; in the fourth, to determine when to make an exception to a primary rule of morality. The example Mill gives of the last is determining when it would not be wrong to tell a lie. Mill does not mention whether someone need ever reckon whether to violate a rule whose general observance and enforcement would cause more happiness, but which is not also generally observed and enforced by moral sanctions. Nor does he mention whether someone need reckon whether his action would conform to such a rule. Mill speaks of using the principle of utility to determine when to make an exception to a rule only if it is not merely a rule whose general observance and enforcement would cause more happiness, but is also a rule which is generally observed and enforced. The only considerations he mentions as to be taken into account against someone's telling a certain lie are undermining reliance on his word, undermining his character, and impairing trust in men's assertions generally. These considerations are relevant only in so far as the rule in question is one that is generally observed.

Of the four sorts of occasions for which Mill speaks of appeal to the principle of utility, he gives examples only of the third and fourth. These examples indicate how he expects such an appeal to be carried out. By the principle of utility, something ought to be done if and only if its consequences would be intrinsically more desirable than those of any alternative; and they would be intrinsically more desirable if and only if it would cause more happiness. A full use of this principle as a test therefore requires reckoning with all the alternatives, and with all the intrinsically desirable and undesirable consequences of each. An exclusive use of this principle as a test requires reckoning with nothing else. In the two examples Mill gives of appeal to the principle of utility, he mentions reckoning with but two alternatives—in one that of saving a certain person's life or not saving it, in the other that of

[64]See *Utilitarianism*, 223; "Whewell," 182.

telling a certain lie or not telling it. A full use of the principle of utility requires reckoning with all intrinsically desirable and undesirable consequences to all sentient beings. In his two examples Mill does not speak of reckoning with consequences to other animals or to all human beings. Elsewhere he writes that in most cases in which someone appeals to the principle of utility "the interest or happiness of some few persons, is all he has to attend to" (220). Use of the principle of utility as a test requires reckoning only with intrinsically desirable and undesirable consequences—only happiness and unhappiness. Mill, however, mentions saving a person's life as the only consequence to be reckoned with in the example he gives of breaking a rule of precedence. The only consequences he mentions to be reckoned with against someone's telling a certain lie are undermining reliance on his word, undermining his character, and impairing trust in men's assertions generally. He also reproaches Bentham for not including among consequences to be reckoned with effects of what a man does on his character.[65] Yet Mill does not hold that the preservation of a man's life is intrinsically desirable or that there is anything intrinsically undesirable about undermining character, about undermining reliance on a man's word, or about impairing general trust in men's assertions. He regards consequences such as these as undesirable only because they in turn would make for less happiness and he speaks of "weighing these conflicting utilities against one another" (223). Instead of a full use of the principle of utility, Mill would agree that reckoning with but a few alternatives and with but a few intrinsically desirable and undesirable consequences of each would be warranted if it would yield a result compatible with full use of the principle. It is not only this that Mill understands by appeal to utility. His examples show that he regards an appeal to utility as being made where what are reckoned with are other desirable and undesirable consequences than happiness and unhappiness.

Still greater latitude is to be observed in the argument which Mill holds is to be given for the desirability of men being compelled generally to observe certain rules. Among such rules he mentions those "which protect every individual from being harmed by others, either directly or by being hindered in his freedom of pursuing his own good," which prevent anyone from "wrongfully withholding from" another "something which is his due," or from depriving him "of some good which he had reasonable ground . . . for counting upon" (256). Although he speaks of such rules as grounded in "general utility" and as "more vital to human well-being than any" others, Mill does not feel called upon to show that use of compulsion to enforce them generally would make for more happiness than would absence of enforcement. He urges instead that men generally have such an intense interest in their enforcement that

[65]See "Bentham," 98; "Remarks on Bentham's Philosophy," 8; "Sedgwick," 56.

"if obedience to them were not the rule, and disobedience the exception, every one would see in every one else a probable enemy, against whom he must be perpetually guarding himself." "It is their observance which alone preserves peace among human beings. . . ."[66] He here argues that the enforcement of such rules is desirable because it is necessary to maintaining relationships among men which in turn are desirable because they are a necessary condition of men achieving to any degree anything desirable. Mill's argument for the desirability of enforcing such rules is thus independent of any view as to what is intrinsically desirable, and therefore of his principle that happiness is the only thing intrinsically desirable.

Since he maintains that the principle of utility is the supreme test of conduct generally, Mill holds that it has application wherever anyone is pondering what to do, even though considerations of right and wrong are not or may not be involved.[67] A man wonders, Should I change my job? Should I go to the mountains for my holiday? Should I invite the Jones for the evening? Should I put on a blue tie this morning? A business considers whether to reduce a certain line of investment. A plumber considers whether he should use copper piping. A municipality hesitates whether to resurface certain roads. Citizens discuss whether their country should reduce certain import tariffs, withdraw its troops from a troubled region, or increase its aid to another country. Mill holds that the answer to any such question is correct if and only if the course of action would maximize happiness. Although Mill is concerned to show that the principle of utility is the supreme test of conduct generally, in *Utilitarianism* he is largely occupied with its role in coping with moral problems. He has far less in general to say about its use in regard to other practical problems. Mill does not maintain that the only motive from which men act is interest in maximizing happiness or that the only principle by which they should test whether something should be done is by whether it would maximize happiness. A man may think that he should do something because he would enjoy doing it, because it is to his interest, because it would afford another enjoyment, because it would be impolite or unconventional not to. Mill does not deny the diversity of considerations employed in determining what an individual or a group should do. Sometimes a political policy is recommended to promote material prosperity, sometimes to promote progress, or freedom or enlightenment, or to relieve certain needs. Although the principle of utility is the supreme test, Mill urges that men cannot avoid using various subordinate principles for determining what should be done, even where questions of right and wrong are not involved. He writes, "all rational creatures go out upon the sea of life with their minds made up on the common questions of right and wrong, as well as on many of the far more

[66]*Utilitarianism*, 255; cf. "Whewell," 192.
[67]See *Logic*, II, 552–6 (VI, xii, 6–7).

difficult questions of wise and foolish. . . . Whatever . . . the fundamental principle . . . we require subordinate principles to apply it by. . . ." (225.)

Mill urges that the happiness of all is more effectively promoted by each pursuing his own happiness, subject to rules required by the good of others, than by each making the good of others his object.[68] He also urges that each can more effectively promote his own happiness not by seeking it but by the active pursuit of ends beyond himself.[69] Whether individuals or groups are engaged in farming, banking, teaching, medicine, or any other distinctive pursuit, Mill urges that it is usually sufficient for them to determine what they should do by reckoning only with what would most effectively promote the end of the pursuit. They are then called upon to consider only "that certain consequences follow from certain causes."[70] The conclusion that a certain thing should be done rests also, of course, on the assumption that the end is desirable. But "in various subordinate arts . . . there is seldom any visible necessity for justifying the end, since in general its desirableness is denied by nobody." Mill mentions two errors to which the adoption of universal practical maxims in any pursuit is subject. One error is that of overlooking that the prescribed mode of action is effective only under certain circumstances. Quite another error is that of overlooking that though it is effective, its "success itself may conflict with some other end, which may possibly chance to be more desirable."[71] Where conflicting desirable ends are affected, Mill speaks of appeal to the principle of utility as called for. Yet for such appeal to be made, Mill does not require that only intrinsically desirable and undesirable consequences be reckoned with. Here too he regards an appeal to utility as being made where what are reckoned with are other desirable and undesirable consequences than happiness and unhappiness.

University of Toronto

D. P. D.

---

[68]*Auguste Comte*, 337.
[69]See *Autobiography* (New York: Columbia University Press, 1924), 100.
[70]*Logic*, II, 554 (VI, xii, 6).
[71]*Ibid.*, 550 (VI, xii, 4).

Textual Introduction

JOHN STUART MILL occupies an important place in the history of moral philosophy, and moral philosophy occupies a similarly important, indeed a central, part in Mill's thought. He wrote, however, no ethical treatise comparable in range and depth to his *Principles of Political Economy* or his *System of Logic*; and while ethical works generally tend to be shorter than works on political economy and logic, one cannot treat Mill's *Utilitarianism*, even apart from length, as commensurate with the *Principles* or the *Logic*. So, accepting *Utilitarianism* as his major ethical work, one must look to other essays if one wishes a comprehensive view of his ethics. In this volume, therefore, *Utilitarianism* is presented, for the first time, in the context of the other significant essays that establish the scope and development of Mill's ethics, and indicate its social and religious affiliations.[1]

A brief glance at the provenance of these essays will, in the light of Professor Priestley's Introduction, help explain their importance and our grouping of them. Three were issued as separate publications—*Utilitarianism*, *Auguste Comte and Positivism*, and *Three Essays on Religion*—but of these just the last appeared only in book form; *Utilitarianism* was first published in three instalments in *Fraser's Magazine*, and *Auguste Comte* in two instalments in the *Westminster Review*.[2] Of the others, four—the major articles

[1]The student who undertakes an exhaustive study of Mill's ethics should look carefully at his *Autobiography*, his *Logic* (especially Book VI), his *Inaugural Address*, and the notes to his edition of his fathers' *Analysis of the Phenomena of the Human Mind*. These are not included here because they find more legitimate places in other volumes of the edition. Many of his other writings are pertinent in lesser ways, and those engaged in detailed research are advised to consult the indexes to the various volumes. Fuller comment on the principles of inclusion and exclusion and of editing procedures in this edition will be found in the Textual Introduction to Volume IV (*Essays on Economics and Society*), xliii ff., and in my "Principles and Methods in the Collected Edition of John Stuart Mill," in John M. Robson, ed., *Editing Nineteenth-Century Texts* (Toronto: University of Toronto Press, 1967), 96–122.

[2]Bibliographic details are given in the headnote to each item. These include details of publication ("not republished" means not republished by Mill in his lifetime); epistolary and biographical information relevant to attribution, dating of the text, and its publication; and the entry from Mill's bibliography. For this last, the page references are to the edition by Ney MacMinn, J. M. McCrimmon, and J. R. Hainds, *Bibliography of the Published Writings of J. S. Mill* (Evanston: Northwestern University Press, 1945), but the readings have been corrected from the manuscript in the British Library of Political and Economic Science.

on Sedgwick, Bentham, Coleridge, and Whewell—appeared in the *Westminster Review* and were reprinted in *Dissertations and Discussions*. The two remaining items in the main text are an appendix to a book not by Mill, Bulwer's *England and the English*, and a review of Blakey from the *Monthly Repository*. (The appended items are discussed below.) It will be seen, if comparison is made with other volumes of essays in this edition, that this one contains a very high percentage of material Mill thought worthy of republication. The significance and history of the items from a textual point of view emerges best when they are grouped in the following way: essays illustrating the development of Mill's utilitarianism; essays begun by Mill with his wife's help in the 1850s; and *Auguste Comte and Positivism*.

ESSAYS ILLUSTRATING THE DEVELOPMENT OF MILL'S UTILITARIANISM

The relevant items here are the first six in the volume (the "Remarks on Bentham's Philosophy," and the reviews of Blakey, Sedgwick, Bentham, Coleridge, and Whewell) and the first two Appendices (the "Preface" to *Dissertations and Discussions*, and Mill's obituary notice of Bentham). The basic unity here is provided by Mill's reassessments of his Benthamite inheritance, as he moves back and forth between eulogy and disparagement, qualifying both, until his general approval is given in his comments on Whewell (and renewed in *Utilitarianism*).[3]

The obituary of Bentham (1832), which appeared anonymously in a Radical weekly, *The Examiner*, is appropriately eulogistic, concentrating in the main on the legal and legislative aspects of Bentham's thought, but hints of criticisms to come are found even here when Bentham's stature as a moralist is in question. At this time Mill was entering his most marked period of assimilation of new ideas, having met the St. Simonians and Coleridge, and formed friendships with Mrs. Taylor (later his wife), Carlyle, and John Sterling.

When, in his Appendix to Bulwer's *England and the English* (1833), he made his most severe attack on Bentham, he was at the height of his reaction against his intellectual heritage. As he says in his *Autobiography*:

To complete the tale of my writings at this period, I may add that in 1833, at the request of Bulwer, who was just then completing his 'England and the English' (a work, at that time, greatly in advance of the public mind), I wrote for him a critical account of Bentham's philosophy, a small part of which he incorporated in his text, and printed the rest (with an honourable acknowledgment), as an

---

[3]A fuller account of his fluctuation will be found in my "John Stuart Mill and Jeremy Bentham, with some Observations on James Mill," in M. MacLure and F. W. Watt, eds., *Essays in English Literature from the Renaissance to the Victorian Age* (Toronto: University of Toronto Press, 1964), 245–68. And cf. Professor Priestley's comments in his Introduction above, *passim*.

appendix. In this, along with the favourable, a part also of the unfavourable side of my estimation of Bentham's doctrines, considered as a complete philosophy, was for the first time put into print.[4]

But he was not willing, in the early 1830s, to acknowledge these opinions as his. To Carlyle he writes (11–12/4/33): "I wish you could see something I have written lately about Bentham & Benthamism—but you can't." After the appearance of Bulwer's book he writes again to Carlyle (2/8/33): "I told you in one of my letters that I had been writing something about Bentham & his philosophy; it was for Bulwer, at his request, for the purposes of this book: contrary to my expectation at that time, he has printed part of this paper *ipsissimis verbis* as an appendix to his book: so you will see it; but I do not acknowledge it, nor mean to do so." And to J. P. Nichol he says (14/10/34): "It is not, and must not be, known to be mine."[5]

The review of Blakey is mainly an assault on the weaknesses of Blakey's understanding and exposition, but it has wider significance, for the basic outline of the important parallel essays on Bentham and Coleridge can be seen in Mill's reference to "the two systems between which, and which only, almost every metaphysician, deserving the name, in all Europe, is now beginning to be convinced that it is necessary to choose," that is, "the association-philosophy as taught by Hartley, and the metaphysics of the German school" (23). And in the last paragraph (29) the importance of secondary moral principles, a theme to which Mill returned again and again, is stressed.

This review was again anonymous, and only in the next essay here reprinted, the review of Sedgwick's *Discourse*, does Mill begin to appear under his own colours. The article was signed "A," not in itself a clear identification, but the authorship was known to a wider group than that of the former items, and the review appeared in a periodical edited by Mill, the *London Review* (later amalgamated with the *Westminster*). In his *Autobiography* (140–1), Mill says that this article, coming as it did in the first number of the *London Review*, and so helping set the tone for his new venture, gave him the opportunity of putting into practice his "scheme of conciliation between the old and the new 'philosophic radicalism.'" Sedgwick's book, he comments, featuring "an intemperate assault on analytic psychology and utilitarian ethics, in the form of an attack on Locke and Paley," had

excited great indignation in my father and others, which I thought it fully deserved. And here, I imagined, was an opportunity of at the same time repelling

---

[4]*Autobiography* (New York: Columbia University Press, 1924), 138–9. In the *Early Draft* of the *Autobiography*, ed. Jack Stillinger (Urbana: University of Illinois Press, 1961), 157, the passage appears without the parenthetical comments.

[5]*Earlier Letters*, ed. Francis E. Mineka, in *Collected Works*, XII (Toronto: University of Toronto Press, 1963), 152, 172, 236.

an unjust attack, and inserting into my defence of Hartleianism and Utilitarianism a number of the opinions which constituted my view of those subjects, as distinguished from that of my old associates. In this I partially succeeded, though my relation to my father would have made it painful to me in any case, and impossible in a review for which he wrote, to speak out my whole mind on the subject at this time.

In the *Early Draft* (158) the final sentence, after "succeeded," reads: "though I could not speak out my whole mind at this time without coming into conflict with my father." This passage replaced a cancelled reading that brings the matter into sharper focus: "though I was obliged to omit two or three pages of comment on what I thought the mistakes of utilitarian moralists, which my father considered as an attack on Bentham & on him. I certainly thought both of them open to it but far less so than some of their followers."

The general judgment in these remarks, dating from 1854–55, is earlier found in a letter to J. P. Nichol (26/11/34), written on completion of the review (though probably before the revisions suggested by James Mill): "I have said a number of things in it which I have never put into print before, and have represented the 'utilitarian theory of morals,' as [Sedgwick] calls it, I think for the first time in its true colours. At all events, I have incidentally represented my own mode of looking at ethical questions; having never yet seen in print any statement of principles on the subject to which I could subscribe."[6]

That his opinion of the review was expressed differently in the Preface to *Dissertations and Discussions*, twenty-five years later, is probably partly because he had been obliged, by his father, "to omit two or three pages of comment" and partly because his own position was more genuinely secure in 1859. In that Preface (493–4 below) he says that his slight revisions have left the articles, in the main, as "memorials of the states of mind in which they were written"; and goes on to explain:

Where what I had written appears a fair statement of part of the truth, but defective inasmuch as there exists another part respecting which nothing, or too little, is said, I leave the deficiency to be supplied by the reader's own thoughts; the rather, as he will, in many cases, find the balance restored in some other part of this collection. Thus, the review of Mr. Sedgwick's *Discourse*, taken by itself, might give an impression of more complete adhesion to the philosophy of Locke, Bentham, and the eighteenth century, than is really the case, and of an inadequate sense of its deficiencies; but that notion will be rectified by the subsequent essays on Bentham and on Coleridge. These, again, if they stood alone, would give just as much too strong an impression of the writer's sympathy with the reaction of the nineteenth century against the eighteenth: but this exaggeration will be corrected by the more recent defence of the 'greatest happiness' ethics against Dr. Whewell.

[6]*Ibid.*, 238.

A glance at the variants in the essay on Sedgwick suggests that this is one of the two articles in *Dissertations and Discussions* in which Mill, aware of the "asperity of tone," revised with a view to retaining "only as much of this strength of expression [resulting from the subject, not from "the smallest feeling of personal ill-will towards my antagonists"], as could not be foregone without weakening the force of the protest" ("Preface," 494, below). This suggestion is supported by a letter to John Sterling of 22 April, 1840, at which time Mill was already beginning to collect articles for republication.[7] "I have softened the asperity of the article on Sedgwick," he says, "& cut out whatever seemed to take an unfair advantage against his opinions, of his deficiencies as an advocate of them." (*Earlier Letters*, XIII, 429.)

We do not know just which revisions were made at what times between 1840 and the publication of *Dissertations and Discussions* in 1859, but the relative frequency of changes in the essays in Volume I (that is, up to and including the "Coleridge," which was first published in March, 1840, just before the letter to Sterling quoted above), when compared with that in Volume II (made up of essays written between 1840 and 1859), suggests that the first revisions, about 1840, were much more thorough than the subsequent ones, which probably were made just before publication, after Harriet Taylor's death.[8]

In any case, many of the changes indicating a softer judgment of Sedgwick's faults were undoubtedly made at the earlier date. An illustration is to be seen at 45^{g-g} and ^{h}: whereas in the version published in 1859 Mill says that Sedgwick "has contented himself with repeating the trivialities he found current," in 1835 he had said that Sedgwick "has repeated the trivialities he found current, not having depth or strength of mind to see beyond them." Other examples of this common type of change may be seen at 39^{y-y}, $^{z-z}$, 45^{d-d}, 69^{b-b}, and 72^{f-f} to 73^{l-l}. The retraction of more serious charges of moral obliquity on Sedgwick's part is illustrated by 70^{n-n}, where Sedgwick's "trick of words" becomes in 1859 his "confusion of ideas" (cf. 71^{w-w} and 72^{z-z}).

Similarly softened judgments on the merits of Cambridge and Oxford,

[7]This notion may well have been prompted by the publication in London early in 1840 of Carlyle's *Critical and Miscellaneous Essays* (published earlier in the United States). In any case, the parallel was in Mill's mind when he approached Parker on 6 April, 1842 (see *Earlier Letters*, XIII, 514), and again on 30 November, 1858, with the suggestion that resulted in the publication of *Dissertations and Discussions*. On the latter occasion he wrote: "I have . . . , prepared for publication, a selection of my articles published in periodicals which I should like to bring out somewhat later in the season. . . . There are enough to make, I should think, two volumes of the size & type of the early editions of Carlyle's Miscellanies: but I have not calculated exactly, and it *may* extend to three." (A.l.s., King's College, Cambridge.) The two volumes of the 1st ed. were published in April, 1859.

[8]For some evidence concerning the date of the revisions of "Coleridge," see the headnote to Appendix D, pp. 503–4 below.

seen at 34^j, 73^{l-l}, and 74^r, should be compared with the footnote on 35, which explains that the article was first published "before the advent of the present comparatively enlightened body of University Reformers." A few changes reflect Mill's logical speculations in the years between the two versions (his *Logic* was first published in 1843): for example, 44^v, ^{w}, $^{a-a}$, and 71^{x-x} (the first three also indicate his changed estimate of the validity of James Mill's view of the uses of history). One should also note Mill's willingness to accept the term "utilitarian": in 1835 the term is said to be Sedgwick's and is given in quotation marks; in 1859 it is accepted without significant qualification (see 36^{n-n}, 52^{i-i}, 65^{d-d}, $^{f-f}$, and cf. the letter to Nichol of 26/11/34 quoted above). An excision of what is probably provocative irony may be seen at 64^{a-a}, where the reading in 1835 is "God has thought fit to furnish us," while in 1859 it is "we have been provided" (cf. 64^{z-z}, and 70^{m-m}; and "Bentham," 93^{u-u}).

Three years after his essay on Sedgwick appeared, Mill published his famous essay on Bentham. His subsequent comment on it in the Preface to *Dissertations and Discussions* (quoted above) is supported by his judgment in his *Autobiography*, where he says that in the article,

while doing full justice to the merits of Bentham, I pointed out what I thought the errors and deficiencies of his philosophy. The substance of this criticism I still think perfectly just; but I have sometimes doubted whether it was right to publish it at that time. I have often felt that Bentham's philosophy, as an instrument of progress, has been to some extent discredited before it had done its work, and that to lend a hand towards lowering its reputation was doing more harm than service to improvement. Now, however, when a counter-action appears to be setting in towards what is good in Benthamism, I can look with more satisfaction on this criticism of its defects, especially as I have myself balanced it by vindications of the fundamental principles of Bentham's philosophy, which are reprinted along with it in the same collection [i.e., "Sedgwick" and "Whewell" in *Dissertations and Discussions*].[9]

The most interesting variants in this essay, as the passage above would suggest, involve Mill's more favourable appraisal of Bentham and Benthamism in the 1850s. Examples, some of them indicating attention to slight nuance, will be seen at 82^{b-b}, 98^{s-s}, 99^{w-w}, 111^{y-y}, and 112^{z-z}, but the most significant is that at 86^{m-m}, which is too long to be quoted here. This variant occurs in Mill's comment on his favourite passage in Bentham, taken from the *Introduction to the Principles of Morals and Legislation*, and quoted or

---

[9]*Autobiography*, 152–3. This passage, revised in 1861 from its earlier version, presents some interesting variants from the *Early Draft*, written 1854–55. The final sentence was added (the *Early Draft* having been written before the publication of *Dissertations and Discussions*); "perfectly" was added before "just"; "much doubted since" became "sometimes doubted" and "at that time" was added; and "in a great measure discredited before it had half done its work" became "to some extent discredited before it had done its work" (*Early Draft*, 166).

referred to in all Mill's major discussions of Bentham.[10] Related changes, illustrating in minor ways the development of his own ethical attitudes, will be seen at 109^{n-n}, 110^{s-s}, 111^{u-u}, and especially 111^{v}.

The roots of Mill's comparison of Bentham and Coleridge in the opening pages of his essay on the latter, probably go back to arguments with Coleridgeans in the London Debating Society. The comparison became explicit in 1834, when, in a letter to Nichol, he says that Coleridge is "the most systematic thinker of our time, without excepting even Bentham." Five years later, after the publication of "Bentham," he tells Sterling that he intends to compose an article on Coleridge "as a counter-pole to the one on Bentham," feeling that the "likeness" of Coleridge "should be taken from the same point of view as that of Bentham."[11] The linking of the two pieces, mentioned again in the Preface to *Dissertations and Discussions*, is also commented on in the *Autobiography*, where Mill says:

In the essay on Coleridge I attempted to characterize the European reaction against the negative philosophy of the eighteenth century: and here, if the effect only of this one paper were to be considered, I might be thought to have erred by giving undue prominence to the favourable side, as I had done in the case of Bentham to the unfavourable. In both cases, the impetus with which I had detached myself from what was untenable in the doctrines of Bentham and of the eighteenth century, may have carried me, though in appearance rather than in reality, too far on the contrary side. But as far as relates to the article on Coleridge, my defence is, that I was writing for Radicals and Liberals, and it was my business to dwell most on that in writers of a different school, from the knowledge of which they might derive most improvement.[12]

Some of the variants in "Coleridge" are evidence of his awareness that in 1840 he had given "undue prominence to the favourable side" of what he calls "the European reaction against the negative philosophy of the eighteenth century". Like most of the other variants, they should be studied in context: see, for example, 134^{n-n}, $^{o-o}$, $^{x-x}$, 137^{m-m}, and 160^{m-m} (and cf. "Bentham," 90^{e-e}, and 109^{l-l}). Lessened "asperity of tone" is seen in the variants to 140n, and Mill's revised assessment of Gladstone (who had moved into the Liberal camp in 1859) is noticeable at 149^{b-b} and 150^{g}. Also worthy of mention are the variants at 157^{a}, where Mill's increased sympathy for socialist criticisms of society is evident; at 130^{f}, where the deletion of the reference to James Mill's *Analysis* as "the greatest accession to abstract

[10]A discussion of Mill's varying treatments of this crucial passage will be found in my "John Stuart Mill and Jeremy Bentham," 263–6. To locate the references to it in the present volume, see the Bibliographic Appendix, 000 below.

[11]*Earlier Letters*, XII, 221 (15/4/34), and XIII, 405–6 (28/9/39). Cf. *ibid.*, XIII, 411.

[12]*Autobiography*, 153. In the *Early Draft* (166) "if the effect only of this one paper were to be considered, I might be thought to have erred" is simply "I erred"; "may have carried me, though in appearance rather than in reality" does not appear; and "my defence is" appears as "the excuse may be made for me".

psychology since Hartley" is more likely a response to the publication of Bain's *The Senses and the Intellect* (1855) and *The Emotions and the Will* (1859) than a depreciation of the *Analysis* (cf. 246n); and at 127^{p-p}, where the added reference to Kant may be the result of a reading (or rereading) of Kant between 1840 and 1859 or, as is more likely, of the reading of Cousin that Mill did for his *Logic*.

The review of Whewell is commented on significantly by Mill only in the Preface to *Dissertations and Discussions* where, as already noted, he remarks that it should correct any exaggerated impression of his "sympathy with the reaction of the nineteenth century against the eighteenth". In fact, his re-assessment of Bentham and utilitarianism was virtually complete in 1852, and the comments in "Whewell" are consonant with those in the *Autobiography* and *Utilitarianism*. As a result—and as a result of the shorter time between the versions—there are fewer variants, and none calling for detailed notice here; attention might be called, however, to the passage on marriage in which 199^{z-z} occurs, where Harriet's influence may well be inferred (as it may also in "Bentham," 113^{i-i}).

Considering together the four essays reprinted in *Dissertations and Discussions*, one finds a total of 638 variants (including those in footnotes), which occur with decreasing frequency as the time between the first publication and the republication lessens.[13] Mill did very little revision for the 2nd ed. of *Dissertations and Discussions* (the one here used for copy-text), only forty-three substantive variants appearing, and these of a minor nature (see, for example, "Coleridge," 134^{r-r}). A rough classification of the variants isolates some 6 per cent as involving a change of opinion or correction of fact (including major expansions or deletions); 3 per cent reflect the difference in time and provenance between the separate publications; 44 per cent arise from qualifications; and the remaining 47 per cent are minor verbal alterations or slight tonal changes (including the removal of italics). The most interesting kinds have already been exemplified, but reference might be made to the change of time indicated at 45n and 85^k, the change in provenance indicated at 74^{s-s}, and, of the many minor qualifications, to those at 41^{l-l} ("all" changed to "much of"), 123^{q-q} ("perfect" to "correct"), and 143^{h-h} ("no" to "scarcely any").

ESSAYS BEGUN IN THE 1850s

The relevant items here are *Utilitarianism* and the *Three Essays on Religion*. Some time after their marriage in 1851, probably towards the end of 1853 when they were together in France, Mill and Harriet drew up a list of

---

[13]There are 237 in "Sedgwick" (5.64 per page of the present text), 178 in "Bentham" (4.56 per page), 195 in "Coleridge" (4.33 per page), and 28 in "Whewell" (.80 per page).

subjects on which they wanted to publish their views. Thinking that one or both of them would not live long, Mill forecast "one large or two small posthumous volumes of Essays, with the Life at their head," which might be ready for publication by Christmas 1855, though, he adds, "not then to be published if we are still alive to improve & enlarge them."[14] They had already composed a draft of the "Life,"[15] though it was to undergo further revision, and Mill on his return to England immediately set to work on the subjects on their list. Having begun with "Nature," he writes to Harriet on 7 Feb., 1854, that that essay is finished, and he is puzzled "what to attempt next." He goes on to say:

I will just copy the list of subjects we made out in the confused order in which we put them down. Differences of character (nation, race, age, sex, temperament). Love. Education of tastes. Religion de l'avenir. Plato. Slander. Foundation of morals. Utility of religion. Socialism. Liberty. Doctrine that causation is will. To these I have now added from your letter, Family, & Conventional.

His own inclination was to go on with the first mentioned,[16] but Harriet preferred that he turn to the "Utility of religion," as he did (see cxxvii–cxxviii below).

This programme adumbrates, at least through suggestion, most of Mill's later writings, but of its detailed working out in the years before Harriet's death not a great deal is known. In her "Introductory Notice" to the *Three Essays on Religion*, Helen Taylor remarks that in addition to "Nature" and "The Utility of Religion," Mill wrote three essays between "1850 and 1858 . . . on Justice, on Utility, and on Liberty. . . . Those on Justice and Utility were afterwards incorporated, with some alterations and additions, into one, and published under the name of *Utilitarianism*." (371 below.) The *terminus a quo* being only roughly given, one need not place full reliance on the *terminus ad quem*; otherwise the account seems reliable. Of the subjects mentioned in the list, it seems likely that "Foundation of morals" and to a lesser extent "Religion de l'avenir" and "Education of tastes" indicate the origins of the essay on Utility that, combined with the essay on Justice, resulted in *Utilitarianism*. Nothing more is known of the essay on Utility,[17] but the origins of the essay on Justice (not mentioned in the list in February, 1854) may be

[14]A.l.s. to Harriet, 29/1/54. With one exception (see n32), all the letters to Harriet here cited are in the Yale University Library.

[15]See Stillinger, *Early Draft*, 5–11.

[16]From the account in his *Logic* (Bk. VI, Chap. v) and hints elsewhere, we can be sure that Mill's thoughts on "Differences of character (nation, race, age, sex, temperament)" were intended to make up his proposed work on "Ethology" that never materialized.

[17]Mill's letter to Harriet of 31/12/54, from Sestri, contains a sentence whose wording suggests that he may have been working on a draft of Chap. ii at that time. "I think that [a corn disease similar to that which destroyed the Irish potato] should be a signal for the universal & simultaneous suicide of the whole human race, suggested by Novalis." Cf. 214 below.

seen in Mill's correspondence with Harriet. On 14 June, 1854, he writes from St. Malo, where he had just arrived from the Isle of Jersey, to say: "I employed the five hours of steamboat partly in conning over the subject of *justice* for the essay . . . ," and the next day consoled himself, in wet weather, by saying that it would at least allow him to write. On the 16th he explains that after posting his last letter, he was able to spend, because of the rain, "a long spell at the Essay on Justice. . . ." At Guingamp, he says on the 19th, he managed an hour's writing, the last for some days. And on the 30th, in the last reference we have, he says: "I do not find the essay on Justice goes on well. I wrote a good long piece of it at Quimper [on the 26th], but it is too metaphysical, & not what is most wanted but I must finish it now in that vein & then strike into another [essay]."

The union of the two essays, and the consequent rewriting, took place not long after Harriet's death, as Mill indicates in his *Autobiography*, saying: ". . . I took from their repository a portion of the unpublished papers which I had written during the last years of our married life, and shaped them, with some additional matter, into the little work entitled 'Utilitarianism'; which was first published, in three parts, in successive numbers of Fraser's Magazine, and afterwards reprinted in a volume."[18] In fact he indicated to Theodor Gomperz as early as August, 1858, before Harriet's death, his intention to publish his papers on utility as "there are not many defences extant of the ethics of utility."[19] On 15 October, 1859, Mill wrote from Avignon to Alexander Bain: "I am employing myself in working up some papers which have been lying by me, with additional matter into a little treatise on Utilitarianism."[20] And again to Bain (14/11/59): "I do not think of publishing my Utilitarianism till next winter at the earliest, though it is now finished, subject to any correction or enlargement which may suggest itself in the interval. It will be but a small book, about a fifth less than the Liberty, if I make no addition to it."[21] He wrote similarly to W. G. Ward (28/11/59) to say that he

---

[18]*Autobiography*, 186–7. It should be noted that here Mill says that these essays were written by himself, and does not describe them as "joint productions" with Harriet.

[19]Lord Stamp, "New Letters of John Stuart Mill," *The Times*, 29 Dec., 1938. Mill's comment is made in connection with his essay on Whewell, republished the next year in *Dissertations and Discussions*, but there can be little doubt (see, e.g., the next footnote) that he was thinking also of his unpublished papers.

[20]Draft, British Library of Political and Economic Science. A cancelled passage in the draft substantially repeats this sentence, but adds, "to be published some time or other, but whether by itself or in a volume of Essays I have not yet determined."

[21]*Letters of John Stuart Mill*, ed. Hugh S. R. Elliot (London: Longmans, Green, 1910), I, 226 (corrected from the autograph draft). The passage continues: "But small books are so much more read than large ones that it is an advantage when one's matter will go into a small space. I have not written it in any hostile spirit towards Xtianity, though undoubtedly both good ethics & good metaphysics will sap Xtianity if it persists in allying itself with bad."

proposed to publish his "little manuscript treatise" when he had kept it "for the length of time . . . desirable & given it such further improvement" as he could.[22]

Bain, who knew Mill's working habits better than anyone else but Harriet and Helen Taylor, comments that the essay was "thoroughly revised in 1860,"[23] and Mill is undoubtedly referring to it in a letter to Henry Fawcett (24/12/60) when he says that since leaving London for Avignon in October, he has "two things finished, one of them a considerable volume [*Considerations on Representative Government*] and [has] made good progress with a third."[24] And *Utilitarianism* was finished in time, as he told Fawcett on 26 September, 1861, for it to appear "in the next three numbers of Fraser."[25] Mill always intended the parts to be united in book form, but there was an unexplained delay. He wrote to Charles Dupont-White on 10 January, 1862: "J'ai laissé mon éditeur le maître de décider le moment de le réimprimer en volume, mais n'ayant rien appris sur ses intentions, je présume que cette réimpression est ajournée."[26] Though the first edition in book form was being printed in February, 1863,[27] as late as 21 January Mill wrote to Samuel Bailey in hesitant terms: "If I reprint them separately as I am thinking of doing I will beg your acceptance of a copy."[28] He selected a cover in March, and the volume was published by Parker in May.

Mill's opinions were quite stable by the time *Utilitarianism* appeared, and though there is a decade between the periodical publication in 1861 and the appearance in 1871 of the 4th ed. (the last in Mill's lifetime, and so used here as copy-text), there are only seventy-four substantive variants (1.35 per page of this edition). Of these, eight may be said to illustrate a change of opinion or fact, one reflects the passage of time (Bain becomes "Professor" in 246n), and twenty-two are qualifications; the rest are minor verbal changes. Of the total, twenty-one were made between the periodical version and the 1st ed. (1863), thirty-seven for the 2nd ed. (1864), eleven for the 3rd ed. (1867), and five for the 4th ed. In fact, almost one-third of the changes were made in the final chapter in the 2nd ed.; the most extensive of these occur in the passage on 244–5 concerning the etymology of the non-

---

[22]*Ibid.*, 231 (draft, Brotherton Library, Leeds).

[23]*John Stuart Mill* (London: Longmans, 1882), 112.

[24]A.l.s., British Library of Political and Economic Science. The "third" is probably *The Subjection of Women*, which was not published until 1869.

[25]*Ibid.*

[26]From Avignon; a.l.s. in possession of M. Pierre-Sadi Carnot. Mill had told Dupont-White in October, 1861, while the articles were appearing in *Fraser's*, that they would be published as a volume.

[27]See the correspondence with Spencer (cited in the Bibliographic Appendix, 557 below) concerning the note at 257–8 below, and Mill's letter to Bain, 13/2/63 (British Library of Political and Economic Science).

[28]*Letters*, ed. Elliot, I, 276 (draft, Brotherton Library, Leeds).

English terms corresponding to "Just." Of the minor changes, one (224^{m-m}) might be mentioned as probably illustrating the printer's common misreading of Mill's "&" for "or".

Actually, one variant which does not occur is potentially more interesting than any that do, for had Mill changed the passage in question much of the subsequent criticism of *Utilitarianism* would have been modified. On 18 March, 1868, writing to Mill about the translations for the German edition he was preparing, Gomperz says:

Let me conclude by expressing my regret that you did not in the later editions of the Utilitarianism remove the stumbling block (to any reader and more especially to a translator) pp. 51–52 1st ed. [234 below] (audible, visible—desirable) which when pointed out to you by me [in 1863, just after the publication of the 1st ed.], you said you would remove. Your argument looks like a verbal quibble, far as it is from being one and has besides to me the serious disadvantage of being utterly untranslatable.

Mill's reply (23 April, 1868) is unfortunately inconclusive:

With regard to the passage you mention in the Utilitarianism I have not had time regularly to rewrite the book & it had escaped my memory that you thought that argument apparently though not really fallacious which proves to me the necessity of, at least, further explanation & development. I beg that in the translation you will kindly reserve the passage to yourself, & please remove the stumbling block, by expressing the real argument in such terms as you think will express it best.[29]

The connection in time between *Utilitarianism* and the first two of the *Three Essays on Religion* is established by Helen Taylor in her "Introductory Notice" to the *Three Essays*, cited above. There, in addition to dating "Nature" and "The Utility of Religion" between 1850 and 1858, she says "Theism" was written between 1868 and 1870. The third essay cannot now be dated more accurately, but one can be more precise about "Nature" and "The Utility of Religion." On 30 August, 1853, during their first separation since marriage, Mill writes to Harriet: "I am very much inclined to take the Essay on Nature again in hand & rewrite it as thoroughly as I did the review of Grote [for the *Edinburgh Review*, 98 (Oct., 1853)]—that is what it wants—it is my old way of working & I do not think I have ever done anything well which was not done in that way."[30] Again separated from Harriet,

[29]Gomperz to Mill, a.l.s. (Johns Hopkins University Library); Mill to Gomperz, draft (*ibid.*) See Adelaide Weinberg, *Theodor Gomperz and John Stuart Mill* (Geneva: Droz, 1963), 51–3. Again unfortunately, Gomperz did not change the passage; see *Das Nützlichkeitsprincip* in *John Stuart Mill's Gesammelte Werke*, I (Leipzig: Fues's Verlag, 1869), 166.

[30]When the essay was first written is not known, but an interesting parallel in thought and word to a well-known passage in "Nature" (see 402 below, and cf. 385) occurs in a letter to Walter Coulson, dated 22 November, 1850, and may suggest that the essay was in hand at that time: "the course of nature, of which so great a part is tyranny &

he writes on 14 January, 1854, to say that as soon as he feels well enough to start writing again he will "finish the rewriting of the paper on Nature," which he began before they left England for the South of France. On the 19th he says: "I have been reading the Essay on Nature as I rewrote the first part of it before we left & I think it very much improved & altogether very passable. I think I could soon finish it equally well." On the 29th, commenting on their plans for a volume or two of essays, perhaps to be published posthumously (see cxxiii above), he writes to Harriet:

The first thing to be done & which I can do immediately towards it is to finish the paper on Nature, & this I mean to set about today, after finishing this letter—being the first Sunday that I have not thought it best to employ in I.H. work [his professional labours at the India House having fallen in arrears during his leave at the end of 1853]. That paper, I mean the part of it rewritten, seems to me on reading it to contain a great deal which we want said, said quite well enough for the volume though not so well as we shall make it when we have time. I hope to be able in two or three weeks to finish it equally well & then to begin something else—but all the other subjects in our list will be much more difficult for me even to begin upon without you to prompt me.

On the 30th, before posting the comments just quoted, Mill received Harriet's letter of the 26th (not extant), on which he remarks: "It is a pleasant coincidence that I should receive her nice say about the 'Nature' just after I have resumed it. I shall put those three beautiful sentences about 'disorder' verbatim into the essay.[31] I wrote a large piece yesterday at intervals . . . & am well pleased with it. I don't think we should make these essays very long, though the subjects are inexhaustible. We want a compact argument first, & if we live to expand it & add a larger dissertation, tant mieux: there is need of both." On 2 February he says: "I have written at the Nature every evening since Sunday & am getting on pretty well with it. I shall not know what to attempt when that is done." Two days later he comments: "By working an hour or two every evening at the Nature I have very nearly finished it: tonight or tomorrow will I believe do everything to it that I am at present capable of doing. There is a pleasure in seeing any fresh thing finished at least so far as to be presentable." And on 7 February he says: "I finished the 'Nature' on Sunday [the 5th] as I expected."

Being puzzled as to what to attempt next, he sent the list of subjects they had agreed on (see cxxiii above). Harriet suggested that he move on to the

---

iniquity—all the things which are punished as the most atrocious crimes when done by human creatures, being the daily doings of nature through the whole range of organic life." (*Letters*, ed. Elliot, I, 156–7; corrected from autograph draft in possession of the Rt. Rev. C. L. Street.)

[31]Presumably these sentences are those (or the basis of those) found at 386.5–9 below, beginning: "Even the love of 'order'. . . ."

"Utility of religion" rather than to an essay on "Differences of character," saying:

About the Essays dear, would not Religion, the Utility of Religion, be one of the subjects you would have most to say on—there is to account for the existence nearly universal of some religion (superstition) by the instincts of fear hope and mystery etc., and throwing over all doctrines and theories, called religion, as devices for power, to show how religion & poetry fill the same want, the craving after higher objects, the consolation of suffering, by hopes of heaven for the selfish, love of God for the tender & grateful—how all this must be superseded by morality deriving its power from sympathies and benevolence and its reward from the approbation of those we respect.

There what a long winded sentence which you would say ten times as well in words half the length.[32]

On 20 February Mill replied: "Your programme of an essay on the utility of religion is beautiful, but it requires you to fill it up—I can try, but a few paragraphs will bring me to the end of all I have got to say on the subject. What would be the use of my outliving you! I could write nothing worth keeping alive for except with your prompting." On 6 March, perhaps having received Harriet's comments, he says: "I have fairly set to at another essay, on the subject you suggested. I wrote several hours at it yesterday, after turning it over mentally many days before—but I cannot work at it here [the India House] yet, as there is another mail in today—luckily a light one." On Sunday, 12 March, he worked on the essay "till near one," and on 20 March he says:

I wrote a good spell at the new Essay yesterday, & hope to get a good deal done to it this week. But I have not yet got to the part of the subject which you so beautifully sketched, having begun with examining the more commonplace view of the subject, the supposed necessity of religion for social purposes as a sanction for morality. I regard the whole of what I am writing or shall write as mere raw material, in what manner & into what to be worked up to be decided between us— & I am much bent upon getting as much of this sort written as possible—but above all I am anxious about the Life, which must be the first thing we go over when we are together.[33]

On 3 April he reports to Harriet (referring to her, as was his custom, in the third person): "I have completed an essay on the usefulness of religion— such a one as I can write though very far inferior to what she could." And again on the 5th, in the last known reference to the essay, he says: "I have done all I can for the subject she last gave me."

It would appear from this evidence that the final form of the essay follows

---

[32]Pencilled a.l., 14–15/2/54, British Library of Political and Economic Science; published, with some variations in reading, in F. A. Hayek, *John Stuart Mill and Harriet Taylor: Their Friendship and Subsequent Marriage* (London: Routledge and Kegan Paul, 1951), 195–6.

[33]A.l.s., King's College, Cambridge.

the original plan, for the first part of which Mill was himself responsible (the introductory section is also almost certainly his), while Harriet's "long winded" and somewhat incoherent sentence served as the basis for the second part, which deals with the effects of religion on the individual. (See 418ff. below, especially 418–20, 421–2.) On such meagre evidence alone can we rely in estimating Harriet's contributions to these "joint productions"; again she appears as the inspirer, suggesting avenues of approach, probably adding words and phrases, but not conceiving the work as a developed whole, or writing any substantial part of it.

There seems now to be no further external evidence concerning dating and the degree of collaboration, or for assessing Helen Taylor's role as editor of the *Three Essays*, which appeared only posthumously, in 1874.[34] At Sothebys' sale on 29 March, 1922, the manuscripts were sold to Atkinson for £1, under the following description: "723. Mill (John Stuart) Utility of Religion, Theism, and Nature. Three Auto. MSS of Essays (3)." Nothing further is known of these, the only recorded manuscripts for any of the essays in the present volume.

The copy-text for the *Three Essays*, since they were published after Mill's death, is that of the 1st ed. (1874); the 2nd (also 1874) and 3rd (1885) eds. being simply reprints. There are, consequently, no variants. The main point to be made about the quotations and references is that the former are infrequent and the latter vague. In this respect they resemble the other essays planned and in part written at the same time, such as *Utilitarianism* or *On Liberty*. It seems likely that Mill, influenced by Harriet, was aiming at a broader audience than in his more technical works and so, except for general reliance on inartistic or extrinsic evidence (to use the rhetorical terms) that would be easily accepted by his audience, put his main argumentative weight on artistic or intrinsic evidence, and consequently cultivated the appeals to *ethos* and *pathos* as well as *logos*.

AUGUSTE COMTE AND POSITIVISM

In his *Autobiography*, having earlier dealt with Comte's influence on his logical speculations and with their correspondence, Mill devotes a full paragraph to explaining his attitude to Comte at the time he composed the two articles that make up *Auguste Comte and Positivism*:

After the completion of the book on Hamilton, I applied myself to a task which a variety of reasons seemed to render specially incumbent upon me; that of giving an account, and forming an estimate, of the doctrines of Auguste Comte. I had contributed more than any one else to make his speculations known in England.

---

[34]It would be useful to know, for example, whether the title, *Three Essays on Religion*, was chosen by Mill or by Helen Taylor.

In consequence chiefly of what I had said of him in my Logic, he had readers and admirers among thoughtful men on this side of the Channel at a time when his name had not yet in France emerged from obscurity. So unknown and unappreciated was he at the time when my Logic was written and published, that to criticize his weak points might well appear superfluous, while it was a duty to give as much publicity as one could to the important contributions he had made to philosophic thought. At the time, however, at which I have now arrived, this state of affairs had entirely changed. His name, at least, was known almost universally, and the general character of his doctrines very widely. He had taken his place in the estimation both of friends and opponents, as one of the conspicuous figures in the thought of the age. The better parts of his speculations had made great progress in working their way into those minds, which, by their previous culture and tendencies, were fitted to receive them: under cover of those better parts those of a worse character, greatly developed and added to in his later writings, had also made some way, having obtained active and enthusiastic adherents, some of them of no inconsiderable personal merit, in England, France, and other countries. These causes not only made it desirable that some one should undertake the task of sifting what is good from what is bad in M. Comte's speculations, but seemed to impose on myself in particular a special obligation to make the attempt. This I accordingly did in two Essays, published in successive numbers of the Westminster Review, and reprinted in a small volume under the title 'Auguste Comte and Positivism.'[35]

As Mill indicates, he wrote the articles on Comte after completing his *Examination of Sir William Hamilton's Philosophy*, but his plans go back to the early 1850s. In 1851 John Chapman, who had just taken over the *Westminster Review*, suggested (evidently prompted by Francis Place) an article on Comte; Mill replied tartly (29/9/51): "I have never had any intention of writing on Comte's book [the *Cours*], nor do I think that a translation or an abridgement of it is likely to be either useful or successful." Three years later, however, after the appearance of Harriet Martineau's English redaction of the *Cours*, Mill took more seriously a renewed suggestion by Chapman. He wrote to Harriet (9/1/54) for her opinion:

Now about reviewing Comte: the reasons *pro* are evident. Those *con* are 1st I don't like to have anything to do with the name or with any publication of H. Martineau. 2dly. The Westr though it will allow I dare say anything else, could not allow me to speak freely about Comte's atheism & I do not see how it is possible to be just to him, when there is so much to attack, without giving him praise on that point of the subject. 3dly. As Chapman is the publisher he doubtless wishes, & expects, an article more laudatory on the whole, than I shd be willing to write. You dearest one will tell me what your perfect judgment & your feeling decide.

Her strong feeling (and judgment) against Harriet Martineau and Comte[36] led her in a letter (not preserved, but written before Mill's letter reached

---

[35]*Autobiography*, 194–5. Earlier discussions of Comte appear on 116–17, 146–9, 156, and 174n.

[36]See Michael St. J. Packe, *The Life of John Stuart Mill* (London: Secker and Warburg, 1954), 277–8.

her) to advise against his proceeding with the review, and he replied (17/1/54):

As for Chapman's request, the *pro* was the great desire I feel to atone for the overpraise I have given Comte & to let it be generally known to those who know me what I think on the unfavourable side about him. The reason that the objection which you feel so strongly & which my next letter afterwards [that quoted above] will have shewn that I feel too, did not completely decide the matter with me, was that Chapman did not want a review of this particular book, but of *Comte*, & I could have got rid of H.M.'s part in a sentence, perhaps without even naming her—I shd certainly have put Comte's own book at the head along with hers & made all the references to *it*. But malgré cela I disliked the connexion & now I dislike it still more, & shall at once write to C. to refuse—putting the delay of an answer upon my long absence so that he may not think I hesitated.

And by 23 January he had written to Chapman refusing.

Not until 1863 did he take up the question again, this time himself opening the matter with Chapman (16/3/63): "M. Littré has nearly ready for publication a life of M. Comte, which would afford a very good occasion for a general estimate of M. Comte and of his philosophy. If you would like to have such an article from me, I would undertake it. I cannot say exactly how soon it could be ready, as I have more than one thing in hand which I should like to finish before commencing it. But I would promise it as early as is possible without a very inconvenient interruption of other things."[37] On 1 August, replying to Chapman's request for an early submission, Mill is even less sanguine about a deadline, pointing out that Littré's volume will perhaps not be published by October. Its earlier appearance, while increasing Mill's desire to write on the subject, led him to another postponement, explained in a letter to Chapman on 6 September:

What I wish to write is an estimate of Comte's philosophy. But the book suggests much to be said about the man himself, his character and career, the conduct of others in relation to him, and various points in the character of his country and of the age, which some of the incidents of his life illustrate. It, therefore, is worth reviewing merely as a biography, independent of the great philosophical questions raised in it; and as the attempt to combine both points of view in one article would not only run to too great a length, but would almost necessarily spoil both, *two* articles seem to be required, one of which, though I should not be unwilling, I have no particular wish to write, while I could not possible set about either before next year.

He suggested, therefore, that if Chapman had someone in mind who could write the biographical article sooner, he would willingly forego the task. Mill was reluctant, he explained (18/9/63), after Chapman asked him to do the

---

[37]This suggestion is adumbrated by a comment to Bain (13/2/63): "Littré writes that he will very shortly publish his life of Comte which I expect will be interesting & I shall perhaps make it an occasion for writing something about Comte, though I do not like being diverted from Hamilton." (Autograph draft, British Library of Political and Economic Science.)

biographical article, because Littré placed both Comte and the French national character in an unfavourable light, and he did not wish to add his voice to the general discrediting of them in England. At this time he intended to treat Robinet's book with Littré's in the first article, and to add Littré's *Paroles de philosophie positive* and de Blignières's volume to Littré's biography for the second; both articles to be finished early in 1864, though not in time for the April number of the *Westminster*, he told Chapman. A week later, however, having read Robinet's book, he felt that he must give up the biographical article:

There is so bitter a feud between those who followed Comte in the last developments of his opinions and those who only went a certain way with him, among whom was Littré; and the two parties differ so widely in their statements of fact, that there is no chance of getting at the truth: and any remarks founded on mere conjecture would be of course utterly valueless, besides the possibility that they might be unjust to one side or the other. I therefore propose to limit myself to one article, which I will set about as soon as I am free from my present occupations and in which I shall pass slightly over Comte's personal history and character, and confine myself in the main to an estimate of his doctrines and method.[38]

In December he was working on Spencer's criticism of Comte's classification of the sciences, so presumably he was preparing the article at that time. He entered into correspondence with Spencer on the question in the spring of 1864, remarking *inter alia*: "I myself owe much more to Comte than you do, though, in my case also, all my principal conclusions had been reached before I saw his book. But in speculative matters (not in practical) I often agree with him where you do not, and, among other subjects, on this particular one, the Classification of the Sciences."[39] By that time, however, he had put the article aside to work on his *Examination of Sir William Hamilton's Philosophy*, which was, as Bain remarks, his main occupation during 1863 and 1864.[40] Picking up the article again in the autumn of 1864 (the *Hamilton* being virtually completed by the end of August), he finished the first draft, but then had to put it aside almost immediately when, early in November, he turned to revisions of his *Principles of Political Economy* for the 5th and People's editions. Only in December[41] was he able to give final form to his plan for treating Comte; on the 12th he wrote to Chapman to say

[38]To Chapman, 25/9/63. (This and the previous letters to Chapman are all at the National Library of Australia, Canberra, except those of 29/9/51 and 1/8/63, which are in the British Library of Political and Economic Science.) Cf. Mill's comment on his proposed essay to d'Eichthal (30/3/64): "il sera peu question de la biographie de Comte; d'autant plus que ceux qui disputent autour de son tombeau sont tellement en désaccord sur les faits, que je désespère d'arriver à la vérité." (A.l.s. in the library of the Arsenal, Paris.)
[39]To Spencer, 3/4/64 (Northwestern University Library).
[40]*John Stuart Mill*, 119.
[41]Letter to Bain, 2/12/64 (autograph draft, Johns Hopkins).

that two articles would after all be needed, one on Comte's *Cours*, and the other on his later speculations.

The first of these [he says] is all written; except two or three references which remain to be put in when I return to England [from Avignon] at the end of January. I can therefore promise it for the April number. But it is very long; sixty pages of the Westminster, if not more [sixty-six, actually]; and I see no possibility of either dividing or shortening it, consistently with its being what I meant it to be. It is for you to judge whether, under these conditions, it will suit the Review. If accepted, as I wish it to be known as mine, I should be glad, if you have no objection, to put my initials.

The second article, he feels "tolerably certain," will be ready for the following number, if Chapman wishes it then. On 4 February, 1865, having finished the first article, he was "well advanced" with the second, and asked Chapman to have twenty copies of the first made up for him to send to friends. He added the reference to Bridges' *General View of Positivism* (a translation of Comte's "Discours préliminaire" to the *Système*) to the second article at this time, remarking to Chapman (9/2/65) that it "gives the pith of Comte's later speculations free from some of their grosser absurdities, and in a form better adapted than any other of his later works for the information and edification of English readers." By 28 February the second article was finished (though not delivered to the printers until after 10 March), and proof of the first returned to the printer with a request for a revise. The revise being returned by 6 March, Mill asked for prepublication copies of the first article so that Littré could have it translated; they were delivered on 25 March. On 11 April he had read proof of the second article, and again asked for a revise (to be sent to Avignon where he was going that evening) and twenty copies.

His interest in the reception of the articles is shown in a request that Chapman let him know of any responses, and in his immediate acceptance of the suggestion that the articles be republished in book form. "I have always contemplated reprinting the articles on Comte as soon as is consistent with the interest of the Review," he writes to Chapman on 20 April, "and if Mr. Trübner—then publisher of the *Westminster*—"wishes to be the publisher, no one has so good a claim. We will therefore consider that as settled." Having returned to England on 30 June at the insistence of the committee seeking his election to parliament for Westminster, Mill outlined to Chapman (28/7/65) his "usual conditions with [his] publishers," half profit for a single edition, with the number of copies being left to the publisher's discretion, and the copyright remaining with the author; he also expressed his wish to revise the articles before they were sent to the printers.[42] The revision,

---

[42]The letters of 12/12/64, 28/2/65, 25/3/65, and 20/4/65 are in the British Library of Political and Economic Science; the others are in Canberra.

"a very slight business," was completed by 22 August, as he told Grote, adding: "The parallel which struck you between Comte in his old age and Plato in his, had impressed itself forcibly on my own mind."[43]

The sale of all Mill's works being greatly promoted by his candidacy and election for Westminster, the Comte sold very quickly; by November Trübner was asking about French and German translations, and by the end of the year was considering stereotyping a new edition (as Longmans was doing with the People's editions of his *Principles, On Liberty,* and *Representative Government*). The arrangements for the 2nd ed. were completed in January, 1866 (while he was again in Avignon), Mill having asked for £70 ("the half profit on the first ed. to be paid when it is all sold & the £70 on the publication of the second"), with the price to be reduced after the sale of the second thousand.[44] When in April Longmans suggested a collected edition of his works, Mill mentioned Trübner's interest in the Comte as a reason for delaying the project, which was eventually dropped.[45]

Of the variants, fifty-one result from changes between the periodical version and the 1st ed., and thirty-six from changes between the 1st and 2nd eds., the majority of the more significant ones coming in the first revision of the first article. A higher percentage than usual results from the change in provenance, mainly because the two essays were combined in book form (see, for example, 265^{b-b}, $^{c-c}$, and ^{d}). The most complicated changes result from the incorporation in the text of the 1st ed. of a passage that had appeared as a long footnote in the periodical version (see 319^{l-l322}). This passage is followed by one introducing a qualification (322^{n-n}), contains another typical qualification (320^{m-m}), and is expanded by a footnote containing further information ($320n$). An interesting example of variants resulting from printer's errors may be seen at 352^{m-m}, where the copy in Mill's library (Somerville College, Oxford) shows a tentative revision not carried out. The relative infrequency of revisions (.82 per page of this edition) reflects the very short time between the separate publications.

PRINCIPLES AND METHODS

As throughout this edition, the copy-text for each item is that of the final version supervised by Mill. Details concerning these texts are given in their headnotes.

Method of Indicating Variants. All the substantive variants are governed by the principles enunciated below, except for a few special cases, in which self-explanatory notes are given in square brackets and italics. "Substantive" here means all changes of text except spelling, capitalization, hyphenation,

---

[43] A.l.s., British Museum.
[44] A.l.s. to Trübner, 9/1/66 (British Library of Political and Economic Science).
[45] A.l.s. to William Longman, 28/4/66 (*ibid.*).

punctuation, demonstrable typographical errors, and such printing-house concerns as type size, etc. With the exception of substitutions of "on" for "upon" (nineteen instances), "though" for "although" (four instances), "an" for "a" before "universal" (four instances; all the foregoing in the 1st ed. of *Dissertations and Discussions*), and "until" for "till" (two instances in the 2nd ed. of *Dissertations*), all substantive variants are recorded. These are of three kinds: addition of a word or words, substitution of a word or words, deletion of a word or words. The following illustrative examples are drawn from "Sedgwick."

Addition of a word or words: see 39[x–x]. In the text, the passage "a true philosopher" appears as "a [x]true[x] philosopher"; the variant note reads "[x–x]+59,67". Here the plus sign indicates that the word "true" was added; the numbers following ("59,67") indicate the editions of this particular text in which the addition appears. The editions are always indicated by the last two numbers of the year of publication: here 59=1859 (the 1st ed. of Volumes I and II of *Dissertations and Discussions*); 67=1867 (the 2nd ed. of these volumes). Information explaining the use of these abbreviations is given in each headnote, as required. Any added editorial information is enclosed in square brackets and italicized.

Placing this example in context, the interpretation is that when first published (1835) the reading was "a philosopher"; in 1859 this was altered to "a true philosopher", and the altered reading was retained in 1867.

Substitution of a word or words: see 39[y–y]. In the text the passage "truths of that small calibre" appears as "truths of [y]that small calibre[y]"; the variant note reads "[y–y]35 the calibre of the *Penny Magazine*". Here the words following the edition indicator are those for which "that small calibre" was substituted; applying the same rules and putting the variant in context, the interpretation is that when first published (1835) the reading was "truths of the calibre of the *Penny Magazine*"; in 1859 this was altered to "truths of that small calibre", and the reading of 1859 was retained in 1867.

In this volume there are very few examples of passages that were altered more than once: an illustrative instance is found in "Bentham" at 98[q–q]. The text reads "[q]which tend to[q] influence"; the variant note reads "[q–q]38 which] 59 which are liable to". Here the different readings, in chronological order, are separated by a square bracket. The interpretation is that the original reading in 1838, "which influence", was altered in 1859 to "which are liable to influence", and in 1867 to "which tend to influence".

Deletion of a word or words: see 39[v]. In the text, a *single* superscript [v] appears *centred* between "the" and "instruments"; the variant note reads "[v]35 mere". Here the word following the edition indicator is the one deleted; applying the same rules and putting the variant in context, the interpretation is that when first published (1835) the reading was "the mere instruments"; in 1859 "mere" was deleted, and the reading of 1859 (as is clear in the text) was retained in 1867.

Variants in Mill's footnotes: see 48n. To avoid four levels of text on the page, a different method has been used to indicate the few changes in the notes supplied by Mill. In the example cited, the final sentence begins "Apparently [35   Evidently] not; he. . . ." Here the interpretation is that in 1835 the sentence began "Evidently not; he. . ."; in 1859 "Apparently" was substituted for "Evidently", and the altered reading was retained in 1867. When necessary, to prevent confusion in reading, the words before and/or after the altered passage are given (see the other variants in the same note).

Dates of footnotes: see 37n. Here the practice is to place immediately after the footnote indicator, in square brackets, the figure indicating the edition in which the footnote first appeared. In the example cited, "[59]" indicates that the note was added in 1859 (and retained in 1867). If no such figure appears, the note is in all versions.

Punctuation and spelling. In general, changes between versions in punctuation and spelling are ignored. Those changes which occur as part of a substantive variant are included in that variant, and the superscript letters in the text are placed exactly with reference to punctuation. Changes between italic and roman type are indicated, except in foreign phrases and titles of works. (In general, italics were removed in *Dissertations and Discussions*; there are forty-four examples in the 1st ed. and ten in the 2nd, in the articles reprinted in this volume.)

Other textual liberties. Some of the titles of Mill's essays have been altered for easier and shorter identification; the full titles in their various forms will be found in the headnotes. The dates added to the titles are those of first publication. The original footnotes to the titles, giving bibliographic information, have—except in the case of the second part of *Auguste Comte and Positivism*—been deleted, and the information given in the headnotes.

Typographical errors have been silently corrected in the text; the note below lists them.[46] Because the original is retained, occasional oddities, not identifiable as typographical errors, such as "resultée" (283.1), "avénement"

[46]Typographical errors in earlier versions are ignored, except when a variant results. The following are corrected (with the erroneous reading first, followed by the corrected reading in square brackets):
21.28 Soames [Soame]
24.24 maintans [maintains]
24.40 past." [past.'] [*altered by style in present ed.*]
34.33 Things [Things,] [*as in* 35, 59]
36.13 excellencies [excellences[[*as in* 35, 59]
38.23 them: [them;] [*as in* 35, 59]
38.24 them; [them:] [*as in* 35, 59]
42.7 following;—[following:—] [*as in* 35, 59]
46.29 unintelligible [unintelligible,] [*as in* 35, 59]
70.6 merely [mere] [*as in* Source, 35, 39]

(287.n8), "lettrès" (352.32), and "depend" (419.8) appear in the text; to avoid annoyance, "[*sic*]" is silently understood in these cases. In the headnotes the quotations from Mill's bibliography, the manuscript of which is a scribal copy, are also silently corrected twice; again, the note below gives the corrections.[47] While the punctuation and spelling of each item are retained, the style has been made uniform: for example, periods are added, when necessary, after such abbreviations as Mr., Dr., and St.; square brackets have been made round; and italic punctuation after italic passages has been made roman.

Also, in accordance with modern practice, all long quotations have been reduced in size, and the quotation marks removed. In consequence, it has been necessary occasionally to add square brackets; there is little opportunity here for confusion, as my editorial insertions (except page references) are in italics. The passage from Locke on 49, although set down, as in the copy-text, includes Mill's quotation marks to facilitate reading. Double quotation marks replace single, and titles have been italicized for works originally published separately, again in accordance with modern practice. Mill's references to sources, and additional editorial references (in square brackets) have been normalized. Where necessary, his references have been silently corrected; a list of the corrections and alterations is given below.[48]

84.n1 I. [I,] [*as in* 38, 59]
86.9 not be [not to be] [*as in* Source, 38]
86.12 and let [that let] [*as in* Source, 38, 59]
120.15 thought is, [thought, is] [*as in* 40, 59]
145.32 reference [reverence] [*as in* 40, 59]
151.n3 *†[‡] [*probably caused by erroneous ommission of footnote in 59*]
161.n3 p., 245 [p. 245]
167.17 inasmueh [inasmuch]
168.19 depositories [depositaries] [*as in* 52]
196.16 Livingstone [Livingston] [*as in* 52]
200.31 done ["done] [*as in* 52]
204.17–18 OF [ON] [*see* 204 *below*]
216.42 deprives [deprive] [*as in* 61, 63, 64, 67]
248.11 though, [though] [*as in* 61, 63, 64, 67]
250.31 stock [stock,] [*as in* 61, 63, 64, 67; in 71 the type has evidently dropped at the end of the line*]
266.22–3 coexistence [co-existences] [*as in* 65, 65¹ *and below on same page*]
267.4 "The [The] [*as in* 65, 65¹]
277.31 contiually [continually]
307.38 M [M.] [*as throughout in* 65, 65¹]
314.14 aad [and] [*error also in* 65¹]
316.35 progress. [progress."] [*as in* 65, 65¹; *altered by style in present ed.*]
328.1 contain [contains] [*as in* 65; 65¹ *also has error*]
352.27 turbulent [turbulent,] [*as in* 65; 65¹ *also has error*]
359.19 there [three] [*as in* 65, 65¹]
484.7 ou [our]

[47]In the headnote on 32 the quotation mark is added before 'Discourse'; similarly on 204 the quotation mark is added before 'Utilitarianism'.

[48]Following the page and line notation, the first reference is to JSM's identification;

Appendices. These items are taken out of the normal chronological order and appended for special reasons. Appendix A, the "Preface" to *Dissertations and Discussions,* is placed here because its comment, while relevant to all the essays in those volumes, has particular reference to four of those here reprinted (the essays on Sedgwick, Bentham, Coleridge, and Whewell). Appendix B, the selection from Mill's obituary of Bentham, although published in a newspaper, has such intimate relevance to his other writings on Bentham that it should appear in the same volume (it will be reprinted in full in the volume of newspaper writings). Appendix C, the account of Bentham in the text of Bulwer's *England and the English,* is included because, as its headnote explains, it is based on material given by Mill to Bulwer. Appendix D, a long passage from "Coleridge" quoted by Mill in Book VI of his *Logic,* gives interesting cross-references in time and subject between the two works.

Appendix E, the Bibliographic Appendix, provides a guide to Mill's quotations, with notes concerning the separate entries, and a list of substantive variants between his quotations and their sources. Excluding citations of statutes, there are references to over 140 publications in the essays in this volume, with quotations from sixty-eight of them. Works by six authors—Blakey, Sedgwick, Coleridge, Bentham, Whewell, and Comte—are reviewed in considerable detail. While there are many references to other moral philosophers, the non-historical nature of these essays is indicated by the infrequency of direct references to works of moral philosophy, and the rarity of quotation from any but those reviewed. As indicated above, there are hardly any direct quotations in *Utilitarianism* and the *Three Essays on*

---

the corrected identification (that which appears in the present text) follows in square brackets. There is no indication of the places where a dash has been substituted for a comma to indicate adjacent pages, where "P." or "Pp." replaces "p." or "pp." (or the reverse), or where the volume number has been added to the reference.

25.35.'—p. 127. '[. . . .]

25.36–7 "—ib. [(II, p. 127.)]

41.11 p. 34 [p. 36]

136.n30 p. 161 [pp. 160–2]

151.n1 p. 75 [pp. 74–5]

151.n2 p. 18 [pp. 18–19]

151.n3 p. 19 [pp. 19–20]

152.n2 pp. 23, 24 [p. 26]

152.n3 p. 29 [pp. 29–30]

152.n4 pp. 31, 32 [pp. 30–2]

155.n9 388 [388–9]

155. n9 *Literary Remains* [*Church and State*]

156.n1 p. 414 [pp. 414–15]

157.n1 p. 414 [p. 413n]

157.n2 p. 414 [pp. 413–14]

158.n1 p. 249 [pp. 249–50]

161.n2 159 [359]

161.n3 Ib [*ie.*, iii] [*Ibid.*, Vol. IV]

174.24 p. 190 [pp. 190–1]

176.8 p. 202 [Pp. 202–3]

181.29 p. 211 [Pp. 210–12]

183.40 p. 215 [Pp. 215–16]

188.12 p. xiii [Pp. xiii–xiv]

190.n9 p. 58 [Pp. 58–9]

192.16 32 [pp. 32–3]

193.14 pp. 138–9 [Pp. 139, 138–9]

198.29 p. 259 [Pp. 259–60]

200.24 ii. 91–94 [Vol. II, p. 93]

200.33 ii. 106 [Vol. II, pp. 105, 106]

287. n28 p. 37 [P. 37n]

295.15 639 [pp. 639–40]

363.n3 pp. 10, 11 [pp. 10–11, 11]

364.n1 11, 12 [*Ibid.*] [*i.e.*, 12]

865.44 substiuted [substituted]

Religion; it should be added that in the latter, as would be expected from the subject, but not from this author, there are many indirect quotations from the Bible.

This Appendix serves as an index to persons, books, and statutes, so references to them are omitted from the Index proper, which has been prepared by R. I. K. Davidson.

ACKNOWLEDGMENTS

AS ALWAYS, I am deeply indebted to the librarians and staff of Somerville College, Oxford, the British Museum, the University of London Library, the Yale University Library, and the British Library of Political and Economic Science. Of those who have helped in various ways in the preparation of the text, I should specially like to thank Mrs. Carolyn Allen, Professor Kathleen Coburn, Professor Sydney Eisen, Dennis Lee, Anne McWhir, Professor Francis E. Mineka, Professor James Moore, James Peddie, Professor Elizabeth Vida, and Dr. Adelaide Weinberg. My thanks also to the staff of the University of Toronto Press, in particular R. M. Schoeffel, the copy-editor, and Francess G. Halpenny, the Managing Editor; and to the Mill Editorial Committee, in particular F. E. L. Priestley and R. F. McRae. Of the manifold ways in which my good wife aided me, I shall mention only the long hours she spent with Auguste Comte, hours from which I profited more than she.

Victoria College

J.M.R.

ESSAYS ON ETHICS, RELIGION AND SOCIETY

REMARKS ON BENTHAM'S PHILOSOPHY

1833

EDITOR'S NOTE

Appendix B in Edward Lytton Bulwer, *England and the English* (London: Bentley, 1833), II, 321–44. Unsigned; not republished. Identified in JSM's bibliography as "The 'Remarks on Bentham's Philosophy' forming one of the Appendices to Bulwer's 'England and the English' " (MacMinn, 33). In the "Advertisement" (dated 9 July, 1833) to his work, Bulwer comments: "to another gentleman, qualified, perhaps before all men living, to judge profoundly of the philosophy of Bentham, I am . . . indebted for considerable aid in the sketch of that remarkable writer's moral and legislative codes which will be found in the Appendix to the second volume . . ." (I, iii). For JSM's attitude toward the Appendix, see the Textual Introduction, cxvi–cxvii above.

In the Somerville College copy of *England and the English* there are pencilled lines opposite passages on 339, 340, 341, and 344; against the passage on "interest" on 14 (in the text below) is written "very good"—these may be Harriet Taylor's markings; they can hardly be JSM's.

Remarks on Bentham's Philosophy

IT IS NO light task to give an abridged view of the philosophical opinions of one, who attempted to place the vast subjects of morals and legislation upon a scientific basis: a mere outline is all that can be attempted.

The first principles of Mr. Bentham's philosophy are these;—that happiness, meaning by that term pleasure and exemption from pain, is the only thing desirable in itself; that all other things are desirable solely as means to that end: that the production, therefore, of the greatest possible happiness, is the only fit purpose of all human thought and action, and consequently of all morality and government; and moreover, that pleasure and pain are the sole agencies by which the conduct of mankind is in fact governed, whatever circumstances the individual may be placed in, and whether he is aware of it or not.

Mr. Bentham does not appear to have entered very deeply into the metaphysical grounds of these doctrines; he seems to have taken those grounds very much upon the showing of the metaphysicians who preceded him. The principle of utility, or as he afterwards called it "the greatest-happiness principle,"[*] stands no otherwise demonstrated in his writings, than by an enumeration of the phrases of a different description which have been commonly employed to denote the rule of life, and the rejection of them all, as having no intelligible meaning, further than as they may involve a tacit reference to considerations of utility. Such are the phrases "law of nature," "right reason," "natural rights," "moral sense." All these Mr. Bentham regarded as mere covers for dogmatism; excuses for setting up one's own *ipse dixit* as a rule to bind other people. "They consist, all of them," says he, "in so many contrivances for avoiding the obligation of appealing to any external standard, and for prevailing upon the reader to accept the author's sentiment or opinion as a reason for itself."[†]

This, however, is not fair treatment of the believers in other moral principles than that of utility. All modes of speech are employed in an ignorant

[*Introduction to the Principles of Morals and Legislation (1789). In *Works*. 11 vols. Ed. John Bowring. Edinburgh: Tait, 1843, Vol. I, p. 1 n.]
[†*Ibid.*, p. 8.]

manner, by ignorant people; but no one who had thought deeply and systematically enough to be entitled to the name of a philosopher, ever supposed that his *own* private sentiments of approbation and disapprobation must necessarily be well-founded, and needed not to be compared with any external standard. The answer of such persons to Mr. Bentham would be, that by an inductive and analytical examination of the human mind, they had satisfied themselves, that what we call our moral sentiments, (that is, the feelings of complacency and aversion we experience when we compare actions of our own or of other people with our standard of right and wrong,) are as much part of the original constitution of man's nature as the desire of happiness and the fear of suffering: That those sentiments do not indeed attach themselves to the same actions under all circumstances, but neither do they, in attaching themselves to actions, follow the law of utility, but certain other general laws, which are the same in all mankind naturally; though education or external circumstances may counteract them, by creating artificial associations stronger than they. No proof indeed can be given that we ought to abide by these laws; but neither can any proof be given, that we ought to regulate our conduct by utility. All that can be said is, that the pursuit of happiness is natural to us; and so, it is contended, is the reverence for, and the inclination to square our actions by, certain general laws of morality.

Any one who is acquainted with the ethical doctrines either of the Reid and Stewart school, or of the German metaphysicians (not to go further back), knows that such would be the answer of those philosophers to Mr. Bentham; and it is an answer of which Mr. Bentham's writings furnish no sufficient refutation. For it is evident, that these views of the origin of moral distinctions are *not*, what he says all such views are, destitute of any precise and tangible meaning; nor chargeable with setting up as a standard the feelings of the particular person. They set up as a standard what are assumed (on grounds which are considered sufficient) to be the instincts of the species, or principles of our common nature as universal and inexplicable as instincts.

To pass judgment on these doctrines, belongs to a profounder and subtler metaphysics than Mr. Bentham possessed. I apprehend it will be the judgment of posterity, that in his views of what, in the felicitous expression of Hobbes, may be called the *philosophia prima*,[*] it has for the most part, even when he was most completely in the right, been reserved for others to *prove* him so. The greatest of Mr. Bentham's defects, his insufficient knowledge and appreciation of the thoughts of other men, shows itself constantly in his grappling with some delusive shadow of an adversary's opinion, and leaving the actual substance unharmed.

[*Thomas Hobbes. "Sive philosophia prima," Part II of *Elementorum philosophiæ Sectio prima, De Corpore*. In *Opera philosophica*. Ed. William Molesworth. London: Bohn, 1839–45, Vol. I, pp. 81 ff.]

After laying down the principle of Utility, Mr. Bentham is occupied through the most voluminous and the most permanently valuable part of his works, in constructing the outlines of practical ethics and legislation, and filling up some portions of the latter science (or rather art) in great detail; by the uniform and unflinching application of his own greatest-happiness principle, from which the eminently consistent and systematic character of his intellect prevented him from ever swerving. In the writings of no philosopher, probably, are to be detected so few contradictions—so few instances of even momentary deviation from the principles he himself has laid down.

It is perhaps fortunate that Mr. Bentham devoted a much larger share of his time and labour to the subject of legislation, than to that of morals; for the mode in which he understood and applied the principle of Utility, appears to me far more conducive to the attainment of true and valuable results in the former, than in the latter of these two branches of inquiry. The recognition of happiness as the only thing desirable in itself, and of the production of the state of things most favourable to happiness as the only rational end both of morals and policy, by no means necessarily leads to the doctrine of expediency as professed by Paley; the ethical canon which judges of the morality of an act or a class of actions, solely by the probable *consequences* of that particular kind of act, supposing it to be generally practised. This is a very small part indeed of what a more enlarged understanding of the "greatest-happiness principle" would require us to take into the account. A certain kind of action, as for example, theft, or lying, would, if commonly practised, occasion certain evil consequences to society: but those evil consequences are far from constituting the entire moral bearings of the vices of theft or lying. We shall have a very imperfect view of the relation of those practices to the general happiness, if we suppose them to exist singly, and insulated. All acts suppose certain dispositions, and habits of mind and heart, which may be in themselves states of enjoyment or of wretchedness, and which must be fruitful in *other* consequences, besides those particular acts. No person can be a thief or a liar without being much else: and if our moral judgments and feelings with respect to a person convicted of either vice, were grounded solely upon the pernicious tendency of thieving and of lying, they would be partial and incomplete; many considerations would be omitted, which are at least equally "germane to the matter;"[*] many which, by leaving them out of our general views, we may indeed teach ourselves a habit of overlooking, but which it is impossible for any of us not to be influenced by, in particular cases, in proportion as they are forced upon our attention.

Now, the great fault I have to find with Mr. Bentham as a moral philosopher, and the source of the chief part of the temporary mischief which in that character, along with a vastly greater amount of permanent good, he must be

[*William Shakespeare. *Hamlet* (ed. Furness), V, ii, 152–3.]

allowed to have produced, is this: that he has practically, to a very great extent, confounded the principle of Utility with the principle of specific consequences, and has habitually made up his estimate of the approbation or blame due to a particular kind of action, from a calculation solely of the consequences to which that very action, if practised generally, would itself lead. He has largely exemplified, and contributed very widely to diffuse, a tone of thinking, according to which any kind of action or any habit, which in its own specific consequences cannot be proved to be necessarily or probably productive of unhappiness to the agent himself or to others, is supposed to be fully justified; and any disapprobation or aversion entertained towards the individual by reason of it, is set down from that time forward as prejudice and superstition. It is not considered (at least, not habitually considered,) whether the act or habit in question, though not in itself necessarily pernicious, may not form part of a *character* essentially pernicious, or at least essentially deficient in some quality eminently conducive to the "greatest happiness." To apply such a standard as this, would indeed often require a much deeper insight into the formation of character, and knowledge of the internal workings of human nature, than Mr. Bentham possessed. But, in a greater or less degree, he, and every one else, judges by this standard: even those who are warped, by some partial view, into the omission of all such elements from their general speculations.

When the moralist thus overlooks the relation of an act to a certain state of mind as its cause, and its connexion through that common cause with large classes and groups of actions apparently very little resembling itself, his estimation even of the consequences of the very act itself, is rendered imperfect. For it may be affirmed with few exceptions, that any act whatever has a tendency to fix and perpetuate the state or character of mind in which itself has originated. And if that important element in the moral relations of the action be not taken into account by the moralist as a cause, neither probably will it be taken into account as a consequence.

Mr. Bentham is far from having altogether overlooked this side of the subject. Indeed, those most original and instructive, though, as I conceive, in their spirit, partially erroneous chapters, on *motives* and on *dispositions*, in his first great work, the Introduction to the *Principles of Morals and Legislation*, open up a direct and broad path to these most important topics. It is not the less true that Mr. Bentham, and many others, following his example, when they came to discuss particular questions of ethics, have commonly, in the superior stress which they laid upon the specific consequences of a class of acts, rejected all contemplation of the action in its general bearings upon the entire moral being of the agent; or have, to say the least, thrown those considerations so far into the background, as to be almost out of sight. And

by so doing they have not only marred the value of many of their speculations, considered as mere philosophical enquiries, but have always run the
risk of incurring, and in many cases have in my opinion actually incurred,
serious practical errors.

This incompleteness, however, in Mr. Bentham's general views, was not
of a nature materially to diminish the value of his speculations through the
greater part of the field of legislation. Those of the bearings of an action,
upon which Mr. Bentham bestowed almost exclusive attention, were also
those with which almost alone legislation is conversant. The legislator enjoins or prohibits an action, with very little regard to the general moral excellence or turpitude which it implies; he looks to the consequences to society
of the particular kind of action; his object is not to render people incapable
of *desiring* a crime, but to deter them from actually *committing* it. Taking
human beings as he finds them, he endeavours to supply such inducements as
will constrain even persons of the dispositions the most at variance with the
general happiness, to practise as great a degree of regard to it in their actual
conduct, as can be obtained from them by such means without preponderant
inconvenience. A theory, therefore, which considers little in an action besides
that action's *own* consequences, will generally be sufficient to serve the purposes of a philosophy of legislation. Such a philosophy will be most apt to
fail in the consideration of the greater social questions—the theory of organic
institutions and general forms of polity; for those (unlike the details of legislation) to be duly estimated, must be viewed as the great instruments of
forming the national character; of carrying forward the members of the community towards perfection, or preserving them from degeneracy. This, as
might in some measure be expected, is a point of view in which, except for
some partial or limited purpose, Mr. Bentham seldom contemplates these
questions. And this signal omission is one of the greatest of the deficiencies by
which his speculations on the theory of government, though full of valuable
ideas, are rendered, in my judgment, altogether inconclusive in their general
results.

To these we shall advert more fully hereafter. As yet I have not acquitted
myself of the more agreeable task of setting forth some part of the services
which the philosophy of legislation owes to Mr. Bentham.

The greatest service of all, that for which posterity will award most honour
to his name, is one that is his exclusively, and can be shared by no one present
or to come; it is the service which can be performed only once for any science,
that of pointing out by what method of investigation it may be *made* a science.
What Bacon did for physical knowledge, Mr. Bentham has done for philosophical legislation. Before Bacon's time, many physical facts had been
ascertained; and previously to Mr. Bentham, mankind were in possession of

many just and valuable detached observations on the making of laws. But he was the first who attempted regularly to deduce all the secondary and intermediate principles of law, by direct and systematic inference from the one great axiom or principle of general utility. In all existing systems of law, those secondary principles or dicta in which the essence of the systems resided, had grown up in detail, and even when founded in views of utility, were not the result of any scientific and comprehensive course of enquiry; but more frequently were purely technical; that is, they had grown out of circumstances purely *historical*, and, not having been altered when those circumstances changed, had nothing left to rest upon but fictions, and unmeaning forms. Take for instance the law of real property; the whole of which continues to this very day to be founded on the doctrine of feudal tenures, when those tenures have long ceased to exist except in the phraseology of Westminster Hall. Nor was the *theory* of law in a better state than the practical systems; speculative jurists having dared little more than to refine somewhat upon the technical maxims of the particular body of jurisprudence which they happened to have studied. Mr. Bentham was the first who had the genius and courage to conceive the idea of bringing back the science to first principles. This could not be done, could scarcely even be attempted, without, as a necessary consequence, making obvious the utter worthlessness of many, and the crudity and want of precision of almost all, the maxims which had previously passed everywhere for principles of law.

Mr. Bentham, moreover, has warred against the errors of existing systems of jurisprudence, in a more direct manner than by merely presenting the contrary truths. The force of argument with which he rent asunder the fantastic and illogical maxims on which the various technical systems are founded, and exposed the flagrant evils which they practically produce, is only equalled by the pungent sarcasm and exquisite humour with which he has derided their absurdities, and the eloquent declamation which he continually pours forth against them, sometimes in the form of lamentation, and sometimes of invective.

This then was the first, and perhaps the grandest achievement of Mr. Bentham; the entire discrediting of all technical systems; and the example which he set of treating law as no peculiar mystery, but a simple piece of practical business, wherein means were to be adapted to ends, as in any of the other arts of life. To have accomplished this, supposing him to have done nothing else, is to have equalled the glory of the greatest scientific benefactors of the human race.

But Mr. Bentham, unlike Bacon, did not merely prophesy a science; he made large strides towards the creation of one. He was the first who conceived with anything approaching to precision, the idea of a Code, or complete body of law; and the distinctive characters of its essential parts,—the

Civil Law, the Penal Law, and the Law of Procedure. On the first two of these three departments he rendered valuable service; the third he actually created. Conformably to the habits of his mind, he set about investigating *ab initio*, a philosophy or science for each of the three branches. He did with the received principles of each, what a good code would do with the laws themselves;—extirpated the bad, substituting others; re-enacted the good, but in so much clearer and more methodical a form, that those who were most familiar with them before, scarcely recognized them as the same. Even upon old truths, when they pass through his hands, he leaves so many of his marks, that often he almost seems to claim the discovery of what he has only systematized.

In creating the philosophy of Civil Law, he proceeded not much beyond establishing on the proper basis some of its most general principles, and cursorily discussing some of the most interesting of its details. Nearly the whole of what he has published on this branch of law, is contained in the *Traités de Législation*, edited by M. Dumont.[*] To the most difficult part, and that which most needed a master-hand to clear away its difficulties, the nomenclature and arrangement of the Civil Code, he contributed little, except detached observations, and criticisms upon the errors of his predecessors. The "Vue Générale d'un Corps Complet de Législation," included in the work just cited, contains almost all which he has given to us on this subject.

In the department of Penal Law, he is the author of the best attempt yet made towards a philosophical classification of offences. The theory of punishments (for which however more had been done by his predecessors, than for any other part of the science of law) he left nearly complete.

The theory of Procedure (including that of the constitution of the courts of justice) he found in a more utterly barbarous state than even either of the other branches; and he left it incomparably the most perfect. There is scarcely a question of practical importance in this most important department, which he has not settled. He has left next to nothing for his successors.

He has shown with the force of demonstration, and has enforced and illustrated the truth in a hundred ways, that by sweeping away the greater part of the artificial rules and forms which obtain in all the countries called civilized, and adopting the simple and direct modes of investigation, which all men employ in endeavouring to ascertain facts for their own private knowledge, it is possible to get rid of at least nine-tenths of the expense, and ninety-nine hundredths of the delay, of law proceedings; not only with no increase, but with an almost incredible diminution, of the chances of erroneous decision. He has also established irrefragably the principles of a good judicial establishment: a division of the country into districts, with *one* judge in each, appointed only for a limited period, and deciding all sorts of cases;

[*3 vols. Paris: Bossange, Mason, and Besson, 1802.]

with a deputy under him, appointed and removable by himself: an appeal lying in all cases whatever, but by the transmission of papers only, to a supreme court or courts, consisting each of only *one* judge, and stationed in the metropolis.

It is impossible within the compass of this sketch, to attempt any further statement of Mr. Bentham's principles and views on the great science which first became a science in his hands.

As an analyst of human nature (the faculty in which above all it is necessary that an ethical philosopher should excel) I cannot rank Mr. Bentham very high. He has done little in this department, beyond introducing what appears to me a very deceptive phraseology, and furnishing a catalogue of the "springs of action,"[*] from which some of the most important are left out.

That the actions of sentient beings are wholly determined by pleasure and pain, is the fundamental principle from which he starts; and thereupon Mr. Bentham creates a *motive*, and an *interest*, corresponding to each pleasure or pain, and affirms that our actions are determined by our *interests*, by the *preponderant* interest, by the *balance* of motives. Now if this only means what was before asserted, that our actions are determined by pleasure and pain, that simple and unambiguous mode of stating the proposition is preferable. But under cover of the obscurer phrase a meaning creeps in, both to the author's mind and the reader's, which goes much farther, and is entirely false: that all our acts are determined by pains and pleasures *in prospect*, pains and pleasures to which we look forward as the *consequences* of our acts. This, as a universal truth, can in no way be maintained. The pain or pleasure which determines our conduct is as frequently one which *precedes* the moment of action as one which follows it. A man *may*, it is true, be deterred, in circumstances of temptation, from perpetrating a crime, by his dread of the punishment, or of the remorse, which he fears he may have to endure *after* the guilty act; and in that case we may say with some kind of propriety, that his conduct is swayed by the balance of motives; or, if you will, of interests. But the case *may* be, and is to the full as likely to be, that he recoils from the very thought of committing the act; the idea of placing himself in such a situation is so painful, that he cannot dwell upon it long enough to have even the physical power of perpetrating the crime. His conduct is determined by pain; but by a pain which precedes the act, not by one which is expected to follow it. Not only *may* this be so, but unless it be so, the man is not really virtuous. The fear of pain *consequent* upon the act, cannot arise, unless there be *deliberation*; and the man as well as "the woman who deliberates," is in imminent danger of being lost.[†] With what propriety shrinking from an action without deliberation, can be called yielding to an

[*See *A Table of the Springs of Action*. London: Hunter, 1817.]
[†Joseph Addison. *Cato*. London: Tonson, 1713, p. 46 (IV, i, 31).]

interest, I cannot see. *Interest* surely conveys, and is intended to convey, the idea of an *end*, to which the conduct (whether it be act or forbearance) is designed as the *means*. Nothing of this sort takes place in the above example. It would be more correct to say that conduct is *sometimes* determined by an *interest*, that is, by a deliberate and conscious aim; and sometimes by an *impulse*, that is, by a feeling (call it an association if you think fit) which has no ulterior end, the act or forbearance becoming an end in itself.

The attempt, again, to *enumerate* motives, that is, human desires and aversions, seems to me to be in its very conception an error. Motives are innumerable: there is nothing whatever which may not become an object of desire or of dislike by association. It may be desirable to distinguish by peculiar notice the motives which are strongest and of most frequent operation; but Mr. Bentham has not even done this. In his list of motives, though he includes sympathy, he omits conscience, or the feeling of duty: one would never imagine from reading him that any human being ever did an act merely because it is right, or abstained from it merely because it is wrong. In this Mr. Bentham differs widely from Hartley, who, although he considers the moral sentiments to be wholly the result of association, does not therefore deny them a place in his system, but includes the feelings of "the moral sense" as one of the six classes into which he divides pleasures and pains.[*] In Mr. Bentham's own mind, deeply imbued as it was with the "greatest-happiness principle," this motive was probably so blended with that of sympathy as to be undistinguishable from it; but he should have recollected that those who acknowledge another standard of right and wrong than happiness, or who have never reflected on the subject at all, have often very strong feelings of moral obligation; and whether a person's standard be happiness or anything else, his attachment to his standard is not necessarily in proportion to his benevolence. Persons of weak sympathies have often a strong feeling of justice; and others, again, with the feelings of benevolence in considerable strength, have scarcely any consciousness of moral obligation at all.

It is scarcely necessary to point out that the habitual omission of so important a spring of action in an enumeration professing to be complete, must tend to create a habit of overlooking the same phenomenon, and consequently making no allowance for it, in other moral speculations. It is difficult to imagine any more fruitful source of gross error; though one would be apt to suppose the oversight an impossible one, without this evidence of its having been committed by one of the greatest thinkers our species has produced. How can we suppose him to be alive to the existence and force of the motive in particular cases, who omits it in a deliberate and comprehensive enumeration of all the influences by which human conduct is governed?

In laying down as a philosophical axiom, that men's actions are always

[*David Hartley. *Observations on Man.* 2 vols. London: Hitch and Austen, 1749, Vol. I, pp. 493–9 (Chap. iv, §6).]

obedient to their interests, Mr. Bentham did no more than dress up the very trivial proposition that all persons do what they feel themselves most disposed to do, in terms which appeared to him more precise, and better suited to the purposes of philosophy, than those more familiar expressions. He by no means intended by this assertion to impute universal selfishness to mankind, for he reckoned the motive of sympathy as an *interest*, and would have included conscience under the same appellation, if that motive had found any place in his philosophy, as a distinct principle from benevolence. He distinguished two kinds of interests, the self-regarding and the social: in vulgar discourse, the name is restricted to the former kind alone.

But there cannot be a greater mistake than to suppose that, because we may ourselves be perfectly *conscious* of an ambiguity in our language, that ambiguity therefore has no effect in perverting our modes of thought. I am persuaded, from experience, that this habit of speaking of all the feelings which govern mankind under the name of *interests*, is almost always in point of fact connected with a tendency to consider *interest* in the vulgar sense, that is, purely self-regarding interest, as exercising, by the very constitution of human nature, a far more exclusive and paramount control over human actions than it really does exercise. Such, certainly, was the tendency of Mr. Bentham's own opinions. Habitually, and throughout his works, the moment he has shown that a man's *selfish* interest would prompt him to a particular course of action, he lays it down without further parley that the man's interest lies that way; and, by sliding insensibly from the vulgar sense of the word into the philosophical, and from the philosophical back into the vulgar, the conclusion which is always brought out is, that the man will act as the selfish interest prompts. The extent to which Mr. Bentham was a believer in the predominance of the selfish principle in human nature, may be seen from the sweeping terms in which, in his *Book of Fallacies*,[*] he expressly lays down that predominance as a philosophical axiom.

"In *every* human breast (rare and short-lived ebullitions, the result of some extraordinarily strong stimulus or excitement, excepted) self-regarding interest is predominant over social interest; each person's own individual interest over the interests of all other persons taken together." (Pp. 392–3.)

In another passage of the same work (p. 363) he says, "Taking the whole of life together, there exists not, *nor ever can exist*, that human being in whose instance any public interest he can have had will not, in so far as depends upon himself, have been sacrificed to his own personal interest. Towards the advancement of the public interest, all that the most public-spirited (which is as much as to say the most virtuous) of men can do, is to do what depends upon himself towards bringing the public interest, that is, his own personal share in the public interest, to a state as nearly approaching to coincidence,

[*London: Hunt, 1824.]

and on as few occasions amounting to a state of repugnance, as possible, with his private interests."

By the promulgation of such views of human nature, and by a general tone of thought and expression perfectly in harmony with them, I conceive Mr. Bentham's writings to have done and to be doing very serious evil. It is by such things that the more enthusiastic and generous minds are prejudiced against all his other speculations, and against the very attempt to make ethics and politics a subject of precise and philosophical thinking; which attempt, indeed, if it were necessarily connected with such views, would be still more pernicious than the vague and flashy declamation for which it is proposed as a substitute. The effect is still worse on the minds of those who are not shocked and repelled by this tone of thinking, for on them it must be perverting to their whole moral nature. It is difficult to form the conception of a tendency more inconsistent with all rational hope of good for the human species, than that which must be impressed by such doctrines, upon any mind in which they find acceptance.

There are, there have been, many human beings, in whom the motives of patriotism or of benevolence have been permanent steady principles of action, superior to any ordinary, and in not a few instances, to any possible, temptations of personal interest. There are, and have been, multitudes, in whom the motive of conscience or moral obligation has been thus paramount. There is nothing in the constitution of human nature to forbid its being so in all mankind. Until it is so, the race will never enjoy one-tenth part of the happiness which our nature is susceptible of. I regard any considerable increase of human happiness, through mere changes in outward circumstances, unaccompanied by changes in the state of the desires, as hopeless; not to mention that while the desires are circumscribed in self, there can be no adequate motive for exertions tending to modify to good ends even those external circumstances. No man's individual share of any public good which he can hope to realize by his efforts, is an equivalent for the sacrifice of his ease, and of the personal objects which he might attain by another course of conduct. The balance can be turned in favour of virtuous exertion, only by the interest of *feeling* or by that of *conscience*—those "social interests," the necessary subordination of which to "self-regarding" is so lightly assumed.

But the power of any one to realize in himself the state of mind, without which his own enjoyment of life can be but poor and scanty, and on which all our hopes of happiness or moral perfection to the species must rest, depends entirely upon his having faith in the actual existence of such feelings and dispositions in others, and in their possibility for himself. It is for those in whom the feelings of virtue are weak, that ethical writing is chiefly needful, and its proper office is to strengthen those feelings. But to be qualified for this task, it is necessary, first to have, and next to show, in every sentence and in every line, a firm unwavering confidence in man's capability of virtue. It is by a sort of sympathetic contagion, or inspiration, that a noble mind assimilates other minds to itself; and no one was ever inspired by one whose own inspiration was not sufficient to give him faith in the possibility of making others feel what *he* feels.

Upon those who *need* to be strengthened and upheld by a really inspired moralist—such a moralist as Socrates, or Plato, or (speaking humanly and not theologically) as Christ; the effect of such writings as Mr. Bentham's, if they be read and believed and their spirit imbibed, must either be hopeless despondency and gloom, or a reckless giving themselves up to a life of that miserable self-seeking, which they are there taught to regard as inherent in their original and unalterable nature.

Mr. Bentham's speculations on politics in the narrow sense, that is, on the theory of government, are distinguished by his usual characteristic, that of beginning at the beginning. He places before himself man in society without a government, and, considering what sort of government it would be advisable to construct, finds that the most expedient would be a representative democracy. Whatever may be the value of this conclusion, the mode in which it is arrived at appears to me to be fallacious; for it assumes that mankind are alike in all times and all places, that they have the same wants and are exposed to the same evils, and that if the same institutions do not suit them, it is only because in the more backward stages of improvement they have not wisdom to see what institutions are most for their good. How to invest certain servants of the people with the power necessary for the protection of person and property, with the greatest possible facility to the people of changing the depositaries of that power, when they think it is abused; such is the only problem in social organization which Mr. Bentham has proposed to himself. Yet this is but a part of the real problem. It never seems to have occurred to him to regard political institutions in a higher light, as the principal means of the social education of a people. Had he done so, he would have seen that the same institutions will no more suit two nations in different stages of civilization, than the same lessons will suit children of different ages. As the degree of civilization already attained varies, so does the kind of social influence necessary for carrying the community forward to the next stage of its progress. For a tribe of North American Indians, improvement means, taming down their proud and solitary self-dependence; for a body of emancipated negroes, it means accustoming them to be self-dependent, instead of being merely obedient to orders: for our semi-barbarous ancestors it would have meant, softening them; for a race of enervated Asiatics it would mean hardening them. How can the same social organization be fitted for producing so many contrary effects?

The prevailing error of Mr. Bentham's views of human nature appears to me to be this—he supposes mankind to be swayed by only a part of the inducements which really actuate them; but of that part he imagines them to be much cooler and more thoughtful calculators than they really are. He has, I think, been, to a certain extent, misled in the theory of politics, by supposing that the submission of the mass of mankind to an established government is mainly owing to a reasoning perception of the necessity of legal protection, and of the common interest of all in a prompt and zealous obedience to the law. He was not, I am persuaded, aware, how very much of the really wonderful acquiescence of mankind in any government which they find established, is the effect of mere habit and imagination, and, therefore, depends upon the preservation of something like continuity of existence in the institutions, and identity in their outward forms; cannot transfer itself easily to new institutions, even though in themselves preferable; and is greatly shaken when there occurs anything like a break in the line of historical duration—anything which can be termed the end of the old constitution and the beginning of a new one.

The constitutional writers of our own country, anterior to Mr. Bentham, had carried feelings of this kind to the height of a superstition; they never considered what was best adapted to their own times, but only what had existed in former times, even in times that had long gone by. It is not very many years since such were the principal grounds on which parliamentary reform itself was defended. Mr. Bentham has done much service in discrediting, as he has done completely, this school of politicians, and exposing the absurd sacrifice of present ends to antiquated means; but he has, I think, himself fallen into a contrary error. The very fact that a certain set of political institutions already exist, have long existed, and have become associated with all the historical recollections of a people, is in itself, as far as it goes, a property which adapts them to that people, and gives them a great advantage over any new institutions in obtaining that ready and willing resignation to what has once been decided by lawful authority, which alone renders possible those innumerable compromises between adverse interests and expectations, without which no government could be carried on for a year, and with difficulty even for a week. Of the perception of this important truth, scarcely a trace is visible in Mr. Bentham's writings.*

*It is necessary, however, to distinguish between Mr. Bentham's practical conclusions, as an English politician of the present day, and his systematic views as a political philosopher. It is to the latter only that the foregoing observations are intended to apply: on the former I am not now called upon to pronounce any opinion. For the just estimation of his merits, the question is not what were his conclusions, but what was his mode of arriving at them. Theoretical views most widely different, may lead to the same practical corollaries: and that part of any system of philosophy which bodies itself forth in directions for immediate practice, must be so small a portion of the whole as to furnish a very insufficient

It is impossible, however, to contest to Mr. Bentham, on this subject or on any other which he has touched, the merit, and it is very great, of having brought forward into notice one of the faces of the truth, and a highly important one. Whether on government, on morals, or on any of the other topics on which his speculations are comparatively imperfect, they are still highly instructive and valuable to any one who is capable of supplying the remainder of the truth; they are calculated to mislead only by the pretension which they invariably set up of being the whole truth, a complete theory and philosophy of the subject. Mr. Bentham was more a thinker than a reader; he seldom compared his ideas with those of other philosophers, and was by no means aware how many thoughts had existed in other minds, which his doctrines did not afford the means either to refute or to appreciate.

---

criterion of the degree in which it approximates to scientific and universal truth. Let Mr. Bentham's opinions on the political questions of the day be as sound or as mistaken as any one may deem them, the fact which is of importance in judging of Mr. Bentham himself is that those opinions rest upon a basis of half-truth. Each enquirer is left to add the other half for himself, and confirm or correct the practical conclusion as the other lights of which he happens to be in possession, allow him.

BLAKEY'S HISTORY OF MORAL SCIENCE

1833

EDITOR'S NOTE

Monthly Repository, VII (Oct., 1833), 661–9. Unsigned; not republished. The title is footnoted: "History of Moral Science. By Robert Blakey, Author of an Essay on Moral Good and Evil. 2 vols. 8vo. [London: Duncan,] 1833." Identified in JSM's bibliography as "A review of Blakey's 'History of Moral Science' in the Monthly Repository for October 1833" (MacMinn, 34). In the brief account in the *Autobiography* (138) of his writings for the *Monthly Repository*, JSM does not mention this article. The writing of it can be dated fairly precisely by JSM's letter (7/9/33) to W. J. Fox, editor of the *Monthly Repository*, in which he says: "I am ashamed to say I can give no hope that Blakey will be ready on Monday [9 Sept.]—though I think part of him will be." Telling Carlyle (5/10/33) which of the articles in the October number are his, JSM writes: "one [is] a review of a foolish book by a man named Blakey, of Morpeth, called a History of Moral Science; for writing which he is utterly unfit, being a man who as you would say, has no eyes, only a pair of *glasses* and I will add, almost *opake* ones." (*Earlier Letters*, XII, 177, 181.)

There are no corrections or alterations in the two Somerville College copies.

Blakey's History of Moral Science

AN AMBITIOUS TITLE, and one which promises much; but the promises of title-pages are so seldom followed by performances! "Moral science" should naturally mean the science of morals. It were something to find that there is a writer alive who believes that such a science exists; and not only exists, but is in such a state of advancement that the time is come to write its history; who, consequently, is not only able to tell us the opinions of others, but has systematic ones of his own. For how should he write the *history* of a science, who has not constructed a consistent scheme of the science in its present state? The historian of moral philosophy must himself have a philosophy of morals; must have surveyed the field of ethics extensively enough, and with sufficient power of concatenation, to have arranged its truths (or whatever present themselves to his mind as such) into a connected series, following and flowing out of one another: thus much, at least, is implied in the name of science. But Mr. Blakey has no such thought. There are few ways in which a mind of little depth or compass is more apt to betray itself than by the use of big words to express small things; whoever does this innocently and without quackery, shows himself to be unfurnished with the larger idea for which he should have reserved his large phrase. By giving the name "History of Moral Science" to a book, which should have been called "Sketch of the Opinions of various Authors on the Foundation of Moral Obligation, with critical Remarks," Mr. Blakey demonstrates how little meaning even the word "Science" has for him, since he considers the whole history of a science to be summed up in the controversial discussions concerning the *first principle* of it.

After a short preamble, and a few loose remarks about "the ancient systems of morality," Mr. Blakey presents us with what professes to be a summary of the opinions of the following writers, concerning the first principle of ethics:—Hobbes, Cudworth, Bishop Cumberland, Locke, Archbishop King, Wollaston, Clarke, Shaftesbury, Mandeville, Bolingbroke and Pope, Soame Jenyns, Hutcheson, a Mr. Thomas Rutherford, Hume, Hartley and Priestley, Lord Kames, Bishop Butler, Dr. Ferguson, Dr. Price, Adam Smith, Paley, Gisborne, Bentham, Godwin, Dugald Stewart, Cogan, Dr. Thomas Brown, and a certain Dr. Dewar. All foreign authors whatever are then disposed of in a single chapter; and two chapters more are employed in promulgating such of the author's own opinions as have not been sufficiently manifested by his strictures on other writers.

Mr. Blakey's statement of the opinions of these various authors deserves the praise of honesty. He never perversely distorts an opinion, in the blindness of prejudice, or to serve a purpose. He generally treats the intentions and talents, even of those from whom he differs most, with justice and liberality. He does not insist upon fastening on them a meaning or consequence which they never contemplated; and he employs but sparingly the favourite weapon of the uncandid and the bigot, imputation of immoral tendency. But our commendation cannot go much further. It is not every man who can give an instructive view of other men's opinions.

There are two modes of writing usefully concerning systems of philosophy: the one, suitable to a mind which is qualified to *judge*; the other, to one which can only *describe*. The intellect which can survey the wanderings of imperfect thinkers from a higher eminence of thought, commanding a view not only of the right track, but of all the by-ways of error, and all the fallacious appearances which seduce the unguarded to deviate into them—such a critic (we use the prostituted word only because we have no other) can not only estimate more justly, but can actually state more clearly and forcibly an author's theory, than the author himself; can really understand it better; because he sees (what the author himself does not see) how the doctrine arose in the author's own mind; of what peculiar position in regard to opportunities of observation, or of what peculiarity of intellect or of disposition, it is the natural consequence. Any thing like this we were not entitled to expect from Mr. Blakey; it supposes a *philosopher*, and such Mr. Blakey is not. But if this was impossible, the next thing to it in usefulness, though at a vast distance, would have been a condensed view of each system, not as it appears to a higher intelligence, but as it appeared to its author; such a statement of the author's train of thought, of the series of his premises and his conclusions, as would be conveyed by a well-made abstract of his principal works, or as would be given by an intelligent disciple thoroughly conversant with his master's doctrines. Mr. Blakey's summaries by no means come up to this idea; they are vague and sketchy, and not only do not, to those who knew the doctrines before, exhibit them in any new light, but give no sufficiently distinct conception of them to those who knew them not. Often the conclusions are exhibited almost without the premises: and on the whole there is little to be learnt even by the merest tyro in philosophy, from these volumes, except a few generalities, and a few forms of expression. He is told in what words philosophers have expressed the results of their speculations, but though he may not be made positively to misunderstand, he is not made thoroughly to *feel*, the meaning in the philosopher's own mind, to which the words are but an index, and often a most imperfect one.

An overweening self-confidence, and contemptuous assumption of superiority, in judging of the intellects of others, would be peculiarly unbecoming in a mind of Mr. Blakey's calibre: and he cannot be accused of those faults; he mostly treats with due respect all who by their speculations have deserved any. To the liberal appreciation of merit which he commonly evinces, there are indeed exceptions; and, unfortunately, in the very cases in which there is most merit to appreciate. But this is a very different thing from arrogance. It is not because an author differs from Mr. Blakey, that Mr. Blakey deems scornfully of him; but because, in addition to differing from Mr. Blakey, he has been cried down by the world—that is to say, the English world. Over-reliance on our own judgment is one thing, over-reliance on the judgment of the world when in unison with our own, is another. The latter is the failing of a weaker, but certainly of a more modest mind. The misfortune is, that the contempt of those who have confidence enough to be scornful only when they are backed by a crowd, is aptest to fall upon those who are most in advance of their age. Mr. Blakey's strongest expressions of disdain are divided between the association-philosophy as taught by Hartley, and the metaphysics of the German school. In other words, the only metaphysical doctrines which he utterly despises, are the two systems between which, and which only, almost every metaphysician, deserving the name, in all Europe, is now beginning to be convinced that it is necessary to choose: the two most perfect forms of the only two theories of the human mind which are, strictly speaking, possible. Both are alike worthless in Mr. Blakey's eyes, because it has been the fashion among English writers to treat both with disrespect, and because he himself understands neither of them. The difference is, he pronounces the one unintelligible, because it is so to him; the other he flatters himself that he sees through and through, and can discern that there is nothing in it.

So little does Mr. Blakey comprehend of the theory which resolves all the phenomena of the mind into ideas of sensation connected together by the law of association, that he does not even see any thing peculiar in the doctrine. Association itself, he will not allow to be a distinct principle or fact in human nature. It is nothing more, he says, than *remembrance*; it has been known in all ages, as the faculty of memory. Just so we may conceive, on the appearance of Newton's *Principia*,[*] some mind of the same character objecting to the theory of *gravitation*, that there was nothing in it but the ancient and familiar fact of *weight*.

If a person, [says Mr. Blakey,] will take the first volume of the treatise *On Man*, and read it carefully over, and whenever he finds the words *association, associates, associating*, &c. let him replace them with the words *memory, remembered, remembrance, connected in his mind*, and he will find that the sense of the

---

[*Isaac Newton. *Philosophiæ Naturalis Principia Mathematica*. London, 1687.]

various passages in which the former class of words are used, will remain as completely the same, when words descriptive of memory are thus employed. (Vol. II, p. 124.)

Not so, Mr. Blakey. *Memory* and *remembrance* only denote the fact that somehow we do remember: *association* denotes that our remembrances (pardon the expression) suggest and recall one another in an order, determined by the order of succession of the *facts remembered*; or rather, determined partly by the order of succession, and partly by the *more or less interesting nature*, of those previous impressions. Cannot Mr. Blakey understand the difference between a *phenomenon*, and the *law* of the phenomenon? The reflexion of light, and of sound, is a fact; that the angle of reflexion is equal to the angle of incidence, is the law of that fact. And this law of nature may be something new to a person, even although he may have heard an echo, and seen his face in a mirror. In like manner a person may know that when we have seen an object or experienced a feeling, we remember it, (which is all that is expressed by the words *faculty of memory*,) and may, notwithstanding, have yet to learn that when we have seen two objects or had two feelings together, we think of them together, and not otherwise; and that the strength of their connexion in our remembrance, depends jointly upon the number of previous conjunctions in fact or in thought, and upon the intensity of the original impressions. Once for all, association is not memory, but the *law* of memory.

Now, the theory of the human mind of which Dr. Hartley was the principal author, maintains that this same law, which is the law of memory, namely, that the order of our thoughts follows the order of our sensations, is not only the law of memory, but the law of imagination, of belief, of reasoning, of the affections, of the will. This may not be true; but it is at least very different from every other theory. But Mr. Blakey knows so little about the Hartleian doctrine, that he propounds as a complete summary of it, the following proposition: The advocates of association state a simple fact, that there is a connexion amongst our ideas. (Vol. II, p. 126.) We exhort him to *read* Hartley; or a more recent work, which has done far more for Hartley's theory, than Hartley himself, Mr. Mill's *Analysis of the Human Mind*.[*]

As a specimen of argumentation which Mr. Blakey considers to be conclusive, we quote the following:

Association is the tendency of one idea to introduce another into the mind. Very well, then; but how do we come to set it down as a general fact, that one set of ideas has an invariable tendency to introduce another set of ideas? By experience, it must be answered. But what is experience? Why, it is the remembrance of that which is past. [Vol. II, pp. 116–17.]

Therefore, association is nothing but memory.

[*James Mill. *Analysis of the Phenomena of the Human Mind*. 2 vols. London: Baldwin and Cradock, 1829.]

We will treat Mr. Blakey with a specimen in return. The pretended science of chemistry is nothing but memory.

Chemistry is the properties of simple substances, and their various compounds. But how do we come to set it down as a general fact, that two substances, as oxygen and hydrogen, being compounded together, form a third substance, water? By experience, it must be answered. But what is experience? Why, it is the *remembrance* of that which is past. In what, therefore, does this chemistry differ from memory?

Mr. Blakey continues—

But to put this matter in as clear a light as possible, let us suppose that A is a present idea in the mind, and that it has a tendency to introduce another idea which has never been in the mind before, and which we will call B. To this tendency of A to introduce B into the mind, is given the name of association. Now how can we assert or deny any thing respecting the tendency of A to introduce B, till we have witnessed A's power over B, and have had B present to the understanding? The very proposition that A has an influence over B implies that we have seen this tendency, and that B must have previously been in the mind, and *consequently an object of memory*. Thus we see then, when we speak about connexions among our ideas, we must consider them as connexions which have been known before; and therefore we ought to infer, that the treating of them comes within the province of memory, and not within any other intellectual power whatever. (Vol. II, p. 117.)

What a paralogism; we might almost call it a bull. Yes, certainly, the *proposition* that A has a tendency to introduce B, implies that we have seen this tendency at some former time, because otherwise we should not know it: but the *fact itself* implies nothing of the kind. When A for the first time introduced B, "which had never been in the mind before," B was *not* an object of memory; although it is so when we have observed and treasured up the occurrence. Because an event must be remembered before it can be talked about, Mr. Blakey imagines that it was a subject of memory when it first happened. It is upon the strength of such reasoning that he assumes such a tone as this:

What a dull and paralyzing effect has the reading of a book in which the principle of the association of ideas forms the philosophical *dramatis personæ* in the piece. . . . There is no way of getting through the book, without violating the rules of politeness by enjoying a smile at the expense of the system. (Vol. II, p. 127.)

With much more of the same sort.

Of foreign authors Mr. Blakey seems to be profoundly ignorant. He affirms that in the majority of cases—

The continental philosophy of human nature presents to a well-constituted mind a repulsive aspect, and is profusely saturated with everything that is impure, ridiculous, profane, whimsical, and pernicious. (Vol. II, p. 300.)

Meaning, we suppose, some *French* writers only, and those only in the eighteenth century. The celebrated theory of Malebranche he states thus, that "all things *should be* seen in God;" (Vol. II, p. 308) and he imagines that *Candide*[*] was written to *support* the doctrines which are put into the mouth of Pangloss! (Vol. II, p. 289.)

At the conclusion of his abstract of the opinions of previous authors, which, it is but justice to say, is in general much fairer, and even more intelligent, than might be supposed from the specimens which we have given, Mr. Blakey sums up the result of the examination in the following words:

> All the systems we have examined may, I conceive, be referred to six distinct heads. 1st. The eternal and immutable nature of all moral distinctions. 2nd. That utility, public or private, is the foundation of moral obligation. 3rd. That all morality is founded upon the will of God. 4th. That a moral sense, feeling, or emotion, is the ground of virtue. 5th. That it is by supposing ourselves in the situation of others, or by a species of sympathetic mechanism, that we derive our notions of good and evil. And 6th, the doctrine of vibrations,* and the association of ideas. (Vol. II, p. 317.)

After declaring that "there are none of these different systems that are not in some degree founded on truth," and that "we cannot resolve all the moral feelings and habits of our nature into one general principle," he assigns, nevertheless, his reasons for preferring to all the other theories the doctrine, "that virtue depends upon the will of God," as made known by revelation. [Vol. II, pp. 319, 320.]

Mr. Blakey's enumeration is illogical: it confounds two distinct, though nearly connected, questions; the *standard* or *test* of moral obligation, and the *origin* of our moral *sentiments*. It is one question what rule we *ought* to obey, and why; another question how our feelings of approbation and disapprobation *actually* originate. The former is the fundamental question of practical morals; the latter is a problem in mental philosophy. Adam Smith's doctrine of *sympathy* which stands fifth, and the doctrine of *association* which stands sixth in Mr. Blakey's list, are theories respecting the nature and origin of our *feelings* of morality. His second and third are theories respecting the *rule* or *law* by which we ought to guide our *conduct*. His first and fourth involve, or may be so understood as to involve, *both* considerations.

These several theories, therefore, are not exclusive of one another. It is possible, for instance, to hold with Hartley, that our *feelings* of morality originate in association, and with Bentham that our *conduct*, in all things which depend on our will, and among the rest, in the cultivation of those

[*Voltaire. *Candide, ou l'optimisme.*]
*The doctrine of *vibrations*, a mere physiological hypothesis, which has no connexion at all with Hartley's theory of association, ought not to have been included in an enumeration of theories of morals. [*JSM's footnote.*]

very feelings, should be guided by *utility*; or with our author, that the will of God is itself the foundation of the obligations of virtue. David Hume seems to have combined the recognition of utility as the standard or test of morality, with the belief of a moral sense, independent of association. Paley has no theory respecting the nature of moral *feelings*, but his notion of the moral *law* is compounded of the second and third of the theories enumerated by our author.

But of all those theories, whether ethical or metaphysical, whether declaring what our *conduct should* be, or what our *feelings are*, none surely is so utterly destitute of plausibility as Mr. Blakey's own doctrine, that virtue is *constituted* by the will of God.

If we believe this, we believe that God does not *declare* what is good, and *command* us to do it, but that God actually *makes* it good. Good is whatever God makes it. What we call evil, is only evil because he has arbitrarily prohibited it. The countless myriads to whom he has never signified his will, are under no moral obligations. This doctrine takes away all motives to yield obedience to God, except those which induce a slave to obey his master. He must be obeyed because he is the stronger. He is not to be obeyed because he is good, for *that* implies a good which he could not have made bad by his mere will. If we had the misfortune to believe that the world is ruled by an evil principle, that there is no God, but only a devil, or that the devil has more power over us than God, we ought by this rule to obey the devil. Mr. Blakey is evidently quite unconscious of these consequences of his theory. But, that they are legitimate consequences who can doubt?

And this theory Mr. Blakey believes to rest upon the authority of scripture.

I venture to affirm, [says he,] that from Genesis to Revelation inclusive, there is not a single passage, which, when fairly examined, claims the attention and homage of mankind upon any other ground than what is implied in the command which accompanies it. (Vol. II, p. 326.)

The scriptures, as Mr. Blakey himself says elsewhere, do not enter into speculative questions; they tell us *what* to do, not *why*. But do they not say perpetually, God is good, God is just, God is righteous, God is holy? And are we to understand by these affirmations nothing at all, but the identical and unmeaning proposition God is himself, or a proposition which has so little to do with morality as this, God is powerful? Has God in short no moral attributes? no attributes but those which the devil is conceived to possess in a smaller degree? and no title to our obedience but such as the devil would have, if there were a devil, and the universe were without God?

Mr. Blakey insists much upon the sublimity of the scriptures, and the perfection of scripture morality; considerations which tell strongly against his own doctrine; for if we are capable of recognising excellence in the commands of the Omnipotent, they must possess excellence independently of his command; and excellence discoverable by us even without revelation; for whatever reason can recognise when found, reason can find. If the morality of the scriptures is admirable because it conduces to happiness, this implies that the production of happiness is a legitimate purpose of morals: if because it accords with our sympathies, *that* implies that morality may be founded on sympathy. If the precepts of scripture have nothing intrinsically good, but are good solely by reason of the power from which they emanate, their character ought to be as mysterious and incomprehensible to us as the ceremonies of magic: nor could there on that supposition be any reason apparent to us, why we are not commanded to hate our neighbour instead of to love him.

Not being of opinion, with Mr. Blakey, that our reception of a philosophic doctrine ought to be determined, not solely by its truth, but by what we imagine respecting the arguments it may afford for or against our religious belief, we ought not, perhaps, to notice the claim which Mr. Blakey sets up for his doctrine, of being peculiarly favourable to the interests of revealed religion. But though such arguments go for nothing with those who can trust themselves to judge of the true and the false, who are resolved to believe the truth, *whatever* may be its consequences, and are not afraid of finding one truth irreconcilable with another; those who are diffident of their own intellectual powers, naturally dread any doctrine which they can be led to think tends to shake from under their feet, the foundation on which they have built all their hopes and purposes. Mr. Blakey, therefore, shall not be allowed the exclusive use of this argument. We tell him that *his* doctrine is more destructive to the foundations of Christianity, than any of the theories of moral obligation which he has enumerated; by taking away altogether its internal evidences, the only ones which are not common to it with a thousand superstitions. In Judea itself, both before and after Christ appeared, numbers of false Christs and charlatans of all descriptions had pretended to work miracles, and had been believed; believed not only by their proselytes, but by those who rejected them, and who ascribed their miraculous powers to the agency of evil spirits. If these impostors sunk, and were heard of no more, while Christianity spread itself over the earth, it was not that greater credence was given to the Christian miracles than to theirs; it was, that the simple-hearted men who gathered themselves round the founder of Christianity, far from believing the doctrines to be excellent because they came from God, believed them to come from God because they felt them to be excellent. The fervour of their love and admiration could not find fit utterance but in the phrase, "he spake as never man spake."[*] Christianity had perished with its founder if Mr. Blakey's theory had been true. The world has acknowledged him as sent of God, has believed him to *be* God, because there *was* a standard of

[*John, 7:46.]

morality by which man could test not the word of man merely, but what was vouched for as the word of God; because of that *internal* evidence, which according to the repeated declarations of Christ himself, ought to have been sufficient. It was out of the hardness of their hearts that they needed signs.[*] Had all been right within, the precepts themselves would have sufficed to prove their own origin.

We have expended more words than were perhaps necessary upon so preposterous a doctrine. Our excuse must be, the infinitely mischievous tendency of a theory of moral duty, according to which God is to be obeyed, not because God is good, nor because it is good to obey him, but from some motive or principle which might have dictated equally implicit obedience to the powers of darkness. Such a philosophy, in proportion as it is realized in men's lives and characters, must extirpate from their minds all reverence, all admiration, and all conscience, and leave them only the abject feelings of a slave.

Such a theory cannot be combated too often; it should be warred against wherever it rears its head. But with regard to most of the other conflicting opinions respecting the primary grounds of moral obligation, it appears to us that a degree of importance is often attached to them, more than commensurate to the influence they really exercise for good or for evil. Doubtless they are important, as all questions in morals are important: a clear conception of the ultimate foundation of morality, is essential to a systematic and scientific treatment of the subject, and to the decision of some of its disputed practical problems. But the most momentous of the differences of opinion on the details of morality, have quite another origin. The real character of any man's ethical system depends not on his first and fundamental principle, which is of necessity so general as to be rarely susceptible of an immediate application to practice; but upon the nature of those secondary and intermediate maxims, *vera illa et media axiomata*, in which, as Bacon observes, real wisdom resides.[†] The grand consideration is, not what any person regards as the ultimate end of human conduct, but through what intermediate ends he holds that his ultimate end is attainable, and should be pursued: and in these there is a nearer agreement between some who differ, than between some who agree, in their conception of the ultimate end. When disputes arise as to any of the secondary maxims, they can be decided, it is true, only by an appeal to first principles; but the necessity of this appeal may be avoided far oftener than is commonly believed; it is surprising how few, in comparison, of the disputed questions of practical morals, require for their determination any premises but such as are common to all philosophic sects.

[*See Mark, 3:5.]
[†*Novum Organum*. In *Works*. Ed. J. Spedding, R. L. Ellis, and D. D. Heath. London: Longman, 1857–74, Vol. I, p. 205.]

SEDGWICK'S DISCOURSE

1835

"Professor Sedgwick's Discourse on the Studies of the University of Cambridge," *D&D*, I (2nd ed., 1867), 95–159, with footnote to title: "London Review, April 1835." Reprinted from the *London Review*, I (Apr., 1835), 94–135, signed "A". Original heading: "Art. V. Professor Sedgwick's Discourse.—State of Philosophy in England. / *A Discourse on the Studies of the University*. By Adam Sedgwick, M.A., F.R.S.; Woodwardian Professor, and Fellow of Trinity College, Cambridge. [London: Parker,] 1834. 3d edit." Identified in JSM's bibliography as "A review of Sedgwick's 'Discourse on the Studies of the University,' headed 'Professor Sedgwick's Discourse—State of Philosophy in England', in the first number of the London Review (April, 1835)" (MacMinn, 43). The article, which he had begun writing by 14 October, 1834, was finished, presumably in an unrevised state, by 26 November (see JSM's letters to J. P. Nichol on those dates, *Earlier Letters*, XII, 235 and 238). See also the footnote to 45 below, which describes a passage as "Written in 1834." For JSM's attitude to this article, and its relation to others in this volume, see the Textual Introduction, cxvii–cxx above.

The following text is collated with that in *D&D* (1st ed.), and that in the *London Review*. In the footnoted variants, *D&D* (2nd ed.) is indicated by "67"; *D&D* (1st ed.) by "59"; the *London Review* by "35". There are no corrections or alterations in the Somerville College copies of *D&D* and the *London Review*.

Sedgwick's Discourse

IF WE WERE ASKED FOR what end, above all others, endowed universities exist, or ought to exist, we should answer—To keep alive philosophy. This, too, is the ground on which, of late years, our own national endowments have chiefly been defended. To educate common minds for the common business of life, a public provision may be useful, but is not indispensable: nor are there wanting arguments, [a] not conclusive, yet of considerable strength, to show that it is undesirable. Whatever individual competition does at all, it commonly does best. All things in which the public are adequate judges of excellence, are best supplied where the stimulus of individual interest is the most active; and that is where pay is in proportion to exertion: not where pay is made sure in the first instance, and the only security for exertion is the superintendence of government; far less where, as in the English universities, even that security has been successfully excluded. But there is an education of which it cannot be pretended that the public are competent judges; the education by which great minds are formed. To rear up minds with aspirations and faculties above the herd, [b] capable of leading on their countrymen to greater achievements in virtue, intelligence, and social well-being; to do this, and likewise so to educate the leisured classes of the community generally, that they may participate as far as possible in the qualities of these superior spirits, and be prepared to appreciate them, and follow in their steps —these are purposes, requiring institutions of education placed above dependence on the immediate pleasure of that very multitude whom they are designed to elevate. These are the ends for which endowed universities are desirable; they are those which all endowed universities profess to aim at; and great is their disgrace, if, having undertaken this task, and claiming credit for fulfilling it, they leave it unfulfilled.

In what manner are these purposes—the greatest which any human institution can propose to itself—purposes which the English Universities must be fit for, or they are fit for nothing—performed by those universities?— *Circumspice.*

In the intellectual pursuits which form great minds, this country was formerly pre-eminent. England once stood at the head of European philosophy. Where stands she now? Consult the general opinion of Europe. The

[a]35   if   [b]35   and

celebrity of England, in the present day, rests upon her docks, her canals, her railroads. In intellect she is distinguished only for a kind of sober good sense, free from extravagance, but also void of lofty aspirations; and for doing all those things which are best done where man most resembles a machine, with the precision of a machine. Valuable qualities, doubtless; but not precisely those by which ᶜmankind raise themselvesᶜ to the perfection of ᵈtheirᵈ nature, or ᵉachieveᵉ greater and greater conquests over the difficulties which encumber ᶠtheirᶠ social arrangements. Ask any reflecting person in France or Germany his opinion of England; whatever may be his own tenets—however friendly his disposition to us—whatever his admiration of our institutions, and ᵍof some parts of our national characterᵍ; however alive to the faults and errors of his own countrymen, the feature which always strikes him in the English mind is the absence of enlarged and commanding views. Every question he finds discussed and decided on its own basis, however narrow, without any light thrown upon it from principles more extensive than itself; and no question discussed at all, unless parliament, or some constituted authority, is to be moved to-morrow or the day after to put it to the vote. Instead of the ardour of research, the eagerness for large and comprehensive inquiry, of the educated part of the French and German youth, what find we? Out of the narrow bounds of mathematical and physical science, not a vestige of a reading and thinking public engaged in the investigation of truth *as* truth, in the prosecution of thought for the sake of thought. Among ʰfewʰ except sectarian religionists—and what they are we all know—is there any interest in the great problem of man's nature and life: among ⁱstill fewerⁱ is there any curiosity respecting the nature and principles of human society, the history or the philosophy of civilization; nor any belief that, from such inquiries, a single important practical consequence can follow. Guizot, the greatest admirer of England among the Continental philosophers, nevertheless remarks that, in England, even great events do not, as they do everywhere else, inspire great ideas.[*] Things, in England, are greater than the men who accomplish them. ⁱ

But perhaps this degeneracy is the effect of some cause over which the universities had no control, and against which they have been ineffectually struggling. If so, those bodies are wonderfully patient of being baffled. Not

[*François Guizot. *Cours d'histoire moderne: Histoire de la civilisation en France*. 5 vols. Paris: Pichon and Didier, 1829–32, Vol. I, pp. 12–13.]

ᶜ⁻ᶜ35	man raises himself	ᵈ⁻ᵈ35	his
ᵉ⁻ᵉ35	achieves	ᶠ⁻ᶠ35	his
ᵍ⁻ᵍ35	even his desire to introduce them into his native country		
ʰ⁻ʰ35	no class	ⁱ⁻ⁱ35	no class whatever

ⁱ35 [*paragraph*] This torpid state of the national mind on the noblest subjects of thought would not be surprising, if in other respects the English were a declining people; if all intellectual energy and manly activity were, as in the later times of the

a word of complaint escapes any of their leading dignitaries—not a hint that their highest endeavours are thwarted, their best labours thrown away; not a symptom of dissatisfaction with the intellectual state of the national mind, save when it discards the boroughmongers, lacks zeal for the Church, or calls for the admission of Dissenters within their precincts. On the contrary, perpetual boasting how perfectly they succeed in accomplishing all that they attempt; endless celebrations of the country's glory and happiness in possessing a youth so taught, so mindful of what they are taught. When any one presumes to doubt whether the universities are all that universities should be, he is not told that they do their best, but that the tendencies of the age are too strong for them; no—he is, with an air of triumph, referred to their fruits, and asked whether an education which has made English gentlemen what we see them, can be other than a good education? All is right so long as no one speaks of taking away their endowments, or encroaching upon their monopoly.* While they are thus eulogizing their own efforts, and the results of their efforts; philosophy—not any particular school of philosophy, but philosophy altogether—speculation of any comprehensive kind, and upon any deep or extensive subject—has been falling more and more into distastefulness and disrepute among the educated classes of England. Have those classes meanwhile learned to slight and despise these authorized teachers of philosophy, or ceased to frequent their schools? Far from it. The universities then may flourish, though the pursuits which are the end and justification of the existence of universities decay. The teacher thrives and is in honour, while that which he affects to teach vanishes from among mankind.

If the above reflections were to occur, as they well might, to an intelligent foreigner, deeply interested in the condition and prospects of English intel-

*[59] Written before the advent of the present comparatively enlightened body of University Reformers.

Roman empire, verging towards extinction. But the direct contrary is the fact. Since the time when the English philosophers gave the law to Europe, England has maintained and added to every other superiority which she possessed. She has advanced immeasurably in wealth, still more immeasurably in power; civilization has spread to the remotest corner of her territory; the manners of her people have been humanized, their tastes refined; they have outstripped all nations in what most distinguishes a civilized people from barbarians, the power of co-operating for a common object; in the diffusion of reading, of philanthropy, of interest in public affairs, no other people in the Old World can be compared with them. While all these changes have been taking place for the better, in the minds and condition of those whom our two great endowed seminaries do *not* educate, there must be some grievous defect in the training of the classes whom those establishments do educate, to account for the low state of all higher pursuits; of the pursuits which the very existence of universities is but a means to the cultivation of —and in which it is the duty of such establishments to send forth their pupils qualified, some to extend the bounds of knowledge itself, and all to enter into its spirit, and turn it to account for the purposes of life.

lect, we may imagine with what avidity he would seize upon the publication before us. It is a discourse on the studies of Cambridge, by a Cambridge Professor, delivered to a Cambridge audience, and published at their request. It contains the opinion of one of the most liberal members of the University on the studies of the place; or, as we should rather say, on the studies which the place recommends, and which some few of its pupils actually prosecute. Mr. Sedgwick is not a mere pedant of a college, who defends the system because he has been formed by the system, and has never learned to see anything but in the light in which the system showed it to him. Though an intemperate [k] , he is not a bigoted, partisan of the body to which he belongs; he can see faults as well as excellences, not merely in their mode of teaching, but in some parts of what they teach. His intellectual pretensions, too, are high. [l]Not[l] of him can it be said that he aspires not to philosophy; he writes in the character of one to whom its loftiest eminences are familiar. Curiosity, therefore, cannot but be somewhat excited to know what he finds to say respecting the Cambridge scheme of education, and what notion may be formed of the place from the qualities he exhibits in himself, one of its [m] favourable specimens.

Whatever be the value of Professor Sedgwick's *Discourse* in the former of these two points of view, in the latter we have found it, on examination, to be a document of considerable importance. The Professor gives his opinion (for the benefit chiefly, he says, of the younger members of the University, but in a manner, he hopes, "not altogether unfitting to other ears"[*]) on the value of several great branches of intellectual culture, and on the spirit in which they should be pursued. Not satisfied with this, he proclaims in his preface another and a still more ambitious purpose—the destruction of what [n]has been termed[n] the Utilitarian theory of morals. "He has attacked the utilitarian theory of morals, not merely because he thinks it founded on false reasoning, but because he also believes that it produces a degrading effect on the temper and conduct of those who adopt it."[†]

This is promising great things: to refute a theory of morals; and to trace its influence on the character and actions of those who embrace it. A better test of capacity for philosophy could not be desired. We shall see how Professor Sedgwick acquits himself of his two-fold task, and what were his qualifications for undertaking it.

From an author's mode of introducing his subject, and laying the outlines of it before the reader, some estimate may generally be formed of his capacity

[*Sedgwick, *Discourse*, p. 8.]
[†*Ibid.*, p. vii.]

[k]35   (witness his replies to Mr. Beverley) [*Four Letters to the Editors of the Leeds Mercury in Reply to R. M. Beverley*. Cambridge: not published, 1836.]
[l-l]35   Nor   [m]35   most   [n-n]35   he terms

for discussing it. In this respect, the indications afforded by Mr. Sedgwick's commencement are not favourable. Before giving his opinion of the studies of the University, he had to tell us what those studies are. They are, first, mathematical and physical science; secondly, the classical languages and literature; thirdly (if some small matter of Locke and Paley deserve so grand a denomination), mental and moral science. For Mr. Sedgwick's purpose, this simple mode of designating these studies would have been sufficiently precise; but if he was determined to hit off their metaphysical characteristics, it should not have been in the following style:—

The studies of this place, as far as they relate to mere human learning, divide themselves into three branches: First, the study of the laws of nature, comprehending all parts of inductive philosophy. Secondly, the study of ancient literature, or, in other words, of those authentic records which convey to us an account of the feelings, the sentiments, and the actions of men prominent in the history of the most famous empires of the ancient world: in these works we seek for examples and maxims of prudence and models of taste. Thirdly, the study of ourselves, considered as individuals and as social beings: under this head are included ethics and metaphysics, moral and political philosophy, and some other kindred subjects of great complexity, hardly touched on in our academic system, and to be followed out in the more mature labours of after life. (P. 10.)

How many errors in expression and classification in one short passage! The "study of the laws of nature" is spoken of as one thing, "the study of ourselves" as another. In studying ourselves, are we not studying the laws of our nature? "All parts of inductive philosophy" are placed under one head; "ethics and metaphysics, moral and political philosophy," under another. Are these no part of inductive philosophy? Of what philosophy, then, are they a part? Is not all philosophy, which is founded upon experience and observation, inductive?* What, again can Mr. Sedgwick mean by calling "ethics" one thing and "moral philosophy" another? Moral philosophy must be either ethics or a branch of metaphysics—either the knowledge of our duty, or the theory of the feelings with which we regard our duty. What a loose description, too, of ancient literature—where no description at all was

*[59] It is just to Mr. Sedgwick to subjoin the following passage from the Preface to a later edition of his *Discourse*:—

"For many years it has been the habit of English writers, more especially those who have been trained at Cambridge, to apply the term *philosophy* only to those branches of exact science that are designated on the Continent by the name of *physics*. As this local use of a general term may lead to a misapprehension of the writer's intentions, it would be well if, in the following pages, the words *inductive philosophy*, and other like phrases, were accompanied with some word limiting their application to the exact physical sciences." [4th ed. Cambridge: Deighton and Parker, 1835, p. ix.]

required. The writings of the ancients are spoken of as if there were nothing in them but the biographies of eminent statesmen.

This want of power to express accurately what is conceived, almost unerringly denotes inaccuracy in the conception itself: such verbal criticism, therefore, [o] is far from unimportant. But the topics of a graver kind, which Mr. Sedgwick's *Discourse* suggests, are fully sufficient to occupy us, and to them we shall henceforth confine ourselves.

The Professor's survey of the studies of the University commences with "the study of the laws of nature," or, to speak a more correct language, the laws of the material universe. Here, to a mind stored with the results of comprehensive thought, there lay open a boundless field of remark, of the kind most useful to the young students of the University. At the stage in education which they are supposed to have reached, the time was come for disengaging their minds from the microscopic contemplation of the details of the various sciences, and elevating them to the idea of Science as a whole—to the idea of human culture as a whole—of the place which those various sciences occupy in the former, and the functions which they perform in the latter. Though an actual analysis would have been impossible, there was room to present, in a rapid sketch, the *results* of an analysis, of [p]the methods[p] of the various physical sciences— [q] the processes by which they severally arrive at truth: the peculiar logic of each science, and the light thrown thereby upon universal logic: the various kinds and degrees of evidence upon which the truths of those sciences rest; how to estimate them; how to adapt our modes of investigation to them: how far the habits of estimating evidence, which these sciences engender, are applicable to other subjects, and to evidence of another kind; how far inapplicable. Hence the transition was easy to the more extensive inquiry, what these physical studies are capable of doing for the mind; which of the habits and powers that constitute a fine intellect those pursuits tend to cultivate; what are those which they do not cultivate, those even (for such there are) which they tend to impede; by what other studies and intellectual exercises, by what general reflections, or course of reading or meditation, those deficiencies may be supplied. The Professor might thus have shown (what it is usual only to declaim about) how highly a familiarity with mathematics, with dynamics, with even experimental physics and natural history, conduces both to [r] strength and [s] soundness of [t] understanding; and yet how possible it is to be master of all these sciences, and to be unable to put two ideas together with a useful result, on any other topic. The youth of

[o]35 as the above,

[p-p]35 what Hobbes and Descartes would have called the *methods** [*footnote:*] **Method*, the *methodus philosophandi*. The employment of the word to denote order and arrangement, is a modern corruption.

[q]35 *i.e.*,

[r]35 the

[s]35 to the

[t]35 a fine

the university might have been taught to set a just value on these attainments, yet to see in them, as branches of general education, what they really are— the early stages in the formation of a *superior* mind; the *v* instruments of a higher culture. Nor would it have been out of place in such a discourse, though perhaps not peculiarly appropriate to this part of it, to have added a few considerations on the tendency of scientific pursuits in general; the influence of habits of analysis and abstraction upon the character:—how, without those habits, the mind is the slave of its own accidental associations, the dupe of every superficial appearance, and fit only to receive its opinions from authority:—on the other hand, how their exclusive *cultivation*, while it strengthens the associations which connect means with ends, effects with causes, tends to weaken many of those upon which our enjoyments and our social feelings depend; and by accustoming the mind to consider, in objects, chiefly the properties on account of which we refer them to classes and give them general names, leaves our conceptions of them as individuals, lame and meagre:—how, therefore, the corrective and antagonist principle to the pursuits which deal with objects only in the abstract, is to be sought in those which deal with them altogether in the concrete, clothed in properties and circumstances: real life in its most varied forms, poetry and art in all their branches.

These, and many kindred topics, a *true* philosopher, standing in the place of Professor Sedgwick, would, as far as space permitted, have illustrated and insisted on. But the Professor's resources supplied him only with a few trite commonplaces, on the high privilege of comprehending the mysteries of the natural world; the value of studies which give a habit of abstraction, and a "power of concentration;" the use of scientific pursuits in saving us from languor and vacuity; with other truths of *that small calibre*. To these he adds, that "the study of the higher sciences is well suited to keep down a spirit of arrogance and intellectual pride," by convincing us of "the narrow limitation of our faculties;"[*] and upon this peg he appends a dissertation on the evidences of design in the universe—a subject on which much originality was not to be hoped for, and the nature of which may be allowed to protect feebleness from any severity of comment.

The Professor's next topic is the classical languages and literature. And here he begins by wondering. *It is a common propensity of writers on

[*Sedgwick, p. 12.]

*u–u*35   great   *v*35   mere
*w–w*35   culture   *x–x*+59,67
*y–y*35   the calibre of the *Penny Magazine*
*z–z*35   This is one of the ways of his profession. Mr. Sedgwick, besides being a professor of geology, is also a clergyman; and it seems to be a propensity inherent in the clerical office

natural theology[z] to erect everything into a wonder. [a]They[a] cannot consider the [b] greatness and wisdom of God, once for all, as proved, but [c]think themselves[c] bound to be finding fresh arguments for it in every chip or stone; and [d]they think[d] nothing a proof of greatness unless [e]they[e] can wonder at it; and to most minds a wonder explained is a wonder no longer. Hence a sort of vague feeling, as if, to [f]their[f] conceptions, God would not be so great if he had made us capable of understanding more of the laws of his universe; and hence a reluctance to admit even the most obvious explanation, lest it should destroy the wonder.

The subject of Professor Sedgwick's wonder is a very simple thing—the manner in which a child acquires a language.

I may recall to your minds, [says he,] the wonderful ease with which a child comprehends the conventional signs of thought formed between man and man—not only learns the meaning of words descriptive of visible things; but understands, by a kind of rational instinct, the meaning of abstract terms, without ever thinking of the faculty by which he comes to separate them from the names of mere objects of sense. The readiness with which a child acquires a language may well be called a rational instinct: for during the time that his knowledge is built up, and that he learns to handle the implements of thought, he knows no more of what passes within himself, that he does of the structure of the eye, or of the properties of light, while he attends to the impressions on his visual sense, and gives to each impression its appropriate name. (P. 33.)

[g]If[g] whatever we do without understanding the machinery by which we do it, be done by a rational instinct, we learn to dance by instinct: since few of the dancing-master's pupils have ever heard of any one of the muscles which his instructions and their own sedulous practice give them the power to use. Do we grow wheat by "a rational instinct," because we know not how the seed germinates in the ground? We know by experience, not by instinct, that it [h]does germinate[h], and on that assurance we sow it. A child learns a language by the ordinary laws of association; by hearing the word spoken, on the various occasions on which the meaning denoted by it has to be conveyed. This mode of acquisition is better adapted for giving a loose and vague, than a precise, conception of the meaning of an abstract term; accordingly, most people's conceptions of the meaning of many abstract terms in common use remain always loose and vague. The rapidity with which [i]children learn[i] a language is not more wonderful than the rapidity with which [j]they learn[j] so much else at an early age. It is a common remark, that we gain more knowl-

[a-a]35   A clergyman   [b]35   infinite
[c-c]35   thinks himself   [d-d]35   he thinks
[e-e]35   he   [f-f]35   his
[g-g]35   This, on its own account, would scarcely require remark: but in illustration of the Professor's metaphysics, of which it is a fair sample, we may observe, that if
[h-h]35   germinates somehow   [i-i]35   a child learns
[j-j]35   he learns

edge in the first few years of life, without labour, than we ever *k*afterwards*k* acquire by the hardest toil, in double the time. There are many causes to account for this; among which it is sufficient to specify, that *l*much of*l* the knowledge we then acquire concerns our most pressing wants, and that our attention to outward impressions is not yet deadened by familiarity, nor distracted, as in grown persons, by a previously accumulated stock of inward *m*feelings and ideas*m*.

Against the general tendency of the Professor's remarks on the cultivation of the ancient languages, *n*there is little to be said*n*. We think with him, that "our fathers have done well in making classical studies an early and prominent part of liberal education" (p. 36). We fully coincide in his opinion, that "the philosophical and ethical works of the ancients deserve a much larger portion of our time than we" (meaning Cambridge) "have hitherto bestowed on them" (p. 39). We commend the liberality (for, in a professor of an English University, the liberality which admits the smallest fault in the university system of tuition deserves to be accounted extraordinary) of the following remarks:—

It is notorious, that during many past years, while verbal criticism has been pursued with so much ardour, the works to which I now allude (coming home, as they do, to the business of life; and pregnant, as they are, with knowledge well fitted to fortify the reasoning powers) have, by the greater number of us, hardly been thought of; and have in no instance been made prominent subjects of academic training. (P. 39.)

I think it incontestably true, that for the last fifty years our classical studies (with much to demand our undivided praise) have been too critical and formal; and that we have sometimes been taught, while straining after an accuracy beyond our reach, to value the husk more than the fruit of ancient learning: and if of late years our younger members have sometimes written prose Greek almost with the purity of Xenophon, or composed iambics in the finished diction of the Attic poets, we may well doubt whether time suffices for such perfection—whether the imagination and the taste might not be more wisely cultivated than by a long sacrifice to what, after all, ends but in verbal imitations.—In short, whether such acquisitions, however beautiful in themselves, are not gained at the expense of something better. This at least is true, that he who forgets that language is but the sign and vehicle of thought, and, while studying the word, knows little of the sentiment—who learns the measure, the garb, and fashion of ancient song, without looking to its living soul or feeling its inspiration—is not one jot better than a traveller in classic land, who sees its crumbling temples, and numbers, with arithmetical precision, their steps and pillars, but thinks not of their beauty, their design, or the living sculptures on their walls—or who counts the stones in the Appian way instead of gazing on the monuments of the 'eternal city.' (Pp. 37–8.)

The illustration which closes the above passage (though, as is often the case with illustrations, it does not illustrate) is rather pretty: a circumstance

*k–k*35,59   after
*m–m*35   ideas and feelings

*l–l*35   all
*n–n*35   we have nothing to say

which we should be sorry not to notice, as, amid much straining, and many elaborate flights of imagination, we have not met with any other instance in which the Professor makes so near an approach to actual eloquence.

We have said that we go all lengths with our author in claiming for classical literature a place in education, at least equal to that commonly assigned to it. But though we think his opinion right, we think most of his reasons wrong. As, for example, the following:—

> With individuals as with nations, the powers of imagination reach their maturity sooner than the powers of reason; and this is another proof that the severer investigations of science ought to be preceded by the study of languages; and especially of those great works of imagination which have become a pattern for the literature of every civilized tongue. (P. 34.)

This *dictum* respecting Imagination and Reason is only not a truism, because it is, as Coleridge would say, a falsism. Does the Professor mean that [o]any "great[o] work of imagination"—the *Paradise Lost*, for instance—could have been produced at an earlier age, or by a less matured or less accomplished mind, than the *Mécanique Céleste*?[*] Does he mean that a learner can appreciate Æschylus or Sophocles before he is old enough to understand Euclid or Lacroix? In nations, again, the assertion, that imagination, in any but the vulgarest sense of the word, attains maturity sooner than reason, is so far from being [p]correct[p], that throughout all history the two have invariably flourished together; have, and necessarily must. Does Mr. Sedgwick think that any great work of imagination ever was, or can be, produced, without great powers of reason? Be the country Greece or Rome, Italy, France, or England, the age of her greatest eminence in poetry and the fine arts has [q] been that of her greatest statesmen, generals, orators, historians, navigators—in one word, thinkers, in every department of active life; not, indeed, of her greatest philosophers, but only because Philosophy is the tardiest product of Reason itself.*

[r]Of the true reasons, and there are most substantial and cogent ones, for

[*Pierre Simon de La Place. *Traité de mécanique céleste*. 5 vols. Paris: Duprat, *et al.*, 1798–1823.]

*In the earlier stages of a nation's culture, the place of philosophy is always pre-occupied by an established religion: all the more interesting questions to which philosophy addresses itself, find a solution satisfactory to the then state of human intellect, ready provided by the received creed. The old religion must have lost its hold on the more cultivated minds, before philosophy is applied to for a solution of the same questions. With the decline of Polytheism came the Greek philosophy; with the decline of Catholicism, the modern.

*o–o*59 "any great [*printer's error?*] *p–p*35 true
*q*35 always
*r–r*35 The true ground for assigning to classical studies a high place in general education—a far higher one, indeed, than to what the Professor calls "the severer investiga-

assigning to classical studies a high place in general education[r], we find not a word in Mr. Sedgwick's tract; but, instead of them, much harping on the value of the writings of antiquity as "patterns" and "models." This is lauding the abuse of classical knowledge as the use; and is a very bad lesson to [s]the "younger[s] members" of the University. The study of the ancient writers has been of unspeakable benefit to the moderns; from which benefit, the attempts at direct imitation of those writers have been no trifling drawback. The necessary effect of imitating "models" is, to set manner above matter. The imitation of the classics has perverted the whole taste of modern Europe on the subject of composition: it has made style a subject of cultivation and of praise, independently of ideas; whereas, by the ancients, style was never thought of but in complete subordination to matter. The ancients [t](in the good times of their literature)[t] would as soon have thought of a coat in the abstract, as of style in the abstract: the merit of a style, in their eyes, was, that it exactly fitted the thought. Their first aim was, by the assiduous study of their subject, to secure to themselves thoughts worth expressing; their next was, to find words which would convey those thoughts with the utmost degree of nicety; and only when this was made sure, did they think of ornament. Their style, therefore, whether ornamented or plain, grows out of their turn of thought; and may be admired, but cannot be imitated, by any one

---

tions of science" (meaning mathematics, and the applications of mathematics) is, that the former cultivate the whole mind, the latter only a narrow corner of it. The subject of the one is but lines and numbers; of the other, human life, from its highest to its homeliest concerns. In the one, the only faculty exercised is ratiocination; and that, too, under circumstances of unusual facility: in the other, there is scarcely a valuable power or habit of the intellect which finds not its appropriate nourishment. We believe, accordingly, that the superiority of scholars over mathematicians, wherever intellects are brought fairly into competition, is borne out by a wide experience. As between the Greek and Roman, and any modern literature, the superiority of the former, as an instrument of education, lies in this—that in all other literatures the various nutriment which is needful for the mind lies scattered, some here, some there, and the same book is seldom food for more than a small part of the character; but in classical literature the whole man drinks from the same fountain; the sense of beauty, the admiration of exalted personal excellence, and the most varied powers of thought, are all nourished and called into action, each in the highest degree, and not separately but simultaneously.

We hold with Mr. Sedgwick, that these languages should be studied in our early years —not because we think, as he almost seems to do, that a young scholar can understand and relish "great works of imagination" before he can learn simple equations—but because the mechanical difficulties are most easily vanquished at an early age; and because the acquisition of a complex and symmetrical language is itself the most valuable discipline, not of the imagination, but of the reason, which a young mind is capable of. The Greek or Latin grammar is a specimen of logical and metaphysical analysis, the place of which in education no other of the ordinary studies of youth could supply.

Of these reasons, substantial and cogent as they are, in recommendation of classical studies

[s–s]35,59   "the younger   [t–t]+59,67

whose turn of thought is different. The instruction which Professor Sedgwick should have given to his pupils, was to follow no models; to attempt no style, but let their thoughts shape out the style best suited to them; to resemble the ancients, not by copying their manner, but by understanding their own subject as well, cultivating their faculties as highly, and taking as much trouble with their work, as the ancients did. All imitation of an author's style, except that which arises from making his thoughts *our* own, is mere affectation and vicious mannerism.

In discussing the value of the ancient languages, Mr. Sedgwick touches upon the importance of ancient history. On this topic, on which so much, and of the most interesting kind, might have been said, he delivers nothing but questionable commonplaces. "History," says he, "is, to our knowledge of man in his social capacity, what physical experiments are to our knowledge of the laws of nature" (p. 42). Common as this notion is, it is a strange one to be held by a professor of physical science; for assuredly no person is satisfied with such evidence in studying the laws of the natural world, as history affords with respect to the laws of political society. The evidence of history, instead of being analogous to that of experiment, leaves the philosophy of society in exactly the state in which physical science was, before the method of experiment was introduced. The Professor should reflect, that we cannot make experiments in history. We are obliged, therefore, as the ancients did in physics, to content ourselves with such experiments as we find made to our hands; and these are so few, and so complicated, that little or nothing can be inferred from them. *v* There is not a fact in history which is not susceptible of as many different explanations as there are possible theories of human affairs. *w* Not only is history not the *source* of political philosophy, but the profoundest political philosophy is requisite to explain history; without it all in history which is worth understanding remains mysterious. Can Mr. Sedgwick *y* explain why the Greeks, in their brief career, so far surpassed their *cotemporaries*, or why the Romans conquered the world? *a*Mr. Sedgwick

---

*u–u*35   your

*v*35   There is a remark of David Hume, of which perhaps Mr. Sedgwick never heard —that the world is yet too young to have a political philosophy. ["Of Civil Liberty," in *Essays and Treatises on Several Subjects.* 2 vols. Edinburgh: Cadell, 1793, Vol. I, pp. 89–90.] If history is to be the basis of it, after ten thousand years the world will still be too young.

*w*35   Whoever knows not this, must be as superficially acquainted with history as with principle; and so, indeed, those who build confidently upon history always are: those who are really versed in it know better in what its value consists.

*x–x*35   foundation

*y*35   , for instance,   *z–z*35   contemporaries

*a–a*35   The real foundation of political wisdom is our experience, not of the men of former ages, whom we cannot know, either themselves or their circumstances, but of those whom and whose circumstances we can know, the people of our own time; and this experience is acquired

mistakes the functions of history in political speculation. History is not the foundation, but the verification, of the social science; it corroborates, and often suggests, political truths, but cannot prove them. The proof of them is drawn from the laws of human nature; ascertained*a* through the study of ourselves by reflection, and of mankind by actual intercourse with them. That what we know of former ages, like what we know of foreign nations, is, with all its *b*imperfections*b*, of much use, by correcting the narrowness incident to personal experience, *c*is undeniable*c* ; but the usefulness of history depends upon its being kept in the second place.

The Professor *d*seems*d* wholly unaware of the importance of accuracy, either in thought or in expression. "In ancient history," says he (p. 42), "we can trace the fortunes of mankind under almost every condition of political and social life." So far is this from being true, that ancient history does not so much as furnish an example of a civilized people in which the bulk of the inhabitants were not slaves. Again, "all the successive actions we contemplate are at such a distance from us, that we can see their true bearings on each other undistorted by that mist of prejudice with which every modern political question is surrounded." We appeal to all who are conversant with the modern writings on ancient history, whether even this is true. The most elaborate Grecian history which we possess* is impregnated with the anti-Jacobin spirit in every line; and the *Quarterly Review* *e* laboured as diligently for many years to vilify the Athenian republic as the American.

Thus far, the faults which we have discovered in Mr. Sedgwick are *f* of omission rather than of commission: or at worst, amount only to this, that he has *g*contented himself with repeating*g* the trivialities he found current *h* . Had there been nothing *i*but this*i* to be said of the remainder of the *Discourse*, we should not have disturbed its peaceful progress to oblivion.

We have now, however, arrived at the opening of that part of Professor Sedgwick's *Discourse* which is most laboured, and for the sake of which all the rest may be surmised to have been written,—his strictures on Locke's *Essay on the Human Understanding*, and Paley's *Principles of Moral Philosophy*. These works comprise what little of ethical and metaphysical instruction is given, or professed to be given, at Cambridge. The remainder of Mr. Sedgwick's *Discourse* is devoted to an attack upon them.

*[67] Written in 1834. [The reference is presumably to William Mitford. *The History of Greece*. 10 vols. London: Cadell and Davies, 1818–20.]

*b–b*35	uncertainties	*c–c*35	we need not be told
*d–d*35	is	*e*35	has
*f*35	faults	*g–g*35	repeated
*h*35	, not having depth or strength of mind to see beyond them		
*i–i*35	worse		

We assuredly have no thought of defending either work as a text-book, still less as the sole text-book, on their respective subjects, in any school of philosophy. Of Paley's work, though it possesses in a high degree some minor merits, we think, on the whole, meanly. Of Locke's *Essay*, the beginning and foundation of the modern analytical psychology, we cannot speak but with the deepest reverence; whether we consider the era which it constitutes in philosophy, the intrinsic value, even at the present day, of its thoughts, or the noble devotion to truth, the beautiful and touching earnestness and simplicity, which he not only manifests in himself, but has the power beyond almost all other philosophical writers of infusing into his reader. His *Essay* should be familiar to every student. But no work, a hundred and fifty years old, can be fit to be the sole, or even the principal work for the instruction of youth in a science like that of Mind. In metaphysics, every new truth sets aside or modifies much of what was previously received as truth. *i* Berkeley's refutation of the doctrine of abstract ideas would of itself necessitate a complete revision of the phraseology of the most valuable parts of Locke's book. And the important speculations originated by Hume and *k*improved*k* by Brown, concerning the nature of our experience, are acknowledged, even by the philosophers who do not adopt in their full extent the conclusions of those writers, to have carried *l* the analysis of our knowledge and of the process of acquiring it, so much beyond the point where Locke left it, as to require that his work should be entirely recast.

Moreover, the book which has changed the face of a science, even when not superseded in its doctrines, is seldom suitable for didactic purposes. It is adapted to the state of mind, not of those who are ignorant of every doctrine, but of those who are instructed in an erroneous doctrine. So far as it is taken up *m*with*m* directly combating the errors which prevailed before it was written, the more completely it has done its work, the more certain it is of becoming superfluous, not to say unintelligible, without a commentary. And even its positive truths are defended against such objections only as were current in its own times, and guarded only against such misunderstandings as the people of those times were likely to fall into. Questions of morals and metaphysics differ from physical questions in this, that their aspect changes with every change *n*in*n* the human mind. At no two periods is the same question embarrassed by the same difficulties, or the same truth in need of the same explanatory comment. The fallacy which is satisfactorily refuted in one age, re-appears in another, in a shape which the arguments formerly used do not precisely meet; and seems to triumph, until some one, with weapons suitable to the altered form of the error, arises and repeats its overthrow.

These remarks are peculiarly applicable to Locke's *Essay*. His doctrines

---

*i*35   Bishop
*k–k*35   perfected   *l*35   on
*m–m*35   in   *n–n*35   of

were new, and had to make their way: he therefore wrote not for learners, but for the learned; for ᵒmenᵒ who were trained in the systems ᵖantecedentᵖ to his—ᵍin thoseᵍ of the Schoolmen or of the Cartesians. He said what he thought necessary to establish his own opinions, and ʳ answered the objections of such objectors as the age afforded; but he could not anticipate all the objections which might be made by a subsequent age: least of all could he anticipate those which would be made now, when his philosophy has long been the prevalent one; when the arguments of objectors have been rendered as far as possible consistent with his principles, and are often such as could not have been thought of until he had cleared the ground by demolishing some received opinion, which no one before him had thought of disputing.*

To attack Locke, therefore, because other arguments than it was necessary

*As an example, and one which is in point to Mr. Sedgwick's attack, let us take Locke's refutation of innate ideas. The doctrine maintained in his time, and against which his arguments are directed, was, that there are ideas which exist in the mind antecedently to experience. Of this theory his refutation is complete, and the error has never again reared its head. But a form of the same doctrine has since arisen, somewhat different from the above, and which could not have been thought of until Locke had established the dependence of all our knowledge upon experience. In this modern theory, it is admitted that experience, or, in other words, impressions received from without, must *precede* the excitement of any ideas in the mind; no ideas, therefore, exist in the mind *antecedently* to experience; but there are some ideas (so the theory contends) which, though experience must precede them, are not *likenesses* of anything which we have experience of, but are only *suggested* or *excited* by it; ideas which are only so far the effects of outward impressions, that they would for ever lie dormant if no outward impressions were ever made. Experience, in short, is a *necessary condition* of those ideas, but not their prototype, or their cause [35   or cause]. One of these ideas, they contend, is, the idea of substance or matter; which is no copy of any sensation; neither, on the other hand, should we ever have had this notion, if we had never had sensation [35, 59   sensations]; but as soon as any sensation is experienced, we are compelled by a law of our nature to form the idea of an external something (which we call matter), [35   something called matter,] and to refer the sensation to this [35   this something] as its exciting cause. Such, it is likewise contended, are [35   is] the idea of duty, and the moral judgments and feelings. We do not bring with us into the world any idea of a criminal act: it is only experience which gives us that idea; but the moment we conceive the act, we instantly, by the constitution of our nature, judge it to be wrong, and frame the idea of an obligation to abstain from it.

This form of the doctrine of innate principles, Locke did not anticipate, and has not supplied the means of completely refuting. Mr. Sedgwick accordingly triumphs over him, as having missed his mark by overlooking the "distinction between innate ideas and innate capacities" (p. 48). If Locke has not adverted to a distinction which probably had [35   which had] never been thought of in his day, others have; and no one who now writes on the subject ever overlooks it. Has Mr. Sedgwick ever read Hartley, or Mill? or even Hume, or Helvetius? Apparently

ᵒ⁻ᵒ35   those   ᵖ⁻ᵖ35   previous
ᵍ⁻ᵍ35   the systems   ʳ35   he

for him to use have become requisite to the support of some of his conclusions, is like reproaching the Evangelists because they did not write Evidences of Christianity. The question is, not what Locke has said, but what would he have said if he had heard all that has since been said against him? *s*Unreasonable*s*, however, as is a criticism on Locke conceived in this spirit, Mr. Sedgwick indulges in another strain of criticism even more *t*unreasonable*t*.

The "greatest fault," he says, of Locke's *Essay*, "is the contracted view it takes of the capacities of man—allowing him, indeed, the faculty of reflecting, and following out trains of thought according to the rules of abstract reasoning; but depriving him both of his powers of imagination and of his moral sense" (p. 57). Several pages are thereupon employed in celebrating "the imaginative powers." And a metaphysician who "discards these powers from his system" (which, according to Mr. Sedgwick, Locke does), is accused of "shutting his eyes to the loftiest qualities of the soul" (p. 49).

Has the Professor so far forgotten the book which he must have read once, and on which he passes judgment with so much authority, as to fancy that it claims to be a treatise on all "the capacities of man?" *u*Can he*u* write in the manner we have just quoted about Locke's book, with the fact looking him in the face from his own pages, that it is entitled *An Essay on the Human Understanding*? Who besides Mr. Sedgwick would look for a treatise on the imagination under such a title? What place, what concern could it have had there?

The one object of Locke's speculations was to ascertain the limits of our knowledge; what questions we may hope to solve, what are beyond our reach. This purpose is *v*announced*v* in the Preface, and manifested in every chapter of the book. He *w*declares*w* that he commenced his inquiries because "in discoursing on a subject very remote from this," it came into his thoughts that "before we set ourselves upon inquiries of that nature, it was necessary to examine our own abilities, and see what objects our understandings were, or were not, fitted to deal with."* The following, from the first chapter of the first book, are a few of the passages in which he describes the scope of his speculations:—

"To inquire into the original, certainty, and extent of human knowledge,

---

[35   Evidently] not; he shows no signs of having read any writer on the side of the question which he attacks, except Locke and Paley, whom he insists upon treating as the representatives of all others who adopt any of their conclusions.

*Preface to Locke's *Essay*. ["The Epistle to the Reader," *Of Human Understanding*, in *Works*, I (London: Tegg, Sharpe, Offor, Robinson, Evans, 1823) xlvi–xlvii.]

s–s35   Absurd
t–t35   absurd still
u–u35   Are words altogether without meaning to the Professor, that he can
v–v35   distinctly declared
w–w35   tells us

together with the grounds and degrees of belief, opinion, and assent." "To consider the *discerning* faculties of man, as they are employed about the objects which they have to do with." "To give an account of the ways whereby our understandings come to attain those notions of things we have," and "set down" some "measures of the certainty of our knowledge, or the grounds of those persuasions which are to be found amongst men." "To search out the bounds between opinion and knowledge, and to examine by what measures, in things whereof we have no certain knowledge, we ought to regulate our assent, and moderate our persuasions." And "by this inquiry into the nature of the understanding," to "discover the powers thereof, how far they reach, to what things they are in any degree proportionate, and where they fail us;" and thereby to "prevail with the busy mind of man to be more cautious in meddling with things exceeding its comprehension, to stop when it is at the utmost extent of its tether, and to sit down in a quiet ignorance of those things which, upon examination, are found to be beyond the reach of our capacities."[*]

And because a philosopher, having placed before himself an undertaking of this magnitude, and of this strictly scientific character, and having his mind full of thoughts which were destined to effect a revolution in the philosophy of the human intellect, does not quit his subject to panegyrize the imagination, he is accused of saying that there is no such thing; or of saying that it is a pernicious thing; or rather (for to this pitch of ingenuity Mr. Sedgwick's criticism reaches) of saying *y*both*y* that there is no such thing, and *z*also*z* that it is a pernicious thing. He "*deprives* man of his powers of imagination;" he "*discards* these powers from his system;" and at the same time he "speaks of those powers only to condemn them;" he "*denounces* the exercise of the imagination as a fraud upon the reason."[†] As well might it be asserted, that Locke denies that man has a body, or condemns the exercise of the body, because he is not constantly proclaiming what a beautiful and glorious thing the body is. Mr. Sedgwick cannot conceive the state of mind of such a man as Locke, who is too entirely absorbed in his subject to be able to turn aside from it every time that an opportunity offers for a flight of rhetoric. With the imagination in its own province, as a source of enjoyment, and a means of educating the feelings, Locke had nothing to do; nor was the subject suited to the character of his mind. He was concerned with imagination, only in the province of pure intellect; and all he had to do with it there, was to warn it off the ground. This Mr. Sedgwick calls "denouncing the exercise of the imagination as a fraud upon the reason," and "regarding men who appeal to the powers of imagination in their proofs and mingle them in their exhortations

[*Locke, *Of Human Understanding*, pp. 1–3.]
[†Sedgwick, pp. 57, 49, 49, 50.]

*x*35   thus,   *y–y*35,59   *both*   *z–z*35,59   *also*

as no better than downright cheats" (p. 50). Locke certainly says that imagination is not proof. Does the Professor then mean—and by his rhapsody about the imagination does he intend us to understand—that imagination *is* proof? But how can we expect clearness of ideas on metaphysical subjects, from a writer who cannot discriminate between the Understanding and the Will? Locke's *Essay* is on the Understanding; Mr. Sedgwick tells us, ^awith^a much finery ^bof language^b, that the imagination is a powerful engine for acting on the will. So is a cat-o'-nine-tails. Is a cat-o'-nine-tails, therefore, one of the sources of human knowledge? "In trying circumstances," says the Professor, "the determination of the will is often more by feeling than by reason" (p. 51). In all circumstances, trying or otherwise, the determination of the will is wholly by feeling. Reason is not an end in itself: it teaches us to know the right ends, and the way to them; but if we desire those ends, this desire is not Reason, but a feeling. Hence the importance of the question, how to give to the imagination that direction which will exercise the most beneficial influence upon the feelings. But the Professor probably meant that "in trying circumstances, the determination" not "of the will," but of the understanding, "is often more by feeling than by reason." Unhappily it is; this is the tendency in human nature, against which Locke warns his readers; and by so warning them, incurs the censure of Mr. Sedgwick.*

The other accusation which the Professor urges against Locke—that of overlooking "the faculties of moral judgment," and "depriving" man of his "moral sense"[*]—will best be considered along with his strictures on Paley's Moral Philosophy; for against Paley, also, the principal charge is that he denies the moral sense.

It is a fact in human nature, that we have moral judgments and moral feelings. We judge certain actions and dispositions to be right, others wrong: this we call approving and disapproving them. We have also feelings of pleasure in the contemplation of the former class of actions and dispositions—feelings of dislike and aversion to the latter; which feelings, as everybody must be

---

*[59] The word Imagination is currently taken in such a variety of senses, that there is some difficulty in making use of it at all without risk of being misunderstood. In one of its acceptations, Imagination is not the auxiliary merely, but the necessary instrument of Reason—namely, by summoning and keeping before the mind a lively and complete *image* of the thing to be reasoned about. The differences which exist among human beings in their capacity of doing this, and the influence which those differences exercise over the soundness and comprehensiveness of their thinking faculties, are topics well worthy of an elaborate discussion. But of this mode of viewing the subject there are no traces in Mr. Sedgwick's *Discourse*.

[*Sedgwick, pp. 52, 57.]

^{a–a}35   amid   ^{b–b}+59,67

conscious, do not exactly resemble any other of our feelings of pain or pleasure.

Such are the phenomena. Concerning their reality there is no dispute. But there are two theories respecting the origin of these phenomena, which have divided philosophers from the earliest ages of philosophy. One is, that the distinction between right and wrong is an ultimate and inexplicable fact; that we perceive this distinction, as we perceive the distinction of colours, by a peculiar faculty; and that the pleasures and pains, the desires and aversions, consequent upon this perception, are all ultimate facts in our nature; as much so as the pleasures and pains, or the desires and aversions, of which sweet or bitter tastes, pleasing or grating sounds, are the object. This is called the theory of the moral sense—or of moral instincts—or of eternal and immutable morality—or of intuitive principles of morality—or by many other names; to the differences between which, those who adopt the theory often attach great importance, but which, for our present purpose, may all be considered as ᶜequivalentᶜ.

The other theory is, that the ideas of right and wrong, and the feelings which attach themselves to those ideas, are not ultimate facts, but may be explained and accounted for; are not the result of any peculiar law of our nature, but of the same laws on which all our other complex ideas and feelings depend: that the distinction between moral and immoral acts is not a peculiar and inscrutable property in the acts themselves, which we perceive by a sense, as we perceive colours by our sense of sight; but flows from the ordinary properties of those actions, for the recognition of which we need no other faculty than our intellects and our bodily senses. And the particular property in actions, which constitutes them moral or immoral, in the opinion of those who hold this theory (all of them, at least, who need ᵈhereᵈ be noticed), is the influence of those actions, and of the dispositions from which they emanate, upon human happiness.

This theory is sometimes called the theory of Utility; and is what Mr. Sedgwick means by "the utilitarian theory of morals."[*]

Maintaining this second theory, Mr. Sedgwick calls "denying the existence of moral feelings" (p. 32). This is, in the first place, misstating the question. Nobody denies the existence of moral feelings. The feelings exist, manifestly exist, and ᵉ cannot be denied. The questions on which there is a difference are—first, whether they are simple or complex feelings, and if complex, of what elementary feelings they are ᶠcomposed:ᶠ which is a question of metaphysics; and secondly, what kind of acts and dispositions are the proper

[*Sedgwick, p. vii.]

ᶜ–ᶜ35   synonymous
ᵉ35   so

ᵈ–ᵈ35   to
ᶠ–ᶠ35   composed?

objects of those *g*feelings;*g* in other words, what is the principle of *h*morals.*h* These questions, and more peculiarly the last, the theory which *i*has been termed utilitarian*i* professes to solve.

Paley adopted this theory. Mr. Sedgwick, who professes the other theory, treats Paley, and all who take Paley's side of the question, with extreme contumely.

We shall show that Mr. Sedgwick has no right to represent Paley as a type of the theory of utility; that he has failed in refuting even Paley; and that the tone of *j*high moral reprobation*j* which he has *k*assumed*k* towards all who adopt that theory is altogether unmerited on their part, and on his, from his extreme ignorance of the subject, peculiarly unbecoming.

Those who maintain that human happiness is the end and test of morality are bound to prove that the principle is true; but not that Paley understood it. *l*No one is*l* entitled to found an argument against a principle, upon the faults or blunders of a particular writer who professed to build his system upon it, without taking notice that the principle may be understood differently, and has in fact been understood differently by other *m*writers.*m* What would be thought of an assailant of Christianity, who should judge of its truth or beneficial tendency from the *n*view*n* taken of it by the Jesuits, or by the Shakers? A doctrine is not judged at all until it is judged in its *o*best*o* form. The principle of utility may be viewed in as many different lights as every other rule or principle may. If it be liable to mischievous misinterpretations, this is true of all very general, and therefore of all first, principles. Whether the ethical creed of a follower of utility will lead him to moral or immoral consequences, depends on what he thinks useful;—just as, with a partizan of the opposite doctrine—that of *p*innate*p* conscience—it depends on what he thinks his conscience enjoins. But either the one theory or the other must be true. Instead, therefore, of cavilling about the abuses and perversions of either, real manliness would consist in accepting the true, with all its liabilities to abuse and perversion; and then bending the whole force of our intellects to the establishment of such secondary and intermediate maxims, as may be guides to the *bonâ fide* inquirer in the application of the principle, and salutary checks to the sophist and the dishonest casuist.

There are faults in Paley's conception of the philosophy of morals, both in its foundations and its subsequent stages, which prevent his book from being an example of the conclusions justly deducible from the doctrine of

*g–g*35   feelings?   *h–h*35   morals?
*i–i*35   Mr. Sedgwick terms "the utilitarian theory"
*j–j*35   insult   *k–k*35   thought fit to assume
*l–l*35   Who can be   *m–m*35   writers?
*n–n*35,59   views   *o–o*35   purest
p–p+59,67

utility, or of the influences of that doctrine, when properly understood, upon the intellect and character.

In the first place, he does not consider utility as itself the source of moral obligation, but as a mere index to the will of God, which he regards as the ultimate groundwork of all morality, and the origin of its binding force. This doctrine (not that utility is an index to the will of God, but that it is an index and nothing else) we consider as highly exceptionable; and having really many of those bad effects on the mind, erroneously ascribed to the principle of utility.

The only view of the connexion between religion and morality which does not annihilate the very idea of the latter, is that which considers the Deity as not qmaking, but recognising and sanctioningq, moral obligation. In the minds of most English rthinkersr down to the middle of the last century, the idea of duty, and that of obedience to God, were so indissolubly united, as to be inseparable even in thought: and when we consider how in those days religious motives and ideas stood in the front of all speculations, it is not wonderful that religion should have been thought to constitute the sessences of all obligations to which it annexed its tsanctiont. To have inquired, Why am I bound to obey God's will? would, to a Christian of that age, have appeared irreverent. It is a question, however, which, as much as any other, requires an answer from a Christian philosopher. "Because he is my Maker" is no answer. Why should I obey my Maker? From gratitude? Then gratitude is in itself obligatory, independently of my Maker's will. From reverence and love? But why is he a proper object of love and reverence? Not because he is my Maker. If I had been made by an evil spirit, for evil purposes, my love and reverence (supposing me to be capable of such feelings) would have been due, not to the evil, but to the good Being. Is it because he is just, righteous, merciful? Then these attributes are in themselves good, independently of his pleasure. If any person has the misfortune to believe that his Creator commands wickedness, more respect is due to him for disobeying such imaginary commands, than for obeying them. If virtue would not be virtue unless the Creator u commanded it—if it derive all its obligatory force from his will—there remains no ground for obeying him except his power; no motive for morality except the selfish one of the hope of heaven, or the selfish and slavish one of the fear of hell.

Accordingly, in strict consistency with this view of the nature of morality, Paley not only represents the proposition that we ought to do good and not harm to mankind, as a mere corollary from the proposition that God wills their good, and not their harm—but represents the motive to virtue, and the

q–q35 *making, but recognizing and sanctioning*
r–r35 philosophers   s–s35 *essence*
t–t35 *sanction*   u35   had

motive which constitutes it virtue, as consisting solely in the hope of heaven and the fear of hell.

It does not, however, follow that Paley believed mankind to have no feelings except selfish ones. He doubtless would have admitted that they are acted upon by other motives, or, in the language of Bentham and Helvetius, that they have other interests, than merely self-regarding ones. But he chose to say that actions done from those other motives are not virtuous. The happiness of mankind, according to him, was the end for which morality was enjoined; yet he would not admit anything to be morality, when the happiness of mankind, or of any of mankind except ourselves, is the inducement of it. He annexed an arbitrary meaning to the word virtue. How he came to think this arbitrary meaning the right one may be a question. ᵛPartly, perhaps,ᵛ by the habit of thinking and talking of morality under the metaphor of a *law*. In the notion of a law, the idea of the command of a superior, enforced by penalties, is of course the main element.

If Paley's ethical system is thus unsound in its foundations, the spirit which runs through the details is no less exceptionable. It is, indeed, such as to prove, that neither the character nor the objects of the writer were those of a philosopher. There is none of the single-minded earnestness for truth, whatever it may be—the intrepid defiance of prejudice, the firm resolve to look all consequences in the face, which the word philosopher supposes, and without which nothing worthy of note was ever accomplished in moral or political philosophy. One sees throughout that he has a particular set of conclusions to come to, and will not, perhaps cannot, allow himself to let in any premises which would interfere with them. His book ʷ is one of a class which has since become very numerous, and is likely to become still more so—an apology for commonplace. Not to lay a solid foundation, and erect an edifice over it suited to the professed ends, but to construct pillars, and insert them ˣunderˣ the existing structure, was Paley's object. He took the doctrines of practical morals which he found current. Mankind were, about that time, ceasing to consider mere use and wont, or even the ordinary special pleading from texts of scripture, as sufficient warrants for ʸthoseʸ common opinions, and were demanding something like a philosophic basis for them. This philosophic basis, Paley, consciously or unconsciously, made it his endeavour to supply. The skill with which his book was adapted to satisfy this want of the time, accounts for the popularity which attended it, notwithstanding the absence of that generous and inspiring tone, which gives so much of their usefulness as well as of their charm to the writings of Plato, and Locke, and Fenelon, and which mankind are accustomed to pretend to admire, whether they really respond to it or not.

ᵛ⁻ᵛ35 Perhaps it was   ʷ35   , in truth,
ˣ⁻ˣ35 *under*   ʸ⁻ʸ35,59   **these**

When an author starts with such an object, it is of little consequence what [z] premises he sets out from. In adopting the principle of utility, Paley, [a]there is[a] no doubt, followed the convictions of his [b]intellect[b]; but if he had started from any other principle, we have as little doubt that he would have arrived at the very same conclusions. These conclusions, namely, the received maxims of his time, were (it would have been strange if they were not) accordant in many [c] points with those which philosophy would have dictated. But had they been accordant on all points, that was not the way in which a philosopher would have dealt with them.

The only deviation from commonplace which has [d] been made an accusation (for all departures from commonplace are made accusations) against Paley's moral system, is that of too readily allowing exceptions to important rules; and this Mr. Sedgwick does not fail to lay hold of, and endeavour, as others have done before him, to fix [e]it[e] upon the principle of utility as [f]an immoral consequence[f]. It is, however, imputable to the very same cause which we have already pointed out. Along with the prevailing maxims, Paley borrowed the prevailing laxity in their application. He had not only to maintain existing doctrines, but to save the credit of existing practices also. He found in his country's morality (especially [g] its political morality), modes of conduct universally prevalent, and applauded by all persons of station and consideration, but which, being acknowledged violations of great [h]moral principles[h], could only be defended as cases of exception, resting on special grounds of expediency; and the only expediency which it was possible to ascribe to them was political expediency—that is, conduciveness to the [i]interest[i] of the [j]ruling powers[j]. To this, and not to the tendencies of the principle of utility, is to be ascribed the lax morality taught by Paley, and justly objected to by Mr. Sedgwick, on the subject of lies, of [k]subscription[k] to articles, of the abuses of influence in the British constitution, and various other topics. The principle of utility leads to no such conclusions. Let us be permitted to add that, if it did, we should not of late years have heard so much in reprobation of it from all manner of persons, and from none more than from the sworn defenders of those very malpractices.

When an inquirer knows beforehand the conclusions which he is to come to, he is not likely to seek far for grounds to rest them upon. Accordingly, the considerations of expediency upon which Paley founds his moral rules, are almost all of the most obvious and vulgar kind. In estimating the consequences of actions, in order to obtain a measure of their morality, there are

[z]35 are the	[a–a]35,59 we have
[b–b]35 understanding	[c]35 , possibly in most,
[d]35,59 ever	[e–e]+59,67
[f–f]35 one of its immoral consequences	[g]35 , in
[h–h]35 principles of morality	[i–i]35,59 interests
[i–i]35 aristocracy	[k–k]35,59 subscriptions

always two sets of considerations involved: the consequences to the outward interests of the parties concerned (including the agent himself); and the consequences to the characters of the same persons, and to their outward interests so far as dependent on their characters. In the estimation of the first of these two classes of considerations, there is in general not much difficulty, nor much room for difference of opinion. The actions which are directly hurtful, or directly useful, to the outward interests of oneself or of other people, are easily distinguished, sufficiently at least for the guidance of a private individual. The rights of individuals, which other individuals ought to respect, over external things, are ˡin generalˡ sufficiently pointed out by a few plain rules, and by the laws of one's country. But it often happens that an essential part of the morality or immorality of an action or a rule of action consists in its influence upon the agent's own mind: upon his susceptibilities of pleasure or pain, upon the general direction of his thoughts, feelings, and imagination, or upon some particular association. Many actions, moreover, produce effects upon the character of other persons besides the agent. In all these cases there will naturally be as much difference in the moral judgments of different persons, as there is in their views of human nature, and of the formation of character. Clear and comprehensive views of education and human culture must therefore precede, and form the basis of, a philosophy of morals; nor can the latter subject ever be understood, but in proportion as the former is so. For this, much yet remains to be done. Even the materials, though abundant, are not complete. Of those which exist, a large proportion have never yet found their way into the writings of philosophers; but are to be gathered, on the one hand, from actual observers of mankind; on the other, from those autobiographers, and from those poets or novelists, who have spoken out unreservedly, from their own experience, any true human feeling. To collect together these materials, and to add to them, will be a labour for successive generations. But Paley, instead of having brought from the philosophy of education and character any new light to illuminate the subject of morals, has not even availed himself of the lights which had already been thrown upon it from that source. He, in fact, had meditated little on this branch of the subject, and had no ideas in relation to it, but the commonest and most superficial. ᵐ

Thus much we have been induced to say, rather from the importance of the subject, than for the sake of a just estimate of Paley, which is a matter of

---

ˡ⁻ˡ+59,67

ᵐ35   [paragraph] What may have been done in this department by the philosophers who have adopted the principle of utility subsequently to Paley, cannot be known, so long as none of them have laid before the world their ethical opinions. But the general laws of the formation of character have to no inquirers been a subject of more attentive investigation; nor, in truth, have the phenomena ever been successfully analyzed into the ultimate elements, but by them.

inferior consequence; still less for the [n]sake of repelling Mr. Sedgwick's onslaught, which[n], as we shall soon see, might have been more summarily disposed of.

Mr. Sedgwick's objections to the principle of utility are of two kinds—first, that it is not true; secondly, that it is dangerous, degrading, and so forth. What he says against its truth, when picked out from a hundred different places, and brought together, would fill about three pages, leaving about twenty consisting of attacks upon its tendency. This already looks [o] ill; for, after all, the truth or falsehood of the principle is the main point. When, of a dissertation on any controverted question, a small part only is employed in proving the author's own opinion, a large part in ascribing odious consequences to the opposite opinion, we are apt to think [p]either[p] that, on the former point, there was not very much to be said [q]; or, if there was, that the author is not very well qualified to say it[q]. One thing is certain; that if an opinion have ever such mischievous consequences, that cannot prevent any thinking person from believing it, if the evidence is in its favour. Unthinking persons, indeed, if they are very solemnly assured that an opinion has mischievous consequences, may be frightened from examining the evidence. When, therefore, we find that this mode of dealing with an opinion is the favourite one—is resorted to in preference to the other, and with greater vehemence, and at greater length—we conclude that it is upon unthinking rather than upon thinking persons that the author calculates upon making an impression; or else, that he himself is one of the former class of persons—that his own judgment is determined, less by evidence presented to his understanding, than by the repugnancy of the opposite opinion to his partialities and affections; and that, perceiving clearly the opinion to be one which it would be painful to him to adopt, he has been easily satisfied with reasons for rejecting it.

All that the Professor says to disprove the principle of utility, and to prove the existence of a moral sense, is found in the following paragraph:—

Let it not be said that our moral sentiments are superinduced by seeing and tracing the consequences of crime. The assertion is not true. The early sense of shame comes before such trains of thought, and is not, therefore, caused by them; and millions, in all ages of the world, have grown up as social beings and moral agents, amenable to the laws of God and man, who never traced or thought of tracing the consequences of their actions, nor ever referred them to any standard of utility. Nor let it be said that the moral sense comes of mere teaching—that right and wrong pass as mere words, first from the lips of the mother to the child, and then from man to man; and that we grow up with moral judgments gradually ingrafted in us from without, by the long-heard lessons of praise and blame, by

[n-n]35 appreciation of Mr. Sedgwick, who
[o]35 but [p-p]+59,67 [q-q]+59,67

the experience of fitness, or the sanction of the law. I repeat that the statement is not true—that our moral perceptions show themselves not in any such order as this. The question is one of feeling; and the moral feelings are often strongest in very early life, before moral rules or legal sanctions have once been thought of. Again, what are we to understand by teaching? Teaching implies capacity: one can be of no use without the other. A faculty of the soul may be called forth, brought to light, and matured; but cannot be created, any more than we can create a new particle of matter, or invent a new law of nature. (Pp. 52–3.)

The substance of the last three sentences is repeated at somewhat greater length shortly after (pp. 54–5), in a passage from which we ʳneedʳ only quote the following words:—"No training (however greatly it may change an individual mind) can create a new faculty, any more than it can give a new organ of sense." In many other parts of the *Discourse*, the same arguments are alluded to, but no new ones are introduced.

Let us, then, examine these arguments.

First, the Professor says, or seems to say, that our moral sentiments cannot be generated by experience of consequences, because a child feels the sense of shame before he has any experience of consequences; and likewise because millions of persons grow up, have moral feelings, and live morally, "who never traced, or thought of tracing, the consequences of their actions," but who yet, it seems, are suffered to go at large, which we thought was not usually the case with persons who never think of the consequences of their actions. The Professor continues—"who never traced, or thought of tracing, the consequences of their actions, nor ever referred them to any standard of utility."

Secondly; ˢ that our moral feelings cannot arise from teaching, because those feelings are often strongest in very early life.

Thirdly; that our moral feelings cannot arise from teaching, because teaching can only call forth a faculty, but cannot create one.

Let us first consider the singular allegation, that the sense of shame in a child precedes all experience of the consequences of actions. Is it not astounding that such an assertion should be ventured upon by any person of sane mind? At what period in a child's life, after it is capable of forming the idea of an action at all, can it be without experience of the consequences of actions? As soon as it has the idea of one person striking another, is it not aware that striking produces pain? As soon as it has the idea of being commanded by its parent, has it not the notion that, by not doing what is commanded, it will excite the parent's displeasure? ᵗ A child's knowledge of the simple fact (one of the earliest he becomes acquainted with), that some acts

ʳ⁻ʳ35   shall   ˢ35   the Professor says,
ᵗ35   Two things manifest themselves throughout the whole passage; extreme ignorance both of children and of grown persons, and an incapacity of making the most obvious distinctions.

produce pain and others pleasure, is called by pompous names, "seeing and tracing the consequences of crime," "trains of thought," "referring actions to a standard," terms which imply continued reflection and large abstractions; and because these terms are absurd when used of a child or an uneducated person, we are to conclude that a child or an uneducated person has no notion that one thing is caused by another. As well might it be said that a child requires an instinct to tell him that he has ten fingers, because he knows it before he has ever thought of "*u*carrying on*u* arithmetical computations."[*] Though a child is not a jurist or a moral philosopher (to whom alone the Professor's phrases would be properly applicable), he has the idea of himself hurting or offending some one, or of some one hurting or annoying him. These are ideas which precede any sense of shame in doing wrong; and it is out of these elements, and not out of abstractions, that the supporters of the theory of utility contend that the idea of wrong, and our feelings of disapprobation *v*of*v* it, are originally formed. Mr. Sedgwick's argument resembles one we often hear, that the principle of utility must be false, because it supposes morality to be founded on the good of society, an idea too complex for the majority of mankind, who look only to the particular persons concerned. Why, none but those who mingle in public transactions, or whose example is likely to have extensive influence, have any occasion to look beyond the particular persons concerned. Morality, for all other people, consists in doing good and refraining from harm, to themselves and to those who immediately surround them. As soon as a child has the idea of voluntarily producing pleasure or pain to any one person, he has an accurate notion of utility. When he afterwards gradually rises to the very complex idea of "society," and learns in what manner his actions may affect the interests of other persons than those who are present to his sight, his conceptions of utility, and of right and wrong founded on utility, undergo a corresponding enlargement, but receive no new element.

Again, if it were ever so true that the sense of shame in a child precedes all knowledge of consequences, what is that to the question respecting a moral sense? *w*Is the sense of shame the same thing*w* with a moral sense? A child is ashamed of doing what he is told is wrong; but so is he also ashamed of doing what he knows is right, if he expects to be laughed at for doing it; he is ashamed of being duller than another child, of being ugly, of being poor, of not having fine clothes, of not being able to run, or wrestle, or box so well as another. He is ashamed of whatever causes him to be thought less of by the persons who surround him. This feeling of shame is accounted for by

[*Cf. Sedgwick, p. 67.]

*u–u*35,59   making
*v–v*35   to
*w–w*35   Has the sense of shame anything to do

obvious associations; but suppose it to be innate, what would that prove in favour of a moral sense? If all that Mr. Sedgwick can show for a moral sense is the sense of shame, *it might well be supposed* that all our moral senti-ments are the result of opinions which come to us from without; since the sense of shame so obviously follows the opinion of others, and, at least in *y* early years, is wholly determined by it.

On the Professor's first argument no more needs *here* be said. His second is the following: that moral feelings cannot "come of mere teaching," because they do not grow up gradually, but are often strongest in very early life.

Now, this is, in the first place, a mistaking of the matter in dispute. *The Professor is not arguing with Mandeville, or with the rhetoricians in Plato.* Nobody *b*, with whom he is concerned,*b* says that moral feelings "come of mere teaching." It is not pretended that they are factitious and artificial asso-ciations, inculcated by parents and teachers purposely to further certain social ends, and no more congenial to our natural feelings than the contrary associations. The idea of the pain of another is naturally painful; the idea of the pleasure of another is naturally pleasurable. From this *fact* in our natural constitution, *d* all our affections both of love and aversion towards human beings, in so far as they are different from those we *e* entertain towards mere inanimate objects which are pleasant or disagreeable to us *f*, are held, by the best teachers of the theory of utility, to originate*f*. In this, the unselfish part of our nature, lies a foundation, even independently of inculcation from without, for the generation of moral feelings.

But if, because it is not inconsistent with the constitution of our nature that moral feelings should grow up independently of teaching, Mr. Sedgwick would infer that they generally do so, or that teaching is not the source of almost all the moral feeling which exists in the world, his assertion is a piece of sentimentality completely at variance with the facts. If by saying that "moral feelings are often strongest in very early life," Mr. Sedgwick means that they are strongest in children, he only proves his *g* ignorance of children. Young children have affections, but *h*not*h* moral feelings; and children whose will is never resisted, never acquire them. There is no selfishness equal to *i*that*i* of children, as every one who is acquainted with children well knows. It is not *j* the hard, cold selfishness of a grown person, for the most affectionate children have it *k*, where their affection is not supplying a counter-impulse*k*;

*x–x*35	we might well suppose	*y*35	our
z–z+59,67		*a–a*+59,67	
b–b+59,67		*c–c*35	foundation
*d*35	arise	*e*35	might
f–f+59,67		*g*35	entire
*h–h*35	no	*i–i*35	the selfishness
*j*35	, indeed,	*k–k*35	equally

but the most selfish of grown persons does not come up to a child in the reckless seizing of any pleasure to himself, regardless of the consequences to others. The pains of others, though naturally painful to us, are not so until we have realized them by an act of imagination, implying voluntary attention; and that no *very young* child ever pays, while under the impulse of a present desire. If a child restrains the indulgence of any wish, it is either from affection or sympathy, which are quite other feelings than those of morality; or else (whatever Mr. Sedgwick may think) because he has been *taught* to do so. And he only learns the habit gradually, and in proportion to the assiduity and skill of the teaching.

The assertion that "moral feelings are often strongest in very early life," is true in no sense but one which confirms what it is brought to refute. The time of life at which moral feelings are apt to be strongest, is the age when we cease to be merely members of our own families, and begin to have intercourse with the world; that is, when the teaching has continued longest in one direction, and has not commenced in any other direction. When we go forth into the world, and meet with teaching, both by precept and example, of an opposite tendency to that which we have been used to, the feeling begins to weaken. Is this a sign of its being wholly independent of teaching? Has a boy quietly educated in *a well-regulated home*, or one who has been at a public school, the strongest moral feelings?

Enough has probably been said on the Professor's second argument. *His third* is, that teaching may strengthen our natural faculties, and call forth those which are powerless because untried; but cannot create a faculty which does not exist; cannot, therefore, have created the moral faculty.

It is surprising that Mr. Sedgwick should not see that his argument begs the question in dispute. To prove that our moral judgments are innate, he assumes that they proceed from a distinct faculty. But this is precisely what the adherents of the principle of utility deny. They contend that the morality of actions is perceived by the same faculties by which we perceive any other of the qualities of actions, namely, our intellects and our senses. They *hold* the capacity of perceiving moral distinctions *to be* no more a *distinct* faculty than the capacity of trying causes, or of making a speech to a jury. This last is a very peculiar power, yet no one says that it must have preexisted in Sir James Scarlett before he was called to the bar, because teaching and practice cannot create a new faculty. They can create a new power; and a faculty is but a finer name for a power. *Mr. Sedgwick loses sight of the very

l–l+59,67

*n–n*35   the parental house

*p–p*35   We proceed to his third. This

*r–r*35   is

*t–t*35   [*in footnote; see JSM's note to* powerless *below*]

*m–m*35,59   *taught*

*o–o*35   We have said enough, we think,

*q–q*35   contend that

*s–s*35   peculiar

meaning of the word faculty—*facultas*. He talks of a faculty "powerless because untried."[*] A power powerless![*]

The only colour for representing our moral judgments as the result of a peculiar part of our nature, is that our feelings of moral approbation and disapprobation are really peculiar feelings. But is it not notorious that peculiar feelings, unlike any others which we have experience of, are created by association every day? What does the Professor think of the feelings of ambition; the desire of power over our fellow-creatures, and the pleasure of its possession and exercise? These are peculiar feelings. But they are obviously generated by the law of association, from the connexion between power over our fellow-creatures and the gratification of almost all our other inclinations. What will the Professor say of the chivalrous point of honour? What of the feelings of envy and jealousy? What of the feelings of ᵘtheᵘ miser to his gold? Who ever looked upon these last as the subject of a distinct natural faculty? Their origin in association is obvious to all the world. Yet they are feelings as peculiar, as unlike any other part of our nature, as the feelings of conscience.

It will hardly be believed that what we have now answered is all that Mr. Sedgwick advances, to prove the principle of utility untrue; yet such is the fact. Let us now see whether he is more successful in proving the pernicious consequences of the principle, and the "degrading effect" which it produces "on the temper and conduct of those who adopt it."[†]

The Professor's talk is more indefinite, and the few ideas he has are more overlaid with declamatory phrases, on this point, than even on the preceding one. We can, however, ᵛ descry through the mist some faint semblance of two tangible objections: one, that the principle of utility is not suited to man's capacity—that if we were ever so desirous of applying it correctly, we should not be capable; the other, that it debases the moral practice of those who

---

[*Sedgwick, p. 55.]

*We cannot help referring the Professor back to Locke, and to that very chapter "On Power" which he singles out for peculiar objurgation. We recommend to his special attention the admirable remarks in that chapter on the abuse of the word "faculty." [*Of Human Understanding*, Bk. II, Chap. xxi, § 6; *Works*, Vol. I, pp. 239–40.] [35   *as* 67 . . . "faculty." [*paragraph*] Mr. Sedgwick falls into the blunder of the prevailing sect among the Schoolmen of the middle ages, the people called the Realists. These people gave to some classes of objects the name *species*, to others not; and then imagined that the classes to which they had given a peculiar name had a peculiar nature. Mr. Sedgwick gives to some of the powers of the mind the name faculties, to others not; and then falls into a like error. He loses sight of the very meaning of the word faculty—*facultas*. He talks of a faculty "powerless because untried." A power powerless!]

[†Sedgwick, p. vii.]

ᵘ⁻ᵘ35   a   ᵛ35   dimly

adopt it—which seems to imply (strange as the assertion is) that ᵂtheᵂ adoption of it as a principle ˣis not consistent with an attemptˣ to apply it correctly.

We must quote Mr. Sedgwick's very words, or it would hardly be believed that we quote him fairly:—

Independently of the bad effects produced on the moral character of man, by a system which makes expediency (in whatever sense the word be used) the test of right and wrong, we may affirm, on a more general view, that the rule itself is utterly unfitted to his capacity. Feeble as man may be, he forms a link in a chain of moral causes, ascending to the throne of God; and trifling as his individual acts may seem, he tries in vain to follow out their consequences as they go down into the countless ages of coming time. Viewed in this light, every act of man is woven into a moral system, ascending through the past—descending to the future—and preconceived in the mind of the Almighty. Nor does this notion, as far as regards ourselves, end in mere quietism and necessity. For we know right from wrong, and have that liberty of action which implies responsibility; and, as far as we are allowed to look into the ways of Providence, it seems compatible with his attributes to use the voluntary acts of created beings, as second causes in working out the ends of his own will. Leaving, however, out of question that stumbling-block which the prescience of God has often thrown in the way of feeble and doubting minds, we are, at least, certain, that man has not foreknowledge to trace the consequences of a single action of his own; and hence that utility (in the highest sense of which the word is capable) is, as a test of right and wrong, unfitted to his understanding, and therefore worthless in its application. (Pp. 63–4.)

Mr. Sedgwick appears to be one of that numerous class who never take the trouble to set before themselves fairly ʸanʸ opinion which they have an aversion to. Who ever said that it was necessary to foresee all the consequences of each individual action, "as they go down into the countless ages of coming time?" Some of the consequences of an action are accidental; others are its natural result, according to the known laws of the universe. The former, for the most part, cannot be foreseen; but the whole course of human life is founded upon the fact that the latter can. In what reliance do we ply our several trades—in what reliance do we buy or sell, eat or drink, write books or read them, walk, ride, speak, think, except on our foresight of the consequences of those actions? The commonest person lives according to maxims of prudence wholly founded on foresight of consequences; and we are told by a wise man from Cambridge, that the foresight of consequences, as a rule to guide ourselves by, is impossible! Our foresight of consequences is not perfect. Is anything else in our constitution perfect? *Est quodam prodire tenus, si non datur ultra: Non possis oculo quantum contendere Lynceus; Non tamen idcirco contemnas lippus*

---

w–w35   their
x–x35   inspires them with a desire *not*
y–y35   any

inungi.[*] If the Professor quarrels with such means of guiding our conduct as *we are gifted with*, it is incumbent on him to show that, in point of fact, *we have been provided* with better. Does the moral sense, allowing its existence, point out any surer practical rules? If so, let us have them in black and white. If nature has given us rules which suffice for our conduct, without any consideration of the probable consequences of our actions, produce them. But no; for two thousand years, nature's moral code has been a topic for declamation, and no one has yet produced a single chapter of it: nothing but a few elementary generalities, which are the mere alphabet of a morality founded upon utility. Hear Bishop Butler, the oracle of the moral-sense school, and whom our author quotes:—

However much men may have disputed about the nature of virtue, and whatever ground for doubt there may be about particulars, yet in general there is an universally acknowledged standard of it. It is that which all ages and all countries have made a profession of in public; it is that which every man you meet puts on the show of; it is that which the primary and fundamental laws of all civil constitutions over the face of the earth make it their business and endeavour to enforce the practice of upon mankind: namely, justice, veracity, and regard to the common good. (P. 130.) [†]

Mr. Sedgwick praises Butler for not being more explanatory.* Did Butler, then, or does Mr. Sedgwick, seriously believe that mankind have not sufficient foresight of consequences to perceive the advantage of "justice, veracity, and regard to the common good?" That, without a peculiar faculty, they would not be able to see that these qualities are useful to them?

When, indeed, the question arises, *what is* justice?—that is, what are those claims of others which we are bound to respect? and *what is* the conduct required by "regard to the common good?" the solutions which we can deduce from our foresight of consequences are not infallible. But let any one try those which he can deduce from the moral sense. Can *he* deduce any? Show us, written in the human heart, any answer to *these*

[*Horace. *Epistle* I, ll. 32, 28–9; in *Opera*. Glasgow: Mundell, 1796.]

[†See Joseph Butler. "Of the Nature of Virtue," in *The Analogy of Religion, Natural and Revealed, to the Constitution and Course of Nature*. London: Knapton, 1736, p. 310.]

*"Here everything," says he, "remains indefinite: yet all the successive propositions have their meaning. The author knew well that the things he had to deal with were indefinite, and that he could not fetter them in the language of a formal definition, without violating their nature. But how small has been the number of moral writers who have understood the real value of this forbearance!" [Sedgwick, pp. 130–1.]

z–z35   God has given us
a–a35   God has thought fit to furnish us   b–b35   we

questions. Bishop Butler gives up the point; and Mr. Sedgwick praises him for doing so. When Mr. Sedgwick wants something definite, to oppose to the indefiniteness of a morality founded on utility, he has recourse not to the moral sense, but to Christianity. With such fairness as this does he hold the *c*balance*c* between the two principles: he supposes his moral-sense man provided with all the guidance which can be derived from a revelation from heaven, and his *d*utilitarian*d* destitute of any such help. When one sees the question so stated, one cannot wonder at any conclusion. Need we say that Revelation, as a means of supplying the uncertainty of human *e*judgment*e*, is as open to one of the two parties as to the other? Need we say that Paley, the very author who, in this *Discourse*, is treated as the representative of *f*the utilitarian system*f*, appeals to Revelation throughout? and *g*obtains*g* no credit from Mr. Sedgwick for it, but the contrary; for Revelation, it seems, may be referred to in aid of the moral sense, but not to assist or rectify our judgments of utility.

The truth, however, is, that Revelation *h*(if by Revelation be meant the New Testament)*h*, as Paley *i* justly observed, *j*enters little into*j* the details of ethics. Christianity does not deliver a code of morals, any more than a code of laws. Its practical morality is altogether indefinite, and was meant to be so. This indefiniteness has been considered by some of the ablest defenders of Christianity as one of its most signal merits, and among the strongest proofs of its divine origin: being the quality which fits it to be an universal religion, and distinguishes it both from the Jewish dispensation, and from all other religions, which as they invariably enjoin, under their most awful sanctions, acts which are only locally or temporarily useful, are in their own nature local and temporary. Christianity, on the contrary, influences *k*the conduct*k* by shaping the character itself: it aims at so elevating and purifying the desires, that there shall be no hindrance to the fulfilment of our duties when recognised; but of what our duties are, at least in regard to outward acts, it says very little but what *l*moralists in general*l* have said. If, therefore, we would have any definite morality at all, we must perforce resort to that "foresight of consequences," of the difficulties of which the Professor has so formidable an idea.

But this talk about uncertainty is mere exaggeration. There *m*would be great*m* uncertainty if each individual had all to do for himself, and only his own experience to guide him. But we are not so situated. Every one directs himself in morality, as in all his conduct, not by his own unaided

*c–c*35	scale	
*e–e*35	reason	
*g–g*35	gets	
*i*35	has	
*k–k*35	our actions only	
*m–m*35	might be	

*d–d*35	"utilitarian"	
*f–f*35	"the utilitarian system"	
h–h+59,67		
*i–i*35	gives little guidance in	
*l–l*35	all moralists	

foresight, but by the accumulated wisdom of all former ages, [n]embodied in[n] traditional aphorisms. So strong is the disposition to submit to the authority of such traditions, and so little danger is there [o], in most conditions of mankind,[o] of erring on the other side, that the absurdest customs are perpetuated through a lapse of ages from no other cause. A hundred millions of human beings think it the most exalted virtue to swing by a hook before an idol, and the most dreadful pollution to drink cow-broth—only because their forefathers thought so. A Turk thinks it the height of indecency for women to [p]be seen[p] in the streets unveiled; and when [q]he is told[q] that in some countries [r]this happens[r] without any evil result, he shakes his head and says, "If you hold butter to the fire it will melt." Did not many generations of the most educated men in Europe believe every line of Aristotle to be infallible? So difficult is it to break loose from a received opinion. The progress of experience, and the growth of the human intellect, succeed but too slowly in correcting and improving traditional opinions. There is little fear, truly, that the mass of mankind should insist upon "tracing the consequences of actions" by their own unaided lights;—they are but too ready to let it be done for them once for all, and to think they have nothing to do with rules of morality (as [s]Tory writers[s] say they have with the laws) but to obey them.

Mr. Sedgwick is master of [t]the stock[t] phrases of those who know nothing of the principle of utility but the name. To act upon rules of conduct, of which utility is recognised as the basis, he calls "waiting for the calculations of utility"—a thing, according to him, in itself immoral, since "to hesitate is to rebel."[*] On the same principle, navigating by rule instead of by instinct might be called waiting for the calculations of astronomy. [u]There seems no absolute necessity for putting off the calculations until the ship[u] is in the middle of the South [v]Sea.[v] Because a sailor has not verified all the computations in the Nautical Almanac, does he therefore "hesitate" to use it?

Thus far Mr. Sedgwick on the difficulties of the principle of utility, when we mean to apply it honestly. [w] But he further charges the principle with having a "debasing" and "degrading" effect.[†]

A word like "debasing," applied to anything which acts upon the mind, may mean several things. It may mean, making us unprincipled; regardless of the rights and feelings of other people. It may mean, making us slavish;

[*Sedgwick, p. 61.]
[†*Ibid.*, p. 63.]

*n–n*35 in the form of
o–o+59,67
*p–p*35 walk
*q–q*35 you tell him
*r–r*35 they do so
*s–s*35 the Tories
*t–t*35 all the hack
*u–u*35 Who puts off his calculations till the vessel
*v–v*35 Sea?
*w*35 It will scarcely be required of us to say more on this part of the question.

spiritless, submissive to injury or insult; incapable of asserting our own rights, and vindicating the just independence of our minds and actions. It may mean, making us cowardly; slothful; incapable of bearing pain, or nerving ourselves to exertion for a worthy object. It may mean, making us narrow-minded; pusillanimous, in Hobbes's sense of the word: [*] too intent upon little things to feel rightly about great ones: incapable of having our imagination fired by a grand object of contemplation; incapable of thinking, feeling, aspiring, or acting, on any but a small scale. An opinion which produced any of these effects upon the mind would be rightly called debasing. But when, without proving, or even in plain terms asserting, that it produces these effects, or any effects which he can make distinctly understood, a man merely says of an opinion that it is debasing,—all he really says is, that he has a *feeling, which he cannot exactly describe, but upon which he values himself, and to which the opinion is in some way or other offensive*. What definite proposition concerning the effect of any doctrine on the mind can be extracted from such a passage as this?—

If expediency be the measure of right, and every one claim the liberty of judgment, virtue and vice have no longer any fixed relations to the moral condition of man, but change with the fluctuations of opinion. Not only are his actions tainted by prejudice and passion, but his rule of life, under this system, must be tainted in like degree—must be brought down to *its* own level: for he will no longer be able, compatibly with his principles, to separate the rule from its application. No high and unvarying standard of morality, which his heart approves, however infirm his practice, will be offered to his thoughts. But his bad passions will continue to do their work in bending him to the earth; and unless he be held upright by the strong power of religion (an extrinsic power which I am not now considering), he will inevitably be carried down, by a degrading standard of action, to a sordid and grovelling life. It may perhaps be said, that we are arguing against a rule, only from its misapprehension and abuse. But we reply, that every precept is practically bad when its abuse is natural and inevitable— that the system of utility brings down virtue from a heavenly throne, and places her on an earthly tribunal, where her decisions, no longer supported by any holy sanction, are distorted by judicial ignorance, and tainted by base passion. (P. 63.)

What does this tell us? First, that if utility be the standard, different persons may have different opinions on morality. This is the talk about uncertainty, which *has been* already disposed of. Next, *a* that where there is uncertainty, men's passions will bias their judgment. Granted; this is one of the evils of our condition, and must be borne with. We do not diminish it by pretending that nature tells us what is right, when nobody ever ventures to set down what

[*Leviathan. In *The English Works of Thomas Hobbes*. Ed. William Molesworth. London: Bohn, 1839–45, Vol. III, p. 79.]

*x–x*35   dislike to the opinion, and that he does not know why, but finding himself dislike it, concludes that it must be very bad
*y–y*Source, 35   his   *z–z*35   we have   *a*35   he says,

nature tells us, nor affects to expound her laws in any way but by an appeal to utility. All that the remainder of the passage does, is to repeat, in various phrases, that Mr. Sedgwick feels such a "standard of action" to be "degrading;" that Mr. Sedgwick feels it to be "sordid" and "grovelling." If so, nobody can compel Mr. Sedgwick to adopt it. If he feels it debasing, no doubt it would be so to him. But until he is able to show some reason why it must be so to others, may we be permitted to suggest, that perhaps the cause of its being so to himself, is only that he does not understand it?

Read this:—

Christianity considers every act grounded on mere worldly consequences as built on a false foundation. The mainspring of every virtue is placed by it in the affections, called into renewed strength by a feeling of self-abasement—by gratitude for an immortal benefit—by communion with God—and by the hopes of everlasting life. Humility is the foundation of the Christian's honour—distrust of self is the ground of his strength—and his religion tells him that every work of man is counted worthless in the sight of heaven, as the means of his pardon or the price of his redemption. Yet it gives him a pure and perfect rule of life; and does not for an instant exempt him from the duty of obedience to his rule: for it ever aims at a purgation of the moral faculties, and a renewal of the defaced image of God; and its moral precepts have an everlasting sanction. And thus does Christian love become an efficient and abiding principle—not tested by the world, but above the world; yet reaching the life-spring of every virtuous deed, and producing in its season a harvest of good and noble works incomparably more abundant than ever rose from any other soil.

The utilitarian scheme starts, on the contrary, with an abrogation of the authority of conscience—a rejection of the moral feelings as the test of right and wrong. From first to last, it is in bondage to the world, measuring every act by a worldly standard, and estimating its value by worldly consequences. Virtue becomes a question of calculation—a matter of profit or loss; and if man gain heaven at all on such a system, it must be by arithmetical details—the computation of his daily work—the balance of his moral ledger. A conclusion such as this offends against the spirit breathing in every page of the book of life; yet is it fairly drawn from the principle of utility. It appears, indeed, not only to have been foreseen by Paley, but to have been accepted by him—a striking instance of the tenacity with which man ever clings to system, and is ready to embrace even its monstrous consequences rather than believe that he has himself been building on a wrong foundation. (Pp. 66–7.)

In a note, he adds,—

The following are the passages here referred to:—

'The Christian religion hath not ascertained *the precise quantity of virtue* necessary to salvation.'

'It has been said, that it can never be a just economy of Providence to admit one part of mankind into heaven, and condemn the other to hell; since there must be very little to choose between the worst man who is received into heaven, and the best who is excluded. And how know we, it might be answered, but that there may be as little to choose in their conditions?' (*Moral Philosophy*, Bk. I, Chap. vii [London: Tegg, 1824, 29, 30].)

In the latter years of his life, Paley would, I believe, have been incapable of uttering or conceiving sentiments such as these.

So that a "purgation of the moral faculties" is necessary: the moral feelings require to be corrected. Yet the moral feelings are "the test of right and wrong;" and whoever "rejects" them as a test, must be called hard names. But we do not want to convict Mr. Sedgwick of inconsistency; we want to get at his meaning. Have we come to it at last? The gravamen of the charge against the principle of utility seems to lie in a word. Utility is a *worldly* standard; and estimates every act by *worldly* consequences.

^bLike most persons who are speaking from their feelings only, on a subject on which they have never seriously thought, the Professor is imposed upon by words. He is carried away by an ambiguity.^b To make his assertion about the *worldliness* of the standard of utility, true, it must be understood in one sense; to make it have the invidious effect which is intended, it must be understood in another. By "worldly," does he mean to ^cimply^c what is commonly meant when ^dthe word is used^d as a reproach—an undue regard to interest in the vulgar sense, our wealth, power, social position, and the like, our command over agreeable outward objects, and over the opinion and good offices of other people? If so, to call utility a worldly standard is ^eto misrepresent the doctrine^e. It is not true that utility estimates actions by this sort of consequences; it estimates them by ^fall^f their consequences. If he means that the principle of utility regards only (to use a scholastic distinction) the *objective* consequences of actions, and omits the *subjective*; attends to the effects on our outward condition, and that of other people, too much—to those on our internal sources of happiness or unhappiness, too little; this criticism is, as we have already remarked, in some degree applicable to Paley; but to charge this blunder upon the principle of utility, would be to say, that if ^git is your rule to^g judge of a thing by ^h its consequences, you will judge only by ^ia portion of them^i. Again, if Mr. Sedgwick meant to speak of a "worldly standard" in contradistinction to a religious standard, and to say that if we adopt the principle of utility, we cannot admit religion as a sanction for it, or cannot attach ^j importance to religious motives or feelings, the assertion would be simply false, and a gross ^kinjustice even to^k Paley. What, therefore, can Mr. Sedgwick mean? ^lMerely^l this: that our actions take place in the world; that

---

^b–b35 The Professor is like other persons whose intellects are not used to grapple with things: all his feelings hang upon words. There is nothing you might not disgust him with, if, by taking advantage even of an ambiguity, you could fasten upon it a bad word.

^c–c35	insinuate	
^e–e35	misrepresentation	
^g–g35	you	
^i–i35	some	
^k–k35	calumny even against	

^d–d35 we use the word
^f–f35 *all*
^h35 all
^j35 the fitting
^l–l35 Simply

their consequences are produced in the world; that *mwe have been placed^m* in the world; and that there, if anywhere, we must earn a place in heaven. The morality founded on utility allows this, certainly: does Mr. Sedgwick's system of morality deny it?

Mark the *nconfusion of ideas^n* involved in this sentence: "Christianity considers every act grounded on mere worldly consequences as built on a false foundation." What is saving a father from death, but saving him from a worldly consequence? What are healing the sick, clothing the naked, sheltering the houseless, but acts which wholly consist in producing a worldly consequence? Confine Mr. Sedgwick to unambiguous words, and he is already answered. What is really true is, that Christianity considers no act as meritorious which is done from mere worldly *motives*; that is, which is in no degree prompted by the desire of our own moral perfection, or of the *oapprobation^o* of a perfect being. These motives, we need scarcely observe, may be equally powerful, whatever be our standard of morality, provided we believe that the Deity approves it.

Mr. Sedgwick is scandalized at the supposition that the place awarded to each of us in the next world will depend on the balance of the good and evil of our lives. According to his notions of justice, we presume, it ought to depend wholly upon one of the two. As usual, Mr. Sedgwick begins by a misapprehension; he neither understands Paley, nor the conclusion which, he says, is "fairly drawn from the principles of utility." Paley held, with *pother^p* Christians, that our place hereafter would be determined by our degree of moral perfection; that is, by the balance, not of our good and evil *qdeeds^q*, which depend upon opportunity and temptation, but of our good and evil *rdispositions^r*; by the intensity and continuity of our *will* to do good; by the strength with which we have *struggled* to be virtuous; not by our accidental lapses, or by the unintended good or evil which has followed from our actions. When Paley said that Christianity has not ascertained "the precise quantity of virtue necessary to salvation," he did not mean the number or kind of beneficial actions; he meant, that Christianity has not decided what positive strength of virtuous inclinations, and what capacity of resisting temptations, will procure acquittal at the tribunal of God. And most *swisely^s* is this left undecided. Nor can there be a solution more consistent with the attributes which Christianity ascribes to the Deity, than Paley's own—that every step *tof advance^t* in *uthe direction of^u* moral perfection, will be something gained towards *v* everlasting welfare.

The remainder of Mr. Sedgwick's argument—if argument it can be called

*m–m*35 God has placed us	*n–n*35 trick of words
*o–o*35 favour	*p–p*35 all
*q–q*35,59 *deeds*	*r–r*35,59 *dispositions*
*s–s*35 rightly	*t–t*35 we gain
u–u+67	*v*35 our

—is a perpetual *ignoratio elenchi*. He lumps up the principle of utility—which is a theory of right and wrong—with the theory, if there be such a theory, of the universal selfishness of mankind. We never know, for many sentences together, which of the two he is arguing against; he never seems to know it himself. He begins a sentence on the one, and ends it on the other. In his mind they seem to be one and the same. Read this:—

Utilitarian philosophy and Christian ethics have in their principles and motives no common bond of union, and ought never to have been linked together in one system: for, palliate and disguise the difference as we may, we shall find at last that they rest on separate foundations; one deriving all its strength from the moral feelings, and the other from the selfish passions of our nature. (P. 67.)

Or this:—

If we suppress the authority of conscience, reject the moral feelings, rid ourselves of the sentiments of honour, and sink (as men too often do) below the influence of religion; and if, at the same time, we are taught to think that utility is the universal test of right and wrong; what is there left within us as an antagonist power to the craving of passion, or the base appetite of worldly gain? In such a condition of the soul, all motive not terminating in mere passion becomes utterly devoid of meaning. On this system, the sinner is no longer abhorred as a rebel against his better nature—as one who profanely mutilates the image of God: he acts only on the principles of other men, but he blunders in calculating the chances of his personal advantage: and thus we deprive virtue of its holiness, and vice of its deformity; humanity of its honour, and language of its meaning; we shut out, as no better than madness or folly, the loftiest sentiments of the heathen as well as of the Christian world; and all that is great or generous in our nature droops under the influence of a cold and withering selfishness. (Pp. 76–7.)

*w*Every line of this passage convicts Mr. Sedgwick of never having taken the trouble to know the meaning of the terms in which the doctrine he so eagerly vilifies is conveyed.*w* What has "calculating the chances of personal advantage" to do with the principle of utility? The object of Mr. Sedgwick is, to represent that principle as leading to the conclusion, that a vicious man is no more a subject of disapprobation than a person who blunders in a question of prudence. If Mr. Sedgwick did but know what the principle of utility is, he would see that it leads to no such conclusion. Some people have been led to that conclusion, not by the principle of utility, but *x*either by the doctrine of philosophical necessity, incorrectly understood, or*x* by a theory of motives, which has been called the selfish theory; and even from that it does not justly follow.

The finery about shutting out "lofty sentiments" scarcely deserves notice.

---

*w–w*35   A writer who heaps abuse in this style upon an opinion, and upon those who profess it, when every word he writes proves that he has never taken the trouble even to know the meaning of the terms in which it is conveyed, is not free from moral culpability.
x–x+59,67

It resembles what ^{y}is said^y in the next page [77] about "suppressing all the kindly emotions which minister to virtue." ^{z}We are far from charging Mr. Sedgwick with^z wilful misrepresentation, but ^{a}this^a is the very next thing to it—misrepresentation in voluntary ignorance. Who proposes to suppress ^{b}any "kindly emotion?"^{b} Human beings, the Professor may be assured, will always love and honour every sentiment, whether "lofty" or otherwise, which is either directly pointed to their good, or tends to raise the mind above the influence of the petty objects for the sake of which mankind injure one another. The Professor is afraid that the sinner will be "no longer abhorred." We imagined that it was not the sinner who should be abhorred, but sin. Mankind, however, are sufficiently ready to abhor whatever is obviously noxious to them. A human being filled with malevolent dispositions, or coldly indifferent to the feelings of his fellow-creatures, will never, the Professor may assure himself, be amiable in their eyes. Whether they will speak of him as "a rebel against his better nature,"—"one who profanely mutilates the image of God," and so on, will depend upon whether they are proficients in commonplace rhetoric. But whatever words they use, rely on it that, while men dread and abhor a wolf or a serpent, which have no better nature, and no image of God to mutilate, they will abhor with infinitely greater intensity a human being who, outwardly resembling themselves, is inwardly their enemy, and, being far more powerful than "toad or asp,"[*] voluntarily cherishes the same ^{c}disposition to mischief^c.

If utility be the standard, "the end," in the Professor's opinion, "will be made to sanctify the means" (p. 78). We answer—just so far as in any other system, and no ^{d}farther^d. In every system of morality, the end, when good, justifies all means which do not conflict with some more important good. On Mr. Sedgwick's own scheme, are there not ends which sanctify actions, in other cases deserving the utmost abhorrence—such, for instance, as taking the life of a fellow-creature in cold blood, in the face of the whole people? According to the principle of utility, the end justifies all means necessary to its attainment, except those which are more mischievous than the end is useful ^{e}; an exception amply sufficient.^{e}

We have now concluded our ^{f}examination^f of Mr. Sedgwick: first, as a commentator on the studies which form part of a liberal education; and

[*John Milton. Sonnet XI, ll. 12–14. In *The Poetical Works*. London: Tonson, 1695, p. 25 of *Poems Upon Several Occasions*.]

y–y35	he says	z–z35	This may not be
a–a35	it	b–b35	a single kindly emotion?
c–c35	dispositions to evil	d–d35	further
e–e35	. What fault can the Professor find with this?		
f–f35	exhibition		

next, as an assailant of the "utilitarian theory of morals." We have shown
that, on the former subject, he has omitted almost everything which ought
to have been said; that almost all which he has said is trivial, and much
of it ^{g}erroneous^g. With regard to the other part of his design, we have
shown that he has not only failed ^{h} to refute the doctrine that human happiness is the foundation of morality, but has, in the attempt, proved himself
not to understand what the doctrine is; ^{i} and to be capable of ^{j}bringing the
most serious charges against^j other men's opinions, and themselves, ^{k}which
even a smattering of the knowledge appropriate to the subject, would have
shown to be groundless^k.

^{l}We by no means affect to consider Mr. Sedgwick as (what he would not
himself claim to be) a sufficient advocate of the cause he has espoused, nor
pretend that his pages contain the best that can be said, or even the best that
has been said, against the theory of utility. That theory numbers among its
enemies, minds of almost every degree of power and intellectual accomplishments; among whom many are capable of making out a much better apparent
case for their opinion. But Mr. Sedgwick's is a fair enough sample of the
popular arguments against the theory; his book has had more readers and
more applauders than a better book would have had, because it is level with
a lower class of capacities: and though, by pointing out its imperfections, we
do little to establish our own opinion, it is something to have shown on how
light grounds, in some cases, men of gravity and reputation arraign the
opinion, and are admired and applauded for so arraigning it.^{l}

The question is not one of pure speculation. Not to mention the importance, to those who are entrusted with the education of the moral sentiments,
of just views respecting their origin and nature; we may remark that, upon
the truth or falseness of the doctrine of a moral sense, it depends whether
morality is a fixed or a progressive body of doctrine. If it be true that man

---

$^{g-g}$35 false
^{h}35 miserably
^{i}35 to be ignorant of almost everything which it is peculiarly incumbent upon a
philosopher to know;
$^{j-j}$35 blackening
$^{k-k}$35 without the slightest pretensions to a knowledge of either
$^{l-l}$35 Such is a man whom general opinion places in the foremost rank of Cambridge minds. Such, if we might judge from this specimen, is Cambridge herself.
It would be unjust, however, even to Cambridge, to assume that she, in reality, produces no minds entitled to look down upon such a specimen of thinking and writing as
this *Discourse*. We trust there are, and that they are ashamed of it. Neither do we
impute to all who reject, even in the most violent manner, the principle of utility, such
a character of intellect as, after the above evidence, we cannot help assigning to Mr.
Sedgwick. We know that there are among them minds of almost every degree of power
and intellectual accomplishments. But we have never heard one of their arguments
which did not appear to us unworthy of such men; and although they are far from
coinciding in all Mr. Sedgwick's sentiments, yet in answering him, we have often, by
implication, answered them.

has a sense given him to determine what is right and wrong, it follows that his moral judgments and feelings cannot be susceptible of any improvement; such as they are they ought to remain. The question, what mankind in general *ought* to think and feel on the subject of their duty, must be determined by observing what, when no interest or passion can be seen to bias them, they think and feel already. *n* According to the theory of utility, on the contrary, the question, what is our duty, is as open to discussion as any other question. Moral doctrines are no more to be received without evidence, *nor* to be sifted less carefully, than any other doctrines. An appeal lies, as on all other subjects, from a received opinion, however generally entertained, to the decisions of cultivated reason. The weakness of human intellect, and all the other infirmities of our nature, are considered to interfere as much with the rectitude of our judgments on morality, as on any other of our concerns; and changes as great are anticipated in our opinions on that subject, as on every other, both from the progress of intelligence, from more authentic and enlarged experience, and from alterations in the condition of the human race, requiring altered rules of conduct.

It deeply concerns the greatest interests of our race, that the only mode of treating ethical questions which *aims* at correcting existing maxims, and rectifying any of the perversions of existing feeling, should not be borne down by clamour. *r* The contemners of analysis have long enough had all the pretension to themselves. They have had the monopoly of the claim to pure, and lofty, and sublime principles; and those who gave reasons to justify their feelings have submitted to be cried down as low, and cold, and degraded. We hope they will submit no longer *s*; and not content with meeting the metaphysics of their more powerful adversaries by profounder metaphysics, will join battle in the field of popular controversy with every antagonist of name and reputation, even when, as in the present case, his name and reputation are his only claims to be heard on such a subject.*s*

*m–m*35   *ought*

*n*35   Accordingly this is an admirable doctrine for those who have hitherto, by education and government, had the framing of the opinions and feelings of mankind mainly in their own hands. A general prejudice may, on this scheme, be at any time erected, by those who are disinterestedly attached to it, or by those whose convenience it suits, into a law of our universal nature. [*paragraph*]

*o–o*35   or

*p–p*35   The question, therefore, is of the utmost importance. And it

*q–q*35   even *aims*

*r*35   All who do not think the morality taught to English gentlemen at English universities perfect, are interested in withstanding the attempt.

*s–s*35   . Our part, at least, shall not be wanting; and whoever shall hereafter deal with this question in Mr. Sedgwick's manner, may expect, if he be a person whose reputation or influence render it needful, a no less unsparing exposure.

BENTHAM

1838

EDITOR'S NOTE

D&D, I (1867), 330–92, with footnote to title: "*London and Westminster Review*, August 1938." Reprinted from *London and Westminster Review*, 7 & 29 (Aug., 1838), 467–506, signed "A" and headed: "Art. XI.—*The Works of Jeremy Bentham*: now first collected, under the supervision of his Executor, John Bowring. Parts I to IV. Tait, Edinburgh. 1838." (These Parts appeared in the full edition in Vols. I and IV; for full details of the contents, see under Bentham, *Works*, in the Bibliographic Appendix, 512 below.) This number of the *London and Westminster* went into a second edition (probably because of this article); in the reprinting JSM added the final footnote (115n), but made no other changes. The second version appeared as an offprint, *An Estimate of Bentham's Philosophy* (London: printed by C. Reynell, 1838), with a title page, new pagination, and the running titles removed, but no other changes (it is still signed "A"). Described in JSM's bibliography as "An article on Bentham, in the London and Westminster Review for August 1838 (No. 6)" (MacMinn, 50).

There are no corrections or alterations in the Somerville College copies of the article, the offprint, and *D&D*. The following text is collated with that in *D&D* (1st ed.); those in the *London and Westminster*, 1st and 2nd eds.; and that of the offprint. In the footnoted variants, *D&D* (2nd ed.) is indicated by "67"; *D&D* (1st ed.) by "59"; and the *London and Westminster* by "38" (in the final footnote, "38²" indicates the 2nd ed. of the *London and Westminster*).

Bentham

THERE ARE two men, recently deceased, to whom their country is indebted
not only for the greater part of the important ideas which have been thrown
into circulation among its thinking men in their time, but for a revolution
in its general modes of thought and investigation. These men, dissimilar in
almost all else, agreed in being closet-students—secluded in a peculiar
degree, by circumstances and character, from the business and intercourse of
the world: and both were, through a large portion of their lives, regarded by
those who took the lead in opinion (when they happened to hear of them)
with feelings akin to contempt. But they were destined to renew a lesson
given to mankind by every age, and always disregarded—to show that speculative philosophy, which to the superficial appears a thing so remote from
the business of life and the outward interests of men, is in reality the thing
on earth which most influences them, and in the long run overbears every
other influence save those which it must itself obey. The writers of whom we
speak have never been read by the multitude; except for the more slight of
their works, their readers have been few: but they have been the teachers
of the teachers; there is hardly to be found in England an individual of any
importance in the world of mind, who (whatever opinions he may have
afterwards adopted) did not first learn to think from one of these two;
and though their influences have but begun to diffuse themselves through
these intermediate channels over society at large, there is already scarcely
a publication of any consequence addressed to the educated classes, which,
if these persons had not existed, would not have been ^a different from what
it is. These men are, Jeremy Bentham and Samuel Taylor Coleridge—the two
great seminal minds of England in their age.

No comparison is intended here between the minds or influences of these
remarkable men: this were impossible unless there were first formed a complete judgment of each, considered apart. It is our intention to attempt, on the
present occasion, an estimate of one of them; the only one, a complete
edition of whose works is yet in progress, and who, in the classification
which may be made of all writers into ^bProgressive^b and Conservative,

belongs to the same division with ourselves. For although they *c* were far too great men to be correctly designated by either appellation exclusively, yet in the main, Bentham was a *dProgressived* philosopher, Coleridge a Conservative one. The influence of the former has made itself felt chiefly *eon minds of the Progressive class;e* of the latter, on *fthose of the Conservative:f* and the two systems of concentric circles which the shock given by them is spreading over the ocean of mind, have only just begun to meet and intersect. The writings of both contain severe lessons to their own side, on many of the errors and faults they are *g* addicted to: but to Bentham it was given to discern more particularly those truths with which existing doctrines and institutions were at variance; to Coleridge, the neglected truths which lay *in* them.

A man of great knowledge of the world, and of the highest reputation for practical talent and sagacity among the official men of his time (himself no follower of Bentham, nor of any partial or exclusive school whatever) once said to us, as the result of his observation, that to Bentham more than to any other source might be traced the questioning spirit, the disposition to demand the *why* of everything, which had gained so much ground and was producing such important consequences in these *htimesh*. The more this assertion is examined, the more true it will be found. Bentham has been in this age and country the great questioner of things established. It is by the influence of the modes of thought with which his writings inoculated a considerable number of thinking men, that the yoke of authority has been broken, and innumerable opinions, formerly received on tradition as incontestable, are put upon their defence, and required to give an account of themselves. Who, before Bentham, (whatever controversies might exist on points of detail) dared to speak disrespectfully, in express terms, of the British Constitution, or the English Law? He did so; and his arguments and his example together encouraged others. We do not mean that his writings caused the Reform Bill, [*] or that the Appropriation Clause [†] owns him as its parent: the changes which have been made, and the greater changes which will be made, in our institutions, are not the work of philosophers, but of the interests and instincts of large portions of society recently grown into strength. But Bentham gave voice to those interests and instincts: until he spoke out, those who found our institutions unsuited to them did not dare to say so, did not

[*2 William IV, c. 45 (7 June, 1832).]
[†See 1&2 Victoria, c. 109 (15 August, 1838).]

*c*38 both	*d–d*38 Movement	
*e–e*38 upon Movement minds,	*f–f*38 Conservative ones;	
*g*38 most	*h–h*38 later days	

dare consciously to think so; they had never heard ⁱthe excellence ofⁱ those
institutions questioned by cultivated men, by men of acknowledged intellect;
and it is not in the nature of uninstructed minds to resist the united authority
of the instructed. Bentham broke the spell. It was not Bentham by his own
writings; it was Bentham through the minds and pens which those writings
fed—through the men in more direct contact with the world, into whom his
spirit passed. If the superstition about ancestorial wisdom has fallen into
decay; if the public are grown familiar with the idea that their laws and
institutions are ʲin great partʲ not the product of intellect and virtue, but of
modern corruption grafted upon ancient barbarism; if the hardiest innovation is no longer scouted ᵏbecauseᵏ it is an innovation—establishments no
longer considered sacred because they are establishments—it will be found
that those who have accustomed the public mind to these ideas have learnt
them in Bentham's school, and that the assault on ancient institutions has
been, and is, carried on for the most part with his weapons. It matters not
although these thinkers, or indeed thinkers of any description, have been but
scantily found among the persons prominently and ostensibly at the head of
the Reform movement. All movements, except ˡdirectlyˡ revolutionary ones,
are headed, not by those who originate them, but by those who know best
how to compromise between the old opinions and the new. The father of
English innovation, both in doctrines and in institutions, is Bentham: he is
the great *subversive*, or, in the language of continental philosophers, the
great *critical*, thinker of his age and country.

We consider this, however, to be not his highest title to fame. Were this
all, he were ᵐonlyᵐ to be ranked among the lowest order of the potentates of
mind—the negative, or destructive philosophers; those who can perceive
what is false, but not what is true; who awaken the human mind to the inconsistencies and absurdities of time-sanctioned opinions and institutions, but
substitute nothing in the place of what they take away. We have no desire to
undervalue the services of such persons: mankind have been deeply indebted
to them; nor will there ever be a lack of work for them, in a world in which
so many false things are believed, in which so many which have been true,
are believed long after they have ceased to be true. The qualities, however,
which fit men for perceiving anomalies, without perceiving the truths which
would rectify them, are not among the rarest of endowments. Courage,
verbal acuteness, command over the forms of argumentation, and a popular
style, will make, out of the shallowest man, with a sufficient lack of reverence,
a ⁿconsiderableⁿ negative philosopher. Such men have never been wanting in

ⁱ-ⁱ+59,67   ʲ-ʲ+59,67
ᵏ-ᵏ38,59 *because*   ˡ-ˡ+59,67
ᵐ-ᵐ+59,67   ⁿ-ⁿ38 first-rate

periods of culture; and the period in which Bentham formed his early impressions was emphatically their reign, in proportion to its barrenness in the more noble products of the human mind. An age of formalism in the Church and corruption in the State, when the most valuable part of the meaning of [o]traditional doctrines[o] had faded from the minds even of those who retained from habit a mechanical belief in them, was the time to raise up all kinds of sceptical philosophy. Accordingly, France had Voltaire, and his school of negative thinkers, and England [p](or rather Scotland)[p] had the profoundest negative thinker on record, David Hume: a man, the peculiarities of whose mind qualified him to detect failure of proof, and want of logical consistency, at a depth which French sceptics, with their comparatively feeble powers of analysis and abstraction, stopt far short of [q], and which German subtlety alone could thoroughly appreciate, or hope to rival.[q]

If Bentham had merely continued the work of Hume, he would scarcely have been heard of in philosophy; for he was far inferior to Hume in Hume's qualities, and was in no respect fitted to excel as a metaphysician. We must not look for subtlety, or the power of recondite analysis, among his intellectual characteristics. In the former quality, few great thinkers have ever been so deficient; and to find the latter, in any considerable measure, in a mind acknowledging any kindred with his, we must have recourse to the late Mr. Mill—a man who united [r] the great qualities of the metaphysicians of the eighteenth century, with others of a different complexion, admirably qualifying him to complete and correct their work. Bentham had not these peculiar gifts; but he possessed others, not inferior, which were not possessed by any of his precursors; which have made him a source of light to a generation which has far outgrown their influence, and, as we called him, the chief subversive thinker of an age which has long lost all that [s]they[s] could subvert.

To speak of him first as a merely negative philosopher—as one who refutes illogical arguments, exposes sophistry, detects contradiction and absurdity; even in that capacity there was a wide field left vacant for him by Hume,

o–o38 spiritual truths p–p+59,67

q–q38 : Hume, the prince of *dilettanti*, from whose writings one will hardly learn that there is such a thing as truth, far less that it is attainable; but only that the *pro* and *con* of everything may be argued with infinite ingenuity, and furnishes a fine intellectual exercise. This absolute scepticism in speculation very naturally brought him round to Toryism in practice; for if no faith can be had in the operations of human intellect, and one side of every question is about as likely as another to be true, a man will commonly be inclined to prefer that order of things which, being no more wrong than every other, he has hitherto found compatible with his private comforts. Accordingly Hume's scepticism agreed very well with the comfortable classes, until it began to reach the uncomfortable: when the discovery was made that, although men could be content to be rich without a faith, men would not be content to be poor without it, and religion and morality came into fashion again as the cheap defence of rent and tithes.

r38 all s–s38 *they*

and which he has occupied to an unprecedented extent; the field of practical abuses. This was Bentham's peculiar province: to this he was called by the whole bent of his disposition: to carry the warfare against absurdity into things practical. His was an essentially practical mind. It was by practical abuses that his mind was first turned to speculation—by the abuses of the profession which was chosen for him, that of the law. He has himself stated what particular abuse first gave that shock to his mind, the recoil of which has made the whole mountain of abuse totter; it was the custom of making the client pay for three attendances in the office of a Master in Chancery, when only one was given. The law, he found, on examination, was full of such things. But were these discoveries of his? No; they were known to every lawyer who *t* practised, to every judge who *u* sat on the bench, and neither before nor for long after did they cause any apparent uneasiness to the consciences of these learned persons, nor hinder them from asserting, whenever occasion offered, in books, in parliament, or on the bench, that the law was the perfection of reason. During so many generations, in each of which thousands of *v* educated young men were successively placed in Bentham's position and with Bentham's opportunities, he alone was found with sufficient moral sensibility and self-reliance to say *w*to himself*w* that these things, however profitable they might be, were frauds, and that between them and himself there should be a gulf fixed. To this rare union of self-reliance and moral sensibility we are indebted for all that Bentham has done. Sent to Oxford by his father at the unusually early age of fifteen—required, on admission, to declare his belief in the Thirty-nine Articles—he felt it necessary to examine them; and the examination suggested scruples, which he sought to get removed, but instead of the satisfaction he expected, was told that it was not for boys like him to set up their judgment against the great men of the Church. After a struggle, he signed; but the impression that he had done an immoral act, never left him; he considered himself to have *x*committed*x* a falsehood, and throughout life he never relaxed in his indignant denunciations of all laws which command such falsehoods, all institutions which attach rewards to *y* them.

By thus carrying the war of criticism and refutation, the conflict with falsehood and absurdity, into the field of practical evils, Bentham, even if he had done nothing else, would have earned an important place in the history of intellect. He carried on the warfare without intermission. To this, not only many of his most piquant chapters, but some of the most finished of his entire works, are entirely devoted: the *Defence of Usury*; the *Book of Fallacies*;

*t*38   ever
*v*38   well]   59   well-
*x–x*38   signed

*u*38   ever
*w–w*38   in his heart
*y*38   the telling of

and the onslaught upon Blackstone, published anonymously under the title of *A Fragment on Government*,[*] which, though a first production, and of a writer afterwards so much ridiculed for his style, excited the highest admiration no less for its composition than for its thoughts, and was attributed by turns to Lord Mansfield, to Lord Camden, and (by Dr. Johnson) to Dunning, one of the greatest masters of style among the lawyers of his day. These writings are altogether original; though of the negative school, they resemble nothing previously produced by negative philosophers; and would have sufficed to create for Bentham, among the subversive thinkers of modern Europe, a place peculiarly his own. But it is not these writings that constitute the real distinction between him and them. There was a deeper difference. It was that they were purely negative thinkers, he was positive: they only assailed error, he made it a point of conscience not to do so until he thought he could plant instead the corresponding truth. Their character was exclusively analytic, his was synthetic. They took for their starting-point the received opinion on any subject, dug round it with their logical implements, pronounced its foundations defective, and condemned it: he began *de novo*, laid his own foundations deeply and firmly, built up his own structure, and *z*bade*z* mankind compare the two; it was when he had solved the problem himself, or thought he had done so, that he declared all other solutions to be erroneous. Hence, what they *a*produced*a* will not last; it must perish, much of it has already perished, with the errors which it exploded: what he did has its own value, by which it must outlast all errors to which it is opposed. Though we may reject, as we often must, his practical conclusions, yet his premises, the collections of facts and observations from which his conclusions were drawn, remain for ever, a part of the materials of philosophy.

A place, therefore, must be assigned to Bentham among the masters of wisdom, the great teachers and permanent intellectual ornaments of the human race. He is among those who have enriched mankind with imperishable gifts; and although these do not transcend all other gifts, nor entitle him to those honours "above all Greek, above all Roman fame,"[†] which by a natural reaction against the neglect and contempt of the *b*ignorant, many*b* of his admirers were once disposed to accumulate upon him, yet to refuse an admiring recognition of what he was, on account of what he was not, is a much worse error, and one which, pardonable in the vulgar, is no longer permitted to any cultivated and instructed mind.

[*Defence of Usury. London: Payne, 1787; The Book of Fallacies. London: Hunt, 1824; A Fragment on Government. London: Payne, 1776.]
[†Alexander Pope. Satires and Epistles of Horace Imitated, "Epistles," Bk. II, Epistle I, l. 26; in Works. New ed. Ed. Joseph Warton, et al. 10 vols. London: Priestley, 1822–25, Vol. IV, p. 149.]

z–z38   bid   a–a38   did   b–b38   world, some few

If we were asked to say, in the fewest possible words, ᶜwhatᶜ we conceive to be Bentham's place among these great intellectual benefactors of humanity; what he was, and what he was not; what kind of service he did and did not render to truth; we should say—he was not a great philosopher, but he was a great reformer in philosophy. He brought into philosophy something which it greatly needed, and for want of which it was at a stand. It was not his doctrines which did this, it was his mode of arriving at them. He introduced into morals and politics those habits of thought and modes of investigation, which are essential to the idea of science; and the absence of which made those departments of inquiry, as physics had been before Bacon, a field of interminable discussion, leading to no result. It was not his ᵈopinionsᵈ, in short, but his ᵉmethodᵉ, that constituted the novelty and the value of what he did; a value beyond all price, even though we should reject the whole, as we unquestionably must a large part, of the opinions themselves.

Bentham's method may be shortly described as the method of ᶠdetailᶠ; of treating wholes by separating them into their parts, abstractions by resolving them into Things,—classes and generalities by distinguishing them into the individuals of which they are made up; and breaking every question into pieces before attempting to solve it. The precise amount of originality of this process, considered as a logical conception—its degree of connexion with the methods of physical science, or with the previous labours of Bacon, Hobbes, or Locke—is not an essential consideration in this place. Whatever originality there was in the method—in the subjects he applied it to, and in the rigidity with which he adhered to it, there was the greatest. Hence his interminable classifications. Hence his elaborate demonstrations of the most acknowledged truths. That murder, incendiarism, robbery, are mischievous actions, he will not take for granted without proof; let the thing appear ever so self-evident, he will know the why and the how of it with the last degree of precision; he will distinguish all the different mischiefs of a crime, whether of the *first*, the *second*, or the *third* order, namely, 1. the evil to the sufferer, and to his personal connexions; 2. the *danger* from example, and the *alarm* or painful feeling of insecurity; and 3. the discouragement to industry and useful pursuits arising from the *alarm*, and the trouble and resources which must be expended in warding off the *danger*. After this enumeration, he will prove ᵍ from the laws of human feeling, that even the first of these evils, the sufferings of the immediate victim, will on the average greatly outweigh the pleasure reaped by the offender; much more when all the other evils are taken into account. Unless this could be proved, he would account the infliction of punishment unwarrantable; and for taking the trouble to prove it formally,

ᶜ–ᶜ38   what
ᵉ–ᵉ38   method
ᵍ38   to you

ᵈ–ᵈ38   opinions
ᶠ–ᶠ38   detail

his defence is, "there are truths which it is necessary to prove, not for their own sakes, because they are acknowledged, but that an opening may be made for the reception of other truths which depend upon them. It is in this manner we provide for the reception of first principles, which, once received, prepare the way for admission of all other truths."* To which may be added, that in this manner also [h] we discipline the mind for practising the same sort of dissection upon questions more complicated and of more doubtful issue.

It is a sound maxim, and one which all close thinkers have felt, but which no one before Bentham ever so consistently applied, that error lurks in generalities: that the human mind is not capable of embracing a complex whole, until it has surveyed and catalogued the parts of which that whole is made up; that abstractions are not [i]realities *per se*[i], but an abridged mode of expressing facts, and that the only practical mode of dealing with them is to trace them back to the facts (whether of experience or of consciousness) of which they are the expression. Proceeding on this principle, Bentham makes short work with the ordinary modes of moral and political reasoning. These, it appeared to him, when hunted to their source, for the most part terminated in *phrases*. In politics, liberty, social order, constitution, law of nature, social compact, &c., were the catch-words: ethics had its analogous ones. Such were the arguments on which the gravest questions of morality and policy were made to turn; not reasons, but allusions to reasons; sacramental expressions, by which a summary appeal was made to some general sentiment of mankind, or to some maxim in familiar use, which might be true or not, but the limitations of which no one had ever critically examined. And this satisfied other people; but not Bentham. He required something more than opinion as a reason for opinion. Whenever he found a *phrase* used as an argument for or against anything, he insisted upon knowing what it meant; whether it appealed to any standard, or gave [i] intimation of any matter of fact relevant to the question; and if he could not find that it did either, he treated it as an attempt on the part of the disputant to impose his own individual sentiment on other people, without giving them a reason for it; a "contrivance for avoiding the obligation of appealing to any external standard, and for prevailing upon the reader to accept of the author's sentiment and opinion as a reason, and that a sufficient one, for itself."[*] Bentham shall speak for himself on this subject: the passage is from his first systematic

*Pt. I, pp. 161–2, of the collected [38 the new] edition ["Essay on the Promulgation of Laws, and the Reasons thereof; with Specimen of a Penal Code," *Works*, Vol. I].

[*Introduction to the Principles of Morals and Legislation, in Works, Vol. I, p. 8.]

[h]38,59 do
[i–i]38 facts   [i]38 any

work, *Introduction to the Principles of Morals and Legislation* [k] , and we could scarcely quote anything more strongly exemplifying both the strength and weakness of his *mode of philosophizing*.

It is curious enough to observe the variety of inventions men have hit upon, and the variety of phrases they have brought forward, in order to conceal from the world, and, if possible, from themselves, this very general and therefore very pardonable self-sufficiency.

1. One man says, he has a thing made on purpose to tell him what is right and what is wrong; and that is called a 'moral sense:' and then he goes to work at his ease, and says, such a thing is right, and such a thing is wrong—why? 'Because my moral sense tells me it is.'

2. Another man comes and alters the phrase: leaving out *moral*, and putting in *common* in the room of it. He then tells you that his common sense tells him what is right and wrong, as surely as the other's moral sense did: meaning by common sense a sense of some kind or other, which, he says, is possessed by all mankind: the sense of those whose sense is not the same as the author's being struck out as not worth taking. This contrivance does better than the other; for a moral sense being a new thing, a man may feel about him a good while without being able to find it out: but common sense is as old as the creation; and there is no man but would be ashamed to be thought not to have as much of it as his neighbours. It has another great advantage: by appearing to share power, it lessens envy; for when a man gets up upon this ground, in order to anathematize those who differ from him, it is not by a *sic volo sic jubeo*, but by a *velitis jubeatis*.

3. Another man comes, and says, that as to a moral sense indeed, he cannot find that he has any such thing: that, however, he has an *understanding*, which will do quite as well. This understanding, he says, is the standard of right and wrong: it tells him so and so. All good and wise men understand as he does: if other men's understandings differ in any part from his, so much the worse for them: it is a sure sign they are either defective or corrupt.

4. Another man says, that there is an eternal and immutable Rule of Right: that that rule of right dictates so and so: and then he begins giving you his sentiments upon anything that comes uppermost: and these sentiments (you are to take for granted) are so many branches of the eternal rule of right.

5. Another man, or perhaps the same man (it is no matter), says that there are certain practices conformable, and others repugnant, to the Fitness of Things; and then he tells you, at his leisure, what practices are conformable, and what repugnant: just as he happens to like a practice or dislike it.

6. A great multitude of people are continually talking of the Law of Nature; and then they go on giving you their sentiments about what is right and what is wrong: and these sentiments, you are to understand, are so many chapters and sections of the Law of Nature.

7. Instead of the phrase, Law of Nature, you have sometimes Law of Reason, Right Reason, Natural Justice, Natural Equity, Good Order. Any of them will do equally well. This latter is most used in politics. The three last are much more tolerable than the others, because they do not very explicitly claim to be anything more than phrases: they insist but feebly upon the being looked upon as so many positive standards of themselves, and seem content to be taken, upon occasion,

---

[k]38   (vol. 1, p. 8, of the present publication)   [l-l]38   system of philosophy

for phrases expressive of the conformity of the thing in question to the proper standard, whatever that may be. On most occasions, however, it will be better to say *utility*: *utility* is clearer, as referring more explicitly to pain and pleasure.

8. We have one philosopher, who says, there is no harm in anything in the world but in telling a lie; and that if, for example, you were to murder your own father, this would only be a particular way of saying, he was not your father. Of course when this philosopher sees anything that he does not like, he says, it is a particular way of telling a lie. It is saying, that the act ought to be done, or may be done, when, *in truth*, it ought not to be done.

9. The fairest and openest of them all is that sort of man who speaks out, and says, I am of the number of the Elect: now God himself takes care to inform the Elect what is right: and that with so good effect, that let them strive ever so, they cannot help not only knowing it but practising it. If therefore a man wants to know what is right and what is wrong, he has nothing to do but to come to me.[*]

Few *m*will contend that this is a perfectly fair representation of the *animus* of those who employ the various phrases so amusingly animadverted on; but that the phrases contain no argument, save what is grounded on the very feelings they are adduced to justify, is a truth which Bentham had the eminent merit of first pointing*m* out.

It is the introduction into the philosophy of human conduct, of this method of detail—of this practice of never reasoning about wholes until they have been resolved into their parts, nor about abstractions until they have been translated into realities—that constitutes the originality of Bentham in philosophy, and makes him the great reformer of the moral and political branch of it. To what he terms the "exhaustive method of classification," which is but one branch of this more general method, he himself ascribes everything original in the systematic and elaborate work from which we have quoted.[†] The generalities of his philosophy itself have little or no novelty: to ascribe any to the doctrine that general utility is the foundation of morality, would imply great ignorance of the history of philosophy, of general literature, and of Bentham's own writings. He derived the idea, as he says himself, from *n* Helvetius; and it was the doctrine no less, of the *o* religious philosophers of that age, prior to Reid and Beattie. We never saw an abler defence of the doctrine of utility than in a book written in refutation of Shaftesbury,

[*Introduction to the Principles of Morals and Legislation, in Works, Vol. I, pp. 8n–9n.]
[†Ibid., p. 101n.]

*m–m*38   , we believe, are now of opinion that these phrases and similar ones have nothing more in them than Bentham saw. But it will be as little pretended, now-a-days, by any person of authority as a thinker, that the phrases can pass as reasons, till after their meaning has been completely analysed, and translated into more precise language: until the standard they appeal to is ascertained, and the *sense* in which, and the *limits* within which, they are admissible as arguments, accurately marked
*n*38   Hume and   *o*38   adversaries of those writers, the

and now little read—Brown's* *Essays on the Characteristics*;[*] and in Johnson's celebrated review of Soame Jenyns,[†] the same doctrine is set forth as that both of the author and of the reviewer. In all ages of philosophy one of its schools has been utilitarian—not only from the time of Epicurus, but long before. It was by mere accident that this opinion became connected in Bentham with his peculiar method. The utilitarian philosophers antecedent to him had no more claims to the method than their antagonists. To refer, for instance, to the Epicurean philosophy, according to the most complete view we have of the moral part of it, by the most accomplished scholar of antiquity, Cicero; we ask any one who has read his philosophical writings, the *De Finibus* for instance, whether the arguments of the Epicureans [p]do not, just as much as those of the Stoics or Platonists, consist of mere[p] rhetorical appeals to common notions, to ἐικότα and σημεῖα instead of τεκμήρια, notions [q]picked up as it were casually, and when true at all, never so narrowly looked into as to ascertain in what sense and under what limitations they are true. The application of a real inductive philosophy to the problems of ethics, is as unknown to the Epicurean moralists as to[q] any of the other schools; they never take a question to pieces, and join issue on a definite point. Bentham certainly did not learn his sifting and anatomizing method from them.

This method Bentham has finally installed in philosophy; has made it henceforth imperative on philosophers of all schools. By it he has formed the intellects of many thinkers, who either never adopted, or have abandoned [r], many[r] of his peculiar opinions. He has taught the method to men of the most opposite schools to his; he has made them perceive that if they do not test their doctrines by the method of detail, their adversaries will. He has thus, it is not too much to say, for the first time introduced precision of thought into moral and political philosophy. Instead of taking up their opinions by intuition, or by ratiocination from premises adopted on a mere

*Author of another book which made no little sensation when it first appeared, —*An Estimate of the Manners* [*and Principles*] *of the Times*. [2 vols. London: Davis and Reymers, 1757–58.]

[*London: Davis, 1752.]

[†Samuel Johnson. "Review of A Free Enquiry," *Works*. London: Buckland, Rivington, 1787, X, 220–58; Soame Jenyns. *A Free Inquiry into the Nature and Origin of Evil*. London: Dodsley, 1757.]

p–p38 are not as perfect a specimen of σκιαμαχία as those of the Stoics or Platonists —vague phrases which different persons may understand in different senses, and no person in any definite sense;

q–q38 never narrowly looked into, and seldom exactly true, or true at all in the sense necessary to support the conclusion. Of any systematic appeal to fact and experience, which might seem to be their peculiar province, the Epicurean moralists are as devoid as

r–r38 most

rough view, and couched in language so vague that it is impossible to say exactly whether they are true or false, philosophers are now forced to understand one another, to break down the generality of their propositions, and join a precise issue in every dispute. This is nothing less than a revolution in philosophy. Its effect is gradually becoming evident in the writings of English thinkers of every variety of opinion, and will be felt more and more in proportion as Bentham's writings are diffused, and as the number of minds to whose formation they contribute is multiplied.

It will naturally be presumed that of the fruits of this great philosophical improvement some portion at least will have been reaped by its author. Armed with such a potent instrument, and wielding it with such singleness of aim; cultivating the field of practical philosophy with such unwearied and such consistent use of a method right in itself, and not adopted by his predecessors; it cannot be but that Bentham by his own inquiries must have accomplished something considerable. And so, it will be found, he has; something not only considerable, but extraordinary; though but little compared with what he has left undone, and far short of what his sanguine and almost boyish fancy made him flatter himself that he had accomplished. His peculiar method, admirably calculated to make clear thinkers, and sure ones to the extent of their materials, has not equal efficacy for making those materials complete. It is a security for accuracy, but not for comprehensiveness; or rather, it is a security for one sort of comprehensiveness, but not for another.

s Bentham's method of laying out his subject is admirable as a preservative against one kind of narrow and partial views. He begins by placing before himself the whole of the field of inquiry to which the particular question belongs, and divides down till he arrives at the thing he is in search of; and thus by successively rejecting all which is *t*not*t* the thing, he gradually works out a definition of what it *u*is*u*. This, which he calls the exhaustive method, is as old as philosophy itself. Plato owes everything to it, and does everything by it; and the use made of it by that great man in his Dialogues, Bacon, in one of those pregnant logical hints scattered through his writings, and so much neglected by most of his pretended followers, pronounces to be the nearest approach to a true inductive method in the ancient philosophy.[*] Bentham was *v*probably not*v* aware that Plato had anticipated him in the process to which he too declared that he owed everything. By the practice of it, his speculations are rendered eminently systematic and consistent; no question, with him, is ever an insulated one; he sees every subject in connexion with

[*Novum Organum, in Works, Vol. I, p. 205.]

s38   It is not to be denied that   t–t38,59   not
u–u38,59   is   v–v38   little

all the other subjects with which in his view it is related, and from which it
requires to be distinguished; and as all that he knows, in the least degree
allied to the subject, has been marshalled in an orderly manner before him,
he does not, like people who use a looser method, forget and overlook a thing
on one occasion to remember it on another. Hence there is probably no
philosopher of so wide a range, in whom there are so few inconsistencies. If
any of the truths which he did not see, had come to be seen by him, he would
have remembered it everywhere and at all times, and would have adjusted
his whole system to it. And this is another admirable quality which he has
impressed upon the best of the minds trained in his habits of thought: when
*w*those minds*w* open to admit new truths, they digest them as fast as they
receive them.

But this system, excellent for keeping before the mind of the thinker all
that he knows, does not make him know enough; it does not make a knowledge of *x*some*x* of the properties of a thing suffice for the whole of it, nor
render a rooted habit of surveying a complex object (though ever so carefully) in only one of its aspects, tantamount to the power of contemplating
it in all. To give this last power, other qualities are required: whether Bentham possessed those other qualities we now have to see.

Bentham's mind, as we have already said, was eminently synthetical. He
begins all his inquiries by supposing nothing to be known on the subject, and
reconstructs all philosophy *ab initio*, without reference to the opinions of his
predecessors. But to build either a philosophy or anything else, there must
be materials. For the philosophy of matter, the materials are the properties
of matter; for moral and political philosophy, the properties of man, and of
man's position in the world. The knowledge which any inquirer possesses of
these properties, constitutes a limit beyond which, as a moralist or a political
philosopher, whatever be his powers of mind, he cannot *y*reach*y*. Nobody's
synthesis can be more complete than his analysis. If in his survey of human
nature and *z* life he has left any element out, then, wheresoever that element
exerts any influence, his conclusions will fail, more or less, in their application. If he has left out many elements, and those very important, his labours
may be highly valuable; he may have largely contributed to that body of
partial truths which, when completed and corrected by one another, constitute practical truth; but the applicability of his system to practice in its own
proper shape will be of an exceedingly limited range.

Human nature and human life are *a*wide subjects*a*, and whoever would
embark in an enterprise requiring a thorough knowledge of them, has need
both of large stores of his own, and of all aids and appliances from elsewhere.

*w–w*38   these minds do
*x–x*38   *some*
*z*38   of human

*y–y*38   go
*a–a*38   a wide subject

His qualifications for success will be proportional to two things: the degree in which his own nature and circumstances furnish him with a correct and complete picture of man's nature and circumstances; and his capacity of deriving light from other minds.

Bentham failed in deriving light from other minds. His writings contain few traces of the accurate knowledge of any *b*schools*b* of thinking but his own; and many proofs of his entire conviction that they could teach him nothing worth knowing. For some of the most illustrious of previous thinkers, his contempt was unmeasured. In almost the only passage of *c*the*c* *Deontology* which, from its style, and from its having before appeared in print, may be known to be Bentham's, Socrates, and Plato are spoken of in terms distressing to his greatest admirers;[*] and the incapacity to appreciate such men, is a fact perfectly in unison with the general habits of Bentham's mind. He had a phrase, expressive of the view he took of all moral speculations to which his method had not been applied, or (which he considered as the same thing) not founded on a recognition of utility as the moral standard; this phrase was "vague generalities.[†] Whatever presented itself to him in such a shape, he dismissed as unworthy of notice, or dwelt upon only to denounce as absurd. He did not heed, or rather the nature of his mind prevented it from occurring to him, that these generalities contained the whole unanalysed experience of the human race.

Unless it can be asserted that mankind did not know anything until logicians taught it *d*to*d* them—that until the last hand has been put to a moral truth by giving it a metaphysically precise expression, all the previous rough-hewing which it has undergone by the common intellect at the suggestion of common wants and common experience is to go for nothing; it must be allowed, that even the originality which can, and the courage which dares, think for itself, is not a more necessary part of the philosophical character than *e*a thoughtful regard*e* for previous thinkers, and for the collective mind of the human race. What has been the opinion of mankind, has been the opinion of persons of all tempers and dispositions, of all partialities and pre-possessions, of all varieties in position, in education, in opportunities of observation and inquiry. No one inquirer is all this; every inquirer is either young or old, rich or poor, sickly or healthy, married or *f*unmarried*f*, meditative or active, a poet or a logician, an ancient or a modern, a man or a woman; and if a thinking person, has, in addition, the accidental peculiarities

[*Ed. John Bowring. 2 vols. London: Longman, Rees, Orme, Brown, Green, & Longman, 1834, Vol. I, p. 39ff.]

[†See *Book of Fallacies*, Pt. IV, Chpt. iii, pp. 230ff.]

*b–b*38   school
d–d+59,67
*f–f*38   single

*c–c*38   Bowring's
*e–e*38   reverence

of his individual modes of thought. Every circumstance which gives a character to the life of a human being, carries with it its peculiar biases; its peculiar facilities for perceiving some things, and for missing or forgetting others. But, from points of view different from his, different things are perceptible; and none are ᵍmoreᵍ likely to have seen what he does not see, ʰthanʰ those who do not see what he sees. The general opinion of mankind is the average of the conclusions of all minds, stripped indeed of their choicest and most recondite thoughts, but freed from their twists and partialities: a net result, in which everybody's particular point of view is represented, nobody's predominant. The collective mind does not penetrate below the surface, but it sees all the surface; which profound thinkers, even by reason of their profundity, ⁱoften fail toⁱ do: their intenser view of a thing in some of its aspects diverting their attention from others.

The hardiest assertor, therefore, of the freedom of private judgment—the keenest detector of the errors of his predecessors, and of the inaccuracies of current modes of thought—is the very person who most needs to fortify the weak side of his own intellect, by ʲ study of the opinions of mankind in all ages and nations, and of the speculations of philosophers of the modes of thought most opposite to his own. It is there that he will find the experiences denied to himself—the remainder of the truth of which he sees but half—the truths, of which the errors he detects are commonly but the exaggerations. If, like Bentham, he brings with him an improved instrument of investigation, the greater is the probability that he will find ready prepared a rich abundance of rough ore, which was merely waiting for that instrument. A man of clear ideas errs grievously if he imagines that whatever is seen confusedly does not exist: it belongs to him, when he meets with such a thing, to dispel the mist, and fix the outlines of the ᵏ vague form which is looming through it.

Bentham's contempt, then, of all other schools of thinkers; his determination to create a philosophy wholly out of the materials furnished by his own mind, and by minds like his own; was his first disqualification as a philosopher. His second, was the incompleteness of his own mind as a representative of universal human nature. In many of the most natural and strongest feelings of human nature he had no sympathy; from many of its graver experiences he was altogether cut off; and the faculty by which one mind understands a mind different from itself, and throws itself into the feelings of that other mind, was denied him by his deficiency of Imagination.

With Imagination in the popular sense, command of imagery and metaphorical expression, Bentham was, to a certain degree, endowed. For want,

ᵍ⁻ᵍ38   so
ⁱ⁻ⁱ38   seldom
ᵏ38   dim

ʰ⁻ʰ38   as
ʲ38   a

indeed, of poetical culture, the images with which his fancy supplied him were seldom beautiful, but they were quaint and humorous, or bold, forcible, and intense: passages might be quoted from him both of playful irony, and of declamatory eloquence, seldom surpassed in the writings of philosophers. The Imagination which he had not, was that to which the name is generally appropriated by the best writers of the present day; that which enables us, by a voluntary effort, to conceive the absent as if it were present, the imaginary as if it were real, and to clothe it in the feelings which, if it were indeed real, it would bring along with it. This is the power by which one human being enters into the mind and circumstances of another. This power constitutes the poet, in so far as he does anything but melodiously utter his own actual feelings. It constitutes the dramatist entirely. It is one of the constituents of the historian; by it we understand other times; by it Guizot interprets to us the middle ages; Nisard, in his beautiful Studies on the later Latin poets,[*] places us in the Rome of the Cæsars; Michelet disengages the distinctive characters of the different races and *l*generations*l* of mankind from the facts of their history. Without it nobody knows even his own nature, further than circumstances have actually tried it and called it out; nor the nature of his fellow-creatures, beyond such generalizations as he may have been enabled to make from his observation of their outward conduct.

By these limits, accordingly, Bentham's knowledge of human nature is bounded. It is wholly empirical; and the empiricism of one who has had little experience. He had neither internal experience nor external; the quiet, even tenor of his life, and his healthiness of mind, conspired to exclude him from both. He never knew prosperity and adversity, passion nor satiety: he never had even the experiences which sickness gives; he lived from childhood to the age of eighty-five in boyish health. He knew no dejection, no heaviness of heart. He never felt life a sore and a weary burthen. He was a boy to the last. Self-consciousness, that dæmon of the men of genius of our time, from Wordsworth to Byron, from Goethe to Chateaubriand, and to which this age owes *m*so much*m* both of its cheerful and its mournful wisdom, never was awakened in him. How much of human nature slumbered in him he knew not, neither can we know. He had never been made alive to the unseen influences which were acting on himself, nor consequently on his fellow-creatures. Other ages and other nations were a blank to him for purposes of instruction. He measured them but by one standard; their knowledge of facts, and their capability to take correct views of utility, and merge all other objects in it. His own lot was cast in a generation of the leanest and barrenest

[*Jean Nisard. *Etudes de mœurs et de critique sur les poètes latins de la décadence*. 3 vols. Brussels: Hauman, 1834.]

*l–l*38   nations   *m–m*38   most

men whom [n]England[n] had yet produced, and he was an old man when a better race came in with the present century. He saw accordingly in man little but what the vulgarest eye can see; recognised no diversities of character but [o]such as[o] he who runs may read. Knowing so little of human feelings, he knew still less of the influences by which those feelings are formed: all the more subtle workings both of the mind upon itself, and of external things upon the mind, escaped him; and no one, probably, who, in a highly instructed age, ever attempted to give a rule to all human conduct, set out with a more limited [p]conception[p] either of the [q]agencies[q] by which human conduct *is*, or of those by which it *should* be, influenced.

This, then, is our idea of Bentham. He was a man both of remarkable endowments for philosophy, and of remarkable deficiencies for it: fitted, beyond almost any man, for drawing from his premises, conclusions not only correct, but sufficiently precise and specific to be practical: but whose general conception of human nature and life, furnished him with an unusually slender stock of premises. It is obvious what would be likely to be achieved by such a man; what a thinker, thus gifted and thus disqualified, could [r]do[r] in philosophy. He could [s], with close and accurate logic, hunt[s] half-truths to their consequences and practical applications, on a scale both of greatness and of minuteness not previously exemplified; and this is the character which posterity will probably assign to Bentham.

We express our sincere and well-considered conviction when we say, that there is hardly anything [t]positive[t] in Bentham's philosophy which is not true: that when his practical conclusions are erroneous, which in our opinion they are very often, it is not because the considerations which he urges are not rational and valid in themselves, but because some more important principle, which he did not perceive, supersedes those considerations, and turns the scale. The bad part of his writings is his resolute denial of all that he does not see, of all truths but those which he recognises. By that alone has he exercised any bad influence upon his age; by that he has, not created a school of deniers, for this is an ignorant prejudice, but put himself at the head of the school which exists always, though it does not always find a great man to give it the sanction of philosophy: thrown the mantle of intellect over the natural tendency of men in all ages to deny [u]or disparage all feelings and mental states[u] of which they have no consciousness in themselves.

The truths which are not Bentham's, which his philosophy takes no account of, are many and important; but his non-recognition of them does

[n–n]38 Europe   [o–o]38 what
[p–p]38 knowledge   [q–q]38 things
[r–r]38 be
[s–s]38 be a systematic and accurately logical half-man; hunting
[t–t]38 *positive*
[u–u]38 the existence of all spiritual influences

not put them out of existence; they are still with us, and it is a comparatively easy task that is reserved for us, to harmonize *those* truths with his. To reject his half of the truth because he overlooked the other half, would be to fall into his error without having his excuse. For our own part, we have a large tolerance for one-eyed men, provided their one eye is a penetrating one: if they saw more, they probably would not see so keenly, nor so eagerly pursue one course of inquiry. Almost all rich veins of original and striking speculation have been opened by systematic *half-thinkers*: though whether these new thoughts drive out others as good, or are peacefully superadded to them, depends on whether these *half-thinkers* are or are not followed in the same track by complete *thinkers*. The field of man's nature and life cannot be too much worked, or in too many directions; until every clod is turned up the work is imperfect; no whole truth is possible but by combining the points of view of all the fractional truths, nor, therefore, until it has been fully seen what each fractional truth can do by itself.

What Bentham's fractional truths could do, there is no such good means of showing as by a review of his philosophy: and such a review, though inevitably a most brief and general one, it is now necessary to attempt.

The first question in regard to any man of speculation is, what is his theory of human life? In the minds of many philosophers, whatever theory they have of this sort is latent, and it would be a revelation to themselves to have it pointed out to them in their writings as others can see it, unconsciously moulding everything to its own likeness. But Bentham always knew his own premises, and made his reader know them: it was not his custom to leave the theoretic grounds of his practical conclusions to conjecture. Few great thinkers have afforded the means of assigning with so much certainty the exact conception which they had formed of man and of man's life.

Man is conceived by Bentham as a being susceptible of pleasures and pains, and governed in all his conduct partly by the different modifications of self-interest, and the passions commonly classed as selfish, partly by sympathies, or occasionally antipathies, towards other beings. And here Bentham's conception of human nature stops. He does not *z* exclude religion; the prospect of divine rewards and punishments he includes under the head of "self-regarding interest," and the devotional feeling under that of sympathy *with* God.[*] But the whole of the impelling or restraining principles,

[*See *Introduction to the Principles of Morals and Legislation*, in *Works*, Vol. I, pp. 56, 52.]

v–v38	these	w–w38	half-minds
x–x38	half-minds	y–y38	minds
z38	, indeed,	a–a38	towards

whether of this ^{b}or of another world^b, which he recognises, are either self-love, or love or hatred towards other ^{c}sentient^c beings. That there might be no doubt of what he thought on the subject, he has not left us to the general evidence of his writings, but has drawn out a *Table of the Springs of Action*, an express enumeration and classification of human motives, with their various names, laudatory, vituperative, and neutral: and this table, to be found in Part I of ^{d}his collected works^d,[*] we recommend to the study of those who would understand his philosophy.

Man is never recognised by him as a being capable of pursuing spiritual perfection as an end; of desiring, for its own sake, the conformity of his own character to his standard of excellence, without hope of good or fear of evil from other source than his own inward consciousness. Even in the more limited form of Conscience, this great fact in human nature escapes him. Nothing is more curious than the absence of recognition in any of his writings of the existence of conscience, as a thing distinct from philanthropy, from affection for God or man, and from self-interest in this world or in the next. There is a studied abstinence from any of the phrases which, in the mouths of others, import the acknowledgment of such a fact.* If we find the words "Conscience," "Principle," "Moral Rectitude," "Moral Duty," in his *Table of the Springs of Action*, it is among the synonymes of the "love of reputation;" with an intimation as to the two former phrases, that they are also sometimes synonymous with the *religious* motive, or the motive of *sympathy*. The feeling of moral approbation or disapprobation properly so called, either towards ourselves or our fellow-creatures, he seems unaware of the existence of; and neither the word *self-respect*, nor the idea to which that word is appropriated, occurs even once, so far as our recollection serves us, in his whole writings.

Nor is it only the moral part of man's nature, in the strict sense of the term—the desire of perfection, or the feeling of an approving or of an accusing conscience—that he overlooks; he but faintly recognises, as a fact in human nature, the pursuit of any other ideal end for its own sake. The sense of *honour*, and personal dignity—that feeling of personal exaltation and

[*_Works_, Vol. I, pp. 195–219.]

*In a passage in the last volume of his book on Evidence, and possibly in one or two other places, the "love of justice" is spoken of as a feeling inherent in almost all mankind. [*Rationale of Judicial Evidence*. Ed. J. S. Mill. 5 vols. London: Hunt and Clarke, 1827, Vol. V, p. 638. Cf. *ibid.*, Vol. I, p. 83.] It is impossible, without explanations now unattainable, to ascertain what sense is to be put upon casual expressions so inconsistent with the general tenor of his philosophy.

$b-b$38   world or the next
$c-c$+59,67 $d-d$38   the present publication

degradation which acts independently of other people's opinion, or even in defiance of it; the love of *beauty*, the passion of the artist; the love of *order*, of congruity, of consistency in all things, and conformity to their end; the love of *power*, not in the limited form of power over other human beings, but abstract power, the power of making our volitions effectual; the love of *action*, the thirst for movement and activity, a principle scarcely of less influence in human life than its opposite, the love of ease:—None of these powerful constituents of human nature are thought worthy of a place among the "Springs of Action;" and though there is possibly no one of them of the existence of which an acknowledgment might not be found in some corner of Bentham's writings, no conclusions are ever founded on the acknowledgment. Man, that most complex being, is a very simple one in his eyes. Even under the head of *sympathy*, his recognition does not extend to the more complex forms of the feeling—the love of *loving*, the need of a sympathising support, or of *e*objects*e* of admiration and reverence. If he thought at all of any of the deeper feelings of human nature, it was but as idiosyncrasies of taste, with which *f*the moralist no more than*f* the legislator had any concern, further than to prohibit such as were mischievous among the actions to which they might chance to lead. To say either that man should, or that he should not, take pleasure in one thing, displeasure in another, appeared to him as much an act of despotism in the moralist as in the political ruler.

It would be most unjust to Bentham to surmise (as narrow-minded and passionate adversaries are apt in such cases to do) that this picture of human nature was copied from himself; that all those constituents of humanity which he rejected from his table of motives, were wanting in his own breast. The unusual strength of his early feelings of virtue, was, as we have seen, the original cause of all his speculations; and a noble sense of morality, and especially of justice, guides and pervades them all. But having been early accustomed to keep before his mind's eye the happiness of mankind (or rather of the whole sentient world), as the only thing desirable in itself, or which rendered anything else desirable, he confounded all disinterested feelings which he found in himself, with the desire of *g*general*g* happiness: just as some religious writers, who loved virtue for its own sake as much perhaps as men could do, habitually confounded their love of virtue with their fear of hell. It would have required greater subtlety than Bentham possessed, to distinguish from each other, feelings which, from long habit, always acted in the same direction; and his want of imagination prevented him from reading the distinction, where it is legible enough, in the hearts of others.

*e–e*38   an object
*f–f*38   neither the moralist nor
*g–g*38   human

Accordingly, he has not been followed in this grand oversight by any of the able men who, from the extent of their intellectual obligations to him, have been regarded as his disciples. They may have followed him in his doctrine of utility, and in his rejection of *ha*^{h} moral sense as *the*^{i} test of right and wrong: but while repudiating it as such, they have, with Hartley, acknowledged it as a fact in human nature; they have endeavoured to account for it, to assign its laws: nor are they justly chargeable either with undervaluing this part of our nature, or with any disposition to throw it into the background of their speculations. If *any*^{j} part of the influence of this cardinal error has extended itself to them, it is circuitously, and through the effect on their minds of other parts of Bentham's doctrines.

Sympathy, the only disinterested motive which Bentham recognised, he felt the inadequacy of, except in certain limited cases, as a security for virtuous action. Personal affection, he well knew, is as liable to operate to the injury of third parties, and requires as much to be kept *under government*^{k}, as any other feeling whatever: and general philanthropy, considered as a motive influencing mankind in general, he estimated at its true value when divorced from the feeling of duty—as the very weakest and most unsteady of all feelings. There remained, as a motive by which mankind are influenced, and by which they may be guided to their good, only personal interest. Accordingly, Bentham's idea of the world is that of a collection of persons pursuing each his separate interest or pleasure, and the prevention of whom from jostling one another more than *is unavoidable, may*^{l} be attempted by hopes and fears derived from three sources—the law, religion, and public opinion. To these three powers, considered as binding human conduct, he gave the name of *sanctions*: the *political* sanction, operating by the rewards and penalties of the law; the *religious* sanction, by those expected from the Ruler of the Universe; and the *popular*, which he characteristically calls also the *moral* sanction, operating through the pains and pleasures arising from the favour or disfavour of our fellow-creatures.[*]

Such is Bentham's theory of the world. And now, in a spirit neither of apology nor of censure, but of calm appreciation, we are to inquire how far this view of human nature and life will carry any one:—how much it will accomplish in morals, and how much in political and social philosophy: what it will do for the individual, and what for society.

It will do nothing for the conduct of the individual, beyond prescribing some of the *more*^{m} obvious dictates of worldly prudence, and outward

[*See *Principles of Morals and Legislation*, Chap. iii, in *Works*, Vol. I, pp. 14–15.]

$^{h-h}$38   the
$^{i-i}$38   some
$^{l-l}$38   can be helped, must
$^{l-l}$38   a
$^{k-k}$38   in check
$^{m-m}$38   most

probity and beneficence. There is no need to expatiate on the deficiencies of a system of ethics which does not pretend to aid individuals in the formation of their own character; which recognises no such wish as that of self-culture, we may even say no such power, as existing in human nature; and if it did recognise, could furnish little assistance to that *ⁿgreat dutyⁿ*, because it overlooks the existence of about half of the whole number of mental feelings which human beings are capable of, including all those of which the direct objects are states of their own mind.

Morality consists of two parts. One of these is self-education; the training, by the human being himself, of his affections and will. That department is a blank in Bentham's system. The other and coequal part, the regulation of his outward actions, must be altogether halting and imperfect without the first; for how can we judge in what manner many an action will affect *ᵒevenᵒ* the worldly interests of ourselves or others, unless we take in, as part of the question, its influence on the regulation of our, or their, affections and desires? A moralist on Bentham's principles may get as far as this, that *ᵖheᵖ* ought not to slay, burn, or steal; but what will be his qualifications for regulating the nicer shades of human behaviour, or for laying down even the greater moralities as to those facts in human life *qwhich tend toq* influence the depths of the character quite independently of any influence on worldly circumstances—such, for instance, as the sexual relations, or those of family in general, or any other social and sympathetic connexions of an intimate kind? The moralities of these questions depend *ʳessentiallyʳ* on considerations *swhich Bentham never so much as took into the account; and when he happened to be in the right, it was always, and necessarily, on wrong or insufficient groundsˢ*.

It is fortunate for the world that Bentham's taste lay rather in the direction of jurisprudential than of properly ethical inquiry. Nothing expressly of the latter kind has been published under his name, except the *Deontology*—a book scarcely ever *ᵗ, in our experience,ᵗ* alluded to by any admirer of Bentham without deep regret that it ever saw the light. We did not expect from Bentham correct systematic views of ethics, or a sound treatment of any question the moralities of which require a profound knowledge of the human heart; but we did *ᵘanticipateᵘ* that the greater moral questions would have been boldly plunged into, and at least a searching criticism produced of the received opinions; we did not expect that the *petite morale* almost alone

---

ⁿ⁻ⁿ38   grand duty of man   ᵒ⁻ᵒ+59,67
ᵖ⁻ᵖ38   we   q⁻q38   which]   59   which are liable to
ʳ⁻ʳ+59,67
ˢ⁻ˢ38   of which Bentham not only was not a competent judge, but which he never even took into the account
ᵗ⁻ᵗ+59,67
ᵘ⁻ᵘ38   expect

would have been treated, and that with the most pedantic minuteness, and on the *quid pro quo* principles which regulate *v*trade*v*. The book has not even the value which would belong to an authentic exhibition of the legitimate consequences of an erroneous line of thought; for the style proves it to have been so entirely rewritten, that it is impossible to tell how much or how little of it is Bentham's. The collected edition, now in progress, will not, it is said, include Bentham's religious writings; these, although we think *w*most of*w* them of exceedingly small value, are at least his, and the world has a right to whatever light they throw upon the constitution of his mind. But the omission of the *Deontology* would be an act of editorial discretion which we should deem entirely justifiable.

If Bentham's theory of life can do so little for the individual, what can it do for society?

It will enable a society which has attained a certain state of spiritual development, and the maintenance of which in that state is otherwise provided for, to prescribe the rules by which it may protect its material interests. It will do nothing (except sometimes as an instrument in the hands of a higher *x*doctrine*x*) for the spiritual interests of society; nor does it suffice of itself even for the material interests. That which alone causes any material interests to exist, which alone enables any body of human beings to exist as a society, is national character: *that* it is, which causes one nation to succeed in *y*what*y* it attempts, another to fail; one nation to understand and aspire to elevated things, another to grovel in mean ones; which makes the greatness of one nation lasting, and dooms another to early and rapid decay. The true teacher of the fitting social arrangements for England, France, or America, is the one who can point out how the English, French, or American character can be improved, and how it has been made what it is. A philosophy of laws and institutions, not founded on a philosophy of national character, is an absurdity. But what could Bentham's opinion be worth on national character? How could he, whose mind contained so few and so poor types of individual character, rise to that higher generalization? All he can do is but to indicate means by which, in any given state of the national mind, the material interests of society can be protected; saving the question, of which others must judge, *z* whether the use of those means would have, on the national character, any injurious influence.

We have arrived, then, at a sort of estimate of what a philosophy like Bentham's can do. It can teach the means of organizing and regulating the merely *business* part of the social arrangements. Whatever can be understood or whatever done without reference to moral influences, his philosophy is equal to; where those influences require to be taken into account, it is at

---

*v–v*38	*trade*	*w–w*+59,67		*x–x*38	principle
*y–y*38	all	*z*38	and not he,		

fault. He committed the mistake of supposing that the [a]business[a] part of human affairs was the whole of them; all at least that the legislator and the moralist had to do with. Not that he disregarded moral influences when he perceived them; but his want of imagination, small experience of human feelings, and ignorance of the filiation and connexion of feelings with one another, made this rarely the case.

The [b]business[b] part is accordingly the only province of human affairs which Bentham has cultivated with any success; into which he has introduced any considerable number of comprehensive and luminous practical principles. That is the field of his greatness; and there he is indeed great. He has swept away the accumulated cobwebs of centuries—he has untied knots which the efforts of the ablest thinkers, age after age, had only drawn tighter; and it is no exaggeration to say of him that over a great part of the field he was the first to shed the light of reason.

We turn with pleasure from what Bentham could not do, to what he did. It is an ungracious task to call a great benefactor of mankind to account for not being a greater—to insist upon the errors of a man who has originated more new truths, has given to the world more sound practical lessons, than it ever received, except in a few glorious instances, from any other individual. The unpleasing part of our work is ended. We are now to show the greatness of the man; the grasp which his intellect took of the subjects with which it was fitted to deal; the giant's task which was before him, and the hero's courage and [c] strength with which he achieved it. Nor let that which he did be deemed of small account because its province was limited: man has but the choice to go a little way in many paths, or a great way in only one. The field of Bentham's labours was like the space between two parallel lines; narrow to excess in one direction, in another it reached to infinity.

Bentham's speculations, as we are already aware, began with law; and in that department he accomplished his greatest triumphs. He found the philosophy of law a chaos, he left it a science: he found the practice of the law an Augean stable, he turned the river into it which is mining and sweeping away mound after mound of its rubbish.

Without [d]joining in[d] the exaggerated invectives against lawyers, which Bentham sometimes permitted [e]to[e] himself, or making one portion of society alone accountable for the fault of all, we may say that circumstances had made English lawyers in a peculiar degree liable to the reproach of Voltaire, who defines lawyers the "conservators of ancient barbarous usages."[*] The

[Voltaire. *La Princesse de Babilone*. In *Oeuvres complètes*. 66 vols. Paris: Renouard, 1817–25, Vol. XL, pp. 157–8.]

[a–a]38 *business*	[b–b]38 *business*
[c]38 hero's	[d–d]38 going into
[e–e]+59,67	

basis of the English law was, and still is, the feudal system. That system, like all those which existed as custom before they were established as law, possessed a certain degree of suitableness to the wants of the society among whom it grew up—that is to say, of a tribe of rude soldiers, holding a conquered people in subjection, and dividing its *spoils* among themselves. Advancing civilization had, however, converted this armed encampment of barbarous warriors in the midst of enemies reduced to slavery, into an industrious, commercial, rich, and free people. The laws which were suitable to the first of these states of society, could have no manner of relation to the circumstances of the second; which could not even have come into existence unless something had been done to adapt those laws to it. But the adaptation was not the result of thought and design; it arose not from any comprehensive consideration of the new state of society and its exigencies. What was done, was done by a struggle of centuries between the old barbarism and the new civilization; between the feudal aristocracy of conquerors, holding fast to the rude system they had established, and the conquered effecting their emancipation. The last was the growing power, but was never strong enough to break its bonds, though ever and anon some weak point gave way. Hence the law came to be like the costume of a full-grown man who had never put off the clothes made for him when he first went to school. Band after band had burst, and, as the rent widened, then, without removing anything except what might drop off of itself, the hole was darned, or patches of fresh law were brought from the nearest shop and stuck on. Hence all ages of English history have given one another *rendezvous* in English law; their several products may be seen all together, not interfused, but heaped one upon another, as *many different* ages of the earth may be read in some perpendicular section of its surface—the deposits of each successive period not substituted but superimposed on those of the preceding. And in the world of law no less than in the physical world, every commotion and conflict of the elements has left its mark behind in some break or irregularity of the strata: every struggle which ever rent the bosom of society is apparent in the disjointed condition of the part of the field of law which covers the spot: nay, the very traps and pitfalls which one contending party set for another are still standing, and the teeth not of hyenas only, but of foxes and all cunning animals, are imprinted on the curious remains found in these antediluvian caves.

In the English law, as in the Roman before it, the adaptations of barbarous laws to the growth of civilized society were made chiefly by stealth. They were generally made by the courts of justice, who could not help reading the new wants of mankind in the cases between man and man which came before them; but who, having no authority to make new laws for those new wants,

*f-f*38   spoil   *g-g*38   *rendezvous*
*h-h*38   all

were obliged to do the work covertly, and evade the jealousy and opposition of an ignorant, prejudiced, and for the most part brutal and tyrannical legislature. Some of the most necessary of these improvements, such as the giving force of law to *trusts*, and the breaking up of *entails*, were effected in actual opposition to the strongly-declared will of Parliament, whose clumsy hands, no match for the astuteness of judges, could not, after repeated trials, manage to make any law which the judges could not find a trick for rendering inoperative. The whole history of the contest about trusts may still be read in the words of a conveyance, as could the contest about entails, till the abolition of fine and recovery by a bill of the present Attorney-General;[*] but dearly did the client pay for the cabinet of historical curiosities which he was obliged to purchase every time that he made a settlement of his estate. The result of this mode of improving social institutions was, that whatever new things were done had to be done in consistency with old forms and names; and the laws were improved with much the same effect as if, in the improvement of agriculture, the plough could only have been introduced by making it look like a spade; or as if, when the primeval practice of ploughing by the horse's tail gave way to the innovation of harness, the tail, for form's sake, had still remained attached to the plough.

When the conflicts were over, and the mixed mass settled down into something like a fixed state, and that state a very profitable and therefore a very agreeable one to lawyers, they, following the natural tendency of the human mind, began to theorize upon it, and, in obedience to necessity, had to digest it and give it a systematic form. It was from this thing of shreds and patches, in which the only part that approached to order or system was the early barbarous part, *already* more than half superseded, that English lawyers had to construct, by induction and abstraction, their philosophy of law; and without the logical habits and general intellectual cultivation which the lawyers of the Roman empire brought to a similar task. Bentham found the philosophy of law what English practising lawyers had made it; a *jumble*, in which *real* and *personal* property, *law* and *equity*, *felony*, *præmunire*, *misprision*, and *misdemeanour*, words without a vestige of meaning when detached from the history of English institutions—mere tide-marks to point out the line which the sea and the shore, in their secular struggles, had adjusted as their mutual boundary—all passed for distinctions inherent in the nature of things; in which every absurdity, every lucrative abuse, had a reason found for it—a reason which only now and then even pretended to be drawn from expediency; most commonly a technical reason, one of mere

[*See 3 & 4 William IV, c. 74 (28 August, 1833).]

*i–i*38   *trusts*   *j–j*38   *entails*
*k–k*38   now   *l–l*38   mess

form, derived from the old barbarous system. While the theory of the law was in this state, to describe what the practice of it was would require the pen of a Swift, or of Bentham himself. The whole progress of a suit at law seemed like a series of contrivances for lawyers' profit, in which the suitors were regarded as the prey; and if the poor were not the helpless victims of every Sir Giles Overreach[*] who could pay the price, they might thank opinion and manners for it, not the law.

It may be fancied by some people that Bentham did an easy thing in merely calling all this absurd, and proving it to be so. But he began the contest a young man, and he had grown old before he had any followers. History will one day refuse to give credit to the intensity of the superstition which, till very lately, protected this mischievous mess from examination or doubt—^{m}passed^m off the charming representations of Blackstone for a just estimate of the English law, and ^{n}proclaimed^n the shame of human reason to be the perfection of it. Glory to Bentham that he has dealt to this superstition its deathblow—that he has been the Hercules of this hydra, the St. George of this pestilent dragon! The honour is all his—nothing but his peculiar qualities could have done it. There were ^{o}wanted^o his indefatigable perseverance, his firm self-reliance, needing no support from other men's opinion; his intensely practical turn of mind, his synthetical habits—above all, his peculiar method. Metaphysicians, armed with vague generalities, had often tried their hands at the subject, and left it no more advanced than they found it. Law is a matter of business; means and ends are the things to be considered in it, not abstractions: vagueness was not to be met by vagueness, but by definiteness and precision: details were not to be encountered with generalities, but with details. Nor could any progress be made, on such a subject, by merely showing that existing things were bad; it was necessary also to show how they might be made better. No great man whom we read of was qualified to do this thing except Bentham. He has done it, once and for ever ^{p}.

Into the ^{q}particulars^q of what Bentham has done we cannot enter: many hundred pages would be required to give a tolerable abstract of it. To sum up our estimate under a few heads. First: he has expelled mysticism from the philosophy of law, and set the example of viewing laws in a practical light, as means to certain definite and precise ends. Secondly: he has cleared up the confusion and vagueness attaching to the idea of law in general, to the idea of a body of laws, and ^{r}the various^r general ideas therein involved. Thirdly: he demonstrated the necessity and practicability of *codification*, or

[*See Philip Massinger. *A New Way to Pay Old Debts*.]

$^{m-m}$38   passing $^{n-n}$38   proclaiming
$^{o-o}$38   wanting
^{p}38   : witness these volumes, and the others by which they are to be followed
$^{q-q}$38   details $^{r-r}$38,59   all the

the conversion of all law into a written and systematically arranged code: not like the Code Napoleon, a code without a single definition, requiring a constant reference to anterior precedent for the meaning of *s* its technical terms; but *t*one*t* containing within itself all that is necessary for its own interpretation, together with a perpetual provision for its own emendation and improvement. He has shown of what parts such a code would consist; the relation of those parts to one another; and by his distinctions and classifications has done very much towards showing what should be, or might be, its nomenclature and arrangement. What he has left undone, he has made it comparatively easy for others to do. Fourthly: he has taken a systematic view* of the exigencies of society for which the civil code is intended to provide, and of the principles of human nature by which its provisions are to be tested: and this view, defective (as we have already intimated) wherever spiritual interests require to be taken into account, is excellent for that large portion of the laws of any country which are designed for the protection of material interests. Fifthly: (to say nothing of the subject of punishment, for which something considerable had been done before) he found the philosophy of judicial procedure, including that of judicial establishments and of evidence, in a more wretched state than even any other part of the philosophy of law; he carried it at once almost to perfection. He left it with every one of its principles established, and little remaining to be done even in the suggestion of practical arrangements.

These assertions in behalf of Bentham may be left, *u* without fear for the result, in the hands of those who are competent to judge of them. There are *v*now*v* even in the highest seats of justice, *w* men to whom the claims made for him will not *x* appear extravagant. Principle after principle of those propounded by him is moreover making its way by infiltration into the understandings most shut against his influence, and driving nonsense and prejudice from one corner of them to another. The reform of the laws of any country according to his principles, can only be gradual, and may be long ere it is accomplished; but the work is in progress, and both parliament and the judges are every year doing something, and often something not inconsiderable, towards the forwarding of it.

It seems proper here to take notice of an accusation sometimes made both against Bentham and against the principle of codification—as if they required one uniform suit of ready-made laws for all times and all states of society.

*See the *Principles of Civil Law*, contained in Part II of his collected works [38 of the present publication]. ["Principles of the Civil Code," *Works*, Vol. I, pp. 297 ff.]

*s*38   all   *t–t*38   a code
*u*38   and now   *v–v*+59,67
*w*38   some   *x*38   now

The doctrine of codification, as the word imports, relates to the form only of the laws, not their substance; it does not concern itself with what the laws should be, but declares that whatever they are, they ought to be systematically arranged, and fixed down to a determinate form of words. To the accusation, so far as it affects Bentham, one of the essays in the *y*collection of his works (then*y* for the first time published in English) is a complete answer: that "On the Influence of Time and Place in Matters of Legislation."[*] It may there be seen that the different exigencies of different nations with respect to law, occupied his attention as systematically as any other portion of the wants which render laws necessary: with the limitations, it is true, which were set to all his speculations by the imperfections of his theory of human nature. For, taking, as we have seen, next to no account of national character and the causes which form and maintain it, he was precluded from considering, except to a very limited extent, the laws of a country as an instrument of national culture: one of their most important aspects, and in which they must of course vary according to the degree and kind of culture already attained; as a tutor gives his pupil different lessons according to the progress already made in his education. The same laws would not have suited our wild ancestors, accustomed to rude independence, and a people of Asiatics bowed down by military despotism: the slave needs to be trained to govern himself, the savage to submit to the government of others. The same laws will not suit the English, who *z*distrust everything which emanates from general principles, and the French, who distrust whatever does not so emanate*z*. Very different institutions are needed to train to the perfection of their nature, or to constitute into a united nation and social polity, an essentially *subjective* people like the *a* Germans, and an essentially *objective* people like those of Northern and Central Italy; the one affectionate and dreamy, the other passionate and worldly; the one trustful and loyal, the other calculating and suspicious; the one not practical enough, the other overmuch; the one wanting individuality, the other fellow-feeling; the one failing for want of exacting enough for itself, the other for want of conceding enough to others. Bentham was little accustomed to look at institutions in their relation to these topics. The effects of this oversight must of course be perceptible throughout his speculations, but we do not think the errors into which it led him very material in the greater part of civil and penal law: it is in the department of constitutional legislation that they were fundamental.

The Benthamic theory of government has made so much noise in the

[*Works*, Vol. I, pp. 169 ff.]

*y–y*38   present collection (now
*z–z*38   place their habitual reliance in themselves, and the French, who place theirs in leaders
*a*38   North-

world of late years; it has held such a conspicuous place among Radical philosophies, and Radical modes of thinking have participated so much more largely than any others in its spirit, that many worthy persons imagine there is no other Radical philosophy extant. Leaving such *b*people*b* to discover their *c*mistake*c* as they may, we shall expend a few words in attempting to discriminate between the truth and error of this celebrated theory.

There are three great questions in government. First, to what authority is it for the good of the people that they should be subject? Secondly, how are they to be induced to obey that authority? The answers to these two questions vary indefinitely, according to the degree and kind of civilization and cultivation already attained by a people, and their peculiar aptitudes for receiving more. Comes next a third question, not liable to so much variation, namely, by what means are the abuses of this authority to be checked? This third question is the only one of the three to which Bentham seriously applies himself, and he gives it the only answer it admits of—Responsibility: responsibility to persons whose interest, whose obvious and recognisable interest, accords with the end in view—good government. This being granted, it is next to be asked, in what body of persons this identity of interest with good government, that is, with the interest of the whole community, is to be found? In nothing less, says Bentham, than the numerical majority: nor, say we, even in the numerical majority itself; of no portion of the community less than all, will the interest coincide, at all times and in all respects, with the interest of all. But, since power given to all, by a representative government, is in fact given to a majority; we are obliged to fall back upon the first of our three questions, namely, under what authority is it for the good of the people that they be placed? And if to this the answer be, under that of a majority among themselves, Bentham's system cannot be questioned. This one assumption being made, his *Constitutional Code*[*] is admirable. That extraordinary power which he possessed, of at once seizing comprehensive principles, and scheming out minute details, is brought into play with surpassing vigour in devising means for preventing rulers from escaping from the control of the majority; for enabling and inducing the majority to exercise that control unremittingly; and for providing them with servants of every desirable endowment, moral and intellectual, compatible with entire subservience to their will.

But *is* this fundamental doctrine of Bentham's political philosophy an universal truth? Is it, at all times and places, good for mankind to be under the absolute authority of the majority of themselves? We say the *d*authority*d*,

[*London: Heward, 1830.]

*b–b*38   persons
*c–c*38   error   *d–d*38   *authority*

not the *political* authority merely, because it is chimerical to suppose that whatever has absolute power over men's bodies will not arrogate it over their minds—will not seek to control (not perhaps by legal penalties, but by the persecutions of society) opinions and feelings which depart from its standard; will not attempt to shape the education of the young by its *f* model, and to extinguish all books, all schools, all combinations of individuals for joint action upon society, which may be attempted for the purpose of keeping alive a spirit at variance with its own. Is it, we say, the proper condition of man, in all ages and nations, to be under the despotism of Public Opinion?

It is very conceivable that such a doctrine should find acceptance from some of the noblest spirits, in a time of reaction against the aristocratic governments of modern Europe; governments founded on the entire sacrifice (except so far as prudence, and sometimes humane feeling interfere) of the community generally, to the self-interest and ease of a few. European reformers have been accustomed to see the numerical majority everywhere unjustly depressed, everywhere trampled upon, or at the best overlooked, by governments; nowhere possessing power enough to extort redress of their most positive grievances, provision for their mental culture, or even to prevent themselves from being taxed avowedly for the pecuniary profit of the ruling classes. To see these things, and to seek to put an end to them, by means (among other things) of giving more political power to the majority, constitutes Radicalism; and it is because so many in this age have felt this wish, and have felt that the realization of it was an object worthy of men's devoting their lives to it, that such a theory of government as Bentham's has found favour with them. But, though to pass from one form of bad government to another be the ordinary fate of mankind, philosophers ought not to make themselves parties to it, by sacrificing one portion of important truth to another.

The numerical majority of any society whatever, must consist of persons all standing in the same social position, and having, in the main, the same pursuits, namely, unskilled manual labourers; and we mean no disparagement to them: whatever we say to their disadvantage, we say equally of a numerical majority of shopkeepers, or of squires. Where there is identity of position and pursuits, there also will be identity of partialities, passions, and prejudices; and to give to any *g*one*g* set of partialities, passions, and prejudices, absolute power, without counter-balance from partialities, passions, and prejudices of a different sort, is the way to render the correction of any of those imperfections hopeless; to make one narrow, mean type of human nature universal and perpetual, and to crush every influence which tends to the further improvement of man's intellectual and moral nature. There must, we know, be some paramount power in society; and that the majority should

e–e38   *political*   f38   own   g–g38   *one* be that power, is on the whole right, not as being just in itself, but as being less unjust than any other footing on which the matter can be placed. But it is necessary that the institutions of society should make provision for keeping up, in some form or other, as a corrective to partial views, and a shelter for freedom of thought and individuality of character, a perpetual and standing Opposition to the will of the majority. All countries which have long continued progressive, or been durably great, have been so because there has been an organized opposition to the ruling power, of whatever kind that power was: plebeians to patricians, clergy to kings, freethinkers to clergy, kings to barons, commons to king and aristocracy. Almost all the greatest men who ever lived have formed part of such an Opposition. Wherever some such quarrel has not been going on—wherever it has been terminated by the complete victory of one of the contending principles, and no new contest has taken the place of the old—society has either [h] hardened into Chinese stationariness, or fallen into dissolution. A centre of resistance, round which all the moral and social elements which the ruling power views with disfavour may cluster themselves, and behind whose bulwarks they may find shelter from the attempts of that power to hunt them out of existence, is as necessary where the opinion of the majority is sovereign, as where the ruling power is a hierarchy or an aristocracy. Where no such *point d'appui* exists, there the human race will inevitably degenerate; and the question, whether the United States, for instance, will in time sink into another China (also a most commercial and industrious nation), resolves itself, to us, into the question, whether such a centre of resistance will gradually evolve itself or not.

These things being considered, we cannot think that Bentham made the most useful employment which might have been made of his great powers, when, not content with enthroning the majority as sovereign, by means of universal suffrage without king or house of lords, he exhausted all the resources of ingenuity in devising means for riveting the yoke of public opinion closer and closer round the necks of all public functionaries, and excluding every possibility of the exercise of the slightest or most temporary influence either by a minority, or by the functionary's own notions of right. Surely when [i]any power has been made the strongest power, enough has been done for it;[i] care is thenceforth wanted rather to prevent that strongest power from swallowing up all others. Wherever all the forces of society act in one single direction, [j]the just claims[j] of the individual human being are in extreme peril. The power of the majority is salutary so far as it is used [k]defensively, not offensively[k]—as its exertion is tempered by respect for the personality of the

[h]38   been
[i-i]38   you have made any power the strongest power, you have done enough for it; your
[j-j]38   there the rights
[k-k]38   *defensively*, not *offensively*

individual, and *l*deference to*l* superiority of cultivated intelligence. If Bentham had employed himself in pointing out the means by which institutions fundamentally democratic might be best adapted to the preservation and strengthening of those two sentiments, he would have done something more permanently valuable, and more worthy of his great intellect. Montesquieu, with the lights of the present age, would have done it; and we are possibly destined to receive this benefit from the Montesquieu of our own times, M. de Tocqueville.

Do we then consider Bentham's political speculations useless? Far from it. We consider them only one-sided. He has brought out into a strong light, has cleared from a thousand confusions and misconceptions, and pointed out with admirable skill the best means of promoting, one of the ideal qualities of a perfect government—identity of interest between the trustees and the community for whom they hold their power in trust. This quality is not attainable in its ideal perfection, and must moreover be striven for with a perpetual eye to all other requisites; but those other requisites must still more be striven for without losing sight of this: and when the slightest postponement is made of it to any other end, the sacrifice, often necessary, is never unattended with evil.* Bentham has pointed out how complete this sacrifice is in modern European societies: how exclusively, partial and sinister interests are the ruling power there, with only such check as is imposed by public opinion—which being thus, in the existing order of things, perpetually apparent as a source of good, he was led by natural partiality to exaggerate its intrinsic excellence. This sinister interest of rulers Bentham hunted through all its disguises, and especially through those which hide it from the men themselves who are influenced by it. The greatest service rendered by him to the philosophy of universal human nature, is, perhaps, his *m*illustration*m* of what he terms "interest-begotten prejudice"—the *n*common*n* tendency of man to make a duty and a virtue of following his self-interest.[*] The idea, it is true, was far from being peculiarly Bentham's: the artifices by which we persuade ourselves that we are not yielding to our selfish inclinations when we are, had attracted the notice of all moralists, and had been probed by religious writers to a depth as much below Bentham's, as their knowledge of the profundities and windings of the human heart was superior to his. But it is selfish interest in the form of class-interest, and the class morality founded thereon, which Bentham has illustrated: the

*[59] For further illustrations of this point, see the Appendix to the present volume. [I.e., *Dissertations and Discussions*, Vol. I, pp. 467–74. See Bibliographic Appendix, p. 548 below.]
[*See, e.g., *A Table of the Springs of Action*, in *Works*, Vol. I, pp. 217–18.]

*l–l*38   reverence for
*m–m*38   illustrations   *n–n*38   inherent

manner in which any set of persons who mix much together, and have a common interest, are apt to make that common interest their standard of virtue, and the social feelings of the members of the class are made to play into the hands of their selfish ones; whence the union so often exemplified in history, between the most heroic personal disinterestedness and the most odious class-selfishness. This was one of Bentham's leading ideas, and almost the only one by which he contributed to the elucidation of history: much of which, except so far as this explained it, must have been entirely inexplicable to him. The idea was given him by Helvetius, whose book, *De l'Esprit*,[*] is one continued and most acute commentary on it; and, together with the other great idea of Helvetius, the influence of circumstances on character, it will make his name live by the side of Rousseau, when [o]most of[o] the other French [p]metaphysicians[p] of the eighteenth century [q]will[q] be extant as such only in literary history.

In the brief view which we have been able to give of Bentham's philosophy, it may surprise the reader that we have said so little about the first principle of it, with which his name is more identified than with anything else; the "principle of utility," or, as he afterwards named it, "the greatest-happiness principle."[†] It is a topic on which much were to be said, if there were room, or if it were in reality necessary for the just estimation of Bentham. On an occasion more suitable for a discussion of the metaphysics of morality, or on which the [r]elucidations[r] necessary to make an opinion on so abstract a subject intelligible could be conveniently given, we should be fully prepared to state what we think on this subject. [s]At present we shall only say, that while, under proper explanations, we entirely agree with Bentham in his principle, we do not hold with him that all right thinking on the details of morals depends on its express assertion.[s] We think utility, or happiness, much too complex and indefinite an end to be sought except through the medium of various secondary ends, concerning which there may be, and often is, agreement among persons who differ in their ultimate standard; and about which there does in fact prevail a much greater unanimity among thinking persons, than might be supposed from their diametrical divergence on the great questions of moral metaphysics. As mankind are much more nearly of one nature, than of one opinion about their own nature, they

[*Claude-Adrien Helvétius. *De l'esprit*. Paris: Durand, 1758.]
[†*Introduction to the Principles of Morals and Legislation*, in *Works*, Vol. I, p. 1n.]

*o–o*38 all
*p–p*38 philosophers
*q–q*38 shall
*r–r*38 explanations
*s–s*38 All we intend to say at present is, that we are much nearer to agreeing with Bentham in his principle, than in the degree of importance which he attached to it.

are ^{t} more easily brought to agree in their intermediate principles, *vera illa et media axiomata*, as Bacon says,[*] than in their first principles: and the attempt to make the bearings of actions upon the ultimate end more evident than they can be made by referring them to the intermediate ends, and to estimate their value by a direct reference to human happiness, generally terminates in attaching most importance, not to those effects which are really the greatest, but to those which can most easily be pointed to and individually identified. Those who adopt utility as a standard can seldom apply it truly except through the secondary principles; those who reject it, generally do no more than erect those secondary principles into first principles. ^{u}It is when two or more of the secondary principles conflict, that a direct appeal to some first principle becomes necessary; and then commences the practical importance of the utilitarian controversy; which is, in other respects,^{u} a question of arrangement and logical subordination rather than of practice; important principally in a purely scientific point of view, for the sake of the systematic unity and coherency of ethical philosophy. ^{v} It is probable, however, that to the principle of utility we owe all that Bentham did; that it was necessary to him to find a first principle which he could receive as self-evident, and to which he could attach all his other doctrines as logical consequences: that to him systematic unity was an indispensable condition of his confidence in his own intellect. And there is something further to be remarked ^{w}. Whether^w happiness be or be not the end to which morality should be referred—that it be referred to an *end* of some sort, and not left in the dominion of vague feeling or inexplicable internal conviction, that it be made a matter of reason and calculation, and not merely of sentiment, is essential to the very idea of moral philosophy; is, in fact, what renders argument or discussion on moral questions possible. That the morality of actions depends on the consequences which they tend to produce, is the doctrine of rational persons of all schools; that the good or evil of those consequences is measured solely by pleasure or pain, is all of the doctrine of the school of utility, which is peculiar to it.

In so far as Bentham's adoption of the principle of utility induced him to fix his attention upon the ^{x}consequences^x of actions as the consideration determining their morality, so far ^{y}he was indisputably^y in the right path:

[*Novum Organum, in Works, Vol. I, p. 205.]

^{t}38   much
$^{u-u}$38   [*paragraph*] We consider, therefore, the utilitarian controversy as
^{v}38   Whatever be our own opinion on the subject, it is from no such source that we look for the great improvements which we believe are destined to take place in ethical doctrine.
$^{w-w}$38   : whether
$^{x-x}$38   *consequences* $^{y-y}$38   at least he was

though to go far in it without wandering, there was needed a greater knowledge of the formation of character, and of the consequences of actions upon the agent's own frame of mind, than Bentham possessed. His want of power to estimate this class of consequences, together with his want of the degree of modest ᶻdeference which, from those who have not competent experience of their own, is due to the experience of others on that part of the subject, greatly limit the value of his speculationsᶻ on questions of practical ethics.

He is chargeable also with another error, which it would be improper to pass over, because nothing has tended more to place him in opposition to the common feelings of mankind, and to give to his philosophy that cold, mechanical, and ungenial air which characterizes the popular idea of a Benthamite. This error, or rather one-sidedness, belongs to him not as a utilitarian, but as a moralist by profession, and in common with almost all professed moralists, whether religious or philosophical: it is that of treating the *moral* view of actions and characters, which is unquestionably the first and most important mode of looking at them, as if it were the ᵃsoleᵃ one: whereas it is only one of three, by all of which our sentiments towards the human being may be, ought to be, and without entirely crushing our own nature cannot but be, materially influenced. Every human action has three aspects: its *moral* aspect, or that of its *right* and *wrong*; its *æsthetic* aspect, or that of its *beauty*; its *sympathetic* aspect, or that of its *loveableness*. The first addresses itself to our reason and conscience; the second to our imagination; the third to our human fellow-feeling. According to the first, we approve or disapprove; according to the second, we admire or despise; according to the third, we love, pity, or dislike. The ᵇmoralityᵇ of an action depends on its foreseeable consequences; its beauty, and its loveableness, or the reverse, depend on the qualities which it is evidence of. Thus, a lie is *wrong*, because its effect is to mislead, and because it tends to destroy the confidence of man in man; it is also *mean*, because it is cowardly—because it proceeds from not daring to face the consequences of telling the truth—or at best is evidence of want of that *power* to compass our ends by straightforward means, which is conceived as properly belonging to every person not deficient in energy or in understanding. The action of Brutus in sentencing his sons was *right*, because it was executing a law essential to the freedom of his country, against persons of whose guilt there was no doubt: it was *admirable*, because it evinced a rare degree of patriotism, courage, and self-control; but there was nothing *loveable* in it; it affords ᶜeitherᶜ no presumption in regard to loveable qualities, ᵈorᵈ a presumption of their deficiency. If one of the sons had engaged in the conspiracy from affection for the other, ᵉhisᵉ action would

---

ᶻ⁻ᶻ38   respect (a far different thing from blind deference) due to the traditional opinions and feelings in which the experience of mankind on that part of the subject lies embodied, render him, we conceive, a most unsafe guide

ᵃ⁻ᵃ38   sole   ᵇ⁻ᵇ38   *morality*   ᶜ⁻ᶜ+59,67
ᵈ⁻ᵈ38   unless   ᵉ⁻ᵉ38   *his*

have been loveable, though neither moral nor admirable. It is not possible for any sophistry to confound these three modes of viewing an action; but it is very possible to adhere to one of them exclusively, and lose sight of the rest. Sentimentality consists in setting the last two of the three above the first; the error of moralists in general, and of Bentham, is to sink the two latter entirely. This is pre-eminently the case with Bentham: he both wrote and felt as if the moral standard ought not only to be paramount (which it ought), but to be alone; as if it ought to be the sole master of all our actions, and even of all our sentiments; as if either to admire or like, or despise or dislike a person for any action which neither does good nor harm, or which does not do a good or a harm proportioned to the sentiment entertained, were an injustice and a prejudice. He carried this so far, that there were certain phrases which, being expressive of what he considered to be this groundless liking or aversion, he could not bear to hear pronounced in his presence. Among these phrases were those of *good* and *bad taste*. He thought it an insolent piece of dogmatism in one person to praise or condemn another *f*in*f* a matter of taste: as if men's likings and dislikings, on things in themselves indifferent, were not *g*full of*g* the most important inferences as to every point of their character; as if a person's tastes did not show him to be wise or a fool, cultivated or ignorant, gentle or rough, *h* sensitive or callous, generous or sordid, benevolent or selfish, conscientious or depraved.

Connected with the same topic are Bentham's peculiar opinions on poetry. Much *i*more has been said than there is any foundation for*i*, about his contempt for the pleasures of imagination, and for the fine arts. Music was throughout life his favourite amusement; painting, sculpture, and the other arts addressed to the eye, he was so far from holding in any contempt, that he occasionally recognises them as means employable for important social ends; though his ignorance of the deeper springs of human character prevented him *j*(as it prevents most Englishmen)*j* from suspecting how profoundly such things enter into the moral nature of man, and into the education both of the individual and of the race. But towards poetry in the narrower sense, that which employs the language of words, he entertained no favour. Words, he thought, were perverted from their proper office when they were employed in uttering anything but precise logical truth. He says, somewhere in his works, that, "quantity of pleasure being equal, push-pin is as good as poetry:"[*] but this is only a paradoxical way of stating what he would equally have said of the things which he most valued and admired. Another aphorism is attributed to him, which is much more characteristic

[*Rationale of Reward*, in *Works*, Vol. II, p. 253.]

f-f38   for
g-g38   pregnant with   h38   polished or coarse,
i-i38   has been said, for which there is no foundation
j-j+59,67

of his view of this subject: "All poetry is misrepresentation."[*] Poetry, he thought, consisted essentially in exaggeration for effect: in proclaiming some one view of a thing very emphatically, and suppressing all the limitations and qualifications. This trait of character seems to us a curious example of what Mr. Carlyle strikingly calls "the completeness of limited men." Here is a philosopher who is happy within his narrow boundary as no man of indefinite range ever was; who flatters himself that he is so completely emancipated from the essential law of poor human intellect, by which it can only see one thing at a time well, that he can even turn round upon the imperfection and lay a solemn interdict upon it. Did Bentham really suppose that it is in ᵏpoetryᵏ only that propositions cannot be exactly true, cannot contain in themselves all the limitations and qualifications with which they require to be taken when applied to practice? We have seen how far his own prose propositions are from realizing this Utopia: and even the attempt to approach ᴵ it would be incompatible not with poetry merely, but with oratory, and ᵐ popular writing of every kind. Bentham's charge is true to the fullest extent; all writing which undertakes to make men ⁿfeelⁿ truths as well as ᵒseeᵒ them, does take up one point at a time, does seek to impress that, to drive that home, to make it sink into and colour the whole mind of the reader or hearer. It is justified in doing so, if the portion of truth which it thus enforces be that which is called for by the occasion. All writing addressed to the feelings has a natural tendency to exaggeration; but Bentham should have remembered that in this, as in many things, we must aim at too much, to be assured of doing enough.

From the same principle in Bentham came the intricate and involved style, which makes his later writings books for the student only, not the general reader. It was from his perpetually aiming at impracticable precision. Nearly all his earlier, and many parts of his later writings, are models, as we have already observed, of light, playful, and popular style: a Benthamiana might be made of passages worthy of Addison or Goldsmith. But in his later years and more advanced studies, he fell into a Latin or German structure of sentence, foreign to the genius of the English language. He could not bear, for the sake of clearness and the reader's ease, to say, as ordinary men are content to do, a little more than the truth in one sentence, and correct it in the next. The whole of the qualifying remarks which ᵖhe intended to makeᵖ, he insisted upon imbedding as parentheses in the very middle of the sentence itself. And thus the sense being so long suspended, and attention being required to the accessory ideas before the principal idea had been properly seized, it became difficult, without some practice, to make out the train of

[*Cf. *Rationale of Reward*, pp. 253–4.]

ᵏ–ᵏ38   poetry
ᵐ38   with
ᵒ–ᵒ38   see

ᴵ38   to
ⁿ–ⁿ38   feel
ᵖ–ᵖ38   were intended to be made

thought. It is fortunate that so many of the most important parts of his writings are free from this defect. We regard it as a *reductio ad absurdum* of his objection to poetry. In trying to write in a manner against which the same objection should not lie, he could stop nowhere short of utter unreadableness, and after all attained no more accuracy than is compatible with opinions as imperfect and one-sided as those of any poet or *q* sentimentalist breathing. Judge then in what state literature and philosophy would be, and what chance they would have of influencing the multitude, if his objection were allowed, and all styles of writing banished which would not stand his test.

We must here close this brief and imperfect view of Bentham and his doctrines; in which many parts of the subject have been entirely untouched, and no part done justice to, but which at least proceeds from an intimate familiarity with his writings, and is *rnearly* the first attempt at an impartial estimate of his character as a philosopher, and of the result of his labours to the world.

After every abatement, and it has been seen whether we have made our abatements sparingly—there remains to Bentham an indisputable place among the great intellectual benefactors of mankind. His writings will long form an indispensable part of the education of the highest order of practical thinkers; and the *scollected editions* of them ought to be in the hands of every one who would either understand his age, or take any beneficial part in the great business of it.*

---

*[38²] Since the first publication of this paper [38² the publication of the first edition of the above article], Lord Brougham's brilliant series of characters has been published, including a sketch of Bentham. [Henry Peter Brougham. "Law Reform: Introduction," in *Speeches of Henry Lord Brougham*. 4 vols. Edinburgh: Black, 1838, II, 285–315.] Lord Brougham's view of Bentham's characteristics agrees in the main points, so far as it goes, with the result of our more minute [38² elaborate] examination, but there is an imputation cast upon Bentham, of a jealous and splenetic disposition in private life, of which we feel called upon to give at once a contradiction and an explanation. It is indispensable to a correct estimate of any of Bentham's dealings with the world, to bear in mind that in everything except abstract speculation he was to the last, what we have called him, essentially a boy. He had the freshness, the simplicity, the confidingness, the liveliness and activity, all the delightful qualities of boyhood, and the weaknesses which are the reverse side of those qualities—the undue importance attached to trifles, the habitual mismeasurement of the practical bearing and value of things, the readiness to be either delighted or offended on inadequate cause. These were the real sources of what was unreasonable in some of his attacks on individuals, and in particular on Lord Brougham, on the subject of his Law Reforms; they were no more the effect of envy or malice, or any really unamiable quality, than the freaks of a pettish child, and are scarcely a fitter subject of censure or criticism.

*q*38   any   *r–r*38   , we believe,   *s–s*38   present collection

COLERIDGE

1840

EDITOR'S NOTE

D&D, I (1867), 393–466, with footnote to title: *"London and Westminster Review,* March 1840." Reprinted from the *London and Westminster Review,* XXXIII (March, 1840), 257–302, signed "A" and headed: "Art. I.—1. *The Literary Remains of Samuel Taylor Coleridge.* Collected and edited by Henry Nelson Coleridge, Esq., M.A. 8vo. [London:] Pickering. 4 vols published. 1836–9. / 2. *Specimens of the Table Talk of Samuel Taylor Coleridge.* Second Edition. 12mo. [London:] Murray, 1836. / 3. I.—*On the Constitution of the Church and State, according to the Idea of Each.* Third Edition. II.—*Lay Sermons:* 1. *The Statesman's Manual.* 2. *"Blessed are ye that sow beside all waters."* Second Edition. By Samuel Taylor Coleridge. Edited from the Author's Corrected Copies; with Notes by Henry Nelson Coleridge, Esq., M.A. 12mo. [London:] Pickering, 1839. / 4. *Aids to Reflection in the Formation of a Manly Character, on the several grounds of Prudence, Morality, and Religion.* Illustrated by Extracts from our Elder Divines, especially from Archbishop Leighton. By S. T. Coleridge. Third Edition. 8vo. [London:] Pickering, 1836. / 5. *The Friend: a Series of Essays, to aid in the Formation of Fixed Principles in Politics, Morals, and Religion; with Literary Amusements interspersed.* By S. T. Coleridge. A new Edition, with the Author's last Corrections, and an Appendix, with a Synoptical Table of the Contents of the Work, by Henry Nelson Coleridge, Esq., M.A. 8vo. 3 vols. [London: Rest Fenner, 1818.] / 6. *Biographia Literaria; or, Biographical Sketches of my Literary Life and Opinions.* By S. T. Coleridge, Esq. 2 vols. 8vo. [London: Rest Fenner, 1817.] / 7. *Memoirs of Samuel Taylor Coleridge.* By James Gillman, Esq. Vol. I. 8vo. [London: Pickering,] 1839."

Identified in JSM's bibliography as "An article on Coleridge, in the London and Westminster Review for March 1840 (No. 65)" (MacMinn, 52). There are no corrections or alterations in the Somerville College copies of the article and *D&D*. The following text is collated with that in *D&D* (1st ed.), and that in the *London and Westminster.* In the footnoted variants, *D&D* (2nd ed.) is indicated by "67"; *D&D* (1st ed.) by "59"; and the *London and Westminster* by "40".

Coleridge

THE NAME OF Coleridge is one of the few English names of our *a* time which are likely to be oftener pronounced, and to become symbolical of more important things, in proportion as the inward workings of the age manifest themselves more and more in outward facts. Bentham excepted, no Englishman of recent date has left his impress so deeply in the opinions and mental tendencies of those among us who attempt to enlighten their practice by philosophical meditation. If it be true, as Lord Bacon affirms, that a knowledge of the speculative opinions of the men between twenty and thirty years of age is the great source of political prophecy,[*1] the existence of Coleridge will show itself by no slight or ambiguous traces in the coming history of our country; for no one has contributed more to shape the opinions of those among its younger men, who can be said to have opinions at all.

The influence of Coleridge, like that of Bentham, extends far beyond those who share in the peculiarities of his religious or philosophical creed. He has been the great awakener in this country of the spirit of philosophy, within the bounds of traditional opinions. He has been, almost as truly as Bentham, "the great questioner of things established;"[†1] for a questioner needs not necessarily be an enemy. By Bentham, beyond all others, men have been led to ask themselves, in regard to any ancient or received opinion, Is it true? and by Coleridge, What is the meaning of it? The one took his stand *b*outside*b* the received opinion, and surveyed it as an entire stranger to it: the other looked at it from within, and endeavoured to see it with the eyes of a believer in it; to discover by what apparent facts it was at first suggested, and by what appearances it has ever since been rendered continually credible —has seemed, to a succession of persons, to be a faithful interpretation of their experience. Bentham judged a proposition true or false as it accorded

[*See Samuel Taylor Coleridge. *First Lay Sermon* (*The Statesman's Manual*), in *On the Constitution of Church and State, and Lay Sermons*. London: Pickering, 1839, p. 216 n. The statement is not Bacon's, but Sir James Steuart's. See his *Inquiry into the Principles of Political Œconomy*. 2 vols. London: Millar and Cadell, 1767, Vol. I, p. 11.]

[†JSM is quoting himself; see above, "Bentham," p. 78.]

*a*40 own   *b–b* 40,59 *outside*

or not with the result of his own inquiries; and did not search very curiously into what might be meant by the proposition, when it obviously did not mean what he thought true. With Coleridge, on the contrary, the very fact that any doctrine had been believed by thoughtful men, and received by whole nations or generations of mankind, was *c* part of the problem to be solved, was one of the phenomena to be accounted for. And as Bentham's short and easy method of referring all to the selfish interests of aristocracies, or priests, or lawyers, or some other species of impostors, could not satisfy a man who saw so much farther into the complexities of the human intellect and feelings—he considered the long or extensive prevalence of any opinion as a presumption that it was not altogether a fallacy; that, to its first authors at least, it was the result of a struggle to express in words something which had a reality to them, though perhaps not to many of those who have since received the doctrine by mere tradition. The long duration of a belief, he thought, is at least proof *d* of an adaptation in it to some portion or other of the human mind; and if, on digging down to the root, we do not find, as is generally the case, some truth, we shall find some natural want or require- ment of human nature which the doctrine in question is fitted to satisfy: among which wants the instincts of selfishness and of credulity have a place, but by no means an exclusive one. From this difference in the points of view of the two philosophers, and from the too rigid adherence of each of his own, it was to be expected that Bentham should continually miss the truth which is in the traditional opinions, and Coleridge that which is out of them, and at variance with them. But it was also likely that each would find, or show the way to finding, much of what the other missed.

It is hardly possible to speak of Coleridge, and his position among his *e*cotemporaries*e*, without reverting to Bentham: they are connected by two of the closest bonds of association—resemblance and contrast. It would be difficult to find two persons of philosophic eminence more exactly the con- trary of one another. Compare their modes of treatment of any subject, and you might fancy them inhabitants of different worlds. They seem to have scarcely a principle or a premise in common. Each of them sees scarcely anything but what the other does not see. Bentham would have regarded Coleridge with a peculiar measure of the good-humoured contempt with which he was accustomed to regard all modes of philosophizing different from his own. Coleridge would probably have made Bentham one of the exceptions to the enlarged and liberal appreciation which (to the credit of *his* mode of philosophizing) he extended to most thinkers of any eminence, from whom he differed. But contraries, as logicians say, are but *quæ in eodem genere maxime distant*, the things which are farthest from one another *f*in the same kind*f*. These two agreed in being the men who, in their age and country,

*c*40   a   *d*40   positive
*e–e*40   contemporaries   *f–f*40   [*in italics*]

did most to enforce, by precept and example, the necessity of a philosophy. They agreed in making it their occupation to recal opinions to first principles; taking no proposition for granted without examining into the grounds of it, and ascertaining that it possessed the kind and degree of evidence suitable to its nature. They agreed in recognising that sound theory is the only foundation for sound practice, and that whoever despises theory, let him give himself what airs of wisdom he may, is self-convicted of being a quack. If a book were to be compiled containing all the best things ever said on the rule-of-thumb school of political craftsmanship, and on the insufficiency for practical purposes of what the mere practical man calls experience, it is difficult to say whether the collection would be more indebted to the writings of Bentham or of Coleridge. They agreed, too, in perceiving that the groundwork of all other philosophy must be laid in the philosophy of the mind. To lay this foundation deeply and strongly, and to raise a superstructure in accordance with it, were the objects to which their lives were devoted. They employed, indeed, for the most part, different materials; but as the materials of both were real observations, the genuine product of experience—the results will in the end be found not hostile, but supplementary, to one another. Of their methods of philosophizing, the same thing may be said: they were different, yet both were legitimate logical processes. In every respect the two men are each other's "completing counterpart:" the strong points of each correspond to the weak points of the other. Whoever could master the premises and combine the methods of both, would possess the entire English philosophy of ᵍtheirᵍ age. Coleridge used to say that every one is born either a Platonist or an Aristotelian:[*] it may be similarly affirmed, that every Englishman of the present day is by implication either a Benthamite or a Coleridgian; holds views of human affairs which can only be proved true on the principles either of Bentham or of Coleridge. In one respect, indeed, the parallel fails. Bentham so improved and added to the system of philosophy he adopted, that for his successors he may almost be accounted its founder; while Coleridge, though he has left on the system he inculcated, such traces of himself as cannot fail to be left by any mind of original powers, was anticipated in all the essentials of his doctrine by the great Germans of the latter half of the last century, and was accompanied in it by the remarkable series of their French expositors and followers. Hence, although Coleridge is to Englishmen the type and the main source of that doctrine, he is the creator rather of the shape in which it has appeared among us, than of the doctrine itself.

The time is yet far distant when, in the estimation of Coleridge, and of his influence upon the intellect of our time, anything like unanimity can be

[*Specimens of the Table Talk of Samuel Taylor Coleridge. Ed. Henry Nelson Coleridge. 2nd ed. London: Murray, 1836.]

ᵍ⁻ᵍ 40,59   his

looked for. As a poet, Coleridge has taken his place. The healthier taste, and more intelligent canons of poetic criticism, which he was himself mainly instrumental in diffusing, have at length assigned to him his proper rank, as one among the great, and (if we look to the powers shown rather than to the amount of actual achievement) among the greatest, names in our literature. But as a philosopher, the class of thinkers has scarcely yet arisen by whom he is to be judged. The limited philosophical public of this country is as yet too exclusively divided between those to whom Coleridge and the views which he promulgated or defended are [h]everything[h], and those to whom they are [i]nothing[i]. A [j]true[j] thinker can only be justly estimated when his thoughts have worked their way into minds formed in a different school; have been wrought and moulded into consistency with all other true and relevant thoughts; when the noisy conflict of half-truths, angrily denying one another, has subsided, and ideas which seemed mutually incompatible, have been found only to require mutual limitations. This time has not yet come for Coleridge. The spirit of philosophy in England, like that of religion, is still rootedly sectarian. Conservative thinkers and Liberals, transcendentalists and admirers of Hobbes and Locke, regard each other as out of the pale of philosophical intercourse; look upon each other's speculations as vitiated by an original taint, which makes all study of them, except for purposes of attack, useless if not mischievous. An error much the same as if Kepler had refused to profit by Ptolemy's or Tycho's observations, because those astronomers believed that the sun moved round the earth; or as if Priestley and Lavoisier, because they differed on the doctrine of phlogiston, had rejected [k]each other's[k] chemical experiments. [l]It is even[l] a still greater error than either of these. For, among the [m] truths long recognised by [n] Continental philosophers, but which very few Englishmen have yet [o]arrived at[o], one is, the importance, in the present imperfect state of mental and social science, of antagonist modes of thought: which, it will one day be felt, are as necessary to one another in speculation, as mutually checking powers are in a political constitution. A clear insight, indeed, into this necessity is the only rational or enduring basis of philosophical tolerance; the only condition under which liberality in matters of opinion can be anything better than a polite synonym for indifference between one opinion and another.

All students of man and society who possess that first requisite for so difficult a study, a due sense of its difficulties, are aware that the besetting danger is not so much of embracing falsehood for truth, as of mistaking part of the truth for the whole. It might be plausibly maintained that in [p]almost[p]

[h-h]40	*all*		[i-i]40	*nothing*
[j-j]40	*great*		[k-k]40	one another's
[l-l]40	Nay, it is		[m]40	*great*
[n]40	the		[o-o]40	found out
[p-p]+59,67				

every one of the leading controversies, past or present, in social philosophy, both sides were in the right in what they affirmed, though wrong in what they denied; and that if either could have been made to take the other's views in addition to its own, little more would have been needed to make its doctrine *q*correct*q*. Take for instance the question how far mankind have gained by civilization. One *r*observer*r* is forcibly stuck by the multiplication of physical comforts; the advancement and diffusion of knowledge; the decay of super-stition; the facilities of mutual intercourse; the softening of manners; the decline of war and personal conflict; the progressive limitation of the tyranny of the strong over the weak; the great works accomplished throughout the globe by the co-operation of multitudes: and he becomes that very common character, the worshipper of "our enlightened age." Another fixes his atten-tion, not upon the value of these advantages, but upon the high price which is paid for them; the relaxation of individual energy and courage; the loss of proud and self-relying independence; the slavery of so large a portion of man-kind to artificial wants; their effeminate shrinking from *s*even*s* the shadow of pain; the dull unexciting monotony of their lives, and the passionless insi-pidity, and absence of any marked individuality, in their characters; the con-trast between the narrow mechanical understanding, produced by a life spent in executing by fixed rules a fixed task, and the varied powers of the man of the woods, whose subsistence and safety depend at each instant upon his capacity of extemporarily adapting means to ends; the demoralizing effect of great inequalities in wealth and social rank; and the sufferings of the great mass of the people of civilized countries, whose wants are scarcely better provided for than those of the savage, while they are bound by a thousand fetters in lieu of the freedom and excitement which are his compensations. *t*One*t* who attends to these things, and to these exclusively, will *u*be apt to*u* infer that *v* savage life is *w*preferable to civilized*w*; that the work of civilization should as far as possible be undone; and from the premises of Rousseau, he will not improbably be led to the practical conclusions of Rousseau's disciple, Robespierre. No two thinkers can be more entirely at variance than the two we have supposed—the worshippers of Civilization and of Independence, of the present and of the remote past. Yet all that is positive in the opinions of either of them is true; and we see how easy it would be to choose one's path, if either half of the truth were the whole of it, and how great may be the difficulty of framing, as it is necessary to do, a set of practical maxims which combine both.

So again, one *x*person*x* sees in a very strong light the need which the great

*q–q*40   perfect
s–s+59,67
*u–u*40   necessarily
*w–w*40   the perfection of human nature

*r–r*40   man
*t–t*40   The man
*v*40   the
*x–x*40   man

mass of mankind have of being ruled over by a degree of intelligence and virtue superior to their own. He is deeply impressed with the mischief done to the uneducated and uncultivated by weaning them of all habits of reverence, appealing to them as a competent tribunal to decide the most ʸintricateʸ questions, and making them think themselves capable, not only of being a light to themselves, but of giving the law to their superiors in culture. He sees, ᶻfurtherᶻ, that cultivation, to be carried beyond a certain point, requires leisure; that leisure is the natural attribute of a hereditary aristocracy; that such a body has all the means of acquiring intellectual and moral superiority; and he needs be at no loss to endow them with abundant motives to it. An aristocracy indeed, being human, are, as he cannot but see, not exempt, any more than their inferiors, from the common need of being controlled and enlightened by a still greater wisdom and goodness than their own. For this, however, his reliance is upon reverence for a Higher above them, sedulously inculcated and fostered by the ᵃ course of their education. We thus see brought together all the elements of a conscientious zealot for an aristocratic government, supporting and supported by an established Christian church. There is truth, and important truth, in this ᵇthinker'sᵇ premises. But there is a ᶜthinkerᶜ of a very different description, in whose premises there is an equal portion of truth. This is he who says, that an average man, even an average member of an aristocracy, if he ᵈcanᵈ postpone the interests of other people to his own calculations or instincts of self-interest, will do so; that all governments ᵉin all ages haveᵉ done so, as far as they were permitted, and generally to a ruinous extent; and that the only possible remedy is a pure democracy, in which the people are their own governors, and can have no selfish interest in oppressing themselves.

Thus it is in regard to every important partial truth; there are always two conflicting modes of thought, one tending to give to that truth too large, the other to give it too small, a place: and the history of opinion is generally an oscillation between these extremes. From the imperfection ᶠofᶠ the human faculties, it seldom happens that, even in the minds of ᵍeminentᵍ thinkers, each partial view of their subject passes for its worth, and none for more than its worth. But even if this just balance exist in the mind of the wiser teacher, it will not exist in his disciples, still less in the general mind. He cannot prevent that which is new in his doctrine, and on which, being new, he is forced to insist the most strongly, from making a disproportionate impression. The impetus necessary to overcome the obstacles which resist all novelties of opinion, seldom fails to carry the public mind almost as far on the contrary

ʸ–ʸ40   difficult
ᵃ40   whole
ᶜ–ᶜ40   man
ᵉ–ᵉ40   have always
ᵍ–ᵍ40   great

ᶻ–ᶻ40   moreover
ᵇ–ᵇ40   man's
ᵈ–ᵈ40   *can*
ᶠ–ᶠ40   inherent in

side of the perpendicular. Thus every excess in either direction determines a corresponding reaction; improvement consisting only in this, that the oscillation, each time, departs rather less widely from the centre, and an ever-increasing tendency is manifested to settle finally in it.

Now the Germano-Coleridgian doctrine is, in our view of the matter, the result of such a reaction. It expresses the revolt of the human mind against the philosophy of the eighteenth century. It is ontological, because that was experimental; conservative, because that was innovative; religious, because so much of that was infidel; concrete and historical, because that was abstract and metaphysical; poetical, because that was matter-of-fact and prosaic. In every respect it flies off in the contrary direction to its predecessor; yet faithful to the general law of improvement last noticed, it is less extreme in its opposition, it denies less of what is true in the doctrine it wars against, than *h*had*h* been the case in any previous philosophic reaction; and in particular, far less than when the philosophy of the eighteenth century triumphed, and so memorably abused its victory, over that which preceded it.

We may begin our consideration of the two systems either at one extreme or the other; with their highest philosophical generalizations, or with their practical conclusions. *i*The former seems preferable*i*, because it is *j*in*j* their highest generalities that the difference between the two systems is most familiarly known.

Every consistent scheme of philosophy requires as its starting-point, a theory respecting the sources of human knowledge, and the objects which the human faculties are capable of taking cognizance of. The prevailing theory in the eighteenth century, on this most comprehensive of questions, was that proclaimed by Locke,[*] and *k*commonly*k* attributed to Aristotle— that all *l* knowledge consists of generalizations from experience. Of nature, or anything whatever external to ourselves, we know, according to this theory, nothing, except the facts which present themselves to our senses, and such other facts as may, by analogy, be inferred from these. There is no knowledge à priori; no truths cognizable by the mind's inward light, and grounded on intuitive evidence. Sensation, and the mind's consciousness of its own acts, are not only the exclusive sources, but the sole materials of our knowledge. From this doctrine, Coleridge, with the German philosophers since Kant (not to go farther back) and most of the English since Reid, strongly dissents. He claims for the human mind a capacity, within certain limits, of perceiving the nature and properties of "Things in themselves." He

[*See. e.g., *Of Human Understanding*, Book II, Chap. i.]

*h–h*40   has
*i–i*40   by
*l*40   our

*i–i*40   We prefer the former
k–k+59,67

distinguishes in the human intellect two faculties, which, in the technical language common to him with the Germans, he calls Understanding and Reason. The former faculty judges of phenomena, or the appearances of things, and forms generalizations from these: to the latter it belongs, by direct intuition, to perceive things, and recognise truths, not cognizable by our senses. These perceptions are not indeed innate, nor could ever have been awakened in us without experience; but they are not copies of it: experience is not their prototype, it is only the occasion by which they are irresistibly suggested. The appearances in nature excite in us, by an inherent law, ideas of those invisible things which are the causes of the visible appearances, and on whose laws those appearances depend: and we then perceive that these things must have pre-existed to render the appearances possible; just as (to use a frequent illustration of Coleridge's) we see, before we know that we have eyes;[*] but when once this is known to us, we perceive that eyes must have pre-existed to enable us to see. Among the truths which are thus known *à priori*, by occasion of experience, but not themselves the subjects of experience, Coleridge includes the fundamental doctrines of religion and ᵐmoralsᵐ, the principles of mathematics, and the ultimate laws even of physical nature; which he contends cannot be proved by experience, though they must necessarily be consistent with it, and would, if we knew them perfectly, enable us to account for all observed facts, and to predict all those which are as yet unobserved.

It is not necessary to remind any one who concerns himself with such subjects, that between the partisans of these two opposite doctrines there reigns a *bellum internecinum*. Neither side is sparing in the imputation of intellectual and moral obliquity to the perceptions, and of pernicious consequences to the creed, of its antagonists. Sensualism is the common term of abuse for the one philosophy, mysticism for the other. The one doctrine is accused of making men beasts, the other lunatics. It is the unaffected belief of numbers on ⁿ one side of the controversy, that their adversaries are actuated by a desire to break loose from moral and religious obligation; and of ᵒ numbers on the other that their opponents are either men fit for Bedlam, or who cunningly pander to the interests of hierarchies and aristocracies, by manufacturing superfine new arguments in favour of old prejudices. It is almost needless to say that those who are freest with these mutual accusations, are seldom those who are most at home in the real intricacies of the question, or who are best acquainted with the argumentative strength of the opposite side, or even of their own. But without going to these extreme lengths, even sober men on both sides take no charitable view of the tendencies of each other's opinions.

[*See, e.g., *The Friend*. 3 vols. London: Rest Fenner, 1818, Vol. I, p. 309 n.]

ᵐ⁻ᵐ40   morality   ⁿ40   the   ᵒ40   equal

It is affirmed that the doctrine of Locke and his followers, that all knowledge is experience generalized, leads by strict logical consequence to atheism: that Hume and other sceptics were right when they contended that it is impossible to prove a God on grounds of experience; and Coleridge ᵖ(like Kant)ᵖ maintains positively, that the ordinary argument for a Deity, from marks of design in the universe, or, in other words, from the resemblance of the order in nature to the effects of human skill and contrivance, is not tenable. It is further said that the same doctrine annihilates moral obligation; reducing morality either to the blind impulses of animal sensibility, or to a calculation of prudential consequences, both equally fatal to its essence. Even science, it is affirmed, loses ᑫtheᑫ character of science in this view of it, and becomes empiricism; a mere enumeration and arrangement of facts, not explaining nor accounting for them: since a fact is only then accounted for when we are made to see in it the manifestation of laws, which, as soon as they are perceived at all, are perceived to be *necessary*. These are the charges brought by the transcendental philosophers against the school of Locke, Hartley, and Bentham. They in their turn allege that the transcendentalists make imagination, and not observation, the criterion of truth; that they lay down principles under which a man may enthrone his wildest dreams in the chair of philosophy, and impose them on mankind as intuitions of the pure reason: which has, in fact, been done in all ages, by all manner of mystical enthusiasts. And even if, with gross inconsistency, the private revelations of any individual ʳBöhmeʳ or Swedenborg be disowned, or, in other words, outvoted (the only means of discrimination which, it is contended, the theory admits of), this is still only substituting, as the test of truth, the dreams of the majority for the dreams of each individual. Whoever form a strong enough party, may at any time set up the immediate perceptions of *their* reason, that is to say, any reigning prejudice, as a truth independent of experience; a truth not only requiring no proof, but to be believed in opposition to all that appears proof to the mere understanding; nay, the more to be believed, because it cannot be put into words and into the logical form of a proposition without a contradiction in terms: for no less authority than this is claimed by some transcendentalists for their *à priori* truths. And thus a ready mode is provided, by which whoever is on the strongest side may dogmatize at his ease, and instead of proving his propositions, may rail at all who deny them, as bereft of "the vision and the faculty divine,"[*] or blinded to its plainest revelations by a corrupt heart.

[*William Wordsworth. "The Excursion," in *The Poetical Works of William Wordsworth*. London: Longman, Rees, Orme, Brown, and Green, 1827, Vol. V, pp. 6–7; Bk. I, l. 78.]

ᵖ⁻ᵖ+59,67   ᑫ⁻ᑫ40 its   ʳ⁻ʳ40,59 Behmen

This is a very temperate statement of what is charged by these two classes of thinkers against each other ˢ. How much of either representation is correct, cannot conveniently be discussed in this place.ˢ In truth, a system of consequences from an opinion, drawn by an adversary, is seldom of much worth. Disputants are rarely sufficiently masters of each other's doctrines, to be good judges ᵗ what is fairly deducible from them, or how a consequence which seems to flow from one part of the theory may or may not be defeated by another part. To combine the different parts of a doctrine with one another, and with all admitted truths, is not indeed a small trouble, ᵘnorᵘ one which a ᵛpersonᵛ is often inclined to take for other people's opinions. Enough if each does it for his own, which he has a greater interest in, and is more disposed to be just to. Were we to search among men's recorded thoughts for the choicest manifestations of human imbecility and prejudice, our specimens would be mostly taken from their opinions of the opinions of one another. Imputations of horrid consequences ought not ʷ to bias the judgment of any person capable of independent thought. Coleridge himself says (in the 25th Aphorism of his *Aids to Reflection*), "He who begins by loving Christianity better than truth, will proceed by loving his own sect or church better than Christianity, and end in loving himself better than all." [*]

As to the fundamental difference of opinion respecting the sources of our knowledge (apart from the corollaries which either party may have drawn from its own principle, or imputed to its opponent's), the question lies far too deep in the recesses of psychology for us to discuss it here. The lists having been open ever since the dawn of philosophy, it is not wonderful that the two parties should have been forced to put on their strongest armour, both of attack and of defence. The question would not so long have remained a question, if the more obvious arguments on either side had been unanswerable. Each ˣpartyˣ has been able to urge in its own favour numerous and striking facts, to ʸreconcile which withʸ the opposite theory has required all the metaphysical resources which that theory could command. It will not be wondered at, then, that we here content ourselves with a bare statement of our opinion. It is, that the truth, on this much-debated question, lies with the school of Locke and of Bentham. The nature and laws of Things in themselves, or of the hidden causes of the phenomena which are the objects of experience, appear to us radically inaccessible to the human faculties. We see no ground for believing that anything can be the object of our knowledge

[*2nd ed. London: Hurst, Chance, 1831, p. 96.]

ˢ⁻ˢ40   , though a grossly exaggerated one of what can be alleged with justice against either.

ᵗ40   of

ᵛ⁻ᵛ40   man

ˣ⁻ˣ40   side

ᵘ⁻ᵘ40   or

ʷ40   , therefore,

ʸ⁻ʸ40   account for which on

except our experience, and what can be inferred from our experience by the analogies of experience itself; nor that there is any idea, feeling, or power in the human mind, which, in order to account for it, requires that its origin should be referred to any other source. We are therefore at issue with Coleridge on the central idea of his philosophy; and we find no need of, and no use for, the *peculiar* technical terminology which he and his masters the Germans have introduced into philosophy, for the double purpose of giving logical precision to doctrines which we do not admit, and of marking a relation between those abstract doctrines and many concrete experimental truths, which this language, in our judgment, serves not to elucidate, but to disguise and obscure. Indeed, but for these peculiarities of language, it would be difficult to understand how the reproach of *mysticism* (by which nothing is meant in common parlance but *unintelligibleness*) has been fixed upon Coleridge and the Germans in the minds of many, to whom doctrines substantially the same, when taught in a manner more superficial and less fenced round against objections, by Reid and Dugald Stewart, have appeared the plain dictates of "common sense," successfully asserted against the subtleties of metaphysics.

Yet, though we think the doctrines of Coleridge and the Germans, in the pure science of mind, erroneous, and have no taste for their peculiar terminology, we are far from thinking that even in respect of this, the least valuable part of their intellectual exertions, those philosophers have lived in vain. The doctrines of the school of Locke stood in need of an entire renovation: to borrow a physiological illustration from Coleridge, they required, like certain secretions of the human body, to be reabsorbed into the system and secreted afresh.[*] In what form did that philosophy generally prevail throughout Europe? In that of the shallowest set of doctrines which perhaps were ever passed off upon a cultivated age as a complete psychological system—the ideology of Condillac and his school; a system which affected to resolve all the phenomena of the human mind into sensation, by a process which essentially consisted in merely *calling* all states of mind, however heterogeneous, by that name; a philosophy now acknowledged to consist solely of a set of verbal generalizations, explaining nothing, distinguishing nothing, leading to nothing. That men should begin by sweeping this *away,* was the first sign that the age of real psychology was about to commence. In England the case, though different, was scarcely better. The philosophy of Locke, as a popular doctrine, had remained *nearly* as it stood in his own book; which, as its title implies, did not pretend to give an account of any

[*_Biographia Literaria_. 2 vols. London: Rest Fenner, 1817, Vol. I, p. 234 n.]

z–z40   new
a–a40   *mysticism*   b–b40   *unintelligibleness*
c–c40   away from them   d–d40   pretty much

but the intellectual part of our nature; which, even within that limited sphere, was but the commencement of a system, and though its errors and defects as such have been exaggerated beyond all just bounds, it did expose many vulnerable points to the searching criticism of the new school. The least imperfect part of it, the purely logical part, had almost dropped out of sight. With respect to those of Locke's doctrines which are properly metaphysical; however the sceptical part of them may have been followed up by others, and carried beyond the point at which he stopped; the only one of his successors who attempted, and achieved, any considerable improvement and extension of the analytical part, and thereby added anything to the explanation of the human mind on Locke's principles, was Hartley. But Hartley's ᵉdoctrinesᵉ, so far as they are true, were so much in advance of the age, and the way had been so little prepared for them by the general tone of thinking which yet prevailed, even under the influence of Locke's writings, that the philosophic world did not deem them worthy of being attended to. Reid and Stewart were allowed to run them down uncontradicted: Brown, though a man of a kindred genius, had evidently never read them; and but for the accident of their being taken up by Priestley, who transmitted them as a kind of heirloom to his Unitarian followers, the name of Hartley might have perished, or survived only as that of a visionary physician, the author of an exploded physiological hypothesis. It perhaps required all the violence of the assaults made by Reid and the German school upon Locke's system, to recall men's minds to Hartley's principles, as alone adequate to the solution, upon that system, of the peculiar difficulties which those assailants pressed upon men's attention as altogether insoluble by it. ᶠ We may here notice that Coleridge, before he adopted his later philosophical views, was an enthusiastic Hartleian; so that his abandonment of the philosophy of Locke cannot be imputed to unacquaintance with the highest form of that philosophy which had yet appeared. That he should pass through that highest form without stopping at it, is itself a strong presumption that there were more difficulties in the question than Hartley had solved. That anything has since been done to solve them we probably owe to the revolution in opinion, of which Coleridge was one of the organs; and even in abstract metaphysics his writings, and those of his school of thinkers, are ᵍone of the richest minesᵍ from whence the opposite school can draw the materials for what has yet to be done to perfect their own theory.

If we now pass from the purely abstract to the concrete and practical doctrines of the two schools, we shall see still more clearly the necessity of the

ᵉ⁻ᵉ40   views
ᶠ40   [footnote:] *The solution of them, so far as it is yet completed, is to be found in a book, in our own opinion, the greatest accession to abstract psychology since Hartley, the *Analysis of the Human Mind*, by the late Mr. Mill.
ᵍ⁻ᵍ40,59   the richest mine

reaction, and the great service rendered to philosophy by its authors. This will be best manifested by a survey of the state of practical philosophy in Europe, as Coleridge and his compeers found it, towards the close of the last century.

The state of opinion in the latter half of the eighteenth century was by no means the same on the Continent of Europe and in our own island; and the difference was still greater in appearance than it was in reality. In the more advanced nations of the Continent, the prevailing philosophy had done its work completely: it had spread itself over every department of human knowledge; it had taken possession of the whole Continental mind: and scarcely one educated person was left who retained any allegiance to the opinions or the institutions of ancient times. In England, the native country of compromise, things had stopped far short of this; the philosophical movement had been brought to a halt in an early stage, and a peace had been patched up by concessions on both sides, between the philosophy of the time and its traditional institutions and creeds. Hence the aberrations of the age were generally, on the Continent, at that period, the extravagances of new opinions; in England, the corruptions of old ones.

To insist upon the deficiencies of the Continental philosophy of the last century, or, as it is commonly termed, the French philosophy, is almost superfluous. That philosophy is indeed as unpopular in this country as its bitterest enemy could desire. If its faults were as well understood as they are much railed at, criticism might be considered to have finished its work. But that this is not yet the case, the nature of the imputations currently made upon the French philosophers, sufficiently proves; many of these being as inconsistent with a just philosophic comprehension of their system of opinions, as with charity towards the men themselves. It is not true, for example, that any of them denied moral obligation, or sought to weaken its force. So far were they from meriting this accusation, that they could not even tolerate the writers who, like Helvetius, ascribed a selfish origin to the feelings of morality, resolving them into a sense of interest. Those writers were as much cried down among the *philosophes* themselves, and what was true and good in them (and there is much that is so) met with as little appreciation, then as now. The error of the philosophers was rather that they trusted too much to those feelings; believed them to be more deeply rooted in human nature than they are; to be not so dependent, as in fact they are, upon collateral influences. They thought them the natural and spontaneous growth of the human heart; so firmly fixed in it, that they would subsist unimpaired, nay invigorated, when the whole system of opinions and observances with which they were habitually intertwined was violently torn away.

To tear away was, indeed, all that these philosophers, for the most part, aimed at: they had no conception that anything else was needful. At their millennium, superstition, priestcraft, error and prejudice of every kind, were to be annihilated; some of them gradually added that despotism and hereditary privileges must share the same fate; and, this accomplished, they never for a moment suspected that all the virtues and graces of humanity could fail to flourish, or that when the noxious weeds were once rooted out, the soil would stand in any need of tillage.

In this they committed the very common error, of mistaking the state of things with which they had always been familiar, for the universal and natural condition of mankind. They were accustomed to see the human race agglomerated in large nations, all (except here and there a madman or a malefactor) yielding obedience more or less strict to a set of laws prescribed by a few of their own number, and to a set of moral rules prescribed by each other's opinion; renouncing the exercise of individual will and judgment, except within the limits imposed by these laws and rules; and acquiescing in the sacrifice of their individual wishes when the point was decided against them by lawful authority; or persevering only in hopes of altering the opinion of the ruling powers. Finding matters to be so generally in this condition, the philosophers apparently concluded that they could not possibly be in any other; and were ignorant, by what a host of civilizing and restraining influences a state of things so repugnant to man's self-will and love of independence has been brought about, and how imperatively it demands the continuance of those influences as the condition of its own existence. The very first element of the social union, obedience to a government of some sort, has not been found so easy a thing to establish in the world. Among a timid and spiritless race, like the inhabitants of the vast plains of tropical countries, passive obedience may be of natural growth; though even there we doubt whether it has ever been found among any people with whom fatalism, or in other words, submission to the pressure of circumstances as the decree of God, did not prevail as a religious doctrine. But the difficulty of inducing a brave and warlike race to submit their individual *arbitrium* to any common umpire, has always been felt to be so great, that nothing short of supernatural power has been deemed adequate to overcome it; and such tribes have always assigned to the first institution of civil society a divine origin. So differently did those judge who knew savage man by actual experience, from those who had no acquaintance with him except in the civilized state. In modern Europe itself, after the fall of the Roman empire, to subdue the feudal anarchy and bring the whole people of any European nation into subjection to government (although Christianity in *h*the*h* most concentrated form *i*of its influence*i* was co-operating *i* in the work) required thrice as many centuries as have elapsed since that time.

*h–h*40   its   *i–i*+59,67   *i*40   with all its influences

Now if these philosophers had known human nature under any other type than that of their own age, and of the particular classes of society among whom they *k*lived*k*, it would have occurred to them, that wherever this habitual submission to law and government has been firmly and durably established, and yet the vigour and manliness of character which resisted its establishment have been in any degree preserved, certain requisites have existed, certain conditions have been fulfilled, of which the following may be regarded as the principal.

First: There has existed, for all who were accounted citizens,—for all who were not slaves, kept down by brute force,—a system of *education*, beginning with infancy and continued through life, of which, whatever else it might include, one main and incessant ingredient was *restraining discipline*. To train the human being in the habit, and thence the power, of subordinating his personal impulses and aims, to what were considered the ends of society; of adhering, against all temptation, to the course of conduct which those ends prescribed; of controlling in himself all the feelings which were liable to militate against those ends, and encouraging all such as tended towards them; this was the purpose, to which every outward motive that the authority directing the system could command, and every inward power or principle which its knowledge of human nature enabled it to evoke, were endeavoured to be rendered instrumental. *l*The entire civil and military policy of the ancient commonwealths was such a system of training: in modern nations its place has been attempted to be supplied principally by religious teaching.*l* And whenever and in proportion as the strictness of *m*the restraining*m* discipline was relaxed, the natural tendency of mankind to anarchy reasserted itself; the State became disorganized from within; mutual conflict for selfish ends, neutralized the energies which were required to keep up the contest against natural causes of evil; and the nation, after a longer or briefer interval of progressive decline, became either the slave of a despotism, or the prey of a foreign invader.

The second condition of permanent political society has been found to be, the existence, in some form or other, of the feeling of allegiance, or loyalty. This feeling may vary in its objects, and is not confined to any particular form of government; but whether in a democracy or in a monarchy, its essence is always the same; viz. that there be in the constitution of the State *something* which is settled, something permanent, and not to be called in question; something which, by general agreement, has a right to be

*k–k*40 moved

*l–l*40 This system of discipline wrought, in the Grecian states, by the conjunct influences of religion, poetry, and law; among the Romans, by those of religion and law; in modern and Christian countries, mainly by religion, with little of the direct agency, but generally more or less of the indirect support and countenance, of law.

*m–m*40 this

where it is, and to be secure against disturbance, whatever else may change. This feeling may attach itself, as among the Jews (and indeed in most of the commonwealths of antiquity), to a common God or gods, the protectors and guardians of their State. Or it may attach itself to certain persons, who are deemed to be, whether by divine appointment, by long prescription, or by the general recognition of their superior capacity and worthiness, the rightful guides and guardians of the rest. Or it may attach itself to laws; to ancient liberties, or ordinances [n]. Or finally (and this is the only shape in which the feeling is likely to exist hereafter) it may attach itself to the principles of individual freedom and political and social equality, as realized in institutions which as yet exist nowhere, or exist only in a rudimentary state.[n] But in all political societies which have had a durable existence, there has been some fixed point; something which men agreed in holding sacred; which [o], wherever freedom of discussion was a recognised principle, it was of course[o] lawful to contest in theory, but which no one could either fear or hope to see shaken in practice; which, in short (except perhaps during some temporary crisis), was in the common estimation placed [p]beyond[p] discussion. And the necessity of this may easily be made evident. A State never is, nor, until mankind are vastly improved, can hope to be, for any long time exempt from internal dissension; for there neither is, nor has ever been, any state of society in which collisions did not occur between the immediate interests and passions of powerful sections of the people. What, then, enables society to weather these storms, and pass through turbulent times without any permanent weakening of the [q]securities for peaceable existence[q]? Precisely this—that however important the interests about which men [r]fell[r] out, the conflict [s]did[s] not affect the fundamental principles of the system of social union which [t]happened[t] to exist; nor threaten large portions of the community with the subversion of that on which they [u]had[u] built their calculations, and with which their hopes and aims [v]had[v] become identified. But when the questioning of these fundamental principles is (not [w]the[w] occasional disease, [x]or salutary medicine,[x] but) the habitual condition of the body politic, and when all the violent animosities are called forth, which spring naturally from such a situation, the State is virtually in a position of civil war; and can never long remain free from it in act and fact.

The third essential condition [y]of stability in political society[y], is a strong

---

[n]–[n]40 ; to the whole or some part of the political, or even of the domestic, institutions of the state.

[o]–[o]40	it might or might not be	[p]–[p]40	*above*
[q]–[q]40	ties which hold it together	[r]–[r]40,59	fall
[s]–[s]40	does	[t]–[t]40	happens
[u]–[u]40	have	[v]–[v]40	have
[w]–[w]40	an	[x]–[x]+59,67	
[y]–[y]40	, which has existed in all durable political societies		

and active principle of ᶻcohesion among the members of the same community or stateᶻ. We need scarcely say that we do not mean ᵃnationality in the vulgar sense of the term;ᵃ a senseless antipathy to foreigners; ᵇan indifference to the general welfare of the human race, or an unjust preference of the supposed interests of our own country;ᵇ ᶜ a cherishing of ᵈbadᵈ peculiarities because they are national; or a refusal to adopt what has been found good by other countries. ᵉ We mean a principle of sympathy, not of hostility; of union, not of separation. We mean a feeling of common interest among those who live under the same government, and are contained within the same natural or historical boundaries. We mean, that one part of the community ᶠdoᶠ not consider themselves as foreigners with regard to another part; that they ᵍset a value on their connexion;ᵍ feel that they are one people, that their lot is cast together, that evil to any of their fellow-countrymen is evil to themselves; and ʰdo not desire selfishly toʰ free themselves from their share of any common inconvenience by severing the connexion. How strong this feeling was in ⁱthoseⁱ ancient commonwealths ⁱwhich attained any durable greatness,ʲ every one knows. How happily Rome, in spite of all her tyranny, succeeded in establishing the feeling of a common country amoung the provinces of her vast and divided empire, will appear when any one who has given due attention to the subject shall take the trouble to point it out.* In modern times

*We are glad to quote a striking passage from Coleridge on this very subject. He is speaking of the misdeeds of England in Ireland; towards which misdeeds this Tory, as he is called (for the Tories, who neglected him in his lifetime, show no little eagerness to give themselves the credit of his name after his death), entertained feelings scarcely surpassed by those which are excited by the masterly exposure for which we have recently been indebted to M. de Beaumont [40 M. de Beaumont's masterly exposure]. [Gustave de Beaumont, *L'Irlande sociale, politique et religieuse*. 2 vols. Paris: Gosselin, 1839.]

"Let us discharge," he says, "what may well be deemed a debt of justice from every well-educated Englishman to his Roman Catholic fellow-subjects of the Sister Island. At least, let us ourselves understand the true cause of the evil as it now exists. To what and to whom is the present state of Ireland mainly to be attributed? This should be the question: and to this I answer aloud, that it is mainly attributable to those who, during a period of little less than a whole century, used as a substitute what Providence had given into their hand as an opportunity; who chose to consider as superseding the most sacred duty, a code of law, which could be excused only on the plea that it enabled them to perform it. To

ᶻ⁻ᶻ40 nationality   ᵃ⁻ᵃ+59,67
ᵇ⁻ᵇ+59,67   ᶜ40 or
ᵈ⁻ᵈ40 absurd
ᵉ40 In all these senses, the nations which have had the strongest national spirit have had the least nationality.
ᶠ⁻ᶠ40 shall
ᵍ⁻ᵍ40 shall cherish the tie which holds them together; shall
ʰ⁻ʰ40 that they cannot selfishly
ⁱ⁻ⁱ40 the   ʲ⁻ʲ+59,67

the countries which have had that feeling in the strongest degree have been the most powerful countries; England, France, and, in proportion to their territory and resources, Holland and Switzerland; while England in her con- nexion with Ireland, is one of the most signal examples of the consequences of its absence. Every Italian knows why Italy is under a foreign yoke; every German knows what maintains despotism in the Austrian empire; the *k*evils*k* of Spain flow as much from the absence of nationality among the Spaniards themselves, as from the presence of it in their relations with foreigners; while the completest illustration of all is afforded by the republics of South America, where the parts of one and the same state adhere so slightly to- gether, that no sooner does any province think itself aggrieved by the general government, than it proclaims itself a separate nation.

These essential requisites of civil society the French philosophers of the eighteenth century unfortunately overlooked. They found, indeed, all three—

---

the sloth and improvidence, the weakness and wickedness, of the gentry, clergy, and governors of Ireland, who persevered in preferring intrigue, violence, and selfish expatriation to a system of preventive and remedial measures, the efficacy of which had been warranted for them alike by the whole provincial history of ancient Rome, *cui pacare subactos summa erat sapientia*, and by the happy results of the few exceptions to the contrary scheme unhappily pursued by their and our ancestors.

I can imagine no work of genius that would more appropriately decorate the dome or wall of a Senate-house, than an abstract of Irish history from the landing of Strongbow to the battle of the Boyne, or to a yet later period, embodied in intelligible emblems—an allegorical history-piece designed in the spirit of a Rubens or a Buonarotti, and with the wild lights, portentous shades, and saturated colours of a Rembrandt, Caravaggio, and Spagnoletti. To complete the great moral and political lesson by the historic contrast, nothing more would be re- quired than by some equally effective means to possess the mind of the spectator with the state and condition of ancient Spain, at less than half a century from the final conclusion of an obstinate and almost unremitting conflict of two hun- dred years by Agrippa's subjugation of the Cantabrians, *omnibus Hispaniæ populis devictis et pacatis*. At the breaking up of the empire the West Goths conquered the country, and made division of the lands. Then came eight centuries of Moorish domination. Yet so deeply had Roman wisdom impressed the fairest characters of the Roman mind, that at this very hour, if we except a compara- tively insignificant portion of Arabic derivatives, the natives throughout the whole Peninsula speak a language less differing from the *Romana rustica*, or provincial Latin of the times of Lucan and Seneca, than any two of its dialects from each other. The time approaches, I trust, when our political economists may study the science of the provincial policy of the ancients in detail, under the auspices of hope, for immediate and practical purposes." (*Church and State* [in *On the Constitution of Church and State, and Lay Sermons*. Ed. Henry Nelson Coleridge. London: Pickering, 1839], pp. 160–2.)

*k–k*40   woes

at least the first and second, and most of what nourishes and invigorates the third—already undermined by the vices of the institutions, and of the men, that were set up as the guardians and bulwarks of them. If innovators, in their theories, disregarded the elementary principles of the social union, Conservatives, in their practice, had set the first example. The existing order of things had ceased to realize those first principles: from the force of circumstances, and from the short-sighted selfishness of its administrators, it had ceased to possess the essential conditions of permanent society, and was therefore tottering to its fall. But the philosophers did not see this. Bad as the existing system was in the days of its decrepitude, according to them it was still worse when it actually did what it now only pretended to do. Instead of feeling that the effect of a bad social order in sapping the necessary foundations of society itself, is *one of the* worst of its many mischiefs, the philosophers saw only, and saw with joy, that it was sapping its own foundations. In the weakening of all government they saw only the weakening of bad government; and thought they could not better employ themselves than in finishing the task so well begun—in *discrediting all that still remained of restraining discipline, because it rested on the ancient and decayed creeds against which they made war*; in unsettling everything which was still considered settled, making men doubtful of the few things of which they still felt certain; and in uprooting what little remained in the people's minds of reverence for anything above them, of respect to any of the limits which custom and prescription had set to the indulgence of each man's fancies or inclinations, or of attachment to any of the things which belonged to them as a nation, and which made them feel their unity as such.

Much of all this was, no doubt, unavoidable, and *n* not justly matter of blame. When the vices of all constituted authorities, added to natural causes of decay, have eaten the heart out of old institutions and beliefs, while at the same time the growth of knowledge, and the altered circumstances of the age, would have required institutions and creeds different from these even if they had remained uncorrupt, we are far from saying that any degree of wisdom on the part of speculative thinkers could avert the political catastrophes, and the subsequent moral anarchy and unsettledness, which we have witnessed and are witnessing. Still less do we pretend that those principles and influences which we have spoken of as the conditions of the permanent existence of the social union, once lost, can ever be, or should be attempted to be, revived in connexion with the same institutions or the same doctrines as before. When society requires to be rebuilt, there is no use in attempting to

*l–l*40   the very
*m–m*40   expelling out of every mind the last vestige of belief in that creed on which all the restraining discipline recognised in the education of European countries still rested, and with which in the general mind it was inseparably associated
*n*40   is

rebuild it on the old plan. By the union of the enlarged views and analytic powers of speculative men with the observation and contriving sagacity of men of practice, better institutions and better doctrines must be elaborated; and until this is done we cannot hope for much improvement in our present condition. The effort to do it in the eighteenth century would have been *o* premature, as the attempts of the Economistes (who, of all persons then living, came nearest to it, and who were the first to form *p*clearly*p* the idea of a Social Science), sufficiently testify. The time was not ripe for doing effectually any other work than that of destruction. But the work of the day should have been so performed as not to impede that of the morrow. No one can calculate what struggles, which the cause of improvement has yet to undergo, might have been spared if the philosophers of the eighteenth century had done anything like justice to the Past. Their mistake was, that they did not acknowledge the historical value of much which had ceased to be useful, nor saw that institutions and creeds, now effete, had rendered essential services to civilization, and still filled a place in the human mind, and in the arrangements of society, which could not without *q*great*q* peril, be left vacant. Their mistake was, that they did not recognise in many of the errors which they assailed, corruptions of important truths, and in many of the institutions most cankered with abuse, necessary elements of civilized society, though in a form and vesture no longer suited to the age; and hence they involved, as far as in them lay, many great truths, in a common discredit with the errors which had grown up around them. *r*They*r* threw away the shell without preserving the kernel; and attempting to new-model society without the binding forces which hold society together, met with such success as might have been anticipated.

Now we claim, in behalf of the philosophers of the reactionary school—of the school to which Coleridge belongs—that exactly what we blame the philosophers of the eighteenth century for not doing, they have done.

Every reaction in opinion, of course brings into view that portion of the truth which was overlooked before. It was natural that a philosophy which anathematized all that had been going on in Europe from Constantine to Luther, or even to Voltaire, should be succeeded by another, at once a severe critic of the new tendencies of society, and an impassioned vindicator of what was good in the past. This is the easy merit of all Tory and Royalist writers. But the peculiarity of the Germano-Coleridgian school is, that they saw beyond the immediate controversy, to the fundamental principles involved in all such controversies. They were the first *s*(except a solitary thinker here and there)*s* who inquired *t*with any comprehensiveness or depth*t* into the

*o*40   essentially
q–*q*40   the utmost
s–*s*+59,67

p–*p*+59,67
r–*r*40   The philosophers
t–*t*40   systematically

inductive laws of the existence and growth of human society. They were the first to bring prominently forward the three requisites which we have enumerated, as essential principles of all permanent forms of social existence, as principles, we say, and not as mere accidental advantages inherent in the particular polity or religion which the writer happened to patronize. They were the first who pursued, philosophically and in the spirit of Baconian investigation, not only this inquiry, but others ulterior and collateral to it. They thus produced, not a piece of party advocacy, but a philosophy of society, in the only form in which it is yet possible, that of a philosophy of history; not a defence of particular ethical or religious doctrines, but a contribution, the largest "yet" made by any class of thinkers, towards the philosophy of human culture.

The brilliant light which has been thrown upon history during the last half century, has proceeded almost wholly from this school. The disrespect in which history was held by the *philosophes* is notorious; one of the soberest of them, D'Alembert we believe, was the author of the wish that all record whatever of past events could be blotted out. And indeed the ordinary mode of writing history, and the ordinary mode of drawing lessons from it, were almost sufficient to excuse this contempt. But the *philosophes* saw, as usual, what was not true, not what was. It is no wonder that ⱽthey who looked onⱽ the greater part of what had been handed down from the past, ʷasʷ sheer hindrances to man's attaining a well-being which would otherwise be of easy attainment, should content themselves with a very superficial study of history. But the case was otherwise with those who regarded the maintenance of society at all, and especially its maintenance in a state of progressive advancement, as a very difficult task, actually achieved, in however imperfect a manner, for a number of centuries, against the strongest obstacles. It was natural that they should feel a deep interest in ascertaining how this had been effected; and should be led to inquire, both what were the requisites of the permanent existence of the body politic, and what were the conditions which had rendered the preservation of these permanent requisites compatible with perpetual and progressive improvement. And hence that series of great writers and thinkers, from Herder to Michelet, by whom history, which was till then "a tale told by an idiot, full of sound and fury, signifying nothing,"[*] has been made a science of causes and effects; who, by making the facts and events of the past have a meaning and an intelligible place in the gradual evolution of humanity, have at once given history, even to the imagination, an interest like romance, and afforded the only means of predicting and

[*William Shakespeare. *Macbeth* (ed. Furness), V, v, 30–2.]

u–u+67
v–v40   men who saw, in   w–w+59,67

guiding the future, by unfolding the agencies which have produced and still maintain the Present.*

The same causes have naturally led the same class of thinkers to do what their predecessors never could have done, for the philosophy of human culture. For the tendency of their speculations compelled them to see in the character of the national education existing in any political society, at once the principal cause of its permanence as a society, and the chief source of its progressiveness: the former by the extent to which that education operated as a system of restraining discipline; the latter by the degree in which it called forth and invigorated the active faculties. Besides, not to have looked upon the culture of the inward man as the problem of problems, would have been incompatible with the belief which ˣmanyˣ of these philosophers entertained in Christianity, and the recognition by all of them of its historical value, and the prime part which it has acted in the progress of mankind. But here, too, let us not fail to observe, they rose to principles, and did not stick in the particular case. The culture of the human being had been carried to no ordinary height, and human nature had exhibited many of its noblest manifestations, not in Christian countries only, but in the ancient world, in Athens,

*There is something at once ridiculous and discouraging in the signs which daily meet us, of the Cimmerian darkness still prevailing in England (wherever recent foreign literature or the speculations of the Coleridgians have not penetrated) concerning the very existence [40   existence] of the views of general history, which have been received throughout the Continent of Europe for the last twenty or thirty years. A writer in *Blackwood's Magazine*, certainly not the least able publication of our day, nor this the least able writer in it, lately announced, with all the pomp and heraldry of triumphant genius, a discovery which was to disabuse the world of an universal prejudice, and create "the philosophy of Roman history." [Thomas De Quincey. "On the True Relations to Civilisation and Barbarism of the Roman Western Empire," *Blackwood's Magazine*, LXVI (Nov., 1839), pp. 644–53.] This is, that the Roman empire perished not from outward violence, but from inward decay; and that the barbarian conquerors were the renovators, not the destroyers of its civilization. Why, there is not a schoolboy in France or Germany who did not possess this writer's discovery before him; the contrary opinion has receded so far into the past, that it must be rather a learned Frenchman or German who remembers that it was ever held [40   held—if indeed it ever *was* held by any cultivated intelligence]. If the writer in *Blackwood* had read a line of Guizot (to go no further than the most obvious sources), he would probably have abstained from making himself very ridiculous, and his country, so far as depends upon him, the laughing-stock of Europe. [40 We would recommend to him, as a sort of ABC, or first spelling lesson in history, Guizot's *Essay on the Municipal Institutions of the Romans* [in *Essais sur l'histoire de France*. 2nd ed. Paris: Brière, 1824, pp. 1–51]. When he is a little older and stronger he may attempt M. Guizot's *Lectures*.] [François P. G. Guizot. *Cours d'histoire moderne*. 5 vols. Paris: Pichon and Didier, 1829–32.]

ˣ-ˣ40   most

Sparta, Rome; nay, even barbarians, as the Germans, or still more unmiti-
gated savages, the wild Indians, and again the Chinese, the Egyptians, the
Arabs, all had their own education, their own culture; a culture which, whatever might be its tendency upon the whole, had been successful in some
respect or other. Every form of polity, every condition of society, whatever
else it had done, had formed its type of national character. What that type
was, and how it had been made what it was, were questions which the metaphysician might overlook, the historical philosopher could not. Accordingly,
the views respecting the various elements of human culture and the causes
influencing the formation of national character, which pervade the writings
of the Germano-Coleridgian school, throw into the shade everything which
had been effected before, or which has been attempted simultaneously by
any other school. Such views are, more than anything else, the characteristic
feature of the Goethian period of German literature; and are richly diffused
through the historical and critical writings of the new French school, as well
as of Coleridge and his followers.

In this long, though most compressed, dissertation on the Continental
philosophy preceding the reaction, and on the nature of the reaction, so far as
directed against that philosophy, we have unavoidably been led to speak
rather of the movement itself, than of Coleridge's particular share in it;
which, from his posteriority in date, was necessarily a subordinate one. And
it would be useless, even did our limits permit, to bring together from the
scattered writings of a man who produced no systematic work, any of the
fragments which he may have contributed to an edifice still incomplete, and
even the general character of which, we can have rendered very imperfectly
intelligible to those who are not acquainted with the *y*thing*y* itself. Our object
is to invite *z* to the study of the original sources, not to supply the place of
such a study. What was peculiar to Coleridge will be better manifested, when
we now proceed to review the state of popular philosophy immediately preceding him in our own island; *a* which was different, in some material respects, from the contemporaneous Continental philosophy.
  In England, the philosophical speculations of the age had not, except in a
few highly metaphysical minds (whose example rather served to deter than
to invite others), taken so audacious a flight, nor achieved anything like so
complete a victory over the counteracting influences, as on the Continent.
There is in the English mind, both in speculation and in practice, a highly
salutary shrinking from all extremes. But as this shrinking is rather an instinct of caution than a result of insight, it is too ready to satisfy itself with
any medium, merely because it is a medium, and to acquiesce in a union of

----

the disadvantages of both extremes instead of their advantages. The circumstances of the age, too, were unfavourable to decided opinions. The repose which followed the great struggles of the Reformation and the Commonwealth; the final victory over Popery and Puritanism, Jacobitism and Republicanism, and the lulling of the controversies which kept speculation and spiritual consciousness alive; the lethargy which came upon all governors and teachers, after their position in society became fixed; and the growing absorption of all classes in material interests—caused a *b*character*b* of mind to diffuse itself, with less of deep inward workings, and less capable of interpreting those it had, than had existed for centuries. The age seemed smitten with an incapacity of producing deep or strong feeling, such *c*as at least*c* could ally itself with meditative habits. There were few poets, and none of a high order; and philosophy fell mostly into the hands of men of a dry prosaic nature, who had not enough of the materials of human feeling in them to be able to imagine any of its more complex and mysterious manifestations; all of which they either left out of their theories, or introduced them with such explanations as no one who had experienced the feelings could receive as adequate. An age like this, an age without earnestness, was the natural era of *d*compromises and half-convictions*d*.

To make out a case for the feudal and ecclesiastical institutions of modern Europe was by no means impossible: they had a meaning, had existed for honest ends, and an honest theory of them might be made. But the administration of those institutions had long ceased to accord with any honest theory. It was impossible to justify them in principle, except on grounds which condemned them in practice; and grounds of which there was at any rate little or no recognition in the philosophy of the eighteenth century. The natural tendency, therefore, of that philosophy, everywhere but in England, was to seek the extinction of those institutions. In England it would doubtless have done the same, had it been strong enough: but as this was beyond its strength, an adjustment was come to between the rival powers. What neither party cared about, the *ends* of existing institutions, the work that was to be done by teachers and governors, was *e* flung overboard. The wages of that work the teachers and governors did care about, and those wages were secured to them. The existing institutions in Church and State were to be preserved inviolate, in outward semblance at least, but were required to be, practically, as much a nullity as possible. The Church continued to "rear her mitred front in courts and palaces,"[*] but not as in the days of Hildebrand or Becket, as the champion of arts against arms, of the serf against the seigneur, peace

[*Edmund Burke. *Reflections on the Revolution in France*. In *Works*. London: Dodsley, 1792, Vol. III, p. 144.]

*b–b*40,59   state
*d–d*40   compromise and halfness

*c–c*40   at least as
*e*40   fairly

against war, or spiritual principles and powers against the domination of animal force. Nor even (as in the days of Latimer and John Knox) as a body divinely commissioned to train *f* the nation in a knowledge of God and obedience to his laws, whatever became of temporal principalities and powers, and whether this end might most effectually be compassed by their assistance or by trampling them under foot. No; but the people of England liked old things, and nobody knew how the place might be filled which the doing away with so conspicuous an institution would leave vacant, and *quieta ne movere* was the favourite doctrine of those times; therefore, on condition of not making too much noise about religion, or taking it too much in earnest, the church was supported, even by philosophers—as a "bulwark against fanaticism," a sedative to the religious spirit, to prevent it from disturbing the harmony of society or the tranquillity of states. The clergy of the establishment thought they had a good bargain on these terms, and kept its conditions very faithfully.

The State, again, was no longer considered, according to the old *g*ideal*g*, as a concentration of the force of all the individuals of the nation in the hands of certain of its members, in order to the accomplishment of whatever could be best accomplished by systematic co-operation. It was found that the State was a bad judge of the wants of society; that it in reality cared very little for them; and when it attempted anything beyond that police against crime, and arbitration of disputes, which are indispensable to social existence, the private sinister interest of some class or individual was usually the prompter of its proceedings. The natural inference would have been that the constitution of the State was somehow not suited to the existing wants of society; having indeed descended, with *h*scarcely any*h* modifications that could be avoided, from a time when the most prominent exigencies of society were quite different. This conclusion, however, was shrunk from; and it required the peculiarities of very recent times, and the speculations of the Bentham school, to produce even any considerable tendency that way. The existing Constitution, and all the arrangements of existing society, continued to be applauded as the best possible. The celebrated theory of the three powers was got up, which made the excellence of our Constitution consist in doing less harm than would be done by any other form of government. Government altogether was regarded as a necessary evil, and was required to hide itself, to make itself as little felt as possible. The cry of the people was not "help us," "guide us," "do for us the things we cannot do, and *i*instruct us, that we may do well*i* those which we can"—and truly such requirements from such rulers would have been a bitter jest: the cry was "let us alone." *j*Power*j* to decide

---

*f*40   up
*h–h*40   no
*i–i*40   Powers [*printer's error?*]

*g–g*40   idea
*i–i*40   show us the way to do

questions of *meum* and *tuum*, to protect society from open violence, and from some of the most dangerous modes of fraud, could not be withheld; these ᵏfunctionsᵏ the Government was left in possession of, and to these it became the expectation of the public that it should confine itself.

Such was the prevailing tone of English belief in temporals; what was it in spirituals? Here too a similar system of compromise had been at work. Those who pushed their philosophical speculations to the denial of the received religious belief, whether they went to the exent of infidelity or only of heterodoxy, met with little encouragement; neither religion itself, nor the received forms of it, were at all shaken by the few attacks which were made upon them from without. The philosophy, however, of the time, made itself felt as effectually in another fashion; it pushed its way *into* religion. The *à priori* arguments for a God were first dismissed. This was indeed inevitable. The internal evidences of Christianity shared nearly the same fate; if not absolutely thrown aside, they fell into the background, and were little thought of. The doctrine of Locke, that we have no *innate* moral sense, perverted into the doctrine that we have no moral sense at all, made it appear that we had not any capacity of judging from the doctrine itself, whether it was worthy to have come from a righteous Being. In forgetfulness of the most solemn warnings of the Author of Christianity, as well as of the Apostle who was the main diffuser of it through the world, belief in his religion was left to stand upon miracles—a species of evidence which, according to the universal belief of the early Christians themselves, was by no means peculiar to true religion: and it is melancholy to see on what frail reeds able defenders of Christianity preferred to rest, rather than upon that better evidence which alone gave to their so-called evidences any value as a collateral confirmation. In the interpretation of Christianity, the palpablest *bibliolatry* prevailed: if (with Coleridge)[*] we may so term that superstitious worship of particular texts, which persecuted Galileo, and, in our own day, anathematized the discoveries of geology. Men whose faith in Christianity rested on the literal infallibility of the sacred volume, ˡshrankˡ in terror from the idea that it could have been included in the scheme of Providence that the human opinions and mental habits of the particular writers should be allowed to mix with and colour their mode of conceiving and of narrating the divine transactions. Yet this slavery to the letter has not only raised every difficulty which envelopes the most unimportant passage in the Bible, into an objection to revelation, but has paralysed many a well-meant effort to bring Christianity home, as a consistent scheme, to human experience and capacities of appre-

[*See, e.g., Samuel Taylor Coleridge. *Literary Remains*. 4 vols. London: Pickering, 1836–39, Vol. III, p. 42.]

ᵏ⁻ᵏ40   , though in stinted measure,   ˡ⁻ˡ40   shrunk

hension; as if there ^{m}was^m much of it which it was more prudent to leave *in nubibus*, lest, in the attempt to make the mind seize hold of it as a reality, some text might be found to stand in the way. It might have been expected that this idolatry of the words of Scripture would at least have saved its doctrines from being tampered with by human notions: but the contrary proved to be the effect; for the vague and sophistical mode of interpreting texts, which was necessary in order to reconcile what was manifestly irre-concilable, engendered a habit of playing fast and loose with Scripture, and finding in ^{n} , or leaving out of it, whatever one pleased. Hence, while Chris-tianity was, in theory and in intention, received and submitted to, with even "prostration of the understanding" before it, much alacrity was in fact displayed in *accommodating* it to the received philosophy, and even to the popular notions of the time. To take only one example, but so signal a one as to be *instar omnium*.[*] If there is any one requirement of Christianity less doubtful than another, it is that of being spiritually-minded; of loving and practising good from a pure love, simply because it is good. But one of the crotchets of the philosophy of the age was, that all virtue is self-interest; and accordingly, in the text-book adopted by the Church (in one of its universities) for instruction in moral philosophy, the reason for doing good is declared to be, that God is stronger than we are, and is able to damn us if we do not. This is no exaggeration of the sentiments of Paley, and hardly even of the crudity of his language.[†]

Thus, on the whole, England had neither the benefits, such as they were, of the new ideas nor of the old. We were just sufficiently under the influences of each, to render the other powerless. We had a Government, which we respected too much to attempt to change it, but not enough to trust it with any power, or look to it for any services that were not compelled. We had a Church, which had ceased to fulfil the honest purposes of a church, but which we made a great point of keeping up as the pretence or *simulacrum* of one. We had a highly spiritual religion (which we were instructed to obey from selfish motives), and the most mechanical and worldly notions on every other subject; and we were so much afraid of being wanting in reverence to each particular syllable of the book which contained our religion, that we let its most important meanings slip through our fingers, and entertained the most grovelling conceptions of its spirit and general purposes. This was not a state of things which could recommend itself to any earnest mind. It was sure in no great length of time to call forth two sorts of men—the one de-manding the extinction of the institutions and creeds which had hitherto

[*Cicero. *Brutus sive de claris oratoribus*, 51.191.]
[†See e.g., *Principles of Moral and Political Philosophy*, pp. 35–6 (Book II, Chap. iii).]

$^{m-m}$40 were ^{n}40 it

existed; the other that they be made a reality: the one pressing the new doctrines to their utmost consequences; the other reasserting the *best* meaning
and purposes of the old. The first type attained its greatest *height* in
Bentham; the last in Coleridge.

We hold that these two sorts of men, who seem to be, and believe themselves to be, enemies, are in reality allies. The powers they wield are opposite
poles of one great force of progression. What was really hateful and contemptible was the state which preceded them, and which each, in its way, has been
striving now for many years to improve. Each ought to hail with rejoicing the
advent of the other. But most of all ought an enlightened Radical or Liberal
to rejoice over such a Conservative as Coleridge. For such a Radical must
know, that the Constitution and Church of England, and the religious
opinions and political maxims professed by their supporters, are not mere
frauds, nor sheer nonsense—have not been got up originally, and all along
maintained, for the sole purpose of picking people's pockets; without aiming
at, or being found conducive to, any honest end during the whole process.
Nothing, of which this is a sufficient account, would have lasted a tithe of
five, eight, or ten centuries, in the most improving period and *(during much
of that period)* the most improving nation *in* the world. These things, we
may depend upon it, were not always without much good in them, however
little of it may now be left: and Reformers ought to hail the man as a brother
Reformer who points out what this good is; what it is *which* we have a
right to expect from things established—which they are bound to do for us,
as the justification of their being established: so that they may be recalled to
it and compelled to do it, or the impossibility of their any longer doing it may
be conclusively manifested. What is any case for reform good for, until it has
passed this test? What mode is there of determining whether a thing is fit to
exist, *without first* considering what purposes it exists for, and whether it
be still capable of fulfilling them?

We have not room here to consider Coleridge's Conservative philosophy
in all its aspects, or in relation to all the quarters from which objections
might be raised against it. We shall consider it with relation to Reformers,
and especially to Benthamites. We would assist them to determine whether
they would have to do with Conservative philosophers or with Conservative
dunces; and whether, since there are Tories, it be better that they should
learn their Toryism from Lord *Eldon*, or even Sir Robert Peel, or from
Coleridge.

Take, for instance, Coleridge's view of the grounds of a Church Establish-

*o–o*40	better	*p–p*40	perfection
q–q+59,67		*r–r*40	of
*s–s*40	that	*t–t*40	but by
*u–u*40	fools	*v–v*40	Roden

ment. His mode of treating any institution is to investigate what he terms the Idea of it, or what in common parlance would be called the principle involved in it. The idea or principle of a national church, and of the Church of England in that character, is, according to him, the reservation of a portion of the land, or of a right to a portion of its produce, as a fund—for what purpose? For the worship of God? For the performance of religious ceremonies? No; for the advancement of knowledge, and the civilization and cultivation of the community. This fund he does not term Church-property, but "the nationality," or national property. He considers it as destined for

the support and maintenance of a permanent class or order, with the following duties. A certain smaller number were to remain at the fountain-heads of the humanities, in cultivating and enlarging the knowledge already possessed, and in watching over the interests of physical and moral science; being likewise the instructors of such as constituted, or were to constitute, the remaining more numerous classes of the order. The members of this latter and far more numerous body were to be distributed throughout the country, so as not to leave even the smallest integral part or division without a resident guide, guardian, and instructor; the objects and final intention of the whole order being these—to preserve the stores and to guard the treasures of past civilization, and thus to bind the present with the past; to perfect and add to the same, and thus to connect the present with the future; but especially to diffuse through the whole community, and to every native entitled to its laws and rights, that quantity and quality of knowledge which was indispensable both for the understanding of those rights, and for the performance of the duties correspondent; finally, to secure for the nation, if not a superiority over the neighbouring states, yet an equality at least, in that character of general civilization, which equally with, or rather more than, fleets, armies, and revenue, forms the ground of its defensive and offensive power.[*]

This organized body, set apart and endowed for the cultivation and diffusion of knowledge, is not, in Coleridge's view, necessarily a religious corporation.

Religion may be an indispensable ally, but is not the essential constitutive end, of that national institute, which is unfortunately, at least improperly, styled the Church; a name which, in its best sense, is exclusively appropriate to the Church of Christ. . . . . The *clerisy* of the nation, or national church in its primary acceptation and original intention, comprehended the learned of all denominations, the sages and professors of the law and jurisprudence, of medicine and physiology, of music, of military and civil architecture, with the mathematical as the common organ of the preceding; in short, all the so-called liberal arts and sciences, the possession and application of which constitute the civilization of a country, as well as the theological. The last was, indeed, placed at the head of all; and of good right did it claim the precedence. But why? Because under the name of theology or divinity were contained the interpretation of languages, the conservation and tradition of past events, the momentous epochs and revolutions of

[*Church and State, pp. 46–7.]

the race and nation, the continuation of the records, logic, ethics, and the determination of ethical science, in application to the rights and duties of men in all their various relations, social and civil; and lastly, the ground-knowledge, the *prima scientia*, as it was named,—philosophy, or the doctrine and discipline of ideas.

Theology formed only a part of the objects, the theologians formed only a portion of the clerks or clergy, of the national Church. The theological order had precedency indeed, and deservedly; but not because its members were priests, whose office was to conciliate the invisible powers, and to superintend the interests that survive the grave; nor as being exclusively, or even principally, sacerdotal or templar, which, when it did occur, is to be considered as an accident of the age, a misgrowth of ignorance and oppression, a falsification of the constitutive principle, not a constituent part of the same. No; the theologians took the lead, because the science of theology was the root and the trunk of the knowledge of civilized man: because it gave unity and the circulating sap of life to all other sciences, by virtue of which alone they could be contemplated as forming collectively the living tree of knowledge. It had the precedency because, under the name theology, were comprised all the main aids, instruments, and materials of national education, the *nisus formativus* of the body politic, the shaping and informing spirit, which, educing or eliciting the latent man in all the natives of the soil, trains them up to be citizens of the country, free subjects of the realm. And, lastly, because to divinity belong those fundamental truths which are the common groundwork of our civil and our religious duties, not less indispensable to a right view of our temporal concerns than to a rational faith respecting our immortal well-being. Not without celestial observations can even terrestrial charts be accurately construtced. (*Church and State*, Chap. v [pp. 48–52].)

The *w*nationalty*w*, or national property, according to Coleridge, "cannot rightfully, and without foul wrong to the nation never has been, alienated from its original purposes," from the promotion of "a continuing and progressive civilization,"[*] to the benefit of individuals, or any public purpose of merely economical or material interest. But the State may withdraw the fund from its actual holders, for the better execution of its *x* purposes. There is no sanctity attached to the means, but only to the ends. The fund is not dedicated to any particular scheme of religion, nor even to religion at all; religion has only to do with it *v*in the character of an*v* instrument of civilization, and in common with all the other instruments.

I do not assert that the proceeds from the *z*nationalty*z* cannot be rightfully vested, except in what we now mean by clergymen and the established clergy. I have everywhere implied the contrary. . . . . In relation to the national church, Christianity, or the Church of Christ, is a blessed accident, a providential boon, a grace of God. . . . . As the olive tree is said in its growth to fertilize the surrounding

[*Ibid*., pp. 54, 46.]

*w–w*67   nationality [*printer's error?*]
*x*40   actual
*v–v*40   as the principal
*z–z*67   nationality [*printer's error?   Cf. w–w above*]

soil, to invigorate the roots of the vines in its immediate neighbourhood, and to improve the strength and flavour of the wines; such is the relation of the Christian and the national Church. But as the olive is not the same plant with the vine, or with the elm or poplar (that is, the State) with which the vine is wedded; and as the vine, with its prop, may exist, though in less perfection, without the olive, or previously to its implantation; even so is Christianity, and à *fortiori* any particular scheme of theology derived, and supposed by its partisans to be deduced, from Christianity, no essential part of the being of the national Church, however conducive or even indispensable it may be to its well-being. (Chap. vi [pp. 53–4, 59–60].)

What *ᵃwouldᵃ* Sir Robert Inglis, or Sir Robert Peel, or Mr. *ᵇSpooner sayᵇ* to such a doctrine as this? Will they thank Coleridge for this advocacy of Toryism? What would become of the three years' debates on the Appropriation Clause,[*] which so disgraced this country before the face of Europe? Will the ends of practical Toryism be much served by a theory under which the Royal Society might claim a part of the Church property with as good right as the bench of bishops, if, by endowing that body like the French Institute, science could be better promoted? a theory by which the State, in the conscientious exercise of its judgment, having decided that the Church of England does not fulfil the object for which the nationalty was intended, might transfer its endowments to any other ecclesiastical body, or to any other body not ecclesiastical, which it deemed more competent to fulfil those objects; might establish any other sect, or all sects, or no sect at all, if *ᶜ* it should deem that in the divided condition of religious opinion in this country, the State can no longer with advantage attempt the complete religious instruction of its people, but must for the present content itself with providing secular instruction, and such religious teaching *ᵈ*, if any,*ᵈ* as all can take part in; leaving each sect to apply to its own communion that which they all agree in considering as the keystone of the arch? We believe this to be the true state of affairs in Great Britain at the present time. We are far from thinking it other than a serious evil. We entirely acknowledge, that in any person fit to be a teacher, the view he takes of religion will be intimately connected with the view he will take of all the greatest things which he has to teach. *ᵉ* Unless the same teachers who give instruction on those other subjects, are at liberty

[*See 1 & 2 Victoria, c.109 (15 August, 1838).]

*a–a*40   says   *b–b*40   Gladstone,
*c*40   after anxious and scrupulous consideration
d+59,67
*e*40   [*footnote:*] *For the illustration of this truth from almost every branch of a liberal education, we may refer the reader to a remarkable pamphlet, entitled *Subscription no Bondage* [Oxford: Parker, 1835], by the Rev. Frederick Maurice; which, though we think it signally unsuccessful in its direct object, the justification of the exclusive regulations of the Universities, contains, like all that author's works, many important truths incidentally illustrated, and a lavish display of the resources of a subtle and accomplished as well as a devoted and earnest mind.

to enter freely on religion, the scheme of education will be, to a certain degree, fragmentary and incoherent. But the State at present has only the option of such an imperfect scheme, or of entrusting the whole business to perhaps the most unfit body *f*for the exclusive charge of it that could be found*f* among persons of any intellectual attainments, namely, the established clergy as at present trained and composed. Such a body would have no chance of being selected as the exclusive administrators of the nationalty, on any foundation but that of divine right; the ground avowedly taken by the only other school of Conservative philosophy which is attempting to raise its head in this country—that of the new Oxford theologians *g* .

Coleridge's merit in this matter consists, as it seems to us, in two things. First, that by setting in a clear light what a national church establishment ought to be, and what, by the very fact of its existence, it must be held to pretend to be, he has pronounced the severest satire upon what in fact it is. There is some difference, truly, between Coleridge's church, in which the schoolmaster forms the first step in the hierarchy, "who, in due time, and under condition of a faithful performance of his arduous duties, should succeed to the pastorate,"* and the Church of England such as we now see. But to say the Church, and mean only the clergy, "constituted," according to Coleridge's conviction, "the first and fundamental apostasy."† He, and the thoughts which have proceeded from him, have done more than would have been effected in thrice the time by Dissenters and Radicals, to make the Church ashamed of the evil of her ways, and to determine that movement of improvement from within, which has begun where it ought to begin, at the Universities and among the younger clergy, and which, if this sect-ridden country is ever to be really taught, must proceed *pari passu* with the assault carried on from without.

Secondly, we honour Coleridge for having rescued from the discredit in which the corruptions of the English Church had involved everything connected with it, and for having vindicated against Bentham and Adam Smith and the whole eighteenth century, the principle of an endowed class, for the cultivation of learning, and for diffusing its results among the community. That such a class is likely to be behind, instead of before, the progress of knowledge, is an induction erroneously drawn from the peculiar circumstances of the last two centuries, and in contradiction to all the rest of modern history. If we have seen *h*much*h* of the abuses of endowments, we have not seen what this country might be made by a proper administration of them, as we trust we shall not see what it would be without them. On this subject we *i*

*[*Church and State,*] p. 57.
†*Literary Remains*, Vol. III, p. 386.

*f-f*40   that could be found for it   *g*40   and Mr Gladstone
*h-h*40   somewhat   *i*40   (that is, the present writer)

are entirely *ᴵatᴵ* one with Coleridge, and with the other great defender of endowed establishments, Dr. Chalmers; and we consider the definitive establishment of this fundamental principle, to be one of the permanent benefits which political science owes to the Conservative philosophers.

Coleridge's theory of the Constitution is not less worthy of notice than his theory of the Church. The Delolme and Blackstone doctrine, the balance of the three powers, he declares he never could elicit one ray of common sense from, no more than from the balance of trade.* There is, however, according to him, an Idea of the Constitution, of which he says—

Because our whole history, from Alfred onwards, demonstrates the continued influence of such an idea, or ultimate aim, in the minds of our forefathers, in their characters and functions as public men, alike in what they resisted and what they claimed; in the institutions and forms of polity which they established, and with regard to those against which they more or less successfully contended; and because the result has been a progressive, though not always a direct or equable, advance in the gradual realization of the idea; and because it is actually, though (even because it is an idea) not adequately, represented in a correspondent scheme of means really existing; we speak, and have a right to speak, of the idea itself as actually existing, that is, as a principle existing in the only way in which a principle can exist—in the minds and consciences of the persons whose duties it prescribes, and whose rights it determines.†

This fundamental idea

is at the same time the final criterion by which all particular frames of government must be tried: for here only can we find the great constructive principles of our representative system: those principles in the light of which it can alone be ascertained what are excrescences, symptoms of distemperature, and marks of degeneration, and what are native growths, or changes naturally attendant on the progressive development of the original germ, symptoms of immaturity, perhaps, but not of disease; or, at worst, modifications of the growth by the defective or faulty, but remediless or only gradually remediable, qualities of the soil and surrounding elements‡

Of these principles he gives the following account:—

It is the chief of many blessings derived from the insular character and circumstances of our country, that our social institutions have formed themselves out of our proper needs and interests; that long and fierce as the birth-struggle and growing pains have been, the antagonist powers have been of our own system, and have been allowed to work out their final balance with less disturbance from external forces than was possible in the Continental States. . . Now, in every country of civilized men, or acknowledging the rights of property, and by means of determined boundaries and common laws united into one people or nation, the two

---

*The Friend, first collected edition (1818), Vol. II, pp. 74–5.
†Church and State, pp. 18–19.
‡Ibid., pp. 19–20. [Note omitted in 59.]

ᴵ–ᴵ40   as [printer's error?]

antagonist powers or opposite interests of the State, under which all other State interests are comprised, are those of *permanence* and of *progression*.[*]

The interest of permanence, or the Conservative interest, he considers to be naturally connected with the land, and with landed property. This doctrine, false in our opinion as an universal principle, is true of England, and of all countries where landed property is accumulated in large masses.

"On the other hand," he says, "the progression of a State, in the arts and comforts of life, in the diffusion of the information and knowledge useful or necessary for all; in short, all advances in civilization, and the rights and privileges of citizens, are especially connected with, and derived from, the four classes,—the mercantile, the manufacturing, the distributive, and the professional."* (We must omit the interesting historical illustrations of this maxim.) "These four last-mentioned classes I will designate by the name of the Personal Interest, as the exponent of all moveable and personal possessions, including skill and acquired knowledge, the moral and intellectual stock in trade of the professional man and the artist, no less than the raw materials, and the means of elaborating, transporting, and distributing them."†

The interest of permanence, then, is provided for by a representation of the landed proprietors; that of progression, by a representation of personal property and of intellectual acquirement: and while one branch of the Legislature, the Peerage, is essentially given over to the former, he considers it a part both of the general theory and of the actual English constitution, that the representatives of the latter should form "the clear and effectual majority of the Lower House;" or if not, that at least, by the added influence of public opinion, they should exercise an effective preponderance there. That "the very weight intended for the effectual counterpoise of the great landholders" has "in the course of events, been shifted into the opposite scale; " that the members for the towns "now constitute a large proportion of the political power and influence of the very class of men whose personal cupidity and whose partial views of the landed interest at large they were meant to keep in check;"—these things he acknowledges: and only suggests a doubt, whether roads, canals, machinery, the press, and other influences favourable to the popular side, do not constitute an equivalent force to supply the deficiency.‡ k

[*Church and State, pp. 23–4.]   *Ibid., p. 26.
†Ibid., pp. 29–30.   ‡Ibid., pp. 30–2.

k40   Whether this be the case or not, let the Corn Laws [see 9 George IV, c. 60] tell; laws more odious to the Personal Interest, as well as to the whole mass of public opinion except the agriculturists alone, than any other abuse of the power of the landed interest is likely to be; and which are steadily supported, not only by the House in which that interest is avowedly predominant, but by two-thirds of that which, according to Coleridge, is destined to keep its selfish views constitutionally in check.

How much better a Parliamentary Reformer, then, is Coleridge, than Lord John Russell, or any Whig who stickles for maintaining this unconstitutional omnipotence of the landed interest. If these became the principles of Tories, we should not wait long for further reform, even in our organic institutions. It is true Coleridge disapproved of the Reform Bill, or rather of the principle, or the no-principle, on which it was supported. He saw in it *(as we may surmise)* the dangers of a change amounting almost to a revolution, without any real tendency to remove those defects in the machine, which alone could justify a change so extensive. And that this is *m* nearly a true view of the matter, all parties seem to be now agreed. The Reform Bill was not calculated *n*greatly*n* to improve the general composition of the Legislature. The good it has done, which is considerable, consists chiefly in this, that being so great a change, it *o*has*o* weakened the superstitious feeling against great changes. Any good, which is contrary to the selfish interest of the dominant class, is *p*still only to be effected by a long and arduous struggle: but*p* improvements which threaten no powerful body in their social importance or in their pecuniary emoluments, are no longer resisted, as they once were, because of their greatness—because of the very benefit which they promised. Witness the speedy passing of the Poor Law Amendment and the Penny Postage Acts.[*]

Meanwhile, though Coleridge's theory is but a mere commencement, not amounting to the first lines of a political philosophy, has the age produced any other theory of government which can stand a comparison with it as to its first principles? Let us take, for example, the Benthamic theory. The principle of this may be said to be, that since the general interest is the object of government, a complete control over the government ought to be given to those whose interest is identical with the general interest. The authors and propounders of this theory were men of extraordinary intellectual powers, and the greater part of what they meant by it is true and important. But *q*when*q* considered as the foundation of a science, it would be difficult to find among theories proceeding from philosophers one *r* less like a philosophical theory, or, in the works of analytical *s*minds*s*, anything more entirely unanalytical. What can a philosopher *t*make of*t* such complex notions as "interest" and "general interest," without breaking them down into the elements of which they are composed? If by men's interest be meant what would appear such to a calculating bystander, judging what would be good for a man

[*4 & 5 William IV, c.76 (14 Aug., 1834); 2 & 3 Victoria, c.52 (17 Aug., 1839).]

l-l+59, 67	*m*40 pretty
*n-n*40,59 materially	*o-o*+59,67
*p-p*40 as little to be looked for as ever. But	
*q-q*40 if	*r*40 looking
*s-s*40 men	*t-t*40 do with

during his whole life, and making no account, or but little, of the gratification of his present passions, his pride, his envy, his vanity, his cupidity, his love of pleasure, his love of ease—it may be questioned whether, in this sense, the interest of an aristocracy, and still more that of a monarch, would not be as accordant with the general interest as that of either the middle or the poorer classes; and if men's interest, in this understanding of it, usually governed their conduct, absolute monarchy would probably be the best form of government. But since men usually do what they like, often being perfectly aware that it is not for their ultimate interest, still more often that it is not for the interest of their posterity; and ^uwhen they do believe that the object they are seeking is permanently good for them,^u almost always overrating its value; it is necessary to consider, not who are they whose permanent interest, but who are they whose immediate interests and habitual feelings, are likely to be most in accordance with the end we seek to obtain. And as that end (the general good) is a very complex state of things, comprising as its component elements many requisites which are neither of one and the same nature, nor attainable by one and the same means—political philosophy must begin by a classification of these elements, in order to distinguish those of them which go naturally together (so that the provision made for one will suffice for the rest), from those which are ordinarily in a state of antagonism, or at least of separation, and require to be provided for apart. This preliminary classification being supposed, things would, in a perfect government, be so ordered, that corresponding to each of the great interests of society, there would be some branch or some integral part of the governing body, so constituted that it should not be merely deemed by philosophers, but ^vshould^v actually and constantly deem itself, to have its strongest interests involved in the maintenance of that one of the ends of society which it is intended to be the guardian of. This, we say, is the thing to be aimed at, the type of perfection in a political constitution. Not that there is a possibility of making more than a limited approach to it in practice. A government must be composed out of the elements already existing in society, and the distribution of power in the constitution cannot vary much or long from the distribution of it in society itself. But wherever the circumstances of society allow any choice, wherever wisdom and contrivance are at all available, this, we conceive, is the principle of guidance; and whatever anywhere exists is imperfect and a failure, just so far as it recedes from this type.

Such a philosophy of government, we need hardly say, is in its infancy: the first step to it, the classification of the exigencies of society, has not been made. Bentham, in his *Principles of Civil Law*,[*] has given a specimen, very useful for many other purposes, but not available, nor intended to be

[*"Principles of the Civil Code," *Works*, Vol. I, pp. 297–364.]

^{u–u}40 (even when ... them)   ^{v–v}+67

so, for founding a theory of representation upon it. For that particular purpose we have seen nothing comparable as far as it goes, notwithstanding its manifest insufficiency, to Coleridge's division of the interests of society into the two antagonist interests of Permanence and Progression. The Continental philosophers have, by a different path, arrived at the same division; and this is about as far, probably, as the science of political institutions has yet reached.

In the details of Coleridge's political opinions there is much good, and much that is questionable, or worse. In political economy especially he writes like an arrant driveller, and it would have been well for his reputation had he never meddled with the subject.* But this department of knowledge can now take care of itself. On other points we meet with far-reaching remarks, and a tone of general feeling sufficient to make a Tory's hair stand on end. Thus, in the work from which we have most quoted, he calls the State policy of the last half-century "a Cyclops with one eye, and that in the back of the head"—its measures "either a series of anachronisms, or a truckling to events instead of the science that should command them."† He styles the great Commonwealthsmen "the stars of that narrow interspace of blue sky between the black clouds of the First and Second Charles's reigns."‡ The *Literary Remains* are full of disparaging remarks on many of the heroes of Toryism and Church-of-Englandism. He sees, for instance, no difference between Whitgift and Bancroft, and Bonner and Gardiner, except that the last were the most consistent—that the former sinned against better knowledge;§ and one of the most poignant of his writings is a character of Pitt, the very reverse of panegyrical.‖ As a specimen of his practical views, we have mentioned his recommendation that the parochial clergy should begin by being schoolmasters. He urges "a different division and subdivision of the kingdom" instead of "the present barbarism, which forms an obstacle to the improvement of the country of much greater magnitude than men are generally aware."# But we must confine ourselves to instances in which he

*Yet even on this subject he has occasionally a just thought, happily expressed; as this: "Instead of the position that all things find, it would be less equivocal and far more descriptive of the fact to say, that things are always finding, their level; which might be taken as the paraphrase or ironical definition of a storm."— *Second Lay Sermon* [in *On the Constitution of Church and State, and Lay Sermons,*] p. 403.

†*Church and State*, p. 69.

‡*Ibid.*, p. 102.

§*Literary Remains*, Vol. II, pp. 388–9.

‖Written in the *Morning Post*, [19 Mar., 1800,] and now (as we rejoice to see) reprinted in Mr. [James] Gillman's biographical memoir. ["Pitt," in *The Life of Samuel Taylor Coleridge*. 2 vols. London: Pickering, 1838, Vol. I, pp. 195–207.]

#*Church and State*, p. 56.

has helped to bring forward great principles, either implied in the old English opinions and institutions, or at least opposed to the new tendencies.

For example, he is at issue with the *let alone* doctrine, or the theory that governments can do ᵂnoᵂ better than to do nothing; a doctrine generated by the manifest selfishness and incompetence of modern European governments, but of which, as a general theory, we may now be permitted to say, that one half of it is true, and the other half false. All who are on a level with their age now readily admit that government ought not to *interdict* men from publishing their opinions, pursuing their employments, or buying and selling their goods, in whatever place or manner they deem the most advantageous. Beyond suppressing force and fraud, governments can seldom, without doing more harm than good, attempt to chain up the free agency of individuals. But does it follow from this that government cannot exercise a free agency of its own?—that it cannot beneficially employ its powers, its means of information, and its pecuniary resources (so far surpassing those of any other association, or of any individual), in promoting the public welfare by a thousand means which individuals would never think of, would have no sufficient motives to attempt, or no sufficient ˣpowerˣ to accomplish? To confine ourselves to one, and that a limited view of the subject: a State ought to be considered as a great benefit society, or mutual insurance company, for helping (under the necessary regulations for preventing abuse) that large proportion of its members who cannot help themselves.

Let us suppose, [says Coleridge,] the negative ends of a State already attained, namely, its own safety by means of its own strength, and the protection of person and property for all its members; there will then remain its positive ends:—1. To make the means of subsistence more easy to each individual: 2. To secure to each of its members the hope of bettering his own condition or that of his children: 3. The development of those faculties which are essential to his humanity, that is to his rational and moral being.*

In regard to the two former ends, he of course does not mean that they can be accomplished merely by making laws to that effect; or that, according to the wild doctrines now afloat, it is the fault of the government if every one has not enough to eat and drink. But he means that government can do something directly, and very much indirectly, to promote even the physical comfort of the people; and that if, besides making a proper use of its own powers, it would exert itself to teach the people what is in theirs, indigence would soon disappear from the face of the earth.

Perhaps, however, the greatest service which Coleridge has rendered to politics in his capacity of a Conservative philosopher, though its fruits are

Second Lay Sermon, pp. 414–15.

w–w40   nothing
x–x40,59   powers [*printer's error?*]

mostly yet to come, is in reviving the idea of a *trust* inherent in landed property. The land, the gift of nature, the source of subsistence to all, and the foundation of everything that influences our physical well-being, cannot be considered a subject of *property,* in the same absolute sense in which men are deemed proprietors of that *in which no one has any interest* but themselves—that which they have actually called into existence by their own bodily exertion. As Coleridge points out, such a notion is altogether of modern growth.

The very idea of individual or private property in our present acceptation of the term, and according to the current notion of the right to it, was originally confined to moveable things; and the more moveable, the more susceptible of the nature of property.*

By the early institutions of Europe, property in land was a public function, created for certain public purposes, and held under condition of their fulfilment; and as such, we predict, under the modifications suited to modern society, it will again come to be considered. In this age, when everything is called in question, and when the foundation of private property itself needs to be argumentatively maintained against *a* plausible and persuasive sophisms, one may easily see the danger of mixing up what is not really tenable with what is—and the impossibility of maintaining an absolute right in an individual to an unrestricted control, a *jus utendi et abutendi*, over an unlimited quantity of the mere raw material of the globe, to which every other person could originally make out as good a natural title as himself. It will certainly not be much longer tolerated that agriculture should be carried on (as Coleridge expresses it) on the same principles as those of trade; "that a gentleman should regard his estate as a merchant his cargo, or a shopkeeper his stock;"† that he should be allowed to deal with it as if it only existed to yield rent to him, not food to the numbers whose hands till it; and should have a right, and a right possessing all the sacredness of property, to turn them out by hundreds and make them perish on the high road, as has been done before now by Irish landlords. We believe it will soon be thought, that a mode of property in land which has brought things to this pass, has existed long enough.

We shall not be suspected (we hope) of recommending a general resumption of landed possessions, or the depriving any one, without compensation, of anything which the law gives him. But we say that when the State allows any one to exercise ownership over more land than suffices to raise by his

Ibid., p. 413 n.
†*Ibid.*, pp. 413–14.

*v–v*40,59   *property*
*z–z*40   which . . . interest in   *a*40   shallow and crude indeed, but

own labour his subsistence and that of his family, it confers on him power over other human beings—power affecting them in their most vital interests; and that no notion of private property can bar the right which the State inherently possesses, to require that the power which it has so given shall not be abused. We say, also, that, by giving this *b*direct*b* power over so large a portion of the community, *c*indirect*c* power is necessarily conferred over all the remaining portion; and this, too, it is the duty of the State to place under proper control. Further, the tenure of land, the various rights connected with it, and the system on which its cultivation is carried on, are points of the utmost importance both to the economical and to the moral well-being of the whole community. And the State fails in one of its highest obligations, unless it takes these points under its particular superintendence; unless, to the full extent of its power, it takes means of providing that the manner in which land is held, the mode and degree of its division, and every other peculiarity which influences the mode of its cultivation, shall be the most favourable possible for making the best use of the land: for drawing the greatest benefit from its productive resources, for securing the happiest existence to those employed on it, and for setting the greatest number of hands free to employ their labour for the benefit of the community in other ways. We believe that these opinions will become, in no very long period, universal throughout Europe. And we gratefully bear *d* testimony to the fact, that the first among us who has given the sanction of philosophy to so great a reform in the popular and current notions, is a Conservative philosopher.

Of Coleridge as a moral and religious philosopher (the character which he presents most prominently in his principal works), there is neither room, nor would it be expedient for us to speak more than generally. On both subjects, few men have ever combined so much earnestness with so catholic and unsectarian a spirit. "We have imprisoned," says he, "our own conceptions by the lines which we have drawn in order to exclude the conceptions of others. *J'ai trouvé que la plupart des sectes ont raison dans une bonne partie de ce qu'elles avancent, mais non pas tant en ce qu'elles nient.*"* That almost all sects, both in philosophy and religion, are right in the positive part of their tenets, though commonly wrong in the negative, is a doctrine which he professes as strongly as the eclectic school in France. Almost all errors he holds to be "truths misunderstood," "half-truths taken as the whole," though not the less, but the more dangerous on that account.† Both the theory and *e* practice

---

**Biographia Literaria*, ed. 1817, Vol. I, pp. 249–50 [the French passage is from G. W. Leibnitz, *Trois Lettres*, in *Œuvres*. Berlin: Eichler, 1840, p. 702].

†*Literary Remains*, Vol. III, p. 145.

*b–b*40 direct		*c–c*40 indirect
*d*40 our		*e*40 the

of enlightened tolerance in matters of opinion, might be exhibited in extracts from his writings more copiously than in those of *almost* any other writer we know; though there are a few (and but a few) exceptions to his own practice of it. In the theory of ethics, he contends against the doctrine of general consequences, and holds that, *for man*, "to obey the simple unconditional commandment of eschewing every act that implies a self-contradiction"—so to act as to "be able, without involving any contradiction, to will that the maxim of thy conduct should be the law of all intelligent beings,—is the one universal and sufficient principle and guide of morality."* Yet even a utilitarian can have little complaint to make of a philosopher who lays it down that "the *outward* object of virtue" is "the greatest producible sum of happiness of all men," and that "happiness in its proper sense is but the continuity and sum-total of the pleasure which is allotted or happens to a man."†

But his greatest object was to bring into harmony Religion and Philosophy. He laboured incessantly to establish that "the Christian faith—in which," says he, "I include every article of belief and doctrine professed by the first reformers in common"—is not only divine truth, but also "the perfection of Human Intelligence."‡ All that Christianity has revealed, philosophy, according to him, can prove, though there is much which it could never have discovered; human reason, once strengthened by Christianity, can evolve all the Christian doctrines from its own sources.§ Moreover, "if infidelity is not to overspread England as well as France,"‖ the Scripture, and every passage of Scripture, must be submitted to this test; inasmuch as "the compatibility of a document with the conclusions of self-evident reason, and with the laws of conscience, is a condition *à priori* of any evidence adequate to the proof of its having been revealed by God;" and this, he says, is no *philosophic* novelty, but a principle "clearly laid down both by Moses and *h* St. Paul."# He thus goes quite as far as the Unitarians in making man's reason and moral feelings a test of revelation; but differs *toto cælo* from them in their rejection of its mysteries, which he regards as the highest philosophic truths, and says that "the Christian to whom, after a long profession of Christianity, the mysteries remain as much mysteries as before, is in the same state as a schoolboy with regard to his arithmetic, to whom the *facit* at the end of the examples in his cyphering-book is the whole ground for his assuming that such and such figures amount to so and so."[*]

The Friend, Vol. I, pp. 256 and 340.   †*Aids to Reflection*, pp. 37 and 39.
‡Preface to the *Aids to Reflection*.   §*Literary Remains*, Vol. I, p. 388.
‖*Ibid.*, Vol. III, p. 263.   #*Ibid.*, Vol. III, p. 293.
[*Ibid.*, Vol. I, pp. 387–8.]

f–f+67   *g–g*40,59   philosophical   *h*Source,40   by

These opinions are not likely to be popular in the religious world, and Coleridge knew it: "I quite calculate,"* said he once, "on my being one day or other holden in worse repute by many Christians than the *i*Unitarians" and even Infidels. "It*i* must be undergone by every one who loves the truth for its own sake beyond all other things." For our part, we are not bound to defend him; and we must admit that, in his attempt to arrive at theology by way of philosophy, we see much straining, and *j*most frequently*j*, as it appears to us, total failure. The question, however, is not whether Coleridge's attempts are *k* successful, but whether it is desirable or not that such attempts should be made. Whatever some religious people may think, philosophy will and must go on, ever seeking to understand whatever can be made understandable; and, whatever some philosophers may think, there is little prospect at present that philosophy will take the place of religion, or that any philosophy will be *l*speedily*l* received in this country, unless supposed not only to be consistent with, but even to yield collateral support to, Christianity. What is the use, then, of treating with contempt the idea of a religious philosophy? *m*Religious philosophies are among the things to be looked for*m*, and our main hope ought to be that *n*they may be such as fulfil*n* the conditions of a philosophy—the very foremost of which is, unrestricted freedom of thought. There is no philosophy possible where fear of consequences is a stronger principle than love of truth; where speculation is paralyzed, either by the belief that conclusions honestly arrived at will be punished by a just and good Being *o*with*o* eternal damnation, or by seeing in every text of Scripture a foregone conclusion, with which the results of inquiry must, at any expense of sophistry and self-deception, be made to quadrate.

From both these withering influences, that have so often made the acutest intellects exhibit specimens of obliquity and imbecility in their theological speculations which have *p*excited*p* the pity of subsequent generations, Coleridge's mind was perfectly free. Faith—the faith which is *q*placed among religious duties*q*—was, in his view, a state of the will and of the affections, not of the understanding. Heresy, in "the literal sense and scriptural import of the word," is, according to him, "wilful error, or belief originating in

Table Talk, 2nd ed., p. 91.

*i-i*40 Unitarians and even infidels. "It   59   "Unitarians" and even "Infidels." It]
67 Unitarians" and even "Infidels." "It] [*as* 67 *clearly represents an attempt to correct the (printer's?) error in 59, the reading of 40 (which is closest to Coleridge's* Unitarians and open infidels. It) *is given above*]
*j-j*40 not unfrequently
*k*40 always
*l-l*40 generally
*m-m*40 We must be looking for a religious philosophy
*n-n*40 it will be such a one as fulfils   *o-o*40 by
*p-p*40,59 made them   *q-q*40 a religious duty

some perversion of the will;" he says, therefore, that there may be orthodox heretics, since indifference to truth may as well be shown on the right side of the question as on the wrong; and denounces, in strong language, the contrary doctrine of the "pseudo-Athanasius," who "interprets Catholic faith by belief,"* an act of the understanding alone. The "true Lutheran doctrine," he says, is, that "neither will truth, as a mere conviction of the understanding, save, nor error condemn. To love truth sincerely is spiritually to have truth; and an error becomes a personal error, not by its aberration from logic or history, but so far as the causes of such error are in the heart, or may be traced back to some antecedent unchristian wish or habit."† "The unmistakable passions of a factionary and a schismatic, the ostentatious display, the ambitious and dishonest arts of a sect-founder, must be superinduced on the false doctrine before the heresy makes the man a heretic."‡

Against the other terror, so fatal to the unshackled exercise of reason on the greatest questions, the view which Coleridge took of the authority of the Scriptures was a preservative. He drew the strongest distinction between the inspiration which he owned in the various writers, and an express dictation by the Almighty of every word they wrote. "The notion of the absolute truth and divinity of every syllable of the text of the books of the Old and New Testament as we have it,"[*] he again and again asserts to be unsupported by the Scripture itself; to be one of those superstitions in which "there is a heart of unbelief;"§ to be, "if possible, still more extravagant" than the Papal infallibility; and declares that the very same arguments are used for both doctrines.‖ God, he believes, informed the minds of the writers with the truths he meant to reveal, and left the rest to their human faculties. He pleaded most earnestly, says his nephew and editor, for this liberty of criticism with respect to the Scriptures, as

the only middle path of safety and peace between a godless disregard of the unique and transcendent character of the Bible, taken generally, and that scheme of interpretation, scarcely less adverse to the pure spirit of Christian wisdom, which wildly arrays our faith in opposition to our reason, and inculcates the sacrifice of the latter to the former; for he threw up his hands in dismay at the language of some of our modern divinity on this point, as if a faith not founded on insight were aught else than a specious name for wilful positiveness; as if the Father of Lights could require, or would accept, from the only one of his creatures whom he had endowed with reason, the sacrifice of fools! . . . . Of the aweless doctrine that God might, if he had so pleased, have given to man a

*Literary Remains, Vol. IV, p. 193.
†Ibid., Vol. III, p. 359.
‡Ibid., Vol. IV, p. 245.
[*Ibid., Vol. II, p. 385.]
§Ibid., Vol. III, p. 229; see also pp. 254, 323, and many other passages in the 3rd and 4th volumes.
‖Ibid., Vol. II, p. 385.

religion which to human intelligence should not be rational, and exacted his faith in it, Coleridge's whole middle and later life was one deep and solemn denial.*

He bewails "bibliolatry" as the pervading error of modern Protestant divinity, and the great stumbling-block of Christianity, and exclaims,† "O might I live but to utter all my meditations on this most concerning point . . . in what sense the Bible may be called the word of God, and how and under what conditions the unity of the Spirit is translucent through the letter, which, read as the letter merely, is the word of this and that pious, but fallible and imperfect, man." It is known that he did live to write down these meditations; and speculations so important will one day, it is devoutly to be hoped, be given to the world.‡

Theological discussion is beyond our province, and it is not for us, ʳ in this place, to judge these sentiments of Coleridge; but it is ˢclear enoughˢ that they are not the sentiments of a bigot, or of one who is to be dreaded by Liberals, lest he should illiberalize the minds of the rising generation of Tories and High-Churchmen. We think the danger is rather lest they should find him vastly too liberal. And yet, now when the most orthodox divines, both in the Church and out of it, find it necessary to explain away the ᵗobviousᵗ sense of the whole first chapter of Genesis, ᵘor failing to do that, consent to disbelieve it provisionally, on the speculation that there may here-after be discovered a sense in which it can be believed,ᵘ one would think the time gone by for expecting to learn from the Bible what it never could have been intended to communicate, and to find in all its statements a literal truth neither necessary nor conducive to what the volume itself declares to be the ends of revelation. Such at least was Coleridge's opinion: and whatever influence such an opinion may have over Conservatives, it cannot do other than make them less bigots, and better philosophers.

But we must close this long essay: long in itself, ᵛthoughᵛ short in its relation to its subject, and to the multitude of topics involved in it. We do not pretend to have given any sufficient account of Coleridge; but we hope we may have proved to some, not previously aware of it, that there is something both in him, and in the school to which he belongs, not unworthy of their better knowledge. We may have done something to show that a Tory philosopher cannot be wholly a Tory, but must often be a better Liberal than

*[Henry Nelson Coleridge,] Preface [pp. xi–xiii] to the 3rd volume of the *Literary Remains*.

†*Literary Remains*, Vol. IV, p. 6.

‡[59] This wish has, to a certain extent, been fulfilled by the publication of the series of letters on the Inspiration of the Scriptures, which bears the not very appropriate name of *Confessions of an Inquiring Spirit*. [London: Pickering, 1840.]

ʳ40 especially   ˢ⁻ˢ40 pretty clear   ᵗ⁻ᵗ40 apparent
ᵘ⁻ᵘ+59,67   ᵛ⁻ᵛ40 but

Liberals themselves; while he is the natural means of rescuing from oblivion truths which Tories have forgotten, and which the prevailing schools of Liberalism never knew.

And even if ^{w} a Conservative philosophy were an absurdity, it is well calculated to drive out a hundred absurdities worse than itself. Let no one think that it is nothing, to accustom ^{x}people^x to give a reason for their opinion, be the opinion ever so untenable, the reason ever so insufficient. A ^{y}person^y accustomed to submit his fundamental tenets to the test of reason, will be more open to the dictates of reason on every other point. Not from him shall we have to apprehend the owl-like dread of light, the drudge-like aversion to change, which were the characteristics of the old unreasoning race of bigots. A man accustomed to contemplate the fair side of Toryism (the side that every attempt at a philosophy of it must bring to view), and to defend the existing system by the display of its capabilities as an engine of public good,—such a man, when he comes to administer the system, will be more anxious than another ^{z}person^z to realize those capabilities, to bring the ^{a} fact a little nearer to the specious theory. "Lord, enlighten thou our enemies," should be the prayer of every true Reformer; sharpen their wits, give acuteness to their perceptions, and consecutiveness and clearness to their reasoning powers: we are in danger from their folly, not from their wisdom; their weakness is what fills us with apprehension, not their strength.

For ourselves, we are not so blinded by our particular opinions as to be ignorant that in this and in every other country ^{b}of Europe^b, the great mass of the owners of ^{c}large^c property, and of all the classes intimately connected with the owners of ^{d}large^d property, are, and must be ^{e}expected to be^e, in the main, Conservative. To suppose that so mighty a body can ^{f} be without immense influence in the commonwealth, or to lay plans for effecting great changes, either spiritual or temporal, in which they are left out of the question, would be ^{g}the height of absurdity^g. Let those who desire such changes, ask themselves if they are content that these classes should be, and remain, to a man, banded against them; and what progress they expect to make, or by what means, unless a process of preparation shall be going on in the minds of these very classes; not by the ^{h}impracticable^h method of converting them from Conservatives into Liberals, but by their being led to adopt one liberal opinion after another, as a part of Conservatism itself. The first step to this, is to inspire them with the desire to systematize and rationalize their own actual creed: and the feeblest attempt to do this has an intrinsic value; far more, then, one which has so much in it, both of moral goodness and true insight, as the philosophy of Coleridge.

^{w}40   we were wrong in this, and

$^{x-x}$40 men	$^{y-y}$40 man	$^{z-z}$40 man
^{a}40 actual	$^{b-b}$+59,67	$^{c-c}$+59,67
$^{d-d}$+59,67	$^{e-e}$+59,67	^{f}40 ever
$^{g-g}$40 weakness itself	$^{h-h}$40 impossible	

WHEWELL ON MORAL PHILOSOPHY

1852

D&D, II (1867), 450–509, with footnote to title: "*Westminster Review*, October 1852.—1. 'Lectures on the History of Moral Philosophy in England.' By William Whewell, D.D., Master of Trinity College, and Professor of Moral Philosophy in the University of Cambridge. 1 vols. 8vo. [London: Parker,] 1852. 2. 'Elements of Morality, including Polity.' By the same Author. 2 vols. 8vo. [London: Parker,] 1845." Reprinted from the *Westminster and Foreign Quarterly Review*, LVIII [n.s. II] (Oct., 1852), 349–85 and headed: "Art. II.—Whewell's Moral Philosophy" with the same bibliographic information as in *D&D*. Identified in JSM's bibliography as "A review of Whewell's Lectures on the History of Moral Philosophy in England, & his Elements of Morality, in the Westminster Review new series No. 4 for October 1852" (MacMinn, 77). For a discussion of the relation between this article and some others in this volume, see the Textual Introduction, cxxii above, and the Preface to *D&D*, 493–4 below. JSM requested offprints of the article from John Chapman, the editor of the *Westminster*, but when only tear-sheets were sent, he refused the further offer of reprinting, saying that he did "not think it worth the expense" as he merely wished to give copies to friends (7 & 9/10/52; A.l.s. at Indiana University). In the one copy he retained he corrected the running-title on 359 from "Association" to "Asceticism" (Somerville College).

The following text is collated with that in *D&D* (2nd ed.), and that in the *Westminster*. In the footnoted variants, *D&D* (2nd ed.) is indicated by "67"; *D&D* (1st ed.) by "59"; and the *Westminster* by "52".

Whewell on Moral Philosophy

IF THE WORTH of Dr. Whewell's writings could be measured by the importance and amplitude of their subjects, no writer of the age could vie with him in merit or usefulness. He has aspired to be not only the historian, but the philosopher and legislator, of almost all the great departments of human knowledge; reducing each to its first principles, and showing how it might be scientifically evolved from these as a connected whole. After endeavouring, in his *History and Philosophy of the Inductive Sciences*,[*] to place physics, and incidentally metaphysics, on a philosophic foundation, he has made an almost equally ambitious attempt on the subjects of morals and government, of which the two works before us are the results. He is thus entitled to the praise of having done his best to wipe off from the two endowed universities, in one of which he holds a high place, the reproach to which they have so long been justly liable, of neglecting the higher regions of philosophy. By his writings and influence, he has been an agent in that revival of speculation on the most difficult and highest subjects, which has been noticeable for some years past within as well as without the pale of Oxford and Cambridge. And inasmuch as mental activity of any kind is better than torpidity, and bad solutions of the great questions of philosophy are preferable to a lazy ignoring of their existence, whoever has taken so active a part as Dr. Whewell in this intellectual movement, may lay claim to considerable merit.

Unfortunately it is not in the nature of bodies constituted like the English Universities, even when stirred up into something like mental activity, to send forth thought of any but one description. There have been universities (those of France and Germany have at some periods been practically conducted on this principle) which brought together into a body the most vigorous thinkers and the ablest teachers, whatever the conclusions to which their thinking might have led them. But in the English Universities no thought can find place, except that which can reconcile itself with orthodoxy.

[*William Whewell. *The History of the Inductive Sciences* (1837). 3rd ed. 3 vols. London: Parker, 1857; *The Philosophy of the Inductive Sciences*. 2 vols. London: Parker, 1840.]

They are ecclesiastical institutions; and it is the essence of all churches to vow adherence to a set of opinions made up and prescribed, it matters little whether three or thirteen centuries ago. Men will some day open their eyes, and perceive how fatal a thing it is that the instruction of those who are intended to be the guides and governors of mankind should be confided to a collection of persons thus pledged. If the opinions they are pledged to were every one as true as any fact in physical science, and had been adopted, not as they almost always are, on trust and authority, but as the result of the most diligent and impartial examination of which the mind of the recipient was capable; even then, the engagement under penalties always to adhere to the opinions once assented to, would debilitate and lame the mind, and unfit it for progress, still more for assisting the progress of others. The person who has to think more of what an opinion leads to, than of what is the evidence of it, cannot be a philosopher, or a teacher of philosophers. Of what value is the opinion on any subject, of a man of whom every one knows that by his profession he must hold that opinion? and how can intellectual vigour be fostered by the teaching of those who, even as a matter of duty, would rather that their pupils were weak and orthodox, than strong with freedom of thought? Whoever thinks that persons thus tied are fitting depositaries of the trust of educating a people, must think that the proper object of intellectual education is not to strengthen and cultivate the intellect, but to make sure of its adopting certain conclusions: that, in short, in the exercise of the thinking faculty, there is something, either religion, or conservatism, or peace, or whatever it be, more important than truth. Not to dilate further on this topic, it is nearly inevitable, that when persons bound by the vows and placed in the circumstances of an established clergy, enter into the paths of higher speculation, and endeavour to make a philosophy, either purpose or instinct will direct them to the kind of philosophy best fitted to prop up the doctrines to which they are pledged. And when these doctrines are so prodigiously in arrear of the general progress of thought, as the doctrines of the Church of England now are, the philosophy resulting will have a tendency not to promote, but to arrest progress.

Without the slightest wish to speak in disparagement of Dr. Whewell's labours, and with no ground for questioning his sincerity of purpose, we think the preceding *remark* thoroughly applicable to his philosophical speculations. We do not say the intention, but certainly the tendency, of his efforts, is to shape the whole of philosophy, physical as well as moral, into a form adapted to serve as a support and a justification to any opinions which happen to be established. A writer who has gone beyond all his predecessors in the manufacture of necessary truths, that is, of propositions which, according to him, may be known to be true independently of proof; who ascribes

*a–a*52 remarks

this self-evidence to the larger generalities of all sciences (however little obvious at first) as soon as they have become familiar—was still more certain to regard all moral propositions familiar to him from his early years as self-evident truths. His *Elements of Morality* could be nothing better than a classification and systematizing of the opinions which he found prevailing among those who had been educated according to the approved methods of his own country; or, let us rather say, an apparatus for converting those prevailing opinions, on matters of morality, into reasons for themselves.

This, accordingly, is what we find in Dr. Whewell's volumes: while we have sought in vain for the numerous minor merits, which *ᵇgiveᵇ* a real scientific value to his previous works. If the *Philosophy of the Inductive Sciences* was, as we think, an erroneous philosophy, it contained much that was not unfit to find place in a better, and was often calculated to suggest deeper thoughts than it possessed of its own. But in the *Elements of Morality* he leaves the subject so exactly as he found it,—the book is so mere a catalogue of received opinions, containing nothing to correct any of them, and little which can work with any potency even to confirm them,—that it can scarcely be counted as anything more than one of the thousand waves on the dead sea of commonplace, affording nothing to invite or to reward a separate examination. We should not, therefore, have felt called upon to concern ourselves specially about it, if Dr. Whewell had not, in his more recent publication, *Lectures on the History of Moral Philosophy in England*, undertaken to characterize and criticise, from his own point of view, all other English writers on moral philosophy; and particularly those who derive their ethical conclusions, not from internal intuition, but from an external standard. So long as he contented himself with giving what we think bad reasons for common opinions, there was not much inducement to interfere with them; but assaults on the only methods of philosophising from which any improvement in ethical opinions can be looked for, ought to be repelled. And in doing this it is necessary to extend our comments to some of Dr. Whewell's substantive opinions also. When he argues in condemnation of any external standard, and especially of utility, or tendency to happiness, as the principle or test of morality, it is material to examine how he gets on without it; how he fares in the attempt to construct a coherent theory of morals on any other basis. We shall make use of his larger work in so far only as it is evidence on this point.

Even with the *Lectures*, considered as giving an account of English speculations on moral philosophy previous to the age of Bentham and Paley, it is not *ᶜour purposeᶜ* to meddle: Hobbes, therefore, and Locke, must be left in the hands of Dr. Whewell, without any attempt either to correct his estimate of their opinions, or to offer any judgment of our own. This historical sketch

*ᵇ–ᵇ*52   gave   *ᶜ–ᶜ*52   necessary suggests, however, one remark of an historical character, not new to any one who is conversant with the writings of English thinkers on ethical subjects. During the greater part of the eighteenth century, the received opinions in religion and ethics were chiefly attacked, as by Shaftesbury, and even by Hume, on the ground of instinctive feelings of virtue, and the theory of a moral taste or sense. As a consequence of this, the defenders of established opinions, both lay and clerical, commonly professed utilitarianism. To the many writers on the side of orthodoxy, of the utilitarian school, mentioned by Dr. Whewell, might be added several, of at least equal note, whom he has omitted; as John Brown, the author of *Essays on the Characteristics*; Soame Jenyns, and his more celebrated reviewer, Dr. Johnson; all of whom, as explicitly as Bentham, laid down the doctrine that utility is the foundation of morals. This series of writers attained its culmination in Paley, whose treatise, proclaiming without evasion or circumlocution, not only expediency as the end, but (a very different doctrine) simple self-interest as the motive, of virtue, and deducing from these premises all the orthodox conclusions, became the text-book of moral philosophy in one of the two Universities of the Church of England. But a change ensued, and the utilitarian doctrine, which had been the favourite theory of the defenders of orthodoxy, began to be used by its assailants. In the hands of the French philosophers, and in those of Godwin and of Bentham,—who, though earlier than Godwin in date, was later in acquiring popular influence,—a moral philosophy founded on utility led to many conclusions very unacceptable to the orthodox. For a whole generation, so effectual a fight was kept up against those conclusions, by bayonets in the field, and prosecutions in the courts of justice, that there seemed no necessity for taking much concern about the premises: but when those carnal weapons fell into disuse, and the spirit ᵈwhichᵈ had wielded them was laid—when the battle of established opinions in Church and State had again to be fought by argument, a demand arose for metaphysics and moral philosophy, of the kind most remote from that which appeared so full of danger to received opinions. Utility was now abjured as a deadly heresy, and the doctrine of *à priori* or self-evident morality, an end in itself, independent of all consequences, became the orthodox theory. Having once entered into this course, and gone in search of a philosophical system to be extracted from the mind itself, without any external evidence, the defenders of orthodoxy were insensibly led to seek their system where it exists in the most elaborate shape—in the German metaphysicians. It was not without reluctance that they found themselves engaged in this path; for German metaphysics in Germany lay under as grave a suspicion of religious scepticism, as the rival philosophy in England or France. But it was found on trial, that philosophy of this cast admitted of easy adaptation, and would

ᵈ⁻ᵈ52   that

bend to the very Thirty-nine Articles; as it is the essence of a philosophy which seeks its evidence in internal conviction, that it bears its testimony with equal ease for any conclusions in favour of which there is a predisposition, and is sceptical with the sceptical, and mystical with the mystical. Accordingly, the tone of religious metaphysics, and of the ethical speculations connected with religion, is now altogether Germanized; and Dr. Whewell, by his writings, has done no little to impress upon the metaphysics of orthodoxy this change of character.

It has always been indistinctly felt that the doctrine of à priori principles is one and the same doctrine, whether applied to the ὄν or the δέον—to the knowledge of truth or to that of duty; that it belongs to the same general tendency of thought, to extract from the mind itself, without any outward standard, principles and rules of morality, and to deem it possible to discover, by mere introspection into our ᵉ minds, the laws of external nature. Both forms of this mode of thought attained a brilliant development in Descartes, the real founder of the modern anti-inductive school of philosophy. The Cartesian tradition was never lost, being kept alive by direct descent through Spinoza, Leibnitz, and Kant, to Schelling and Hegel; but the speculations of Bacon and Locke, and the progress of the experimental sciences, gave a long period of predominance to the philosophy of experience; and though many followed out that philosophy into its natural alliances, and acknowledged not only observation and experiment as rulers of the speculative world, but utility of the practical, others thought that it was scientifically possible to separate the two opinions, and professed themselves Baconians in the physical department, remaining Cartesians in the moral. It will probably be thought by posterity to be the principal merit of the German metaphysicians of the last and present age, that they have proved the impossibility of resting on this middle ground of compromise; and have convinced all thinkers of any force, that if they adhere to the doctrine of à priori principles of morals, they must follow Descartes and Hegel in ascribing the same character to the principles of physics.

On the present occasion, it is only with the moral branch of the subject that we have to deal; and we shall begin by showing in what manner Dr. Whewell states the question between us.

Schemes of morality, that is, modes of deducing the rules of human action, are of two kinds:—those which assert it to be the law of human action to aim at some external object, (external, that is, to the mind which aims,) as, for example, those which in ancient or modern times have asserted pleasure, or utility, or the greatest happiness of the greatest number, to be the true end of human action; and those which would regulate human action by an internal principle or relation, as conscience or a moral faculty, or duty, or rectitude, or the superiority of

ᵉ52   own

reason to desire. These two kinds of schemes may be described respectively as *dependent* and *independent* morality. Now, it is here held that independent morality is the true scheme. We maintain, with Plato, that reason has a natural and rightful authority over desire and affection; with Butler, that there is a difference of kind in our principles of action; with the general voice of mankind, that we must do what is right, at whatever cost of pain and loss. We deny the doctrine of the ancient Epicureans, that pleasure is the supreme good; of Hobbes, that moral rules are only the work of men's mutual fear; of Paley, that what is expedient is right, and that there is no difference among pleasures except their intensity and duration; and of Bentham, that the rules of human action are to be obtained by casting up the pleasures which actions produce. But though we thus take our stand upon the ground of independent morality, as held by previous writers, we hope that we are (by their aid mainly) able to present it in a more systematic and connected form than has yet been done. ("Introductory Lecture," [*Lectures on the History of Moral Philosophy in England,*] pp. ix–x.)

There is in this mode of stating the question, great unfairness to the doctrine of "dependent morality," as Dr. Whewell terms it, though the word independent is *ffully* as applicable to it as to the intuition doctrine. He appropriates to his own side of the question all the expressions, such as conscience, duty, rectitude, with which the reverential feelings of mankind towards moral ideas are associated, and cries *gout*, *I* am for these noble things, *you* are for pleasure, or utility. We cannot accept this as a description of the matter in issue. Dr. Whewell is assuming to himself what belongs quite as rightfully to his antagonists. We are as much for conscience, duty, rectitude, as Dr. Whewell. The terms, and all the feelings connected with them, are as much a part of the ethics of utility as of *hthat ofh* intuition. The point in dispute is, what acts are the proper objects of those *ifeelings*; *iwhether we* ought to take the feelings as we find them, as accident or design has made them, or whether the tendency of actions to promote happiness affords a test to which the feelings of morality should *iconform.i* In the same spirit, Dr. Whewell announces it as *his* opinion, as the side *he* takes in this great controversy, "that we must do what is right, at whatever cost of pain and loss." As if this was not everybody's opinion: as if it was not the very meaning of the word right. The matter in debate is, what *is* right, not whether what is right ought to be done. Dr. Whewell represents his opponents as denying an identical proposition, in order that he may claim a monopoly of high principle for his own opinions. The same unfairness pervades the whole phraseology. It is not only Dr. Whewell who "maintains, with Plato, that reason has a rightful authority over desire and affection." Everybody maintains it; only, what *is* reason? and by what rule is it to guide and govern the desires and affections? The description of Bentham, as obtaining his rule of

f–f52   quite
g–g+59,67   h–h+59,67
i–i52   feelings?   j–j52   conform?

conduct by "casting up the pleasures which actions produce," ought to be "casting up the pleasures and pains which actions produce:" a very different thing.

As might be expected from the historical character of the *Lectures*, the discussion of opinions mostly assumes the form of criticism on writers. Dr. Whewell's objections to utility, or the "greatest happiness," as the standard of morals, are chiefly contained in his animadversions on Paley and on Bentham. It would be quite open to a defender of the principle of utility, to refuse encumbering himself with a defence of either of those authors. The principle is not bound up with what they have said in its behalf, nor with the degree of felicity which they may have shown in applying it. As for Paley, we resign him without compunction to the tender mercies of Dr. Whewell. It concerns Dr. Whewell more than ourselves to uphold the reputation of a writer, who, whatever principle of morals he professed, seems to have had no object but to insert it as a foundation underneath the existing set of opinions, ethical and political; who, when he had laid down utility as the fundamental axiom, and the recognition of general rules as the condition of its application, took his leave of scientific analysis, and betook himself to picking up utilitarian reasons by the wayside, in proof of all accredited doctrines, and in defence of most tolerated practices. Bentham was a moralist of another stamp. With him, the first use to be made of his ultimate principle, was to erect on it, as a foundation, secondary or middle principles, capable of serving as premises for a body of ethical doctrine not derived from existing opinions, but fitted to be their test. Without such middle principles, an universal principle, either in science or in morals, serves for little but a thesaurus of commonplaces for the discussion of questions, instead of a means of deciding them. If Bentham has been regarded by subsequent adherents of a morality grounded on the "greatest happiness," as in a peculiar sense the founder of that system of ethics, it is not because, as Dr. Whewell imagines (p. 190), he either thought himself, or was thought by others, to be the "discoverer of the principle," but because he was the first who, keeping clear of the direct and indirect influences of all doctrines inconsistent with it, deduced a set of subordinate generalities from utility alone, and by these consistently tested all particular questions. This great service, previously to which a scientific doctrine of ethics on the foundation of utility was impossible, has been performed by Bentham (though with a view to the exigencies of legislation more than to those of morals) in a manner, as far as it goes, eminently meritorious, and so as to indicate clearly the way to complete the scheme. We must at the same time qualify our approbation by adding, not that his practical conclusions *k*in morals*k* were often wrong, for we think that as far as they went they were mostly right; but that there

k–k+59,67

were large deficiencies and hiatuses in his scheme of human nature and life, and a consequent want of breadth and comprehension in his secondary principles, which led him often to deduce just conclusions from premises so narrow as to provoke many minds to a rejection of what was nevertheless truth. It is by his *method* chiefly that Bentham, as we think, justly earned a position in moral science analogous to that of Bacon in physical. It is because he was the first to enter into the right mode of working ethical problems, though he worked many of them, as Bacon did physical, on insufficient data. Dr. Whewell's shafts, however, seldom touch Bentham where he is really vulnerable; they are mostly aimed at his strong points.

Before commencing his attack on Bentham's opinions, Dr. Whewell gives a sketch of his life. In this there is an apparent desire to be just to Bentham, as far as the writer's opinions allow. But there is in some of the strictures a looseness of expression, *l*scarcely*l* excusable in an extemporaneous lecture, and still less in a printed book. "He [Bentham] showed very early that peculiar one-sidedness in his mode of asserting and urging his opinions, which made him think all moderation with regard to his opponents superfluous and absurd" (p. 189). What is here called "one-sidedness in his mode of asserting and urging his opinions," must mean one-sidedness in the opinions themselves. It could not be Bentham's "mode of asserting his opinions," that "made him think" whatever he did think. This is as if any one should say, "his speaking only English made him unable to understand French," or "his peculiar habit of fighting made him think it superfluous and absurd to keep the peace." Again (pp. 190–1), "Bentham appears to have been one of those persons to whom everything which passes through their own thoughts assumes quite a different character and value from that which the same thing had when it passed through the thoughts of other persons." If a thought in a person's own mind did not assume a different character from what the same thought had in other minds, people might as well think by deputy.

A more serious injustice to Bentham is that of citing, as is constantly done in this volume, the book called *Deontology*, as the authentic exposition of Bentham's philosophy of morals. Dr. Whewell would, no doubt, justify this by saying that the book in question is the only treatise expressly and exclusively on morals, which we have from Bentham. It is true that we have no other; but the *Deontology* was not, and does not profess to be written by Bentham. *m* Still less ought that book to be represented as the embodiment of the opinions and mental characteristics of all who share Bentham's general conception of ethics. After charging the compiler of the *Deontology* with

---

*l–l*52   not
*m*52   We cannot acknowledge any one as the authorized expositor of Bentham's unwritten opinions.

profound ignorance, and saying that it is almost "superfluous to notice mis-statements so gross and partiality so blind," Dr. Whewell adds that "such misrepresentations and such unfairness are the usual style of controversy of him [Bentham] and his disciples; and it is fit that we, in entering upon the consideration of their writings, should be aware of this."[*] Who are the persons here included under the name of Bentham's "disciples," we are not enabled to judge; nor are we aware that Bentham ever had any disciples, in Dr. Whewell's sense of the term. As far as our means of observation have gone, which ⁿin this matterⁿ are considerably greater than Dr. Whewell's, those who, from the amount of their intellectual obligations to Bentham, would be the most likely to be classed by Dr. Whewell as Benthamites, were and are persons in an unusual degree addicted to judging and thinking for themselves; persons remarkable for learning willingly from all masters, but swearing blind fealty to none. It is also a fact, with which Dr. Whewell cannot be altogether unacquainted, that among them there have been men of the widest and most accurate acquirements in history and philosophy, against whom the accusation of ignorance of the opinions which they controverted would be as unfounded as the imputation of blind partiality. We protest against including them and Bentham in an imaginary sect, of which the *Deontology* is to be considered the gospel. Bentham's merits or demerits must stand on what is contained in the books written by himself.

Among these, the one in which the doctrine of utility is expressly dis-cussed, and contrasted with the various ethical doctrines opposed to it, is the *Introduction to the Principles of Morals and Legislation,* published in 1789. On this Dr. Whewell comments as follows:—

The first chapter of this work is 'On the Principle of Utility:' the second 'On Principles adverse to that of Utility.' These adverse principles are stated to be two: The Principle of Asceticism, and the Principle of Sympathy. [Bentham calls it the Principle of Sympathy and Antipathy, which is already a considerable difference.] The principle of asceticism is that principle which approves of actions in proportion as they tend to *diminish* human happiness, and, conversely, dis-approves of them as they tend to augment it. The principle of sympathy is that which approves or disapproves of certain actions 'merely because a man finds himself disposed to approve or disapprove of them, holding up that approbation or disapprobation as a sufficient reason for itself, and disclaiming the necessity of looking out for any extrinsic ground.' And these two principles are, it seems, according to Bentham's view, the only principles which are, or which can be, opposed to the principle of utility!

Now it is plain that these are not only not fair representations of any principles ever held by moralists, or by any persons speaking gravely and deliberately, but that they are too extravagant and fantastical to be accepted even as caricatures of any such principles. For who ever approved of actions because they tend to

[*Whewell, *Lectures,* p. 200.]

n-n+59,67

make mankind miserable? or who ever said anything which could, even in an intelligible way of exaggeration, be so represented? . . . But who then are the ascetic school who are thus ridiculed? We could not, I think, guess from the general description thus given; but from a note, it appears that he had the Stoical philosophers and the religious ascetics in his mind. With regard to the Stoics, it would of course be waste of time and thought to defend them from such coarse buffoonery as this, which does not touch their defects, whatever these may be, [&c.] (Pp. 202–3.)

Not solely for the due estimation of Bentham, but for the right understanding of the utilitarian controversy, it is important to know what the truth is, respecting the points here in issue between Bentham and Dr. Whewell.

Undoubtedly no one has set up, in opposition to the "greatest happiness" principle, a "greatest unhappiness" principle, as the standard of virtue. But it was Bentham's business not merely to discuss the avowed principles of his opponents, but to draw out those which, without being professed as principles, were implied in detail, or were essential to support the judgments passed in particular cases. His own doctrine being that the increase of pleasure and the prevention of pain were the proper ends of all moral rules, he had for his opponents all who contended that pleasure could ever be an evil or pain a good in itself, apart from its consequences. Now this, whatever Dr. Whewell may say, the religious ascetics really did. They held that self-mortification, or even self-torture, practised for its own sake, and not for the sake of any useful end, was meritorious. It matters not that they may have expected to be rewarded for these merits by consideration in this world, or by the favour of an invisible tyrant in a world to come. So far as this life was concerned, their doctrine required it to be supposed that pain was a thing to be sought, and pleasure to be avoided. Bentham generalized this into a maxim, which he called the principle of asceticism. The Stoics did not go so far as the ascetics; they stopped half-way. They did not say that pain is a good, and pleasure an evil. But they said, and boasted of saying, that pain is no evil, and pleasure no good: and this is all, and more than all, that Bentham imputes to them, as may be seen by any one who reads that chapter of his book. This, however, was enough to place them, equally with the ascetics, in direct opposition to Bentham, since they denied his supreme end to be an end at all. And hence he classed them and the ascetics together, as professing the direct negation of the utilitarian standard.

In the other division of his opponents he placed those who, though they did not deny pleasure to be a good and pain an evil, refused to consider the pain or the pleasure which an action or a class of actions tends to produce, as the criterion of its morality. As the former category of opponents were described by Bentham as followers of the "principle of asceticism," so he described these as followers of "the principle of sympathy and antipathy;" not because they had themselves generalized their principle of judgment, or would have acknowledged it when placed undisguised before them; but because, at the bottom of what they imposed on themselves and others as reasons, he could find nothing else; because they all, in one phrase or another, placed the test of right and wrong in a feeling of approbation or disapprobation, thus making the feeling its own reason and its own justification. This portion of Bentham's doctrine can only be fairly exhibited in his own words.

It is manifest that this [the principle of sympathy and antipathy] is rather a principle in name than in reality; it is not a positive principle of itself, so much as a term employed to signify the negation of all principle. What one expects to find in a principle is something that points out some external consideration as a means of warranting and guiding the internal sentiments of approbation and disapprobation: this expectation is but ill fulfilled by a proposition which does neither more nor less than hold up each of these sentiments as a ground and standard for itself.

In looking over the catalogue of human actions (says a partisan of this principle) in order to determine which of them are to be marked with the seal of disapprobation, you need but to take counsel of your own feelings; whatever you find in yourself a propensity to condemn, is wrong for that very reason. For the same reason it is also meet for punishment: in what proportion it is adverse to utility, or whether it be adverse to utility at all, is a matter that makes no difference. In that same proportion also is it meet for punishment: if you hate much, punish much; if you hate little, punish little: punish as you hate. If you hate not at all, punish not at all: the fine feelings of the soul are not to be overborne and tyrannized by the harsh and rugged dictates of political utility.

The various systems that have been formed concerning the standard of right and wrong, may all be reduced to the principle of sympathy and antipathy. One account may serve for all of them. They consist, all of them, in so many contrivances for avoiding the obligation of appealing to any external standard, and for prevailing upon the reader to accept of the author's sentiment or opinion as a reason for itself. The phrase is different, but the principle the same.

It is curious enough to observe the variety of inventions men have hit upon, and the variety of phrases they have brought forward, in order to conceal from the world, and if possible from themselves, this very general, and therefore very pardonable self-sufficiency.

One man says, he has a thing made on purpose to tell him what is right and what is wrong, and that it is called a *moral sense*; and then he goes to work at his ease, and says, such a thing is right, and such a thing is wrong—why? 'because my moral sense tells me it is.'

Another man comes and alters the phrase; leaving out *moral*, and putting in *common* in the room of it. He then tells you, that his common sense teaches him what is right and wrong, as much as the other's moral sense did: meaning, by common sense, a sense of some kind or other, which, he says, is possessed by all mankind; the sense of those, whose sense is not the same as the author's, being struck out of the account as not worth taking. This contrivance does better than the other; for a moral sense being a new thing, a man may feel about him a good while without being able to find it out; but common sense is as old as the creation; and there is no man but would be ashamed to be thought not to have as much of it as his neighbours. It has another great advantage; by appearing to share power, it lessens envy: for when a man gets up upon this ground, in order to anathematize those who differ from him, it is not by a *sic volo sic jubeo*, but by a *velitis jubeatis*.

Another man comes, and says, that as to a moral sense indeed, he cannot find that he has any such thing; that, however, he has an *understanding*, which will do quite as well. This understanding, he says, is the standard of right and wrong: it tells him so and so. All good and wise men understand as he does: if other men's understandings differ in any point from his, so much the worse for them; it is a sure sign they are either defective or corrupt.

Another man says, that there is an eternal and immutable rule of right; that that rule of right dictates so and so; and then he begins giving you his sentiments upon anything that comes uppermost; and these sentiments (you are to take for granted) are so many branches of the eternal rule of right.

Another man, or perhaps the same man (it's no matter), says, that there are certain practices conformable, and others repugnant, to the fitness of things; and then he tells you, at his leisure, what practices are conformable and what repugnant; just as he happens to like a practice or dislike it.

A great multitude of people are continually talking of the law of nature; and then they go on giving you their sentiments about what is right and what is wrong; and these sentiments, you are to understand, are so many chapters and sections of the law of nature.

We have one philosopher who says, there is no harm in anything in the world but in telling a lie; and that if, for example, you were to murder your own father, this would only be a particular way of saying, he was not your father. Of course, when this philosopher sees anything that he does not like, he says, it is a particular way of telling a lie. It is saying, that the act ought to be done, or may be done, when, *in truth*, it ought not to be done. (Chap. ii.) [*]

To this Dr. Whewell thinks it a sufficient answer to call it extravagant ridicule, and to ask, "Who ever asserted that he approved or disapproved of actions merely because he found himself disposed to do so, and that this was reason sufficient in itself for his moral judgments?"[†] Dr. Whewell will find that this by no means disposes of Bentham's doctrine. Bentham did not mean that people "ever asserted" that they approved or condemned actions only because they felt disposed to do so. He meant that they do it without asserting it; that they find certain feelings of approbation and disapprobation in themselves, take for granted that these feelings are the right ones, and when called on to say anything in justification of their approbation or disapprobation, produce phrases which mean nothing but the fact of the approbation or disapprobation itself. If the hearer or reader feels in the same way, the phrases pass muster; and a great part of all the ethical reasoning in books and in the world is of this sort. All this is not only true, but cannot consistently be denied by those who, like Dr. Whewell, consider the moral feelings as their own justification. Dr. Whewell will doubtless say that the feelings they appeal to are not their own individually, but a part of universal human nature. Nobody denies that they say so: a feeling of liking or aversion to an action, confined to an individual, would have no chance of being accepted as a

[*Introduction to the Principles of Morals and Legislation, Works, Vol. I, pp. 8, 8n–9n.]

[†Whewell, Lectures, p. 205.]

reason. The appeal is always to something which is assumed to belong to all mankind. But it is not of much consequence whether the feeling which is set up as its own standard is the feeling of an individual human being, or of a multitude. A feeling is not proved to be right, and exempted from the neccssity of justifying itself, because the writer or speaker is not only conscious of it in himself, but expects to find it in other people; because instead of saying "I," he says "you and I." If it is alleged that the intuitive school require, as an authority for the feeling, that it should *in fact* be universal, we deny it. They assume the utmost latitude of arbitrarily determining whose votes deserve to be counted. They either ignore the existence of dissentients, or leave them out of the account, on the pretext that they have the feeling which they deny having, or if not, that they ought to have it. This falsification of the universal suffrage which is ostensibly appealed to, is not confined, as is often asserted, to cases in which the only dissentients are barbarous tribes. The same measure is dealt out to whole ages and nations, the most conspicuous for the cultivation and development of their mental faculties; and to individuals among the best and wisest of their respective countries. The explanation of the matter is, the inability of persons in general to conceive that feelings of right and wrong, which have been deeply implanted in their minds by the teaching they have from infancy received from all around them, can be sincerely thought by any one else to be mistaken or misplaced. This is the mental infirmity which Bentham's philosophy tends especially to correct, and Dr. Whewell's to perpetuate. Things which were really believed by all mankind, and for which all were convinced that they had the unequivocal evidence of their senses, have been proved to be false: as that the sun rises and sets. Can immunity from similar error be claimed for the moral feelings? when all experience shows that those feelings are eminently artificial, and the product of culture; that even when reasonable, they are no more spontaneous than the growth of corn and wine (which are quite as natural), and that the most senseless and pernicious feelings can as easily be raised to the utmost intensity by inculcation, as hemlock and thistles could be reared to luxuriant growth by sowing them instead of wheat. Bentham, therefore, did not judge too severely a kind of ethics whereby any implanted sentiment which is tolerably general may be erected into a moral law, binding, under penalties, on all mankind. The contest between the morality which appeals to an external standard, and that which grounds itself on internal conviction, is the contest of progressive morality against stationary—of reason and argument against the deification of mere opinion and habit. The doctrine that the existing order of things is the natural order, and that, being natural, all innovation upon it is criminal, is as vicious in morals, as it is now at last admitted to be in physics, and in society and government.

Let us now consider Dr. Whewell's objections to utility as the foundation of ethics.

Let it be taken for granted, as a proposition which is true, if the terms which it involves be duly understood, that actions are right and virtuous in proportion as they promote the happiness of mankind; the actions being considered upon the whole, and with regard to all their consequences. Still, I say, we cannot make this truth the basis of morality, for two reasons: first, we cannot calculate all the consequences of any action, and thus cannot estimate the degree in which it promotes human happiness; second, happiness is derived from moral elements, and therefore we cannot properly derive morality from happiness. The calculable happiness resulting from actions cannot determine their virtue: first, because the resulting happiness is not calculable; and secondly, because the virtue is one of the things which determine the resulting happiness. (P. 210.)

The first of these arguments is an irrelevant truism. "We cannot calculate *all* the consequences of any action." If Dr. Whewell can point out any department of human affairs in which we can do *all* that would be desirable, he will have found something new. But because we cannot foresee everything, is there no such thing as foresight? Does Dr. Whewell mean to say that no estimate can be formed of consequences, which can be any guide for our conduct, unless we can calculate *all* consequences? that because we cannot predict every effect which may follow from a person's death, we cannot know that the liberty of murder would be destructive to human happiness? Dr. Whewell, in his zeal against the morality of consequences, commits the error of proving too much. Whether morality is or is not a question of consequences, he cannot deny that prudence is; and if there is such a thing as prudence, it is because the consequences of actions *can* be calculated. Prudence, indeed, depends on a calculation of the consequences of individual actions, while for the establishment of moral rules it is only necessary to calculate the consequences of classes of actions—a much easier matter. It is certainly a very effectual way of proving that morality does not depend on expediency, to maintain that there is no such thing as expediency—that we have no means of knowing whether anything is expedient or not. Unless Dr. Whewell goes this length, to what purpose is what he says about the uncertainty of consequences? Uncertain or certain, we are able to guide ourselves by them, otherwise human life could not exist. And there is hardly any one concerned in the business of life, who has not daily to decide questions of expediency far more knotty than those which Dr. Whewell so coolly pronounces to be insoluble.

But let us examine more closely what Dr. Whewell finds to say for the proposition, that "if we ask whether a given action will increase or diminish the total amount of human happiness, it is impossible to answer with any degree of certainty."

Take ordinary cases. I am tempted to utter a flattering falsehood: to gratify some sensual desire contrary to ordinary moral rules. How shall I determine, on the greatest happiness principle, whether the act is virtuous, or the contrary? In the first place, the direct effect of each act is to give pleasure, to another by flattery, to myself by sensual gratification; and pleasure is the material of happiness, in the scheme we are now considering. But by the flattering lie I promote falsehood, which is destructive of confidence, and so, of human comfort. Granted that I do this in some degree—although I may easily say that I shall never allow myself to speak falsely, except when it will give pleasure; and thus I may maintain that I shall not shake confidence in any case in which it is of any value. But granted that I do, in some degree, shake the general fabric of mutual human confidence by my flattering lie,—still the question remains, *how much* I do this: whether in such a degree as to overbalance the pleasure, which is the primary and direct consequence of the act. How small must be the effect of my solitary act upon the whole scheme of human action and habit! how clear and decided is the direct effect of increasing the happiness of my hearer! And in the same way we may reason concerning the sensual gratification. Who will know it? Who will be influenced by it of those who do know it? What appreciable amount of pain will it produce in its consequences, to balance the palpable pleasure, which, according to our teachers, is the only real good? It appears to me that it is impossible to answer these questions in any way which will prove, on these principles, mendacious flattery, and illegitimate sensuality, to be vicious and immoral. They may possibly produce, take in all their effects, a balance of evil; but if they do, it is by some process which we cannot trace with any clearness, and the result is one which we cannot calculate with any certainty, or even probability; and therefore, on this account, because the resulting evil of such falsehood and sensuality is not calculable or appreciable, we cannot, by calculation of resulting evil, show falsehood and sensuality to be vices. And the like is true of other vices; and, on this ground, the construction of a scheme of morality on Mr. Bentham's plan is plainly impossible. (Pp. 210–12.)

Dr. Whewell supposes his self-deceiving utilitarian to be very little master of his own principles. If the effect of a "solitary act upon the whole scheme of human action and habit" is small, the addition which the accompanying pleasure makes to the general mass of human happiness is small likewise. So small, in the great majority of cases, are both, that we have no scales to weigh them against each other, taken singly. We must look at them multiplied, and in large masses. The portion of the tendencies of an action which belong to it not individually, but as a violation of a general rule, are as certain and as calculable as any other consequences; °only° they must be examined not in the individual case, but in classes of cases. Take, for example, the case of murder. There are many persons to kill whom would be to remove men who are a cause of no good to any human being, of cruel physical and moral suffering to ᵖseveralᵖ, and whose whole influence tends to increase the mass of unhappiness and vice. Were such a man to be assassinated, the balance of traceable consequences would be greatly in favour of the act. The counter-consideration, on the principle of utility, is, that unless

o–o52 but   p–p52 many

persons were punished for killing, and taught not to kill; that if it were thought allowable for any one to put to death at pleasure any human being whom he believes that the world would be well rid of, nobody's life would be safe. To this Dr. Whewell answers—

How does it appear that the evil, that is, the pain, arising from violating a general rule once, is too great to be overbalanced by the pleasurable consequences of that single violation? The actor says, I acknowledge the general rule—I do not deny its value; but I do not intend that this one act should be drawn into consequence. (Pp. 212–13.)

But it does not depend on him whether or not it shall be drawn into consequence. If one person may break through the rule on his own judgment, the same liberty cannot be refused to others; and since no one could rely on the rule's being observed, the rule would cease to exist. If a hundred infringements would produce all the mischief implied in the abrogation of the rule, a hundredth part of that mischief must be debited to each one of the infringements, though we may not be able to trace it home individually. And this hundredth part will generally far outweigh any good qexpected to ariseq from the individual act. We say generally, not universally; for the admission of exceptions to rules is a necessity equally felt in all systems of morality. To take an obvious instance, the rule against homicide, the rule against deceiving, the rule against taking advantage of superior physical strength, and various other important moral rules, are suspended against enemies in the field, and partially against malefactors in private life: in each case suspended as far as is required by the peculiar nature of the case. That the moralities arising from the special circumstances of the action may be so important as to overrule those arising from the class of acts to which it belongs, perhaps to take it out of the category of virtues into that of crimes, or *vice versâ*, is a liability common to all ethical systems.

And here it may be observed that Dr. Whewell, in his illustration drawn from flattering lies, gives to the side he advocates a colour of rigid adherence to principle, which the fact does not bear out. Is none of the intercourse of society carried on by those who hold the common opinions, by means of what is here meant by "flattering lies?" Does no one of Dr. Whewell's way of thinking say, or allow it to be thought, that he is glad to see a visitor whom he wishes away? Does he never ask acquaintances or relatives to stay when he would prefer them to go, or invite them when he hopes that they will refuse? Does he never show any interest in persons and things he cares nothing for, or send people away believing in his friendly feeling, to whom his real feeling is indifference, or even dislike? Whether these things are right, we are not now going to discuss. For our part, we think that flattery should be only permitted to those who can flatter without lying, as all persons of sympathiz-

q-q52 resulting

ing feelings and quick perceptions can. At all events, the existence of exceptions to moral rules is no stumbling-block peculiar to the principle of utility.
The essential is, that the exception should be itself a general rule; so that,
being of definite extent, and not leaving the expediencies to the partial judgment of the agent in the individual case, it may not shake the stability of the
wider rule in the cases to which the reason of the exception does not extend.
This is an ample foundation for "the construction of a scheme of morality."
With respect to the means of inducing people to conform in their actions to
the scheme so formed, the utilitarian system depends, like all other schemes
of morality, on the external motives supplied by law and opinion, and the
internal feelings produced by education or reason. It is thus no worse off in
this respect than any other scheme—we might rather say, much better;
inasmuch as people are likely to be more willing to conform to rules when a
reason is given for them.

Dr. Whewell's second argument against the happiness principle is, that
the morality of actions cannot depend on the happiness they produce, because
the happiness depends on the morality.

> Why should a man be truthful and just? Because acts of veracity and justice,
> even if they do not produce immediate gratification to him and his friends in
> other ways (and it may easily be that they do not), at least produce pleasure in
> this way, that they procure him his own approval and that of all good men. To us
> this language is intelligible and significant; but the Benthamite must analyze it
> further. What does it mean according to him? A man's own approval of his act,
> means that he thinks it virtuous. And therefore the matter stands thus. He (being
> a Benthamite) thinks it virtuous, because it gives him pleasure; and it gives him
> pleasure because he thinks it virtuous. This is a vicious circle, quite as palpable
> as any of those in which Mr. Bentham is so fond of representing his adversaries
> as revolving. And in like manner with regard to the approval of others. The action
> is virtuous, says the Benthamite, because it produces pleasure; namely, the
> pleasure arising from the approval of neighbours; they approve it and think it
> virtuous, he also says, because it gives pleasure. The virtue depends upon the
> pleasure, the pleasure depends upon the virtue. Here again is a circle from which
> there is no legitimate egress. We may grant that, taking into account all the
> elements of happiness—the pleasures of self-approval—of peace of mind and
> harmony within us, and of the approval of others—of the known sympathy of
> all good men;—we may grant that, including these elements, virtue always does
> produce an overbalance of happiness; but then we cannot make this moral truth
> the basis of morality, because we cannot extricate the happiness and the virtue
> the one from the other, so as to make the first, the happiness, the foundation of
> the second, the virtue. (Pp. 215–16.)

In Dr. Whewell's first argument against utility, he was obliged to assert
that it is impossible for human beings to know that some actions are useful
and others hurtful. In the present, he forgets against what principle he is
combating, and draws out an elaborate argument against something else.
What he now appears to be contending against, is the doctrine (whether

really held by any one or not), that the test of morality is the greatest happiness of the agent himself. It argues total ignorance of Bentham, to represent him as saying that an action is virtuous because it produces "the approbation of neighbours," and as making so "fluctuating" a thing as "public opinion," and such a "loose and wide abstraction as education," the "basis of morality." When Bentham talks of public opinion in connexion with morality, he is not talking of the "basis of morality" at all. He was the last person to found the morality of actions upon anybody's opinion of them. He founded it upon facts: namely, upon the observed tendencies of the actions. Nor did he ever dream of defining morality to be the self-interest of the agent. His "greatest happiness principle" was the greatest happiness of mankind, and of all sensitive beings. When he talks of education, and of "the popular or moral sanction," meaning the opinion of our fellow-creatures, it is not as constituents or tests of virtue, but as *motives* to it; as means of making the self-interest of the individual *accord* with the greatest happiness principle.*

Dr. Whewell's remark, therefore, that the approval of our fellow-creatures, presupposing moral ideas, cannot be the foundation of morality, has no application against Bentham, nor against the principle of utility. It may, however, be pertinently remarked, that the moral ideas which this approval presupposes, are no other than those of utility and hurtfulness. There is no great stretch of hypothesis in supposing that in proportion as mankind are aware of the tendencies of actions to produce happiness or misery, they will like and commend the first, abhor and reprobate the second. How these

---

*It is curious that while Dr. Whewell here confounds the Happiness theory of Morals with the theory of Motives sometimes called the Selfish System, and attacks the latter as Bentham's, under the name of the former, Dr. Whewell himself, in his larger work, adopts the Selfish theory. Happiness, he says (meaning, as he explains, our own happiness), is "our being's end and aim;" we cannot desire anything else unless by identifying it with our happiness. (*Elements*, Vol. I, p. 359). To this we should have nothing to object, if by identification was meant that what we desire unselfishly must first, by a mental process, become an actual part of what we seek as our own happiness; that the good of others becomes our pleasure because we have learnt to find pleasure in it: this is, we think, the true philosophical account of the matter. But we do not understand this to be Dr. Whewell's meaning: for in an argument to prove that there is no virtue without religion, he says that religion alone can assure us of the identity of happiness with duty. [*Ibid.*, pp. 359–60.] Now, if the happiness connected with duty were the happiness we find *in* our duty, self-consciousness would give us a full account of this, without religion. The happiness, therefore, which Dr. Whewell means, must consist, not in the thing itself, but in a reward appended to it: and when he says that there can be no morality unless we believe that happiness is identical with duty, and that we cannot believe this apart from "the belief in God's government of the world," [*ibid.*, Vol. II, p. 3] he must mean that no one would act virtuously unless he believed that God would reward him for it. In Dr. Whewell's view of morality, therefore, disinterestedness has no place.

feelings of natural complacency and natural dread and aversion directed towards actions, come to assume the peculiar character of what we term *moral* feelings, is not a question of ethics but of metaphysics, and very fit to be discussed in its proper place. Bentham did not concern himself with it. He left it to other thinkers. It sufficed him that the perceived influence of actions on human happiness is cause enough, both in reason and in fact, for strong feelings of favour to some actions and of hatred towards others. From the sympathetic reaction of these feelings in the imagination and self-consciousness of the agent, naturally arise the more complex feelings of self-approbation and self-reproach, or, to avoid all disputed questions, we will merely say of satisfaction and dissatisfaction with ourselves. All this must be admitted, whatever else may be denied. Whether the greatest happiness is the principle of morals or not, people do desire their own happiness, and do consequently like the conduct in other people which they think promotes it, and dislike that which visibly endangers it. This is absolutely all that Bentham postulates. Grant this, and you have his popular sanction, and its reaction on the agent's own mind, two influences tending, in proportion to mankind's enlightenment, to keep the conduct of each in the line which promotes the general happiness. Bentham thinks that there is no other true morality than this, and that the so-called moral sentiments, whatever their origin or composition, should be trained to act in this direction only. And Dr. Whewell's attempt to find anything illogical or incoherent in this theory, only proves that he does not yet understand it.

Dr. Whewell puts the last hand to his supposed refutation of Bentham's principle, by what he thinks a crushing *reductio ad absurdum*. The reader might make a hundred guesses before discovering what this is. We have not yet got over our astonishment, not at Bentham, but at Dr. Whewell. See, he says, to what consequences your greatest-happiness principle leads! Bentham says that it is as much a moral duty to regard the pleasures and pains of other animals as those of human beings. We cannot resist quoting the admirable passage which Dr. Whewell cites from Bentham, with the most *naïf* persuasion that everybody will regard it as reaching the last pitch of paradoxical absurdity.

Under the Gentoo and Mahometan religion the interests of the rest of the animal kingdom seem to have met with some attention. Why have they not, universally, with as much as those of human creatures, allowance made for the difference in point of sensibility? Because the laws that are, have been the work of mutual fear; a sentiment which the less rational animals have not had the same means as man has of turning to account. Why ought they not? No reason can be given. The day may come when the rest of the animal creation may acquire those rights which never could have been withholden from them but by the hand of tyranny. It may come one day to be recognised that the number of the legs, the villosity of the skin, or the termination of the *os sacrum*, are reasons insufficient for abandoning a sensitive being to the caprice of a tormentor. What else is it that should trace the insuperable line? Is it the faculty of reason, or perhaps the faculty of discourse? But a full-grown horse or dog is beyond comparison a more rational, as well as a more conversable animal, than an infant of a day, a week, or even a month old. But suppose the case were otherwise, what would it avail? The question is not, can they reason? nor, can they speak? but, can they suffer?[*]

This noble anticipation, in 1780, of the better morality of which a first dawn has been seen in the laws enacted nearly fifty years afterwards against cruelty to animals, is in Dr. Whewell's eyes the finishing proof that the morality of happiness is absurd!

The pleasures of animals are elements of a very different order from the pleasures of man. We are bound to endeavour to augment the pleasures of men, not only because they are pleasures, but because they are human pleasures. We are bound to men by the universal tie of humanity, of human brotherhood. We have no such tie to animals. [*Lectures*, p. 223.]

This then is Dr. Whewell's noble and disinterested ideal of virtue. Duties, according to him, are only duties to ourselves and our like.

We are to be *humane* to them, because we are *human*, not because we and they alike feel *animal* pleasures. . . . The morality which depends upon the increase of pleasure alone, would make it our duty to increase the pleasure of pigs or of geese rather than that of men, if we were sure that the pleasures we could give them were greater than the pleasures of men. . . . . It is not only not an obvious, but to most persons not a tolerable doctrine, that we may sacrifice the happiness of men provided we can in that way produce an overplus of pleasure to cats, dogs, and hogs. (Pp. 223–5.)

It is "to most persons" in the Slave States of America not a tolerable doctrine that we may sacrifice any portion of the happiness of white men for the sake of a greater amount of happiness to black men. It would have been intolerable five centuries ago "to most persons" among the feudal nobility, to hear it asserted that the greatest pleasure or pain of a hundred serfs ought not to give way to the smallest of a nobleman. According to the standard of Dr. Whewell, the slavemasters and the nobles were right. They too felt themselves "bound" by a "tie of brotherhood" to the white men and to the nobility, and felt no such tie to the negroes and serfs. And if a feeling on moral subjects is right because it is natural, their feeling was justifiable. Nothing is more natural to human beings, nor, up to a certain point in cultivation, more universal, than to estimate the pleasures and pains of others as deserving of regard exactly in proportion to their likeness to ʳourselvesʳ. These superstitions of selfishness had the characteristics by which Dr.

[*Bentham, *Introduction to the Principles of Morals and Legislation*, in *Works*, Vol. I, pp. 142n–143n; quoted by Whewell, *Lectures*, p. 224.]

ʳ⁻ʳ52   themselves

Whewell recognises his moral rules; and his opinion on the rights of animals shows that in this case at least he is consistent. We are perfectly willing to stake the whole question on this one issue. Granted that any practice causes more pain to animals than it gives pleasure to *man*[s]; is that practice moral or immoral? And if, exactly in proportion as human beings raise their heads out of the slough of selfishness, they do not with one voice answer "immoral," let the morality of the principle of utility be for ever condemned.

There cannot be a fitter transition than this subject affords, from the Benthamic standard of ethics to that of Dr. Whewell. It is not enough to object to the morality of utility. It is necessary also to show that there is another and a better morality. This is what Dr. Whewell proposes to himself in his Introductory Lecture, and in the whole of his previous work, *Elements of Morality*. We shall now, therefore, proceed to examine Dr. Whewell's achievements as the constructor of a scientific foundation for the theory of morals.

"The moral rule of human action," Dr. Whewell says, is that "we must do what is right." (*Lectures*, p. xi.) Here, at all events, is a safe proposition; since to deny it would be a contradiction in terms. But what is meant by "right?" According to Dr. Whewell, "what we must do." This, he says, is the very definition of right.

The definition of *rightful*, or of the adjective *right*, is, I conceive, contained in the maxim which I have already quoted as proceeding from the general voice of mankind: namely this, that we must do what is right at whatever cost. That an action is right, is a reason for doing it, which is paramount to all other reasons, and overweighs them all when they are on the contrary side. It is painful; but it is right: therefore we must do it. It is a loss; but it is right: therefore we must do it. It is unkind; but it is right: therefore we must do it. These are self-evident [he might have said identical] propositions. That a thing is right, is a *supreme* reason for doing it. *Right* implies this supreme, unconquerable reason; and does this especially and exclusively. No other word does imply such an irresistible cogency in its effect, except in so far as it involves the same notion. What we *ought* to do, what we *should* do, that we *must* do, though it bring pain and loss. But why? *Because* it is *right*. The expressions all run together in their meaning. And this *supreme* rule, that we must do what is right, is also the *moral* rule of human action. (Pp. x–xi.)

Right means that which we *must* do, and the rule of action is, that we must do what is right; that we must do that which we must do. This we will call vicious circle the first. But let us not press hardly on Dr. Whewell at this stage; perhaps he only means that the foundation of morals is the conviction that there is *something* which we must do at all risks; and he admits that we have still to find what this something is. "What *is* right; what it is that we ought to do, we must have some means of determining, in order to complete our moral scheme." (P. xi.)

Attempting then to pick out Dr. Whewell's leading propositions, and exhibit them in connexion, we find, first, that "the supreme rule of human action, Rightness," ought to control the desires and affections, or otherwise that these are "to be regulated so that they may be right." (Pp. xii–xiii.) This does not help towards showing what *is* right.

But secondly, we come to a "condition which is obviously requisite." In order that the desires and affections which relate to "other men" may be right, "they must conform to this primary and universal condition, that they do not violate the *rights* of others. This condition may not be sufficient, but it is necessary." (Pp. xiii–xiv.)

This promises something. In tracing to its elements the idea of Right, the adjective, we are led to the prior, and it is to be presumed more elementary idea, of Rights, the substantive. But now, what are rights? and how came they to be rights?

Before answering these questions, Dr. Whewell gives a classification of rights "commonly recognised among men." [P. xiv.] He says, they are of five sorts, "those of person, property, family, state, and contract." (P. xv.) But how do we discover that they are rights? and what is meant by calling them rights? Much to our surprise, Dr. Whewell refers us, on both these points, to the law. And he asks, "in what manner do we rise from mere legal rights to moral rightness?" and replies, "we do so in virtue of this principle: that the supreme rule of man's actions must be a rule which has authority over the whole of man; over his intentions as well as his actions; over his affections, his desires, his habits, his thoughts, his wishes." [P. xv.] We must not only not violate the rights of others, but we must not desire to violate them. "And thus we rise from legal obligation to moral duty; from legality to virtue; from blamelessness in the forum of man to innocence in the court of conscience." [P. xvi.]

And this Dr. Whewell actually gives as his scheme of morality. His rule of right is, to infringe no rights conferred by the law, and to cherish no dispositions which could make us desire such infringements! According to this, the early Christians, the religious reformers, the founders of all free governments, Clarkson, Wilberforce, and all enemies of the rights of slaveowners, must be classed among the wicked. If this is Dr. Whewell's morality, it is the very Hobbism which he reprobates, and this in its worst sense. But though Dr. Whewell says that this is his morality, he presently unsays it.

Our morality is not derived from the special commands of existing laws, but from the fact that laws exist, and from our classification of their subjects. Personal safety, property, contracts, family and civil relations, are everywhere the subjects of law, and are everywhere protected by law; therefore we judge that these things must be the subjects of morality, and must be reverently regarded by morality. But we are not thus bound to approve of all the special appointments with regard to those subjects, which may exist at a given time in the laws of a given country. On the contrary, we may condemn the laws as being contrary to morality. We cannot frame a morality without recognising property, and property exists through law; but yet the law of property, in a particular country, may be at variance with that moral purpose for which, in our eyes, laws exist. Law is the foundation and necessary condition of justice; but yet laws may be unjust, and when unjust ought to be changed. (P. xvii.)

The practical enormities consequent on Dr. Whewell's theory are thus got rid of; but when these are gone, there is nothing of the theory left. He undertook to explain how we may know what is right. It appeared at first that he was about to give a criterion, when he said that it is not right to violate legal rights. According to this, when we want to know what is right, we have to consult the law, and see what rights it recognises. But now it seems that these rights may be contrary to right; and all we can be sure of is, that it is right there should be rights of some sort. And we learn that, after all, it is for a "moral purpose" that in Dr. Whewell's opinion "laws exist." So that while the meaning of *ought* is that we ought to respect rights, it is a previous condition that these rights must be such as *ought* to be respected. Morality must conform to law, but law must first conform to morality. This is vicious circle the second. Dr. Whewell has broken out of the first; he has made, this time, a larger sweep; the curve he describes is wider, but it still returns into itself.

An adherent of "dependent morality" would say that, instead of deriving right from rights, we must have a rule of right before it can be decided what ought to be rights; and that, both in law and in morals, the rights which ought to exist are those which for the general happiness it is expedient should exist. And Dr. Whewell anticipates that some one may even do him what he thinks the injustice of supposing this to be his opinion. He introduces an objector as saying, "that by making our morality begin from rights, we really do found it upon expediency, notwithstanding our condemnation of systems so founded. For, it may be said, rights such as property exist only because they are expedient." Dr. Whewell hastens to repel this imputation; and here is his theory. "We reply as before, that rights are founded on the whole nature of man, in such a way that he cannot have a human existence without them. He is a moral being, and must have rights, *because morality cannot exist where rights are not.*" [Pp. xviii–xix.] Was ever an unfortunate metaphysician driven into such a corner? We wanted to know what morality is, and Dr. Whewell said that it is conforming to rights. We ask how he knows that there are rights, and he answers, because otherwise there could be no morality. This is vicious circle the third, and the most wonderful of the three. The Indians placed their elephant on the back of a tortoise, but they did not at the same time place the tortoise on the back of the elephant.

Dr. Whewell has failed in what it was impossible to succeed in. Every attempt to dress up an appeal to intuition in the forms of reasoning, must break down in the same manner. The system must, from the conditions of the case, revolve in a circle. If morality is not to gravitate to any end, but to hang self-balanced in space, it is useless attempting to suspend one point of it upon another point. The fact of moral rules supposes a certain assemblage of ideas. It is to no purpose detaching these ideas one from another, and saying that one of them must exist because another does. Press the moralist a step farther, and he can only say that the other must exist because of the first. The house must have a centre because it has wings, and wings because it has a centre. But the question was about the whole house, and how it comes to exist. It would be much simpler to say plainly, that it exists because it exists. This is what Dr. Whewell is in the end obliged to come to; and he would have saved himself a great deal of bad logic, if he had begun with it.*

So much as to the existence of moral rules: now as to what they are.

We do not rest our rules of action upon the tendency of actions to produce the happiness of others, or of mankind in general; because we cannot solve a problem so difficult as to determine which of two courses of action will produce the greatest amount of human happiness: and we see a simpler and far more satisfactory mode of deducing such rules; namely, by considering that there must be such rules; that they must be rules for man; for man living among men; and for the whole of man's being. Since we are thus led directly to moral rules, by the consideration of the internal condition of man's being, we cannot think it wise to turn away from this *method,* and to try to determine such rules by reference to an obscure and unmanageable external condition, the amount of happiness produced. (P. xx.)

If these were not Dr. Whewell's own words, we should expect to be charged, as he charges Bentham, with caricature. This is given as a scientific statement of the proper mode of discovering what are the rules of morality! We are to "deduce such rules" from four considerations. First, "that there must be such rules;" a necessary preliminary, certainly. If we are to build a wall, it is because it has been previously decided that there must be a wall.

*In Dr. Whewell's larger work, we find him resorting, after all, to an "external object" as the ultimate ground for acknowledging any moral rules whatever. He there says, that "the reason for doing what is absolutely right, is that it is the will of God, through whom the condition and destination of mankind are what they are." (*Elements*, Vol. I, p. 225.) In the *Lectures*, however, he admits that this renders nugatory the ascribing any moral attributes to God. "If we make holiness, justice, and purity, the mere result of God's commands, we can no longer find any force in the declaration that God is holy, just, and pure; since the assertion then becomes merely an empty identical proposition." (Pp. 58–9.) We hope that this indicates a change of opinion since the publication of the earlier work.

*t–t*52   method (!)

But we must know what the wall is for; what end it is intended to serve; or we shall not know what sort of wall is required. What end are moral rules intended to serve? No end, according to Dr. Whewell. They do not exist for the sake of an end. To have them is part of man's nature, like (it is Dr. Whewell's own illustration) the circulation of the blood. It is now then to be inquired *what* rules are part of our nature. This is to be discovered from three things: that they must be "rules for man; for man living among men; and for the whole of man's being." This is only saying over again, in a greater number of words, what we want, not how we are to find it. First, they must be "rules for man;" but we are warned not to suppose that this means for man's benefit; it only means that they are for man to obey. This leaves us exactly where we were before. Next, they are for "man living among men," that is, for the conduct of man to men: but *how* is man to conduct himself to men? Thirdly, they are "for the whole of man's being;" that is, according to Dr. Whewell's explanation, they are for the regulation of our desires as well as of our actions; but what we wanted to know was, *how* we are to regulate our desires and our actions? Of the four propositions given as premises from which all moral rules are to be deduced, not one points to any difference between one kind of moral rules and another. Whether the rule is to love or to hate our neighbour, it will equally answer all Dr. Whewell's conditions. These are the premises which are more "simple and satisfactory" than such "obscure and unmanageable" propositions, so utterly impossible to be assured of, as that some actions are favourable, and others injurious, to human happiness! Try a parallel case. Let it be required to find the principles of the art of navigation. Bentham says, we must look to an "external end;" getting from place to place on the water. No, says Dr. Whewell, there is a "simpler and more satisfactory" mode, viz. to consider that there must be such an art; that it must be for a ship; for a ship at sea; and for all the parts of a ship. Would Dr. Whewell prevail on any one to suppose that these considerations made it unnecessary to consider, with Bentham, what a ship is intended to do?

This account is all we get from Dr. Whewell, in the *Lectures*, of the mode of discovering and recognising the rules of morality. But perhaps he succeeds better in doing the thing, than in explaining how it ought to be done. At all events, having written two volumes of *Elements of Morality*, he must have performed this feat, either well or ill; he must have found a way of "deducing moral rules." We will now, therefore, dismiss Dr. Whewell's generalities, and try to estimate his method, not by what he says about it, but by what we see him doing when he carries it into practice.

We turn, then, to his *Elements of Morality*, and to the third chapter of that work, which is entitled, "Moral Rules exist necessarily." And here we at once find something well calculated to surprise us. That moral rules must

exist, was, it may be remembered, the first of Dr. Whewell's four fundamental axioms; and has been presented hitherto as a law of human nature,
requiring no proof. It must puzzle some of his pupils to find him here proving
it; and still more, to find him proving it from utility.

In enumerating and describing, as we have done, certain desires as among the
most powerful springs of human action, we have stated that man's life is scarcely
tolerable if these desires are not in some degree gratified; that man cannot be at
all satisfied without some security in such gratification; that without property,
which gratifies one of these desires, man's free agency cannot exist; that without
marriage, which gratifies another, there can be no peace, comfort, tranquillity,
or order. And the same may be said of all those springs of actions which we
enumerated as mental desires. Without some provision for the tranquil gratification of these desires, society is disturbed, unbalanced, painful. The gratification
of such desires must be a part of the order of the society. There must be rules
which direct the course and limits of such gratification. Such rules are necessary
for the peace of society. (*Elements*, Vol. I, pp. 32–3.)

This is a very different mode of treating the subject from that which we
observed in the *Lectures*. We are now among reasons: good or bad they may
be, but still reasons. Moral rules are here spoken of as means to an end. We
now hear of the peace and comfort of society; of making man's life tolerable;
of the satisfaction and gratification of human beings; of preventing a disturbed and painful state of society. This is utility—this is pleasure and pain.
When real reasons are wanted, the repudiated happiness-principle is always
the resource. It is true, this is soon followed by a recurrence to the old topics,
of the necessity of rules "for the action of man as man," and the impossibility
to "conceive man as man without conceiving him as subject to rules." [Vol.
I, p. 33.] But any meaning it is possible to find in these phrases (which is not
much) is all reflected from the utilitarian reasons given just before. Rules
are necessary, because mankind would have no security for any of the things
which they value, for anything which gives them pleasure or shields them
from pain, unless they could rely on one another for doing, and in particular
for abstaining from, certain acts. And it is true, that man could not be conceived "as man," that is, with the average human intelligence, if he were
unable to perceive so obvious an utility.

Almost all the *generalia* of moral philosophy prefixed to the *Elements* are
in like manner derived from utility. For example: that the desires, until subjected to general rules, bring mankind into conflict and opposition; but that,
when general rules are established, the feelings which gather round these
"are sources not of opposition, but of agreement;" that they "tend to make
men unanimous; and that such rules with regard to the affections and desires
as tend to control the repulsive and confirm the attractive forces which
operate in human society; such as tend to unite men, to establish concord,

unanimity, sympathy, agree with that which is the character of moral rules." (Vol. I, p. 35.) This is Benthamism—even approaching to Fourierism.

And again, in attempting a classification and definition of virtues, and a parallel one of duties corresponding to them. The definitions of both the one and the other are deduced from utility. After classing virtues under the several heads of benevolence, justice, truth, purity, and order, Benevolence is defined as "desire of the good of all men;" and in a wider sense, as the "absence of all the affections which tend to separate men, and the aggregate of the affections which unite them." (Vol. I, pp. 137–8.) Justice, as "the desire that each person should have his own." (P. 138.) Truth is defined "an agreement of the verbal expression with the thought," and is declared to be a duty because "lying and deceit tend to separate and disunite men, and to make all actions implying mutual dependence, that is, all social action and social life, impossible." (Pp. 139, 138–9.) Purity is defined "the control of the appetites by the moral sentiments and the reason." [P. 139.] Order, as a conformity of our internal dispositions to the laws and to moral rules (why not rather to good laws, and good moral rules?) All these definitions, though very open to criticism in detail, are in principle utilitarian.* Though Dr. Whewell will not recognise the promotion of happiness as the ultimate principle, he deduces his secondary principles from it, and supports his propositions by utilitarian reasons as far as they will go. He is chiefly distinguished from utilitarian moralists of the more superficial kind, by this, that he ekes out his appeals to utility with appeals to "our idea of man as man;" and when reasons fail, or are not sufficiently convincing, then "all men think," or "we cannot help feeling," serves as a last resort, and closes the discussion.

Of this hybrid character is the ethics of Dr. Whewell's *Elements of Morality*. And in this he resembles all other writers of the intuitive school of ^umorals^u. They are none of them frankly and consistently intuitive. To use

---

*The enumeration of duties does not always follow accurately the definition of the corresponding virtues. For example, the definition of purity is one which suits temperance, "the control of the appetites by the moral sentiments and the reason:" but the scheme of duties set forth under this head is rather as if the definition had been "the conformity of the appetites to the moral opinions and customs of the country." It is remarkable that a writer who uses the word purity so much out of its common meaning as to make it synonymous with temperance, should charge Bentham, (*Lectures*, p. 208,) because he employs the word in another of its acknowledged senses, with arbitrarily altering its signification. Bentham understands by the purity of a pleasure, its freedom from admixture of pain: as we speak of pure gold, pure water, pure truth, of things purely beneficial or purely mischievous: meaning, in each case, freedom from alloy with any other ingredient.

*u–u*52 morality

a happy expression of Bentham in a different case, they draw from a double fountain—utility, and internal conviction; the tendencies of actions, and the feelings with which mankind regard them. This is not a matter of choice with these writers, but of necessity. It arises from the nature of the morality of internal conviction. Utility, as a standard, is capable of being carried out singly and consistently; a moralist can deduce from it his whole system of ethics, without calling to his assistance any foreign principle. It is not so with one who relies on moral intuition; for where will he find his moral intuitions? How many ethical propositions can be enumerated, of which the most reckless assertor will venture to affirm that they have the adhesion of all mankind? Dr. Whewell declares unhesitatingly that the moral judgment of mankind, when it is unanimous, must be right. "What are universally held as virtues, must be dispositions in conformity with this [the supreme] law: what are universally reckoned vices, must be wrong." [Vol. I, p. 164.] This is saying much, when we consider the worth, in other matters nearly allied to these, of what is complimentarily called the general opinion of mankind; when we remember what grovelling superstitions, what witchcraft, magic, astrology, what oracles, ghosts, what gods and demons scattered through all nature, were once universally believed in, and still are so by the majority of the human race. But where are these unanimously recognised vices and virtues to be found? Practices the most revolting to the moral feelings of some ages and nations do not incur the smallest censure from others; and it is doubtful whether there is a single virtue which is held to be a virtue by all nations *, in the same sense, and with the same reservations*. There are, indeed, some moralities of an utility so unmistakeable, so obviously indispensable to the common purposes of life, that as general rules mankind could no more differ about them than about the multiplication table; but even here, there is the widest difference of sentiment about the exceptions. The universal voice of mankind, so often appealed to, is universal only in its discordance. What passes for it is merely the voice of the majority, or, failing that, of any large number having a strong feeling on the subject; especially if it be a feeling of which they cannot give any account, and which, as it is not consciously grounded on any reasons, is supposed to be better than reasons, and of higher authority. With Dr. Whewell, a strong feeling, shared by most of those whom he thinks worth counting, is always an *ultima ratio* from which there is no appeal. He forgets that as much might have been pleaded, and in many cases might still be pleaded, in defence of the absurdest superstitions.

It seems to be tacitly supposed that however liable mankind are to be wrong in their opinions, they are generally right in their feelings, and especially in their antipathies. On the contrary, there is nothing which it is

–+59,67

more imperative that they should be required to justify by reasons. The antipathies of mankind are mostly derived from three sources. One of these is an impression, true or false, of utility. They dislike what is painful or dangerous, or what is apparently so. These antipathies, being grounded on the happiness principle, must be required to justify themselves by it. The second class of antipathies are against what they are taught, or imagine, to be displeasing to some visible or invisible power, capable of doing them harm, and whose wrath, once kindled, may be wreaked on those who tolerated, as well as on those who committed, the offence. The third kind of antipathies, often as strong as either of the others, are directed towards mere differences of opinion, or of taste. Any of the three, when nourished by education, and deriving confidence from mutual encouragement, assumes to common minds the character of a moral feeling. But to pretend that any such antipathy, were it ever so general, gives the smallest guarantee of its own justice and reasonableness, or has any claim to be binding on those who do not partake in the sentiment, is as irrational as to adduce the belief in ghosts or witches as a proof of their real existence. I am not bound to abstain from an action because another person dislikes it, however he may dignify his dislike with the name of disapprobation.

We cannot take *w* leave of Dr. Whewell's strictures on Bentham, without adverting to some observations made by him on Bentham's character as a jurist rather than as a moralist. In this capacity Dr. Whewell does more justice to Bentham, than in the department of moral philosophy. But he finds fault with him for two things: first, for not sufficiently recognising what Dr. Whewell calls the historical element of legislation; and imagining "that to a certain extent his schemes of law might be made independent of local conditions." [*Lectures*, p. 254.] *x* Dr. Whewell admits it to be part of Bentham's doctrine, that different countries must to a certain extent have different laws; and is aware that he wrote an *Essay on the Influence of Time and Place in Matters of Legislation*; but thinks him wrong in maintaining that there should be a general plan, of which the details only should be modified by local circumstances; and contends, that different countries require different ground-plans of legislation.

There is in every national code of law a necessary and fundamental historical element; not a few supplementary provisions which may be added or adapted to the local circumstances after the great body of the code has been constructed: not a few touches of local colouring to be put in after the picture is almost painted: but an element which belongs to law from its origin, and penetrates to its roots: a part of the intimate structure; a cast in the original design. The national views of personal status; property, and the modes of acquisition; bargains, and the modes of concluding them; family, and its consequences; government, and its origin; these affect even the most universal aspects and divisions of

*w*52   our   *x*52   It is true,

penal offences; these affect still more every step of the expository process which the civil law applies to rights in defining penal offences. (*Lectures*, p. 254.)

What Dr. Whewell designates by the obscure and misleading expression, "an historical element," and accuses Bentham of paying too little regard to, is the existing opinions and feelings of the people. These may, without doubt, in some sense be called historical, as being partly the product of their previous history; but whatever attention is due to those opinions and feelings in legislation, is due to them not as matter of history, but as social forces in present being. Now Bentham, in common with all other rational persons, admitted that a legislator is obliged to have regard to the opinions and feelings of the people to be legislated for; but with this difference, that he did not look upon those opinions and feelings as affecting, in any great degree, what was desirable to be done, but only what could be done. Take one of Dr. Whewell's instances, "the national views of personal status." The "national views" may regard slavery as a legitimate condition of human beings, and Mr. Livingston, in legislating for Louisiana, may have been obliged to recognise slavery as a fact, and to make provision for it, and for its consequences, in his code of laws; but he was bound to regard the equality of human beings as the foundation of his legislation, and the concession to the "historical element" as a matter of temporary expediency; and while yielding to the necessity, to endeavour, by all the means in his power, to educate the nation into better things. And so of the other subjects mentioned by Dr. Whewell—property, contracts, family, and government. The fact that, in any of these matters, a people prefer some particular mode of legislation, on historical grounds—that is, because they have been long used to it,—is no proof of any original adaptation in it to their nature or circumstances, and goes a very little way in recommendation of it as for their benefit now. But it may be a very important element in determining what the legislator can do, and still more, the manner in which he should do it: and in both these respects Bentham allowed it full weight. What he is at issue with Dr. Whewell upon, is in deeming it right for the legislator to keep before his mind an ideal of what he would do if the people for whom he made laws were entirely devoid of prejudice or accidental prepossession: while Dr. Whewell, by placing their prejudices and accidental prepossessions "at the basis of the system," [*Lectures*, p. 255,] enjoins legislation not in simple recognition of existing popular feelings, but in obedience to them.

The other objection made by Dr. Whewell to Bentham as a writer on legislation, (for we omit the criticism on his classification of offences, as too much a matter of detail for the present discussion,) is that he does not fully recognise "the moral object of law" (p. 257). Dr. Whewell says, in phraseology which we considerably abridge, that law ought not only to preserve and gratify man, but to improve and teach him: not only to take care of him as an animal, but to raise him to a moral life. Punishment, therefore, he says, "is to be, not merely a means of preventing suffering, but is also to be a moral lesson." [*Ibid.*] But Bentham, as Dr. Whewell is presently forced to admit, says the same: and in fact carries this doctrine so far, as to maintain that legal punishment ought sometimes to be attached to acts for the mere purpose of stigmatizing them, and turning the popular sentiment against them. No one, more than Bentham, recognises that most important, but most neglected, function of the legislator, the office of an instructor, both moral and intellectual. But he receives no credit for this from Dr. Whewell, except that of being false to his principles; for Dr. Whewell seems to reckon it an impertinence in anybody to recognise morality as a good, who thinks, as Bentham does, that it is a means to an end. If any one who believes that the moral sentiments should be guided by the happiness of mankind, proposes that moral sentiments, so guided, should be cultivated and fostered, Dr. Whewell treats this as a deserting of utilitarian principles, and borrowing or stealing from his.

As an example of "Bentham's attempt to exclude morality, as such, in his legislation," Dr. Whewell refers to "what he says respecting the laws of marriage, and especially in favour of a liberty of divorce by common consent."[*] As this is the only opportunity Dr. Whewell gives his readers, of comparing his mode of discussing a specific moral question with Bentham's, we shall devote a few words to it.

Having quoted from Bentham the observation that a government which interdicts divorce "takes upon itself to decide that it understands the interests of individuals better than they do themselves,"[†] Dr. Whewell answers, that this is an objection to all laws: that in many other cases, "government, both in its legislation and administration, does assume that it understands the interests of individuals, *and the public interest as affected by them*, better than they do themselves."[‡] The words which we have put in italics, adroitly change the question. Government is entitled to assume that it will take better care than individuals of the public interest, but not better care of their own interest. It is one thing for the legislator to dictate to individuals what they shall do for their own advantage, and another thing to protect the interest of other persons who may be injuriously affected by their acts. Dr. Whewell's own instances *v*suffice:*v* "What is the meaning of restraints imposed for the sake of public health, cleanliness, and comfort? Why are not individuals left to do what they like with reference to such matters? Plainly because carelessness, ignorance, indolence, would prevent their doing what is most for their

[*Whewell, *Lectures*, p. 258.]
[†Bentham, "Principles of the Civil Code," in *Works*, Vol. I, p. 355.]
[‡Whewell, *Lectures*, p. 258.]

v-*v*52 suffice us.

own interest." (P. 258.) Say rather, would lead them to do what is contrary to the interest of other people. The proper object of sanitary laws is not to compel people to take care of their own health, but to prevent them from endangering that of others. To prescribe by law, what they should do for their own health alone, would by most people be justly regarded as something very like tyranny.

Dr. Whewell continues:—

But is Mr. Bentham ready to apply consistently the principle which he thus implies, that in such matters individuals are the best judges of their own interests? Will he allow divorce to take place whenever the two parties agree in desiring it? . . . Such a facility of divorce as this, leaves hardly any difference possible between marriage and concubinage. If a pair may separate when they please, why does the legislator take the trouble to recognise their living together? [P. 259.]

Apply this to other cases. If a man can pay his tailor when he and his tailor choose, why does the law take the trouble to recognise them as debtor and creditor? Why recognise, as partners in business, as landlords and tenants, as servants and employers, people who are not tied to each other for life?

Dr. Whewell finds what he thinks an inconsistency in Bentham's view of the subject. He thus describes Bentham's opinions.

Marriage for life is, he [Bentham] says, the most natural marriage: if there were no laws except the ordinary law of contracts, this would be the most ordinary arrangement. So far, good. But Mr. Bentham, having carried his argument so far, does not go on with it. What conclusion are we to suppose him to intend? This arrangement would be very *general* without law, therefore the legislator should pass a law to make it *universal*? . . . No. The very next sentence is employed in showing the absurdity of making the engagement one from which the parties cannot liberate themselves by mutual consent. And there is no attempt to reduce these arguments, or their results, to a consistency. (Pp. 259–60.)

Dr. Whewell's ideas of inconsistency seem to be peculiar. Bentham, he says, is of opinion, that in the majority of cases it is best for the happiness of married persons that they should remain together. Is it so? (says Dr. Whewell)—then why not force them to remain together, even when it would be best for their happiness to separate?

Try again parallel cases. In choosing a profession, a sensible person will fix on one in which he will find it agreeable to remain; therefore, it should not be lawful to change a profession once chosen. A landlord, when he has a good tenant, best consults his own interest by not changing him; therefore, all tenancy should be for life. Electors who have found a good representative will probably do wisely in re-electing him; therefore, members of parliament should be irremovable.

Dr. Whewell intended to show into what errors Bentham was led, by treating the question of marriage apart from "moral grounds." Yet part of his complaint is that Bentham does consider moral grounds, which, according to Dr. Whewell, he has no right to do. If one married person maltreats the other to procure consent to a divorce,—

> Bentham's decision is, that liberty should be allowed to the party maltreated and not to the other. . . . Now to this decision I have nothing to object: but I must remark, that the view which makes it tolerable is, its being a decision on moral grounds, such as Mr. Bentham would not willingly acknowledge. The man may not take advantage of his own wrong: *that* is a maxim which quite satisfies *us*. But Mr. Bentham, who only regards wrong as harm, would, I think, find it difficult to satisfy the man that he was fairly used. [P. 261.]

Mr. Bentham would have found it difficult to conceive that any one attempting to criticise his philosophy could know so little of its elements. Dr. Whewell wonders what the reason can be, on Bentham's principles, for not allowing a man to benefit by his own wrong. Did it never occur to him, that it is to take away from the man his inducement to commit the wrong?

Finally, Dr. Whewell says, "No good rule can be established on this subject without regarding the marriage union in a moral point of view; without assuming it as one great object of the law to elevate and purify men's idea of marriage; to lead them to look upon it as an entire union of interests and feelings, enjoyments and hopes, between the two parties." [P. 262.] We cannot agree in the doctrine that it should be an object of the law to "lead men to look upon" marriage as being what it is not. Neither Bentham nor any one who thinks with him would deny that this entire union is the completest ideal of marriage; but it is bad philosophy to speak of a relation as if it always *was* the best thing that it possibly can be, and then infer that when it is notoriously not such, as in an immense majority of cases, and even when it is the extreme contrary, as in a *considerable* minority, it should nevertheless be treated exactly as if the fact corresponded with the theory. The liberty of divorce is contended for, because marriages are not what Dr. Whewell says they should be looked upon as being; because a choice made by an inexperienced person, and not allowed to be corrected, cannot, except by a happy accident, realize the conditions essential to this complete union.

We give these observations not as a discussion of the question, but of Dr. Whewell's treatment of it; as part of the comparison which he invites his readers to institute between his method and that of Bentham. Were it our object to confirm the general character we have given of Dr. Whewell's philosophy, by a survey in detail of the morality laid down by him, the two volumes of *Elements* afford abundant materials. We could show that Dr. Whewell not only makes no improvement on the old moral doctrines, but

z–z52 large

attempts to set up afresh several of them which have been loosened or thrown down by the stream of human progress.

Thus we find him everywhere inculcating, as one of the most sacred duties, reverence for superiors, even when personally undeserving (Vol. I, pp. 176–7), and obedience to existing laws, even when bad. "The laws of the state are to be observed even when they enact slavery." (Vol. I, p. 351.) "The morality of the individual," he says, (Vol. I, p. 58), "depends on his not violating the law of his nation." It is not even the spirit of the law, but the letter (Vol. I, p. 213), to which obedience is due. The law, indeed, is accepted by Dr. Whewell as the fountain of rights; of those rights which it is the primary moral duty not to infringe. And mere custom is of almost equal authority with express enactment. Even in a matter so personal as marriage, the usage and practice of the country is to be a paramount law. "In some countries, the marriage of the child is a matter usually managed by the parents; in such cases, it is the child's duty to bring the affections, as far as possible, into harmony with the custom." (Vol. I, p. 211.) "Reverence and affection" towards "the constitution of each country," he holds (Vol. II, p. 204) as "one of the duties of a citizen."

Again, Dr. Whewell affirms, with a directness not usually ventured on in these days by persons of his standing and importance, that to disbelieve either a providential government of the world, or revelation, is morally criminal; for that "men are blameable in disbelieving truths after they have been promulgated, though they are ignorant without blame before the promulgation." (Vol. II, p. 93.) This is the very essence of religious intolerance, aggravated by the fact, that among the persons thus morally stigmatized are notoriously included many of the best men who ever lived. He goes still further, and lays down the principle of intolerance in its broad generality, saying, that "the man who holds false opinions" is morally condemnable "when he has had the means of knowing the truth" (Vol. II, p. 102); that it is "his duty to think rationally," (*i.e.* to think the same as Dr. Whewell): that it is to no purpose his saying that he has "done all he could to arrive at truth, since a man has never done *all he can* to arrive at truth." (Vol. II, pp. 105, 106.) If a man has never done all he can, neither has his judge done all he can; and the heretic may have more *a*grounds*a* for believing his opinion true, than the judge has for affirming it to be false. But the judge is on the side of received opinions, which, according to Dr. Whewell's standard, makes all right.

It is not, however, our object to criticise Dr. Whewell as a teacher of the details of morality. Our design goes no farther than to illustrate his controversy with Bentham respecting its first principle. It may, perhaps, be thought that Dr. Whewell's arguments against the philosophy of utility are too feeble

*a–a*52   ground

to require so long a refutation. But feeble arguments easily pass for convincing, when they are on the same side *as* the prevailing sentiment; and readers in general are so little acquainted with that or any other system of moral philosophy, that they take the word of anybody, especially an author in repute, who professes to inform them what it is; and suppose that a doctrine must be indeed absurd, to which mere truisms are offered as a sufficient reply. It was, therefore, not unimportant to show, by a minute examination, that Dr. Whewell has misunderstood and misrepresented the philosophy of utility, and that his attempts to refute it, and to construct a moral philosophy without it, have been equally failures.

*b–b*52   with

UTILITARIANISM

1861

EDITOR'S NOTE

4th ed. London: Longmans, Green, Reader, and Dyer, 1871. Revised and reprinted from 3rd ed. (London: Longmans, Green, Reader and Dyer, 1867), 2nd ed. (London: Longman, Green, Longman, Roberts, and Green, 1864), 1st ed. (London: Parker, Son, and Bourn, 1863), and *Fraser's Magazine*, LXIV (Oct., 1861), 391–406 [Chaps. i–ii], *ibid.* (Nov., 1861), 525–34 [Chaps. iii–iv], *ibid.* (Dec., 1861), 658–73 [Chap. v]. The articles in *Fraser's* were identified as "by John Stuart Mill." Described in JSM's bibliography as "An Essay in five Chapters entitled 'Utilitarianism' published in the three numbers of Fraser's Magazine for October, November and December 1861. Reprinted as a separate work early in 1863." (MacMinn, 93.) For a further account of the place of the work in relation to the other essays in this volume, see the Textual Introduction, cxxii–cxxvi above.

The following text is collated with those of the 1st, 2nd, and 3rd eds., and that in *Fraser's*. In the footnoted variants, the 4th ed. is indicated by "71"; the 3rd by "67"; the 2nd by "64"; the 1st by "63"; and *Fraser's* by "61". There are no copies of relevant editions in Somerville College. In all versions the title of Chap. v begins "On the . . ."; the Tables of Contents, however, except for 63, give "Of the. . . ." Here "On" is accepted.

CHAPTER I

General Remarks

THERE ARE few circumstances among those which make up the present condition of human knowledge, more unlike what might have been expected, or more significant of the backward state in which speculation on the most important subjects still lingers, than the little progress which has been made in the decision of the controversy respecting the criterion of right and wrong. From the dawn of philosophy, the question concerning the *summum bonum*, or, what is the same thing, concerning the foundation of morality, has been accounted the main problem in speculative thought, has occupied the most gifted intellects, and divided them into sects and schools, carrying on a vigorous warfare against one another. And after more than two thousand years the same discussions continue, philosophers are still ranged under the same contending banners, and neither thinkers nor mankind at large seem nearer to being unanimous on the subject, than when the youth Socrates listened to the old Protagoras, and asserted (if Plato's dialogue be grounded on a real conversation) the theory of utilitarianism against the popular morality of the so-called sophist.

It is true that similar confusion and uncertainty, and in some cases similar discordance, exist respecting the first principles of all the sciences, not excepting that which is deemed the most certain of them, mathematics; without much impairing, generally indeed without impairing at all, the trustworthiness of the conclusions of those sciences. An apparent anomaly, the explanation of which is, that the detailed doctrines of a science are not usually deduced from, nor depend for their evidence upon, what are called its first principles. Were it not so, there would be no science more precarious, or whose conclusions were more insufficiently made out, than algebra; which derives none of its certainty from what are commonly taught to learners as its elements, since these, as laid down by some of its most eminent teachers, are as full of fictions as English law, and of mysteries as theology. The truths which are ultimately accepted as the first principles of a science, are really the last results of metaphysical analysis, practised on the elementary notions with which the science is conversant; and their relation to the science is not that of foundations to an edifice, but of roots to a tree, which may perform their office equally well though they be never dug down to and exposed to light. But though in science the particular truths precede the general theory, the contrary might be expected to be the case with a practical art, such as morals or legislation. All action is for the sake of some end, and rules of action, it seems natural to suppose, must take their whole character and colour from the end to which they are subservient. When we engage in a pursuit, a clear and precise conception of what we are pursuing would seem to be the first thing we need, instead of the last we are to look forward to. A test of right and wrong must be the means, one would think, of ascertaining what is right or wrong, and not a consequence of having already ascertained it.

The difficulty is not avoided by having recourse to the popular theory of a natural faculty, a sense or instinct, informing us of right and wrong. For—besides that the existence of such a moral instinct is itself one of the matters in dispute—those believers in it who have any pretensions to philosophy, have been obliged to abandon the idea that it discerns what is right or wrong in the particular case in hand, as our other senses discern the sight or sound actually present. Our moral faculty, according to all those of its interpreters who are entitled to the name of thinkers, supplies us only with the general principles of moral judgments; it is a branch of our reason, not of our sensitive faculty; and must be looked to for the abstract doctrines of morality, not for perception of it in the concrete. The intuitive, no less than what may be termed the inductive, school of ethics, insists on the necessity of general laws. They both agree that the morality of an individual action is not a question of direct perception, but of the application of a law to an individual case. They recognise also, to a great extent, the same moral laws; but differ as to their evidence, and the source from which they derive their authority. According to the one opinion, the principles of morals are evident *à priori*, requiring nothing to command assent, except that the meaning of the terms be understood. According to the other doctrine, right and wrong, as well as truth and falsehood, are questions of observation and experience. But both hold equally that morality must be deduced from principles; and the intuitive school affirm as strongly as the inductive, that there is a science of morals. Yet they seldom attempt to make out a list of the *à priori* principles which are to serve as the premises of the science; still more rarely do they make any effort to reduce those various principles to one first principle, or common ground of obligation. They either assume the ordinary precepts of morals as of *à priori* authority, or they lay down as the common groundwork of those maxims, some generality much less obviously authoritative than the maxims themselves, and which has never succeeded in gaining popular acceptance. Yet to support their pretensions there ought either to be some one fundamental principle or law, at the root of all morality, or if there be several, there should be a determinate order of precedence among them;

and the one principle, or the rule for deciding between the various principles when they conflict, ought to be self-evident.

To inquire how far the bad effects of this deficiency have been mitigated in practice, or to what extent the moral beliefs of mankind have been vitiated or made uncertain by the absence of any distinct recognition of an ultimate standard, would imply a complete survey and criticism of past and present ethical doctrine. It would, however, be easy to show that whatever steadiness or consistency these moral beliefs have attained, has been mainly due to the tacit influence of a standard not recognised. Although the non-existence of an acknowledged first principle has made ethics not so much a guide as a consecration of men's actual sentiments, still, as men's sentiments, both of favour and of aversion, are greatly influenced by what they suppose to be the effects of things upon their happiness, the principle of utility, or as Bentham latterly called it, the greatest happiness principle, has had a large share in forming the moral doctrines even of those who most scornfully reject its authority. Nor is there any school of thought which refuses to admit that the influence of actions on happiness is a most material and even pre-dominant consideration in many of the details of morals, however unwilling to acknowledge it as the fundamental principle of morality, and the source of moral obligation. I might go much further, and say that to all those *à priori* moralists who deem it necessary to argue at all, utilitarian arguments are indispensable. It is not my present purpose to criticize these thinkers; but I cannot help referring, for illustration, to a systematic treatise by one of the most illustrious of them, the *Metaphysics of Ethics*, by Kant. This re-markable man, whose system of thought will long remain one of the land-marks in the history of philosophical speculation, does, in the treatise in question, lay down an universal first principle as the origin and ground of moral obligation; it is this:—"So act, that the rule on which thou actest would admit of being adopted as a law by all rational beings."[*] But when he begins to deduce from this precept any of the actual duties of morality, he fails, almost grotesquely, to show that there would be any contradiction, any logical (not to say physical) impossibility, in the adoption by all rational beings of the most outrageously immoral rules of conduct. All he shows is that the *consequences* of their universal adoption would be such as no one would choose to incur.

On the present occasion, I shall, without further discussion of the other theories, attempt to contribute something towards the understanding and appreciation of the Utilitarian or Happiness theory, and towards such proof as it is susceptible of. It is evident that this cannot be proof in the ordinary and popular meaning of the term. Questions of ultimate ends are not amenable to direct proof. Whatever can be proved to be good, must be so by being

[*See *Grundlegung zur Metaphysik der Sitten*. Riga: Hartknoch, 1797, p. 52.]

shown to be a means to something admitted to be good without proof. The medical art is proved to be good, by its conducing to health; but how is it possible to prove that health is good? The art of music is good, for the reason, among others, that it produces pleasure; but what proof is it possible to give that pleasure is good? If, then, it is asserted that there is a comprehensive formula, including all things which are in themselves good, and that what ever else is good, is not so as an end, but as a *mean*, the formula may be accepted or rejected, but is not a subject of what is commonly understood by proof. We are not, however, to infer that its acceptance or rejection must depend on blind impulse, or arbitrary choice. There is a larger meaning of the word proof, in which this question is as amenable to it as any other of the disputed questions of philosophy. The subject is within the cognizance of the rational faculty; and neither does that faculty deal with it solely in the way of intuition. Considerations may be presented capable of determining the intellect either to give or withhold its assent to the doctrine; and this is equivalent to proof.

We shall examine presently of what nature are these considerations; in what manner they apply to the case, and what rational grounds, therefore, can be given for accepting or rejecting the utilitarian formula. But it is a preliminary condition of rational acceptance or rejection, that the formula should be correctly understood. I believe that the very imperfect notion ordinarily formed of its meaning, is the chief obstacle which impedes its reception; and that could it be cleared, even from only the grosser misconceptions, the question would be greatly simplified, and a large proportion of its difficulties removed. Before, therefore, I attempt to enter into the philosophical grounds which can be given for assenting to the utilitarian standard, I shall offer some illustrations of the doctrine itself; with the view of showing more clearly what it is, distinguishing it from what it is not, and disposing of such of the practical objections to it as either originate in, or are closely connected with, mistaken interpretations of its meaning. Having thus prepared the ground, I shall afterwards endeavour to throw such light as I can upon the question, considered as one of philosophical theory.

*a–a*61   means

CHAPTER II

What Utilitarianism Is

A PASSING REMARK is all that needs be given to the ignorant blunder of sup-posing that those who stand up for utility as the test of right and wrong, use the term in that restricted and merely colloquial sense in which utility is opposed to pleasure. An apology is due to the philosophical opponents of utilitarianism, for even the momentary appearance of confounding them with any one capable of so absurd a misconception; which is the more extra-ordinary, inasmuch as the contrary accusation, of referring everything to pleasure, and that too in its grossest form, is another of the common charges against utilitarianism: and, as has been pointedly remarked by an able writer, the same sort of persons, and often the very same persons, denounce the theory "as impracticably dry when the word utility precedes the word pleasure, and as too practicably voluptuous when the word pleasure precedes the word utility." Those who know anything about the matter are aware that every writer, from Epicurus to Bentham, who maintained the theory of utility, meant by it, not something to be contradistinguished from pleasure, but pleasure itself, together with exemption from pain; and instead of oppos-ing the useful to the agreeable or the ornamental, have always declared that the useful means these, among other things. Yet the common herd, including the herd of writers, not only in newspapers and periodicals, but in books of weight and pretension, are perpetually falling into this shallow mistake. Having caught up the word utilitarian, while knowing nothing whatever about it but its sound, they habitually express by it the rejection, or the neglect, of pleasure in some of its forms; of beauty, of ornament, or of amuse-ment. Nor is the term thus ignorantly misapplied solely in disparagement, but occasionally in compliment; as though it implied superiority to frivolity and the mere pleasures of the moment. And this perverted use is the only one in which the word is popularly known, and the one from which the new generation are acquiring their sole notion of its meaning. Those who intro-duced the word, but who had for many years discontinued it as a distinctive appellation, may well feel themselves called upon to resume it, if by doing so they can hope to contribute anything towards rescuing it from this utter degradation.*

*The author of this essay has reason for believing himself to be the first person

The creed which accepts as the foundation of morals, Utility, or the Greatest Happiness Principle, holds that actions are right in proportion as they tend to promote happiness, wrong as they tend to produce the reverse of happiness. By happiness is intended pleasure, and the absence of pain; by unhappiness, pain, and the privation of pleasure. To give a clear view of the moral standard set up by the theory, much more requires to be said; in particular, what things it includes in the ideas of pain and pleasure; and to what extent this is left an open question. But these supplementary explanations do not affect the theory of life on which this theory of morality is grounded— namely, that pleasure, and freedom from pain, are the only things desirable as ends; and that all desirable things (which are as numerous in the utilitarian as in any other scheme) are desirable either for the pleasure inherent in themselves, or as means to the promotion of pleasure and the prevention of pain.

Now, such a theory of life excites in many minds, and among them in some of the most estimable in feeling and purpose, inveterate dislike. To suppose that life has (as they express it) no higher end than pleasure—no better and nobler object of desire and pursuit—they designate as utterly mean and grovelling; as a doctrine worthy only of swine, to whom the followers of Epicurus were, at a very early period, contemptuously likened; and modern holders of the doctrine are occasionally made the subject of equally polite comparisons by its German, French, and English assailants.

When thus attacked, the Epicureans have always answered, that it is not they, but their accusers, who represent human nature in a degrading light; since the accusation supposes human beings to be capable of no pleasures except those of which swine are capable. If this supposition were true, the charge could not be gainsaid, but would then be no longer an imputation; for if the sources of pleasure were precisely the same to human beings and to swine, the rule of life which is good enough for the one would be good enough for the other. The comparison of the Epicurean life to that of beasts is felt as degrading, precisely because a beast's pleasures do not satisfy a human being's conceptions of happiness. Human beings have faculties more elevated than the animal appetites, and when once made conscious of them, do not regard anything as happiness which does not include their gratifica-

---

who brought the word utilitarian into use. He did not invent it, but adopted it from a passing expression in Mr. [John] Galt's *Annals of the Parish* [Edinburgh: Blackwood, 1821, p. 286]. After using it as a designation for several years, he and others abandoned it from a growing dislike to anything resembling a badge or watchword of sectarian distinction. But as a name for one single opinion, not a set of opinions—to denote the recognition of utility as a [61   the] standard, not any particular way of applying it—the term supplies a want in the language, and offers, in many cases, a convenient mode of avoiding tiresome circumlocution.

tion. I do not, indeed, consider the Epicureans to have been by any means faultless in drawing out their scheme of consequences from the utilitarian principle. To do this in any sufficient manner, many Stoic, as well as Christian elements require to be included. But there is no known Epicurean theory of life which does not assign to the pleasures of the intellect, of the feelings and imagination, and of the moral sentiments, a much higher value as pleasures than to those of mere sensation. It must be admitted, however, that utilitarian writers in general have placed the superiority of mental over bodily pleasures chiefly in the greater permanency, safety, uncostliness, &c., of the former—that is, in their circumstantial advantages rather than in their intrinsic nature. And on all these points utilitarians have fully proved their case; but they might have taken the other, and, as it may be called, higher ground, with entire consistency. It is quite compatible with the principle of utility to recognise the fact, that some *kinds* of pleasure are more desirable and more valuable than others. It would be absurd that while, in estimating all other things, quality is considered as well as quantity, the estimation of pleasures should be supposed to depend on quantity alone.

If I am asked, what I mean by difference of quality in pleasures, or what makes one pleasure more valuable than another, merely as a pleasure, except its being greater in amount, there is but one possible answer. Of two pleasures, if there be one to which all or almost all who have experience of both give a decided preference, irrespective of any feeling of moral obligation to prefer it, that is the more desirable pleasure. If one of the two is, by those who are competently acquainted with both, placed so far above the other that they prefer it, even though knowing it to be attended with a greater amount of discontent, and would not resign it for any quantity of the other pleasure which their nature is capable of, we are justified in ascribing to the preferred enjoyment a superiority in quality, so far outweighing quantity as to render it, in comparison, of small account.

Now it is an unquestionable fact that those who are equally acquainted with, and equally capable of appreciating and enjoying, both, do give a most marked preference to the manner of existence which employs their higher faculties. Few human creatures would consent to be changed into any of the lower animals, for a promise of the fullest allowance of a beast's pleasures; no intelligent human being would consent to be a fool, no instructed person would be an ignoramus, no person of feeling and conscience would be selfish and base, even though they should be persuaded that the fool, the dunce, or the rascal is better satisfied with his lot than they are with theirs. They would not resign what they possess more than he, for the most complete satisfaction of all the desires which they have in common with him. If they ever fancy they would, it is only in cases of unhappiness so extreme, that to escape from it they would exchange their lot for almost any other, however undesirable in their own eyes. A being of higher faculties requires more to make him happy, is capable probably of more acute suffering, and *b*is*b* certainly accessible to it at more points, than one of an inferior type; but in spite of these liabilities, he can never really wish to sink into what he feels to be a lower grade of existence. We may give what explanation we please of this unwillingness; we may attribute it to pride, a name which is given indiscriminately to some of the most and to some of the least estimable feelings of which mankind are capable; we may refer it to the love of liberty and personal independence, an appeal to which was with the Stoics one of the most effective means for the inculcation of it; to the love of power, or to the love of excitement, both of which do really enter into and contribute to it: but its most appropriate appellation is a sense of dignity, which all human beings possess in one form or other, and in some, though by no means in exact, proportion to their higher faculties, and which is so essential a part of the happiness of those in whom it is strong, that nothing which conflicts with it could be, otherwise than momentarily, an object of desire to them. Whoever supposes that this preference takes place at a sacrifice of happiness—that the superior being, in anything like equal circumstances, is not happier than the inferior —confounds the two very different ideas, of happiness, and content. It is indisputable that the being whose capacities of enjoyment are low, has the greatest chance of having them fully satisfied; and a highly-endowed being will always feel that any happiness which he can look for, as the world is constituted, is imperfect. But he can learn to bear its imperfections, if they are at all bearable; and they will not make him envy the being who is indeed unconscious of the imperfections, but only because he feels not at all the good which those imperfections qualify. It is better to be a human being dissatisfied than a pig satisfied; better to be Socrates dissatisfied than a fool satisfied. And if the fool, or the pig, *c*is*c* of a different opinion, it is because they only know their own side of the question. The other party to the comparison knows both sides.

It may be objected, that many who are capable of the higher pleasures, occasionally, under the influence of temptation, postpone them to the lower. But this is quite compatible with a full appreciation of the intrinsic superiority of the higher. Men often, from infirmity of character, make their election for the nearer good, though they know it to be the less valuable; and this no less when the choice is between two bodily pleasures, than when it is between bodily and mental. They pursue sensual indulgences to the injury of health, though perfectly aware that health is the greater good. It may be further objected, that many who begin with youthful enthusiasm for everything noble, as they advance in years sink into indolence and selfishness. But I do not believe that those who undergo this very common change, voluntarily

b–b+67,71   *c–c*61,63   are

choose the lower description of pleasures in preference to the higher. I believe that before they devote themselves exclusively to the one, they have already become incapable of the other. Capacity for the nobler feelings is in most natures a very tender plant, easily killed, not only by hostile influences, but by mere want of sustenance; and in the majority of young persons it speedily dies away if the occupations to which their position in life has devoted them, and the society into which it has thrown them, are not favourable to keeping that higher capacity in exercise. Men lose their high aspirations as they lose their intellectual tastes, because they have not time or opportunity for indulging them; and they addict themselves to inferior pleasures, not because they deliberately prefer them, but because they are either the only ones to which they have access, or the only ones which they are any longer capable of enjoying. It may be questioned whether any one who has remained equally susceptible to both classes of pleasures, ever knowingly and calmly preferred the lower; though many, in all ages, have broken down in an ineffectual attempt to combine both.

From this verdict of the only competent judges, I apprehend there can be no appeal. On a question which is the best worth having of two pleasures, or which of two modes of existence is the most grateful to the feelings, apart from its moral attributes and from its consequences, the judgment of those who are qualified by knowledge of both, or, if they differ, that of the majority among them, must be admitted as final. And there needs be the less hesitation to accept this judgment respecting the quality of pleasures, since there is no other tribunal to be referred to even on the question of quantity. What means are there of determining which is the acutest of two pains, or the intensest of two pleasurable sensations, except the general suffrage of those who are familiar with both? Neither pains nor pleasures are homogeneous, and pain is always heterogeneous with pleasure. What is there to decide whether a particular pleasure is worth purchasing at the cost of a particular pain, except the feelings and judgment of the experienced? When, therefore, those feelings and judgment declare the pleasures derived from the higher faculties to be preferable *in kind*, apart from the question of intensity, to those of which the animal nature, disjoined from the higher faculties, is susceptible, they are entitled on this subject to the same regard.

I have dwelt on this point, as being a necessary part of a perfectly just conception of Utility or Happiness, considered as the directive rule of human conduct. But it is by no means an indispensable condition to the acceptance of the utilitarian standard; for that standard is not the agent's own greatest happiness, but the greatest amount of happiness altogether; and if it may possibly be doubted whether a noble character is always the happier for its nobleness, there can be no doubt that it makes other people happier, and that the world in general is immensely a gainer by it. Utilitarianism, therefore, could only attain its end by the general cultivation of nobleness of character, even if each individual were only benefited by the nobleness of others, and his own, so far as happiness is concerned, were a sheer deduction from the benefit. But the bare enunciation of such an absurdity *d*as this last,*d* renders refutation superfluous.

According to the Greatest Happiness Principle, as above explained, the ultimate end, with reference to and for the sake of which all other things are desirable (whether we are considering our own good or that of other people), is an existence exempt as far as possible from pain, and as rich as possible in enjoyments, both in point of quantity and quality; the test of quality, and the rule for measuring it against quantity, being the preference felt by those who, in their opportunities of experience, to which must be added their habits of self-consciousness and self-observation, are best furnished with the means of comparison. This, being, according to the utilitarian opinion, the end of human action, is necessarily also the standard of morality; which may accordingly be defined, the rules and precepts for human conduct, by the observance of which an existence such as has been described might be, to the greatest extent possible, secured to all mankind; and not to them only, but, so far as the nature of things admits, to the whole sentient creation.

Against this doctrine, however, arises another class of objectors, who say that happiness, in any form, cannot be the rational purpose of human life and action; because, in the first place, it is unattainable: and they contemptuously ask, What right hast thou to be happy? a question which Mr. Carlyle clenches by the addition, What right, a short time ago, hadst thou even *to be*?[*] Next, they say, that men can do *without* happiness; that all noble human beings have felt this, and could not have become noble but by learning the lesson of Entsagen, or renunciation; which lesson, thoroughly learnt and submitted to, they affirm to be the beginning and necessary condition of all virtue.

The first of these objections would go to the root of the matter were it well founded; for if no happiness is to be had at all by human beings, the attainment of it cannot be the end of morality, or of any rational conduct. Though, even in that case, something might still be said for the utilitarian theory; since utility includes not solely the pursuit of happiness, but the prevention or mitigation of unhappiness; and if the former aim be chimerical, there will be all the greater scope and more imperative need for the latter, so long at least as mankind think fit to live, and do not take refuge in the simultaneous act of suicide recommended under certain conditions by Novalis.[†] When, how-

---

[*Thomas Carlyle. *Sartor Resartus*. 2nd ed. Boston: Munroe, 1837, p. 197.]
[†See Thomas Carlyle. "Novalis," *Critical and Miscellaneous Essays*. 5 vols. London: Fraser, 1840, Vol. II, pp. 286, 288.]
    d–d+63,64,67,71

ever, it is thus positively asserted to be impossible that human life should be happy, the assertion, if not something like a verbal quibble, is at least an exaggeration. If by happiness be meant a continuity of highly pleasurable excitement, it is evident enough that this is impossible. A state of exalted pleasure lasts only moments, or in some cases, and with some intermissions, hours or days, and is the occasional brilliant flash of enjoyment, not its permanent and steady flame. Of this the philosophers who have taught that happiness is the end of life were as fully aware as those who taunt them. The happiness which they meant was not a life of rapture; but moments of such, in an existence made up of few and transitory pains, many and various pleasures, with a decided predominance of the active over the passive, and having as the foundation of the whole, not to expect more from life than it is capable of bestowing. A life thus composed, to those who have been fortunate enough to obtain it, has always appeared worthy of the name of happiness. And such an existence is even now the lot of many, during some considerable portion of their lives. The present wretched education, and wretched social arrangements, are the only real hindrance to its being attainable by almost all.

The objectors perhaps may doubt whether human beings, if taught to consider happiness as the end of life, would be satisfied with such a moderate share of it. But great numbers of mankind have been satisfied with much less. The main constituents of a satisfied life appear to be two, either of which by itself is often found sufficient for the purpose: tranquillity, and excitement. With much tranquillity, many find that they can be content with very little pleasure: with much excitement, many can reconcile themselves to a considerable quantity of pain. There is assuredly no inherent impossibility in enabling even the mass of mankind to unite both; since the two are so far from being incompatible that they are in natural alliance, the prolongation of either being a preparation for, and exciting a wish for, the other. It is only those in whom indolence amounts to a vice, that do not desire excitement after an interval of repose; it is only those in whom the need of excitement is a disease, that feel the tranquillity which follows excitement dull and insipid, instead of pleasurable in direct proportion to the excitement which preceded it. When people who are tolerably fortunate in their outward lot do not find in life sufficient enjoyment to make it valuable to them, the cause generally is, caring for nobody but themselves. To those who have neither public nor private affections, the excitements of life are much curtailed, and in any case dwindle in value as the time approaches when all selfish interests must be terminated by death: while those who leave after them objects of personal affection, and especially those who have also cultivated a fellow-feeling with the collective interests of mankind, retain as lively an interest in life on the eve of death as in the vigour of youth and health. Next to selfishness, the principal cause which makes life unsatisfactory, is want of mental cultivation.

A cultivated mind—I do not mean that of a philosopher, but any mind to which the fountains of knowledge have been opened, and which has been taught, in any tolerable degree, to exercise its faculties—finds sources of inexhaustible interest in all that surrounds it; in the objects of nature, the achievements of art, the imaginations of poetry, the incidents of history, the ways of mankind past and present, and their prospects in the future. It is possible, indeed, to become indifferent to all this, and that too without having exhausted a thousandth part of it; but only when one has had from the beginning no moral or human interest in these things, and has sought in them only the gratification of curiosity.

Now there is absolutely no reason in the nature of things why an amount of mental culture sufficient to give an intelligent interest in these objects of contemplation, should not be the inheritance of every one born in a civilized country. As little is there an inherent necessity that any human being should be a selfish egotist, devoid of every feeling or care but those which centre in his own miserable individuality. Something far superior to this is sufficiently common even now, to give ample earnest of what the human species may be made. Genuine private affections, and a sincere interest in the public good, are possible, though in unequal degrees, to every rightly brought up human being. In a world in which there is so much to interest, so much to enjoy, and so much also to correct and improve, every one who has this moderate amount of moral and intellectual requisites is capable of an existence which may be called enviable; and unless such a person, through bad laws, or subjection to the will of others, is denied the liberty to use the sources of happiness within his reach, he will not fail to find this enviable existence, if he escape the positive evils of life, the great sources of physical and mental suffering—such as indigence, disease, and the unkindness, worthlessness, or premature loss of objects of affection. The main stress of the problem lies, therefore, in the contest with these calamities, from which it is a rare good fortune entirely to escape; which, as things now are, cannot be obviated, and often cannot be in any material degree mitigated. Yet no one whose opinion deserves a moment's consideration can doubt that most of the great positive evils of the world are in themselves removable, and will, if human affairs continue to improve, be in the end reduced within narrow limits. Poverty, in any sense implying suffering, may be completely extinguished by the wisdom of society, combined with the good sense and providence of individuals. Even that most intractable of enemies, disease, may be indefinitely reduced in dimensions by good physical and moral education, and proper control of noxious influences; while the progress of science holds out a promise for the future of still more direct conquests over this detestable foe. And every advance in that direction relieves us from some, not only of the chances which cut short our own lives, but, what concerns us still more, which deprive us of those in whom our happiness is wrapt up. As for vicissitudes of fortune, and other disappointments connected with worldly circumstances, these are principally the effect either of gross imprudence, of ill-regulated desires, or of bad or imperfect social institutions. All the grand sources, in short, of human suffering are in a great degree, many of them almost entirely, conquerable by human care and effort; and though their removal is grievously slow—though a long succession of generations will perish in the breach before the conquest is completed, and this world becomes all that, if will and knowledge were not wanting, it might easily be made—yet every mind sufficiently intelligent and generous to bear a part, however small and unconspicuous, in the endeavour, will draw a noble enjoyment from the contest itself, which he would not for any bribe in the form of selfish indulgence consent to be without.

And this leads to the true estimation of what is said by the objectors concerning the possibility, and the obligation, of learning to do without happiness. Unquestionably it is possible to do without happiness; it is done involuntarily by nineteen-twentieths of mankind, even in those parts of our present world which are least deep in barbarism; and it often has to be done voluntarily by the hero or the martyr, for the sake of something which he prizes more than his individual happiness. But this something, what is it, unless the happiness of others, or some of the requisites of happiness? It is noble to be capable of resigning entirely one's own portion of happiness, or chances of it: but, after all, this self-sacrifice must be for some end; it is not its own end; and if we are told that its end is not happiness, but virtue, which is better than happiness, I ask, would the sacrifice be made if the hero or martyr did not believe that it would earn for others immunity from similar sacrifices? Would it be made, if he thought that his renunciation of happiness for himself would produce no fruit for any of his fellow creatures, but to make their lot like his, and place them also in the condition of persons who have renounced happiness? All honour to those who can abnegate for themselves the personal enjoyment of life, when by such renunciation they contribute worthily to increase the amount of happiness in the world; but he who does it, or professes to do it, for any other purpose, is no more deserving of admiration than the ascetic mounted on his pillar. He may be an inspiriting proof of what men *can* do, but assuredly not an example of what they *should*.

Though it is only in a very imperfect state of the world's arrangements that any one can best serve the happiness of others by the absolute sacrifice of his own, yet so long as the world is in that imperfect state, I fully acknowledge that the readiness to make such a sacrifice is the highest virtue which can be found in man. I will add, that in this condition of the world, paradoxical as the assertion may be, the conscious ability to do without happiness gives the best prospect of realizing such happiness as is attainable. For nothing except that consciousness can raise a person above the chances of life, by making him feel that, let fate and fortune do their worst, they have not power to subdue him: which, once felt, frees him from excess of anxiety concerning the evils of life, and enables him, like many a Stoic in the worst times of the Roman Empire, to cultivate in tranquillity the sources of satisfaction accessible to him, without concerning himself about the uncertainty of their duration, any more than about their inevitable end.

Meanwhile, let utilitarians never cease to claim the morality of self-devotion as a possession which belongs by as good a right to them, as either to the Stoic or to the Transcendentalist. The utilitarian morality does recognise in human beings the power of sacrificing their own greatest good for the good of others. It only refuses to admit that the sacrifice is itself a good. A sacrifice which does not increase, or tend to increase, the sum total of happiness, it considers as wasted. The only self-renunciation which it applauds, is devotion to the happiness, or to some of the means of happiness, of others; either of mankind collectively, or of individuals within the limits imposed by the collective interests of mankind.

I must again repeat, what the assailants of utilitarianism seldom have the justice to acknowledge, that the happiness which forms the utilitarian standard of what is right in conduct, is not the agent's own happiness, but that of all concerned. As between his own happiness and that of others, utilitarianism requires him to be as strictly impartial as a disinterested and benevolent spectator. In the golden rule of Jesus of Nazareth, we read the complete spirit of the ethics of utility. To do as *one* would be done by, and to love *one's* neighbour as *oneself*, constitute the ideal perfection of utilitarian morality. As the means of making the nearest approach to this ideal, utility would enjoin, first, that laws and social arrangements should place the happiness, or (as speaking practically it may be called) the interest, of every individual, as nearly as possible in harmony with the interest of the whole; and secondly, that education and opinion, which have so vast a power over human character, should so use that power as to establish in the mind of every individual an indissoluble association between his own happiness and the good of the whole; especially between his own happiness and the practice of such modes of conduct, negative and positive, as regard for the universal happiness prescribes: so that not only he may be unable to conceive the possibility of happiness to himself, consistently with conduct opposed to the general good, but also that a direct impulse to promote the general good may be in every individual one of the habitual motives of action, and the sentiments connected therewith may fill a large and prominent place in every human being's sentient existence. If the impugners of the utilitarian morality

e–e61,63   you   f–f61,63   your   g–g61,63   yourself represented it to their own minds in this its true character, I know not what recommendation possessed by any other morality they could possibly affirm to be wanting to it: what more beautiful or more exalted developments of human nature any other ethical system can be supposed to foster, or what springs of action, not accessible to the utilitarian, such systems rely on for giving effect to their mandates.

The objectors to utilitarianism cannot always be charged with representing it in a discreditable light. On the contrary, those among them who entertain anything like a just idea of its disinterested character, sometimes find fault with its standard as being too high for humanity. They say it is exacting too much to require that people shall always act from the inducement of promoting the general interests of society. But this is to mistake the very meaning of a standard of morals, and ^{h}to^h confound the rule of action with the motive of it. It is the business of ethics to tell us what are our duties, or by what test we may know them; but no system of ethics requires that the sole motive of all we do shall be a feeling of duty; on the contrary, ninety-nine hundredths of all our actions are done from other motives, and rightly so done, if the rule of duty does not condemn them. It is the more unjust to utilitarianism that this particular misapprehension should be made a ground of objection to it, inasmuch as utilitarian moralists have gone beyond almost all others in affirming that the motive has nothing to do with the morality of the action, though much with the worth of the agent. He who saves a fellow creature from drowning does what is morally right, whether his motive be duty, or the hope of being paid for his trouble: he who betrays the friend that trusts him, is guilty of a crime, even if his object be to serve another friend to whom he is under greater obligations.* But to speak only of actions

*[64] An opponent, whose intellectual and moral fairness it is a pleasure to acknowledge (the Rev. J. Llewellyn Davies), has objected to this passage, saying, "Surely the rightness or wrongness of saving a man from drowning does depend very much upon the motive with which it is done. Suppose that a tyrant, when his enemy jumped into the sea to escape from him, saved him from drowning simply in order that he might inflict upon him more exquisite tortures, would it tend to clearness to speak of that rescue as 'a morally right action?' Or suppose again, according to one of the stock illustrations of ethical inquiries, that a man betrayed a trust received from a friend, because the discharge of it would fatally injure that friend himself or some one belonging to him, would utilitarianism compel one to call the betrayal 'a crime' as much as if it had been done from the meanest motive?"

I submit, that he who saves another from drowning in order to kill him by torture afterwards, does not differ only in motive from him who does the same thing from duty or benevolence; the act itself is different. The rescue of the man is, in the case supposed, only the necessary first step of an act far more atrocious than leaving him to drown would have been. Had Mr. Davies said, "The

$h-h+67,71$

done from the motive of duty, and in direct obedience to principle: it is a misapprehension of the utilitarian mode of thought, to conceive it as implying that people should fix their minds upon so wide a generality as the world, or society at large. The great majority of good actions are intended, not for the benefit of the world, but for that of individuals, of which the good of the world is made up; and the thoughts of the most virtuous man need not on these occasions travel beyond the particular persons concerned, except so far as is necessary to assure himself that in benefiting them he is not violating the rights—that is, the legitimate and authorized expectations—of any one else. The multiplication of happiness is, according to the utilitarian ethics, the object of virtue: the occasions on which any person (except one in a thousand) has it in his power to do this on an extended scale, in other words, to be a public benefactor, are but exceptional; and on these occasions alone is he called on to consider public utility; in every other case, private utility, the interest or happiness of some few persons, is all he has to attend to. Those alone the influence of whose actions extends to society in general, need concern themselves habitually about so large an object. In the case of abstinences indeed—of things which people forbear to do, from moral considerations, though the consequences in the particular case might be beneficial—it would be unworthy of an intelligent agent not to be consciously aware that the action is of a class which, if practised generally, would be generally injurious, and that this is the ground of the obligation to abstain from it. The amount of regard for the public interest implied in this recognition, is no greater than is demanded by every system of morals; for they all enjoin to abstain from whatever is manifestly pernicious to society.

The same considerations dispose of another reproach against the doctrine of utility, founded on a still grosser misconception of the purpose of a standard of morality, and of the very meaning of the words right and wrong. It is often affirmed that utilitarianism renders men cold and unsympathizing; that it chills their moral feelings towards individuals; that it makes them regard only the dry and hard consideration of the consequences of actions,

---

rightness or wrongness of saving a man from drowning does depend very much" —not upon the motive, but—"upon the *intention*," no utilitarian would have differed from him. Mr. Davies, by an oversight too common not to be quite venial, has in this case confounded the very different ideas of Motive and Intention. There is no point which utilitarian thinkers (and Bentham pre-eminently) have taken more pains to illustrate than this. The morality of the action depends entirely upon the intention—that is, upon what the agent *wills to do*. But the motive, that is, the feeling which makes him will so to do, when it [64, 67   if it] makes no difference in the act, makes none in the morality: though it makes a great difference in our moral estimation of the agent, especially if it indicates a good or a bad habitual *disposition*—a bent of character from which useful, or from which hurtful actions are likely to arise.

not taking into their moral estimate the qualities from which those actions emanate. If the assertion means that they do not allow their judgment respecting the rightness or wrongness of an action to be influenced by their opinion of the qualities of the person who does it, this is a complaint not against utilitarianism, but against having any standard of morality at all; for certainly no known ethical standard decides an action to be good or bad because it is done by a good or a bad man, still less because done by an amiable, a brave, or a benevolent man, or the contrary. These considerations are relevant, not to the estimation of actions, but of persons; and there is nothing in the utilitarian theory inconsistent with the fact that there are other things which interest us in persons besides the rightness and wrongness of their actions. The Stoics, indeed, with the paradoxical misuse of language which was part of their system, and by which they strove to raise themselves above all concern about anything but virtue, were fond of saying that he who has that has everything; that he, and only he, is rich, is beautiful, is a king. But no claim of this description is made for the virtuous man by the utilitarian doctrine. Utilitarians are quite aware that there are other desirable possessions and qualities besides virtue, and are perfectly willing to allow to all of them their full worth. They are also aware that a right action does not necessarily indicate a virtuous character, and that actions which are blameable often proceed from qualities entitled to praise. When this is apparent in any particular case, it modifies their estimation, not certainly of the act, but of the agent. I grant that they are, notwithstanding, of opinion, that in the long run the best proof of a good character is good actions; and resolutely refuse to consider any mental disposition as good, of which the predominant tendency is to produce bad conduct. This makes them unpopular with many people; but it is an unpopularity which they must share with every one who regards the distinction between right and wrong in a serious light; and the reproach is not one which a conscientious utilitarian need be anxious to repel.

If no more be meant by the objection than that many utilitarians look on the morality of actions, as measured by the utilitarian standard, with too exclusive a regard, and do not lay sufficient stress upon the other beauties of character which go towards making a human being loveable or admirable, this may be admitted. Utilitarians who have cultivated their moral feelings, but not their sympathies nor their artistic perceptions, do fall into this mistake; and so do all other moralists under the same conditions. What can be said in excuse for other moralists is equally available for them, namely, that if there is to be any error, it is better that it should be on that side. As a matter of fact, we may affirm that among utilitarians as among adherents of other systems, there is every imaginable degree of rigidity and of laxity in the application of their standard: some are even puritanically rigorous, while

others are as indulgent as can possibly be desired by sinner or by sentimentalist. But on the whole, a doctrine which brings prominently forward
the interest that mankind have in the repression and prevention of conduct
which violates the moral law, is likely to be inferior to no other in turning
the sanctions of opinion against such violations. It is true, the question,
What does violate the moral law? is one on which those who recognise different standards of morality are likely now and then to differ. But difference
of opinion on moral questions was not first introduced into the world by
utilitarianism, while that doctrine does supply, if not always an easy, at all
events a tangible and intelligible mode of deciding such differences.

It may not be superfluous to notice a few more of the common misappre-
hensions of utilitarian ethics, even those which are so obvious and gross that
it might appear impossible for any person of candour and intelligence to fall
into them: since persons, even of considerable mental endowments, often
give themselves so little trouble to understand the bearings of any opinion
against which they entertain a prejudice, and men are in general so little
conscious of this voluntary ignorance as a defect, that the vulgarest misunderstandings of ethical doctrines are continually met with in the deliberate
writings of persons of the greatest pretensions both to high principle and to
philosophy. We not uncommonly hear the doctrine of utility inveighed
against as a *godless* doctrine. If it be necessary to say anything at all against
so mere an assumption, we may say that the question depends upon what
idea we have formed of the moral character of the Deity. If it be a true belief
that God desires, above all things, the happiness of his creatures, and that
this was his purpose in their creation, utility is not only not a godless doctrine,
but more profoundly religious than any other. If it be meant that utilitarianism does not recognise the revealed will of God as the supreme law of
morals, I answer, that an utilitarian who believes in the perfect goodness and
wisdom of God, necessarily believes that whatever God has thought fit to
reveal on the subject of morals, must fulfil the requirements of utility in a
supreme degree. But others besides utilitarians have been of opinion that
the Christian revelation was intended, and is fitted, to inform the hearts and
minds of mankind with a spirit which should enable them to find for themselves what is right, and incline them to do it when found, rather than to tell
them, except in a very general way, what it is: and that we need a doctrine
of ethics, carefully followed out, to *interpret* to us the will of God. Whether
this opinion is correct or not, it is superfluous here to discuss; since whatever
aid religion, either natural or revealed, can afford to ethical investigation, is
as open to the utilitarian moralist as to any other. He can use it as the testimony of God to the usefulness or hurtfulness of any given course of action,

by as good a right as others can use it for the indication of a transcendental law, having no connexion with usefulness or with happiness.

Again, Utility is often summarily stigmatized as an immoral doctrine by giving it the name of Expediency, and taking advantage of the popular use of that term to contrast it with Principle. But the Expedient, in the sense in which it is opposed to the Right, generally means that which is expedient for the particular interest of the agent himself; as when a minister sacrifices the *interest* of his country to keep himself in place. When it means anything better than this, it means that which is expedient for some immediate object, some temporary purpose, but which violates a rule whose observance is expedient in a much higher degree. The Expedient, in this sense, instead of being the same thing with the useful, is a branch of the hurtful. Thus, it would often be expedient, for the purpose of getting over some momentary embarrassment, or attaining some object immediately useful to ourselves or others, to tell a lie. But inasmuch as the cultivation in ourselves of a sensitive feeling on the subject of veracity, is one of the most useful, and the enfeeblement of that feeling one of the most hurtful, things to which our conduct can be instrumental; and inasmuch as any, even unintentional, deviation from truth, does that much towards weakening the trustworthiness of human assertion, which is not only the principal support of all present social well-being, but the insufficiency of which does more than any one thing that can be named to keep back civilization, virtue, everything on which human happiness on the largest scale depends; we feel that the violation, for a present advantage, of a rule of such transcendant expediency, is not expedient, and that he who, for the sake of a convenience to himself or to some other individual, does what depends on him to deprive mankind of the good, and inflict upon them the evil, involved in the greater or less reliance which they can place in each other's word, acts the part of one of their worst enemies. Yet that even this rule, sacred as it is, admits of possible exceptions, is acknowledged by all moralists; the chief of which is when the withholding of some fact (as of information from a malefactor, or of bad news from a person dangerously ill) would *preserve some one* (especially *a person* other than oneself) from great and unmerited evil, and when the withholding can only be effected by denial. But in order that the exception may not extend itself beyond the need, and may have the least possible effect in weakening reliance on veracity, it ought to be recognised, and, if possible, its limits defined; and if the principle of utility is good for anything, it must be good for weighing these conflicting utilities against one another, and marking out the region within which one or the other preponderates.

*i–i*61,63   interests
*j–j*61,63,64   save an individual   *k–k*61,63,64   an individual

Again, defenders of utility often find themselves called upon to reply to such objections as this—that there is not time, previous to action, for calculating and weighing the effects of any line of conduct on the general happiness. This is exactly as if any one were to say that it is impossible to guide our conduct by Christianity, because there is not time, on every occasion on which anything has to be done, to read through the Old and New Testaments. The answer to the objection is, that there has been ample time, namely, the whole past duration of the human species. During all that time mankind have been learning by experience the tendencies of actions; on which experience all the prudence, as well as all the morality of life, ^{l}is^l dependent. People talk as if the commencement of this course of experience had hitherto been put off, and as if, at the moment when some man feels tempted to meddle with the property or life of another, he had to begin considering for the first time whether murder ^{m}and^m theft are injurious to human happiness. Even then I do not think that he would find the question very puzzling; but, at all events, the matter is now done to his hand. It is truly a whimsical supposition that if mankind were agreed in considering utility to be the test of morality, they would remain without any agreement as to what *is* useful, and would take no measures for having their notions on the subject taught to the young, and enforced by law and opinion. There is no difficulty in proving any ethical standard whatever to work ill, if we suppose universal idiocy to be conjoined with it; but on any hypothesis short of that, mankind must by this time have acquired positive beliefs as to the effects of some actions on their happiness; and ^{n}the^n beliefs which have thus come down are the rules of morality for the multitude, and for the philosopher until he has succeeded in finding better. That philosophers might easily do this, even now, on many subjects; that the received code of ethics is by no means of divine right; and that mankind have still much to learn as to the effects of actions on the general happiness, I admit, or rather, earnestly maintain. The corollaries from the principle of utility, like the precepts of every practical art, admit of indefinite improvement, and, in a progressive state of the human mind, their improvement is perpetually going on. But to consider the rules of morality as improvable, is one thing; to pass over the intermediate generalizations entirely, and endeavour to test each individual action directly by the first principle, is another. It is a strange notion that the acknowledgment of a first principle is inconsistent with the admission of secondary ones. To inform a traveller respecting the place of his ultimate destination, is not to forbid the use of landmarks and direction-posts on the way. The proposition that happiness is the end and aim of morality, does not mean that no road ought to be laid down to that goal, or that persons going thither should not be advised to

$^{l-l}$61,63,64   are
$^{m-m}$61   or [*printer's error?*] $^{n-n}$67   their [*printer's error?*]

take one direction rather than another. Men really ought to leave off talking a kind of nonsense on this subject, which they would neither talk nor listen to on other matters of practical concernment. Nobody argues that the art of navigation is not founded on astronomy, because sailors cannot wait to calculate the Nautical Almanack. Being rational creatures, they go to sea with it ready calculated; and all rational creatures go out upon the sea of life with their minds made up on the common questions of right and wrong, as well as on many of the far more difficult questions of wise and foolish. And this, as long as foresight is a human quality, it is to be presumed they will continue to do. Whatever we adopt as the fundamental principle of morality, we require subordinate principles to apply it by: the impossibility of doing without them, being common to all systems, can afford no argument against any one in particular: but gravely to argue as if no such secondary principles could be had, and as if mankind had remained till now, and always must remain, without drawing any general conclusions from the experience of human life, is as high a pitch, I think, as absurdity has ever reached in philosophical controversy.

The remainder of the stock arguments against utilitarianism mostly consist in laying to its charge the common infirmities of human nature, and the general difficulties which embarrass conscientious persons in shaping their course through life. We are told than an utilitarian will be apt to make his own particular case an exception to moral rules, and, when under temptation, will see an utility in the breach of a rule, greater than he will see in its observance. But is utility the only creed which is able to furnish us with excuses for evil doing, and means of cheating our own conscience? They are afforded in abundance by all doctrines which recognise as a fact in morals the existence of conflicting considerations; which all doctrines do, that have been believed by sane persons. It is not the fault of any creed, but of the complicated nature of human affairs, that rules of conduct cannot be so framed as to require no exceptions, and that hardly any kind of action can safely be laid down as either always obligatory or always condemnable. There is no ethical creed which does not temper the rigidity of its laws, by giving a certain latitude, under the moral responsibility of the agent, for accommodation to peculiarities of circumstances; and under every creed, at the opening thus made, self-deception and dishonest casuistry get in. There exists no moral system under which there do not arise unequivocal cases of conflicting obligation. These are the real difficulties, the knotty points both in the theory of ethics, and in the conscientious guidance of personal conduct. They are overcome practically with greater or with less success according to the intellect and virtue of the individual; but it can hardly be pretended that any one will be the less qualified for dealing with them, from possessing an ultimate standard to which conflicting rights and duties can be referred.

If utility is the ultimate source of moral obligations, utility may be invoked to decide between them when their demands are incompatible. Though the application of the standard may be difficult, it is better than none at all: while in other systems, the moral laws all claiming independent authority, there is no common umpire entitled to interfere between them; their claims to precedence one over another rest on little better than sophistry, and unless determined, as they generally are, by the unacknowledged influence of considerations of utility, afford a free scope for the action of personal desires and partialities. We must remember that only in these cases of conflict between secondary principles is it requisite that first principles should be appealed to. There is no case of moral obligation in which some secondary principle is not involved; and if only one, there can seldom be any real doubt which one it is, in the mind of any person by whom the principle itself is recognised.

CHAPTER III

Of the Ultimate Sanction
of the Principle of Utility

THE QUESTION is often asked, and properly so, in regard to any supposed moral standard—What is its sanction? what are the motives to obey it? or more specifically, what is the source of its obligation? whence does it derive its binding force? It is a necessary part of moral philosophy to provide the answer to this question; which, though frequently assuming the shape of an objection to the utilitarian morality, as if it had some special applicability to that above others, really arises in regard to all standards. It arises, in fact, whenever a person is called on to *adopt* a standard, or refer morality to any basis on which he has not been accustomed to rest it. For the customary morality, that which education and opinion have consecrated, is the only one which presents itself to the mind with the feeling of being *in itself* obligatory; and when a person is asked to believe that this morality *derives* its obligation from some general principle round which custom has not thrown the same halo, the assertion is to him a paradox; the supposed corollaries seem to have a more binding force than the original theorem; the superstructure seems to stand better without, than with, what is represented as its foundation. He says to himself, I feel that I am bound not to rob or murder, betray or deceive; but why am I bound to promote the general happiness? If my own happiness lies in something else, why may I not give that the preference?

If the view adopted by the utilitarian philosophy of the nature of the moral sense be correct, this difficulty will always present itself, until the influences which form moral character have taken the same hold of the principle which they have taken of some of the consequences—until, by the improvement of education, the feeling of unity with our fellow creatures shall be (what it cannot be °doubted° that Christ intended it to be) as deeply rooted in our character, and to our own consciousness as completely a part of our nature, as the horror of crime is in an ordinarily well-brought up young person. In the mean time, however, the difficulty has no peculiar application to the doctrine of utility, but is inherent in every attempt to analyse morality and reduce

°–°61,63   denied

it to principles; which, unless the principle is already in men's minds invested with as much sacredness as any of its applications, always seems to divest them of a part of their sanctity.

The principle of utility either has, or there is no reason why it might not have, all the sanctions which belong to any other system of morals. Those sanctions are either external or internal. Of the external sanctions it is not necessary to speak at any length. They are, the hope of favour and the fear of displeasure from our fellow creatures or from the Ruler of the Universe, along with whatever we may have of sympathy or affection for them, or of love and awe of Him, inclining us to do his will independently of selfish consequences. There is evidently no reason why all these motives for observance should not attach themselves to the utilitarian morality, as completely and as powerfully as to any other. Indeed, those of them which refer to our fellow creatures are sure to do so, in proportion to the amount of general intelligence; for whether there be any other ground of moral obligation than the general happiness or not, men do desire happiness; and however imperfect may be their own practice, they desire and commend all conduct in others towards themselves, by which they think their happiness is promoted. With regard to the religious motive, if men believe, as most profess to do, in the goodness of God, those who think that conduciveness to the general happiness is the essence, or even only the criterion, of good, must necessarily believe that it is also that which God approves. The whole force therefore of external reward and punishment, whether physical or moral, and whether proceeding from God or from our fellow men, together with all that the capacities of human nature admit, of disinterested devotion to either, become available to enforce the utilitarian morality, in proportion as that morality is recognised; and the more powerfully, the more the appliances of education and general cultivation are bent to the purpose.

So far as to external sanctions. The internal sanction of duty, whatever our standard of duty may be, is one and the same—a feeling in our own mind; a pain, more or less intense, attendant on violation of duty, which in properly-cultivated moral natures rises, in the more serious cases, into shrinking from it as an impossibility. This feeling, when disinterested, and connecting itself with the pure idea of duty, and not with some particular form of it, or with any of the merely accessory circumstances, is the essence of Conscience; though in that complex phenomenon as it actually exists, the simple fact is in general all encrusted over with collateral associations, derived from sympathy, from love, and still more from fear; from all the forms of religious feeling; from the recollections of childhood and of all our past life; from self-esteem, desire of the esteem of others, and occasionally even self-abasement. This extreme complication is, I apprehend, the origin of the sort of mystical character which, by a tendency of the human mind of which there are many other examples, is apt to be attributed to the idea of moral obligation, and which leads people to believe that the idea cannot possibly attach itself to any other objects than those which, by a supposed mysterious law, are found in our present experience to excite it. Its binding force, however, consists in the existence of a mass of feeling which must be broken through in order to do what violates our standard of right, and which, if we do nevertheless violate that standard, will probably have to be encountered afterwards in the form of remorse. Whatever theory we have of the nature or origin of conscience, this is what essentially constitutes it.

The ultimate sanction, therefore, of all morality (external motives apart) being a subjective feeling in our own minds, I see nothing embarrassing to those whose standard is utility, in the question, what is the sanction of that particular standard? We may answer, the same as of all other moral standards —the conscientious feelings of mankind. Undoubtedly this sanction has no binding efficacy on those who do not possess the feelings it appeals to; but neither will these persons be more obedient to any other moral principle than to the utilitarian one. On them morality of any kind has no hold but through the external sanctions. Meanwhile the feelings exist, a fact in human nature, the reality of which, and the great power with which they are capable of acting on those in whom they have been duly cultivated, are proved by experience. No reason has ever been shown why they may not be cultivated to as great intensity in connexion with the utilitarian, as with any other rule of morals.

There is, I am aware, a disposition to believe that a person who sees in moral obligation a transcendental fact, an objective reality belonging to the province of "Things in themselves," is likely to be more obedient to it than one who believes it to be entirely subjective, having its seat in human consciousness only. But whatever a person's opinion may be on this point of Ontology, the force he is really urged by is his own subjective feeling, and is exactly measured by its strength. No one's belief that Duty is an objective reality is stronger than the belief that God is so; yet the belief in God, apart from the expectation of actual reward and punishment, only operates on conduct through, and in proportion to, the subjective religious feeling. The sanction, so far as it is disinterested, is always in the mind itself; and the notion therefore of the transcendental moralists must be, that this sanction will not exist *in* the mind unless it is believed to have its root out of the mind; and that if a person is able to say to himself, This which is restraining me, and which is called my conscience, is only a feeling in my own mind, he may possibly draw the conclusion that when the feeling ceases the obligation ceases, and that if he find the feeling inconvenient, he may disregard it, and endeavour to get rid of it. But is this danger confined to the utilitarian morality? Does the belief that moral obligation has its seat outside the mind make the feeling of it too strong to be got rid of? The fact is so far otherwise, that all moralists admit and lament the ease with which, in the generality of minds, conscience can be silenced or stifled. The question, Need I obey my conscience? is quite as often put to themselves by persons who never heard of the principle of utility, as by its adherents. Those whose conscientious feelings are so weak as to allow of their asking this question, if they answer it affirmatively, will not do so because they believe in the transcendental theory, but because of the external sanctions.

It is not necessary, for the present purpose, to decide whether the feeling of duty is innate or implanted. Assuming it to be innate, it is an open question to what objects it naturally attaches itself; for the philosophic supporters of that theory are now agreed that the intuitive perception is of principles of morality, and not of the details. If there be anything innate in the matter, I see no reason why the feeling which is innate should not be that of regard to the pleasures and pains of others. If there is any principle of morals which is intuitively obligatory, I should say it must be that. If so, the intuitive ethics would coincide with the utilitarian, and there would be no further quarrel between them. Even as it is, the intuitive moralists, though they believe that there are other intuitive moral obligations, do already believe this to be one; for they unanimously hold that a large *portion* of morality turns upon the consideration due to the interests of our fellow creatures. Therefore, if the belief in the transcendental origin of moral obligation gives any additional efficacy to the internal sanction, it appears to me that the utilitarian principle has already the benefit of it.

On the other hand, if, as is my own belief, the moral feelings are not innate, but acquired, they are not for that reason the less natural. It is natural to man to speak, to reason, to build cities, to cultivate the ground, though these are acquired faculties. The moral feelings are not indeed a part of our nature, in the sense of being in any perceptible degree present in all of us; but this, un-happily, is a fact admitted by those who believe the most strenuously in their transcendental origin. Like the other acquired capacities above referred to, the moral faculty, if not a part of our nature, is a natural outgrowth from it; capable, like them, in a certain small degree, of springing up spontaneously; and susceptible of being brought by cultivation to a high degree of develop-ment. Unhappily it is also susceptible, by a sufficient use of the external sanc-tions and of the force of early impressions, of being cultivated in almost any direction: so that there is hardly anything so absurd or so mischievous that it may not, by means of these influences, be made to act on the human mind with all the authority of conscience. To doubt that the same potency might be given by the same means to the principle of utility, even if it had no foundation in human nature, would be flying in the face of all experience.

But moral associations which are wholly of artificial creation, when intel-lectual culture goes on, yield by degrees to the dissolving force of analysis:

and if the feeling of duty, when associated with utility, would appear equally arbitrary; if there were no leading department of our nature, no powerful class of sentiments, with which that association would harmonize, which would make us feel it congenial, and incline us not only to foster it in others (for which we have abundant interested motives), but also to cherish it in ourselves; if there were not, in short, a natural basis of sentiment for utilitarian morality, it might well happen that this association also, even after it had been implanted by education, might be analysed away.

But there *is* this basis of powerful natural sentiment; and this it is which, when once the general happiness is recognised as the ethical standard, will constitute the strength of the utilitarian morality. This firm foundation is that of the social feelings of mankind; the desire to be in unity with our fellow creatures, which is already a powerful principle in human nature, and happily one of those which tend to become stronger, even without express inculcation, from the influences of advancing civilization. The social state is at once so natural, so necessary, and so habitual to man, that, except in some unusual circumstances or by an effort of voluntary abstraction, he never conceives himself otherwise than as a member of a body; and this association is riveted more and more, as mankind are further removed from the state of savage independence. Any condition, therefore, which is essential to a state of society, becomes more and more an inseparable part of every person's conception of the state of things which he is born into, and which is the destiny of a human being. Now, society between human beings, except in the relation of master and slave, is manifestly impossible on any other footing than that the interests of all are to be consulted. Society between equals can only exist on the understanding that the interests of all are to be regarded equally. And since in all states of civilization, every person, except an absolute monarch, has equals, every one is obliged to live on these terms with somebody; and in every age some advance is made towards a state in which it will be impossible to live permanently on other terms with anybody. In this way people grow up unable to conceive as possible to them a state of total disregard of other people's interests. They are under a necessity of conceiving themselves as at least abstaining from all the grosser injuries, and (if only for their own protection) living in a state of constant protest against them. They are also familiar with the fact of co-operating with others, and proposing to themselves a collective, not an individual, interest, as the aim (at least for the time being) of their actions. So long as they are co-operating, their ends are identified with those of others; there is at least a temporary feeling that the interests of others are their own interests. Not only does all strengthening of social ties, and all healthy growth of society, give to each individual a stronger personal interest in practically consulting the welfare of others; it also leads him to identify his *feelings* more and more with their good, or at least with an ever greater degree of practical consideration for it.

He comes, as though instinctively, to be conscious of himself as a being who *of course* pays regard to others. The good of others becomes to him a thing naturally and necessarily to be attended to, like any of the physical conditions of our existence. Now, whatever amount of this feeling a person has, he is urged by the strongest motives both of interest and of sympathy to demonstrate it, and to the utmost of his power encourage it in others; and even if he has none of it himself, he is as greatly interested as any one else that others should have it. Consequently, the smallest germs of the feeling are laid hold of and nourished by the contagion of sympathy and the influences of education; and a complete web of corroborative association is woven round it, by the powerful agency of the external sanctions. This mode of conceiving ourselves and human life, as civilization goes on, is felt to be more and more natural. Every step in political improvement renders it more so, by removing the sources of opposition of interest, and levelling those inequalities of legal privilege between individuals or classes, owing to which there are large portions of mankind whose happiness it is still practicable to disregard. In an improving state of the human mind, the influences are constantly on the increase, which tend to generate in each individual a feeling of unity with all the rest; which [p]feeling[p], if perfect, would make him never think of, or desire, any beneficial condition for himself, in the benefits of which they are not included. If we now suppose this feeling of unity to be taught as a religion, and the whole force of education, of institutions, and of opinion, directed, as it once was in the case of religion, to make every person grow up from infancy surrounded on all sides both by the profession and [q]by[q] the practice of it, I think that no one, who can realize this conception, will feel any misgiving about the sufficiency of the ultimate sanction for the Happiness morality. To any ethical student who finds the realization difficult, I recommend, as a means of facilitating it, the second of M. Comte's two principal works, the [r]*Système*[r] *de Politique Positive.*[*] I entertain the strongest objections to the system of politics and morals set forth in that treatise; but I think it has superabundantly shown the possibility of giving to the service of humanity, even without the aid of belief in a Providence, both the [s]psychical[s] power and the social efficacy of a religion; making it take hold of human life, and colour all thought, feeling, and action, in a manner of which the greatest ascendancy ever exercised by any religion may be but a type and foretaste; and of which the danger is, not that it should be insufficient, but that it should be so excessive as to interfere unduly with human freedom and individuality.

[***Système de politique positive, ou Traité de sociologie, instituant la Religion de l'humanité*. 4 vols. Paris: Mathias, 1851–54.]

p–p+64,67,71
q–q+64,67,71
*r–r*61,63 *Traité*
*s–s*61,63 psychological

Neither is it necessary to the feeling which constitutes the binding force of the utilitarian morality on those who recognise it, to wait for those social influences which would make its obligation felt by mankind at large. In the comparatively early state of human advancement in which we now live, a person cannot indeed feel that entireness of sympathy with all others, which would make any real discordance in the general direction of their conduct in life impossible; but already a person in whom the social feeling is at all developed, cannot bring himself to think of the rest of his fellow creatures as struggling rivals with him for the means of happiness, whom he must desire to see defeated in their object in order that he may succeed in his. The deeply-rooted conception which every individual even now has of himself as a social being, tends to make him feel it one of his natural wants that there should be harmony between his feelings and aims and those of his fellow creatures. If differences of opinion and of mental culture make it impossible for him to share many of their actual feelings—perhaps make him denounce and defy those feelings—he still needs to be conscious that his real aim and theirs do not conflict; that he is not opposing himself to what they really wish for, namely, their own good, but is, on the contrary, promoting it. This feeling in most individuals is much inferior in strength to their selfish feelings, and is often wanting altogether. But to those who have it, it possesses all the characters of a natural feeling. It does not present itself to their minds as a superstition of education, or a law despotically imposed by the power of society, but as an attribute which it would not be well for them to be without. This conviction is the ultimate sanction of the greatest-happiness morality. This it is which makes any mind, of well-developed feelings, work with, and not against, the outward motives to care for others, afforded by what I have called the external sanctions; and when those sanctions are wanting, or act in an opposite direction, constitutes in itself a powerful internal binding force, in proportion to the sensitiveness and thoughtfulness of the character; since few but those whose mind is a moral blank, could bear to lay out their course of life on the plan of paying no regard to others except so far as their own private interest compels.

CHAPTER IV

Of What Sort of Proof the
Principle of Utility Is Susceptible

IT HAS already been remarked, that questions of ultimate ends do not admit of proof, in the ordinary acceptation of the term. To be incapable of proof by reasoning is common to all first principles; to the first premises of our knowledge, as well as to those of our conduct. But the former, being matters of fact, may be the subject of a direct appeal to the faculties which judge of fact—namely, our senses, and our internal consciousness. Can an appeal be made to the same faculties on questions of practical ends? Or by what other faculty is cognizance taken of them?

Questions about ends are, in other words, questions what things are desirable. The utilitarian doctrine is, that happiness is desirable, and the only thing desirable, as an end; all other things being only desirable as means to that end. What ought to be required of this doctrine—what conditions is it requisite that the doctrine should fulfil—to make good its claim to be believed?

The only proof capable of being given that an object is visible, is that people actually see it. The only proof that a sound is audible, is that people hear it: and so of the other sources of our experience. In like manner, I apprehend, the sole evidence it is possible to produce that anything is desirable, is that people do actually desire it. If the end which the utilitarian doctrine proposes to itself were not, in theory and in practice, acknowledged to be an end, nothing could ever convince any person that it was so. No reason can be given why the general happiness is desirable, except that each person, so far as he believes it to be attainable, desires his own happiness. This, however, being a fact, we have not only all the proof which the case admits of, but all which it is possible to require, that happiness is a good: that each person's happiness is a good to that person, and the general happiness, therefore, a good to the aggregate of all persons. Happiness has made out its title as *one* of the ends of conduct, and consequently one of the criteria of morality.

But it has not, by this alone, proved itself to be the sole criterion. To do that, it would seem, by the same rule, necessary to show, not only that people desire happiness, but that they never desire anything else. Now it is palpable that they do desire things which, in common language, are decidedly distinguished from happiness. They desire, for example, virtue, and the absence of vice, no less really than pleasure and the absence of pain. The desire of virtue is not as universal, but it is as authentic a fact, as the desire of happiness. And hence the opponents of the utilitarian standard deem that they have a right to infer that there are other ends of human action besides happiness, and that happiness is not the standard of approbation and disapprobation.

But does the utilitarian doctrine deny that people desire virtue, or maintain that virtue is not a thing to be desired? The very reverse. It maintains not only that virtue is to be desired, but that it is to be desired disinterestedly, for itself. Whatever may be the opinion of utilitarian moralists as to the original conditions by which virtue is made virtue; however they may believe (as they do) that actions and dispositions are only virtuous because they promote another end than virtue; yet this being granted, and it having been decided, from considerations of this description, what *is* virtuous, they not only place virtue at the very head of the things which are good as means to the ultimate end, but they also recognise as a psychological fact the possibility of its being, to the individual, a good in itself, without looking to any end beyond it; and hold, that the mind is not in a right state, not in a state conformable to Utility, not in the state most conducive to the general happiness, unless it does love virtue in this manner—as a thing desirable in itself, even although, in the individual instance, it should not produce those other desirable consequences which it tends to produce, and on account of which it is held to be virtue. This opinion is not, in the smallest degree, a departure from the Happiness principle. The ingredients of happiness are very various, and each of them is desirable in itself, and not merely when considered as swelling an aggregate. The principle of utility does not mean that any given pleasure, as music, for instance, or any given exemption from pain, as for example health, are to be looked upon as means to a collective something termed happiness, and to be desired on that account. They are desired and desirable in and for themselves; besides being means, they are a part of the end. Virtue, according to the utilitarian doctrine, is not naturally and originally part of the end, but it is capable of becoming so; and in those who love it disinterestedly it has become so, and is desired and cherished, not as a means to happiness, but as a part of their happiness.

To illustrate this farther, we may remember that virtue is not the only thing, originally a means, and which if it were not a means to anything else, would be and remain indifferent, but which by association with what it is a means to, comes to be desired for itself, and that too with the utmost intensity. What, for example, shall we say of the love of money? There is nothing originally more desirable about money than about any heap of glittering pebbles. Its worth is solely that of the things which it will buy; the desires for other things than itself, which it is a means of gratifying. Yet the love of money is not only one of the strongest moving forces of human life, but money is, in many cases, desired in and for itself; the desire to possess it is often stronger than the desire to use it, and goes on increasing when all the desires which point to ends beyond it, *t* to be compassed by it, are falling off. It *u*may be then*u* said truly, that money is desired not for the sake of an end, but as part of the end. From being a means to happiness, it has come to be itself a principal ingredient of the individual's conception of happiness. The same may be said of the majority of the great objects of human life—power, for example, or *v*fame*v*; except that to each of these there is a certain amount of immediate pleasure annexed, which has at least the semblance of being naturally inherent in them; a thing which cannot be said of money. Still, however, the strongest natural attraction, both of power and of *w*fame*w*, is the immense aid they give to the attainment of our other wishes; and it is the strong association thus generated between them and all our objects of desire, which gives to the direct desire of them the intensity it often assumes, so as in some characters to surpass in strength all other desires. In these cases the means have become a part of the end, and a more important part of it than any of the things which they are means to. What was once desired as an instrument for the attainment of happiness, has come to be desired for its own sake. In being desired for its own sake it is, however, desired as *part* of happiness. The person is made, or thinks he would be made, happy by its mere possession; and is made unhappy by failure to obtain it. The desire of it is not a different thing from the desire of happiness, any more than the love of music, or the desire of health. They are included in happiness. They are some of the elements of which the desire of happiness is made up. Happiness is not an abstract idea, but a concrete whole; and these are some of its parts. And the utilitarian standard sanctions and approves their being so. Life would be a poor thing, very ill provided with sources of happiness, if there were not this provision of nature, by which things originally indifferent, but conducive to, or otherwise associated with, the satisfaction of our primitive desires, become in themselves sources of pleasure more valuable than the primitive pleasures, both in permanency, in the space of human existence that they are capable of covering, and even in intensity.

Virtue, according to the utilitarian conception, is a good of this description. There was no original desire of it, or motive to it, save its conduciveness to pleasure, and especially to protection from pain. But through the association thus formed, it may be felt a good in itself, and desired as such with as great intensity as any other good; and with this difference between it and the

*t*61   and
*v–v*61   glory

*u–u*61   may then be] 63   may, then, be
*w–w*61   glory

love of money, of power, or of ˣfameˣ, that all of these may, and often do, render the individual noxious to the other members of the society to which he belongs, whereas there is nothing which makes him so much a blessing to them as the cultivation of the disinterested love of virtue. And consequently, the utilitarian standard, while it tolerates and approves those other acquired desires, up to the point beyond which they would be more injurious to the general happiness than promotive of it, enjoins and requires the cultivation of the love of virtue up to the greatest strength possible, as being above all things important to the general happiness.

It results from the preceding considerations, that there is in reality nothing desired except happiness. Whatever is desired otherwise than as a means to some end beyond itself, and ultimately to happiness, is desired as itself a part of happiness, and is not desired for itself until it has become so. Those who desire virtue for its own sake, desire it either because the consciousness of it is a pleasure, or because the consciousness of being without it is a pain, or for both reasons united; as in truth the pleasure and pain seldom exist separately, but almost always together, the same person feeling pleasure in the degree of virtue attained, and pain in not having attained more. If one of these ʸgaveʸ him no pleasure, and the other no pain, he would not love or desire virtue, or would desire it only for the other benefits which it might produce to himself or to persons whom he cared for.

We have now, then, an answer to the question, of what sort of proof the principle of utility is susceptible. If the opinion which I have now stated is psychologically true—if human nature is so constituted as to desire nothing which is not either a part of happiness or a means of happiness, we can have no other proof, and we require no other, that these are the only things desirable. If so, happiness is the sole end of human action, and the promotion of it the test by which to judge of all human conduct; from whence it necessarily follows that it must be the criterion of morality, since a part is included in the whole.

And now to decide whether this is really so; whether mankind do desire nothing for itself but that which is a pleasure to them, or of which the absence is a pain; we have evidently arrived at a question of fact and experience, dependent, like all similar questions, upon evidence. It can only be determined by practised self-consciousness and self-observation, assisted by observation of others. I believe that these sources of evidence, impartially consulted, will declare that desiring a thing and finding it pleasant, aversion to it and thinking of it as painful, are phenomena entirely inseparable, or rather two parts of the same phenomenon; in strictness of language, two different modes of naming the same psychological fact: that to think of an object as desirable (unless for the sake of its consequences), and to think of it as

ˣ–ˣ61   glory   ʸ–ʸ61   give [printer's error?]

pleasant, are one and the same thing; and that to desire anything, except in proportion as the idea of it is pleasant, is a physical and metaphysical impossibility.

So obvious does this appear to me, that I expect it will hardly be disputed: and the objection made will be, not that desire can possibly be directed to anything ultimately except pleasure and exemption from pain, but that the will is a different thing from desire; that a person of confirmed virtue, or any other person whose purposes are fixed, carries out his purposes without any thought of the pleasure he has in contemplating them, or expects to derive from their fulfilment; and persists in acting on them, even though these pleasures are much diminished, by changes in his character or decay of his passive sensibilities, or are outweighed by the pains which the pursuit of the purposes may bring upon him. All this I fully admit, and have stated it elsewhere,[*] as positively and emphatically as any one. Will, the active phenomenon, is a different thing from desire, the state of passive sensibility, and though originally an offshoot from it, may in time take root and detach itself from the parent stock; so much so, that in the case of an habitual purpose, instead of willing the thing because we desire it, we often desire it only because we will it. This, however, is but an instance of that familiar fact, the power of habit, and is nowise confined to the case of virtuous actions. Many indifferent things, which men originally did from a motive of some sort, they continue to do from habit. Sometimes this is done unconsciously, the consciousness coming only after the action: at other times with conscious volition, but volition which has became habitual, and is put ᶻintoᶻ operation by the force of habit, in opposition perhaps to the deliberate preference, as often happens with those who have contracted habits of vicious or hurtful indulgence. Third and last comes the case in which the habitual act of will in the individual instance is not in contradiction to the general intention prevailing at other times, but in fulfilment of it; as in the case of the person of confirmed virtue, and of all who pursue deliberately and consistently any determinate end. The distinction between will and desire thus understood, is an authentic and highly important psychological fact; but the fact consists solely in this— that will, like all other parts of our constitution, is amenable to habit, and that we may will from habit what we no longer desire for itself, or desire only because we will it. It is not the less true that will, in the beginning, is entirely produced by desire; including in that term the repelling influence of pain as well as the attractive one of pleasure. Let us take into consideration, no longer the person who has a confirmed will to do right, but him in whom that virtuous will is still feeble, conquerable by temptation, and not to be

[*See *A System of Logic*. 8th ed. 2 vols. London: Longmans, Green, Reader, and Dyer, 1872, Vol. II, pp. 428–9 (Book VI, Chap. ii, § 4).]

ᶻ–ᶻ61,63,64,67   in

fully relied on; by what means can it be strengthened? How can the will to be virtuous, where it does not exist in sufficient force, be implanted or awakened? Only by making the person *desire* virtue—by making him think of it in a pleasurable light, or of its absence in a painful one. It is by associating the doing right with pleasure, or the doing wrong with pain, or by eliciting and impressing and bringing home to the person's experience the pleasure naturally involved in the one or the pain in the other, that it is possible to call forth that will to be virtuous, which, when confirmed, acts without any thought of either pleasure or pain. Will is the child of desire, and passes out of the dominion of its parent only to come under that of habit. That which is the result of habit affords no presumption of being intrinsically good; and there would be no reason for wishing that the purpose of virtue should become independent of pleasure and pain, were it not that the influence of the pleasurable and painful associations which prompt to virtue is not sufficiently to be depended on for unerring constancy of action until it has acquired the support of habit. Both in feeling and in conduct, habit is the only thing which imparts certainty; and it is because of the importance to others of being able to rely absolutely on one's feelings and conduct, and to oneself of being able to rely on one's own, that the will to do right ought to be cultivated into this habitual independence. In other words, this state of the will is a means to good, not intrinsically a good; and does not contradict the doctrine that nothing is a good to human beings but in so far as it is either itself pleasurable, or a means of attaining pleasure or averting pain.

But if this doctrine be true, the principle of utility is proved. Whether it is so or not, must now be left to the consideration of the thoughtful reader.

CHAPTER V

On the Connexion between
Justice and Utility

IN ALL AGES of speculation, one of the strongest obstacles to the reception of the doctrine that Utility or Happiness is the criterion of right and wrong, has been drawn from the idea of Justice. The powerful sentiment, and apparently clear perception, which that word recals with a rapidity and certainty resembling an instinct, have seemed to the majority of thinkers to point to an inherent quality in things; to show that the Just must have an existence in Nature as something absolute—generically distinct from every variety of the Expedient, and, in idea, opposed to it, though (as is commonly acknowledged) never, in the long run, disjoined from it in fact.

In the case of this, as of our other moral sentiments, there is no necessary connexion between the question of its origin, and that of its binding force. That a feeling is bestowed on us by Nature, does not necessarily legitimate all its promptings. The feeling of justice might be a peculiar instinct, and might yet require, like our other instincts, to be controlled and enlightened by a higher reason. If we have intellectual instincts, leading us to judge in a particular way, as well as animal instincts that prompt us to act in a particular way, there is no necessity that the former should be more infallible in their sphere than the latter in theirs: it may as well happen that wrong judgments are occasionally suggested by those, as wrong actions by these. But though it is one thing to believe that we have natural feelings of justice, and another to acknowledge them as an ultimate criterion of conduct, these two opinions are very closely connected in point of fact. Mankind are always predisposed to believe that any subjective feeling, not otherwise accounted for, is a revelation of some objective reality. Our present object is to determine whether the reality, to which the feeling of justice corresponds, is one which needs any such special revelation; whether the justice or injustice of an action is a thing intrinsically peculiar, and distinct from all its other qualities, or only a combination of certain of those qualities, presented under a peculiar aspect. For the purpose of this inquiry, it is practically important to consider whether the feeling itself, of justice and injustice, is *sui generis* like our sensations of colour and taste, or a derivative feeling, formed by a combination of others. And this it is the more essential to examine, as people are in general willing enough to allow, that objectively the dictates of justice coincide with a part of the field of General Expediency; but inasmuch as the subjective mental feeling of Justice is different from that which commonly attaches to simple expediency, and, except in *a* extreme cases of the latter, is far more imperative in its demands, people find it difficult to see, in Justice, only a particular kind or branch of general utility, and think that its superior binding force requires a totally different origin.

To throw light upon this question, it is necessary to attempt to ascertain what is the distinguishing character of justice, or of injustice: what is the quality, or whether there is any quality, attributed in common to all modes of conduct designated as unjust (for justice, like many other moral attributes, is best defined by its opposite), and distinguishing them from such modes of conduct as are disapproved, but without having that particular epithet of disapprobation applied to them. If, in everything which men are accustomed to characterize as just or unjust, some one common attribute or collection of attributes is always present, we may judge whether this particular attribute or combination of attributes would be capable of gathering round it a sentiment of that peculiar character and intensity by virtue of the general laws of our emotional constitution, or whether the sentiment is inexplicable, and requires to be regarded as a special provision of Nature. If we find the former to be the case, we shall, in resolving this question, have resolved also the main problem: if the latter, we shall have to seek for some other mode of investigating it.

To find the common attributes of a variety of objects, it is necessary to begin by surveying the objects themselves in the concrete. Let us therefore advert successively to the various modes of action, and arrangements of human affairs, which are classed, by universal or widely spread opinion, as Just or as Unjust. The things well known to excite the sentiments associated with those names, are of a very multifarious character. I shall pass them rapidly in review, without studying any particular arrangement.

In the first place, it is mostly considered unjust to deprive any one of his personal liberty, his property, or any other thing which belongs to him by law. Here, therefore, is one instance of the application of the terms just and unjust in a perfectly definite sense, namely, that it is just to respect, unjust to violate, the *legal rights* of any one. But this judgment admits of several exceptions, arising from the other forms in which the notions of justice and injustice present themselves. For example, the person who suffers the deprivation may (as the phrase is) have *forfeited* the rights which he is so deprived of:

*a*61,63   the

a case to which we shall return presently. But also,

Secondly; the legal rights of which he is deprived, may be rights which *ought* not to have belonged to him; in other words, the law which confers on him these rights, may be a bad law. When it is so, or when (which is the same thing for our purpose) it is supposed to be so, opinions will differ as to the justice or injustice of infringing it. Some maintain that no law, however bad, ought to be disobeyed by an individual citizen; that his opposition to it, if shown at all, should only be shown in endeavouring to get it altered by competent authority. This opinion (which condemns many of the most illustrious benefactors of mankind, and would often protect pernicious institutions against the only weapons which, in the state of things existing at the time, have any chance of succeeding against them) is defended, by those who hold it, on grounds of expediency; principally on that of the importance, to the common interest of mankind, of maintaining inviolate the sentiment of submission to law. Other persons, again, hold the directly contrary opinion, that any law, judged to be bad, may blamelessly be disobeyed, even though it be not judged to be unjust, but only inexpedient; while others would confine the licence of disobedience to the case of unjust laws: but again, some say, that all laws which are inexpedient are unjust; since every law imposes some restriction on the natural liberty of mankind, which restriction is an injustice, unless legitimated by tending to their good. Among these diversities of opinion, it seems to be universally admitted that there may be unjust laws, and that law, consequently, is not the ultimate criterion of justice, but may give to one person a benefit, or impose on another an evil, which justice condemns. When, however, a law is thought to be unjust, it seems always to be regarded as being so in the same way in which a breach of law is unjust, namely, by infringing somebody's right; which, as it cannot in this case be a legal right, receives a different appellation, and is called a moral right. We may say, therefore, that a second case of injustice consists in taking or withholding from any person that to which he has a *moral right*.

Thirdly, it is universally considered just that each person should obtain that (whether good or evil) which he *deserves*; and unjust that he should obtain a good, or be made to undergo an evil, which he does not deserve. This is, perhaps, the clearest and most emphatic form in which the idea of justice is conceived by the general mind. As it involves the notion of desert, the question arises, what constitutes desert? Speaking in a general way, a person is understood to deserve good if he does right, evil if he does wrong; and in a more particular sense, to deserve good from those to whom he does or has done good, and evil from those to whom he does or has done evil. The precept of returning good for evil has never been regarded as a case of the fulfilment of justice, but as one in which the claims of justice are waved, in obedience to other considerations.

Fourthly, it is confessedly unjust to *break faith* with any one: to violate an engagement, either express or implied, or disappoint expectations raised by our own conduct, at least if we have raised those expectations knowingly and voluntarily. Like the other obligations of justice already spoken of, this one is not regarded as absolute, but as capable of being overruled by a stronger obligation of justice on the other side; or by such conduct on the part of the person concerned as is deemed to absolve us from our obligation to him, and to constitute a *forfeiture* of the benefit which he has been led to expect.

Fifthly, it is, by universal admission, inconsistent with justice to be *partial*; to show favour or preference to one person over another, in matters to which favour and preference do not properly apply. Impartiality, however, does not seem to be regarded as a duty in itself, but rather as instrumental to some other duty; for it is admitted that favour and preference are not always censurable, and indeed the cases in which they are condemned are rather the exception than the rule. A person would be more likely to be blamed than applauded for giving his family or friends no superiority in good offices over strangers, when he could do so without violating any other duty; and no one thinks it unjust to seek one person in preference to another as a friend, connexion, or companion. Impartiality where rights are concerned is of course obligatory, but this is involved in the more general obligation of giving to every one his right. A tribunal, for example, must be impartial, because it is bound to award, without regard to any other consideration, a disputed object to the one of two parties who has the right to it. There are other cases in which impartiality means, being solely influenced by desert; as with those who, in the capacity of judges, preceptors, or parents, administer reward and punishment as such. There are cases, again, in which it means, being solely influenced by consideration for the public interest; as in making a selection among candidates for a government employment. Impartiality, in short, as an obligation of justice, may be said to mean, being exclusively influenced by the considerations which it is supposed ought to influence the particular case in hand; and resisting the solicitation of any motives which prompt to conduct different from what those considerations would dictate.

Nearly allied to the idea of impartiality, is that of *equality*; which often enters as a component part both into the conception of justice and into the practice of it, and, in the eyes of many persons, constitutes its essence. But in this, still more than in any other case, the notion of justice varies in different persons, and always conforms in its variations to their notion of utility. Each person maintains that equality is the dictate of justice, except where he thinks that expediency requires inequality. The justice of giving equal protection to the rights of all, is maintained by those who support the most outrageous inequality in the rights themselves. Even in slave countries it is theoretically admitted that the rights of the slave, such as they are, ought to be as sacred as those of the master; and that a tribunal which fails to enforce them with equal strictness is wanting in justice; while, at the same time, institutions which leave to the slave scarcely any rights to enforce, are not deemed unjust, because they are not deemed inexpedient. Those who think that utility requires distinctions of rank, do not consider it unjust that riches and social privileges should be unequally dispensed; but those who think this inequality inexpedient, think it unjust also. Whoever thinks that government is necessary, sees no injustice in as much inequality as is constituted by giving to the magistrate powers not granted to other people. Even among those who hold levelling doctrines, there are as many questions of justice as there are differences of opinion about expediency. Some Communists consider it unjust that the produce of the labour of the community should be shared on any other principle than that of exact equality; others think it just that those should receive most whose [b]needs[b] are greatest; while others hold that those who work harder, or who produce more, or whose services are more valuable to the community, may justly claim a larger quota in the division of the produce. And the sense of natural justice may be plausibly appealed to in behalf of every one of these opinions.

Among so many diverse applications of the term Justice, which yet is not regarded as ambiguous, it is a matter of some difficulty to seize the mental link which holds them together, and on which the moral sentiment adhering to the term essentially depends. Perhaps, in this embarrassment, some help may be derived from the history of the word, as indicated by its etymology.

In most, if not in all, languages, the etymology of the word which corresponds to Just, points [c] to an origin connected [d]either with positive law, or with that which was in most cases the primitive form of law—authoritative custom[d]. *Justum* is a form of *jussum*, that which has been ordered. [e]*Jus* is of the same origin.[e] Δίκαιον comes [f] from δίκη, [g]of which the principal meaning, at least in the historical ages of Greece, was[g] a suit at law. [h]Originally, indeed, it meant only the mode or *manner* of doing things, but it early came to mean the *prescribed* manner; that which the recognised authorities, patriarchal, judicial, or political, would enforce.[h] *Recht*, from which came *right* and *righteous*, is synonymous with law. [i]The original meaning indeed of *recht* did not point to law, but to physical straightness; as *wrong* and its Latin equivalents meant twisted or *tortuous*; and from this it is argued that right did not originally mean law, but on the contrary law meant right. But however this may be, the fact that *recht* and *droit* became restricted in their meaning to positive law, although much which is not [i]required[i] by law is

[b-b]61,63   wants
[c]61,63   distinctly
[e-e]+64,67,71
[g-g]+64,67,71
[i-i]+64,67,71

[d-d]61,63   with the ordinances of law
[f]61,63   directly
[h-h]+64,67,71
[i-i]+67,71   [*printer's error?*]

equally necessary to moral straightness or rectitude, is as significant of the original character of moral ideas as if the derivation had been the reverse way.[i] The courts of justice, the administration of justice, are the courts and the administration of law. *La justice*, in French, is the established term for judicature. [k] There can, I think, be no doubt that the *idée mère*, the primitive element, in the formation of the notion of justice, was conformity to law. It constituted the entire idea among the Hebrews, up to the birth of Christianity; as might be expected in the case of a people whose laws attempted to embrace all subjects on which precepts were required, and who believed those laws to be a direct emanation from the Supreme Being. But other nations, and in particular the Greeks and Romans, who knew that their laws had been made originally, and still continued to be made, by men, were not afraid to admit that those men might make bad laws; might do, by law, the same things, and from the same motives, which, if done by individuals without the sanction of law, would be called unjust. And hence the sentiment of injustice came to be attached, not to all violations of law, but only to violations of such laws as *ought* to exist, including such as ought to exist but do not; and to laws themselves, if supposed to be contrary to what ought to be law. In this manner the idea of law and of its injunctions was still predominant in the notion of justice, even when the laws actually in force ceased to be accepted as the standard of it.

It is true that mankind consider the idea of justice and its obligations as applicable to many things which neither are, nor is it desired that they should be, regulated by law. Nobody desires that laws should interfere with the whole [l]detail[l] of private life; yet every one allows that in all daily conduct a person may and does show himself to be either just or unjust. But even here, the idea of the breach of what ought to be law, still lingers in a modified shape. It would always give us pleasure, and chime in with our feelings of fitness, that acts which we deem unjust should be punished, though we do not always think it expedient that this should be done by the tribunals. We forego that gratification on account of incidental inconveniences. We should be glad to see just conduct enforced and injustice repressed, even in the minutest details, if we were not, with reason, afraid of trusting the magistrate with so unlimited an amount of power over individuals. When we think that a person is bound in justice to do a thing, it is an ordinary form of language to say, that he ought to be compelled to do it. We should be gratified to see the obligation enforced by anybody who had the power. If we see that its enforcement by law would be inexpedient, we lament the

[k]61,63 I am not committing the fallacy imputed with some show of truth to Horne Tooke, of assuming that a word must still continue to mean what it originally meant. Etymology is slight evidence of what the idea now signified is, but the very best evidence of how it sprang up.

[l]–[l]61 details [*printer's error?*]

impossibility, we consider the impunity given to injustice as an evil, and strive to make amends for it by bringing a strong expression of our own and the public disapprobation to bear upon the offender. Thus the idea of legal constraint is still the generating idea of the notion of justice, though under-going several transformations before that notion, as it exists in an advanced state of society, becomes complete.

The above is, I think, a true account, as far as it goes, of the origin and progressive growth of the idea of justice. But we must observe, that it con-tains, as yet, nothing to distinguish that obligation from moral obligation in general. For the truth is, that the idea of penal sanction, which is the essence of law, enters not only into the conception of injustice, but into that of any kind of wrong. We do not call anything wrong, unless we mean to imply that a person ought to be punished in some way or other for doing it; if not by law, by the opinion of his fellow creatures; if not by opinion, by the re-proaches of his own conscience. This seems the real turning point of the distinction between morality and simple expediency. It is a part of the notion of Duty in every one of its forms, that a person may rightfully be compelled to fulfil it. Duty is a thing which may be *exacted* from a person, as one exacts a debt. Unless we think that it *might* be exacted from him, we do not call it his duty. Reasons of prudence, or the interest of other people, may militate against actually exacting it; but the person himself, it is clearly understood, would not be entitled to complain. There are other things, on the contrary, which we wish that people should do, which we like or admire them for doing, perhaps dislike or despise them for not doing, but yet admit that they are not bound to do; it is not a case of moral obligation; we do not blame them, that is, we do not think that they are proper objects of punishment. How we come by these ideas of deserving and not deserving punishment, will appear, perhaps, in the sequel; but I think there is no doubt that this dis-tinction lies at the bottom of the notions of right and wrong; that we call any conduct wrong, or employ, instead, some other term of dislike or disparage-ment, according as we think that the person ought, or ought not, to be punished for it; and we *say that* it would be right to do so and so, or merely that it would be desirable or laudable, according as we would wish to see the person whom it concerns, compelled, or only persuaded and exhorted, to act in that manner.*

This, therefore, being the characteristic difference which marks off, not

*See this point enforced and illustrated by Professor [61   Mr.] Bain, in an admirable chapter (entitled "The Ethical Emotions, or the Moral Sense"), of the second of the two treatises composing his elaborate and profound work on the Mind. [Alexander Bain. *The Emotions and the Will*. London: Parker, 1859.]

m–m61,63   may   n–n61,63   say,

justice, but morality in general, from the remaining provinces of Expediency and Worthiness; the character is still to be sought which distinguishes justice from other branches of morality. Now it is known that ethical writers divide moral duties into two classes, denoted by the ill-chosen expressions, duties of perfect and of imperfect obligation; the latter being those in which, though the act is obligatory, the particular occasions of performing it are left to our choice; as in the case of charity or beneficence, which we are indeed bound to practise, but not towards any definite person, nor at any prescribed time. In the more precise language of philosophic jurists, duties of perfect obligation are those duties in virtue of which a correlative *right* resides in some person or persons; duties of imperfect obligation are those moral obligations which do not give birth to any right. I think it will be found that this distinction exactly coincides with that which exists between justice and the other obligations of morality. In our survey of the various popular acceptations of justice, the term appeared generally to involve the idea of a personal right— a claim on the part of one or more individuals, like that which the law gives when it confers a proprietary or other legal right. Whether the injustice consists in depriving a person of a possession, or in breaking faith with him, or in treating him worse than he deserves, or worse than other people who have no greater claims, in each case the supposition implies two things—a wrong done, and some assignable person who is wronged. Injustice may also be done by treating a person better than others; but the wrong in this case is to his competitors, who are also assignable persons. It seems to me that this feature in the case—a right in some person, correlative to the moral obligation—constitutes the specific difference between justice, and generosity or beneficence. Justice implies something which it is not only right to do, and wrong not to do, but which some individual person can claim from us as his moral right. No one has a moral right to our generosity or beneficence, because we are not morally bound to practise those virtues towards any given individual. And it will be found with respect to this as °with respect° to every correct definition, that the instances which seem to conflict with it are those which most confirm it. For if a moralist attempts, as some have done, to make out that mankind generally, though not any given individual, have a right to all the good we can do them, he at once, by that thesis, includes generosity and beneficence within the category of justice. He is obliged to say, that our utmost exertions are *due* to our fellow creatures, thus assimilating them to a debt; or that nothing less can be a sufficient *return* for what society does for us, thus classing the case as one of gratitude; both of which are acknowledged cases of justice. Wherever there is a right, the case is one of justice, and not of the virtue of beneficence: and whoever does not place the distinction between justice and morality in general where we have now

o–o+64,67,71

placed it, will be found to make no distinction between them at all, but to merge all morality in justice.

Having thus endeavoured to determine the distinctive elements which enter into the composition of the idea of justice, we are ready to enter on the inquiry, whether the feeling, which accompanies the idea, is attached to it by a special dispensation of nature, or whether it could have grown up, by any known laws, out of the idea itself; and in particular, whether it can have originated in considerations of general expediency.

I conceive that the sentiment itself does not arise from anything which would commonly, or correctly, be termed an idea of expediency; but that though the sentiment does not, whatever is moral in it does.

We have seen that the two essential ingredients in the sentiment of justice are, the desire to punish a person who has done harm, and the knowledge or belief that there is some definite individual or individuals to whom harm has been done.

Now it appears to me, that the desire to punish a person who has done harm to some individual, is a spontaneous outgrowth from two sentiments, both in the highest degree natural, and which either are or resemble instincts; the impulse of self-defence, and the feeling of sympathy.

It is natural to resent, and to repel or retaliate, any harm done or attempted against ourselves, or against those with whom we sympathize. The origin of this sentiment it is not necessary here to discuss. Whether it be an instinct or a result of intelligence, it is, we know, common to all animal nature; for every animal tries to hurt those who have hurt, or who it thinks are about to hurt, itself or its young. Human beings, on this point, only differ from other animals in two particulars. First, in being capable of sympathizing, not solely with their offspring, or, like some of the more noble animals, with some superior animal who is kind to them, but with all human, and even with all sentient, beings. Secondly, in having a more developed intelligence, which gives a wider range to the whole of their sentiments, whether self-regarding or sympathetic. By virtue of his superior intelligence, even apart from his superior range of sympathy, a human being is capable of apprehending a community of interest between himself and the human society of which he forms a part, such that any conduct which threatens the security of the society generally, is threatening to his own, and calls forth his instinct (if instinct it be) of self-defence. The same superiority of intelligence, joined to the power of sympathizing with human beings generally, enables him to attach himself to the collective idea of his tribe, his country, or mankind, in such a manner that any act hurtful to them ᵖrousesᵖ his instinct of sympathy, and urges him to resistance.

The sentiment of justice, in that one of its elements which consists of the

ᵖ⁻ᵖ61,63   , raises [*printer's error?*]

desire to punish, is thus, I conceive, the natural feeling of retaliation or vengeance, rendered by intellect and sympathy applicable to those injuries, that is, to those hurts, which wound us through, or in common with, society at large. This sentiment, in itself, has nothing moral in it; what is moral is, the exclusive subordination of it to the social sympathies, so as to wait on and obey their call. For the natural feeling *q*tends to*q* make us resent indiscriminately whatever any one does that is disagreeable to us; but when moralized by the social feeling, it only acts in the directions conformable to the general good: just persons resenting a hurt to society, though not otherwise a hurt to themselves, and not resenting a hurt to themselves, however painful, unless it be of *r*the*r* kind which society has a common interest with them in the repression of.

It is no objection against this doctrine to say, that when we feel our sentiment of justice outraged, we are not thinking of society at large, or of any collective interest, but only of the individual case. It is common enough certainly, though the reverse of commendable, to feel resentment merely because we have suffered pain; but a person whose resentment is really a moral feeling, that is, who considers whether an act is blameable before he allows himself to resent it—such a person, though he may not say expressly to himself that he is standing up for the interest of society, certainly does feel that he is asserting a rule which is for the benefit of others as well as for his own. If he is not feeling this—if he is regarding the act solely as it affects him individually—he is not consciously just; he is not concerning himself about the justice of his actions. This is admitted even by anti-utilitarian moralists. When Kant (as before remarked)[*] propounds as the fundamental principle of morals, "So act, that thy rule of conduct might be adopted as a law by all rational beings," he virtually acknowledges that the interest of mankind collectively, or at least of mankind indiscriminately, must be in the mind of the agent when conscientiously deciding on the morality of the act. Otherwise he uses words without a meaning: for, that a rule even of utter selfishness could not *possibly* be adopted by all rational beings —that there is any insuperable obstacle in the nature of things to its adoption—cannot be even plausibly maintained. To give any meaning to Kant's principle, the sense put upon it must be, that we ought to shape our conduct by a rule which all rational beings might adopt *with benefit to their *s*collective interest*s*.

To recapitulate: the idea of justice supposes two things; a rule of conduct, and a sentiment which sanctions the rule. The first must be supposed common to all mankind, and intended for their good. The other (the sentiment)

[*P. 207 *above*.]

*q–q*61,63   would   *r–r*61   a   *s–s*61   *interests* is a desire that punishment may be suffered by those who infringe the rule. There is involved, in addition, the conception of some definite person who suffers by the infringement; whose rights (to use the expression appropriated to the case) are violated by it. And the sentiment of justice appears to me to be, the animal desire to repel or retaliate a hurt or damage to oneself, or to those with whom one sympathizes, widened so as to include all persons, by the human capacity of enlarged sympathy, and the human conception of intelligent self-interest. *From the latter elements, the feeling derives its morality; from the former, its peculiar impressiveness, and energy of self-assertion.*

I have, throughout, treated the idea of a *right* residing in the injured person, and violated by the injury, not as a separate element in the composition of the idea and sentiment, but as one of the forms in which the other two elements clothe themselves. These elements are, a hurt to some assignable person or persons on the one hand, and a demand for punishment on the other. An examination of our own minds, I think, will show, that these two things include all that we mean when we speak of violation of a right. When we call anything a person's right, we mean that he has a valid claim on society to protect him in the possession of it, either by the force of law, or by that of education and opinion. If he has what we consider a sufficient claim, on whatever account, to have something guaranteed to him by society, we say that he has a right to it. If we desire to prove that anything does not belong to him by right, we think this done as soon as it is admitted that society ought not to take measures for securing it to him, but should leave *it* to chance, or to his own exertions. Thus, a person is said to have a right to what he can earn in fair professional competition; because society ought not to allow any other person to hinder him from endeavouring to earn in that manner as much as he can. But he has not a right to three hundred a-year, though he may happen to be earning it; because society is not called on to provide that he shall earn that sum. On the contrary, if he owns ten thousand pounds three per cent stock, he *has* a right to three hundred a-year; because society has come under an obligation to provide him with an income of that amount.

To have a right, then, is, I conceive, to have something which society ought to defend me in the possession of. If the objector goes on to *ask why it ought,* I can give him no other reason than general utility. If that expression does not seem to convey a sufficient feeling of the strength of the obligation, nor to account for the peculiar energy of the *feeling*, it is because *there goes to the composition of the sentiment, not a rational only but also an animal element, the thirst for retaliation; and this thirst derives its intensity, as well as its moral justification, from* the extraordinarily important and impressive kind of utility which is concerned. The interest involved is that of security, to every one's feelings the most vital of all interests. *Nearly all* other earthly benefits are needed by one person, not needed by another; and many of them can, if necessary, be cheerfully foregone, or replaced by something else; but security no human being can possibly do without; on it we depend for all our immunity from evil, and for the whole value of all and every good, beyond the passing moment; since nothing but the gratification of the instant could be of any worth to us, if we could be deprived of everything the next instant by whoever was momentarily stronger than ourselves. Now this most indispensable of all necessaries, after physical nutriment, cannot be had, unless the machinery for providing it is kept unintermittedly in active play. Our notion, therefore, of the claim we have on our fellow-creatures to join in making safe for us the very groundwork of our existence, gathers feelings round it so much more intense than those concerned in any of the more common cases of utility, that the difference in degree (as is often the case in psychology) becomes a real difference in kind. The claim assumes that character of absoluteness, that apparent infinity, and incommensurability with all other considerations, which constitute the distinction between the feeling of right and wrong and that of ordinary expediency and inexpediency. The feelings concerned are so powerful, and we count so positively on finding a responsive feeling in others (all being alike interested), that *ought* and *should* grow into *must*, and recognised indispensability becomes a moral necessity, analogous to physical, and often not inferior to it in binding force.

If the preceding analysis, or something resembling it, be not the correct account of the notion of justice; if justice be totally independent of utility, and be a standard *per se*, which the mind can recognise by simple introspection of itself; it is hard to understand why that internal oracle is so ambiguous, and why so many things appear either just or unjust, according to the light in which they are regarded.

We are continually informed that Utility is an uncertain standard, which every different person interprets differently, and that there is no safety but in the immutable, ineffaceable, and unmistakeable dictates of Justice, which carry their evidence in themselves, and are independent of the fluctuations of opinion. One would suppose from this that on questions of justice there could be no controversy; that if we take that for our rule, its application to any given case could leave us in as little doubt as a mathematical demonstration. So far is this from being the fact, that there is as much difference of opinion, and as *fierce* discussion, about what is just, as about what is useful to society. Not only have different nations and individuals different notions

*v–v*61,63   All   *z–z*61,63   much of justice, but, in the mind of one and the same individual, justice is not some one rule, principle, or maxim, but many, which do not always coincide in their dictates, and in choosing between which, he is guided either by some extraneous standard, or by his own personal predilections.

For instance, there are some who say, that it is unjust to punish any one for the sake of example to others; that punishment is just, only when intended for the good of the sufferer himself. Others maintain the extreme reverse, contending that to punish persons who have attained years of discretion, for their own benefit, is despotism and injustice, since if the matter at issue is solely their own good, no one has a right to control their own judgment of it; but that they may justly be punished to prevent evil to others, this being *an* exercise of the legitimate right of self-defence. Mr. Owen, again, affirms that it is unjust to punish at all; for the criminal did not make his own character; his education, and the circumstances which *surround* him, have made him a criminal, and for these he is not responsible. All these opinions are extremely plausible; and so long as the question is argued as one of justice simply, without going down to the principles which lie under justice and are the source of its authority, I am unable to see how any of these reasoners can be refuted. For, in truth, every one of the three builds upon rules of justice confessedly true. The first appeals to the acknowledged injustice of singling out an individual, and making him a sacrifice, without his consent, for other people's benefit. The second relies on the acknowledged justice of self-defence, and the admitted injustice of forcing one person to conform to another's notions of what constitutes his good. The Owenite invokes the admitted principle, that it is unjust to punish any one for what he cannot help. Eact is triumphant so long as he is not compelled to take into consideration any other maxims of justice than the one he has selected; but as soon as their several maxims are brought face to face, each disputant seems to have exactly as much to say for himself as the others. No one of them can carry out his own notion of justice without trampling upon another equally binding. These are difficulties; they have always been felt to be such; and many devices have been invented to turn rather than to overcome them. As a refuge from the last of the three, men imagined what they called the freedom of the will; fancying that they could not justify punishing a man whose will is in a thoroughly hateful state, unless it be supposed to have come into that state through no influence of anterior circumstances. To escape from the other difficulties, a favourite contrivance has been the fiction of a contract, whereby at some unknown period all the members of society engaged to obey the laws, and consented to be punished for any disobedience to them; thereby giving to their legislators the right, which it is assumed they would not otherwise have had, of punishing them, either for their own good or for

*a–a*61,63,64   the   *b–b*61,63,64,67   surrounded

that of society. This happy thought was considered to get rid of the whole difficulty, and to legitimate the infliction of punishment, in virtue of another received maxim of justice, *volenti non fit injuria*;[*] that is not unjust which is done with the consent of the person who is supposed to be hurt by it. I need hardly remark, that even if the consent were not a mere fiction, this maxim is not superior in authority to the others which it is brought in to supersede. It is, on the contrary, an instructive specimen of the loose and irregular manner in which supposed principles of justice grow up. This particular one evidently came into use as a help to the coarse exigencies of courts of law, which are sometimes obliged to be content with very uncertain presumptions, on account of the greater evils which would often arise from any attempt on their part to cut finer. But even courts of law are not able to adhere consistently to the maxim, for they allow voluntary engagements to be set aside on the ground of fraud, and sometimes on that of mere mistake or misinformation.

Again, when the legitimacy of inflicting punishment is admitted, how many conflicting conceptions of justice come to light in discussing the proper apportionment of ᶜpunishmentᶜ to offences. No rule on ᵈthisᵈ subject recommends itself so strongly to the primitive and spontaneous sentiment of justice, as the *lex talionis*, an eye for an eye and a tooth for a tooth. Though this principle of the Jewish and of the Mahomedan law has been generally abandoned in Europe as a practical maxim, there is, I suspect, in most minds, a secret hankering after it; and when retribution accidentally falls on an offender in that precise shape, the general feeling of satisfaction evinced, bears witness how natural is the sentiment to which this repayment in kind is acceptable. With many the test of justice in penal infliction is that the punishment should be proportioned to the offence; meaning that it should be exactly measured by the moral guilt of the culprit (whatever be their standard for measuring moral guilt) : the consideration, what amount of punishment is necessary to deter from the offence, having nothing to do with the question of justice, in their estimation: while there are others to whom that consideration is all in all; who maintain that it is not just, at least for man, to inflict on a fellow-creature, whatever may be his offences, any amount of suffering beyond the least that will suffice to prevent him from repeating, and others from imitating, his misconduct.

To take another example from a subject already once referred to. In a co-operative industrial association, is it just or not that talent or skill should give a title to superior remuneration? On the negative side of the question it is argued, that whoever does the best he can, deserves equally well, and

[*See Ulpian. *Corpus Juris Civilis Romani, Digesta.* Lib. XLVII, Tit. x, 1, §5.]

ᶜ⁻ᶜ61,63,64   punishments   ᵈ⁻ᵈ61,63   the

ought not in justice to be put in a position of inferiority for no fault of his own; that superior abilities have already advantages more than enough, in the admiration they excite, the personal influence they command, and the internal sources of satisfaction attending them, without adding to these a superior share of the world's goods; and that society is bound in justice rather to make compensation to the less favoured, for this unmerited inequality of advantages, than to aggravate it. On the contrary side it is contended, that society receives more from the more efficient labourer; that his services being more useful, society owes him a larger return for them; that a greater share of the joint result is actually his work, and not to allow his claim to it is a kind of robbery; that if he is only to receive as much as others, he can only be justly required to produce as much, and to give a smaller amount of time and *exertion*, proportioned to his superior efficiency. Who shall decide between these appeals to conflicting principles of justice? Justice has in this case two sides to it, which it is impossible to bring into harmony, and the two disputants have chosen opposite sides; the one looks to what it is just that the individual should receive, the other to what it is just that the community should give. Each, from his own point of view, is unanswerable; and any choice between them, on grounds of justice, must be perfectly arbitrary. Social utility alone can decide the preference.

How many, again, and how irreconcileable, are the standards of justice to which reference is made in discussing the repartition of taxation. One opinion is, that payment to the State should be in numerical proportion to pecuniary means. Others think that justice dictates what they term graduated taxation; taking a higher percentage from those who have more to spare. In point of natural justice a strong case might be made for disregarding means altogether, and taking the same absolute sum (whenever it could be got) from every one: as the subscribers to a mess, or to a club, all pay the same sum for the same privileges, whether they can all equally afford it or not. Since the protection (it might be said) of law and government is afforded to, and is equally required by, all, there is no injustice in making all buy it at the same price. It is reckoned justice, not injustice, that a dealer should charge to all customers the same price for the same article, not a price varying according to their means of payment. This doctrine, as applied to taxation, finds no advocates, because it conflicts *f* strongly with *gmen's*g feelings of humanity and *h*perceptions*h* of social expediency; but the principle of justice which it invokes is as true and as binding as those which can be appealed to against it. Accordingly, it exerts a tacit influence on the line of defence employed for other modes of assessing taxation. People feel obliged to argue that the State does more for the rich than for the poor, as a justification for its taking more from them:

e–e61   exertions [*printer's error?*]   f61,63   so
g–g63   man's [*printer's error?*]   h–h+67,71

though this is in reality not true, for the rich would be far better able to protect themselves, in the absence of law or government, than the poor, and indeed would probably be successful in converting the poor into their slaves. Others, again, so far defer to the same conception of justice, as to maintain that all should pay an equal capitation tax for the protection of their persons (these being of equal value to all), and an unequal tax for the protection of their property, which is unequal. To this others reply, that the all of one man is as valuable to him as the all of another. From these confusions there is no other mode of extrication than the utilitarian.

Is, then, the difference between the Just and the Expedient a merely imaginary distinction? Have mankind been under a delusion in thinking that justice is a more sacred thing than policy, and that the latter ought only to be listened to after the former has been satisfied? By no means. The exposition we have given of the nature and origin of the sentiment, recognises a real distinction; and no one of those who profess the most sublime contempt for the consequences of actions as an element in their morality, attaches more importance to the distinction than I do. While I dispute the pretensions of any theory which sets up an imaginary standard of justice not grounded on utility, I account the justice which is grounded on utility to be the chief part, and incomparably the most sacred and binding part, of all morality. Justice is a name for certain classes of moral rules, which concern the essentials of human well-being more nearly, and are therefore of more absolute obligation, than any other rules for the guidance of life; and the notion which we have found to be of the essence of the idea of justice, that of a right residing in an individual, implies and testifies to this more binding obligation.

The moral rules which forbid mankind to hurt one another (in which we must never forget to include wrongful interference with each other's freedom) are more vital to human well-being than any maxims, however important, which only point out the best mode of managing some department of human affairs. They have also the peculiarity, that they are the main element in determining the whole of the social feelings of mankind. It is their observance which alone preserves peace among human beings: if obedience to them were not the rule, and disobedience the exception, every one would see in every one else *a probable* enemy, against whom he must be perpetually guarding himself. What is hardly less important, these are the precepts which mankind have the strongest and the most direct inducements for impressing upon one another. By merely giving to each other prudential instruction or exhortation, they may gain, or think they gain, nothing: in inculcating on each other the duty of positive beneficence they have an unmistakeable interest, but far less in degree: a person may possibly not need the benefits of

*–*61,63   an

others; but he always needs that they should not do him hurt. Thus the moralities which protect every individual from being harmed by others, either directly or by being hindered in his freedom of pursuing his own good, are at once those which he himself has most at heart, and those which he has the strongest interest in publishing and enforcing by word and deed. It is by a person's observance of these, that his fitness to exist as one of the fellowship of human beings, is tested and decided; for on that depends his being a nuisance or not to those with whom he is in contact. Now it is these moralities primarily, which compose the obligations of justice. The most marked cases of injustice, and those which give the tone to the feeling of repugnance which characterizes the sentiment, are acts of wrongful aggression, or wrongful exercise of power over some one; the next are those which consist in wrongfully withholding from him something which is his due; in both cases, inflicting on him a positive hurt, either in the form of direct suffering, or of the privation of some good which he had reasonable ground, either of a physical or of a social kind, for counting upon.

The same powerful motives which command the observance of these primary moralities, enjoin the punishment of those who violate them; and as the impulses of self-defence, of defence of others, and of vengeance, are all called forth against such persons, retribution, or evil for evil, becomes closely connected with the sentiment of justice, and is universally included in the idea. Good for good is also one of the dictates of justice; and this, though its social utility is evident, and though it carries with it a natural human feeling, has not at first sight that obvious connexion with hurt or injury, which, existing in the most elementary cases of just and unjust, is the source of the characteristic intensity of the sentiment. But the connexion, though less obvious, is not less real. He who accepts benefits, and denies a return of them when needed, inflicts a real hurt, by disappointing one of the most natural and reasonable of expectations, and one which he must at least tacitly have encouraged, otherwise the benefits would seldom have been conferred. The important rank, among human evils and wrongs, of the disappointment of expectation, is shown in the fact that it constitutes the principal criminality of two such highly immoral acts as a breach of friendship and a breach of promise. Few hurts which human beings can sustain are greater, and none wound more, than when that on which they habitually and with full assurance relied, fails them in the hour of need; and few wrongs are greater than this mere withholding of good; none excite more resentment, either in the person suffering, or in a sympathizing spectator. The principle, therefore, of giving to each what they deserve, that is, good for good as well as evil for evil, is not only included within the idea of Justice as we have defined it, but is a proper object of that intensity of sentiment, which places the Just, in human estimation, above the simply Expedient.

Most of the maxims of justice current in the world, and commonly appealed to in its transactions, are simply instrumental to carrying into effect the principles of justice which we have now spoken of. That a person is only responsible for what he has done voluntarily, or could voluntarily have avoided; that it is unjust to condemn any person unheard; that the punishment ought to be proportioned to the offence, and the like, are maxims intended to prevent the just principle of evil for evil from being perverted to the infliction of evil without that justification. The greater part of these common maxims have come into use from the practice of courts of justice, which have been naturally led to a more complete recognition and elaboration than was likely to suggest itself to others, of the rules necessary to enable them to fulfil their double function, of inflicting punishment when due, and of awarding to each person his right.

That first of judicial virtues, impartiality, is an obligation of justice, partly for the reason last mentioned; as being a necessary condition of the fulfilment of the other obligations of justice. But this is not the only source of the exalted rank, among human obligations, of those maxims of equality and impartiality, which, both in popular estimation and in that of the most enlightened, are included among the precepts of justice. In one point of view, they may be considered as corollaries from the principles already laid down. If it is a duty to do to each according to his deserts, returning good for good as well as repressing evil by evil, it necessarily follows that we should treat all equally well (when no higher duty forbids) who have deserved equally well of ^{j}us^j, and that society should treat all equally well who have deserved equally well of ^{k}it^k, that is, who have deserved equally well absolutely. This is the highest abstract standard of social and distributive justice; towards which all institutions, and the efforts of all virtuous citizens, should be made in the utmost possible degree to converge. But this great moral duty rests upon a still deeper foundation, being a direct emanation from the first principle of morals, and not a mere logical corollary from secondary or derivative doctrines. It is involved in the very meaning of Utility, or the Greatest-Happiness Principle. That principle is a mere form of words without rational signification, unless one person's happiness, supposed equal in degree (with the proper allowance made for kind), is counted for exactly as much as another's. Those conditions being supplied, Bentham's dictum, "everybody to count for one, nobody for more than one,"[*] might be written under the principle of utility as an explanatory commentary.* The equal claim of everybody to

[*Cf. *Plan of Parliamentary Reform*, in *Works*, Vol. III, p. 459.]

*This implication, in the first principle of the utilitarian scheme, of perfect impartiality between persons, is regarded by Mr. Herbert Spencer (in his *Social Statics* [London: Chapman, 1851, p. 94]) as a disproof of the pretensions of

$^{j-j}$61,63 *us* $^{k-k}$61,63,64,67 *it*

happiness in the estimation of the moralist and the legislator, involves an equal claim to all the means of happiness, except in so far as the inevitable conditions of human life, and the general interest, in which that of every individual is included, set limits to the maxim; and those limits ought to be strictly construed. As every other maxim of justice, so this, is by no means applied or held applicable universally; on the contrary, as I have already remarked, it bends to every person's ideas of social expediency. But in whatever case it is deemed applicable at all, it is held to be the dictate of justice. All persons are deemed to have a *right* to equality of treatment, except when some recognised social expediency requires the reverse. And hence all social inequalities which have ceased to be considered expedient, assume the character not of simple inexpediency, but of injustice, and appear so tyrannical, that people are apt to wonder how they ever could have been tolerated; forgetful that they themselves perhaps tolerate other inequalities under an equally mistaken notion of expediency, the correction of which would make

---

utility to be a sufficient guide to [61   be the foundation of] right; since (he says) the principle of utility presupposes the anterior principle, that everybody has an equal right to happiness. It may be more correctly described as supposing that equal amounts of happiness are equally desirable, whether felt by the same or by different persons. This, however, is not a presupposition [61, 63, 64   *pre*supposition]; not a premise needful to support the principle of utility, but the very principle itself; for what is the principle of utility, if it be not that "happiness" and "desirable" are synonymous terms? If there is any anterior principle implied, it can be no other than this, that the truths [61   rules] of arithmetic are applicable to the valuation of happiness, as of all other measurable quantities.

[63] Mr. Herbert Spencer, in a private communication on the subject of the preceding Note, objects to being considered an opponent of Utilitarianism, and states that he regards happiness as the ultimate end of morality; but deems that end only partially attainable by empirical generalizations from the observed results of conduct, and completely attainable only by deducing, from the laws of life and the conditions of existence, what kinds of action necessarily tend to produce happiness, and what kinds to produce unhappiness. [See Herbert Spencer. *Autobiography*. London: Williams and Norgate, 1904, Vol. II, pp. 87–90.] With the exception of the word "necessarily," I have no dissent to express from this doctrine; and (omitting that word) I am not aware that any modern advocate of utilitarianism is of a different opinion. Bentham, certainly, to whom in the *Social Statics* [pp. 21–3] Mr. Spencer particularly referred, is, least of all writers, chargeable with unwillingness to deduce the effect of actions on happiness from the laws of human nature and the universal conditions of human life. The common charge against him is of relying too exclusively upon such deductions, and declining altogether to be bound by the generalizations from specific experience which Mr. Spencer thinks that utilitarians generally confine themselves to. My own opinion (and, as I collect, Mr. Spencer's) is, that in ethics, as in all other branches of scientific study, the consilience of the results of both these processes, each corroborating and verifying the other, is requisite to give to any general proposition the kind and degree of evidence which constitutes scientific proof.

that which they approve seem quite as monstrous as what they have at last learnt to condemn. The entire history of social improvement has been a series of transitions, by which one custom or institution after another, from being a supposed primary necessity of social existence, has passed into the rank of an universally stigmatized injustice and tyranny. So it has been with the distinctions of slaves and freemen, nobles and serfs, patricians and ple-beians; and so it will be, and in part already is, with the aristocracies of colour, race, and sex.

It appears from what has been said, that justice is a name for certain moral requirements, which, regarded collectively, stand higher in the scale of social utility, and are therefore of more paramount obligation, than any others; though particular cases may occur in which some other social duty is so important, as to overrule any one of the general maxims of justice. Thus, to save a life, it may not only be allowable, but a duty, to steal, or take by force, the necessary food or medicine, or to kidnap, and compel to officiate, the only qualified medical practitioner. In such cases, as we do not call any-thing justice which is not a virtue, we usually say, not that justice must give way to some other moral principle, but that what is just in ordinary cases is, by reason of that other principle, not just in the particular case. By this useful accommodation of language, the character of indefcasibility attributed to justice is kept up, and we are saved from the necessity of maintaining that there can be laudable injustice.

The considerations which have now been adduced resolve, I conceive, the only real difficulty in the utilitarian theory of morals. It has always been evident that all cases of justice are also cases of expediency: the difference is in the peculiar sentiment which attaches to the former, as contradistinguished from the latter. If this characteristic sentiment has been sufficiently accounted for; if there is no necessity to assume for it any peculiarity of origin; if it is simply the natural feeling of resentment, moralized by being made co-exten-sive with the demands of social good; and if this feeling not only does but ought to exist in all the classes of cases to which the idea of justice corre-sponds; that idea no longer presents itself as a stumbling-block to the utilita-rian ethics. Justice remains the appropriate name for certain social utilities which are vastly more important, and therefore more absolute and imperative, than any others are as a class (though not more so than others may be in parti-cular cases); and which, therefore, ought to be, as well as naturally are, guarded by a sentiment not only different in degree, but also in kind; distin-guished from the milder feeling which attaches to the mere idea of promoting human pleasure or convenience, at once by the more definite nature of its commands, and by the sterner character of its sanctions.

AUGUSTE COMTE AND POSITIVISM

1865

2nd ed. London: Trübner, 1866. Reprinted from 1st ed., *ibid.*, 1865; and from *Westminster and Foreign Quarterly Review,* LXXXIII (Apr., 1865), 339–405 [Part I], and *ibid.*, LXXXIV (July, 1865), 1–42 [Part II], these two articles signed "J.S.M." The former is headed: "Art. I.—The Positive Philosophy of Auguste Comte. / 1. *Cours de Philosophie Positive.* Par Auguste Comte, Répétiteur d'Analyse transcendante et de Mécanique rationnelle à l'Ecole Polytechnique, et Examinateur des Candidats qui se destinent à cette Ecole. Deuxième Edition, augmentée d'une Préface par E. Littré, et d'une Table alphabétique des matières. [6 vols.] Paris: [Baillière,] 1864. / 2. *Auguste Comte et la Philosophie Positive.* Par. E. Littré. Paris: [Hachette,] 1863." The second is headed: "Art. I. —Later Speculations of Auguste Comte," and lists the works reviewed as in the footnote to 328 below, giving Comte as the author of the first four books.

Identified in JSM's bibliography as "Two articles on Comte's Philosophy in the Westminster Review for April and July 1865, afterwards reprinted and published by Trübner as a volume entitled 'Auguste Comte and Positivism' " (MacMinn, 95). For further discussion of the writing of the work and its relation to other essays in this volume, see the Textual Introduction, cxxix–cxxxiv above.

The following text is collated with that of the 1st ed., and that in the *Westminster.* In the footnoted variants, the 2nd ed. is indicated by "66"; the 1st by "65¹"; the *Westminster* by "65". There are no changes or corrections in the offprints of the articles or in the two copies of the 2nd ed. in the Somerville College Library, but several corrections are found in the copy of the 1st ed. The following typographical errors, all of which were corrected in the 2nd ed. (and hence are not listed in the Textual Introduction above), are marked for correction: 290.40 "we" corrected to "he", 320.n4 "with" corrected to "into", 320.n11 "part" corrected to "fact", 338.39 "then" corrected to "them", 345.33 the "a" before "private life" deleted. Two errors in 65 that were partially altered in 65¹, and altered again in 66 are marked in the Somerville College copy of the 1st ed.: 296.12 "of" altered to "to" (see 296^{c-c}), and 342.39 "it all he" altered to "all it" (see 342^{e-e}). At 338.12 the correction indicated ("others" for "other") is retained as a variant because the earlier form is found in 65 as well as 65¹; so is that at 352.34 ("desirous" for "desiring") because the incomplete correction was not adopted. Finally, the change indicated in the Somerville copy at 332.38 ("evoked" for "invoked") is accepted in the text below, though the change was not made in 66. One substantive variant occurs in the posthumous 3rd ed. (London: Trübner, 1882) and therefore in the paperback photographic reproduction of that edition (Ann Arbor: University of Michigan Press, 1961): at 351.39 the reading in 1882 is "it is supposed" rather than "as he calculates". The minor changes in the list of publications listed in the second part between 65¹ and 66 are not here indicated (JSM gives the identification of Comte as "Auteur du Système de Philosophie Positive" in the first title, and as "Auteur du Système de Philosophie Positive et du Système de Politique Positive" in the next three titles; the common eighteenth-century spelling, "Systême" rather than "Système", found in the list in 65 is retained in 65¹ at the second appearance of the word in the fourth title).

PART I

The Cours de Philosophie Positive*

FOR SOME TIME much has been said, in England and on the Continent, concerning "Positivism" and "the Positive Philosophy." Those phrases, which during the life of the eminent thinker who introduced them had made their way into no writings or discussions but those of his very few direct disciples, have emerged from the depths and manifested themselves on the surface of the philosophy of the age. It is not very widely known what they represent, but it is understood that they represent something. They are symbols of a recognized mode of thought, and one of sufficient importance to induce almost all who now discuss the great problems of philosophy, or survey from any elevated point of view the opinions of the age, to take what is termed the Positivist view of things into serious consideration, and define their own position, more or less friendly or hostile, in regard to it. Indeed, though the mode of thought expressed by the terms Positive and Positivism is widely spread, the words themselves are, as usual, better known through the enemies of that mode of thinking than through its friends; and more than one thinker who never called himself or his opinions by those appellations, and carefully guarded himself against being confounded with those who did, finds himself, sometimes to his displeasure, though generally by a tolerably correct instinct, classed with Positivists, and assailed as a Positivist. This change in the bearings of philosophic opinion commenced in England earlier than in France, where a philosophy of a contrary kind had been more widely cultivated, and had taken a firmer hold on the speculative minds of a generation formed by Royer-Collard, Cousin, Jouffroy, and their compeers. The great treatise of M. Comte was scarcely mentioned in French literature or criticism, when it was already working powerfully on the minds of many British students and thinkers. But agreeably to the usual course of things in France, the new tendency, when it set in, set in more strongly. Those who call themselves Positivists are indeed not numerous; but all French writers who adhere to the common philosophy, now feel it necessary to begin by fortifying their position against "the Positivist school." And the mode of thinking thus designated is already manifesting its importance by one of the most unequivocal signs, the appearance of thinkers who attempt a compromise or *juste*

[*2nd ed. 6 vols. Preface, E. Littré. Paris: Baillière, 1864.]

milieu between it and its opposite. The acute critic and metaphysician M. Taine, and the distinguished chemist M. Berthelot, are the authors of the two most conspicuous of these attempts.[*]

The time, therefore, seems to have come, when every philosophic thinker not only ought to form, but may usefully express, a judgment respecting this intellectual movement; endeavouring to understand what it is, whether it is essentially a wholesome movement, and if so, what is to be accepted and what rejected of the direction given to it by its most important movers. There cannot be a more appropriate *a*mode of discussing these points than in the form of*a* a critical examination of the philosophy of Auguste Comte; for which the appearance of a new edition of his fundamental treatise, with a preface by the most eminent, in every point of view, of his professed disciples, M. Littré, affords a good opportunity. The name of M. Comte is more identified than any other with this mode of thought. He is the first who has attempted its complete systematization, and the scientific extension of it to all objects of human knowledge. And in doing this he has displayed a quantity and quality of mental power, and achieved an amount of success, which have not only won but retained the high admiration of thinkers as radically and strenuously opposed as it is possible to be, to nearly the whole of his later tendencies, and to many of his earlier opinions. It would have been a mistake had such thinkers busied themselves in the first instance with drawing attention to what they regarded as errors in his great work. Until it had taken the place in the world of thought which belonged to it, the important matter was not to criticise it, but to help in making it known. To have put those who neither knew nor were capable of appreciating the greatness of the book, in possession of its vulnerable points, would have indefinitely retarded its progress to a just estimation, and was not needful for guarding against any serious inconvenience. While a writer has few readers, and no influence except on independent thinkers, the only thing worth considering in him is what he can teach us: if there be anything in which he is less wise than we are already, it may be left unnoticed until the time comes when his errors can do harm. But the high place which M. Comte has now assumed among European thinkers, and the increasing influence of his principal work, while they make it a more hopeful task than before to impress and enforce the strong points of his philosophy, have rendered it, for the first time, not inopportune to discuss his mistakes. Whatever errors he may have fallen into are now in a position to be injurious, while the free exposure of them can no longer be so.

[*See Hippolyte Taine. *Le positivisme anglaise, Etude sur Stuart Mill.* Paris: Baillière, 1864; Marcelin-Pierre-Eugène Berthelot. "La science idéale et la science positive," *Revue des Deux Mondes*, 2e sér., 48 (Nov., 1863), 442–59.]

*a–a*65   form for the discussion of these points than

We propose, then, to pass in review the main principles of M. Comte's philosophy; *b*commencing with*b* the great treatise by which, in this country, he is chiefly known, and *c*postponing consideration of*c* the writings of the last ten years of his life, except for the occasional illustration of detached points. When we extend our examination to these later productions, *d* we shall have, in the main, to reverse our judgment. Instead of recognizing, as in the *Cours de Philosophie Positive*, an essentially sound view of philosophy, with a few capital errors, it is in their general character that we deem the subsequent speculations false and misleading, while in the midst of this wrong general tendency, we find a crowd of valuable thoughts, and suggestions of thought, in detail. For the present we put out of the question this signal anomaly in M. Comte's intellectual career. We shall consider only the principal gift which he has left to the world, his clear, full, and comprehensive exposition, and in part creation, of what he terms the Positive Philosophy: endeavouring to sever what in our estimation is true, from the much less which is erroneous, in that philosophy as he conceived it, and distinguishing, as we proceed, the part which is specially his, from that which belongs to the philosophy of the age, and is the common inheritance of thinkers. This last discrimination has been partially made in a late pamphlet, by Mr. Herbert Spencer, in vindication of his own independence of thought: but this does not diminish the utility of doing it, with a less limited purpose, here; especially as Mr. Spencer rejects nearly all which properly belongs to M. Comte, and in his abridged mode of statement does scanty justice to what he rejects.[*] The separation is not difficult, even on the direct evidence given by M. Comte himself, who, far from claiming any originality not really belonging to him, was eager to connect his own most original thoughts with every germ of anything similar which he observed in previous thinkers.

The fundamental doctrine of a true philosophy, according to M. Comte, and the character by which he defines Positive Philosophy, is the following: —We have no knowledge of anything but Phænomena; and our knowledge of phænomena is relative, not absolute. We know not the essence, nor the real mode of production, of any fact, but only its relations to other facts in the way of succession or of similitude. These relations are constant; that is, always the same in the same circumstances. The constant resemblances which link phænomena together, and the constant sequences which unite them as antecedent and consequent, are termed their laws. The laws of phænomena are all we know respecting them. Their essential nature, and

[*The Classification of the Sciences. London: Williams and Norgate, 1864; see esp. pp. 29–31, 34–42.]

*b–b*65   confining ourselves for the present to
*c–c*65   leaving out of consideration
*d*65   as we hope hereafter to do,

their ultimate causes, either efficient or final, are unknown and inscrutable to us.

M. Comte claims no originality for this conception of human knowledge. He avows that it has been virtually acted on from the earliest period by all who have made any real contribution to science, and became distinctly present to the minds of speculative men from the time of Bacon, Descartes, and Galileo, whom he regards as collectively the founders of the Positive Philosophy. As he says, the knowledge which mankind, even in the earliest ages, chiefly pursued, being that which they most needed, was *fore*knowledge: "savoir, pour prévoir." When they sought for the cause, it was mainly in order to control the effect, or if it was uncontrollable, to foreknow and adapt their conduct to it. Now, all foresight of phænomena, and power over them, depend on knowledge of their sequences, and not upon any notion we may have formed respecting their origin or inmost nature. We foresee a fact or event by means of facts which are signs of it, because experience has shown them to be its antecedents. We bring about any fact, other than our own muscular contractions, by means of some fact which experience has shown to be followed by it. All foresight, therefore, and all intelligent action, have only been possible in proportion as men have successfully attempted to ascertain the successions of phænomena. Neither foreknowledge, nor the knowledge which is practical power, can be acquired by any other means.

The conviction, however, that knowledge of the successions and co-existences of phænomena is the sole knowledge accessible to us, could not be arrived at in a very early stage of the progress of thought. Men have not even now left off hoping for other knowledge, nor believing that they have attained it; and that, when attained, it is, in some undefinable manner, greatly more precious than mere knowledge of sequences and co-existences. The true doctrine was not seen in its full clearness even by Bacon, though it is the result to which all his speculations tend: still less by Descartes. It was, however, *e*apprehended with considerable correctness*e* by Newton.* But it was probably first conceived in its entire generality by Hume, who carries it a step further than Comte, maintaining not merely that the only causes of phænomena which can be known to us are other phænomena, their invariable antecedents, but that there is no other kind of causes: cause, as he interprets it, *means* the invariable antecedent. This is the only part of Hume's doctrine which was contested by his great adversary, Kant; who, maintaining as strenuously as Comte that we know nothing of Things in themselves, of Noumena, of real Substances and real Causes, yet peremptorily asserted their

*See the Chapter on Efficient Causes in Reid's *Essays on the Active Powers* [*of Man.* Edinburgh: Bell, 1788], which is avowedly grounded on Newton's ideas.

*e–e*65,65[1]   correctly apprehended

existence. But neither does Comte question this: on the contrary, all his language implies it. Among the direct successors of Hume, the writer who has best stated and defended Comte's fundamental doctrine is Dr. Thomas Brown. The doctrine and spirit of Brown's philosophy are entirely Positivist, and no better introduction to Positivism than the early part of his *Lectures*[*] has yet been produced. Of living thinkers we do not speak; but the same great truth formed the groundwork of all the speculative philosophy of Bentham, and pre-eminently of James Mill: and Sir William Hamilton's famous doctrine of the Relativity of human knowledge has guided many to it, though we cannot credit Sir William Hamilton himself with having understood the principle, or been willing to assent to it if he had.

The foundation of M. Comte's philosophy is thus in no way peculiar to him, but the general property of the age, however far as yet from being universally accepted even by thoughtful minds. The philosophy called Positive is not a recent invention of M. Comte, but a simple adherence to the traditions of all the great scientific minds whose discoveries have made the human race what it is. M. Comte has never presented it in any other light. But he has made the doctrine his own by his manner of treating it. To know rightly what a thing is, we require to know, with equal distinctness, what it is not. To enter into the real character of any mode of thought we must understand what other modes of thought compete with it. M. Comte has taken care that we should do so. The modes of philosophizing which, according to him, dispute ascendancy with the Positive, are two in number, both of them anterior to it in date; the Theological, and the Metaphysical.

We use the words Theological, Metaphysical, and Positive, because they are chosen by M. Comte as a vehicle for M. Comte's ideas. Any philosopher whose thoughts another person undertakes to set forth, has a right to require that it should be done by means of his own nomenclature. They are not, however, the terms we should ourselves choose. In all languages, but especially in English, they excite ideas other than those intended. The words Positive and Positivism, in the meaning assigned to them, are ill fitted to take root in English soil; while Metaphysical suggests, and suggested even to M. Comte, much that in no way deserves to be included in his denunciation. The term Theological is less wide of the mark, though the use of it as a term of condemnation implies, as we shall see, a greater reach of negation than need be included in the Positive creed. Instead of the Theological we should prefer to speak of the Personal, or Volitional explanation of *f*facts*f*; instead of Metaphysical, the Abstractional or Ontological: and the meaning of Positive would be less ambiguously expressed in the objective aspect by Phænomenal,

[*Thomas Brown. *Lectures on the Philosophy of the Human Mind*. 4 vols. Edinburgh: Tait, 1820.]

*f-f*65,65[1]   nature

in the subjective by Experiential. But M. Comte's opinions are best stated in his own phraseology; several of them, indeed, can scarcely be presented in some of their bearings without it.

The Theological, which is the original and spontaneous form of thought, regards the facts of the universe as governed not by invariable laws of sequence, but by single and direct volitions of beings, real or imaginary, possessed of life and intelligence. In the infantile state of reason and experience, individual objects are looked upon as animated. The next step is the conception of invisible beings, each of whom superintends and governs an entire class of objects or events. The last merges this multitude of divinities in a single God, who made the whole universe in the beginning, and guides and carries on its phænomena by his continued action, or, as others think, only modifies them from time to time by special interferences.

The mode of thought which M. Comte terms Metaphysical, accounts for phænomena by ascribing them, not to volitions either sublunary or celestial, but to realized abstractions. In this stage it is no longer a god that causes and directs each of the various agencies of nature: it is a power, or a force, or an occult quality, considered as real existences, inherent in but distinct from the concrete bodies in which they reside, and which they in a manner animate. Instead of Dryads presiding over trees, producing and regulating their phænomena, every plant or animal has now a Vegetative Soul, the θρεπτίκη ψυχή of Aristotle.[*] At a later period the Vegetative Soul has become a Plastic Force, and still later, a Vital Principle. Objects now do all that they do because it is their Essence to do so, or by reason of an inherent Virtue. Phænomena are accounted for by supposed tendencies and propensities of the abstraction Nature; which, though regarded as impersonal, is figured as acting on a sort of motives, and in a manner more or less analogous to that of conscious beings. Aristotle affirms a tendency of nature towards the best, which helps him to a theory of many natural phænomena. The rise of water in a pump is attributed to Nature's horror of a vacuum. The fall of heavy bodies, and the ascent of flame and smoke, are construed as attempts of each to get to its *natural* place. Many important consequences are deduced from the doctrine that Nature has no breaks (non habet saltum). In medicine the curative force (vis medicatrix) of Nature furnishes the explanation of the reparative processes which modern physiologists refer each to its own particular agencies and laws.

Examples are not necessary to prove to those who are acquainted with the past phases of human thought, how great a place both the theological and the metaphysical interpretations of phænomena have historically occupied, as well in the speculations of thinkers as in the familiar conceptions of the multitude. Many had perceived before M. Comte that neither of these

[*De Anima, 415a, 23.]

modes of explanation was final: the warfare against both of them could scarcely be carried on more vigorously than it already was, early in the seventeenth century, by Hobbes. Nor is it unknown to any one who has followed the history of the various physical sciences, that the positive explanation of facts has substituted itself, step by step, for the theological and metaphysical, as the progress of inquiry brought to light an increasing number of the invariable laws of phænomena. In these respects M. Comte has not originated anything, but has taken his place in a fight long since engaged, and on the side already in the main victorious. The generalization which belongs to himself, and in which he had not, to the best of our knowledge, been at all anticipated, is, that every distinct class of human conceptions passes g through all these stages, beginning with the theological, and proceeding through the metaphysical to the positive: the metaphysical being a mere state of transition, but an indispensable one, from the theological mode of thought to the positive, which is destined finally to prevail, by the universal recognition that all phænomena without exception are governed by invariable laws, with which no volitions, either natural or supernatural, interfere. This general theorem is completed by the addition, that the theological mode of thought has three stages, Fetichism, Polytheism, and Monotheism: the successive transitions being prepared, and indeed caused, by the gradual uprising of the two rival modes of thought, the metaphysical and the positive, and in their turn preparing the way for the ascendancy of these; first and temporarily of the metaphysical, finally of the positive.

This generalization is the most fundamental of the doctrines which originated with M. Comte; and the survey of history, which occupies the two largest volumes of the six composing his work, is a continuous exemplification and verification of the law. How well it accords with the facts, and how vast a number of the greater historical phænomena it explains, is known only to those who have studied its exposition, where alone it can be found—in these most striking and instructive volumes. As this theory is the key to M. Comte's other generalizations, all of which are more or less dependent on it; as it forms the backbone, if we may so speak, of his philosophy, and, unless it be true, he has accomplished little; we cannot better employ part of our space than in clearing it from misconception, and giving the explanations necessary to remove the obstacles which prevent many competent persons from assenting to it.

It is proper to begin by relieving the doctrine from a religious prejudice. The doctrine condemns all theological explanations, and replaces them, or thinks them destined to be replaced, by theories which take no account of anything but an ascertained order of phænomena. It is inferred that if this change were completely accomplished, mankind would cease to refer the

g65   necessarily

constitution of Nature to an intelligent will, or to believe at all in a Creator and supreme Governor of the world. This supposition is the more natural, as M. Comte was avowedly of that opinion. He indeed disclaimed, with some acrimony, dogmatic atheism, and even says (in a later work, but the earliest contains nothing at variance with it) that the hypothesis of design has much greater verisimilitude than that of a blind mechanism. But conjecture, founded on analogy, did not seem to him a basis to rest a theory on, in a mature state of human intelligence. He deemed all real knowledge of a commencement inaccessible to us, and the inquiry into it an overpassing of the essential limits of our mental faculties. To this point, however, those who accept his theory of the progressive stages of opinion are not obliged to follow him. The Positive mode of thought is not necessarily a denial of the supernatural; it merely throws back that question to the origin of all things. If the universe had a beginning, its beginning, by the very conditions of the case, was supernatural; the laws of nature cannot account for their own origin. The Positive philosopher is free to form his opinion on the subject, according to the weight he attaches to the analogies which are called marks of design, and to the general traditions of the human race. The value of these evidences is indeed a question for Positive philosophy, but it is not one upon which Positive philosophers must necessarily be agreed. It is one of M. Comte's mistakes that he never allows of open questions. Positive Philosophy maintains that within the existing order of the universe, or rather of the part of it known to us, the direct determining cause of every phænomenon is not supernatural but natural. It is compatible with this to believe, that the universe was created, and even that it is continuously governed, by an Intelligence, provided we admit that the intelligent Governor adheres to fixed laws, which are only modified or counteracted by other laws of the same dispensation, and are never either capriciously or providentially departed from. Whoever regards all events as parts of a constant order, each one being the invariable consequent of some antecedent condition, or combination of conditions, accepts fully the Positive mode of thought: whether he acknowledges or not an universal antecedent on which the whole system of nature was originally consequent, and whether that universal antecedent is conceived as an Intelligence or not.

There is a corresponding misconception to be corrected respecting the Metaphysical mode of thought. In repudiating metaphysics, M. Comte did not interdict himself from analyzing or criticising any of the abstract conceptions of the mind. He was not ignorant (though he sometimes seemed to forget) that such analysis and criticism are a necessary part of the scientific process, and accompany the scientific mind in all its operations. What he condemned was the habit of conceiving these mental abstractions as real entities, which could exert power, produce phænomena, and the enunciation of which could be regarded as a theory or explanation of facts. Men of the present day with difficulty believe that so absurd a notion was ever really entertained, so repugnant is it to the mental habits formed by long and assiduous cultivation of the positive sciences. But those sciences, however widely cultivated, have never formed the basis of intellectual education in any society. It is with philosophy as with religion: men marvel at the absurdity of other people's tenets, while exactly parallel absurdities remain in their own, and the same man is unaffectedly astonished that words can be mistaken for things, who is treating other words as if they were things every time he opens his mouth to discuss. No one, unless entirely ignorant of the history of thought, will deny that the mistaking of abstractions for realities pervaded speculation all through antiquity and the middle ages. The mistake was generalized and systematized in the famous Ideas of Plato. The Aristotelians carried it on. Essences, quiddities, virtues residing in things, were accepted as a *bonâ fide* explanation of phænomena. Not only abstract qualities, but the concrete names of genera and species, were mistaken for objective existences. It was believed that there were General Substances corresponding to all the familiar classes of concrete things: a substance Man, a substance Tree, a substance Animal, which, and not the individual objects so called, were directly denoted by those names. The real existence of Universal Substances was the question at issue in the famous controversy of the later middle ages between Nominalism and Realism, which is one of the turning points in the history of thought, being its first struggle to emancipate itself from the dominion of verbal abstractions. The Realists were the stronger party, but though the Nominalists for a time succumbed, the doctrine they rebelled against fell, after a short interval, with the rest of the scholastic philosophy. But while universal substances and substantial forms, being the grossest kind of realized abstractions, were the soonest discarded, Essences, Virtues, and Occult Qualities long survived them, and were first completely extruded from real existence by the Cartesians. In Descartes' conception of science, all physical phænomena were to be explained by matter and motion, that is, not by abstractions but by invariable physical laws: though his own explanations were many of them hypothetical, and turned out to be erroneous. Long after him, however, fictitious entities (as they are happily termed by Bentham)[*] continued to be imagined as means of accounting for the more mysterious phænomena; above all in physiology, where, under great varieties of phrase, mysterious *forces* and *principles* were the explanation, or substitute for explanation, of the phænomena of organized beings. To modern philosophers these fictions are merely the abstract names of the classes of phænomena which correspond to them; and it is one of the

[*See, e.g., *Introduction to the Principles of Morals and Legislation*, in *Works*, Vol. I, p. 53n.]

puzzles of philosophy, how mankind, after inventing a set of mere names to keep together certain combinations of ideas or images, could have so far forgotten their own act as to invest these creations of their will with objective reality, and mistake the name of a phænomenon for its efficient cause. What was a mystery from the purely dogmatic point of view, is cleared up by the historical. These abstract words are indeed now mere names of phænomena, but were not so in their origin. To us they denote only the phænomena, because we have ceased to believe in what else they once designated; and the employment of them in explanation is to us evidently, as M. Comte says, the naïf reproduction of the phænomenon as the reason for itself: but it was not so in the beginning. The metaphysical point of view was not a perversion of the positive, but a transformation of the theological. The human mind, in framing a class of objects, did not set out from the notion of a name, but from that of a divinity. The realization of abstractions was not the embodiment of a word, but the gradual disembodiment of a Fetish.

The primitive tendency or instinct of mankind is to assimilate all the agencies which they perceive in Nature, to the only one of which they are directly conscious, their own voluntary activity. Every object which seems to originate power, that is, to act without being first visibly acted upon, to communicate motion without having first received it, they [h]invest, or are disposed to invest, with[h] life, consciousness, will. This first rude conception of nature can scarcely, however, have been at any time extended to all phænomena. The simplest observation, without which the preservation of life would have been impossible, must have pointed out many uniformities in nature, many objects which, under given circumstances, acted exactly like one another: and whenever this was observed, men's natural and untutored faculties led them to form the similar objects into a class, and to think of them together: of which it was a natural consequence to refer effects, which were exactly alike, to a single will, rather than to a number of wills precisely accordant. But this single will could not be the will of the objects themselves, since they were many: it must be the will of an invisible being, apart from the objects, and ruling them from an unknown distance. This is Polytheism. We are not aware that in any tribe of savages or negroes who have been observed, Fetishism has been found totally unmixed with Polytheism, and it is probable that the two coexisted from the earliest period at which the human mind was capable of forming objects into classes. Fetishism proper gradually becomes limited to objects possessing a marked individuality. A particular mountain or river is worshipped bodily (as it is even now by the Hindoos and the South Sea Islanders) as a divinity in itself, not the mere residence of one, long after invisible gods have been imagined as rulers of all the great classes of phænomena, even intellectual and moral, as war, love, wisdom, beauty, &c. The worship of the earth (Tellus or Pales) and of the

[h–h]65,651   suppose to possess

various heavenly bodies, was prolonged into the heart of Polytheism. Every scholar knows, though *littérateurs* and men of the world do not, that in the full vigour of the Greek religion, the Sun and Moon, not a god and goddess thereof, were sacrificed to as deities—older deities than Zeus and his descendants, belonging to the earlier dynasty of the Titans (which was the mythical version of the fact that their worship was older), and these deities had a distinct set of fables or legends connected with them. The father of Phaëthon and the lover of Endymion were not Apollo and Diana, whose identification with the Sungod and the Moongoddess was a late invention. Astrolatry, which, as M. Comte observes, is the last form of Fetishism, survived the other forms, partly because its objects, being inaccessible, were not so soon discovered to be in themselves inanimate, and partly because of the persistent spontaneousness of their apparent motions.

As far as Fetishism reached, and as long as it lasted, there was no abstraction, or classification of objects, and no room consequently for the metaphysical mode of thought. But as soon as the voluntary agent, whose will governed the phænomenon, ceased to be the physical object itself, and was removed to an invisible position, from which he or she superintended an entire class of natural agencies, it began to seem impossible that this being should exert his powerful activity from a distance, unless through the medium of something present on the spot. Through the same Natural Prejudice which made Newton unable to conceive the possibility of his own law of gravitation without a subtle ether filling up the intervening space, and through which the attraction could be communicated—from this same natural infirmity of the human mind, it seemed indispensable that the god, at a distance from the object, must act through something residing in it, which was the immediate agent, the god having imparted to the intermediate something the power whereby it influenced and directed the object. When mankind felt a need for naming these imaginary entities, they called them the *nature* of the object, or its *essence*, or *virtues* residing in it, or by many other different names. These metaphysical conceptions were regarded as intensely real, and at first as mere instruments in the hands of the appropriate deities. But the habit being acquired of ascribing not only substantive existence, but real and efficacious agency, to the abstract entities, the consequence was that when belief in the deities declined and faded away, the entities were left standing, and a semblance of explanation of phænomena, equal to what existed before, was furnished by the entities alone, without referring them to any volitions. When things had reached this point, the metaphysical mode of thought had completely substituted itself for the theological.

Thus did the different successive states of the human intellect, even at an early stage of its progress, overlap one another, the Fetishistic, the Polytheistic, and the Metaphysical modes of thought coexisting even in the same minds, while the belief in invariable laws, which constitutes the Positive mode of thought, was slowly winning its way beneath them all, as observation and experience disclosed in one class of phænomena after another the laws to which they are really subject. It was this growth of positive knowledge which principally determined the next transition in the theological conception of the universe, from Polytheism to Monotheism.

It cannot be doubted that this transition took place very tardily. The conception of a unity in Nature, which would admit of attributing it to a single will, is far from being natural to man, and only finds admittance after a long period of discipline and preparation, the obvious appearances all pointing to the idea of a government by many conflicting principles. We know how high a degree both of material civilization and of moral and intellectual development preceded the conversion of the leading populations of the world to the belief in one God. The superficial observations by which Christian travellers have persuaded themselves that they found their own Monotheistic belief in some tribes of savages, have always been contradicted by more accurate knowledge: those who have read, for instance, Mr. Kohl's *Kitchi-gami*,[*] know what to think of the Great Spirit of the American Indians, who belongs to a well-defined system of Polytheism, interspersed with large remains of an original Fetishism. We have no wish to dispute the matter with those who believe that Monotheism was the primitive religion, transmitted to our race from its first parents in uninterrupted tradition. By their own acknowledgment, the tradition was lost by all the nations of the world except a small and peculiar people, in whom it was miraculously kept alive, but who were themselves continually lapsing from it, and in all the earlier parts of their history did not hold it at all in its full meaning, but admitted the real existence of other gods, though believing their own to be the most powerful, and to be the Creator of the world. A greater proof of the unnaturalness of Monotheism to the human mind before a certain period in its development, could not well be required.* The highest form of Monotheism, Christianity, has persisted to the present time in giving partial satisfaction to the mental dispositions that lead to Polytheism, by admitting into its theology the thoroughly polytheistic conception of a devil. When Monotheism, after many centuries, made its way to the Greeks and Romans from the small corner of the world where it existed, we know how the notion of dæmons facilitated

---

[*Johann Kohl. *Kitschi-Gami, oder Erzählungen vom Obern See.* Bremen: Schünemann, 1859.]

*[66] How unreal the most rigidly monotheistic religion is found to be in the minds of a people not rendered capable of it by positive knowledge, may be seen in any authentic account of popular Mahomedanism. The Fellah of the Nile valley believes, indeed, that "there is no God but God;" but he lives in the perpetual presence and dread of an infinity of other supernatural beings, whom he firmly believes to be crossing his path and endangering his interests in every hour of every day of his life.

its reception, by making it unnecessary for Christians to deny the existence of the gods previously believed in, it being sufficient to place them under the absolute power of the new God, as the gods of Olympus were already under that of Zeus, and as the local deities of all the subjugated nations had been subordinated by conquest to the divine patrons of the Roman State.

In whatever mode, natural or supernatural, we choose to account for the early Monotheism of the Hebrews, there can be no question that its reception by the Gentiles was only rendered possible by the slow preparation which the human mind had undergone from the philosophers. In the age of the Cæsars nearly the whole educated and cultivated class had outgrown the polytheistic creed, and though individually liable to returns of the superstition of their childhood, were predisposed (such of them as did not reject all religion whatever) to the acknowledgment of one Supreme Providence. It is vain to object that Christianity did not find the majority of its early proselytes among the educated class: since, except in Palestine, its teachers and propagators were mainly of that class—many of them, like St. Paul, well versed in the mental culture of their time; and they had evidently found no intellectual obstacle to the new doctrine in their own minds. We must not be deceived by the recrudescence, at a much later date, of a metaphysical Paganism in the Alexandrian and other philosophical schools, provoked not by attachment to Polytheism, but by distaste for the political and social ascendancy of the Christian teachers. The fact was, that Monotheism had become congenial to the cultivated mind: and a belief which has gained the cultivated minds of any society, unless put down by force, is certain, sooner or later, to reach the multitude. Indeed the multitude itself had been prepared for it, as already hinted, by the more and more complete subordination of all other deities to the supremacy of Zeus; from which the step to a single Deity, surrounded by a host of angels, and keeping in recalcitrant subjection an army of devils, was by no means difficult.

By what means, then, had the cultivated minds of the Roman Empire been educated for Monotheism? By the growth of a practical feeling of the invariability of natural laws. Monotheism had a natural adaptation to this belief, while Polytheism naturally and ⁱalmostⁱ necessarily conflicted with it. As men could not easily, and in fact never did, suppose that beings so powerful had their power absolutely restricted, each to its special department, the will of any divinity might always be frustrated by another: and unless all their wills were in complete harmony (which would itself be the most difficult to credit of all cases of invariability, and would require beyond anything else the ascendancy of a Supreme Deity) it was impossible that the course of any of the phænomena under their government could be invariable. But if, on the contrary, all the phænomena of the universe were under the exclusive and uncontrollable influence of a single will, it was an admissible supposition that this will might be always consistent with itself, and might choose to conduct each class of its operations in an invariable manner. In proportion, therefore, as the invariable laws of phænomena revealed themselves to observers, the theory which ascribed them all to one will began to grow plausible; but must still have appeared improbable until it had come to seem likely that invariability was the common rule of all nature. The Greeks and Romans at the Christian era had reached a point of advancement at which this supposition had become probable. The admirable height to which geometry had already been carried, had familiarized the educated mind with the conception of laws absolutely invariable. The logical analysis of the intellectual processes by Aristotle had shown a similar uniformity of law in the realm of mind. In the concrete external world, the most imposing phænomena, those of the heavenly bodies, which by their power over the imagination had done most to keep up the whole system of ideas connected with supernatural agency, had been ascertained to take place in so regular an order as to admit of being predicted with a precision which to the notions of those days must have appeared perfect. And though an equal degree of regularity had not been discerned in natural phænomena generally, even the most empirical observation had ascertained so many cases of an uniformity *almost* complete, that inquiring minds were eagerly on the look-out for further indications pointing in the same direction; and vied with one another in the formation of theories which, though hypothetical and essentially premature, it was hoped would turn out to be correct representations of invariable laws governing large classes of phænomena. When this hope and expectation became general, they were already a great encroachment on the original domain of the theological principle. Instead of the old conception, of events regulated from day to day by the unforeseen and changeable volitions of a legion of deities, it seemed more and more probable that all the phænomena of the universe took place according to rules which must have been planned from the beginning; by which conception the function of the gods seemed to be limited to forming the plans, and setting the machinery in motion: their subsequent office appeared to be reduced to a sinecure, or if they continued to reign, it was in the manner of constitutional kings, bound by the laws to which they had previously given their assent. Accordingly, the pretension of philosophers to explain physical phænomena by physical causes, or to predict their occurrence, was, up to a very late period of Polytheism, regarded as a sacrilegious insult to the gods. Anaxagoras was banished for it *i*(according to some authorities, even sentenced to death)*i*; Aristotle had to fly for his life; and the mere unfounded suspicion of it contributed greatly to the condemnation of Socrates. We are too well acquainted with this form of the religious sentiment even now, to have any difficulty in comprehending what must have been its violence then. It was inevitable that philosophers should be anxious to get rid of at least *these* gods, and so escape from the particular fables which stood immediately in their way; accepting a notion of divine government which harmonized better with the lessons they learnt from the study of nature, and a God concerning whom no mythos, as far as they knew, had yet been invented.

*k*And indeed*k*, when the idea became prevalent that the constitution of every part of Nature had been planned from the beginning, and continued to take place as it had been planned, this was itself a striking feature of resemblance extending through all Nature, and affording a presumption that the whole was the work, not of many, but of the same hand. It must have appeared vastly more probable that there should be one indefinitely fore-seeing Intelligence and immovable Will, than hundreds and thousands of such. The philosophers had not at that time the arguments which might have been grounded on universal laws not yet suspected, such as the law of gravita-tion and the laws of heat; but there was a multitude, obvious even to them, of analogies and homologies in natural phænomena, which suggested unity of plan; and a still greater number were raised up by their active fancy, aided by their premature scientific theories, all of which aimed at interpreting some phænomenon by the analogy of others supposed to be better known; assuming, indeed, a much greater similarity among the various processes of Nature, than ampler experience has since shown to exist. The theological mode of thought thus advanced from Polytheism to Monotheism through the direct influence of the Positive mode of thought, not yet aspiring to complete speculative ascendancy. But, inasmuch as the belief in the invaria-bility of natural laws was still imperfect even in highly cultivated minds, and in the merest infancy in the uncultivated, it gave rise to the belief in one God, but not in an immovable one. For many centuries the God believed in was flexible by entreaty, was incessantly ordering the affairs of mankind by direct volitions, and continually reversing the course of nature by miraculous interpositions; and this is believed still, wherever the invariability of law has established itself in men's convictions as a general, but not as an universal truth.

In the change from Polytheism to Monotheism, the Metaphysical mode of thought contributed its part, affording great aid to the up-hill struggle which the Positive spirit had to maintain against the prevailing form of the Theo-logical. M. Comte, indeed, has considerably exaggerated the share of the Metaphysical spirit in this mental revolution, since by a lax use of terms he credits the Metaphysical mode of thought with all that is due to dialectics and negative criticism—to the exposure of inconsistencies and absurdities in the

*k–k*65,65[1]   Again

received religions. But this operation is quite independent of the Metaphysical mode of thought, and was no otherwise connected with it than in being very generally carried on by the same minds (Plato is a brilliant example), since the most eminent efficiency in it does not necessarily depend on the possession of positive scientific knowledge. *The* Metaphysical spirit strictly so called, did *however* contribute largely to the advent of Monotheism. The conception of impersonal entities, interposed between the governing deity and the phænomena, and forming the machinery through which these are immediately produced, is not repugnant, as the theory of direct supernatural volitions is, to the belief in invariable laws. The entities not being, like the gods, framed after the exemplar of men—being neither, like them, invested with human passions, nor supposed, like them, to have power beyond the phænomena which are the special department of each, there was no fear of offending them by the attempt to foresee and define their action, or by the supposition that it took place according to fixed laws. The popular tribunal which condemned Anaxagoras had evidently not risen to the metaphysical point of view. Hippocrates, who was concerned only with a select and instructed class, could say with impunity, speaking of what were called the god-inflicted diseases, that to his mind they were neither more nor less god-inflicted than all others. The doctrine of abstract entities was a kind of instinctive conciliation between the observed uniformity of the facts of nature, and their dependence on arbitrary volition; since it was easier to conceive a single volition as setting a machinery to work, which afterwards went on of itself, than to suppose an inflexible constancy in so capricious and changeable a thing as volition must then have appeared. But though the régime of abstractions was in strictness compatible with Polytheism, it demanded Monotheism as the condition of its free development. The received Polytheism being only the first remove from Fetishism, its gods were too closely mixed up in the daily details of phænomena, and the habit of propitiating them and ascertaining their will before any important action of life was too inveterate, to admit, without the strongest shock to the received system, the notion that they did not habitually rule by special interpositions, but left phænomena in all ordinary cases to the operation of the essences or peculiar natures which they had first implanted in them. Any modification of Polytheism which would have made it fully compatible with the Metaphysical conception of the world, would have been more difficult to effect than the transition to Monotheism, as Monotheism was at first conceived.

We have given, in our own way, and at some length, this important portion of M. Comte's view of the evolution of human thought, as a sample of the manner in which his theory corresponds with and interprets historical facts, and also to obviate some objections to it, grounded on an imperfect compre-

*l–l*65,65¹ But the   *m–m*+66

hension, or rather on a mere first glance. Some, for example, think the doctrine of the three successive stages of speculation and belief, inconsistent with the fact that they all three existed contemporaneously; much as if the natural succession of the hunting, the nomad, and the agricultural state could be refuted by the fact that there are still hunters and nomads. That the three states were contemporaneous, that they all began before authentic history, and still coexist, is M. Comte's express statement: as well as that the advent of the two later modes of thought was the very cause which disorganized and is gradually destroying the primitive one. The Theological mode of explaining phænomena was once universal, with the exception, doubtless, of the familiar facts which, being even then seen to be controllable by human will, belonged already to the Positive mode of thought. The first and easiest generalizations of common observation, anterior to the first traces of the scientific spirit, determined the birth of the Metaphysical mode of thought; and every further advance in the observation of nature, gradually bringing to light its invariable laws, determined a further development of the Metaphysical spirit at the expense of the Theological, this being the only medium through which the conclusions of the Positive mode of thought and the premises of the Theological could be temporarily made compatible. At a later period, when the real character of the positive laws of nature had come to be in a certain degree understood, and the theological idea had assumed, in scientific minds, its final character, that of a God governing by general laws, the positive spirit, having now no longer need of the fictitious medium of imaginary entities, set itself to the easy task of demolishing the instrument by which it had risen. But though it destroyed the actual belief in the objective reality of these abstractions, that belief has left behind it vicious tendencies of the human mind, which are still far enough from being extinguished, and which we shall presently have occasion to characterize.

The next point on which we have to touch is one of greater importance than it seems. If all human speculation had to pass through the three stages, we may presume that its different branches, having always been very unequally advanced, could not pass from one stage to another at the same time. There must have been a certain order of succession in which the different sciences would enter, first into the metaphysical, and afterwards into the purely positive stage; and this order M. Comte proceeds to investigate. The result is his remarkable conception of a scale of subordination of the sciences, being the order of the logical dependence of those which follow on those which precede. It is not at first obvious how a mere classification of the sciences can be not merely a help to their study, but itself an important part of a body of doctrine; the classification, however, is a very important part of M. Comte's philosophy.

He first distinguishes between the abstract and the concrete sciences. The abstract sciences have to do with the laws which govern the elementary facts of Nature; laws on which all phænomena actually realized must of course depend, but which would have been equally compatible with many other combinations than those which actually come to pass. The concrete sciences, on the contrary, concern themselves only with the particular combinations of phænomena which are found in existence. For example; the minerals which compose our planet, or are found in it, have been produced and are held together by the laws of mechanical aggregation and by those of chemical union. It is the business of the abstract sciences, Physics and Chemistry, to ascertain these laws: to discover how and under what conditions bodies may become aggregated, and what are the possible modes and results of chemical combination. The great majority of these aggregations and combinations take place, so far as we are aware, only in our laboratories; with these the concrete science, Mineralogy, has nothing to do. Its business is with those aggregates, and those chemical compounds, which form themselves, or have at some period been formed, in the natural world. Again, Physiology, the abstract science, investigates, by such means as are available to it, the general laws of organization and life. Those laws determine what living beings are possible, and maintain the existence and determine the phænomena of those which actually exist: but they would be equally capable of maintaining in existence plants and animals very different from these. The concrete sciences, Zoology and Botany, confine themselves to species which really exist, or can be shown to have really existed: and do not concern themselves with the mode in which even these would comport themselves under all circumstances, but only under those which really take place. They set forth the actual mode of existence of plants and animals, the phænomena which they in fact present: but they set forth all of these, and take into simultaneous consideration the whole real existence of each species, however various the ultimate laws on which it depends, and to whatever number of different abstract sciences these laws may belong. The existence of a date tree, or of a lion, is ^{n}a^n joint result of many natural laws, physical, chemical, biological, and even astronomical. Abstract science deals with these laws separately, but considers each of them in all its aspects, all its possibilities of operation: concrete science considers them only in combination, and so far as they exist and manifest themselves in the animals or plants of which we have experience. The distinctive attributes of the two are summed up by M. Comte in the expression, that concrete science relates to Beings, or Objects, abstract science to Events.*

*Mr. Herbert Spencer, who also distinguishes between abstract and concrete sciences, employs the terms in a different sense from that explained above. [See
$^{n-n}$65   the

The concrete sciences are inevitably later in their development than the abstract sciences on which they depend. Not that they begin later to be studied; on the contrary, they are the earliest cultivated, since in our abstract investigations we necessarily set out from spontaneous facts. But though we may make empirical generalizations, we can form no scientific theory of concrete phænomena until the laws which govern and explain them are first known; and those laws are the subject of the abstract sciences. In consequence, there is not one of the concrete studies (unless we count astronomy among them) which has received, up to the present time, its final scientific constitution, or can be accounted a science, except in a very loose sense, but only materials for science: partly from insufficiency of facts, but more, because the abstract sciences, except those at the very beginning of the scale, have not attained the degree of perfection necessary to render real concrete sciences possible.

Postponing, therefore, the concrete sciences, as not yet formed, but only tending towards formation, the abstract sciences remain to be classed. These, as marked out by M. Comte, are six in number; and the principle which he proposes for their classification is admirably in accordance with the conditions of our study of Nature. It might have happened that the different classes of phænomena had depended on laws altogether distinct; that in changing

---

The Classification of the Sciences, pp. 6 ff.] He calls a science abstract when its truths are merely ideal; when, like the truths of geometry, they are not exactly true of real things—or, like the so-called law of inertia (the persistence in direction and velocity of a motion once impressed) are "involved" in experience but never actually seen in it, being always more or less completely frustrated. Chemistry and biology he includes, on the contrary, among concrete sciences, because chemical combinations and decompositions, and the physiological action of tissues, do actually take place (as our senses testify) in the manner in which the scientific propositions state them to take place. We will not discuss the logical or philological propriety of either use of the terms abstract and concrete, in which two-fold point of view very few of the numerous acceptations of these words are entirely defensible: but of the two distinctions M. Comte's answers to by far the deepest and most vital difference. Mr. Spencer's is open to the radical objection, that it classifies truths not according to their subject-matter or their mutual relations, but according to an unimportant difference in the manner in which we come to know them. Of what consequence is it that the law of inertia (considered as an exact truth) is not generalized from our direct perceptions, but inferred by combining with the movements which we see, those which we should see if it were not for the disturbing causes? In either case we are equally certain that it *is* an exact truth: for every dynamical law is perfectly fulfilled even when it seems to be counteracted. There must, we should think, be many truths in physiology (for example) which are only known by a similar indirect process; and Mr. Spencer would hardly detach these from the body of the science, and call them abstract and the remainder concrete.

from one to another subject of scientific study, the student left behind all the laws he previously knew, and passed under the dominion of a totally new set of uniformities. The sciences would then have been wholly independent of one another; each would have rested entirely on its own inductions, and if deductive at all, would have drawn its deductions from premises exclusively furnished by itself. The fact, however, is otherwise. The relation which really subsists between different kinds of phænomena, enables the sciences to be arranged in such an order, that in travelling through them we do not pass out of the sphere of any laws, but merely take up additional ones at each step. In this order M. Comte proposes to arrange them. He classes the sciences in an ascending series, according to the degree of complexity of their phæno- mena; so that each science depends on the truths of all those which precede it, with the addition of peculiar truths of its own.

Thus, the truths of number are true of all things, and depend only on their own laws; the science, therefore, of Number, consisting of Arithmetic and Algebra, may be studied without reference to any other science. The truths of Geometry presuppose the laws of Number, and a more special class of laws peculiar to extended bodies, but require no others: Geometry, there- fore, can be studied independently of all sciences except that of Number. Rational Mechanics presupposes, and depends on, the laws of number and those of extension, and along with them another set of laws, those of Equi- librium and Motion. The truths of Algebra and Geometry nowise depend on these last, and would have been true if these had happened to be the reverse of what we find them: but the phænomena of equilibrium and motion cannot be understood, nor even stated, without assuming the laws of number and extension, such as they actually are. The phænomena of Astronomy depend on these three classes of laws, and on the law of gravitation besides; which last has no influence on the truths of number, geometry, or mechanics. Physics (badly named in common English parlance Natural Philosophy) presupposes the three mathematical sciences, and also astronomy; since all terrestrial phænomena are affected by influences derived from the motions of the earth and of the heavenly bodies. Chemical phænomena depend (besides their own laws) on all the preceding, those of physics among the rest, espe- cially on the laws of heat and electricity; physiological phænomena, on the laws of physics and chemistry, and their own laws in addition. The phæno- mena of human society obey laws of their own, but do not depend solely upon these: they depend upon all the laws of organic and animal life, together with those of inorganic nature, these last influencing society not only through their influence on life, but by determining the physical conditions under which society has to be carried on. "Chacun de ces degrés successifs exige des inductions qui lui sont propres; mais elles ne peuvent jamais devenir systématiques que sous l'impulsion déductive resultée de tous les ordres moins compliqués."*

Thus arranged by M. Comte in a series, of which each term represents an advance in speciality beyond the term preceding it, and (what necessarily accompanies increased speciality) an increase of complexity—a set of phæ-nomena determined by a more numerous combination of laws; the sciences stand in the following order: 1st, Mathematics; its three branches following one another on the same principle, Number, Geometry, Mechanics. 2nd, Astronomy. 3rd, Physics. 4th, Chemistry. 5th, Biology. 6th, Sociology, or the Social Science, the phænomena of which depend on, and cannot be under-stood without, the principal truths of all the other sciences. The subject matter and contents of these various sciences are obvious of themselves, with the exception of Physics, which is a group of sciences rather than a single science, and is again divided by M. Comte into five departments: Barology, or the science of weight; Thermology, or that of heat; Acoustics, Optics, and Electrology. These he attempts to arrange on the same principle of increasing speciality and complexity, but they hardly admit of such a scale, and M. Comte's mode of placing them varied at different periods. All the five being essentially independent of one another, he attached little importance to their order, except that barology ought to come first, as the connecting link with astronomy, and electrology last, as the transition to chemistry.

If the best classification is that which is grounded on the properties most important for our purposes, this classification will stand the test. By placing the sciences in the order of the complexity of their subject matter, it presents them in the order of their difficulty. Each science proposes to itself a more arduous inquiry than those which precede it in the series; it is therefore likely to be susceptible, even finally, of a less degree of perfection, and will certainly arrive later at the degree attainable by it. In addition to this, each science, to establish its own truths, needs those of all the sciences anterior to it. The only means, for example, by which the physiological laws of life could have been ascertained, was by distinguishing, among the multifarious and complicated facts of life, the portion which physical and chemical laws cannot account for. Only by thus isolating the effects of the peculiar organic laws, did it become possible to discover what these are. It follows that the order in which the sciences succeed one another in the series, cannot but be, in the main, the historical order of their development; and is the only order in which they can rationally be studied. For this last there is an additional reason: since the more special and complete sciences require not only the truths of the simpler and more general ones, but still more their methods. The scientific

*Système de Politique Positive, [ou, Traité de sociologie, instituant la Religion de l'humanité. 4 vols. Paris: Mathias, 1851–54], Vol. II, p. 36.

intellect, both in the individual and in the race, must learn in the more elementary studies that art of investigation and those canons of proof which are to be put in practice in the more elevated. No intellect is properly qualified for the higher part of the scale, without due practice in the lower.

Mr. Herbert Spencer, in his essay entitled "The Genesis of oScienceo,"* and more recently in a pamphlet on "the Classification of the Sciences," has criticised and condemned M. Comte's classification, and proposed a more elaborate one of his own: and M. Littré, in his valuable biographical and philosophical work on M. Comte (*Auguste Comte et la Philosophie Positive*),[*] has at some length criticised the criticism. Mr. Spencer is one of the small number of persons who by the solidity and encyclopedical character of their knowledge, and their power of co-ordination and concatenation, may claim to be the peers of M. Comte, and entitled to a vote in the estimation of him. But after giving to his animadversions the respectful attention due to all that comes from Mr. Spencer, we cannot find that he has made out any case. It is always easy to find fault with a classification. There are a hundred possible ways of arranging any set of objects, and something may almost always be said against the best, and in favour of the worst of them. But the merits of a classification depend on the purposes to which it is instrumental. We have shown the purposes for which M. Comte's classification is intended. Mr. Spencer has not shown that it is ill adapted to those purposes: and we cannot perceive that his own answers any ends equally important. His chief objection is that if the more special sciences need the truths of the more general ones, the latter also need some of those of the former, and have at times been stopped in their progress by the imperfect state of sciences which follow long after them in M. Comte's scale; so that, the dependence being mutual, there is a *consensus*, but not an ascending scale or hierarchy of the sciences.[†] That the earlier sciences derive help from the later is undoubtedly true; it is part of M. Comte's theory, and amply exemplified in the details of his work. When he affirms that one science historically precedes another, he does not mean that the perfection of the first precedes the humblest commencement of those which follow. Mr. Spencer does not distinguish between the empirical stage of the cultivation of a branch of knowledge, and the scientific stage. The commencement of every study consists in gathering together unanalyzed facts, and treasuring up such spontaneous generalizations as present themselves to natural sagacity. In

*[66] In the first series of his *Essays, Scientific, Political, and Speculative*. [London: Longman, Brown, Green, Longmans, and Roberts, 1858.]
[*Paris: Hachette, 1863, pp. 284 ff.]
[†"The Genesis of Science," pp. 172 ff.]

o–o65   Sciences [*printer's error?*]

this stage any branch of inquiry can be carried on independently of every other; and it is one of M. Comte's own remarks that the most complex, in a scientific point of view, of all studies, the latest in his series, the study of man as a moral and social being, since from its absorbing interest it is cultivated more or less by every one, and pre-eminently by the great practical minds, acquired at an early period a greater stock of just though unscientific observations than the more elementary sciences. It is these empirical truths that the later and more special sciences lend to the earlier; or, at most, some extremely elementary scientific truth, which happening to be easily ascertainable by direct experiment, could be made available for carrying a previous science already founded, to a higher stage of development; a re-action of the later sciences on the earlier which M. Comte not only fully recognized, but attached great importance to systematizing.*

But though detached truths relating to the more complex order of phænomena may be empirically observed, and a few of them even scientifically established, contemporaneously with an early stage of some of the sciences anterior in the scale, such detached truths, as M. Littré justly remarks, do not constitute a science. What is known of a subject, only becomes a science when it is made a connected body of truth; in which the relation between the general principles and the details is definitely made out, and each particular truth can be recognized as a case of the operation of wider laws. This point

---

*The strongest case which Mr. Spencer produces of a scientifically ascertained law, which, though belonging to a later science, was necessary to the scientific formation of one occupying an earlier place in M. Comte's series, is the law of the accelerating force of gravity; which M. Comte places in Physics, but without which the Newtonian theory of the celestial motions could not have been discovered, nor could even now be proved. [Spencer, "The Genesis of Science," pp. 178–9.] This fact, as is judiciously remarked by M. Littré, is not valid against the plan of M. Comte's classification, but discloses a slight error in the detail. [Littré, Comte, p. 294.] M. Comte should not have placed the laws of terrestrial gravity under Physics. They are part of the general theory of gravitation, and belong to astronomy. Mr. Spencer has hit one of the weak points in M. Comte's scientific scale; weak however only because left unguarded. Astronomy, the second of M. Comte's abstract sciences, answers to his own definition of a concrete science. M. Comte however was only wrong in overlooking a distinction. There *is* an abstract science of astronomy, namely, the theory of gravitation, which would equally agree with and explain the facts of a totally different solar system from the one of which our earth forms a part. The actual facts of our own system, the dimensions, distances, velocities, temperatures, physical constitution [65   composition], &c., of the sun, earth, and planets, are properly the subject of a concrete science, similar to natural history; but the concrete is more inseparably united to the abstract science than in any other case, since the few celestial facts really accessible to us are nearly all required for discovering and proving the law of gravitation as an universal property of bodies, and have therefore an indispensable place in the abstract science as its fundamental data.

of progress, at which the study passes from ᵖtheᵖ preliminary state of mere preparation, into a science, cannot be reached by the more complex studies until it has been attained by the simpler ones. A certain regularity of recurrence in the celestial appearances was ascertained empirically before much progress had been made in geometry; but astronomy could no more be a science until geometry was a highly advanced one, than the rule of three could have been practised before addition and subtraction. The truths of the simpler sciences are a part of the laws to which the phænomena of the more complex sciences conform: and are not only a necessary element in their explanation, but must be so well understood as to be traceable through complex combinations, before the special laws which co-exist and co-operate with them can be brought to light. This is all that M. Comte affirms, and enough for his purpose.* He no doubt occasionally indulges in more unqualified expressions than can be completely justified, regarding the logical perfection of the construction of his series, and its exact correspondence with the historical evolution of the sciences; exaggerations confined to language, and which the details of his exposition often correct. But he is sufficiently near the truth, in both respects, for every practical purpose† Minor inaccuracies

*The only point at which the general principle of the series fails in its application, is the subdivision of Physics; and as there is no real subordination among the different branches [65, 65¹ Physics; and there, as the subordination of the different branches scarcely exists], their order is of little consequence. Thermology, indeed, is altogether an exception to the principle of decreasing generality, heat, as Mr. Spencer truly says, being as universal as gravitation. ["Genesis of Science," p. 219.] But the place of Thermology is marked out, within certain narrow limits, by the ends of the classification, though not by its principle. The desideratum is, that every science should precede those which cannot be scientifically constituted or rationally studied until it is known. It is as a means to this end, that the arrangement of the phænomena in the order of their dependence on one another is important. Now, though heat is as universal a phænomenon as any which external nature presents, its laws do not affect, in any manner important to us, the phænomena of Astronomy, and operate in the other branches of Physics only as slight modifying agencies, the consideration of which may be postponed to a rather advanced stage. But the phaenomena of Chemistry and Biology depend on them often for their very existence. The ends of the classification require therefore that Thermology should precede Chemistry and Biology, but do not demand that it should be thrown farther back. On the other hand, those same ends, in another point of view, require that it should be subsequent to Astronomy, for reasons not of doctrine but of method: Astronomy being the best school of the true art of interpreting Nature, by which Thermology profits like other sciences, but which it was ill adapted to originate.

†The philosophy of the subject is perhaps nowhere so well expressed as in the *Système de Politique Positive* (Vol. III, p. 41). "Conçu logiquement, l'ordre suivant lequel nos principales théories accomplissent l'évolution fondamentale résulte nécessairement de leur dépendance mutuelle. Toutes les sciences peuvent,

must often be forgiven even to great thinkers. Mr. Spencer, in the very writings in which he criticises M. Comte, affords signal instances of them.*

Combining the doctrines, that every science is in a less advanced state as it occupies a higher place in the ascending scale, and that all the sciences pass through the three stages, theological, metaphysical, and positive, it follows that the more special a science is, the tardier is it in effecting each

---

sans doute, être ébauchées à la fois: leur usage pratique exige même cette culture simultanée. Mais elle ne peut concerner que les inductions propres à chaque classe de spéculations. Or cet essor inductif ne saurait fournir des principes suffisants qu'envers les plus simples études. Partout ailleur, ils ne peuvent être établis qu'en subordonnant chaque genre d'inductions scientifiques à l'ensemble des déductions émanées des domaines moins compliqués, et dès-lors moins dépendants. Ainsi nos diverses théories reposent dogmatiquement les unes sur les autres, suivant un ordre invariable, qui doit régler historiquement leur avénement décisif, les plus indépendantes ayant toujours dû se développer plus tôt."

*"Science," says Mr. Spencer in his "Genesis," "while purely inductive is purely qualitative. . . . All quantitative prevision is reached deductively; induction can achieve only qualitative prevision." [Pp. 163–4.] Now, if we remember that the very first accurate quantitative law of physical phænomena ever established, the law of the accelerating force of gravity, was discovered and proved by Galileo partly at least [65   Galileo strictly] by experiment; that the quantitative laws on which the whole theory of the celestial motions is grounded, were generalized by Kepler from direct comparison of observations; that the quantitative law of the condensation of gases by pressure, the law of Boyle and Mariotte, was arrived at by direct experiment; that the proportional quantities in which every known substance combines chemically with every other, were ascertained by innumerable experiments, from which the general law of chemical equivalents, now the ground of the most exact quantitative previsions, was an inductive generalization; we must conclude that Mr. Spencer has committed himself to a general proposition, which a very slight consideration of truths perfectly known to him would have shown to be unsustainable.

Again, in the very pamphlet in which Mr. Spencer defends himself against the supposition of being a disciple of M. Comte (*The Classification of the Sciences*, p. 37n), he speaks of "M. Comte's adherent, Mr. Buckle." Now, except in the opinion common to both, that history may be made a subject of science, the speculations of these two thinkers are not only different, but run in different channels, M. Comte applying himself principally to the laws of evolution common to all mankind, Mr. Buckle almost exclusively to the diversities: and it may be affirmed without presumption, that they neither saw the same truths, nor fell into the same errors, nor defended their opinions, either true or erroneous, by the same arguments. Indeed, it is one of the surprising things in the case of Mr. Buckle as of Mr. Spencer, that being a man of kindred genius, of the same wide range of knowledge, and devoting himself to speculations of the same kind, he profited so little by M. Comte.

These oversights prove nothing against the general accuracy of Mr. Spencer's acquirements. They are mere lapses of inattention, such as thinkers who attempt speculations requiring that vast multitudes of facts should be kept in recollection at once, can scarcely hope always to avoid.

transition, so that a completely positive state of an earlier science has often coincided with the metaphysical state of the one next to it, and a purely theological state of those ᵠfurtherᵠ on. This statement correctly represents the general course of the facts, though requiring allowances in the detail. Mathematics, for example, from the very beginning of its cultivation, can hardly at any time have been in the theological state, though exhibiting many traces of the metaphysical. No one, probably, ever believed that the will of a god kept parallel lines from meeting, or made two and two equal to four; or ever prayed to the gods to make the square of the hypothenuse equal to more or less than the sum of the squares of the sides. The most devout believers have recognized in propositions of this description, a class of truths independent of the divine omnipotence. Even among the truths which popular philosophy calls by the misleading name of Contingent, the few which are at once exact and obvious were probably, from the very first, excepted from the theological explanation. M. Comte observes, after Adam Smith, that we are not told in any age or country of a god of Weight.[*] It was otherwise with Astronomy: the heavenly bodies were believed not merely to be moved by gods, but to be gods themselves: and when this theory was exploded, their movements were explained by metaphysical conceptions; such as a tendency of Nature to perfection, in virtue of which these sublime bodies, being left to themselves, move in the most perfect orbit, the circle. Even Kepler was full of fancies of this description, which only terminated when Newton, by unveiling the real physical laws of the celestial motions, closed the metaphysical period of astronomical science. As M. Comte remarks, our power of foreseeing phæ-nomena, and our power of controlling them, are the two things which destroy the belief of their being governed by changeable wills. In the case of phæno-mena which science has not yet taught us either to foresee or to control, the theological mode of thought has not ceased to operate: men still pray for rain, or for success in war, or to avert a shipwreck or a pestilence, but not to put back the stars in their courses, to abridge the time necessary for a journey, or to arrest the tides. Such vestiges of the primitive mode of thought linger in the more intricate departments of sciences which have attained a high degree of positive development. The metaphysical mode of explanation, being less antagonistic than the theological to the idea of invariable laws, is still slower in being entirely discarded. M. Comte finds remains of it in the sciences which are the most completely positive, with the single exception of astronomy, ʳeven mathematics not having, he thinks, altogether freed itselfʳ from them: which is not wonderful, when we see at how very recent a

[*Cours, Vol. IV, p. 491; Adam Smith. "History of Astronomy," §3, in Essays on Philosophical Subjects. London: Cadell and Davies, 1795, p. 25.]

ᵠ⁻ᵠ65   farther
ʳ⁻ʳ65, 65¹   mathematics itself not being, he thinks, altogether free

date mathematicians have been able to give the really positive interpretation of their own symbols.* We have already however had occasion to notice M. Comte's propensity to use the term metaphysical in cases containing nothing that truly answers to his definition of the word. For instance, he considers chemistry as tainted with the metaphysical mode of thought by the notion of chemical affinity. He thinks that the chemists who said that bodies combine because they have an affinity for each other, believed in a mysterious entity residing in bodies and inducing them to combine. On any other supposition, he thinks the statement could only mean that bodies combine because they combine. But it really meant more. It was the abstract expression of the doctrine, that bodies have an invariable tendency to combine with one thing in preference to another: that the tendencies of different substances to combine are fixed quantities, of which the greater always prevails over the less, so that if A detaches B from C in one case it will do so in every other; which was called having a greater attraction, or, more technically, a greater affinity for it. This was not a metaphysical theory, but a positive generalization, which accounted for a great number of facts, and would have kept its place as a law of nature, had it not been disproved by the discovery of cases in which though A detached B from C in some circumstances, C detached it from A in others, showing the law of elective chemical combination to be a less simple one than had at first been supposed. In this case, therefore, M. Comte made a mistake: and he will be found to have made many similar ones. But in the science next after chemistry, biology, the empty mode of explanation by scholastic entities, such as a plastic force, a vital principle, and the like, has been kept up even to the present day. The German physiology of the school of Oken, notwithstanding his acknowledged genius, is almost as metaphysical as Hegel, and there is in France a quite recent revival of the Animism of Stahl. These metaphysical explanations, besides their inanity, did serious harm, by directing the course of positive scientific inquiry into wrong channels. There was indeed nothing to prevent investigating the mode of action of the supposed plastic or vital force by observation and experiment; but the phrases gave currency and coherence to a false abstraction and generalization, setting inquirers to look out for one cause of complex phenomena which undoubtedly depended on many.

According to M. Comte, chemistry entered into the positive stage with Lavoisier, in the latter half of the last century (in a subsequent treatise he places the date a generation earlier); and biology at the beginning of the present, when Bichat drew the fundamental distinction between nutritive or vegetative and properly animal life, and referred the properties of organs to

*We refer particularly to the mystical metaphysics connected with the negative sign, imaginary quantities, infinity and infinitesimals, &c., all cleared up and put on a rational footing in the highly philosophical treatises of Professor De Morgan.

the general laws of the component tissues. The most complex of all sciences, the Social, had not, he maintained, become positive at all, but was the subject of an ever-renewed and barren contest between the theological and the metaphysical modes of thought. To make this highest of the sciences positive, and thereby complete the positive character of all human speculations, was the principal aim of his labours, and he believed himself to have accomplished it in the last three volumes of his Treatise. But the term Positive is not, any more than Metaphysical, always used by M. Comte in the same meaning. There never can have been a period in any science when it was not in some degree positive, since it always professed to draw conclusions from experience and observation. M. Comte would have been the last to deny that previous to his own speculations, the world possessed a multitude of truths, of greater or less certainty, on social subjects, the evidence of which was obtained by inductive or deductive processes from observed sequences of phænomena. Nor could it be denied that the best writers on subjects upon which so many men of the highest mental capacity had employed their powers, had accepted ˢthe positive point of view as thoroughlyˢ, and rejected the theological and metaphysical as decidedly, as M. Comte himself. Montesquieu; even Macchiavelli; ᵗTurgot,ᵗ Adam Smith, and the political economists universally, both in France and in England; Bentham, and all thinkers initiated by him,—had a full conviction that social phænomena conform to invariable laws, the discovery and illustration of which was their great object as speculative thinkers. All that can be said is, that those philosophers did not get so far as M. Comte in discovering the methods best adapted to bring these laws to light. It was not, therefore, reserved for M. Comte to make sociological inquiries positive. But what he really meant by making a science positive, is what we will call, with M. Littré, giving it its final scientific constitution; in other words, discovering or proving, and pursuing to their consequences, those of its truths which are fit to form the connecting links among the rest: truths which are to it what the law of gravitation is to astronomy, what the elementary properties of the tissues are to physiology, and we will add (though M. Comte did not) what the laws of association are to psychology. This is an operation which, when accomplished, puts an end to the empirical period, and enables the science to be conceived as a co-ordinated and coherent body of doctrine. This is what had not yet been done for sociology; and the hope of effecting it was, from his early years, the prompter and incentive of all M. Comte's philosophic labours.

It was with a view to this that he undertook that wonderful systematization of the philosophy of all the antecedent sciences, from mathematics to physiology, which, if he had done nothing else, would have stamped him, in all

ˢ–ˢ65,65¹   as thoroughly the positive point of view
ᵗ–ᵗ+66

minds competent to appreciate it, as one of the principal thinkers of the age. To make its nature intelligible to those who are not acquainted with it, we must explain what we mean by the philosophy of a science, as distinguished from the science itself. The proper meaning of philosophy we take to be, what *u*, in the main,*u* the ancients understood by it—the scientific knowledge of Man, as an intellectual, moral, and social being. Since his intellectual faculties include his knowing faculty, the science of Man includes everything that man can know, so far as regards his mode of knowing it: in other words, the whole doctrine of the conditions of human knowledge. The philosophy of a Science thus comes to mean the science itself, considered not as to its results, the truths which it ascertains, but as to the processes by which the mind attains them, the marks by which it recognizes them, and the co-ordinating and methodizing of them with a view to the greatest clearness of conception and the fullest and readiest availability for use: in one word, the logic of the science. M. Comte has accomplished this for the first five of the fundamental sciences, with a success which can hardly be too much admired. We never reopen even the least admirable part of this survey, the volume on chemistry and biology (which was behind the actual state of those sciences when first written, and is far in the rear of them now), without a renewed sense of the great reach of its speculations, and a conviction that the way to a complete rationalizing of those sciences, still very imperfectly conceived by most who cultivate them, has been shown nowhere so successfully as there.

Yet, for a correct appreciation of this great philosophical achievement, we ought to take account of what has not been accomplished, as well as of what has. Some of the chief deficiencies and infirmities of M. Comte's system of thought will be found, as is usually the case, in close connexion with its greatest successes.

The philosophy of Science consists of two principal parts; the methods of investigation, and the requisites of proof. The one points out the roads by which the human intellect arrives at conclusions, the other the mode of testing their evidence. The former if complete would be an Organon of Discovery, the latter of Proof. It is to the first of these that M. Comte principally confines himself, and he treats it with a degree of perfection hitherto unrivalled. Nowhere is there anything comparable, in its kind, to his survey of the resources which the mind has at its disposal for investigating the laws of phænomena; the circumstances which render each of the fundamental modes of exploration suitable or unsuitable to each class of phænomena; the extensions and transformations which the process of investigation has to undergo in adapting itself to each new province of the field of study; and the especial gifts with which every one of the fundamental sciences enriches the

u–u+66

method of positive inquiry, each science in its turn being the best fitted to bring to perfection one process or another. These, and many cognate subjects, such as the theory of Classification, and the proper use of scientific Hypotheses, M. Comte has treated with a completeness of insight which leaves little to be desired. Not less admirable is his survey of the most comprehensive truths that had been arrived at by each science, considered as to their relation to the general sum of human knowledge, and their logical value as aids to its further progress. But after all this, there remains a further and distinct question. We are taught the right way of searching for results, but when a result has been reached, how shall we know that it is true? How assure ourselves that the process has been performed correctly, and that our premises, whether consisting of generalities or of particular facts, really prove the conclusion we have grounded on them? On this question M. Comte throws no light. He supplies no test of proof. As regards deduction, he neither recognizes the syllogistic system of Aristotle and his successors (the insufficiency of which is as evident as its utility is real) nor proposes any other in lieu of it: and of induction he has no canons whatever. He does not seem to admit the possibility of any general criterion by which to decide whether a given inductive inference is correct or not. Yet he does not, with Dr. Whewell, regard an inductive theory as proved if it accounts for the facts: on the contrary, he sets himself in the strongest opposition to those scientific hypotheses which, like the luminiferous ether, are not susceptible of direct proof, and are accepted on the sole evidence of their aptitude for explaining phænomena. He maintains that no hypothesis is legitimate unless it is susceptible of verification, and that none ought to be accepted as true unless it can be shown not only that it accords with the facts, but that its falsehood would be inconsistent with them. He therefore needs a test of inductive proof; and in assigning none, he seems to give up as impracticable the main problem of Logic properly so called. At the beginning of his treatise he speaks of a doctrine of Method, apart from particular applications, as conceivable, but not needful: method, according to him, is learnt only by seeing it in operation, and the logic of a science can only usefully be taught through the science itself. Towards the end of the work, he assumes a more decidedly negative tone, and treats the very conception of studying Logic otherwise than in its applications as chimerical. He got on, in his subsequent writings, to considering it as wrong. This indispensable part of Positive Philosophy he not only left to be supplied by others, but did all that depended on him to discourage them from attempting it.

This hiatus in M. Comte's system is not unconnected with a defect in his original conception of the subject matter of scientific investigation, which has been generally noticed, for it lies on the surface, and is more apt to be exaggerated than overlooked. It is often said of him that he rejects the study of causes. This is not, in the correct acceptation, true, for it is only questions of ultimate origin, and of Efficient as distinguished from what are called Physical causes, that he rejects. The causes that he regards as inaccessible are causes which are not themselves phænomena. Like other people he admits the study of causes, in every sense in which one physical fact can be the cause of another. But he has an objection to the *word* cause; he will only consent to speak of Laws of Succession: and depriving himself of the use of a word which has a Positive meaning, he misses the meaning it expresses. He sees no difference between such generalizations as Kepler's laws, and such as the theory of gravitation. He fails to perceive the real distinction between the laws of succession and coexistence which thinkers of a different school call Laws of Phænomena, and those of what they call the action of Causes: the former exemplified by the succession of day and night, the latter by the earth's rotation which ᵛproducesᵛ it. The succession of day and night is as much an invariable sequence, as the alternate exposure of opposite sides of the earth to the sun. Yet day and night are not the causes of one another; why? Because their sequence, though invariable in our experience, is not unconditionally so: those facts only succeed each other, provided that the presence and absence of the sun succeed each other, and if this alternation were to cease, we might have either day or night unfollowed by one another. There are thus two kinds of uniformities of succession, the one unconditional, the other conditional on the first: laws of causation, and other successions dependent on those laws. All ultimate laws are laws of causation, and the only universal law beyond the pale of mathematics is the law of universal causation, namely, that every phænomenon has a phænomenal cause; has some phænomenon other than itself, or some combination of phænomena, on which it is invariably and unconditionally consequent. It is on the universality of this law that the possibility rests of establishing a canon of Induction. A general proposition inductively obtained is only then proved to be true, when the instances on which it rests are such that if they have been correctly observed, the falsity of the generalization would be inconsistent with the constancy of causation; with the universality of the fact that the phænomena of nature take place according to invariable laws of succession.* It is probable, therefore, that M. Comte's determined abstinence from the word and

*Those who wish to see this idea followed out, are referred to *A System of Logic, Ratiocinative and Inductive* [Vol. I, pp. 373 ff; Bk. III, Chap. v.]. It is not irrelevant to state that M. Comte, soon after the publication of that work, expressed, both in a letter (published in M. Littré's volume [*Comte*, pp. 448 ff.]) and in print, his high approval of it (especially of the Inductive part) as a real contribution to the construction of the Positive Method. But we cannot discover that he was indebted to it for a single idea, or that it influenced, in the smallest particular, the course of his subsequent speculations.

ᵛ—ᵛ65,65¹   causes

the idea of Cause, had much to do with his inability to conceive an Inductive Logic, by diverting his attention from the only basis upon which it could be founded.

We are afraid it must also be said, though shown only by slight indications in his fundamental work, and coming out in full evidence only in his later writings—that M. Comte, at bottom, was not so solicitous about completeness of proof as becomes a positive philosopher, and that the unimpeachable objectivity, as he would have called it, of a conception—its exact correspondence to the realities of outward fact—was not, with him, an indispensable condition of adopting it, if it was subjectively useful, by affording facilities to the mind for grouping phænomena. This appears very curiously in his chapters on the philosophy of Chemistry. He recommends, as a judicious use of "the degree of liberty left to our intelligence by the end and purpose of positive science,"[*] that we should accept as a convenient generalization the doctrine that all chemical composition is between two elements only; that every substance which our analysis decomposes, let us say into four elements, has for its immediate constituents two hypothetical substances, each compounded of two simpler ones. There would have been nothing to object to in this as a scientific hypothesis, assumed tentatively as a means of suggesting experiments by which its truth *may* be tested. With this for its destination, the conception would have been legitimate and philosophical; the more so, as, if confirmed, it would have afforded an explanation of the fact that some substances which analysis shows to be composed of the same elementary substances in the same proportions, differ in their general properties, as for instance, sugar and gum.* And if, besides affording a reason for difference between things which differ, the hypothesis had afforded a reason for agreement between things which agree; if the *two immediate constituents into which the quaternary compound was resolved*, could have been so chosen as to bring *the case* within the analogies of some known class of binary compounds (which it is easy to suppose possible, and which in some particular instances actually happens);† the universality of binary composi-

[*Cours, Vol. III, p. 81.]

*The force, however, of this last consideration has been much weakened by the progress of discovery since M. Comte left off studying chemistry; it being now probable that most if not all substances, even elementary, are susceptible of *allotropic* forms; as in the case of oxygen and ozone, the two forms of phosphorus, &c.

†Thus; by considering prussic acid as a compound of hydrogen and cyanogen rather than of hydrogen and the elements of cyanogen (carbon and nitrogen), it is assimilated to a whole class of acid compounds between hydrogen and other substances, and a reason is thus found for its agreeing in their acid properties.

*w–w*65   might
*x–x*65,651   intermediate link by which the quaternary compound was resolved into two binary ones
*y–y*65,651   each of them

tion would have been a successful example of an hypothesis in anticipation of a positive theory, to give a direction to inquiry which might end in its being either proved or abandoned. But M. Comte evidently thought that even though it should never be proved—however many cases of chemical composition might always remain in which the theory was still as hypothetical as at first—so long as it was not actually disproved (which it is scarcely in the nature of the case that it should ever be) it would deserve to be retained, for its mere convenience in bringing a large body of phænomena under a general conception. In a *résumé* of the general ᶻprinciplesᶻ of the positive method at the end of the work, he claims, in express terms, an unlimited license of adopting "without any vain scruple" hypothetical conceptions of this sort; "in order to satisfy, within proper limits, our just mental inclinations, which always turn, with an instinctive predilection, towards simplicity, continuity, and generality of conceptions, while always respecting the reality of external laws in so far as accessible to us" (Vol. VI, pp. 639–40). "The most philosophic point of view leads us to conceive the study of natural laws as destined to represent the external world so as to give as much satisfaction to the essential inclinations of our intelligence, as is consistent with the degree of exactitude commanded by the aggregate of our practical wants" (*ibid.*, p. 642). Among these "essential inclinations" he includes not only our "instinctive predilection for order and harmony," [*ibid.*] which makes us relish any conception, even fictitious, that helps to reduce phænomena to system; but even our feelings of taste, "les convenances purement esthétiques," which, he says, have a legitimate part in the employment of the "genre de liberté resté facultatif pour notre intelligence." [*Ibid.*, pp. 646–7.] After the due satisfaction of our "most eminent mental inclinations," there will still remain "a considerable margin of indeterminateness, which should be made use of to give a direct gratification to our *besoin* of ideality, by embellishing our scientific thoughts, without injury to their essential reality" (*ibid.*, p. 647). In consistency with all this, M. Comte warns thinkers against too severe a scrutiny of the exact truth of scientific laws, and stamps with "severe reprobation" those who break down "by too minute an investigation" generalizations already made, without being able to substitute others (*ibid.*, p. 639): as in the case of Lavoisier's general theory of chemistry, which would have made that science more satisfactory than at present to "the instinctive inclinations of our intelligence" if it had turned out true, but unhappily it did not [Vol. III, pp. 131 ff.]. These mental dispositions in M. Comte account for his not having found or sought a logical criterion of proof; but they are scarcely consistent with his inveterate hostility to the hypothesis of the luminiferous ether [Vol. II, p. 302], which certainly gratifies our "predilection for order and harmony," not to say our "besoin d'idéalité," in no ordinary degree. This notion of the "destination" of the study of natural

ᶻ–ᶻ65 principle [*printer's error?*]

laws is to our minds a complete dereliction of the essential principles which form the Positive conception of science; and contained the germ of the perversion of his own philosophy which marked his later years *a* . It might be interesting, but *b*not worth while here*b*, to attempt to penetrate to the just thought which misled M. Comte, for there is almost always a grain of truth in the errors of an original and powerful mind.

There is another grave aberration in M. Comte's view of the method of positive science, which though not more unphilosophical than the last mentioned, is of greater practical importance. He rejects totally, as an invalid process, psychological observation properly so called, or in other words, internal consciousness, at least as regards our intellectual operations. He gives no place in his series *c*to the science of*c* Psychology, and always speaks of it with contempt. The study of mental phænomena, or, as he expresses it, of moral and intellectual functions [Vol. III, p. 530], has a place in his scheme, under the head of Biology, but only as a branch of physiology. Our knowledge of the human mind must, he thinks, be acquired by observing other people. How we are to observe other people's mental operations, or how interpret the signs of them without having learnt what the signs mean by knowledge of ourselves, he does not state. But it is clear to him that we can learn very little about the feelings, and nothing at all about the intellect, by self-observation. Our intelligence can observe all other things, but not itself: we cannot observe ourselves observing, or observe ourselves reasoning: and if we could, attention to this reflex operation would annihilate its object, by stopping the process observed.

There is little need for an elaborate refutation of a fallacy respecting which the only wonder is that it should impose on any one. Two answers may be given to it. In the first place, M. Comte might be referred to experience, and to the writings of his countryman M. Cardaillac and our own Sir William Hamilton, for proof that the mind can not only be conscious of, but attend to, more than one, and even a considerable number, of impressions at once.* It is true that attention is weakened by being divided; and this forms a special difficulty in psychological observation, as psychologists (Sir William Hamilton in particular) have fully recognized; but a difficulty is not an impossibility. Secondly, it might have occurred to M. Comte that a fact may be studied through the medium of memory, not at the very moment of our perceiving it, but the moment after: and this is really the mode in which our

---

*According to Sir William Hamilton, as many as six; but numerical precision in such matters is out of the question, and it is probable that different minds have the power in different degrees. [See Hamilton. *Lectures on Metaphysics and Logic*. Edinburgh: Blackwood, 1859–60, Vol. I, p. 254.]

*a*65   , and which we propose on a future occasion to describe and characterise
*b–b*65,65¹   scarcely worth while
*c–c*65   of the sciences to]   65¹   of the science of [*printer's error?*]

best knowledge of our intellectual acts is generally acquired. We reflect on what we have been doing, when the act is past, but when its impression in the memory is still fresh. Unless in one of these ways, we could not have acquired the knowledge, which nobody denies us to have, of what passes in our minds. M. Comte would scarcely have affirmed that we are not aware of our own intellectual operations. We know of our observings and our reasonings, either at the very time, or by memory the moment after; in either case, by direct knowledge, and not (like things done by us in a state of somnambulism) merely by their results. This simple fact destroys the whole of M. Comte's argument. Whatever we are directly aware of, we can directly observe.

And what Organon for the study of "the moral and intellectual functions" does M. Comte offer, in lieu of the direct mental observation which he repudiates? We are almost ashamed to say, that it is Phrenology! [Vol. III, p. 539 n.] Not, indeed, he says, as a science formed, but as one still to be created; for he rejects almost all the special organs imagined by phrenologists, and accepts only their general division of the brain into the three regions of the propensities, the sentiments, and the intellect,* and the subdivision of the latter region between the organs of meditation and those of observation. Yet this mere first outline of an apportionment of the mental functions among different organs, he regards as extricating the mental study of man from the metaphysical stage, and elevating it to the positive. The condition of mental science would be sad indeed if this were its best chance of being positive; for the later course of physiological observation and speculation has not tended to confirm, but to discredit, the phrenological hypothesis. And even if that hypothesis were true, psychological observation would still be necessary; for how is it possible to ascertain the correspondence between two things, by observation of only one of them? To establish a relation between mental functions and cerebral conformations, requires not only a parallel system of observations applied to each, but (as M. Comte himself, with some inconsistency, acknowledges) an analysis of the mental faculties, "des diverses facultés élémentaires," (Vol. III, p. 573), conducted without any reference to the physical conditions, since the proof of the theory would lie in the correspondence between the division of the brain into organs and that of the mind into faculties, each shown by separate evidence. To accomplish this analysis requires direct psychological study carried to a high pitch of perfection; it being necessary, among other things, to investigate the degree in which mental character is created by circumstances, since no one supposes that cerebral conformation does all, and circumstances nothing. The phrenological study of Mind thus supposes as its necessary preparation the whole of the Association psychology. Without, then, rejecting any aid which study

*Or, as afterwards corrected by him, the appetites and emotions, the active capacities, and the intellectual faculties; "le cœur," "le caractère," and "l'esprit." [Système, Vol. I, pp. 682 ff.]

of the brain and nerves can afford to psychology (and it has afforded, and will yet afford, much), we may affirm that M. Comte has done nothing for the constitution of the positive method of mental science. He refused to profit by the very valuable commencements made by his predecessors, especially by Hartley, Brown, and James Mill (if indeed any of those philosophers were known to him), and left the psychological branch of the positive method, as well as psychology itself, to be put in their true position as a part of Positive Philosophy by successors who duly placed themselves at the twofold point of view of physiology and psychology, Mr. Bain and Mr. Herbert Spencer. This great mistake is not a mere hiatus in M. Comte's system, but the parent of serious errors in his attempt to create a Social Science. He is indeed very skilful in estimating the effect of circumstances in moulding the general character of the human race; were he not, his historical theory could be of little worth: but in appreciating the influence which circumstances exercise, through psychological laws, in producing diversities of character, collective or individual, he is sadly at fault.

After this summary view of M. Comte's conception of Positive Philosophy, it remains to give some account of his more special and equally ambitious attempt to create the Science of Sociology, or, as he expresses it, to elevate the study of social phænomena to the positive state.

He regarded all who profess any political opinions as hitherto divided between the adherents of the theological and those of the metaphysical mode of thought: the former deducing all their doctrines from divine ordinances, the latter from abstractions. This assertion, however, cannot be intended in the same sense as when the terms are applied to the sciences of inorganic nature; for it is impossible that acts evidently proceeding from the human will could be ascribed to the agency (at least immediate) of either divinities or abstractions. No one ever regarded himself or his fellow-man as a mere piece of machinery worked by a god, or as the abode of an entity which was the true author of what the man himself appeared to do. True, it was believed that the gods, or God, could move or change human wills, as well as control their consequences, and prayers were offered to them accordingly, rather as able to overrule the spontaneous course of things, than as at each instant carrying it on. On the whole, however, the theological and metaphysical conceptions, in their application to sociology, had reference not to the production of phænomena, but to the rule of duty, and conduct in life. It is this which was based, either on a divine will, or on abstract mental conceptions, which, by an illusion of the rational faculty, were invested with objective validity. On the one hand, the established rules of morality were everywhere referred to a divine origin. In the majority of countries the entire civil and criminal law was looked upon as revealed from above; and it is to the petty military communities which escaped this delusion, that man is indebted for being now a progressive being. The fundamental institutions of the state were almost everywhere believed to have been divinely established, and to be still, in a greater or less degree, of divine authority. The divine right of certain lines of kings to rule, and even to rule absolutely, was but lately the creed of the dominant party in most countries of Europe; while the divine right of popes and bishops to dictate men's beliefs (and not respecting the invisible world alone) is still striving, though under considerable difficulties, to rule mankind. When these opinions began to be out of date, a rival theory presented itself to take their place. There were, in truth, many such theories, and to some of them the term metaphysical, in M. Comte's sense, cannot justly be applied. All theories in which the ultimate standard of institutions and rules of action was the happiness of mankind, and observation and experience the guides (and some such there have been in all periods of free speculation), are entitled to the name Positive, whatever, in other respects, their imperfections may be. But these were a small minority. M. Comte was right in affirming that the prevailing schools of moral and political speculation, when not theological, have been metaphysical. They affirmed that moral rules, and even political institutions, were not means to an end, the general good, but corollaries evolved from the conception of Natural Rights. This was especially the case in all the countries in which the ideas of publicists were the offspring of the Roman Law. The legislators of opinion on these subjects, when not theologians, were lawyers: and the Continental lawyers followed the Roman jurists, who followed the Greek metaphysicians, in acknowledging as the ultimate source of right and wrong in morals, and consequently in institutions, the imaginary law of the imaginary being Nature. The first systematizers of morals in Christian Europe, on any other than a purely theological basis, the writers on International Law, reasoned wholly from these premises, and transmitted them to a long line of successors. This mode of thought reached its culmination in Rousseau, in whose hands it became as powerful an instrument for destroying the past, as it was impotent for directing the future. The complete victory which this philosophy gained, in speculation, over the old doctrines, was temporarily followed by an equally complete practical triumph, the French Revolution: when, having had, for the first time, a full opportunity of developing its tendencies, and showing what it could not do, it failed so conspicuously as to determine a partial reaction to the doctrines of feudalism and Catholicism. Between these and the political metaphysics (metapolitics as Coleridge called it) [*] of the Revolution, society has since oscillated; raising up in the process a hybrid intermediate party, termed Conservative, or the party of Order, which has no doctrines of its own, but attempts to hold the scales even between the

[*The Friend, Vol. I, p. 309n.]

two others, borrowing alternately the arguments of each, to use as weapons against whichever of the two seems at the moment most likely to prevail.

Such, reduced to a very condensed form, is M. Comte's ᵈversionᵈ of the state of European opinion on politics and society. An Englishman's criticism would be, that it describes well enough the general division of political opinion in France and the countries which follow her lead, but not in England, or the communities of English origin: in all of which, divine right died out with the Jacobites, and the law of nature and natural rights have never been favourites even with the extreme popular party, who preferred to rest their claims on the historical traditions of their own country, and on maxims drawn from its law books, and since they outgrew this standard, almost always base them on general expediency. In England, the preference of one form of government to another seldom turns on anything but the practical consequences which it produces, or which are expected from it. M. Comte can point to little of the nature of metaphysics in English politics, except "la metaphysique constitutionnelle,"[*] a name he chooses to give to the conventional fiction by which the occupant of the throne is supposed to be the source from whence all power emanates, while nothing can be further from the belief or intention of anybody than that such should really be the case. Apart from this, which is a matter of forms and words, and has no connexion with any belief except belief in the proprieties, the severest criticism can find nothing either worse or better, in the modes of thinking either of our conservative or of our liberal party, than a particularly shallow and flimsy kind of positivism. The working classes indeed, or some portion of them, perhaps still rest their claim to universal suffrage on abstract right, in addition to more substantial reasons, and thus far and no farther does metaphysics prevail in the region of English politics. But politics is not the ᵉentireᵉ art of social existence: ethics is ᶠa stillᶠ deeper and more vital part of it: and in that, as much in England as elsewhere, the current opinions are still divided between the theological mode of thought and the metaphysical. What is the whole doctrine of Intuitive Morality, which reigns supreme wherever the idolatry of Scripture texts has abated and the influence of Bentham's philosophy has not reached, but the metaphysical state of ethical science? What else, indeed, is the whole à priori philosophy, in morals, jurisprudence, psychology, logic, even physical science, for it does not always keep its hands off that, the oldest domain of observation and experiment? It has the universal diagnostic of the metaphysical mode of thought, in the Comtean sense of the word; that of erecting a mere creation of the mind into a test or *norma* of external truth, and presenting the abstract expression of the beliefs already entertained, as the

[*Cours, Vol. IV, p. 86.]

ᵈ–ᵈ65   exposition
ᵉ–ᵉ65   whole   ᶠ–ᶠ65   still a [*printer's error?*]

reason and evidence which justifies them. Of those who still adhere to the old opinions we need not speak; but when one of the most vigorous as well as boldest thinkers that English speculation has yet produced, full of the true scientific spirit, Mr. Herbert Spencer, places in the front of his philosophy the doctrine that the ultimate test of the truth of a proposition is the inconceivableness of its negative; when, following in the steps of Mr. Spencer, an able expounder of positive philosophy like Mr. Lewes, in his meritorious and by no means superficial work on Aristotle, after laying, very justly, the blame of almost every error of the ancient thinkers on their neglecting to *verify* their opinions, announces that there are two kinds of verification, the Real and the Ideal, the ideal test of truth being that its negative is unthinkable, and by the application of that test judges that gravitation must be universal even in the stellar regions, because in the absence of proof to the contrary, "the idea of matter without gravity is unthinkable;"[*]—when those from whom it was least to be expected thus set up acquired necessities of thought in the minds of one or two generations as evidence of real necessities in the universe, we must admit that the metaphysical mode of thought still rules the higher philosophy, even in the department of inorganic nature, and far more in all that relates to man as a moral, intellectual, and social being.

But, while M. Comte is so far in the right, we often, as already intimated, find him using the name metaphysical to denote certain practical conclusions, instead of a particular kind of theoretical premises. Whatever goes by the different names of the revolutionary, the radical, the democratic, the liberal, the free-thinking, the sceptical, or the negative and critical school or party in religion, politics, or philosophy, all passes with him under the designation of metaphysical, and whatever he has to say about it forms part of his description of the metaphysical school of social science. He passes in review, one after another, what he deems the leading doctrines of the revolutionary school of politics, and dismisses them all as mere instruments of attack upon the old social system, with no permanent validity as social truth.

He assigns only this humble rank to the first of all the articles of the liberal creed, "the absolute right of free examination, or the dogma of unlimited liberty of conscience."[†] As far as this doctrine only means that opinions, and their expression, should be exempt from *legal* restraint, either in the form of prevention or of penalty, M. Comte is a firm adherent of it: but the *moral* right of every human being, however ill-prepared by the necessary instruction and discipline, to erect himself into a judge of the most intricate as well as the most important questions that can occupy the human intellect, he resolutely denies. "There is no liberty of conscience," he said in

[*George Henry Lewes. *Aristotle: A Chapter from the History of Science.* London: Smith, Elder, 1864, p. 126.]

[†*Cours*, Vol. IV, p. 43.]

302   ESSAYS ON ETHICS, RELIGION AND SOCIETY

an early work, "in astronomy, in physics, in chemistry, even in physiology, in the sense that every one would think it absurd not to accept in confidence the principles established in those sciences by the competent persons. If it is otherwise in politics, the reason is merely because, the old doctrines having gone by and the new ones not being yet formed, there are not properly, during the interval, any established opinions."[*] When first mankind outgrew the old doctrines, an appeal from doctors and teachers to the outside public was inevitable and indispensable, since without the toleration and encouragement of discussion and criticism from all quarters, it would have been impossible for any new doctrines to grow up. But in itself, the practice of carrying the questions which more than all others require special knowledge and preparation, before the incompetent tribunal of common opinion, is, he contends, radically irrational, and will and ought to cease when once mankind have again made up their minds to a system of doctrine. The prolongation of this provisional state, producing an ever-increasing divergence of opinions, is already, according to him, extremely dangerous, since it is only when there is a tolerable unanimity respecting the rule of life, that a real moral control can be established over the self-interest and passions of individuals. Besides which, when every man is encouraged to believe himself a competent judge of the most difficult social questions, he cannot be prevented from thinking himself competent also to the most important public duties, and the baneful competition for power and official functions spreads constantly downwards to a lower and lower grade of intelligence. In M. Comte's opinion, the peculiarly complicated nature of sociological studies, and the great amount of previous knowledge and intellectual discipline requisite for them, together with the serious consequences that may be produced by even temporary errors on such subjects, render it necessary in the case of ethics and politics, still more than of mathematics and physics, that whatever legal liberty may exist of questioning and discussing, the opinions of mankind should really be formed for them by an exceedingly small number of minds of the highest class, trained to the task by the most thorough and laborious mental preparation: and that the questioning of their conclusions by any one, not of an equivalent grade of intellect and instruction, should be accounted equally presumptuous, and more blamable, than the attempts occasionally made by sciolists to refute the Newtonian astronomy. All this is, in a sense, true: but we confess our sympathy with those who feel towards it like the man in the story, who being asked whether he admitted that six and five make eleven, refused to give an answer until he knew what use was to be made of it. The doctrine is one of a class of truths which, unless completed by other truths, are so liable to perversion, that we may fairly decline

[*Système de politique positive. Paris: Saint-Simon, 1824, p. 14.]

to take notice of them except in connexion with some definite application. In justice to M. Comte it should be said that he does not wish this intellectual dominion to be exercised over an ignorant people. Far from him is the thought of promoting the allegiance of the mass to scientific authority by withholding from them scientific knowledge. He holds it the duty of society to bestow on every one who grows up to manhood or womanhood as complete a course of instruction in every department of science, from mathematics to sociology, as can possibly be made general: and his ideas of what is possible in that respect are carried to a length to which few are prepared to follow him. There is something startling, though, when closely looked into, not Utopian or chimerical, in the amount of positive knowledge of the most varied kind which he believes may, by good methods of teaching, be made the common inheritance of all persons with ordinary faculties who are born into the world: not the mere knowledge of results, to which, except for the practical arts, he attaches only secondary value, but knowledge also of the mode in which those results were attained, and the evidence on which they rest, so far as it can be known and understood by those who do not devote their lives to its study.

We have stated thus fully M. Comte's opinion on the most fundamental doctrine of liberalism, because it is the clue to much of his general conception of politics. If his object had only been to exemplify by that doctrine the purely negative character of the principal liberal and revolutionary schools of thought, he need not have gone so far: it would have been enough to say, that the mere liberty to hold and express any creed, cannot itself *be* that creed. Every one is free to believe and publish that two and two make ten, but the important thing is to know that they make four. M. Comte has no difficulty in making out an equally strong case against the other principal tenets of what he calls the revolutionary school; since all that they generally amount to is, that something ought not to be: which cannot possibly be the whole truth, and which M. Comte, in general, will not admit to be even part of it. Take for instance the doctrine which denies to governments any initiative in social progress, restricting them to the function of preserving order, or in other words keeping the peace: an opinion which, so far as grounded on so-called rights of the individual, he justly regards as purely metaphysical; but does not recognize that it is also widely held as an inference from the laws of human nature and human affairs, and therefore, whether true or false, as a Positive doctrine. Believing with M. Comte that there are no absolute truths in the political art, nor indeed in any art whatever, we agree with him that the *laisser faire* doctrine, stated without large qualifications, is both unpractical and unscientific; but it does not follow that those who assert it are not, nineteen times out of twenty, practically nearer the truth than those who deny it. The doctrine of Equality meets no better fate at M. Comte's hands. He regards it as the erection into an absolute dogma of a mere protest against the inequalities which came down from the middle ages, and ᵍanswerᵍ no legitimate end in modern society. He observes, that mankind in a normal state, having to act together, are necessarily, in practice, organized and classed with some reference to their unequal aptitudes, natural or acquired, which demand that some should be under the direction of others: scrupulous regard being at the same time had to the fulfilment towards all, of "the claims rightfully inherent in the dignity of a human being; the aggregate of which, still very insufficiently appreciated, will constitute more and more the principle of universal morality as applied to daily use. . . . . a grand moral obligation, which has never been directly denied since the abolition of slavery" (Vol. IV, p. 54). There is not a word to be said against these doctrines: but the practical question is one which M. Comte never even entertains—viz., when, after being properly educated, people are left to find their places for themselves, do they not spontaneously class themselves in a manner much more conformable to their unequal or dissimilar aptitudes, than governments or social institutions are likely to do it for them? The Sovereignty of the People, again,— that metaphysical axiom which in France and the rest of the Continent has so long been the theoretic basis of radical and democratic politics,—he regards as of a purely negative character, signifying the right of the people to rid themselves by insurrection of a social order that has become oppressive; but, when erected into a positive principle of government, which condemns indefinitely all superiors to "an arbitrary dependence upon the multitude of their inferiors," he considers it as a sort of "transportation to ʰpeoplesʰ of the divine right so much reproached to kings" (*ibid.*, pp. 55–6). On the doctrine as a metaphysical dogma or an absolute principle, this criticism is just; but there is also a Positive doctrine, without any pretension to being absolute, which claims the direct participation of the governed in their own government, not as a natural right, but as a means to important ends, under the conditions and with the limitations which those ends impose. The general result of M. Comte's criticism on the revolutionary philosophy, is that he deems it not only incapable of aiding the necessary reorganization of society, but a serious impediment thereto, by setting up, on all the great interests of mankind, the mere negation of authority, direction, or organization, as the most perfect state, and the solution of all problems: the extreme point of this aberration being reached by Rousseau and his followers, when they extolled the savage state, as an ideal from which civilization was only a degeneracy, more or less marked and complete.

The state of sociological speculation being such as has been described— divided between a feudal and theological school, now effete, and a demo-

ᵍ–ᵍ65   answered   ʰ–ʰ65   people [*plural in Comte*]

cratic and metaphysical one, of no value except for the destruction of the former; the problem, how to render the social science positive, must naturally have presented itself, more or less distinctly, to superior minds. M. Comte examines and criticises, for the most part justly, some of the principal efforts which have been made by individual thinkers for this purpose. But the weak side of his philosophy comes out prominently in his strictures on the only systematic attempt yet made by any body of thinkers, to constitute a science, not indeed of social phænomena generally, but of one great class or division of them. We mean, of course, political economy, which (with a reservation in favour of the speculations of Adam Smith as valuable preparatory studies for science) he deems unscientific, unpositive, and a mere branch of metaphysics, that comprehensive category of condemnation in which he places all attempts at positive science which are not in his opinion directed by a right scientific method. Any one acquainted with the writings of political economists need only read his few pages of animadversions on them (Vol. IV, pp. 193–205), to learn how extremely superficial M. Comte can sometimes be. He affirms that they have added nothing really new to the original *aperçus* of Adam Smith; when every one who has read them knows that they have added so much as to have changed the whole aspect of the science, besides rectifying and clearing up in the most essential points the *aperçus* themselves. He lays an almost puerile stress, for the purpose of disparagement, on the discussions about the meaning of words which are found in the best books on political economy, as if such discussions were not an indispensable accompaniment of the progress of thought, and abundant in the history of every physical science. On the whole question he has but one remark of any value, and that he misapplies; namely, that the study of the conditions of national wealth as a detached subject is unphilosophical, because, all the different aspects of social phænomena acting and reacting on one another, they cannot be rightly understood apart: which by no means proves that the material and industrial phænomena of society are not, even by themselves, susceptible of useful generalizations, but only that these generalizations must necessarily be relative to a given form of civilization and a given stage of social advancement. This, we apprehend, is what no political economist would deny. None of them pretend that the laws of wages, profits, values, prices, and the like, set down in their treatises, would be *i*strictly true, or many of them true at all,*i* in the savage state (for example), or in a community composed of masters and slaves. But they do think, with good reason, that whoever understands the political economy of a country with the complicated and manifold civilization of the nations of Europe, can deduce without difficulty the political economy of any other state of society, with

*i-i*65   true

the particular circumstances of which he is equally well acquainted.* We do not pretend that political economy has never been prosecuted or taught in a contracted spirit. As often as a study is cultivated by narrow minds, they will draw from it narrow conclusions. If a political economist is deficient in general knowledge, he will exaggerate the importance and universality of the limited class of truths which he knows. All kinds of scientific men are liable to this imputation, and M. Comte is never weary of urging it against them; reproaching them with their narrowness of mind, the petty scale of their thoughts, their incapacity for large views, and the stupidity of those they occasionally attempt beyond the bounds of their own subjects. Political economists do not deserve these reproaches more than other classes of positive inquirers, but less than most. The principal error of narrowness with which they are frequently chargeable, is that of regarding, not any economical doctrine, but their present experience of mankind, as of universal validity; mistaking temporary or local phases of human character for human nature itself; having no faith in the wonderful pliability of the human mind; deeming it impossible, in spite of the strongest evidence, that the earth can produce human beings of a different type from that which is familiar to them in their own age, or even, perhaps, in their own country. The only security against this narrowness is a liberal mental cultivation, and all it proves is that a person is not likely to be a good political economist who is nothing else.

Thus far, we have had to do with M. Comte, as a sociologist, only in his critical capacity. We have now to deal with him as a constructor—the author of a sociological system. The first question is that of the Method proper to the study. His view of this is highly instructive.

The Method proper to the Science of Society must be, in substance, the same as in all other sciences; the interrogation and interpretation of experience, by the twofold process of Induction and Deduction. But its mode of practising these operations has features of peculiarity. In general, Induction furnishes to science the laws of the elementary facts, from which, when known, those of the complex combinations are thought out deductively: specific observation of complex phænomena yields no general laws, or only empirical ones; its scientific function is to verify the laws obtained by deduc-

---

*M. Littré, who, though a warm admirer, and accepting the position of a disciple of M. Comte, is singularly free from his errors, makes the equally ingenious and just remark, that Political Economy corresponds in social science to the theory of the nutritive functions in biology, which M. Comte, with all good physiologists, thinks it not only permissible but a great and fundamental improvement to treat, in the first place, separately, as the necessary basis of the higher branches of the science: although the nutritive functions can no more be withdrawn in fact from the influence of the animal and human attributes, than the economical phænomena of society from that of the political and moral. [See Littré, Comte, p. 674.]

tion. This mode of philosophizing is not adequate to the exigencies of sociological investigation. In social phænomena the elementary facts are feelings and actions, and the laws of these are the laws of human nature, social facts being the results of human acts and situations. Since, then, the phænomena of man in society result from his nature as an individual being, it might be thought that the proper mode of constructing a positive Social Science must be by deducing it from the general laws of human nature, using the facts of history merely for verification. Such, accordingly, has been the conception of social science by many of those who have endeavoured to render it positive, particularly by the school of Bentham. M. Comte considers this as an error. We may, he says, draw from the universal laws of human nature some conclusions (though even these, we think, rather precarious) concerning the very earliest stages of human progress, of which there are either no, or very imperfect, historical records. But as society proceeds in its development, its phænomena are determined, more and more, not by the simple tendencies of universal human nature, but by the accumulated influence of past generations over the present. The human beings themselves, on the laws of whose nature the facts of history depend, are not abstract or universal but historical human beings, already shaped, and made what they are, by human society. This being the case, no powers of deduction could enable any one, starting from the mere conception of the Being Man, placed in a world such as the earth may have been before the commencement of human agency, to predict and calculate the phænomena of his development such as they have in fact proved. If the facts of history, empirically considered, had not given rise to any generalizations, a deductive study of history could never have reached higher than more or less plausible conjecture. By good fortune (for the case might easily have been otherwise) the history of our species, looked at as a comprehensive whole, does exhibit a determinate course, a certain order of development: though history alone cannot prove this to be a necessary law, as distinguished from a temporary accident. Here, therefore, begins the office of Biology (or, as we should say, of Psychology) in the social science. The universal laws of human nature are part of the data of sociology, but in using them we must reverse the method of the deductive physical sciences: for while, in these, specific experience commonly serves to verify laws arrived at by deduction, in sociology it is specific experience which suggests the laws, and deduction which verifies them. If a sociological theory, collected from historical evidence, contradicts the established general laws of human nature; if (to use M. Comte's instances) it implies, in the mass of mankind, any very decided natural bent, either in a good or in a bad direction; if it supposes that the reason, in average human beings, predominates over the desires, or the disinterested desires over the personal; we may know that history has been misinterpreted, and that the theory is false. On the other hand, if laws of social phænomena, empirically generalized from history, can when once suggested be affiliated to the known laws of human nature; if the direction actually taken by the developments and changes of human society, can be seen to be such as the properties of man and of his dwelling-place made antecedently probable, the empirical generalizations are raised into positive laws, and Sociology becomes a science.

Much has been said and written for centuries past, by the practical or empirical school of politicians, in condemnation of theories founded on principles of human nature, without an historical basis; and the theorists, in their turn, have successfully retaliated on the practicalists. But we know not any thinker who, before M. Comte, had penetrated to the philosophy of the matter, and placed the necessity of historical studies as the foundation of sociological speculation on the true footing. From this time any political thinker who fancies himself able to dispense with a connected view of the great facts of history, as a chain of causes and effects, must be regarded as below the level of the age; while the vulgar mode of using history, by looking in it for parallel cases, as if any cases were parallel, or as if a single instance, or even many instances not compared and analyzed, could reveal a law, will be more than ever, and irrevocably, discredited.

The inversion of the ordinary relation between Deduction and Induction is not the only point in which, according to M. Comte, the Method proper to Sociology differs from that of the sciences of inorganic nature. The common order of science proceeds from the details to the whole. The method of Sociology should proceed from the whole to the details. There is no universal principle for the order of study, but that of proceeding from the known to the unknown; finding our way to the facts at whatever point is most open to our observation. In the phænomena of the social state, the collective phænomenon is more accessible to us than the parts of which it is composed. This is already, in a great degree, true of the mere animal body. It is essential to the idea of an organism, and it is even more true of the social organism than of the individual. The state of every part of the social whole at any time, is intimately connected with the contemporaneous state of all the others. Religious belief, philosophy, science, the fine arts, the industrial arts, commerce, navigation, government, all are in close mutual dependence on one another, insomuch that when any considerable change takes place in one, we may know that a parallel change in all the others has preceded or will follow it. The progress of society from one general state to another is not an aggregate of partial changes, but the product of a single impulse, acting through all the partial agencies, and can therefore be most easily traced by studying them together. Could it even be detected in them separately, its true nature could not be understood except by examining them in the *ensemble*. In constructing, therefore, a theory of society, all the different aspects of the social organization must be taken into consideration at once.

Our space is not consistent with inquiring into all the limitations of this doctrine. It requires many of which M. Comte's theory takes no account. There is one, in particular, dependent on a scientific artifice familiar to students of science, especially of the applications of mathematics to the study of nature. When an effect depends on several variable conditions, some of which change less, or more slowly, than others, we are often able to determine, either by reasoning or by experiment, what would be the law of variation of the effect if its changes depended only on some of the conditions, the remainder being supposed constant. The law so found will be sufficiently near the truth for all times and places in which the latter set of conditions do not vary greatly, and will be a basis to set out from when it becomes necessary to allow for the variations of those conditions also. Most of the conclusions of social science applicable to practical use are of this description. M. Comte's system makes no room for them. We have seen how he deals with the part of them which are the most scientific in character, the generalizations of political economy.

There is one more point in the general philosophy of sociology requiring notice. Social phænomena, like all others, present two aspects, the statical, and the dynamical; the phænomena of equilibrium, and those of motion. The statical aspect is that of the laws of social existence, considered abstractedly from progress, and confined to what is common to the progressive and the stationary state. The dynamical aspect is that of social progress. The statics of society is the study of the conditions of existence and permanence of the social state. The dynamics studies the laws of its evolution. The first is the theory of the *consensus*, or interdependence of social phænomena. The second is the theory of their filiation.

The first division M. Comte, in his great work, treats in a much more summary manner than the second; and it forms, to our thinking, the weakest part of the treatise. He can hardly have seemed even to himself to have originated, in the statics of society, anything new,* unless his revival of the Catholic idea of a Spiritual Power may be so considered. The remainder, with the exception of detached thoughts, in which even his feeblest productions are always rich, is trite, while in our judgment far from being always true.

He begins by a statement of the general properties of human nature which

*Indeed his claim to be the creator of Sociology does not extend to this branch of the science; on the contrary, he, in a subsequent work [*Système*, Vol. II, p. 351], expressly declares that the real founder of it was Aristotle, by whom the theory of the conditions of social existence was carried as far towards perfection as was possible in the absence of any theory of Progress. Without going quite this length, we think it hardly possible to appreciate too highly the merit of those early efforts, beyond which little progress had been made, until a very recent period, either in ethical or in political science.

make social existence possible. Man has a spontaneous propensity to the society of his fellow-beings, and seeks it instinctively, for its own sake, and not out of regard to the advantages it procures for him, which, in many conditions of humanity, must appear to him very problematical. Man has also a certain, though moderate, amount of natural benevolence. On the other hand, these social propensities are by nature weaker than his selfish ones; and the social state, being mainly kept in existence through the former, involves an habitual antagonism between the two. Further, our wants of all kinds, from the purely organic upwards, can only be satisfied by means of labour, nor does bodily labour suffice, without the guidance of intelligence. But labour, especially when prolonged and monotonous, is naturally hateful, and mental labour the most irksome of all; and hence a second antagonism, which must exist in all societies whatever. The character of the society is principally determined by the degree in which the better incentive, in each of these cases, makes head against the worse. In both the points, human nature is capable of great amelioration. The social instincts may approximate much nearer to the strength of the personal ones, though never entirely coming up to it; the aversion to labour in general, and to intellectual labour in particular, may be much weakened, and the predominance of the inclinations over the reason greatly diminished, though never completely destroyed. The spirit of improvement results from the increasing strength of the social instincts, combined with the growth of an intellectual activity, which guiding the personal propensities, inspires each individual with a deliberate desire to improve his condition. The personal instincts left to their own guidance, and the indolence and apathy natural to mankind, are the sources which mainly feed the spirit of Conservation. The struggle between the two spirits is an universal incident of the social state.

The next of the universal elements in human society is family life; which M. Comte regards as originally the sole, and always the principal, source of the social feelings, and the only school open to mankind in general, in which unselfishness can be learnt, and the feelings and conduct demanded by social relations be made habitual. M. Comte takes this opportunity of declaring his opinions on the proper constitution of the family, and in particular of the marriage institution. They are of the most orthodox and conservative sort. M. Comte adheres not only to the popular Christian, but to the Catholic view of marriage in its utmost strictness, and rebukes Protestant nations for having tampered with the indissolubility of the engagement, by permitting divorce. He admits that the marriage institution has been, in various respects, beneficially modified with the advance of society, and that we may not yet have reached the last of these modifications; but strenuously maintains that such changes cannot possibly affect what he regards as the essential principles of the institution—the irrevocability of the engagement, and the complete subordination of the wife to the husband, and of women generally to men; which are precisely the great vulnerable points of the existing constitution of society on this important subject. It is unpleasant to have to say it of a philosopher, but the incidents of his life which have been made public by his biographers afford an explanation of one of these two opinions: he had quarrelled with his wife.* At a later period, under the influence of circumstances equally personal, his opinions and feelings respecting women were very much modified, without becoming more rational: in his final scheme of society, instead of being treated as grown children, they were exalted into goddesses: honours, privileges, and immunities, were lavished on them, only not simple justice. On the other question, the irrevocability of marriage, M. Comte must receive credit for impartiality, since the opposite doctrine would have better suited his personal convenience: but we can give him no other credit, for his argument is not only futile but refutes itself. He says that with liberty of divorce, life would be spent in a constant succession of experiments and failures; and in the same breath congratulates himself on the fact, that modern manners and sentiments have in the main prevented the baneful effects which the toleration of divorce in Protestant countries might have been expected to produce. He did not perceive that if modern habits and feelings have successfully resisted what he deems the tendency of a less rigorous marriage law, it must be because modern habits and feelings are inconsistent with the perpetual series of new trials which he dreaded. If there are tendencies in human nature which seek change and variety, there are others which demand fixity, in matters which touch the daily sources of happiness; and one who had studied history as much as M. Comte, ought to have known that ever since the nomad mode of life was exchanged for the agricultural, the latter tendencies have been always gaining ground on the former. All experience testifies that regularity in domestic relations is almost in direct proportion to industrial civilization. Idle life, and military life with its long intervals of idleness, are the conditions to which either sexual profligacy, or prolonged vagaries of imagination on that subject, are congenial. Busy men have no time for them, and have too much other occupation for their thoughts: they require that home should be a place of rest, not of incessantly renewed excitement and disturbance. In the condition, therefore, into which modern society has passed, there is no probability that marriages would often be contracted without a sincere desire on both sides that they should be permanent. That this has been the case hitherto in countries where divorce was permitted, we have on M. Comte's own showing: and everything

---

*It is due to them both to say, that he continued to express, in letters which have been published, a high opinion of her, both morally and intellectually; and her persistent and strong concern for his interests and his fame is attested both by M. Littré and by his own correspondence. [See Littré, *Comte*, pp. 466 ff.]

leads us to believe that the power, if granted elsewhere, would in general be used only for its legitimate purpose—for enabling those who, by a blameless or excusable mistake, have lost their first throw for domestic happiness, to free themselves (with due regard for all interests concerned) from the burthensome yoke, and try, under more favourable auspices, another chance. Any further discussion of these great social questions would evidently be incompatible with the nature and limits of the present paper.

Lastly, a phænomenon universal in all societies, and constantly assuming a wider extension as they advance in their progress, is the co-operation of mankind one with another, by the division of employments and interchange of commodities and services; a communion which extends to nations as well as individuals. The economic importance of this spontaneous organization of mankind as joint workers with and for one another, has often been illustrated. Its moral effects, in connecting them by their interests, and as a more remote consequence, by their sympathies, are equally salutary. But there are some things to be said on the other side. The increasing specialization of all employments; the division of mankind into innumerable small fractions, each engrossed by an extremely minute fragment of the business of society, is not without inconveniences, as well moral as intellectual, which, if they could not be remedied, would be a serious abatement from the benefits of advanced civilization. The interests of the whole—the bearings of things on the ends of the social union—are less and less present to the minds of men who have so contracted a sphere of activity. The insignificant detail which forms their whole occupation—the infinitely minute wheel they help to turn in the machinery of society—does not arouse or gratify any feeling of public spirit, or unity with their fellow-men. Their work is a mere tribute to physical necessity, not the glad performance of a social office. This lowering effect of the extreme division of labour tells most of all on those who are set up as the lights and teachers of the rest. A man's mind is as fatally narrowed, and his feelings towards the great ends of humanity as miserably stunted, by giving all his thoughts to the classification of a few insects or the resolution of a few equations, as to sharpening the points or putting on the heads of pins. The "dispersive speciality"[*] of the present race of scientific men, who, unlike their predecessors, have a positive aversion to enlarged views, and seldom either know or care for any of the interests of mankind beyond the narrow limits of their pursuit, is dwelt on by M. Comte as one of the great and growing evils of the time, and the one which most retards moral and intellectual regeneration. To contend against it is one of the main purposes towards which he thinks the forces of society should be directed. The obvious remedy is a large and liberal general education, preparatory to all special pursuits: and this is M. Comte's opinion: but the education of youth

[*Cours, Vol. IV, p. 430.]

is not in his estimation enough: he requires an agency set apart for obtruding upon all classes of persons through the whole of life, the paramount claims of the general interest, and the comprehensive ideas that demonstrate the mode in which human actions promote or impair it. In other words, he demands a moral and intellectual authority, charged with the duty of guiding men's opinions and enlightening and warning their consciences; a Spiritual Power, whose judgments on all matters of high moment should deserve, and receive, the same universal respect and deference which is paid to the united ʲjudg-mentʲ of astronomers in matters astronomical. The very idea of such an authority implies that an unanimity has been attained, at least in essentials, among moral and political thinkers, corresponding or approaching to that which already exists in the other sciences. There cannot be this unanimity, until the true methods of positive science have been applied to all subjects, as completely as they have been applied to the study of physical science: to this, however, there is no real obstacle; and when once it is accomplished, the same degree of accordance will naturally follow. The undisputed authority which astronomers possess in astronomy, will be possessed on the great social questions by Positive Philosophers; to whom will belong the spiritual government of society, subject to two conditions: that they be entirely inde-pendent, within their own sphere, of the temporal government, and that they be peremptorily excluded from all share in it, receiving instead the entire conduct of education.

This is the leading feature in M. Comte's conception of a regenerated society; and however much this ideal differs from that which is implied more or less confusedly in the negative philosophy of the last three centuries, we hold the amount of truth in the two to be about the same. M. Comte has got hold of half the truth, and the so-called liberal or revolutionary school pos-sesses the other half; each sees what the other does not see, and seeing it exclusively, draws consequences from it which to the other appear mis-chievously absurd. It is, without doubt, the necessary condition of mankind to receive most of their opinions on the authority of those who have specially studied the matters to which they relate. The wisest can act on no other rule, on subjects with which they are not themselves thoroughly conversant; and the mass of mankind have always done the like on all the great subjects of thought and conduct, acting with implicit confidence on opinions of which they did not know, and were often incapable of understanding, the grounds, but on which as long as their natural guides were unanimous they fully relied, growing uncertain and sceptical only when these became divided, and teachers who as far as they could judge were equally competent, professed contradictory opinions. Any doctrines which come recommended by the nearly universal verdict of instructed minds will no doubt continue to be, as

ʲ–ʲ65   judgments [*printer's error?*]

they have hitherto been, accepted without misgiving by the rest. The difference is, that with the wide diffusion of scientific education among the whole people, demanded by M. Comte, their faith, however implicit, would not be that of ignorance: it would not be the blind submission of dunces to men of knowledge, but the intelligent deference of those who know much, to those who know still more. It is those who have some knowledge of astronomy, not those who have none at all, who best appreciate how prodigiously more Lagrange or Laplace knew than themselves. This is what can be said in favour of M. Comte. On the contrary side it is to be said, that in order that this salutary ascendancy over opinion should be exercised by the most eminent thinkers, it is not necessary that they should be associated and organized. The ascendancy will come of itself when the unanimity is attained, without which it is neither desirable nor possible. It is because astronomers agree in their teaching that astronomy is trusted, and not because there is an Academy of Sciences or a Royal Society issuing decrees or passing resolutions. A constituted moral authority can only be required when the object is not merely to promulgate and diffuse principles of conduct, but to direct the detail of their application; to declare and inculcate, not duties, but each person's duty, as was attempted by the spiritual authority of the middle ages. From this extreme application of his principle M. Comte does not shrink. A function of this sort, no doubt, may often be very usefully discharged by individual members of the speculative class; but if entrusted to any organized body, would involve nothing less than a spiritual despotism. This however is what M. Comte really contemplated, though it would practically nullify that peremptory separation of the spiritual from the temporal power, which he justly deemed essential to a wholesome state of society. Those whom an irresistible public opinion invested with the right to dictate or control the acts of rulers, though without the means of backing their advice by force, would have all the real power of the temporal authorities, without their labours or their responsibilities. M. Comte would probably have answered that the temporal rulers, having the whole legal power in their hands, would certainly not pay to the spiritual authority more than a very limited obedience: which amounts to saying that the ideal form of society which he sets up, is only fit to be an ideal because it cannot possibly be realized.

That education should be practically directed by the philosophic class, when there is a philosophic class who have made good their claim to the place in opinion hitherto filled by the clergy, would be natural and indispensable. But that all education should be in the hands of a centralized authority, whether composed of clergy or of philosophers, and be consequently all framed on the same model, and directed to the perpetuation of the same type, is a state of things which instead of becoming more acceptable, will assuredly be more repugnant to mankind, with every step of their progress in the unfettered exercise of their highest faculties. We shall see, ^{k}in the Second Part^k, the evils with which the conception of the new Spiritual Power is pregnant, coming out into full bloom in the more complete development which M. Comte gave to the idea in his later years.

After this unsatisfactory attempt to trace the outline of Social Statics, M. Comte passes to a topic on which he is much more at home—the subject of his most eminent speculations; Social Dynamics, or the laws of the evolution of human society.

Two questions meet us at the outset: Is there a natural evolution in human affairs? and is that evolution an improvement? M. Comte resolves them both in the affirmative by the same answer. The natural progress of society consists in the growth of our human attributes, comparatively to our animal and our purely organic ones: the progress of our humanity towards an ascendancy over our animality, ever more nearly approached though incapable of being completely realized. This is the character and tendency of human development, or of what is called civilization; and the obligation of seconding this movement—of working in the direction of it—is the nearest approach which M. Comte makes in this treatise to a general principle or standard of morality.

But as our more eminent, and peculiarly human, faculties are of various orders, moral, intellectual, and æsthetic, the question presents itself, is there any one of these whose development is the predominant agency in the evolution of our species? According to M. Comte, the main agent in the progress of mankind is their intellectual development. Not because the intellectual is the most powerful part of our nature, for, limited to its inherent strength, it is one of the weakest: but because it is the guiding part, and acts not with its own strength alone, but with the united force of all parts of our nature which it can draw after it. In a social state the feelings and propensities cannot act with their full power, in a determinate direction, unless the speculative intellect places itself at their head. The passions are, in the individual man, a more energetic power than a mere intellectual conviction; but the passions tend to divide, not to unite, mankind: it is only by a common belief that passions are brought to work together, and become a collective force instead of forces neutralizing one another. Our intelligence is first awakened by the stimulus of our animal wants and of our stronger and coarser desires; and these for a long time almost exclusively determine the direction in which our intelligence shall work: but once roused to activity, it assumes more and more the management of the operations of which stronger impulses are the prompters, and constrains them to follow its lead, not by its own strength, but because in the play of antagonistic forces, the path it points out is (in scientific phraseology) the direction of least resistance. Personal interests

$^{k-k}$65   on a future occasion

and feelings, in the social state, can only obtain the maximum of satisfaction by means of co-operation, and the necessary condition of co-operation is a common belief. All human society, consequently, is grounded on a system of fundamental opinions, which only the speculative faculty can provide, and which, when provided, directs our other impulses in their mode of seeking their gratification. And hence the history of opinions, and of the speculative faculty, has always been the leading element in the history of mankind.

This doctrine has been combated by Mr. Herbert Spencer, in the pamphlet already referred to; and we will quote, in his own words, the theory he propounds in opposition to it:—

Ideas do not govern and overthrow the world; the world is governed or overthrown by feelings, to which ideas serve only as guides. The social mechanism does not rest finally upon opinions, but almost wholly upon character. Not intellectual anarchy, but moral antagonism, is the cause of political crises. All social phænomena are produced by the totality of human emotions and beliefs, of which the emotions are mainly predetermined, while the beliefs are mainly postdetermined. Men's desires are chiefly inherited; but their beliefs are chiefly acquired, and depend on surrounding conditions; and the most important surrounding conditions depend on the social state which the prevalent desires have produced. The social state at any time existing, is the resultant of all the ambitions, self-interest, fears, reverences, indignations, sympathies, &c., of ancestral citizens and existing citizens. The ideas current in this social state must, on the average, be congruous with the feelings of citizens, and therefore, on the average, with the social state these feelings have produced. Ideas wholly foreign to this social state cannot be evolved, and if introduced from without, cannot get accepted—or, if accepted, die out when the temporary phase of feeling which caused their acceptance ends. Hence, though advanced ideas, when once established, act upon society and aid its further advance, yet the establishment of such ideas depends on the fitness of society for receiving them. Practically, the popular character and the social state determine what ideas shall be current; instead of the current ideas determining the social state and the character. The modification of men's moral natures, caused by the continuous discipline of social life, which adapts them more and more to social relations, is therefore the chief proximate cause of social progress.*

A great part of these statements would have been acknowledged as true by M. Comte, and belong as much to his theory as to Mr. Spencer's. The re-action of all other mental and social elements upon the intellectual not only is fully recognized by him, but his philosophy of history makes great use of it, pointing out that the principal intellectual changes could not have taken place unless changes in other elements of society had preceded; but also showing that these were themselves consequences of prior intellectual changes. It will not be found, on a fair examination of what M. Comte has written, that he has overlooked any of the truth that there is in Mr. Spencer's

*Of the Classification of the Sciences, pp. 37–8.

theory. He would not indeed have said (what Mr. Spencer apparently wishes us to say) that the effects which can be historically traced, for example to religion, were not produced by the belief in God, but by reverence and fear of him. He would have said that the reverence and fear presuppose the belief: that a God must be believed in before he can be feared or reverenced. The whole influence of the belief in a God upon society and civilization, depends on the powerful human sentiments which are ready to attach themselves to the belief; and yet the sentiments are only a social force at all, through the definite direction given to them by that or some other intellectual conviction; nor did the sentiments spontaneously throw up the belief in a God, since in themselves they were equally capable of gathering round some other object. Though it is true that men's passions and interests often dictate their opinions, or rather decide their choice among the two or three forms of opinion which the existing condition of human intelligence renders possible, this disturbing cause is confined to morals, politics, and religion; and it is the intellectual movement in other regions than these, which is at the root of all the great changes in human affairs. It was not human emotions and passions which discovered the motion of the earth, or detected the evidence of its antiquity; which exploded Scholasticism, and inaugurated the exploration of nature; which invented printing, paper, and the mariner's compass. Yet the Reformation, the English and French Revolutions, and still greater moral and social changes yet to come, are direct consequences of these and similar discoveries. Even alchemy and astrology were not believed because people thirsted for gold and were anxious to pry into the future, for these desires are as strong now as they were then: but because alchemy and astrology were conceptions natural to a particular stage in the growth of human knowledge, and consequently determined during that stage the particular means whereby the passions which always exist, sought their gratification. To say that men's intellectual beliefs do not determine their conduct, is like saying that the ship is moved by the steam and not by the steersman. The steam indeed is the motive power; the steersman, left to himself, could not advance the vessel a single inch; yet it is the steersman's will and the steersman's knowledge which decide in what direction it shall move and whither it shall go.

Examining next what is the natural order of intellectual progress among mankind, M. Comte observes, that as their general mode of conceiving the universe must give its character to all their conceptions of detail, the determining fact in their intellectual history must be the natural succession of theories of the universe; which, it has been seen, consists of three stages, the theological, the metaphysical, and the positive. The passage of mankind through these stages, including the successive modifications of the theological conception by the rising influence of the other two, is, to M. Comte's mind, the most decisive fact in the evolution of humanity. Simultaneously, however, there has been going on throughout history a parallel movement in the purely temporal department of things, consisting of the gradual decline of the military mode of life (originally the chief occupation of all freemen) and its replacement by the industrial. M. Comte maintains that there is a necessary connexion and interdependence between this historical sequence and the other: and he easily shows that the progress of industry and that of positive science are correlative; man's power to modify the facts of nature evidently depending on the knowledge he has acquired of their laws. We do not think him equally successful in showing a natural connexion between the theological mode of thought and the military system of society: but since they both belong to the same age of the world—since each is, in itself, natural and inevitable, and they are together modified and together undermined by the same cause, the progress of science and industry, M. Comte is justified in considering them as linked together, and the movement by which mankind emerge from them as a single evolution.

These propositions having been laid down as the first principles of social dynamics, M. Comte proceeds to verify and apply them by a connected view of universal history. This survey nearly fills two large volumes, above a third of the work, in all of which there is scarcely a sentence that does not add an idea. We regard it as by far his greatest achievement, except his review of the sciences, and in some respects more striking even than that. We wish it were practicable in the compass of an essay like the present, to give even a faint conception of the extraordinary merits of this historical analysis. It must be read to be appreciated. Whoever disbelieves that the philosophy of history can be made a science, should suspend his judgment until he has read these volumes of M. Comte. We do not affirm that they would certainly change his opinion; but we would strongly advise him to give them a chance.

We shall not attempt the vain task of abridgment. A few words are all we can give to the subject. M. Comte confines himself to the main stream of human progress, looking only at the races and nations that led the van, and regarding as the successors of a people not their actual descendants, but those who took up the thread of progress after them. His object is to characterize truly, though generally, the successive states of society through which the advanced guard of our species has passed, and the filiation of these states on one another—how each grew out of the preceding and was the parent of the following state. A more detailed explanation, taking into account minute differences and more special and local phænomena, M. Comte does not aim at, though he does not avoid it when it falls in his path. Here, as in all his other speculations, we meet occasional misjudgments, and his historical correctness in minor matters is now and then at fault; but we may well wonder that it is not oftener so, considering the vastness of the field, and a passage in one of his prefaces in which he says of himself that he *rapidly* amassed the materials for his great enterprise (Vol. VI, p. 34). This expression in his mouth does not imply what it would in that of the majority of men, regard being had to his rare capacity of prolonged and concentrated mental labour: and it is wonderful that he so seldom gives cause to wish that his collection of materials had been less "rapid." But (as he himself remarks) in an inquiry of this sort the vulgarest facts are the most important. A movement common to all mankind—to all of them at least who do move—must depend on causes affecting them all; and these, from the scale on which they operate, cannot require abstruse research to bring them to light: they are not only seen, but best seen, in the most obvious, most universal, and most undisputed phænomena. Accordingly M. Comte lays no claim to new views respecting the mere facts of history; he takes them as he finds them, builds almost exclusively on those concerning which there is no dispute, and only tries what positive results can be obtained by combining them. Among the vast mass of historical observations which he has grouped and co-ordinated, if we have found any errors they are in things which do not affect his main conclusions. The chain of causation by which he connects the spiritual and temporal life of each era with one another and with the entire series, will be found, we think, in all essentials, irrefragable. When local or temporary disturbing causes have to be taken into the account as modifying the general movement, criticism has more to say. But this will only become important when the attempt is made to write the history or delineate the character of some given society on M. Comte's principles.

¹Such doubtful statements, or misappreciations of states of society, as we have remarked, are confined to cases which stand more or less apart from the principal line of development of the progressive societies. For instance, he makes greatly too much of what, with many other Continental thinkers, he calls the Theocratic state. He regards this as a natural, and at one time almost an universal, stage of social progress, though admitting that it either never existed or speedily ceased in the two ancient nations to which mankind are chiefly indebted for being permanently progressive. We hold it doubtful if there ever existed what M. Comte means by a theocracy. There was indeed no lack of societies in which, the civil and penal law being supposed to have been divinely revealed, the priests were its authorized interpreters. But this is the case even in Mussulman countries, the extreme opposite of theocracy. By a theocracy we understand to be meant, and we understand M. Comte to mean, a society founded on caste, and in which the speculative, necessarily identical with the priestly caste, has the temporal government in its hands or under its control. We believe that no such state of things ever existed in the societies commonly cited as theocratic. There is

*1-1*322**65**   [*in footnote to* principles.]

no reason to think that in any of them, the king, or chief of the government, was ever, unless by occasional usurpation, a member of the priestly caste.* It was not so in Israel, even in the time of the Judges; Jephtha, for example, was a Gileadite, of the tribe of Manasseh, and a military captain, as all governors in such an age and country needed to be. Priestly rulers only present themselves in two anomalous cases, of which next to nothing is known: the Mikados of Japan and the Grand Lamas of Thibet: in neither of which instances was the general constitution of society one of caste, and in the latter of them the priestly sovereignty is as nominal as it has become in the former. India is the typical specimen of the institution of caste—the only case in which we are certain that it ever really existed, for its existence anywhere else is a matter of *m*more or less probable*m* inference in the remote past. But in India, where the importance of the sacerdotal order was greater than in any other recorded state of society, the king not only was not a priest, but, consistently with the religious law, could not be one: he belonged to a different caste. The Brahmins were invested with an exalted character of sanctity, and an enormous amount of civil privileges; the king was enjoined to have a council of Brahmin advisers; but practically he took their advice or disregarded it exactly as he pleased. As is observed by the historian who first threw the light of reason on Hindoo society,† the king, though in dignity,

*[65¹] In the case of Egypt we admit that there may be cited against us the authority of Plato, in whose *Politicus* [290e] it is said that the king of Egypt must be a member of the priestly caste, or if by usurpation a member of any other caste acquired the sovereignty he must be initiated into the sacerdotal order. But Plato was writing of a state of things which already belonged to the past; nor have we any assurance that his information on Egyptian institutions was authentic and accurate. Had the king been necessarily or commonly a member of the priestly order, it is most improbable that the careful Herodotus, of whose comprehensive work an entire book [Book II] was devoted to a minute account of Egypt and its institutions, and who collected his information from Egyptian priests in the country itself, would have been ignorant of a fact so important, and tending so much to exalt the dignity of the priesthood, who were much more likely to affirm it falsely to Plato than to withhold the knowledge of it if true from Herodotus. Not only is Herodotus silent respecting any such law or custom, but he thinks it needful to mention that in one particular instance the king (by name Sethôs) was a priest, which he would scarcely have done if this had been other than an exceptional case. It is likely enough that a king of Egypt would learn the hieratic character, and would not suffer any of the mysteries of law or religion which were in the keeping of the priests to be withheld from him; and this was very probably all the foundation which existed for the assertion of the Eleatic stranger in Plato's dialogue.

†[James] Mill, *History of British India* [3 vols. London: Baldwin, Cradock, and Jay, 1817], Bk. II, Chap. iii [Vol. I, pp. 122–32, esp. 132]. [65 *included in parentheses in long footnote here indicated by* ˡ⁻ˡ.]

*m–m*65   doubtful

to judge by the written code, he seemed vastly inferior to the Brahmins, had always the full power of a despotic monarch: the reason being that he had the command of the army, and the control of the public revenue. There is no case known to authentic history in which either of these belonged to the sacerdotal caste. Even in the cases most favourable to them, the priesthood had no voice in temporal affairs, except the "consultative"[*] voice which M. Comte's theory allows to every spiritual power. His collection of materials must have been unusually "rapid" in this instance, for he regards almost all the societies of antiquity, except the Greek and Roman, as theocratic, even Gaul under the Druids, and Persia under Darius; admitting, however, that in these two countries, when they emerge into the light of history, the theocracy had already been much broken down by military usurpation. By what evidence he could have proved that it ever existed, we confess ourselves unable to divine.

The only other imperfection worth noticing here, which we find in M. Comte's view of history, is that he has a very insufficient understanding of the peculiar phænomena of English development; though he recognizes, and on the whole correctly estimates, its exceptional character in relation to the general European movement. His failure consists chiefly in want of appreciation of Protestantism; which, like almost all thinkers, even unbelievers, who have lived and thought exclusively in a Catholic atmosphere, he sees and knows only on its negative side, regarding the Reformation as a mere destructive movement, stopped short in too early a stage. He does not seem to be aware that Protestantism has any positive influences, other than the general ones of Christianity; and misses one of the most important facts connected with it, its remarkable efficacy, as contrasted with Catholicism, in cultivating the intelligence and conscience of the individual believer. Protestantism, when not merely professed but actually taken into the mind, makes a demand on the intelligence; the mind is expected to be active, not passive, in the reception of it. The feeling of a direct responsibility of the individual immediately to God, is almost wholly a creation of Protestantism. Even when Protestants were nearly as persecuting as Catholics (quite as much so they never were); even when they held as firmly as Catholics that salvation depended on having the true belief, they still maintained that the belief was not to be accepted from a priest, but to be sought and found by the believer, at his eternal peril if he failed; and that no one could answer to God for him, but that he had to answer for himself. The avoidance of fatal error thus became in a great measure a question of culture; and there was the strongest inducement to every believer, however humble, to seek culture and to profit by it. In those Protestant countries, accordingly, whose Churches were not, as the Church of England always was, principally political institutions—in

[*Cours, Vol. V, p. 219.]

Scotland, for instance, and the New England States—an amount of education was carried down to the poorest of the people, of which there is no other example; every peasant expounded the Bible to his family (many to their neighbours), and had a mind practised in meditation and discussion on all the points of his religious creed. The food may not have been the most nourishing, but we cannot be blind to the sharpening and strengthening exercise which such great topics gave to the understanding—the discipline in abstraction and reasoning which such mental occupation brought down to the humblest layman, and one of the consequences of which was the privilege long enjoyed by Scotland of supplying the greater part of Europe with professors for its universities, and educated and skilled workmen for its practical arts.[l]

[n]This, however, notwithstanding its importance, is, in a comprehensive view of universal history, only a matter of detail. We find no fundamental errors in M. Comte's general conception of history. He[n] is singularly exempt from most of the twists and exaggerations which we are used to find in almost all thinkers who meddle with speculations [o]of this character[o]. Scarcely any of them is so free (for example) from the opposite errors of ascribing too much or too little influence to accident, and to the qualities of individuals. The vulgar mistake of supposing that the course of history has no tendencies of its own, and that great events usually proceed from small causes, or that kings, or conquerors, or the founders of philosophies and religions, can do with society what they please, no one has more completely avoided or more tellingly exposed. But he is equally free from the error of those who ascribe all to general causes, and imagine that neither casual circumstances, nor governments by their acts, nor individuals of genius by their thoughts, materially accelerate or retard human progress. This is the mistake which pervades the instructive writings of the thinker who in England and in our own times bore the nearest, though a very remote, resemblance to M. Comte—the lamented Mr. Buckle; who, had he not been unhappily cut off in an early stage of his labours, and before the complete maturity of his powers, would probably have thrown off an error, the more to be regretted as it gives a colour to the prejudice which regards the doctrine of the invariability of natural laws as identical with fatalism. Mr. Buckle also fell into another mistake which M. Comte avoided, that of regarding the intellectual as the only progressive element in man, and the moral as too much the same at all times to affect even the annual average of crime. M. Comte shows, on the contrary, a most acute sense of the causes which elevate or lower the general level of moral excellence; and deems intellectual progress in no other way so beneficial as by creating a standard to guide the

[n-n]65   M. Comte
[o-o]65   on history

moral sentiments of mankind, and a mode of bringing those sentiments effectively to bear on conduct.

M. Comte is equally free from the error of considering any practical rule or doctrine that can be laid down in politics as universal and absolute. All political truth he deems strictly relative, implying as its correlative a given state or situation of society. This conviction is now common to him with all thinkers who are on a level with the age, and comes so naturally to any intelligent reader of history, that the only wonder is how men could have been prevented from reaching it sooner. It marks one of the principal differences between the political philosophy of the present time and that of the past; but M. Comte adopted it when the opposite mode of thinking was still general, and there are few thinkers to whom the principle owes more in the way of comment and illustration.

Again, while he sets forth the historical succession of systems of belief and forms of political society, and places in the strongest light those imperfections in each which make it impossible that any of them should be final, this does not make him for a moment unjust to the men or the opinions of the past. He accords with generous recognition the gratitude due to all who, with whatever imperfections of doctrine or even of conduct, contributed materially to the work of human improvement. In all past modes of thought and forms of society he acknowledged a useful, in many a necessary, office, in carrying mankind through one stage of improvement into a higher. The theological spirit in its successive forms, the metaphysical in its principal varieties, are honoured by him for the services they rendered in bringing mankind out of pristine savagery into a state in which more advanced modes of belief became possible. His list of heroes and benefactors of mankind includes, not only every important name in the scientific movement, from Thales ᵖof Miletusᵖ to Fourier the mathematician and Blainville the biologist, and in the æsthetic from Homer to Manzoni, but the most illustrious names in the annals of the various religions and philosophies, and the really great politicians in all states of society.* Above all, he has the most

*At a somewhat later period M. Comte drew up what he termed a Positivist Calendar, in which every day was dedicated to some benefactor of humanity (generally with the addition of a similar but minor luminary, to be celebrated in the room of his principal each bissextile year). In this no kind of human eminence, really useful, is omitted, except that which is merely negative and destructive. On this principle (which is avowed) the French *philosophes* as such are excluded, those only among them being admitted who, like Voltaire and Diderot, had claims to admission on other grounds: and the Protestant religious reformers are left out entirely, with the curious exception of George Fox—who is included, we presume, in consideration of his Peace principles. [See *Catéchisme positiviste*. Paris: Comte, Carilian-Gœury, and Dalmont, 1852, facing p. 332.]

ᵖ–ᵖ+65¹,66

profound admiration for the services rendered by Christianity, and by the Church of the middle ages. His estimate of the Catholic period is such as the majority of Englishmen (from whom we take the liberty to differ) would deem exaggerated, if not absurd. The great men of Christianity, from St. Paul to St. Francis of Assisi, receive his warmest homage: nor does he forget the greatness even of those who lived and thought in the centuries in which the Catholic Church, having stopt short while the world had gone on, had become a hindrance to progress instead of a promoter of it; such men as Fénélon and St. Vincent de Paul, Bossuet and Joseph de Maistre. A more comprehensive, and, in the primitive sense of the term, more catholic, sympathy and reverence towards real worth, and every kind of service to humanity, we have not met with in any thinker. Men who would have torn each other in pieces, who even tried to do so, if each usefully served in his own way the interests of mankind, are all hallowed to him.

Neither is his a cramped and contracted notion of human excellence, which cares only for certain forms of development. He not only personally appreciates, but rates high in moral value, the creations of poets and artists in all departments, deeming them, by their mixed appeal to the sentiments and the understanding, admirably fitted to educate the feelings of abstract thinkers, and enlarge the intellectual horizon of people of the world.* He regards the law of progress as applicable, in spite of appearances, to poetry and art as much as to science and politics. The common impression to the contrary he ascribes solely to the fact, that the perfection of æsthetic creation requires as its condition a consentaneousness in the feelings of mankind, which depends for its existence on a fixed and settled state of opinions: while the last five centuries have been a period not of settling, but of unsettling and decomposing, the most general beliefs and sentiments of mankind. The numerous monuments of poetic and artistic genius which the modern mind has produced even under this great disadvantage, are (he maintains) sufficient proof what great productions it will be capable of, when one harmonious vein of sentiment shall once more thrill through the whole of society, as in the days of Homer, of Æschylus, of Phidias, and even of Dante.

After so profound and comprehensive a view of the progress of human society in the past, of which the future can only be a prolongation, it is natural to ask, to what use does he put this survey as a basis of practical recommendations? Such recommendations he certainly makes, though, in the present Treatise, they are of a much less definite character than in his later writings. But we miss a necessary link; there is a break in the otherwise

---

*He goes still further and deeper in a subsequent work. "L'art ramène doucement à la réalité les contemplations trop abstraites du théoricien, tandis qu'il pousse noblement le praticien aux spéculations désintéressées." *Système de Politique Positive*, Vol. I, p. 287.

close concatenation of his speculations. We fail to see any scientific connexion between his theoretical explanation of the past progress of society, and his proposals for future improvement. The proposals are not, as we might expect, recommended as that towards which human society has been tending and working through the whole of history. It is thus that thinkers have usually proceeded, who formed theories for the future, grounded on historical analysis of the past. Tocqueville, for example, and others, finding, as they thought, through all history, a steady progress in the direction of social and political equality, argued that to smooth this transition, and make the best of what is certainly coming, is the proper employment of political foresight. We do not find M. Comte supporting his recommendations by a similar line of argument. They rest as completely, each on its separate reasons of supposed utility, as with philosophers who, like Bentham, theorize on politics without any historical basis at all. The only bridge of connexion which leads from his historical speculations to his practical conclusions, is the inference, that since the old powers of society, both in the region of thought and of action, are declining and destined to disappear, leaving only the two rising powers, positive thinkers on the one hand, leaders of industry on the other, the future necessarily belongs to these: spiritual power to the former, temporal to the latter. As a specimen of historical forecast this is very deficient; for are there not the masses as well as the leaders of industry? and is not theirs also a growing power? Be this as it may, M. Comte's conceptions of the mode in which these growing powers should be organized and used, are grounded on anything rather than on history. And we cannot but remark a singular anomaly in a thinker of M. Comte's calibre. After the ample evidence he has brought forward of the slow growth of the sciences, all of which except the mathematico-astronomical couple are still, as he justly thinks, in a very early stage, it yet appears as if, to his mind, the mere institution of a positive science of sociology were tantamount to its completion; as if all the diversities of opinion on the subject, which set mankind at variance, were solely owing to its having been studied in the theological or the metaphysical manner, and as if when the positive method which has raised up real sciences on other subjects of knowledge, is similarly employed on this, divergence would at once cease, and the entire body of positive social inquirers would exhibit as much agreement in their doctrines as those who cultivate any of the sciences of inorganic life. Happy would be the prospects of mankind if this were so. A time such as M. Comte reckoned upon may come; unless something stops the progress of human improvement, it is sure to come: but after an unknown duration of hard thought and violent controversy. The period of decomposition, which has lasted, on his own computation, from the beginning of the fourteenth century to the present, is not yet terminated: the shell of the old edifice will remain standing until there is another ready to replace it; and the new synthesis is barely begun, nor is even the preparatory analysis completely finished. On other occasions M. Comte is very well aware that the Method of a science is not the science itself, and that when the difficulty of discovering the right processes has been overcome, there remains a still greater difficulty, that of applying them. This, which is true of all sciences, is truest of all in Sociology. The facts being more complicated, and depending on a greater concurrence of forces, than in any other science, the difficulty of treating them deductively is proportionally increased, while the wide difference between any one case and every other in some of the circumstances which affect the result, makes the pretence of direct induction usually no better than empiricism. It is therefore, out of all proportion, more uncertain than in any other science, whether two inquirers equally competent and equally disinterested will take the same view of the evidence, or arrive at the same conclusion. When to this intrinsic difficulty is added the infinitely greater extent to which personal or class interests and predilections interfere with impartial judgment, the hope of such accordance of opinion among sociological inquirers as would obtain, in mere deference to their authority, the universal assent which M. Comte's scheme of society requires, must be adjourned to an indefinite distance.

M. Comte's own theory is an apt illustration of these difficulties, since, though prepared for these speculations as no one had ever been prepared before, his views of social regeneration even in the rudimentary form in which they appear above-ground in this treatise (not to speak of the singular system into which he afterwards enlarged them) are such as perhaps no other person of equal knowledge and capacity would agree in. Were those views as true as they are questionable, they could not take effect until the unanimity among positive thinkers, to which he looked forward, shall have been attained; since the mainspring of his system is a Spiritual Power composed of positive philosophers, which only the previous attainment of the unanimity in question could call into existence. A few words will sufficiently express the outline of his scheme. A corporation of philosophers, receiving a modest support from the state, surrounded by reverence, but peremptorily excluded not only from all political power or employment, but from all riches, and all occupations except their own, are to have the entire direction of education: together with, not only the right and duty of advising and reproving all persons respecting both their public and their private life, but also a control (whether authoritative or only moral is not defined) over the speculative class itself, to prevent them from wasting time and ingenuity on inquiries and speculations of no value to mankind (among which he includes many now in high estimation), and compel them to employ all their powers on the investigations which may be judged, at the time, to be the most urgently important to the general welfare. The temporal government which is to coexist with this spiritual authority, consists of an aristocracy of capitalists, whose dignity and authority are to be in the ratio of the degree of generality of their conceptions and operations—bankers at the summit, merchants next, then manufacturers, and agriculturists at the bottom of the scale. No representative system, or other popular organization, by way of counterpoise to this governing power, is ever contemplated. The checks relied upon for preventing its abuse, are the counsels and remonstrances of the Spiritual Power, and unlimited liberty of discussion and comment by all classes of inferiors. Of the mode in which either set of authorities should fulfil the office assigned to it, little is said in this treatise: but the general idea is, while regulating as little as possible by law, to make the pressure of opinion, directed by the Spiritual Power, so heavy on every individual, from the humblest to the most powerful, as to render legal obligation, in as many cases as possible, needless. Liberty and spontaneity on the part of individuals form no part of the scheme. M. Comte looks on them with as great jealousy as any scholastic pedagogue, or ecclestiastical director of consciences. Every particular of conduct, public or private, is to be open to the public eye, and to be kept, by the power of opinion, in the course which the Spiritual corporation shall judge to be the most right.

This is not a sufficiently tempting picture to have much chance of making converts rapidly, and the objections to the scheme are too obvious to need stating. Indeed, it is only thoughtful persons to whom it will be credible, that speculations leading to this result can deserve the attention necessary for understanding them. *q*We propose in the next Essay to*q* examine them as part of the elaborate and coherent system of doctrine, which M. Comte afterwards put together for the reconstruction of society. Meanwhile the reader will gather, from what has been said, that M. Comte has not, in our opinion, created Sociology. Except his analysis of history, to which there is much to be added, but which we do not think likely to be ever, in its general features, superseded, he has done nothing in Sociology which does not require to be done over again, and better. Nevertheless, he has greatly advanced the study. Besides the great stores of thought, of various and often of eminent merit, with which he has enriched the subject, his conception of its method is so much truer and more profound than that of any one who preceded him, as to constitute an era in its cultivation. If it cannot be said of him that he has created a science, it may be said truly that he has, for the first time, made the creation possible. This is a great achievement, and, with the extraordinary merit of his historical analysis, and of his philosophy of the physical sciences, is enough to immortalize his name. But his renown with posterity would probably have been greater than it is now likely to be, if after showing the way in which the social science should be formed, he had not flattered himself that he had formed it, and that it was already sufficiently solid for attempting to build upon its foundation the entire fabric of the Political Art.

*q-q*65   Their further consideration must be deferred until we can

PART II

The Later Speculations of M. Comte*

THE ʳappendedʳ list of publications contains the materials for knowing and estimating what M. Comte termed his second career, in which the *savant*, historian, and philosopher of his fundamental treatise, came forth transfigured as the High Priest of the Religion of Humanity. They include all his writings ˢnot purely scientific,ˢ except the *Cours de Philosophie Positive*: for his early productions, and the occasional publications of his later life, are reprinted as Preludes or Appendices to the treatises here enumerated, or in Dr. Robinet's volume, which, as well as that of M. Littré, also contains copious extracts from his correspondence.

In the concluding pages of his great systematic work, M. Comte had announced four other treatises as in contemplation: on Politics; on the Philosophy of Mathematics; on Education, a project subsequently enlarged to include the systematization of Morals; and on Industry, or the action of man upon external nature. Our list comprises the only two of these which he lived to execute. It further contains a brief exposition of his final doctrines, in the form of a Dialogue, or, as he terms it, a Catechism, of which a transla-

*1. *Système de Politique Positive, ou Traité de Sociologie, instituant la Religion de l'Humanité*. 4 vols. 8vo. Paris: [Mathias,] 1851–1854.

2. *Catéchisme Positiviste, ou Sommaire Exposition de la Religion Universelle, en onze Entretiens Systématiques entre une Femme et un Prêtre de l'Humanité*. 1 vol. 12mo. Paris: [Comte, Carilian-Gœury and Dalmont,] 1852.

3. *Appel aux Conservateurs*. Paris: [Comte, Dalmont,] 1855 (brochure).

4. *Synthèse Subjective, ou Système Universel des Conceptions propres à l'Etat Normal de l'Humanité*. Tome Premier, contenant le Système de Logique Positive, ou Traité de Philosophie Mathématique. 8vo. Paris: [Comte, Dalmont,] 1856.

5. *Auguste Comte et la Philosophie Positive*. Par E. Littré. 1 vol. 8vo. Paris: [Hachette,] 1863.

6. *Exposition Abrégée et Populaire de la Philosophie et de la Religion Positives*. Par Célestin de Blignières, ancien élève de l'Ecole Polytechnique. 1 vol. 12mo. Paris: [Chamerot,] 1857.

7. *Notice sur l'Œuvre et sur la Vie d'Auguste Comte*. Par le Docteur Robinet, son Médecin, et l'un de ses treize Exécuteurs Testamentaires. 1 vol. 8vo. Paris: [Dunod,] 1860.

ʳ⁻ʳ65 above [*i.e., at head of article*]   ˢ⁻ˢ+66

tion has been published by his principal English adherent, Mr. Congreve.[*]
There has also appeared very recently, under the title of *A General View of
Positivism*,[†] a translation by Dr. Bridges, of the Preliminary Discourse in
six chapters, prefixed to the *Système de Politique Positive*. The ᵗlastᵗ three
books on our list are the productions of disciples in different degrees. M.
Littré, the only thinker of established reputation who accepts that character,
is a disciple only of the *Cours de Philosophie Positive*, and can see the weak
points even in that.[‡] Some of them he has discriminated and discussed
with great judgment: and the merits of his volume, both as a sketch of
M. Comte's life and an appreciation of his doctrines, would well deserve a
fuller notice than we are able to give it here. M. de Blignières is a far more
thorough adherent; so much so, that the reader of his singularly well and
attractively written condensation and popularization of his master's doctrines, does not easily discover in what it falls short of that unqualified
acceptance which alone, it would seem, could find favour with M. Comte.
For he ended by casting off M. de Blignières, as he had previously cast off
M. Littré, and every other person who, having gone with him a certain
length, refused to follow him to the end. The author of the last work in our
enumeration, Dr. Robinet, is a disciple after M. Comte's own heart; one
whom no difficulty stops, and no absurdity startles. But it is far from our disposition to speak otherwise than respectfully of Dr. Robinet and the other
earnest men, who maintain ᵘroundᵘ the tomb of their master an organized
co-operation for the diffusion of doctrines which they believe destined to
regenerate the human race. Their enthusiastic veneration for him, and devotion to the ends he pursued, do honour alike to them and to their teacher,
and are an evidence of the personal ascendancy he exercised over those who
approached him; an ascendancy which for a time carried away even M. Littré,
as he confesses, to a length which his calmer judgment does not now
approve.[§]

These various writings raise many points of interest regarding M. Comte's
personal history, and some, not without philosophic bearings, respecting his
mental habits: from all which matters we shall abstain, with the exception
of two, which he himself proclaimed with great emphasis, and a knowledge
of which is almost indispensable to an apprehension of the characteristic
difference between his second career and his first. It should be known that

[*Richard Congreve, trans. *The Catechism of Positive Religion*. London:
Chapman, 1858.]
[†John H. Bridges, trans. *A General View of Positivism*. London: Trübner,
1865.]
[‡See Littré, *Auguste Comte*, Préface.]
[§*Ibid.*]

ᵗ⁻ᵗ65,65¹ remaining   ᵘ⁻ᵘ65 around

during his later life, and even before completing his first great treatise, M. Comte adopted a rule, to which he very rarely made any exception: to abstain systematically, not only from newspapers or periodical publications, even scientific, but from all reading whatever, except a few favourite poets in the ancient and modern European languages. This abstinence he practised for the sake of mental health; by way, as he said, of "*hygiène cérébrale.*"[*] We are far from thinking that the practice has nothing whatever to recommend it. For most thinkers, doubtless, it would be a very unwise one; but we will not affirm that it may not sometimes be advantageous to a mind of the peculiar quality of M. Comte's—one that can usefully devote itself to following out to the remotest developments a particular line of meditations, of so arduous a kind that the complete concentration of the intellect upon its own thoughts is almost a necessary condition of success. When a mind of this character has laboriously and conscientiously laid in beforehand, as M. Comte had done, an ample stock of materials, he may be justified in thinking that he will contribute most to the mental wealth of mankind by occupying himself solely in working upon these, without distracting his attention by continually taking in more matter, or keeping a communication open with other independent intellects. The practice, therefore, may be legitimate; but no one should adopt it without being aware of what he loses by it. He must resign the pretension of arriving at the whole truth on the subject, whatever it be, of his meditations. That he should effect this, even on a narrow subject, by the mere force of his own mind, building on the foundations of his predecessors, without aid or correction from his *con-temporaries*, is simply impossible. He may do eminent service by elaborating certain sides of the truth, but he must expect to find that there are other sides which have wholly escaped his attention. However great his powers, everything that he can do without the aid of incessant remindings from other thinkers, is merely provisional, and will require a thorough revision. He ought to be aware of this, and accept it with his eyes open, regarding himself as a pioneer, not a constructor. If he thinks that he can contribute most towards the elements of the final synthesis by following out his own original thoughts as far as they will go, leaving to other thinkers, or to himself at a subsequent time, the business of adjusting them to the thoughts by which they ought to be accompanied, he is right in doing so. But he deludes himself if he imagines that any conclusions he can arrive at, while he practises M. Comte's rule of *hygiène cérébrale*, can possibly be definitive.

Neither is such a practice, in a hygienic point of view, free from the gravest dangers to the philosopher's own mind. When once he has persuaded himself

[*Cours, Vol. VI, p. 34.]

*v–v*65   cotemporaries

that he can work out the final truth on any subject, exclusively from his own sources, he is apt to lose all measure or standard by which to be apprized when he is departing from common sense. Living only with his own thoughts, he gradually forgets the aspect they present to minds of a different mould from his own; he looks at his conclusions only from the point of view which suggested them, and from which they naturally appear perfect; and every consideration which from other points of view might present itself, either as an objection or as a necessary modification, is to him as if it did not exist. When his merits come to be recognised and appreciated, and especially if he obtains disciples, the intellectual infirmity soon becomes complicated with a moral one. The natural result of the position is a gigantic self-confidence, not to say self-conceit. That of M. Comte is colossal. Except here and there in an entirely self-taught thinker, who has no high standard with which to compare himself, we have met with nothing approaching to it. As his thoughts grew more extravagant, his self-confidence grew more outrageous. The height it ultimately attained must be seen, in his writings, to be believed.

The other circumstance of a personal nature which it is impossible not to notice, because M. Comte is perpetually referring to it as the origin of the great superiority which he ascribes to his later as compared with his earlier speculations, is the "moral regeneration" which he underwent from "une angélique influence" and "une incomparable passion privée."[*] He formed a passionate attachment to a lady whom he describes as uniting everything which is morally with much that is intellectually admirable, and his relation to whom, besides the direct influence of her character upon his own, gave him an insight into the true sources of human happiness, which changed his whole conception of life. This attachment, which always remained pure, gave him but one year of passionate enjoyment, the lady having been cut off by death at the end of that short period; but the adoration of her memory survived, and became, as we shall see, the type of his conception of the sympathetic culture proper for all human beings. The change thus effected in his personal character and sentiments, manifested itself at once in his speculations; which, from having been only a philosophy, now aspired to become a religion; and from having been as purely, and almost rudely, scientific and intellectual, as was compatible with a character always enthusiastic in its admirations and in its ardour for *human* improvement, became from this time what, for want of a better name, may be called sentimental; but sentimental in a way of its own, very curious to contemplate. In considering the system of religion, politics, and morals, which in his later writings M. Comte constructed, it is not unimportant to bear in mind the nature of the personal

[*See *Système*, Vol. I, Préface, p. 6; Vol. IV, p. 546; Vol. II, p. xxxi.]

w–w+66

experience and inspiration to which he himself constantly attributed this phasis of his philosophy. But as we shall have much more to say against, than in favour of, the conclusions to which he was in this manner conducted, it is right to declare that, from the evidence of his writings, we really believe the moral influence of Madame Clotilde de Vaux upon his character to have been of the ennobling as well as softening character which he ascribes to it. Making allowance for the effects of his exuberant growth in self-conceit, we perceive almost as much improvement in his feelings, as deterioration in his speculations, compared with those of the *Philosophie Positive*. Even the speculations are, in some secondary aspects, improved through the beneficial effect of the improved feelings; and might have been more so, if, by a rare good fortune, the object of his attachment had been qualified to exercise as improving an influence over him intellectually as morally, and if he could have been contented with something less ambitious than being the supreme moral legislator and religious pontiff of the human race.

When we say that M. Comte has erected his philosophy into a religion, the word religion must not be understood in its ordinary sense. He made no change in the purely negative attitude which he maintained towards theology: his religion is without a God. In saying this, we have done enough to induce nine-tenths of all readers, at least in our own country, to avert their faces and close their ears. To have no religion, though scandalous enough, is an idea they are partly used to: but to have no God, and to talk of religion, is to their feelings at once an absurdity and an impiety. Of the remaining tenth, a great proportion, perhaps, will turn away from anything which calls itself by the name of religion at all. Between the two, it is difficult to find an audience who can be induced to listen to M. Comte without an insurmountable prejudice. But, to be just to any opinion, it ought to be considered, not exclusively from an opponent's point of view, but from that of the mind which propounds it. Though conscious of being in an extremely small minority, we venture to think that a religion may exist without belief in a God, and that a religion without a God may be, even to Christians, an instructive and profitable object of contemplation.

What, in truth, are the conditions necessary to constitute a religion? There must be a creed, or conviction, claiming authority over the whole of human life; a belief, or set of beliefs, deliberately adopted, respecting human destiny and duty, to which the believer inwardly acknowledges that all his actions ought to be subordinate. Moreover, there must be a sentiment connected with this creed, or capable of being evoked by it, sufficiently powerful to give it in fact, the authority over human conduct to which it lays claim in theory. It is a great advantage (though not absolutely indispensable) that this sentiment should crystallize, as it were, round a concrete object; if possible a really existing one, though, in all the more important cases, only ideally present. Such an object Theism and Christianity offer to the believer: but the condition may be fulfilled, if not in a manner strictly equivalent, by another object. It has been said that whoever believes in "the Infinite nature of Duty,"[*] even if he believe in nothing else, is religious. M. Comte believes in what is meant by the infinite nature of duty, but he refers the obligations of duty, as well as all sentiments of devotion, to a concrete object, at once ideal and real; the Human Race, conceived as a continuous whole, including the past, the present, and the future. This great collective existence, this "Grand Etre," as he terms it, though the feelings it can excite are necessarily very different from those which direct themselves towards an ideally perfect Being, has, as he forcibly urges, this advantage in respect to us, that it really needs our services, which Omnipotence cannot, in any genuine sense of the term, be supposed to do: and M. Comte says, that assuming the existence of a Supreme Providence (which he is as far from denying as from affirming), the best, and even the only, way in which we can rightly worship or serve Him, is by doing our utmost to love and serve that other Great Being, whose inferior Providence has bestowed on us all the benefits that we owe to the labours and virtues of former generations. It may not be consonant to usage to call this a religion; but the term so applied has a meaning, and one which is not adequately expressed by any other word. Candid persons of all creeds may be willing to admit, that if a person has an ideal object, his attachment and sense of duty towards which are able to control and discipline all his other sentiments and propensities, and prescribe to him a rule of life, that person has a religion: and though every one naturally prefers his own religion to any other, all must admit that if the object of this attachment, and of this feeling of duty, is the aggregate of our fellow-creatures, this Religion of the Infidel cannot, in honesty and conscience, be called an intrinsically bad one. Many, indeed, may be unable to believe that this object is capable of gathering round it feelings sufficiently strong: but this is exactly the point on which a doubt can hardly remain in an intelligent reader of M. Comte: and we join with him in contemning, as equally irrational and mean, the conception of human nature as incapable of giving its love and devoting its existence to any object which cannot afford in exchange an eternity of personal enjoyment.

The power which may be acquired over the mind by the idea of the general interest of the human race, both as a source of emotion and as a motive to conduct, many have perceived; but we know not if any one, before M. Comte, realized so fully as he has done, all the majesty of which that idea is susceptible. It ascends into the unknown recesses of the past, embraces the manifold present, and descends into the indefinite and unforeseeable future. Forming a collective Existence without assignable beginning or end, it

[*Thomas Carlyle. *Sartor Resartus*, p. 170 (Book II, Chap. vii).]

appeals to that feeling of the Infinite, which is deeply rooted in human nature, and which seems necessary to the imposingness of all our highest conceptions. Of the vast unrolling web of human life, the part best known to us is irrevocably past; this we can no longer serve, but can still love: it comprises for most of us the far greater number of those who have loved us, or from whom we have received benefits, as well as the long series of those who, by their labours and sacrifices for mankind, have deserved to be held in everlasting and grateful remembrance. As M. Comte truly says, the highest minds, even now, live in thought with the great dead, far more than with the living; and, next to the dead, with those ideal human beings yet to come, whom they are never destined to see. If we honour as we ought those who have served mankind in the past, we shall feel that we are also working for those benefactors by serving that to which their lives were devoted. And when reflection, guided by history, has taught us the intimacy of the connexion of every age of humanity with every other, making us see in the earthly destiny of mankind the playing out of a great drama, or the action of a prolonged epic, all the generations of mankind become indissolubly united into a single image, combining all the power over the mind of the idea of Posterity, with our best feelings towards the living world which surrounds us, and towards the predecessors who have made us what we are. That the ennobling power of this grand conception may have its full efficacy, we should, with M. Comte, regard the Grand Etre, Humanity, or Mankind, as composed, in the past, solely of those who, in every age and variety of position, have played their part worthily in life. It is only as thus restricted that the aggregate of our species becomes an object deserving our veneration. The unworthy members of it are best dismissed from our habitual thoughts; and the imperfections which adhered through life, even to those of the dead who deserve honourable remembrance, should be no further borne in mind than is necessary not to falsify our conception of facts. On the other hand, the Grand Etre in its completeness ought to include not only all whom we venerate, but all sentient beings to which we owe duties, and which have a claim on our attachment. M. Comte, therefore, incorporates into the ideal object whose service is to be the law of our life, not our own species exclusively, but, in a subordinate degree, our humble auxiliaries, those animal races which enter into real society with man, which attach themselves to him, and voluntarily co-operate with him, like the noble dog who gives his life for his human friend and benefactor. For this M. Comte has been subjected to unworthy ridicule, but there is nothing truer or more honourable to him in the whole body of his doctrines. The strong sense he always shows of the worth of the inferior animals, and of the duties of mankind towards them, is one of the very finest traits of his character.

We, therefore, not only hold that M. Comte was justified in the attempt to develope his philosophy into a religion, and had realized the essential conditions of one, but that all other religions are made better in proportion as, in their practical result, they are brought to coincide with that which he aimed at constructing. But, unhappily, the next thing we are obliged to do, is to charge him with making a complete mistake at the very outset of his operations—with fundamentally misconceiving the proper office of a rule of life. He committed the error which is often, but falsely, charged against the whole class of utilitarian moralists; he required that the test of conduct should also be the exclusive motive to it. Because the good of the human race is the ultimate standard of right and wrong, and because moral discipline consists in cultivating the utmost possible repugnance to all conduct injurious to the general good, M. Comte infers that the good of others is the only inducement on which we should allow ourselves to act; and that we should endeavour to starve the whole of the desires which point to our personal satisfaction, by denying them all gratification not strictly required by physical necessities. The golden rule of morality, in M. Comte's religion, is to live for others, "vivre pour autrui."[*] To do as we would be done by, and to love our neighbour as ourself, are not sufficient for him: they partake, he thinks, of the nature of personal calculations. We should endeavour not to love ourselves at all. We shall not succeed in it, but we should make the nearest approach to it possible. Nothing less will satisfy him, as towards humanity, than the sentiment which one of his favourite writers, Thomas à Kempis, addresses to God: Amem te plus quam me, nec me nisi propter te.[†] All education and all moral discipline should have but one object, to make altruism (a word of his own coining)[‡] predominate over egoism. If by this were only meant that egoism is bound, and should be taught, always to give way to the well-understood interests of enlarged altruism, no one who acknowledges any morality at all would object to the proposition. But M. Comte, taking his stand on the biological fact that organs are strengthened by exercise and atrophied by disuse, and firmly convinced that each of our elementary inclinations has its distinct cerebral organ, thinks it the grand duty of life not only to strengthen the social affections by constant habit and by referring all our actions to them, but, as far as possible, to deaden the personal passions and propensities by desuetude. Even the exercise of the intellect is required to obey as an authoritative rule the dominion of the social feelings over the intelligence (du cœur sur l'esprit).[§] The physical and other personal instincts are to be mortified far beyond the demands of bodily health, which indeed the morality of the future is not to insist much upon, for fear

[*See *Système*, Vol. I, title page.]
[†*De Imitatione Christi*, Lib. III, Cap. v.]
[‡See, e.g., *Catéchisme*, pp. 21–2.]
[§See, e.g., *ibid*., p. 19.]

of encouraging "les calculs personnels."[*] M. Comte condemns only such austerities as, by diminishing the vigour of the constitution, make us less capable of being useful to others. Any indulgence, even in food, not necessary to health and strength, he condemns as immoral.[†] All gratifications except those of the affections, are to be tolerated only as "inevitable infirmities."[‡] Novalis said of Spinoza that he was a God-intoxicated man:[§] M. Comte is a morality-intoxicated man. Every question with him is one of morality, and no motive but that of morality is permitted.

The explanation of this we find in an original mental twist, very common in French thinkers, and by which M. Comte was distinguished beyond them all. He could not dispense with what he called "unity." It was for the sake of Unity that a religion was, in his eyes, desirable. Not in the mere sense of Unanimity, but in a far wider one. A religion must be something by which to "systematize" human life. His definition of it, in the *Catéchisme*, is

the state of complete unity which distinguishes our existence, at once personal and social, when all its parts, both moral and physical, converge habitually to a common destination . . . Such a harmony, individual and collective, being incapable of complete realization in an existence so complicated as ours, this definition of religion characterizes the immovable type towards which tends more and more the aggregate of human efforts. Our happiness and our merit consist especially in approaching as near as possible to this unity, of which the gradual increase constitutes the best measure of real improvement, personal or social.[‖]

To this theme he continually returns, and argues that this unity or harmony among all the elements of our life is not consistent with the predominance of the personal propensities, since these drag us in different directions; it can only result from the subordination of them all to the social feelings, which may be made to act in a uniform direction by a common system of convictions, and which differ from the personal inclinations in this, that we all naturally encourage them in one another, while, on the contrary, social life is a perpetual restraint upon the selfish propensities.

The *fons errorum* in M. Comte's later speculations is this inordinate demand for "unity" and "systematization." This is the reason why it does not suffice to him that all should be ready, in case of need, to postpone their personal interests and inclinations to the requirements of the general good: he demands that each should regard as vicious any care at all for his personal interests, except as a means to the good of others—should be ashamed

[*Système, Vol. I, p. 97.]
[†See Catéchisme, pp. 269, 271 ff.]
[‡See Système, Vol. I, p. 222.]
[§See Thomas Carlyle. "Novalis," Critical and Miscellaneous Essays, Vol. II, p. 296.]
[‖Catéchisme, pp. 2–3.]

of it, should strive to cure himself of it, because his existence is not "systema-tized," is not in "complete unity," as long as he cares for more than one thing. The strangest part of the matter is, that this doctrine seems to M. Comte to be axiomatic. That all perfection consists in unity, he apparently considers to be a maxim which no sane man thinks of questioning. It never seems to enter into his conceptions that any one could object *ab initio*, and ask, why this universal systematizing, systematizing, systematizing? Why is it neces-sary that all human life should point but to one object, and be cultivated into a system of means to a single end? May it not be the fact that mankind, who after all are made up of single human beings, obtain a greater sum of happiness when each pursues his own, under the rules and conditions required by the good of the rest, than when each makes the good of the rest his only ˣobjectˣ, and allows himself no personal pleasures not indispensable to the preservation of his faculties? The regimen of a blockaded town should be cheerfully submitted to when high purposes require it, but is it the ideal perfection of human existence? M. Comte sees none of these difficulties. The only true happiness, he affirms, is in the exercise of the affections. He had found it so for a whole year, which was enough to enable him to get to the bottom of the question, and to judge whether he could do without every-thing else. Of course the supposition was not to be heard of that any other person could require, or be the better for, what M. Comte did not value. "Unity" and "systematization" absolutely demanded that all other people should model themselves after M. Comte. It would never do to suppose that there could be more than one road to human happiness, or more than one ingredient in it.

The most prejudiced must admit that this religion without theology is not chargeable with ʸ relaxation of moral restraints. On the contrary, it pro-digiously exaggerates them. It makes the same ethical mistake as the theory of Calvinism, that every act in life should be done for the glory of God, and that whatever is not a duty is a sin. It does not perceive that between the region of duty and that of sin there is an intermediate space, the region of positive worthiness. It is not good that persons should be bound, by other people's opinion, to do everything that they would deserve praise for doing. There is a standard of altruism to which all should be required to come up, and a degree beyond it which is not obligatory, but meritorious. It is incum-bent on every one to restrain the pursuit of his personal objects within the limits consistent with the essential interests of others. What those limits are, it is the province of ethical science to determine; and to keep all individuals and aggregations of individuals within them, is the proper office of punish-ment and of moral blame. If in addition to fulfilling this obligation, persons

ˣ–ˣ651   subject [*printer's error?*]
ʸ65   any

make the good of others a direct object of disinterested exertions, postponing or sacrificing to it even innocent personal indulgences, they deserve gratitude and honour, and are fit objects of moral praise. So long as they are in no way compelled to this conduct by any external pressure, there cannot be too much of it; but a necessary condition is its spontaneity; since the notion of a happiness for all, procured by the self-sacrifice of each, if the abnegation is really felt to be a sacrifice, is a contradiction. Such spontaneity by no means excludes sympathetic encouragement; but the encouragement should take the form of making self-devotion pleasant, not that of making everything else painful. The object should be to stimulate services to humanity by their natural rewards; not to render the pursuit of our own good in any other manner impossible, by visiting it with the reproaches of *other* and of our own conscience. The proper office of those sanctions is to enforce upon every one, the conduct necessary to give all other persons their fair chance: conduct which chiefly consists in not doing them harm, and not impeding them in anything which without harming others does good to themselves. To this must of course be added, that when we either expressly or tacitly undertake to do more, we are bound to keep our promise. And inasmuch as every one, who avails himself of the advantages of society, leads others to expect from him all such positive good offices and disinterested services as the moral improvement attained by mankind has rendered customary, he deserves moral blame if, without just cause, he disappoints that expectation. Through this principle the domain of moral duty *a*, in an improving society,*a* is always widening. When what once was uncommon virtue becomes common virtue, it comes to be numbered among obligations, while a degree exceeding what has grown common, remains simply meritorious.

M. Comte is accustomed to draw most of his ideas of moral cultivation from the discipline of the Catholic Church. Had he followed that guidance in the present case, he would have been less wide of the mark. For the distinction which we have drawn was fully recognized by the sagacious and far-sighted men who *b*constructed*b* the Catholic ethics. It is even one of the stock reproaches against Catholicism, that it has two standards of morality, and does not make obligatory on all Christians the highest rule of Christian perfection. It has one standard which, faithfully acted up to, suffices for salvation, another and a higher which when realized constitutes a saint. M. Comte, perhaps unconsciously, for there is nothing that he would have been more unlikely to do if he had been aware of it, has taken a leaf out of the book of the despised Protestantism. Like the extreme Calvinists, he requires that all believers shall be saints, and damns them (after his own fashion) if they are not.

*z–z*65,65[1]   others [*printer's error; corrected in Somerville College copy of* 65[1]]
a–a+66   *b–b*65,65[1]   created

Our conception of human life is different. We do not conceive life to be so rich in enjoyments, that it can afford to forego the cultivation of all those which address themselves to what M. Comte terms the egoistic propensities. On the contrary, we believe that a sufficient gratification of these, short of excess, but up to the measure which renders the enjoyment greatest, is almost always favourable to the benevolent affections. The moralization of the personal enjoyments we deem to consist, not in reducing them to the smallest possible amount, but in cultivating the habitual wish to share them with others, and with all others, and scorning to desire anything for oneself which is incapable of being so shared. There is only one passion or inclination which is permanently incompatible with this condition—the love of domination, or superiority, for its own sake; which implies, and is grounded on, the equivalent depression of other people. As a rule of conduct, to be enforced by moral sanctions, we think no more should be attempted than to prevent people from doing harm to others, or omitting to do such good as they have undertaken. Demanding no more than this, society, in any tolerable circumstances, obtains much more; for the natural activity of human nature, shut out from all noxious directions, will expand itself in useful ones. This is our conception of the moral rule prescribed by the religion of Humanity. But above this standard there is an unlimited range of moral worth, up to the most exalted heroism, which should be fostered by every positive encouragement, though not converted into an obligation. It is as much a part of our scheme as of M. Comte's, that the direct cultivation of altruism, and the subordination of egoism to it, far beyond the point of absolute moral duty, should be one of the chief aims of education, both individual and collective. We even recognize the value, for this end, of ascetic discipline, in the original Greek sense of the word. We think with Dr. Johnson, that he who has never denied himself anything which is not wrong, cannot be fully trusted for denying himself everything which is so. We do not doubt that children and young persons will one day be again systematically disciplined in self-mortification; that they will be taught, as in antiquity, to control their appetites, to brave dangers, and submit voluntarily to pain, as simple exercises in education. Something has been lost as well as gained by no longer giving to every citizen the training necessary for a soldier. Nor can any pains taken be too great, to form the habit, and develop the desire, of being useful to others and to the world, by the practice, independently of reward and of every personal consideration, of positive virtue beyond the bounds of prescribed duty. No efforts should be spared to associate the pupil's self-respect, and his desire of the respect of others, with service rendered to Humanity; when possible, collectively, but at all events, what is always possible, in the persons of its individual members. There are many remarks and precepts in M. Comte's volumes, which, as no less pertinent to our conception of morality than to his, we fully accept. For example; without admitting that to make "calculs personnels" is contrary to morality, we agree with him in the opinion, that the principal hygienic precepts should be inculcated, not solely or principally as maxims of prudence, but as a matter of duty to others, since by squandering our health we disable ourselves from rendering to our fellow-creatures the services to which they are entitled.[*] As M. Comte truly says, the prudential motive is by no means fully sufficient for the purpose, even physicians often disregarding their own precepts. The personal penalties of neglect of health are commonly distant, as well as more or less uncertain, and require the additional and more immediate sanction of moral responsibility. M. Comte, therefore, in this instance, is, we conceive, right in principle; though we have not the smallest doubt that he would have gone into extreme exaggeration in practice, and would have wholly ignored the legitimate liberty of the individual to judge for himself respecting his own bodily conditions, with due relation to the sufficiency of his means of knowledge, and taking the responsibility of the result.

Connected with the same considerations is another idea of M. Comte, which has great beauty and grandeur in it, and the realization of which, within the bounds of possibility, would be a cultivation of the social feelings on a most essential point. It is, that every person who lives by any useful work, should be habituated to regard himself not as an individual working for his private benefit, but as a public functionary;[†] and his wages, of whatever sort, ^cnot as^c the remuneration or purchase-money of his labour, which should be given freely, but as the provision made by society to enable him to carry it on, and to replace the materials and products which have been consumed in the process. M. Comte observes,[‡] that in modern industry every one in fact works much more for others than for himself, since his productions are to be consumed by others, and it is only necessary that his thoughts and imagination should adapt themselves to the real state of the fact. The practical problem, however, is not quite so simple, for a strong sense that he is working for others may lead to nothing better than feeling himself necessary to them, and instead of freely giving his commodity, may only encourage him to put a high price upon it. What M. Comte really means is that we should regard working for the benefit of others as a good in itself; that we should desire it for its own sake, and not for the sake of remuneration, which cannot justly be claimed for doing what we like: that the proper return for a service to society is the gratitude of society: and that the moral claim of any one in regard to the provision for his personal wants, is not a

[*See, e.g., *Système*, Vol. I, pp. 667–8.]
[†See, e.g., *ibid.*, p. 363.]
[‡*Catéchisme*, pp. 20–1.]

^{c–c}65,65¹   as not

question of *quid pro quo* in respect to his co-operation, but of how much the circumstances of society permit to be assigned to him, consistently with the just claims of others. To this opinion we entirely subscribe. The rough method of settling the labourer's share of the produce, ^d the competition of the market, may represent a practical necessity, but certainly not a moral ideal. Its defence is, that civilization has not hitherto been equal to organizing anything better than this first rude approach to an equitable distribution. Rude as it is, we for the present go less wrong by leaving the thing to settle itself, than by settling it artificially in any mode which has yet been tried. But in whatever manner that question may ultimately be decided, the true moral and social idea of Labour is in no way affected by it. Until labourers and employers perform the work of industry in the spirit in which soldiers perform that of an army, industry will never be moralized, and military life will remain, what, in spite of the anti-social character of its direct object, it has hitherto been—the chief school of moral co-operation.

Thus far of the general idea of M. Comte's ethics and religion. We must now say something of the details. Here we approach the ludicrous side of the subject: but we shall unfortunately have to relate other things far more really ridiculous.

There cannot be a religion without a *cultus*. We use this term for want of any other, for its nearest equivalent, worship, suggests a different order of ideas. We mean by it, a set of systematic observances, intended to cultivate and maintain the religious sentiment. Though M. Comte justly appreciates the superior efficacy of acts, in keeping up and strengthening the feeling which prompts them, over any mode whatever of mere expression, he takes pains to organize the latter also with great minuteness. He provides an equivalent both for the private devotions, and for the public ceremonies, of other faiths. The reader will be surprised to learn, that the former consists of prayer. But prayer, as understood by M. Comte, does not mean asking; it is a mere outpouring of feeling; and for this view of it he claims the authority of the Christian mystics. It is not to be addressed to the Grand Etre, to collective Humanity; though he occasionally carries metaphor so far as to style this a goddess. The honours to collective Humanity are reserved for the public celebrations. Private adoration is to be addressed to it in the persons of worthy individual representatives, who may be either living or dead, but must in all cases be women; for women, being the *sexe aimant*,[*] represent the best attribute of humanity, that which ought to regulate all human life, nor can Humanity possibly be symbolized in any form but that of a woman. The objects of private adoration are the mother, the wife, and the daughter, representing severally the past, the present, and the future, and

[*Système, Vol. II, p. 313.]
^d65   by

calling into active exercise the three social sentiments, veneration, attachment, and kindness. We are to regard them, whether dead or alive, as our guardian angels, "les vrais anges gardiens."[*] If the last two have never existed, or if, in the particular case, any of the three types is too faulty for the office assigned to it, their place may be supplied by some other type of womanly excellence, even by one merely historical. Be the object living or dead, the adoration (as we understand it) is to be addressed only to the idea. The prayer consists of two parts; a commemoration, followed by an effusion. By a commemoration M. Comte means an effort of memory and imagination, summoning up with the utmost possible vividness the image of the object: and every artifice is exhausted to render the image as life-like, as close to the reality, as near an approach to actual hallucination, as is consistent with sanity. This degree of intensity having been, as far as practicable, attained, the effusion follows. Every person should compose his own form of prayer, which should be repeated not mentally only, but orally, and may be added to or varied for sufficient cause, but never arbitrarily. It may be interspersed with passages from the best poets, when they present themselves spontaneously, as giving a felicitous expression to the adorer's own feeling. These observances M. Comte practised to the memory of his Clotilde, and he enjoins them on all true believers. They are to occupy two hours of every day, divided into three parts; at rising, in the middle of the working hours, and in bed at night. The first, which should be in a kneeling attitude, will commonly be the longest, and the second the shortest. The third is to be extended as nearly as possible to the moment of falling asleep, that its effect may be felt in disciplining even the dreams.

The public *cultus* consists of a series of celebrations or festivals, eighty-four in the year, so arranged that at least one occurs in every week. They are devoted to the successive glorification of Humanity itself; of the various ties, political and domestic, among mankind; of the successive stages in the past evolution of our species; and of the several classes into which M. Comte's polity divides mankind. M. Comte's religion has, moreover, nine Sacraments; consisting in the solemn consecration, by the priests of Humanity, with appropriate exhortations, of all the great transitions in life; the entry into life itself, and into each of its successive stages: education, marriage, the choice of a profession, and so forth. Among these is death, which receives the name of transformation, and is considered as a passage from objective existence to subjective—to living in the memory of our fellow-creatures. Having no eternity of objective existence to offer, M. Comte's religion gives *e*it all it*e* can, by holding out the hope of subjective immortality—of existing in the remembrance and in the posthumous adoration of mankind at large,

[*See, e.g., *Catéchisme*, pp. 184–5.]

*e–e*65   all it] 65¹   it all he [*printer's error; corrected in Somerville College copy of* 65¹] if we have done anything to deserve remembrance from them; at all events, of those whom we loved during life; and when they too are gone, of being included in the collective adoration paid to the Grand Etre. People are to be taught to look forward to this as a sufficient recompense for the devotion of a whole life to the service of Humanity. Seven years after death, comes the last Sacrament: a public judgment, by the priesthood, on the memory of the defunct. This is not designed for purposes of reprobation, but of honour, and any one may, by declaration during life, exempt himself from it. If judged, and found worthy, he is solemnly incorporated with the Grand Etre, and his remains are transferred from the civil to the religious place of sepulture: "le bois sacré qui doit entourer chaque temple de l'Humanité."[*]

This brief abstract gives no idea of the minuteness of M. Comte's prescriptions, and the extraordinary height to which he carries the mania for regulation by which Frenchmen are distinguished among Europeans, and M. Comte among Frenchmen. It is this which throws an irresistible air of ridicule over the whole subject. There is nothing really ridiculous in the devotional practices which M. Comte recommends towards a cherished memory or an ennobling ideal, when they come unprompted from the depths of the individual feeling; but there is something ineffably ludicrous in enjoining that everybody shall practise them three times daily for a period of two hours, not because his feelings require them, but for the premeditated purpose of getting his feelings up. The ludicrous, however, in any of its shapes, is a phænomenon with which M. Comte seems to have been totally unacquainted. There is nothing in his writings from which it could be inferred that he knew of the existence of such things as wit and humour. The only writer *distinguished for either, of* whom he shows any admiration, is Molière, and him he admires not for his wit but for his wisdom. We notice this without intending any reflection on M. Comte; for a profound conviction raises a person above the feeling of ridicule. But there are passages in his writings which, it really seems to us, could have been written by no man who had ever laughed. We will give one of these instances. Besides the regular prayers, M. Comte's religion, like the Catholic, has need of forms which can be applied to casual and unforeseen occasions. These, he says, must in general be left to the believer's own choice; but he suggests as a very suitable one the repetition of "the fundamental formula of Positivism," viz., "l'amour pour principe, l'ordre pour base, et le progrès pour but."[†] Not content, however, with an equivalent for the Paters and Aves of Catholicism, he must have one for the sign of the cross also; and he thus delivers himself:* "Cette expansion peut être perfectionnée par des signes universels. . . . Afin de

[*Système, Vol. IV, p. 130.]
[†See ibid., Vol. I, title page.]
*Ibid., Vol. IV, p. 100.

*-*65 possessed of either, for

mieux développer l'aptitude nécessaire de la formule positiviste à représenter toujours la condition humaine, il convient ordinairement de l'énoncer en touchant successivement les principaux organes que la théorie cérébrale assigne à ses trois éléments." This *may* be a very appropriate mode of expressing one's devotion to the Grand Etre: but any one who had appreciated its effect on the profane reader, would have thought it judicious to keep it back till a considerably more advanced stage in the propagation of the Positive Religion.

As M. Comte's religion has a *cultus*, so also it has a clergy, who are the pivot of his entire social and political system. Their nature and office will be best shown by describing his ideal of political society in its normal state, with the various classes of which it is composed.

The necessity of a Spiritual Power, distinct and separate from the temporal government, is the essential principle of M. Comte's political scheme; as it may well be, since the Spiritual Power is the only counterpoise he provides or tolerates, to the absolute dominion of the civil rulers. Nothing can exceed his combined detestation and contempt for government by assemblies, and for parliamentary or representative institutions in any form. They are an expedient, in his opinion, only suited to a state of transition, and even that nowhere but in England. The attempt to naturalize them in France, or any Continental nation, he regards as mischievous quackery. Louis Napoleon's usurpation is absolved, is made laudable to him, because it overthrew a representative government. Election of superiors by inferiors, except as a revolutionary expedient, is an abomination in his sight. Public functionaries of all kinds should name their successors, subject to the approbation of their own superiors, and giving public notice of the nomination so long beforehand as to admit of discussion, and the timely revocation of a wrong choice. But, by the side of the temporal rulers, he places another authority, with no power to command, but only to advise and remonstrate. The family being, in his mind as in that of Frenchmen generally, the foundation and essential type of all society, the separation of the two powers commences there. The spiritual, or moral and religious power, in ᵍaᵍ family, is the women of it. The positivist family is composed of the "fundamental couple,"[*] their children, and the parents of the man, if alive. The whole government of the household, except as regards the education of the children, resides in the man; and even over that he has complete power, but should forbear to exert it. The part assigned to the women is to improve the man through his affections, and to bring up the children, who, until the age of fourteen, at which scientific instruction begins, are to be educated wholly by their mother. That women may be better fitted for these functions, they are peremptorily excluded from

[**Système*, Vol. IV, p. 293.]

ᵍ⁻ᵍ65   the

all others. No woman is to work for her living. Every woman is to be supported by her husband or her male relations, and if she has none of these, by the State. She is to have no powers of government, even domestic, and no property. Her legal rights of inheritance are preserved to her, that her feelings of duty may make her voluntarily forego them. There are to be no marriage portions, that women may no longer be sought in marriage from interested motives. Marriages are to be rigidly indissoluble, except for a single cause. It is remarkable that the bitterest enemy of divorce among all philosophers, nevertheless allows it, in a case which the laws of England, and of other countries reproached by him with tolerating divorce, do not admit: namely, when one of the parties has been sentenced to an infamizing punishment, involving loss of civil rights. It is monstrous that condemnation, even for life, to a felon's punishment, should leave an unhappy victim bound to, and in the wife's case under the legal authority of, the culprit. M. Comte could feel for the injustice in this special case, because it chanced to be the unfortunate situation of his Clotilde. Minor degrees of unworthiness may entitle the innocent party to a legal separation, but without the power of re-marriage. Second marriages, indeed, are not permitted by the Positive Religion. There is to be no impediment to them by law, but morality is to condemn them, and every couple who are married religiously as well as civilly are to make a vow of eternal widowhood, "le veuvage éternel."[*] This absolute monogamy is, in M. Comte's opinion, essential to the complete fusion between two beings, which is the essence of marriage; and moreover, eternal constancy is required by the posthumous adoration, which is to be continuously paid by the survivor to one who, though objectively dead, still lives "subjectively." The domestic spiritual power, which resides in the women of the family, is chiefly concentrated in the most venerable of them, the husband's mother, while alive. It has an auxiliary in the influence of age, represented by the husband's father, who is supposed to have passed the period of retirement from active life, fixed by M. Comte (for he fixes everything) at sixty-three; at which age the head of the family gives up the reins of authority to his son, retaining only a consultative voice.

This domestic Spiritual Power, being principally moral, and confined to private life, requires the support and guidance of an intellectual power exterior to it, the sphere of which will naturally be wider, extending also to public life. This consists of the clergy, or priesthood, for M. Comte is fond of borrowing the consecrated expressions of Catholicism to denote the nearest equivalents which his own system affords. The clergy are the theoretic or philosophical class, and are supported by an endowment from the State, voted periodically, but administered by themselves. Like women, they are to be excluded from all riches, and from all participation in power (except the

[*See, e.g., *Système*, Vol. IV, p. 128.]

*h*undivided dominion*h* of each over his own household). They are neither to inherit, nor to receive emolument from any of their functions, or from their writings or teachings of any description, but are to live solely on their small salaries. This M. Comte deems necessary to the complete disinterestedness of their *i*counsel*i*. To have the confidence of the masses, they must, like the masses, be poor. Their exclusion from political and from all other practical occupations is indispensable for the same reason, and for others equally peremptory. Those occupations are, he contends, incompatible with the habits of mind necessary to philosophers. A practical position, either private or public, chains the mind to specialities and details, while a philosopher's business is with general truths and connected views (vues d'ensemble).[*] These, again, require an habitual abstraction from details, which unfits the mind for judging well and rapidly of individual cases. The same person cannot be both a good theorist and a good practitioner or ruler, though practitioners and rulers ought to have a solid theoretic education. The two kinds of function must be absolutely exclusive of one another: to attempt them both, is inconsistent with fitness for either. But as men may mistake their vocation, up to the age of thirty-five they are allowed to change their career.

To the clergy is entrusted the theoretic or scientific instruction of youth. The medical art also is to be in their hands, since no one is fit to be a physician who does not study and understand the whole man, moral as well as physical. M. Comte has a contemptuous opinion of the existing race of physicians, who, he says, deserve no higher name than that of veterinaires, since they concern themselves with man only in his animal, and not in his human character.[†] In his last years, M. Comte (as we learn from Dr. Robinet's volume) indulged in the wildest speculations on medical science, declaring all maladies to be one and the same disease, the disturbance or destruction of "l'unité cérébrale."[‡] The other functions of the clergy are moral, much more than intellectual. They are the spiritual directors, and venerated advisers, of the active or practical classes, including the political. They are the mediators in all social differences; between the labourers, for instance, and their employers. They are to advise and admonish on all important violations of the moral law. Especially, it devolves on them to keep the rich and powerful to the performance of their moral duties towards their inferiors. If private remonstrance fails, public denunciation is to follow: in extreme cases they may proceed to the length of excommunication, which, though it only operates through opinion, yet if it carries opinion with it, may, as M. Comte complacently observes, be of such powerful efficacy, that the richest man

[*See *Synthèse*, p. 524.]
[†*Catéchisme*, p. 247.]
[‡See Robinet, *Notice*, pp. 527–37.]

*h-h*65,65¹ absolute power   *i-i*65 counsels

may be driven to produce his subsistence by his own manual labour, through the impossibility of inducing any other person to work for him.[*] In this as in all other cases, the priesthood depends for its authority on carrying with it the mass of the people—those who, possessing no accumulations, live on the wages of daily labour; popularly but incorrectly termed the working classes, and by French writers, in their Roman law phraseology, proletaires. These, therefore, who are not allowed the smallest political rights, are incorporated into the Spiritual Power, of which they form, after women and the clergy, the third element.

It remains to give an account of the Temporal Power, composed of the rich and the employers of labour, two classes who in M. Comte's system are reduced to one, for he allows of no idle rich. A life made up of mere amusement and self-indulgence, though not interdicted by law, is to be deemed so disgraceful, that nobody with the smallest sense of shame would choose to be guilty of it. Here, we think, M. Comte has lighted on a true principle, towards which the tone of opinion in modern Europe is more and more tending, and which is destined to be one of the constitutive principles of regenerated society. We believe, for example, with him, that in the future there will be no class of landlords living at ease on their rents, but every landlord will be a capitalist trained to agriculture, himself superintending and directing the cultivation of his estate. No one but he who guides the work, should have the control of the tools. In M. Comte's system, the rich, as a rule, consist of the "captains of industry:"[†] but the rule is not entirely without exception, for M. Comte recognizes other useful modes of employing riches. In particular, one of his favourite ideas is that of an order of Chivalry, composed of the most generous and self-devoted of the rich, voluntarily dedicating themselves, like knights-errant of old, to the redressing of wrongs, and the protection of the weak and oppressed. He remarks, that oppression, in modern life, can seldom reach, or even venture to attack, the life or liberty of its victims (he forgets the case of domestic tyranny), but only their pecuniary means, and it is therefore by the purse chiefly that individuals can usefully interpose, as they formerly did by the sword. The occupation, however, of nearly all the rich, will be the direction of labour, and for this work they will be educated. Reciprocally, it is in M. Comte's opinion essential, that all directors of labour should be rich. Capital (in which he includes land) should be concentrated in a few holders, so that every capitalist may conduct the most extensive operations which one mind is capable of superintending. This is not only demanded by good economy, in order to take the utmost advantage of a rare kind of practical ability, but it necessarily follows from the principle of M. Comte's

[*Catéchisme, p. 254.]

[†See Thomas Carlyle. Past and Present. London: Chapman and Hall, 1843, Bk. IV, Chap. iv (chapter title).]

scheme, which regards a capitalist as a public functionary. M. Comte's conception of the relation of capital to society is essentially that of Socialists, but he would bring about by education and opinion, what they aim at effecting by positive institution. The owner of capital is by no means to consider himself its absolute proprietor. Legally he is not to be controlled in his dealings with it, for power should be in proportion to responsibility: but it does not belong to him for his own use; he is merely entrusted by society with a portion of the accumulations made by the past providence of mankind, to be administered for the benefit of the present generation and of posterity, under the obligation of preserving them unimpaired, and handing them down, more or less augmented, to *those who are to come*. He is not entitled to dissipate them, or divert them from the service of Humanity to his own pleasures. Nor has he a moral right to consume on himself the whole even of his profits. He is bound in conscience, if they exceed his reasonable wants, to employ the surplus in improving either the efficiency of his operations, or the physical and mental condition of his labourers. The portion of his gains which he may appropriate to his own use, must be decided by himself, under accountability to opinion; and opinion ought not to look very narrowly into the matter, nor hold him to a rigid reckoning for any moderate indulgence of luxury or ostentation; since under the great responsibilities that will be imposed on him, the position of an employer of labour will be so much less desirable, to any one in whom the instincts of pride and vanity are not strong, than the "heureuse insouciance" of a labourer, that those instincts must be to a certain degree indulged, or no one would undertake the office. With this limitation, every employer is a mere administrator of his possessions, for his work-people and for society at large. If he indulges himself lavishly, without reserving an ample remuneration for all who are employed under him, he is morally culpable, and will incur sacerdotal admonition. This state of things necessarily implies that capital should be in few hands, because, as M. Comte observes, without great riches, the obligations which society ought to impose, could not be fulfilled without an amount of personal abnegation that it would be hopeless to expect. If a person is conspicuously qualified for the conduct of an industrial enterprise, but destitute of the fortune necessary for undertaking it, M. Comte recommends that he should be enriched by subscription, or, in cases of sufficient importance, by the State. Small landed proprietors and capitalists, and the middle classes altogether, he regards as a parasitic growth, destined to disappear, the best of the body becoming large capitalists, and the remainder proletaires. Society will consist only of rich and poor, and it will be the business of the rich to make the best possible lot for the poor. The remuneration of the labourers will continue, as at present, to be a matter of voluntary arrangement between them and their employers, the last resort

*–*65,65[1]   our successors

on either side being refusal of co-operation, "refus de concours,"[*] in other words, a strike or a lock-out; with the sacerdotal order for mediators in case of need. But though wages are to be an affair of free contract, their standard is not to be the competition of the market, but the application of the products in equitable proportion between the wants of the labourers and the wants and dignity of the employer. As it is one of M. Comte's principles that a question cannot be usefully proposed without an attempt at a solution, he gives his ideas from the beginning as to what the normal income of a labouring family should be. They are on such a scale, that until some great extension shall have taken place in the scientific resources of mankind, it is no wonder he thinks it necessary to limit as much as possible the number of those who are to be supported by what is left of the produce. In the first place the labourer's dwelling, which is to consist of seven rooms, is, with all that it contains, to be his own property: it is the only landed property he is allowed to possess, but every family should be the absolute owner of all things which are destined for its exclusive use. Lodging being thus independently provided for, and education and medical attendance being secured gratuitously by the general arrangements of society, the pay of the labourer is to consist of two portions, the one monthly, and of fixed amount, the other weekly, and proportioned to the produce of his labour. The former M. Comte fixes at 100 francs (£ 4) for a month of 28 days; being £ 52 a year: and the rate of piece-work should be such as to make the other part amount to an average of seven francs (5s. 6d.) per working day.[†]

Agreeably to M. Comte's rule, that every public functionary should appoint his successor, the capitalist has unlimited power of transmitting his capital by gift or bequest, after his own death or retirement. In general it will be best bestowed entire upon one person, unless the business will advantageously admit of subdivision. He will naturally leave it to one or more of his sons, if sufficiently qualified; and rightly so, hereditary being, in M. Comte's opinion, preferable to acquired wealth, as being usually more generously administered. But, merely as his sons, they have no moral right to it. M. Comte here recognizes another of the principles, on which we believe that the constitution of regenerated society will rest. He maintains (as others in the present generation have done) that the father owes nothing to his son, except a good education, and pecuniary aid sufficient for an advantageous start in life: that he is entitled, and may be morally bound, to leave the bulk of his fortune to some other properly selected person or persons, whom he judges likely to make a more beneficial use of it. This is the first of three important points, in which M. Comte's theory of the family, wrong as we deem it in its foundations, is in advance of prevailing theories and existing

[*Système, Vol. IV, p. 334.]
[†Ibid., p. 341.]

institutions. The second is the re-introduction of adoption, not only in default of children, but to fulfil the purposes, and satisfy the sympathetic wants, to which such children as there are may happen to be inadequate. The third is a most important point—the incorporation of domestics as substantive members of the family. There is hardly any part of the present constitution of society more essentially vicious, and morally injurious to both parties, than the relation between masters and servants. To make this a really human and a moral relation, is one of the principal desiderata in social improvement. The feeling of the vulgar of all classes, that domestic service has anything in it peculiarly mean, is a feeling than which there is none meaner. In the feudal ages, youthful nobles of the highest rank though themselves honoured by officiating in what is now called a menial capacity, about the persons of superiors of both sexes, for whom they felt respect: and, as M. Comte observes, there are many families who can in no other way so usefully serve Humanity, as by ministering to the bodily wants of other families, called to functions which require the devotion of all their thoughts. We will add, by way of supplement to M. Comte's doctrine, that much of the daily physical work of a household, even in opulent families, if silly notions of degradation, common to all ranks, did not interfere, might very advantageously be performed by the family itself, at least by its younger members; to whom it would give healthful exercise of the bodily powers, which has now to be sought in modes far less useful, and also a familiar acquaintance with the real work of the world, and a moral willingness to take their share of its burthens, which, in the great majority of the better-off classes, do not now get cultivated at all.

We have still to speak of the directly political functions of the rich, or, as M. Comte terms them, the patriciate.[*] The entire political government is to be in their hands. First, however, the existing nations are to be broken up into small republics, the largest not exceeding the size of Belgium, Portugal, or Tuscany; any larger nationalities being incompatible with the unity of wants and feelings, which is required, not only to give due strength to the sentiment of patriotism (always strongest in small states), but to prevent undue compression; for no territory, M. Comte thinks, can without oppression be governed from a distant centre. Algeria, therefore, is to be given up to the Arabs, Corsica to its inhabitants, and France proper is to be, before the end of the century, divided into seventeen republics, corresponding to the number of considerable towns: Paris, however, (need it be said?) succeeding to Rome as the religious metropolis of the world. Ireland, Scotland, and Wales, are to be separated from England, which is of course to detach itself from all its transmarine dependencies. In each state thus constituted, the powers of government are to be vested in a triumvirate of the three principal bankers, who are to take the foreign, home, and financial depart-

[*Système, Vol. IV, p. 345.]

ments respectively. How they are to conduct the government and remain bankers, does not clearly appear; but it must be intended that they should combine both offices, for they are to receive no pecuniary remuneration for the political one. Their power is to amount to a dictatorship (M. Comte's own word):[*] and he is hardly justified in saying that he gives political power to the rich, since he gives it over the rich and every one else, to three individuals of the number, not even chosen by the rest, but named by their predecessors. As a check on the dictators, there is to be complete freedom of speech, writing, printing, and voluntary association; and all important acts of the government, except in cases of emergency, are to be announced sufficiently long beforehand to ensure ample discussion. This, and the ᵏinfluenceᵏ of the Spiritual Power, are the only guarantees provided against misgovernment. When we consider that the complete dominion of every nation of mankind is thus handed over to only four men—for the Spiritual Power is to be under the absolute and undivided control of a single Pontiff for the whole human race—one is appalled at the picture of entire subjugation and slavery, which is recommended to us as the last and highest result of the evolution of Humanity. But the conception rises to the terrific, when we are told the mode in which the single High Priest of Humanity is intended to use his authority. It is the most warning example we know, into what frightful aberrations a powerful and comprehensive mind may be led by the exclusive following out of a single idea.

The single idea of M. Comte, on this subject, is that the intellect should be wholly subordinated to the feelings; or, to translate the meaning out of sentimental into logical language, that the exercise of the intellect, as of all our other faculties, should have for its sole object the general good. Every other employment of it should be accounted not only idle and frivolous, but morally culpable. Being indebted wholly to Humanity for the cultivation to which we owe our mental powers, we are bound in return to consecrate them wholly to her service. Having made up his mind that this ought to be, there is with M. Comte but one step to concluding that the Grand Pontiff of Humanity must take care that it ˡshallˡ be; and on this foundation he organizes an elaborate system for the total suppression of all independent thought. He does not, indeed, invoke the arm of the law, or call for any prohibitions. The clergy are to have no monopoly. Any one else may cultivate science if he can, may write and publish if he can find readers, may give private instruction if anybody consents to receive it. But since the sacerdotal body will absorb into itself all but those whom it deems either intellectually or morally unequal to the vocation, all rival teachers will, as he calculates, be so discredited beforehand, that their competition will not be formidable. Within the body

[*Ibid., p. 346.]

ᵏ⁻ᵏ651   influences [printer's error?]   ˡ⁻ˡ65   shall itself, the High Priest has it in his power to make sure that there shall be no opinions, and no exercise of mind, but such as he approves; for he alone decides the duties and local residence of all its members, and can even eject them from the body. Before electing to be under this rule, we feel a natural curiosity to know in what manner it is to be exercised. Humanity has only yet had one Pontiff, whose mental qualifications for the post are not likely to be often surpassed, M. Comte himself. It is of some importance to know what are the ideas of this High Priest, concerning the moral and religious government of the human intellect.

One of the doctrines which M. Comte most strenuously enforces in his later writings is, that during the preliminary evolution of humanity, terminated by the foundation of Positivism, the free development of our forces of all kinds was the important matter, but that from this time forward the principal need is to regulate them. Formerly the danger was of their being insufficient, but henceforth, of their being abused. Let us express, in passing, our entire dissent from this doctrine. Whoever thinks that the wretched education which mankind as yet receive, calls forth their mental powers (except those of a select few) in a sufficient or even tolerable degree, must be very easily satisfied: and the abuse of them, far from becoming proportionally greater as knowledge and mental capacity increase, becomes rapidly less, provided always that the diffusion of those qualities keeps pace with their growth. The abuse of intellectual power is only to be dreaded, when society is divided between a few highly cultivated intellects and an ignorant and stupid multitude. But mental power is a thing which M. Comte does not want —or wants infinitely less than he wants submission and obedience. Of all the ingredients of human nature, he continually says, the intellect most needs to be disciplined and reined-in. It is the most turbulent, "le plus perturbateur,"[*] of all the mental elements; more so than even the selfish instincts. Throughout the whole modern transition, beginning with ancient Greece (for M. Comte tells us that we have always been in a state of revolutionary transition since then), the intellect has been in a state of systematic insurrection against "le cœur."[†] The metaphysicians and literati (lettrès), after helping to pull down the old religion and social order, are rootedly hostile to the construction of the new, ᵐdesiringᵐ only to prolong the existing scepticism and intellectual anarchy, which secure to them a cheap social ascendancy, without the labour of earning it by solid scientific preparation.[‡] The

[*Synthèse, p. 71.]
[†See, e.g., Système, Vol. I, p. 290; Vol. III, p. 288.]
[‡See, e.g., Catéchisme, pp. 375–80; Système, Vol. IV, pp. 497–8, 540.]

ᵐ–ᵐ65   and desire] 65¹   and desiring [printer's error; in the Somerville College copy of 65¹ desirous is substituted for desiring, but this incomplete change was not adopted]

scientific class, from whom better might have been expected, are, if possible, worse. Void of enlarged views, despising all that is too large for their comprehension, devoted [n]each exclusively[n] to his special science, contemptuously indifferent to moral and political interests, their sole aim is to acquire an easy reputation, and in France (through paid Academies and professorships) personal lucre, by pushing their sciences into idle and useless inquiries (speculations oiseuses),[*] of no value to the real interests of mankind, and tending to divert the thoughts from them. One of the duties most incumbent on opinion and on the Spiritual Power, is to stigmatize as immoral, and effectually suppress, these useless employments of the speculative faculties. All exercise of thought should be abstained from, which has not some beneficial tendency, some actual utility to mankind. M. Comte, of course, is not the man to say that it must be a merely material utility. If a speculation, though it has no doctrinal, has a logical value—if it throws any light on universal Method—it is still more deserving of cultivation than if its usefulness was merely practical: but, either as method or as doctrine, it must bring forth fruits to Humanity, otherwise it is not only contemptible, but criminal.

That there is a portion of truth at the bottom of all this, we should be the last to deny. No respect is due to any employment of the intellect which does not tend to the good of mankind. It is precisely on a level with any idle amusement, and should be condemned as waste of time, if carried beyond the limit within which amusement is permissible. And whoever devotes powers of thought which could render to Humanity services it urgently needs, to speculations and studies which it could dispense with, is liable to the discredit attaching to a well-grounded suspicion of caring little for Humanity. But who can affirm positively of any speculations, guided by right scientific methods, on subjects really accessible to the human faculties, that they are incapable of being of any use? Nobody knows what knowledge will prove to be of use, and what is destined to be useless. The most that can be said is that some kinds are of more certain, and above all, of more present utility than others. How often the most important practical results have been the remote consequence of studies which no one would have expected to lead to them! Could the mathematicians, who, in the schools of Alexandria, investigated the properties of the ellipse, have foreseen that nearly two thousand years afterwards their speculations would explain the solar system, and a little later would enable ships safely to circumnavigate the earth? Even in M. Comte's opinion, it is well for mankind that, in those early days, knowledge was thought worth pursuing for its own sake. Nor has the "foundation of Positivism," we imagine, so far changed the conditions of human existence, that

[*See, e.g., *Système*, Vol. I, p. 476.]

[n]–[n]65,65[1]   exclusively each

it should now be criminal to acquire, by observation and reasoning, a knowledge of the facts of the universe, leaving to posterity to find a use for it. Even in the last two or three years, has not the discovery of new metals, which may prove important even in the practical arts, arisen from one of the investigations which M. Comte most unequivocally condemns as idle, the research into the internal constitution of the sun? How few, moreover, of the discoveries which have changed the face of the world, either were or could have been arrived at by investigations aiming directly at the object! Would the mariner's compass ever have been found by direct efforts for the improvement of navigation? Should we have reached the electric telegraph by any amount of striving for a means of instantaneous communication, if Franklin had not identified electricity with lightning, and Ampère with magnetism? The most apparently insignificant archæological or geological fact, is often found to throw a light on human history, which M. Comte, the basis of whose social philosophy is history, should be the last person to disparage. The direction of the entrance to the °three great Pyramids° of Ghizeh, by showing the position of the circumpolar stars at the time when ᵖthey wereᵖ built, is the best evidence we even now have of the immense antiquity of Egyptian civilization.* The one point on which M. Comte's doctrine has some colour of reason, is the case of sidereal astronomy: so little knowledge of it being really accessible to us, and the connexion of that little with any terrestrial interests being, according to all our means of judgment, infinitesimal. It is certainly difficult to �q imagine�q how any considerable benefit to humanity can be derived from a knowledge of the motions of the double stars: should these ever become important to us it will be in so prodigiously remote an age, that we can afford to remain ignorant of them until, at least, all our moral, political, and social difficulties have been settled. Yet the discovery that gravitation extends even to those remote regions, gives some additional strength to the conviction of the universality of natural laws; and the habitual meditation on such vast objects and distances is not without an æsthetic usefulness, by kindling and exalting the imagination, the worth of which in itself, and even its reaction on the intellect, M. Comte is quite capable of appreciating. He would reply, however, that there are better means of accomplishing these purposes. In the same spirit he condemns the study even of the solar system, when extended to any planets but those which are visible to the naked eye, and which alone exert an appreciable gravitative influence on the earth. Even the perturbations he thinks it idle to study, beyond a mere general conception of them, and thinks that astronomy may well limit its domain to the motions and

*[65¹] See Sir John Herschel's *Outlines of Astronomy* [London: Longman, Brown, Green, and Longmans, 1849], § 319 [pp. 191–2].

o–o65   great Pyramid   p–p65   it was   q–q65   conceive

mutual action of the earth, sun, and moon. He looks for a similar expurgation of all the other sciences. In one passage he expressly says that the greater part of the researches which are really accessible to us are idle and useless. He would pare down the dimensions of all the sciences as narrowly as possible. He is continually repeating that no science, as an abstract study, should be carried further than is necessary to lay the foundation for the science next above it, and so ultimately for moral science, the principal purpose of them all. Any further extension of the mathematical and physical sciences should be merely "episodic;"[*] limited to what may from time to time be demanded by the requirements of industry and the arts; and should be left to the industrial classes, except when they find it necessary to apply to the sacerdotal order for some additional development of scientific theory. This, he evidently thinks, would be a rare contingency, most physical truths sufficiently concrete and real for practice being empirical. Accordingly in estimating the number of clergy necessary for France, Europe, and our entire planet (for his forethought extends thus far), he proportions it solely to their moral and religious attributions (overlooking, by the way, even their medical); and leaves nobody with any time to cultivate the sciences, except abortive candidates for the priestly office, who having been refused admittance into it for insufficiency in moral excellence or in strength of character, may be thought worth retaining as "pensioners"[†] of the sacerdotal order, on account of their theoretic abilities.

It is no exaggeration to say, that M. Comte gradually acquired a real hatred for scientific and all purely intellectual pursuits, and was bent on retaining no more of them than was strictly indispensable. The greatest of his anxieties is lest people should reason, and seek to know, more than enough. He regards all abstraction and all reasoning as morally dangerous, by developing an inordinate pride (orgueil), and still more, by producing dryness (sécheresse).[‡] Abstract thought, he says, is not a wholesome occupation for more than a small number of human beings, nor of them for more than a small part of their time. Art, which calls the emotions into play along with and more than the reason, is the only intellectual exercise really adapted to human nature. It is nevertheless indispensable that the chief theories of the various abstract sciences, together with the modes in which those theories were historically and logically arrived at, should form a part of universal education: for, first, it is only thus that the methods can be learnt, by which to attain the results sought by the moral and social sciences: though we cannot perceive that M. Comte got at his own moral and social results by

[*See *Système*, Vol. IV, p. 193.]
[†*Ibid.*, p. 225.]
[‡*Synthèse*, p. 69.]

those processes. Secondly, the principal truths of the subordinate sciences are necessary to the systematization (still systematization!) of our conceptions, by binding together our notions of the world in a set of propositions, which are coherent, and ʳareʳ a sufficiently correct representation of fact for our practical wants. Thirdly, a familiar knowledge of the invariable laws of natural phenomena is a great elementary lesson of submission, which, he is never weary of saying, is the first condition both of morality and of happiness. For these reasons, he would cause to be taught, from the age of fourteen to that of twenty-one, to all persons, rich and poor, girls or youths, a knowledge of the whole series of abstract sciences, such as none but the most highly instructed persons now possess, and of a far more systematic and philosophical character than is usually possessed even by them. (N.B.— They are to learn, during the same years, Greek and Latin, having previously, between the ages of seven and fourteen, learnt the five principal modern languages, to the degree necessary for reading, with due appreciation, the chief poetical compositions in each.) [*] But they are to be taught all this, not only without encouraging, but stifling as much as possible, the examining and questioning spirit. The disposition which should be encouraged is that of receiving all on the authority of the teacher. The Positivist faith, even in its scientific part, is *la foi démontrable*, but ought by no means to be *la foi toujours démontrée*.[†] The pupils have no business to be over-solicitous about proof. The teacher should not even present the proofs to them in a complete form, or as proofs. The object of instruction is to make them understand the doctrines themselves, perceive their mutual connexion, and form by means of them a consistent and *systematized* conception of nature. As for the demonstrations, it is rather desirable than otherwise that even theorists should forget them, retaining only the results. Among all the aberrations of scientific men, M. Comte thinks none greater than the pedantic anxiety they show for complete proof, and perfect rationalization of scientific processes. It ought to be enough that the doctrines afford an explanation of phænomena, consistent with itself and with known facts, and that the processes are justified by their fruits. This over-anxiety for proof, he complains, is breaking down, by vain scruples, the knowledge which seemed to have been attained; witness the present state of chemistry. The demand of proof for what has been accepted by Humanity, is itself a mark of "distrust, if not hostility, to the sacerdotal order"[‡] (the naïveté of this would be charming, if it were not deplorable), and is a revolt against the traditions of the human race. So early had the new High Priest adopted the feelings and taken up the

[*See *Système*, Vol. I, pp. 172 ff.]
[†*Synthèse*, p. 93.]
[‡*Ibid.*, p. 278.]

ʳ⁻ʳ+65¹,66

inheritance of the old. One of his favourite aphorisms is the strange one, that the living are more and more governed by the dead.[*] As is not uncommon with him, he introduces the dictum in one sense, and uses it in another. What he at first means by it, is that as civilization advances, the sum of our possessions, physical and intellectual, is due in a decreasing proportion to ourselves, and in an increasing one to our progenitors. The use he makes of it is, that we should submit ourselves more and more implicitly to the authority of previous generations, and suffer ourselves less and less to doubt their judgment, or test by our own reason the grounds of their opinions. The unwillingness of the human intellect and conscience, in their present state of "anarchy," to sign their own abdication, he calls "the insurrection of the living against the dead."[†] To this complexion has Positive Philosophy come at last!

Worse, however, remains to be told. M. Comte selects a hundred volumes of science, philosophy, poetry, history, and general knowledge, which he deems a sufficient library for every positivist, even of the theoretic order, and actually proposes a systematic holocaust of books in general—it would almost seem of all books except these.[‡] Even that to which he shows most indulgence, poetry, except the very best, is to *share this* fate, with the reservation of select passages, on the ground that, poetry being intended to cultivate our instinct of ideal perfection, any kind of it that is less than the best is worse than none. This imitation of the error, we will call it the crime, of the early Christians—and in an exaggerated form, for even they destroyed only those writings of pagans or heretics which were directed against themselves— is the one thing in M. Comte's projects which merits real indignation. When once M. Comte has decided, all evidence on the other side, nay, the very historical evidence on which he grounded his decision, had better perish. When mankind have enlisted under his banner, they must burn their ships. There is, though in a less offensive form, the same overweening presumption in a suggestion he makes, that all species of animals and plants which are useless to man should be systematically rooted out. As if any one could presume to assert that the smallest weed may not, as knowledge advances, be found to have some property serviceable to man. When we consider that the united power of the whole human race cannot reproduce a species once eradicated —that what is once done, in the extirpation of races, can never be repaired; one can only be thankful that amidst all which the past rulers of mankind have to answer for, they have never come up to the measure of the great regenerator of Humanity; mankind have not yet been under the rule of one

[*See, e.g., *Catéchisme*, p. 32; *Système*, Vol. III, p. xxxiv.]
[†*Synthèse*, p. 278.]
[‡*Système*, Vol. IV, pp. 269–70; *Catéchisme*, p. 179.]

*–*65,651   undergo a similar

who assumes that he knows all there is to be known, and that when he has put himself at the head of humanity, the book of human knowledge may be closed.

Of course M. Comte does not make this assumption consistently. He does not imagine that he actually possesses all knowledge, but only that he is an infallible judge what knowledge is worth possessing. He does not believe that mankind have reached in all directions the extreme limits of useful and laudable scientific inquiry. He thinks there is a large scope for it still, in adding to our power over the external world, but chiefly in perfecting our own physical, intellectual, and moral nature. He holds that all our mental strength should be economized, for the pursuit of this object in the mode leading most directly to the end. With this view, some one problem should always be selected, the solution of which would be more important than any other to the interests of humanity, and upon this the entire intellectual resources of the theoretic mind should be concentrated, until it is either resolved, or has to be given up as insoluble: after which mankind should go on to another, to be pursued with similar exclusiveness. The selection of this problem of course rests with the sacerdotal order, or in other words, with the High Priest. We should then see the whole speculative intellect of the human race simultaneously at work on one question, by orders from above, as a French minister of public instruction once boasted that a million of boys were saying the same lesson during the same half-hour in every town and village of France. The reader will be anxious to know, how much better and more wisely the human intellect will be applied under this absolute monarchy, and to what degree this system of government will be preferable to the present anarchy, in which every theorist does what is intellectually right in his own eyes. M. Comte has not left us in ignorance on this point. He gives us ample means of judging. The Pontiff of Positivism informs us what problem, in his opinion, should be selected before all others for this united pursuit.

What this problem is, we must leave those who are curious on the subject to learn from the treatise itself. When they have done so, they will be qualified to form their own opinion of the amount of advantage which the general good of mankind would be likely to derive, from exchanging the present "dispersive speciality" and "intellectual anarchy" for the subordination of the intellect to the *cœur*, personified in a High Priest, prescribing a single problem for the undivided study of the theoretic mind.

We have given a sufficient general idea of M. Comte's plan for the regeneration of human society, by putting an end to anarchy, and "systematizing" human thought and conduct under the direction of feeling. But an adequate conception will not have been formed of the height of his self-confidence, until something more has been told. Be it known, then, that M. Comte by no means proposes this new constitution of society for realization in the remote future. A complete plan of measures of transition is ready prepared, and he determines the year, before the end of the present century, in which the new spiritual and temporal powers will be installed, and the régime of our maturity will begin. He did not indeed calculate on converting to Positivism, within that time, more than a thousandth part of all the heads of families in Western Europe and its offshoots beyond the Atlantic. But he fixes the time necessary for the complete political establishment of Positivism at thirty-three years, divided into three periods, of seven, five, and twenty-one years respectively. At the expiration of seven, the direction of public education in France would be placed in M. Comte's hands. In five years more, the Emperor Napoleon, or his successor, will resign his power to a provisional triumvirate, composed of three eminent proletaires of the positivist faith; for proletaires, though not fit for permanent rule, are the best agents of the transition, being the most free from the prejudices which are the chief obstacle to it. These rulers will employ the remaining twenty-one years in preparing society for its final constitution; and after duly installing the Spiritual Power, and effecting the decomposition of France into the seventeen republics before mentioned, will give over the temporal government of each to the normal dictatorship of the three bankers. A man may be deemed happy, but scarcely modest, who had such boundless confidence in his own powers of foresight, and expected so complete a triumph of his own ideas on the reconstitution of society within the possible limits of his lifetime. If he could live (he said) to the age of Fontenelle, or of Hobbes, or even of Voltaire, he should see all this realized, or as good as realized. He died, however, at sixty, without leaving any disciple sufficiently advanced to be appointed his successor. There is now a College, and a Director, of Positivism; but Humanity no longer possesses a High Priest.

What more remains to be said may be despatched more summarily. Its interest is philosophic rather than practical. In his four volumes of *Politique Positive*, M. Comte revises and re-elaborates the scientific and historical expositions of his first treatise. His object is to systematize (again to systematize) knowledge from the human or subjective point of view, the only one, he contends, from which a real synthesis is possible. For (he says) the knowledge attainable by us of the laws of the universe is at best fragmentary, and incapable of reduction to a real unity. An objective synthesis, the dream of Descartes and the best thinkers of old, is impossible.[*] The laws of the real world are too numerous, and the manner of their working into one another too intricate, to be, as a general rule, correctly traced and represented by our reason. The only connecting principle in our knowledge is its relation to our wants, and it is upon that we must found our systematization. The answer to this is, first, that there is no necessity for an universal synthesis;

[*See, e.g., *Système*, Vol. I, p. 420; Vol. IV, p. 211.]

and secondly, that the same arguments may be used against the possibility of a complete subjective, as of a complete objective systematization. A subjective synthesis must consist in the arrangement and co-ordination of all useful knowledge, on the basis of its relation to human wants and interests. But those wants and interests are, like the laws of the universe, extremely multifarious, and the order of preference among them in all their different gradations (for it varies according to the degree of each) cannot be cast into precise general propositions. M. Comte's subjective synthesis consists only in eliminating from the sciences everything that he deems useless, and presenting as far as possible every theoretical investigation as the solution of a practical problem. To this, however, he cannot consistently adhere; for, in every science, the theoretic truths are much more closely connected with one another than with the human purposes which they eventually serve, and can only be made to cohere in the intellect by being, to a great degree, presented as if they were truths of pure reason, irrespective of any practical application.

There are many things eminently characteristic of M. Comte's second career, in this revision of the results of his first. Under the head of Biology, and for the better combination of that science with Sociology and Ethics, he found that he required a new system of Phrenology, being justly dissatisfied with that of Gall and his successors. Accordingly he set about constructing one *à priori*, grounded on the best enumeration and classification he could make of the elementary faculties of our intellectual, moral, and animal nature; to each of which he assigned an hypothetical place in the skull, the most conformable that he could to the few positive facts on the subject which he considered as established, and to the general presumption that functions which react strongly on one another must have their organs adjacent: leaving the localities avowedly to be hereafter verified, by anatomical and inductive investigation. There is considerable merit in this attempt, though it is liable to obvious criticisms, of the same nature as his own upon Gall. But the characteristic thing is, that while presenting all this as hypothesis waiting for verification, he could not have taken its truth more completely for granted if the verification had been made. In all that he afterwards wrote, every detail of his theory of the brain is as unhesitatingly asserted, and as confidently built upon, as any other doctrine of science. This is his first great attempt in the "Subjective Method," which, originally meaning only the subordination of the pursuit of the truth to human uses, had already come to mean drawing truth itself from the fountain of his own mind. He had become, on the one hand, almost indifferent to proof, provided he attained theoretic coherency, and on the other, serenely confident that even the guesses which originated with himself could not but come out true.

There is one point in his later view of the sciences, which appears to us a decided improvement on his earlier. He adds to the six fundamental sciences of his original scale, a seventh under the name of Morals, forming the highest step of the ladder, immediately after Sociology: remarking that it might, with still greater propriety, be termed Anthropology, being the science of individual human nature, a study, when rightly understood, more special and complicated than even that of Society. For it is obliged to take into consideration the diversities of constitution and temperament (la réaction cérébrale des viscères végétatifs) the effects of which, still very imperfectly understood, are highly important in the individual, but in the theory of society may be neglected, because, differing in different persons, they neutralize one another on the large scale.[*] This is a remark worthy of M. Comte in his best days; and the science thus conceived is, as he says, the true scientific foundation of the art of Morals (and indeed of the art of human life), which, therefore, may, both philosophically and didactically, be properly combined with it.

His philosophy of general history is recast, and in many respects changed; we cannot but say, greatly for the worse. He gives much greater development than before to the Fetishistic, and to what he terms the Theocratic, periods.[†] To the Fetishistic view of nature he evinces a partiality, which appears strange in a Positive philosopher. But the reason is that Fetish-worship is a religion of the feelings, and not at all of the intelligence. He regards it as cultivating universal love: as a practical fact it cultivates much rather universal fear. He looks upon Fetishism as much more akin to Positivism than any of the forms of Theology, inasmuch as these consider matter as inert, and moved only by forces, natural and supernatural, exterior to itself: while Fetishism resembles Positivism in conceiving matter as spontaneously active, and errs only by not distinguishing activity from life. As if the superstition of the Fetishist consisted only in believing that the objects which produce the phænomena of nature involuntarily, produce them voluntarily. The Fetishist thinks not merely that his Fetish is alive, but that it can help him in war, can cure him of diseases, can grant him prosperity, or afflict him with all the contrary evils. Therein consists the lamentable effect of Fetishism— its degrading and prostrating influence on the feelings and conduct, its conflict with all genuine experience, and antagonism to all real knowledge of nature.

M. Comte had also no small sympathy with the Oriental theocracies, as he calls the sacerdotal castes, who indeed often deserved it by their early services to intellect and civilization; by the aid they gave to the establishment of regular government, the valuable though empirical knowledge they accumulated, and the height to which they helped to carry some of the useful arts. M. Comte admits that they became oppressive, and that the prolongation of

[*See *Système*, Vol. II, pp. 437 ff.]
[†*Ibid.*, pp. 84 ff.]

their ascendancy came to be incompatible with further improvement. But he ascribes this to their having arrogated to themselves the temporal government, which, so far as we have any authentic information, they never did. The reason why the sacerdotal corporations became oppressive, was because they were organized: because they attempted the "unity" and "systematization" so dear to M. Comte, and allowed no science and no speculation, except with their leave and under their direction. M. Comte's sacerdotal order, which, in his system, has all the power that ever they had, would be oppressive in the same manner; with no variation but that which arises from the altered state of society and of the human mind.

M. Comte's partiality to the theocracies is strikingly contrasted with his dislike of the Greeks, whom as a people he thoroughly detests, for their undue addiction to intellectual speculation, and considers to have been, by an inevitable fatality, morally sacrificed to the formation of a few great scientific intellects,—principally Aristotle, Archimedes, Apollonius, and Hipparchus. Any one who knows Grecian history as it can now be known, will be amazed at M. Comte's travestie of it, in which the vulgarest historical prejudices are accepted and exaggerated, to illustrate the mischiefs of intellectual culture left to its own guidance.

There is no need to analyze further M. Comte's second view of universal history. The best chapter ^{t}, to our mind,^{t} is that on the Romans,[*] to whom, because they were greater in practice than in theory, and for centuries worked together in obedience to a social sentiment (though only that of their country's aggrandizement), M. Comte is as favourably affected, as he is inimical to all but a small selection of eminent thinkers among the Greeks. The greatest blemish in this chapter is the ^{u}prodigious over-estimation^u of Julius Cæsar, whom M. Comte regards as one of the most illustrious characters in history, and of the greatest practical benefactors of mankind. Cæsar had many eminent qualities, but what he did to deserve such praise we are at a loss to discover, except subverting a free government: that merit, however, with M. Comte, goes a great way. It did not, in his former days, suffice to rehabilitate Napoleon, whose name and memory he regarded with a bitterness highly honourable to himself, and whose career he deemed one of the greatest calamities in modern history. But in his later writings these sentiments are considerably mitigated: he regards Napoleon as a more estimable "dictator" than Louis Philippe, and thinks that his greatest error was re-establishing the Academy of Sciences![†] That this should be said by M. Comte, and said of Napoleon, measures the depth to which his moral standard had fallen.

[*Système, Vol. III, Chap. v.]
[†Ibid., Vol. IV, pp. 388 ff.]

$^{t-t}$+66 $^{u-u}$65,65^1 idolatry

The last volume which he published, that on the Philosophy of Mathematics,[*] is in some respects a still sadder picture of intellectual degeneracy than those which preceded it. After the admirable résumé of the subject in the first volume of his first great work, we expected something of the very highest order when he returned to the subject for a more thorough treatment of it. But, being the commencement of a Synthèse Subjective, it contains, as might be expected, a great deal that is much more subjective than mathematical. Nor of this do we complain: but we little imagined of what nature this subjective matter was to be. M. Comte here joins together the two ideas, which, of all that he has put forth, are the most repugnant to the fundamental principles of Positive Philosophy. One of them is that on which we have just commented, the assimilation between Positivism and Fetishism. The other, of which we took notice in a former article, was the "liberté facultative" of shaping our scientific conceptions to gratify the demands not solely of objective truth, but of intellectual and æsthetic suitability.[†] It would be an excellent thing, M. Comte thinks, if science could be deprived of its *sécheresse*, and directly associated with sentiment. Now it is impossible to prove that the external world, and the bodies composing it, are not endowed with feeling, and voluntary agency. It is therefore highly desirable that we should educate ourselves into imagining that they are. Intelligence it will not do to invest them with, for some distinction must be maintained between simple activity and life. But we may suppose that they feel what is done to them, and desire and will what they themselves do. Even intelligence, which we must deny to them in the present, may be attributed to them in the past. Before man existed, the earth, at that time an intelligent being, may have exerted

its physico-chemical activity so as to improve the astronomical order by changing its principal coefficients. Our planet may be supposed to have rendered its orbit less excentric, and thereby more habitable, by planning a long series of explosions, analogous to those from which, according to the best hypotheses, comets proceed. Judiciously reproduced, similar shocks may have rendered the inclination of the earth's axis better adapted to the future wants of the Grand Etre. *A fortiori* the Earth may have modified its own figure, which is only beyond our intervention because our spiritual ascendancy has not at its disposal a sufficient material force.

The like may be conceived as having been done by each of the other planets, in concert, possibly, with the Earth and with one another.

In proportion as each planet improved its own condition, its life exhausted itself by excess of innervation; but with the consolation of rendering its self-devotion more efficacious, when the extinction of its special functions, first animal, and finally vegetative, reduced it to the universal attributes of feeling and activity.*

[*See the *Synthèse subjective*.]
[†See above, p. 294; the reference is to the *Cours*, Vol. III, p. 81.]
Synthèse, pp. 10–11, 11.

This stuff, though he calls it fiction, he soon after speaks of as belief (croyance), to be greatly recommended, as at once satisfying our natural curiosity, and "perfecting our unity" (again unity!) ᵛ"by supplying"ᵛ the gaps in our scientific notions with poetic fictions, and developing sympathetic emotions and æsthetic inspirations: the world being conceived as aspiring to second mankind in ameliorating the universal order under the impulse of the Grand Etre."[*] And he obviously intends that we should be trained to make these fantastical inventions permeate all our associations, until we are incapable of conceiving the world and Nature apart from them, and they become equivalent to, and are in fact transformed into, real beliefs.

Wretched as this is, it is singularly characteristic of M. Comte's later mode of thought. A writer might be excused for introducing into an avowed work of fancy this dance of the planets, and conception of an animated Earth. If finely executed, he might even be admired for it. No one blames a poet for ascribing feelings, purposes, and human propensities to flowers. Because a conception might be interesting, and perhaps edifying, in a poem, M. Comte would have it imprinted on the inmost texture of every human mind in ordinary prose. If the imagination were not taught its prescribed lesson equally with the reason, where would be Unity? "It is important that the domain of fiction should become as *systematic* as that of demonstration, in order that their mutual harmony may be conformable to their respective destinations, both equally directed towards the continual increase of *unity*, personal and social."*

Nor is it enough to have created the Grand Fétiche (so he actually proposes to call the Earth),[†] and to be able to include it and all concrete existence in our adoration along with the Grand Etre. It is necessary also to extend Positivist Fetishism to purely abstract existence; to "animate" the laws as well as the facts of nature. It is not sufficient to have made physics sentimental, mathematics must be made so too. This does not at first seem easy; but M. Comte finds the means of accomplishing it. His plan is, to make Space also an object of adoration, under the name of the Grand Milieu, and consider it as the representative of Fatality in general. "The final *unity* disposes us to cultivate sympathy by developing our gratitude to whatever serves the Grand Etre. It must dispose us to venerate the Fatality on which reposes the whole aggregate of our existence."[‡] We should conceive this Fatality as having a fixed seat, and that seat must be considered to be Space, which should be conceived as possessing feeling, but not activity or intelligence. And in our abstract speculations we should imagine all our conceptions as located in free Space. Our images of all sorts, down to our geometrical

[*Synthèse, p. 12.] *Ibid.
[†Ibid., p. 14.] [‡Ibid., p. 15.]
ᵛ⁻ᵛ65 by "supplying

diagrams, and even our ciphers and algebraic symbols, should always be figured to ourselves as written in space, and not on paper or any other material substance. M. Comte adds that they should be conceived as green on a white ground.[*]

We cannot go on any longer with this *w* . In spite of it all, the volume on mathematics is full of profound thoughts, and will be very suggestive to those who take up the subject after M. Comte. What deep meaning there is, for example, in the idea that the infinitesimal calculus is a conception analogous to the corpuscular hypothesis in physics; which last M. Comte has always considered as a logical artifice; not an opinion respecting matters of fact. The assimilation, as it seems to us, throws a flood of light on both conceptions; on the physical one still more than the mathematical. We might extract many ideas of similar, though none perhaps of equal, suggestiveness. But mixed with these, what pitiable *niaiseries*! One of his great points is the importance of the "moral and intellectual properties of numbers."[†] He cultivates a superstitious reverence for some of them. The first three are sacred, *les nombres sacrés*: One being the type of all Synthesis, Two of all Combination, which he now says *is* always binary (in his first treatise he only said that we may usefully represent it to ourselves as being so), and Three of all Progression, which not only requires three terms, but, as he now maintains, never ought to have any more.[‡] To these sacred numbers all our mental operations must be made, as far as possible, to adjust themselves. Next to them, he has a great partiality for the number seven; for these whimsical reasons: "Composed of two progressions followed by a synthesis, or of one progression between two couples, the number seven, coming next after the sum of the three sacred numbers, determines the largest group which we can distinctly imagine. Reciprocally, it marks the limit of the divisions which we can directly conceive in a magnitude of any kind."[§] The number seven, therefore, must be foisted in wherever possible, and among other things, is to be made the basis of numeration, which is hereafter to be septimal instead of decimal: producing all the inconvenience of a change of system, not only without getting rid of, but greatly aggravating, the disadvantages of the existing one. But then, he says, it is absolutely necessary that the basis of numeration should be a prime number. All other people think it absolutely necessary that it should not, and regard the present basis as only objectionable in not being divisible enough. But M. Comte's puerile predilection for prime numbers almost passes belief. His reason is that they are the type of irreducibility: each of them is a kind of ultimate arithmetical fact. This, to any one who knows M. Comte in his later aspects, is amply sufficient. Nothing can exceed

[*Ibid., p. 119.]
[‡Synthèse, p. 108.]
*w*65   trash

[†Système, Vol. I, p. 542.]
[§Ibid., p. 127.]

his delight in anything which says to the human mind, Thus far shalt thou go and no farther. If prime numbers are precious, doubly prime numbers are doubly so; meaning those which are not only themselves prime numbers, but the number which marks their place in the series of prime numbers is a prime number. Still greater is the dignity of trebly prime numbers; when the number marking the place of this second number is also prime. The number thirteen fulfils these conditions: it is a prime number, it is the seventh prime number, and seven is the fifth prime number.[*] Accordingly he has an outrageous partiality to the number thirteen. Though one of the most inconvenient of all small numbers, he insists on introducing it everywhere.

These strange conceits are connected with a highly characteristic example of M. Comte's frenzy for regulation. He cannot bear that anything should be left unregulated: there ought to be no such thing as hesitation; nothing should remain arbitrary, for *l'arbitraire*[†] is always favourable to egoism. Submission to artificial prescriptions is as indispensable as to natural laws, and he boasts that under the reign of sentiment, human life may be made equally, and even more, regular than the courses of the stars. But the great instrument of exact regulation for the details of life is numbers: fixed numbers, therefore, should be introduced into all our conduct. M. Comte's first application of this system was to the correction of his own literary style. Complaint had been made, not undeservedly, that in his first great work, especially in the latter part of it, the sentences and paragraphs were long, clumsy, and involved. To correct this fault, of which he was aware, he imposed on himself the following rules. No sentence was to exceed two lines of his manuscript, equivalent to five of print. No paragraph was to consist of more than seven sentences. He further applied to his prose writing the rule of French versification which forbids a *hiatus* (the concourse of two vowels), not allowing it to himself even at the break between two sentences or two paragraphs; nor did he permit himself ever to use the same word twice, either in the same sentence or in two consecutive sentences, though belonging to different paragraphs: with the exception of the monosyllabic auxiliaries.* All this is well enough, especially the first two precepts, and a good way of breaking through a bad habit. But M. Comte persuaded himself that any arbitrary restriction, though in no way emanating from, and therefore necessarily disturbing, the natural order and proportion of the thoughts, is a benefit in itself, and tends to improve style. If it renders composition vastly more difficult, he rejoices at it, as tending to confine writing to superior minds. Accordingly, in the *Synthèse Subjective*, he institutes the following "plan for all compositions of importance." "Every volume really capable of forming

[*Synthèse, p. 111.]
[†Ibid., p. 107.]
* Preface [p. ix] to the fourth volume of the *Système*.

a distinct treatise" should consist of "seven chapters, besides the introduction and the conclusion; and each of these should be composed of three parts." Each third part of a chapter should be divided into

seven sections, each composed of seven groups of sentences, separated by the usual break of line. Normally formed, the section offers a central group of seven sentences, preceded and followed by three groups of five: the first section of each part reduces to three sentences three of its groups, symmetrically placed; the last section gives seven sentences to each of its extreme groups. These rules of composition make prose approach to the regularity of poetry, when combined with my previous reduction of the maximum length of a sentence to two manuscript or five printed lines, that is, 250 letters.

Normally constructed, great poems consist of thirteen cantos, decomposed into parts, sections, and groups like my chapters, saving the complete equality of the groups and of the sections.

"This difference of structure between volumes of poetry and of philosophy is more apparent than real, for the introduction and the conclusion of a poem should comprehend six of its thirteen cantos," leaving, therefore, the cabalistic number seven for the body of the poem. And all this regulation not being sufficiently meaningless, fantastic, and oppressive, he invents an elaborate system for compelling each of his sections and groups to begin with a letter of the alphabet, determined beforehand, the letters being selected so as to compose words having "a synthetic or sympathetic signification," and as close a relation as possible to the section or part to which they are appropriated.[*]

Others may laugh, but we could far rather weep at this melancholy decadence of a great intellect. M. Comte used to reproach his early English admirers with maintaining the "conspiracy of silence"[†] concerning his later performances. The reader can now judge whether such reticence is not more than sufficiently explained by tenderness for his fame, and a conscientious fear of bringing undeserved discredit on the noble speculations of his earlier career.

M. Comte was accustomed to consider Descartes and Leibnitz as his principal precursors, and the only great philosophers (among many thinkers of high philosophic capacity) in modern times. It was to their minds that he considered his own to bear the nearest resemblance. Though we have not so lofty an opinion of any of the three as M. Comte had, we think the assimilation just: these were, of all recorded thinkers, the two who bore most resemblance to M. Comte. They were like him in earnestness, like him, though scarcely equal to him, in confidence in themselves; they had the same extraordinary power of concatenation and co-ordination; they enriched human knowledge with great truths and great conceptions of method; they

[*Synthèse, pp. 755–7.]   [†Ibid., p. xxxvi.]

were, of all great scientific thinkers, the most consistent, and for that reason often the most absurd, because they *shrank* from no consequences, however contrary to common sense, to which their premises appeared to lead. Accordingly their names have come down to us associated with grand thoughts, with most important discoveries, and also with some of the most extravagantly wild and ludicrously absurd conceptions and theories which ever were solemnly propounded by thoughtful men. We think M. Comte as great as either of these philosophers, and hardly more extravagant. Were we to speak our whole mind, we should call him superior to them: *though* not intrinsically, *yet* by the exertion of equal intellectual power in a more advanced state of human preparation; but also in an age less tolerant of palpable absurdities, and to which those he has committed, if not in themselves greater, at least appear more ridiculous.

$x-x$65   shrunk
$y-y+$65^1,66
$z-z$65   but

THREE ESSAYS ON RELIGION

1874

EDITOR'S NOTE

London: Longmans, Green, Reader, and Dyer, 1874. As this volume was posthumously published, edited by Helen Taylor, there is no entry in JSM's bibliography, and the essays are not mentioned in his *Autobiography*. For comment on the writing of the essays, and their relation to the other essays in this volume, see the Textual Introduction, cxxii–cxix above.

There are no corrections or alterations in the Somerville College copies, although Helen Taylor has written "1st Ed." on the title page of the 1874 ed., probably when the 2nd ed. was in preparation. The 2nd ed. (1874) and 3rd ed. (1885) are simply reprints of the 1st, without changes.

Introductory Notice

THE THREE following Essays on Religion were written at considerable intervals of time, without any intention of forming a consecutive series, and must not therefore be regarded as a connected body of thought, excepting in so far as they exhibit the Author's deliberate and exhaustive treatment of the topics under consideration.

The two first of these three Essays were written between the years 1850 and 1858, during the period which intervened between the publication of the *Principles of Political Economy*, and that of the work on Liberty; during which interval three other Essays—on Justice, on Utility, and on Liberty—were also composed. Of the five Essays written at that time, three have already been given to the public by the Author. That on Liberty was expanded into the now well-known work bearing the same title. Those on Justice and Utility were afterwards incorporated, with some alterations and additions, into one, and published under the name of *Utilitarianism*. The remaining two—on Nature and on the Utility of Religion—are now given to the public, with the addition of a third—on Theism—which was produced at a much later period. In these two first Essays indications may easily be found of the date at which they were composed; among which indications may be noted the absence of any mention of the works of Mr. Darwin and Sir Henry Maine in passages where there is coincidence of thought with those writers, or where subjects are treated which they have since discussed in a manner to which the Author of these Essays would certainly have referred had their works been published before these were written.

The last Essay in the present volume belongs to a different epoch; it was written between the years 1868 and 1870, but it was not designed as a sequel to the two Essays which now appear along with it, nor were they intended to appear all together. On the other hand it is certain that the Author considered the opinions expressed in these different Essays, as fundamentally consistent. The evidence of this lies in the fact that in the year 1873, after he had completed his Essay on Theism, it was his intention to have published the Essay on Nature at once, with only such slight revision as might be judged necessary in preparing it for the press, but substantially in its present form. From this it is apparent that his manner of thinking had undergone no substantial change. Whatever discrepancies, therefore, may seem to remain after a really careful comparison between different passages, may be set down either to the fact that the last Essay had not undergone the many revisions which it was the Author's habit to make peculiarly searching and thorough; or to that difference of tone, and of apparent estimate of the relative weight of different considerations, which results from taking a wider view and including a larger number of considerations in the estimate of the subject as a whole, than in dealing with parts of it only.

The fact that the Author intended to publish the Essay on Nature in 1873 is sufficient evidence, if any is needed, that the volume now given to the public was not withheld by him on account of reluctance to encounter whatever odium might result from the free expression of his opinions on religion. That he did not purpose to publish the other two Essays at the same time, was in accord with the Author's habit in regard to the public utterance of his religious opinions. For at the same time that he was peculiarly deliberate and slow in forming opinions, he had a special dislike to the utterance of half-formed opinions. He declined altogether to be hurried into premature decision on any point to which he did not think he had given sufficient time and labour to have exhausted it to the utmost limit of his own thinking powers. And, in the same way, even after he had arrived at definite conclusions, he refused to allow the curiosity of others to force him to the expression of them before he had bestowed all the elaboration in his power upon their adequate expression, and before, therefore, he had subjected to the test of time, not only the conclusions themselves, but also the form into which he had thrown them. The same reasons, therefore, that made him cautious in the spoken utterance of his opinion in proportion as it was necessary to be at once precise and comprehensive in order to be properly understood, which in his judgment was pre-eminently the case in religious speculation, were the reasons that made him abstain from publishing his Essay on Nature for upwards of fifteen years, and might have led him still to withhold the others which now appear in the same volume.

From this point of view it will be seen that the Essay on Theism has both greater value and less than any other of the Author's works. The last considerable work which he completed, it shows the latest state of the Author's mind, the carefully balanced result of the deliberations of a lifetime. On the other hand, there had not been time for it to undergo the revision to which from time to time he subjected most of his writings before making them public. Not only therefore is the style less polished than that of any other of his published works, but even the matter itself, at least in the exact shape it here assumes, has never undergone the repeated examination which it certainly would have passed through before he would himself have given it to the world.

HELEN TAYLOR

Nature

NATURE, natural, and the group of words derived from them, or allied to them in etymology, have at all times filled a great place in the thoughts and taken a strong hold on the feelings of mankind. That they should have done so is not surprising, when we consider what the words, in their primitive and most obvious signification, represent; but it is unfortunate that a set of terms which play so great a part in moral and metaphysical speculation, should have acquired many meanings different from the primary one, yet sufficiently allied to it to admit of confusion. The words have thus become entangled in so many foreign associations, mostly of a very powerful and tenacious character, that they have come to excite, and to be the symbols of, feelings which their original meaning will by no means justify; and which have made them one of the most copious sources of false taste, false philosophy, false morality, and even bad law.

The most important application of the Socratic Elenchus, as exhibited and improved by Plato, consists in dissecting large abstractions of this description; fixing down to a precise definition the meaning which as popularly used they merely shadow forth, and questioning and testing the common maxims and opinions in which they bear a part. It is to be regretted that among the instructive specimens of this kind of investigation which Plato has left, and to which subsequent times have been so much indebted for whatever intellectual clearness they have attained, he has not enriched posterity with a dialogue περὶ φύσεως. If the idea denoted by the word had been subjected to his searching analysis, and the popular commonplaces in which it figures had been submitted to the ordeal of his powerful dialectics, his successors probably would not have rushed, as they speedily did, into modes of thinking and reasoning of which the fallacious use of that word formed the corner stone; a kind of fallacy from which he was himself singularly free.

According to the Platonic method which is still the best type of such investigations, the first thing to be done with so vague a term is to ascertain precisely what it means. It is also a rule of the same method, that the meaning of an abstraction is best sought for in the concrete—of an universal in the particular. Adopting this course with the word Nature, the first question must be, what is meant by the "nature" of a particular object? as of fire, of water, or of some individual plant or animal? Evidently the *ensemble* or aggregate of its powers or properties: the modes in which it acts on other things (counting among those things the senses of the observer) and the modes in which other things act upon it; to which, in the case of a sentient being, must be added, its own capacities of feeling, or being conscious. The Nature of the thing means all this; means its entire capacity of exhibiting phenomena. And since the phenomena which a thing exhibits, however much they vary in different circumstances, are always the same in the same circumstances, they admit of being described in general forms of words, which are called the *laws* of the thing's nature. Thus it is a law of the nature of water that under the mean pressure of the atmosphere at the level of the sea, it boils at 212° Fahrenheit.

As the nature of any given thing is the aggregate of its powers and properties, so Nature in the abstract is the aggregate of the powers and properties of all things. Nature means the sum of all phenomena, together with the causes which produce them; including not only all that happens, but all that is capable of happening; the unused capabilities of causes being as much a part of the idea of Nature, as those which take effect. Since all phenomena which have been sufficiently examined are found to take place with regularity, each having certain fixed conditions, positive and negative, on the occurrence of which it invariably happens; mankind have been able to ascertain, either by direct observation or by reasoning processes grounded on it, the conditions of the occurrence of many phenomena; and the progress of science mainly consists in ascertaining those conditions. When discovered they can be expressed in general propositions, which are called laws of the particular phenomenon, and also, more generally, Laws of Nature. Thus, the truth that all material objects tend towards one another with a force directly as their masses and inversely as the square of their distance, is a law of Nature. The proposition that air and food are necessary to animal life, if it be as we have good reason to believe, true without exception, is also a law of nature, though the phenomenon of which it is the law is special, and not, like gravitation, universal.

Nature, then, in this its simplest acceptation, is a collective name for all facts, actual and possible: or (to speak more accurately) a name for the mode, partly known to us and partly unknown, in which all things take place. For the word suggests, not so much the multitudinous detail of the phenomena, as the conception which might be formed of their manner of existence as a mental whole, by a mind possessing a complete knowledge of them: to which conception it is the aim of science to raise itself, by successive steps of generalization from experience.

Such, then, is a correct definition of the word Nature. But this definition corresponds only to one of the senses of that ambiguous term. It is evidently inapplicable to some of the modes in which the word is familiarly employed. For example, it entirely conflicts with the common form of speech by which Nature is opposed to Art, and natural to artificial. For in the sense of the word Nature which has just been defined, and which is the true scientific sense, Art is as much Nature as anything else; and everything which is artificial is natural—Art has no independent powers of its own: Art is but the employment of the powers of Nature for an end. Phenomena produced by human agency, no less than those which as far as we are concerned are spontaneous, depend on the properties of the elementary forces, or of the elementary substances and their compounds. The united powers of the whole human race could not create a new property of matter in general, or of any one of its species. We can only take advantage for our purposes of the properties which we find. A ship floats by the same laws of specific gravity and equilibrium, as a tree uprooted by the wind and blown into the water. The corn which men raise for food, grows and produces its grain by the same laws of vegetation by which the wild rose and the mountain strawberry bring forth their flowers and fruit. A house stands and holds together by the natural properties, the weight and cohesion of the materials which compose it: a steam engine works by the natural expansive force of steam, exerting a pressure upon one part of a system of arrangements, which pressure, by the mechanical properties of the lever, is transferred from that to another part where it raises the weight or removes the obstacle brought into connexion with it. In these and all other artificial operations the office of man is, as has often been remarked, a very limited one; it consists in moving things into certain places. We move objects, and by doing this, bring some things into contact which were separate, or separate others which were in contact: and by this simple change of place, natural forces previously dormant are called into action, and produce the desired effect. Even the volition which designs, the intelligence which contrives, and the muscular force which executes these movements, are themselves powers of Nature.

It thus appears that we must recognize at least two principal meanings in the word Nature. In one sense, it means all the powers existing in either the outer or the inner world and everything which takes place by means of those powers. In another sense, it means, not everything which happens, but only what takes place without the agency, or without the voluntary and intentional agency, of man. This distinction is far from exhausting the ambiguities of the word; but it is the key to most of those on which important consequences depend.

Such, then, being the two principal senses of the word Nature; in which of these is it taken, or is it taken in either, when the word and its derivatives are used to convey ideas of commendation, approval, and even moral obligation?

It has conveyed such ideas in all ages. *Naturam sequi* was the fundamental principle of morals in many of the most admired schools of philosophy. Among the ancients, especially in the declining period of ancient intellect and thought, it was the test to which all ethical doctrines were brought. The Stoics and the Epicureans, however irreconcilable in the rest of their systems, agreed in holding themselves bound to prove that their respective maxims of conduct were the dictates of nature. Under their influence the Roman jurists, when attempting to systematize jurisprudence, placed in the front of their exposition a certain *Jus Naturale*, "quod natura", as Justinian declares in the *Institutes*, "omnia animalia docuit":[*] and as the modern systematic writers not only on law but on moral philosophy, have generally taken the Roman jurists for their models, treatises on the so-called Law of Nature have abounded; and references to this Law as a supreme rule and ultimate standard have pervaded literature. The writers on International Law have done more than any others to give currency to this style of ethical specula-tion; inasmuch as having no positive law to write about, and yet being anxious to invest the most approved opinions respecting international morality with as much as they could of the authority of law, they endeavoured to find such an authority in Nature's imaginary code. The Christian theology during the period of its greatest ascendancy, opposed some, though not a complete, hindrance to the modes of thought which erected Nature into the criterion of morals, inasmuch as, according to the creed of most denominations of Christians (though assuredly not of Christ) man is by nature wicked. But this very doctrine, by the reaction which it provoked, has made the deistical moralists almost unanimous in proclaiming the divinity of Nature, and set-ting up its fancied dictates as an authoritative rule of action. A reference to that supposed standard is the predominant ingredient in the vein of thought and feeling which was opened by Rousseau, and which has infiltrated itself most widely into the modern mind, not excepting that portion of it which calls itself Christian. The doctrines of Christianity have in every age been largely accommodated to the philosophy which happened to be prevalent, and the Christianity of our day has borrowed a considerable part of its colour and flavour from sentimental deism. At the present time it cannot be said that Nature, or any other standard, is applied as it was wont to be, to deduce rules of action with juridical precision, and with an attempt to make its appli-cation co-extensive with all human agency. The people of this generation do not commonly apply principles with any such studious exactness, nor own such binding allegiance to any standard, but live in a kind of confusion of many standards; a condition not propitious to the formation of steady moral convictions, but convenient enough to those whose moral opinions sit lightly on them, since it gives them a much wider range of arguments for defending the doctrine of the moment. But though perhaps no one could now be found

[*Lib. I, Tit. ii.]

who like the institutional writers of former times, adopts the so-called Law of Nature as the foundation of ethics, and endeavours consistently to reason from it, the word and its cognates must still be counted among those which carry great weight in moral argumentation. That any mode of thinking, feeling, or acting, is "according to nature" is usually accepted as a strong argument for its goodness. If it can be said with any plausibility that "nature enjoins" anything, the propriety of obeying the injunction is by most people considered to be made out: and conversely, the imputation of being contrary to nature, is thought to bar the door against any pretension on the part of the thing so designated, to be tolerated or excused; and the word unnatural has not ceased to be one of the most vituperative epithets in the language. Those who deal in these expressions, may avoid making themselves responsible for any fundamental theorem respecting the standard of moral obligation, but they do not the less imply such a theorem, and one which must be the same in substance with that on which the more logical thinkers of a more laborious age grounded their systematic treatises on Natural Law.

Is it necessary to recognize in these forms of speech, another distinct meaning of the word Nature? Or can they be connected, by any rational bond of union, with either of the two meanings already treated of? At first it may seem that we have no option but to admit another ambiguity in the term. All inquiries are either into what is, or into what ought to be: science and history belonging to the first division, art, morals and politics to the second. But the two senses of the word Nature first pointed out, agree in referring only to what is. In the first meaning, Nature is a collective name for everything which is. In the second, it is a name for everything which is of itself, without voluntary human intervention. But the employment of the word Nature as a term of ethics seems to disclose a third meaning, in which Nature does not stand for what is, but for what ought to be; or for the rule or standard of what ought to be. A little consideration, however, will show that this is not a case of ambiguity; there is not here a third sense of the word. Those who set up Nature as a standard of action do not intend a merely verbal proposition; they do not mean that the standard, whatever it be, should be *called* Nature; they think they are giving some information as to what the standard of action really is. Those who say that we ought to act according to Nature do not mean the mere identical proposition that we ought to do what we ought to do. They think that the word Nature affords some external criterion of what we should do; and if they lay down as a rule for what ought to be, a word which in its proper signification denotes what is, they do so because they have a notion, either clearly or confusedly, that what is, constitutes the rule and standard of what ought to be.

The examination of this notion, is the object of the present Essay. It is proposed to inquire into the truth of the doctrines which make Nature a test of right and wrong, good and evil, or which in any mode or degree attach merit or approval to following, imitating, or obeying Nature. To this inquiry the foregoing discussion respecting the meaning of terms, was an indispensable introduction. Language is as it were the atmosphere of philosophical investigation, which must be made transparent before anything can be seen through it in the true figure and position. In the present case it is necessary to guard against a further ambiguity, which though abundantly obvious, has sometimes misled even sagacious minds, and of which it is well to take distinct note before proceeding further. No word is more commonly associated with the word Nature, than Law; and this last word has distinctly two meanings, in one of which it denotes some definite portion of what is, in the other, of what ought to be. We speak of the law of gravitation, the three laws of motion, the law of definite proportions in chemical combination, the vital laws of organized beings. All these are portions of what is. We also speak of the criminal law, the civil law, the law of honour, the law of veracity, the law of justice; all of which are portions of what ought to be, or of somebody's suppositions, feelings, or commands respecting what ought to be. The first kind of laws, such as the laws of motion, and of gravitation, are neither more nor less than the observed uniformities in the occurrence of phenomena: partly uniformities of antecedence and sequence, partly of concomitance. These are what, in science, and even in ordinary parlance, are meant by laws of nature. Laws in the other sense are the laws of the land, the law of nations, or moral laws; among which, as already noticed, is dragged in, by jurists and publicists, something which they think proper to call the Law of Nature. Of the liability of these two meanings of the word to be confounded there can be no better example than the first chapter of Montesquieu;[*] where he remarks, that the material world has its laws, the inferior animals have their laws, and man has his laws; and calls attention to the much greater strictness with which the first two sets of laws are observed, than the last; as if it were an inconsistency, and a paradox, that things always are what they are, but men not always what they ought to be. A similar confusion of ideas pervades the writings of Mr. George Combe, from whence it has overflowed into a large region of popular literature, and we are now continually reading injunctions to obey the physical laws of the universe, as being obligatory in the same sense and manner as the moral. The conception which the ethical use of the word Nature implies, of a close relation if not absolute identity between what is and what ought to be, certainly derives part of its hold on the mind from the custom of designating what is, by the expression "laws of nature," while the same word Law is also used, and even more familiarly and emphatically, to express what ought to be.

When it is asserted, or implied, that Nature, or the laws of Nature, should

[*_De l'esprit des lois_. 2 vols. Geneva: Barrilot, 1748.]

be conformed to, is the Nature which is meant, Nature in the first sense of the term, meaning all which is—the powers and properties of all things? But in this signification, there is no need of a recommendation to act according to nature, since it is what nobody can possibly help doing, and equally whether he acts well or ill. There is no mode of acting which is not conformable to Nature in this sense of the term, and all modes of acting are so in exactly the same degree. Every action is the exertion of some natural power, and its effects of all sorts are so many phenomena of nature, produced by the powers and properties of some of the objects of nature, in exact obedience to some law or laws of nature. When I voluntarily use my organs to take in food, the act, and its consequences, take place according to laws of nature: if instead of food I swallow poison, the case is exactly the same. To bid people conform to the laws of nature when they have no power but what the laws of nature give them—when it is a physical impossibility for them to do the smallest thing otherwise than through some law of nature, is an absurdity. The thing they need to be told is, what particular law of nature they should make use of in a particular case. When, for example, a person is crossing a river by a narrow bridge to which there is no parapet, he will do well to regulate his proceedings by the laws of equilibrium in moving bodies, instead of conforming only to the law of gravitation, and falling into the river.

Yet, idle as it is to exhort people to do what they cannot avoid doing, and absurd as it is to prescribe as a rule of right conduct what agrees exactly as well with wrong; nevertheless a rational rule of conduct *may* be constructed out of the relation which it ought to bear to the laws of nature in this widest acceptation of the term. Man necessarily obeys the laws of nature, or in other words the properties of things, but he does not necessarily *guide* himself by them. Though all conduct is in conformity to laws of nature, all conduct is not grounded on knowledge of them, and intelligently directed to the attainment of purposes by means of them. Though we cannot emancipate ourselves from the laws of nature as a whole, we can escape from any particular law of nature, if we are able to withdraw ourselves from the circumstances in which it acts. Though we can do nothing except through laws of nature, we can use one law to counteract another. According to Bacon's maxim, we can obey nature in such a manner as to command it.[*] Every alteration of circumstances alters more or less the laws of nature under which we act; and by every choice which we make either of ends or of means, we place ourselves to a greater or less extent under one set of laws of nature instead of another. If, therefore, the useless precept to follow nature were changed into a precept to study nature; to know and take heed of the properties of the things we have to deal with, so far as these properties are capable of forwarding or obstructing any given purpose; we should have arrived at the first principle of all

[*Novum Organum, Works, Vol. IV, p. 47.]

intelligent action, or rather at the definition of intelligent action itself. And a confused notion of this true principle, is, I doubt not, in the minds of many of those who set up the unmeaning doctrine which superficially resembles it. They perceive that the essential difference between wise and foolish conduct consists in attending, or not attending, to the particular laws of nature on which some important result depends. And they think, that a person who attends to a law of nature in order to shape his conduct by it, may be said to obey it, while a person who practically disregards it, and acts as if no such law existed, may be said to disobey it: the circumstance being overlooked, that what is thus called disobedience to a law of nature is obedience to some other or perhaps to the very law itself. For example, a person who goes into a powder magazine either not knowing, or carelessly omitting to think of, the explosive force of gunpowder, is likely to do some act which will cause him to be blown to atoms in obedience to the very law which he has disregarded.

But however much of its authority the "Naturam sequi" doctrine may owe to its being confounded with the rational precept "Naturam observare," its favourers and promoters unquestionably intend much more by it than that precept. To acquire knowledge of the properties of things, and make use of the knowledge for guidance, is a rule of prudence, for the adaptation of means to ends; for giving effect to our wishes and intentions whatever they may be. But the maxim of obedience to Nature, or conformity to Nature, is held up not as a simply prudential but as an ethical maxim; and by those who talk of *jus naturæ*, even as a law, fit to be administered by tribunals and enforced by sanctions. Right action, must mean something more and other than merely intelligent action: yet no precept beyond this last, can be connected with the word Nature in the wider and more philosophical of its acceptations. We must try it therefore in the other sense, that in which Nature stands distinguished from Art, and denotes, not the whole course of the phenomena which come under our observation, but only their spontaneous course.

Let us then consider whether we can attach any meaning to the supposed practical maxim of following Nature, in this second sense of the word, in which Nature stands for that which takes place without human intervention. In Nature as thus understood, is the spontaneous course of things when left to themselves, the rule to be followed in endeavouring to adapt things to our use? But it is evident at once that the maxim, taken in this sense, is not merely, as it is in the other sense, superfluous and unmeaning, but palpably absurd and self-contradictory. For while human action cannot help conforming to Nature in the one meaning of the term, the very aim and object of action is to alter and improve Nature in the other meaning. If the natural course of things were perfectly right and satisfactory, to act at all would be a gratuitous meddling, which as it could not make things better, must make them worse. Or if action at all could be justified, it would only be when in direct obedience to instincts, since these might perhaps be accounted part of the spontaneous order of Nature; but to do anything with forethought and purpose, would be a violation of that perfect order. If the artificial is not better than the natural, to what end are all the arts of life? To dig, to plough, to build, to wear clothes, are direct infringements of the injunction to follow nature.

Accordingly it would be said by every one, even of those most under the influence of the feelings which prompt the injunction, that to apply it to such cases as those just spoken of, would be to push it too far. Everybody professes to approve and admire many great triumphs of Art over Nature: the junction by bridges of shores which Nature had made separate, the draining of Nature's marshes, the excavation of her wells, the dragging to light of what she has buried at immense depths in the earth; the turning away of her thunderbolts by lightning rods, of her inundations by embankments, of her ocean by breakwaters. But to commend these and similar feats, is to acknowledge that the ways of Nature are to be conquered, not obeyed: that her powers are often towards man in the position of enemies, from whom he must wrest, by force and ingenuity, what little he can for his own use, and deserves to be applauded when that little is rather more than might be expected from his physical weakness in comparison to those gigantic powers. All praise of Civilization, or Art, or Contrivance, is so much dispraise of Nature; an admission of imperfection, which it is man's business, and merit, to be always endeavouring to correct or mitigate.

The consciousness that whatever man does to improve his condition is in so much a censure and a thwarting of the spontaneous order of Nature, has in all ages caused new and unprecedented attempts at improvement to be generally at first under a shade of religious suspicion; as being in any case uncomplimentary, and very probably offensive to the powerful beings (or, when polytheism gave place to monotheism, to the all-powerful Being) supposed to govern the various phenomena of the universe, and of whose will the course of nature was conceived to be the expression. Any attempt to mould natural phenomena to the convenience of mankind might easily appear an interference with the government of those superior beings: and though life could not have been maintained, much less made pleasant, without perpetual interferences of the kind, each new one was doubtless made with fear and trembling, until experience had shown that it could be ventured on without drawing down the vengeance of the Gods. The sagacity of priests showed them a way to reconcile the impunity of particular infringements with the maintenance of the general dread of encroaching on the divine administration. This was effected by representing each of the principal human inventions as the gift and favour of some God. The old religions also afforded many resources for consulting the Gods, and obtaining their express permission for what would otherwise have appeared a breach of their prerogative. When oracles had ceased, any religion which recognized a revelation afforded expedients for the same purpose. The Catholic religion had the resource of an infallible Church, authorized to declare what exertions of human spontaneity were permitted or forbidden; and in default of this, the case was always open to argument from the Bible whether any particular practice had expressly or by implication been sanctioned. The notion remained that this liberty to control Nature was conceded to man only by special indulgence, and as far as required by his necessities; and there was always a tendency, though a diminishing one, to regard any attempt to exercise power over nature, beyond a certain degree, and a certain admitted range, as an impious effort to usurp divine power, and dare more than was permitted to man. The lines of Horace in which the familiar arts of shipbuilding and navigation are reprobated as *vetitum nefas*,[*] indicate even in that sceptical age a still unexhausted vein of the old sentiment. The intensity of the corresponding feeling in the middle ages is not a precise parallel, on account of the superstition about dealing with evil spirits with which it was complicated: but the imputation of prying into the secrets of the Almighty long remained a powerful weapon of attack against unpopular inquirers into nature; and the charge of presumptuously attempting to defeat the designs of Providence, still retains enough of its original force to be thrown in as a make-weight along with other objections when there is a desire to find fault with any new exertion of human forethought and contrivance. No one, indeed, asserts it to be the intention of the Creator that the spontaneous order of the creation should not be altered, or even that it should not be altered in any new way. But there still exists a vague notion that though it is very proper to control this or the other natural phenomenon, the general scheme of nature is a model for us to imitate: that with more or less liberty in details, we should on the whole be guided by the spirit and general conception of nature's own ways: that they are God's work, and as such perfect; that man cannot rival their unapproachable excellence, and can best show his skill and piety by attempting, in however imperfect a way, to reproduce their likeness; and that if not the whole, yet some particular parts of the spontaneous order of nature, selected according to the speaker's predilections, are in a peculiar sense, manifestations of the Creator's will; a sort of finger posts pointing out the direction which things in general, and therefore our voluntary actions, are intended to take. Feelings of this sort, though repressed on ordinary occasions by the contrary current of life, are ready to break out whenever custom is silent, and the native promptings of the mind have nothing opposed to them but reason: and appeals are continually made to them by rhetoricians, with the effect, if not

[*Horace. *Carmina* I, iii, ll. 25–6; in *Opera*, p. 9.]

of convincing opponents, at least of making those who already hold the opinion which the rhetorician desires to recommend, better satisfied with it. For in the present day it probably seldom happens that any one is persuaded to approve any course of action because it appears to him to bear an analogy to the divine government of the world, though the argument tells on him with great force, and is felt by him to be a great support, in behalf of anything which he is already inclined to approve.

If this notion of imitating the ways of Providence as manifested in Nature, is seldom expressed plainly and downrightly as a maxim of general application, it also is seldom directly contradicted. Those who find it on their path, prefer to turn the obstacle rather than to attack it, being often themselves not free from the feeling, and in any case afraid of incurring the charge of impiety by saying anything which might be held to disparage the works of the Creator's power. They therefore, for the most part, rather endeavour to show, that they have as much right to the religious argument as their opponents, and that if the course they recommend seems to conflict with some part of the ways of Providence, there is some other part with which it agrees better than what is contended for on the other side. In this mode of dealing with the great *à priori* fallacies, the progress of improvement clears away particular errors while the causes of errors are still left standing, and very little weakened by each conflict: yet by a long series of such partial victories precedents are accumulated, to which an appeal may be made against these powerful prepossessions, and which afford a growing hope that the misplaced feeling, after having so often learnt to recede, may some day be compelled to an unconditional surrender. For however offensive the proposition may appear to many religious persons, they should be willing to look in the face the undeniable fact, that the order of nature, in so far as unmodified by man, is such as no being, whose attributes are justice and benevolence, would have made, with the intention that his rational creatures should follow it as an example. If made wholly by such a Being, and not partly by beings of very different qualities, it could only be as a designedly imperfect work, which man, in his limited sphere, is to exercise justice and benevolence in amending. The best persons have always held it to be the essence of religion, that the paramount duty of man upon earth is to amend himself: but all except monkish quietists have annexed to this in their inmost minds (though seldom willing to enunciate the obligation with the same clearness) the additional religious duty of amending the world, and not solely the human part of it but the material; the order of physical nature.

In considering this subject it is necessary to divest ourselves of certain preconceptions which may justly be called natural prejudices, being grounded on feelings which, in themselves natural and inevitable, intrude into matters with which they ought to have no concern. One of these feelings is the astonishment, rising into awe, which is inspired (even independently of all religious sentiment) by any of the greater natural phenomena. A hurricane; a mountain precipice; the desert; the ocean, either agitated or at rest; the solar system, and the great cosmic forces which hold it together; the boundless firmament, and to an educated mind any single star; excite feelings which make all human enterprises and powers appear so insignificant, that to a mind thus occupied it seems insufferable presumption in so puny a creature as man to look critically on things so far above him, or dare to measure himself against the grandeur of the universe. But a little interrogation of our own consciousness will suffice to convince us, that what makes these phenomena so impressive is simply their vastness. The enormous extension in space and time, or the enormous power they exemplify, constitutes their sublimity; a feeling in all cases, more allied to terror than to any moral emotion. And though the vast scale of these phenomena may well excite wonder, and sets at defiance all idea of rivalry, the feeling it inspires is of a totally different character from admiration of excellence. Those in whom awe produces admiration may be æsthetically developed, but they are morally uncultivated. It is one of the endowments of the imaginative part of our mental nature that conceptions of greatness and power, vividly realized, produce a feeling which though in its higher degrees closely bordering on pain, we prefer to most of what are accounted pleasures. But we are quite equally capable of experiencing this feeling towards maleficent power; and we never experience it so strongly towards most of the powers of the universe, as when we have most present to our consciousness a vivid sense of their capacity of inflicting evil. Because these natural powers have what we cannot imitate, enormous might, and overawe us by that one attribute, it would be a great error to infer that their other attributes are such as we ought to emulate, or that we should be justified in using our small powers after the example which Nature sets us with her vast forces.

For, how stands the fact? That next to the greatness of these cosmic forces, the quality which most forcibly strikes every one who does not avert his eyes from it, is their perfect and absolute recklessness. They go straight to their end, without regarding what or whom they crush on the road. Optimists, in their attempts to prove that "whatever is, is right,"[*] are obliged to maintain, not that Nature ever turns one step from her path to avoid trampling us into destruction, but that it would be very unreasonable in us to expect that she should. Pope's "Shall gravitation cease when you go by?"[†] may be a just rebuke to any one who should be so silly as to expect common human morality from nature. But if the question were between two men, instead of

[*Alexander Pope. *Essay on Man*, Epistle I, l. 294; in *Works*. New ed. Ed. Joseph Warton, *et al*. London: Priestley, 1822–25, Vol. III, p. 47.]

[†*Ibid.*, Epistle IV, l. 128; Vol. III, p. 134.]

between a man and a natural phenomenon, that triumphant apostrophe would be thought a rare piece of impudence. A man who should persist in hurling stones or firing cannon when another man "goes by," and having killed him should urge a similar plea in exculpation, would very deservedly be found guilty of murder.

In sober truth, nearly all the things which men are hanged or imprisoned for doing to one another, are nature's every day performances. Killing, the most criminal act recognized by human laws, Nature does once to every being that lives; and in a large proportion of cases, after protracted tortures such as only the greatest monsters whom we read of ever purposely inflicted on their living fellow-creatures. If, by an arbitrary reservation, we refuse to account anything murder but what abridges a certain term supposed to be allotted to human life, nature also does this to all but a small percentage of lives, and does it in all the modes, violent or insidious, in which the worst human beings take the lives of one another. Nature impales men, breaks them as if on the wheel, casts them to be devoured by wild beasts, burns them to death, crushes them with stones like the first christian martyr, starves them with hunger, freezes them with cold, poisons them by the quick or slow venom of her exhalations, and has hundreds of other hideous deaths in reserve, such as the ingenious cruelty of a Nabis or a Domitian never surpassed. All this, Nature does with the most supercilious disregard both of mercy and of justice, emptying her shafts upon the best and noblest indifferently with the meanest and worst; upon those who are engaged in the highest and worthiest enterprises, and often as the direct consequence of the noblest acts; and it might almost be imagined as a punishment for them. She mows down those on whose existence hangs the well-being of a whole people, perhaps the prospects of the human race for generations to come, with as little compunction as those whose death is a relief to themselves, or a blessing to those under their noxious influence. Such are Nature's dealings with life. Even when she does not intend to kill, she inflicts the same tortures in apparent wantonness. In the clumsy provision which she has made for that perpetual renewal of animal life, rendered necessary by the prompt termination she puts to it in every individual instance, no human being ever comes into the world but another human being is literally stretched on the rack for hours or days, not unfrequently issuing in death. Next to taking life (equal to it according to a high authority) is taking the means by which we live; and Nature does this too on the largest scale and with the most callous indifference. A single hurricane destroys the hopes of a season; a flight of locusts, or an inundation, desolates a district; a trifling chemical change in an edible root, starves a million of people. The waves of the sea, like banditti seize and appropriate the wealth of the rich and the little all of the poor with the same accompaniments of stripping, wounding, and killing as their human antitypes. Everything in short, which the worst men commit either against life or property is perpetrated on a larger scale by natural agents. Nature has Noyades more fatal than those of Carrier; her explosions of fire damp are as destructive as human artillery; her plague and cholera far surpass the poison cups of the Borgias. Even the love of "order" which is thought to be a following of the ways of Nature, is in fact a contradiction of them. All which people are accustomed to deprecate as "disorder" and its consequences, is precisely a counterpart of Nature's ways. Anarchy and the Reign of Terror are overmatched in injustice, ruin, and death, by a hurricane and a pestilence.

But, it is said, all these things are for wise and good ends. On this I must first remark that whether they are so or not, is altogether beside the point. Supposing it true that contrary to appearances these horrors when perpetrated by Nature, promote good ends, still as no one believes that good ends would be promoted by our following the example, the course of Nature cannot be a proper model for us to imitate. Either it is right that we should kill because nature kills; torture because nature tortures; ruin and devastate because nature does the like; or we ought not to consider at all what nature does, but what it is good to do. If there is such a thing as a *reductio ad absurdum*, this surely amounts to one. If it is a sufficient reason for doing one thing, that nature does it, why not another thing? If not all things, why anything? The physical government of the world being full of the things which when done by men are deemed the greatest enormities, it cannot be religious or moral in us to guide our actions by the analogy of the course of nature. This proposition remains true, whatever occult quality of producing good may reside in those facts of nature which to our perceptions are most noxious, and which no one considers it other than a crime to produce artificially.

But, in reality, no one consistently believes in any such occult quality. The phrases which ascribe perfection to the course of nature can only be considered as the exaggerations of poetic or devotional feeling, not intended to stand the test of a sober examination. No one, either religious or irreligious, believes that the hurtful agencies of nature, considered as a whole, promote good purposes, in any other way than by inciting human rational creatures to rise up and struggle against them. If we believed that those agencies were appointed by a benevolent Providence as the means of accomplishing wise purposes which could not be compassed if they did not exist, then everything done by mankind which tends to chain up these natural agencies or to restrict their mischievous operation, from draining a pestilential marsh down to curing the toothache, or putting up an umbrella, ought to be accounted impious; which assuredly nobody does account them, notwithstanding an undercurrent of sentiment setting in that direction which is occasionally perceptible. On the contrary, the improvements on which the civilized part of mankind most pride themselves, consist in more successfully warding off those natural calamities which if we really believed what most people profess to believe, we should cherish as medicines provided for our earthly state by infinite wisdom. Inasmuch too as each generation greatly surpasses its predecessors in the amount of natural evil which it succeeds in averting, our condition, if the theory were true, ought by this time to have become a terrible manifestation of some tremendous calamity, against which the physical evils we have learnt to overmaster, had previously operated as a preservative. Any one, however, who acted as if he supposed this to be the case, would be more likely, I think, to be confined as a lunatic, than reverenced as a saint.

It is undoubtedly a very common fact that good comes out of evil, and when it does occur, it is far too agreeable not to find people eager to dilate on it. But in the first place, it is quite as often true of human crimes, as of natural calamities. The fire of London, which is believed to have had so salutary an effect on the healthiness of the city, would have produced that effect just as much if it had been really the work of the "furor papisticus" so long commemorated on the Monument. The deaths of those whom tyrants or persecutors have made martyrs in any noble cause, have done a service to mankind which would not have been obtained if they had died by accident or disease. Yet whatever incidental and unexpected benefits may result from crimes, they are crimes nevertheless. In the second place, if good frequently comes out of evil, the converse fact, evil coming out of good, is equally common. Every event public or private, which, regretted on its occurrence, was declared providential at a later period on account of some unforeseen good consequence, might be matched by some other event, deemed fortunate at the time, but which proved calamitous or fatal to those whom it appeared to benefit. Such conflicts between the beginning and the end, or between the event and the expectation, are not only as frequent, but as often held up to notice, in the painful cases as in the agreeable; but there is not the same inclination to generalize on them; or at all events they are not regarded by the moderns (though they were by the ancients) as similarly an indication of the divine purposes: men satisfy themselves with moralizing on the imperfect nature of our foresight, the uncertainty of events, and the vanity of human expectations. The simple fact is, human interests are so complicated, and the effects of any incident whatever so multitudinous, that if it touches mankind at all, its influence on them is, in the great majority of cases, both good and bad. If the greater number of personal misfortunes have their good side, hardly any good fortune ever befel any one which did not give either to the same or to some other person, something to regret: and unhappily there are many misfortunes so overwhelming that their favourable side, if it exist, is entirely overshadowed and made insignificant; while the corresponding statement can seldom be made concerning blessings. The effects too of every cause depend so much on the circumstances which accidentally accompany it, that many cases are sure to occur in which even the total result is markedly opposed to the predominant tendency: and thus not only evil has its good and good its evil side, but good often produces an overbalance of evil and evil an overbalance of good. This, however, is by no means the general tendency of either phenomenon. On the contrary, both good and evil naturally tend to fructify, each in its own kind, good producing good, and evil, evil. It is one of Nature's general rules, and part of her habitual injustice, that "to him that hath shall be given, but from him that hath not, shall be taken even that which he hath."[*] The ordinary and predominant tendency of good is towards more good. Health, strength, wealth, knowledge, virtue, are not only good in themselves but facilitate and promote the acquisition of good, both of the same and of other kinds. The person who can learn easily, is he who already knows much: it is the strong and not the sickly person who can do everything which most conduces to health; those who find it easy to gain money are not the poor but the rich; while health, strength, knowledge, talents, are all means of acquiring riches, and riches are often an indispensable means of acquiring these. Again, e converso, whatever may be said of evil turning into good, the general tendency of evil is towards further evil. Bodily illness renders the body more susceptible of disease; it produces incapacity of exertion, sometimes debility of mind, and often the loss of means of subsistence. All severe pain, either bodily or mental, tends to increase the susceptibilities of pain for ever after. Poverty is the parent of a thousand mental and moral evils. What is still worse, to be injured or oppressed, when habitual, lowers the whole tone of the character. One bad action leads to others, both in the agent himself, in the bystanders, and in the sufferers. All bad qualities are strengthened by habit, and all vices and follies tend to spread. Intellectual defects generate moral, and moral, intellectual; and every intellectual or moral defect generates others, and so on without end.

That much applauded class of authors, the writers on natural theology, have, I venture to think, entirely lost their way, and missed the sole line of argument which could have made their speculations acceptable to any one who can perceive when two propositions contradict one another. They have exhausted the resources of sophistry to make it appear that all the suffering in the world exists to prevent greater—that misery exists, for fear lest there should be misery: a thesis which if ever so well maintained, could only avail to explain and justify the works of limited beings, compelled to labour under conditions independent of their own will; but can have no application to a Creator assumed to be omnipotent, who, if he bends to a supposed necessity, himself makes the necessity which he bends to. If the maker of the world *can* all that he will, he wills misery, and there is no escape from the conclusion. The more consistent of those who have deemed themselves qualified to "vin-

[*Matthew, 25:29.]

dicate the ways of God to man"[*] have endeavoured to avoid the alternative by hardening their hearts, and denying that misery is an evil. The goodness of God, they say, does not consist in willing the happiness of his creatures, but their virtue; and the universe, if not a happy, is a just, universe. But waving the objections to this scheme of ethics, it does not at all get rid of the difficulty. If the Creator of mankind willed that they should all be virtuous, his designs are as completely baffled as if he had willed that they should all be happy: and the order of nature is constructed with even less regard to the requirements of justice than to those of benevolence. If the law of all creation were justice and the Creator omnipotent, then in whatever amount suffering and happiness might be dispensed to the world, each person's share of them would be exactly proportioned to that person's good or evil deeds; no human being would have a worse lot than another, without worse deserts; accident or favouritism would have no part in such a world, but every human life would be the playing out of a drama constructed like a perfect moral tale. No one is able to blind himself to the fact that the world we live in is totally different from this; insomuch that the necessity of redressing the balance has been deemed one of the strongest arguments for another life after death, which amounts to an admission that the order of things in this life is often an example of injustice, not justice. If it be said that God does not take sufficient account of pleasure and pain to make them the reward or punishment of the good or the wicked, but that virtue is itself the greatest good and vice the greatest evil, then these at least ought to be dispensed to all according to what they have done to deserve them; instead of which, every kind of moral depravity is entailed upon multitudes by the fatality of their birth; through the fault of their parents, of society, or of uncontrollable circumstances, certainly through no fault of their own. Not even on the most distorted and contracted theory of good which ever was framed by religious or philosophical fanaticism, can the government of Nature be made to resemble the work of a being at once good and omnipotent.

The only admissible moral theory of Creation is that the Principle of Good *cannot* at once and altogether subdue the powers of evil, either physical or moral; could not place mankind in a world free from the necessity of an incessant struggle with the maleficent powers, or make them always victorious in that struggle, but could and did make them capable of carrying on the fight with vigour and with progressively increasing success. Of all the religious explanations of the order of nature, this alone is neither contradictory to itself, nor to the facts for which it attempts to account. According to it, man's duty would consist, not in simply taking care of his own interests by obeying irresistible power, but in standing forward a not ineffectual auxiliary to a Being of perfect beneficence; a faith which seems much better

[*Alexander Pope. *Essay on Man*, Epistle I, l. 16; in *Works*, Vol. III, p. 11.]

adapted for nerving him to exertion than a vague and inconsistent reliance on an Author of Good who is supposed to be also the author of evil. And I venture to assert that such has really been, though often unconsciously, the faith of all who have drawn strength and support of any worthy kind from trust in a superintending Providence. There is no subject on which men's practical belief is more incorrectly indicated by the words they use to express it, than religion. Many have derived a base confidence from imagining themselves to be favourites of an omnipotent but capricious and despotic Deity. But those who have been strengthened in goodness by relying on the sympathizing support of a powerful and good Governor of the world, have, I am satisfied, never really believed that Governor to be, in the strict sense of the term, omnipotent. They have always saved his goodness at the expense of his power. They have believed, perhaps, that he could, if he willed, remove all the thorns from their individual path, but not without causing greater harm to some one else, or frustrating some purpose of greater importance to the general well-being. They have believed that he could do any one thing, but not any combination of things: that his government, like human government, was a system of adjustments and compromises; that the world is inevitably imperfect, contrary to his intention.* And since the exertion of all his power to make it as little imperfect as possible, leaves it no better than it is, they cannot but regard that power, though vastly beyond human estimate, yet as in itself not merely finite, but extremely limited. They are bound, for example, to suppose that the best he could do for his human creatures was to make an immense majority of all who have yet existed, be born (without any fault of their own) Patagonians, or Esquimaux, or something nearly as brutal and degraded, but to give them capacities which by being cultivated for very many centuries in toil and suffering, and after many of the best specimens of the race have sacrificed their lives for the purpose, have at last enabled some chosen portions of the species to grow into something better, capable of being improved in centuries more into something really good, of which

---

*This irresistible conviction comes out in the writings of religious philosophers, in exact proportion to the general clearness of their understanding. It nowhere shines forth so distinctly as in Leibnitz's famous *Théodicée* [*Essais de théodicée sur la bonté de Dieu, la liberté de l'homme, et l'origine du mal.* Amsterdam: Troyel, 1710], so strangely mistaken for a system of optimism, and, as such, satirized by Voltaire [in *Candide*] on grounds which do not even touch the author's argument. Leibnitz does not maintain that this world is the best of all imaginable, but only of all possible worlds; which, he argues, it cannot but be, inasmuch as God, who is absolute goodness, has chosen it and not another. In every page of the work he tacitly assumes an abstract possibility and impossibility, independent of the divine power: and through his pious feelings make him continue to designate that power by the word Omnipotence, he so explains that term as to make it mean, power extending to all that is within the limits of that abstract possibility.

hitherto there are only to be found individual instances. It may be possible to believe with Plato that perfect goodness, limited and thwarted in every direction by the intractableness of the material, has done this because it could do no better.[*] But that the same perfectly wise and good Being had absolute power over the material, and made it, by voluntary choice, what it is; to admit this might have been supposed impossible to any one who has the simplest notions of moral good and evil. Nor can any such person, whatever kind of religious phrases he may use, fail to believe, that if Nature and Man are both the works of a Being of perfect goodness, that Being intended Nature as a scheme to be amended, not imitated, by Man.

But even though unable to believe that Nature, as a whole, is a realization of the designs of perfect wisdom and benevolence, men do not willingly renounce the idea that some part of Nature, at least, must be intended as an exemplar, or type; that on some portion or other of the Creator's works, the image of the moral qualities which they are accustomed to ascribe to him, must be impressed; that if not all which is, yet something which is, must not only be a faultless model of what ought to be, but must be intended to be our guide and standard in rectifying the rest. It does not suffice them to believe, that what tends to good is to be imitated and perfected, and what tends to evil is to be corrected: they are anxious for some more definite indication of the Creator's designs; and being persuaded that this must somewhere be met with in his works, undertake the dangerous responsibility of picking and choosing among them in quest of it. A choice which except so far as directed by the general maxim that he intends all the good and none of the evil, must of necessity be perfectly arbitrary; and if it leads to any conclusions other than such as can be deduced from that maxim, must be, exactly in that proportion, pernicious.

It has never been settled by any accredited doctrine, what particular departments of the order of nature shall be reputed to be designed for our moral instruction and guidance; and accordingly each person's individual predilections, or momentary convenience, have decided to what parts of the divine government the practical conclusions that he was desirous of establishing, should be recommended to approval as being analogous. One such recommendation must be as fallacious as another, for it is impossible to decide that certain of the Creator's works are more truly expressions of his character than the rest; and the only selection which does not lead to immoral results, is the selection of those which most conduce to the general good, in other words, of those which point to an end which if the entire scheme is the expression of a single omnipotent and consistent will, is evidently not the end intended by it.

There is however one particular element in the construction of the world,

[*Plato. *Statesman*, 273c.]

which to minds on the look-out for special indication of the Creator's will, has appeared, not without plausibility, peculiarly fitted to afford them; viz. the active impulses of human and other animated beings. One can imagine such persons arguing that when the Author of Nature only made circumstances, he may not have meant to indicate the manner in which his rational creatures were to adjust themselves to those circumstances; but that when he implanted positive stimuli in the creatures themselves, stirring them up to a particular kind of action, it is impossible to doubt that he intended that sort of action to be practised by them. This reasoning, followed out consistently, would lead to the conclusion that the Deity intended, and approves, whatever human beings do; since all that they do being the consequence of some of the impulses with which their Creator must have endowed them, all must equally be considered as done in obedience to his will. As this practical conclusion was shrunk from, it was necessary to draw a distinction, and to pronounce that not the whole, but only parts of the active nature of mankind point to a special intention of the Creator in respect to their conduct. These parts it seemed natural to suppose, must be those in which the Creator's hand is manifested rather than the man's own: and hence the frequent antithesis between man as God made him, and man as he has made himself. Since what is done with deliberation seems more the man's own act, and he is held more completely responsible for it than for what he does from sudden impulse, the considerate part of human conduct is apt to be set down as man's share in the business, and the inconsiderate as God's. The result is the vein of sentiment so common in the modern world (though unknown to the philosophic ancients) which exalts instinct at the expense of reason; an aberration rendered still more mischievous by the opinion commonly held in conjunction with it, that every, or almost every, feeling or impulse which acts promptly without waiting to ask questions, is an instinct. Thus almost every variety of unreflecting and uncalculating impulse receives a kind of consecration, except those which, though unreflecting at the moment, owe their origin to previous habits of reflection: these, being evidently not instinctive, do not meet with the favour accorded to the rest; so that all unreflecting impulses are invested with authority over reason, except the only ones which are most probably right. I do not mean, of course, that this mode of judgment is even pretended to be consistently carried out: life could not go on if it were not admitted that impulses must be controlled, and that reason ought to govern our actions. The pretension is not to drive Reason from the helm but rather to bind her by articles to steer only in a particular way. Instinct is not to govern, but reason is to practise some vague and unassignable amount of deference to Instinct. Though the impression in favour of instinct as being a peculiar manifestation of the divine purposes, has not been cast into the form of a consistent general theory, it remains a standing prejudice, capable of being stirred up into hostility to reason in any case in which the dictate of the rational faculty has not acquired the authority of prescription.

I shall not here enter into the difficult psychological question, what are, or are not instincts: the subject would require a volume to itself. Without touching upon any disputed theoretical points, it is possible to judge how little worthy is the instinctive part of human nature to be held up as its chief excellence—as the part in which the hand of infinite goodness and wisdom is peculiarly visible. Allowing everything to be an instinct which anybody has ever asserted to be one, it remains true that nearly every respectable attribute of humanity is the result not of instinct, but of a victory over instinct; and that there is hardly anything valuable in the natural man except capacities—a whole world of possibilities, all of them dependent upon eminently artificial discipline for being realized.

It is only in a highly artificialized condition of human nature that the notion grew up, or, I believe, ever could have grown up, that goodness was natural: because only after a long course of artificial education did good sentiments become so habitual, and so predominant over bad, as to arise unprompted when occasion called for them. In the times when mankind were nearer to their natural state, cultivated observers regarded the natural man as a sort of wild animal, distinguished chiefly by being craftier than the other beasts of the field; and all worth of character was deemed the result of a sort of taming; a phrase often applied by the ancient philosophers to the appropriate discipline of human beings. The truth is that there is hardly a single point of excellence belonging to human character, which is not decidedly repugnant to the untutored feelings of human nature.

If there be a virtue which more than any other we expect to find, and really do find, in an uncivilized state, it is the virtue of courage. Yet this is from first to last a victory achieved over one of the most powerful emotions of human nature. If there is any one feeling or attribute more natural than all others to human beings, it is fear; and no greater proof can be given of the power of artificial discipline than the conquest which it has at all times and places shown itself capable of achieving over so mighty and so universal a sentiment. The widest difference no doubt exists between one human being and another in the facility or difficulty with which they acquire this virtue. There is hardly any department of human excellence in which difference of original temperament goes so far. But it may fairly be questioned if any human being is naturally courageous. Many are naturally pugnacious, or irascible, or enthusiastic, and these passions when strongly excited may render them insensible to fear. But take away the conflicting emotion, and fear reasserts its dominion: consistent courage is always the effect of cultivation. The courage which is occasionally though by no means generally found among tribes of savages, is as much the result of education as that of the

Spartans or Romans. In all such tribes there is a most emphatic direction of the public sentiment into every channel of expression through which honour can be paid to courage and cowardice held up to contempt and derision. It will perhaps be said, that as the expression of a sentiment implies the sentiment itself, the training of the young to courage presupposes an originally courageous people. It presupposes only what all good customs presuppose— that there must have been individuals better than the rest, who set the customs going. Some individuals, who like other people had fears to conquer, must have had strength of mind and will to conquer them for themselves. These would obtain the influence belonging to heroes, for that which is at once astonishing and obviously useful never fails to be admired: and partly through this admiration, partly through the fear they themselves excite, they would obtain the power of legislators, and could establish whatever customs they pleased.

Let us next consider a quality which forms the most visible, and one of the most radical of the moral distinctions between human beings and most of the lower animals; that of which the absence, more than of anything else, renders men bestial; the quality of cleanliness. Can anything be more entirely artificial? Children, and the lower classes of most countries, seem to be actually fond of dirt: the vast majority of the human race are indifferent to it: whole nations of otherwise civilized and cultivated human beings tolerate it in some of its worst forms, and only a very small minority are consistently offended by it. Indeed the universal law of the subject appears to be, that uncleanliness offends only those to whom it is unfamiliar, so that those who have lived in so artificial a state as to be unused to it in any form, are the sole persons whom it disgusts in all forms. Of all virtues this is the most evidently not instinctive, but a triumph over instinct. Assuredly neither cleanliness nor the love of cleanliness is natural to man, but only the capacity of acquiring a love of cleanliness.

Our examples have thus far been taken from the personal, or as they are called by Bentham, the self regarding virtues, because these, if any, might be supposed to be congenial even to the uncultivated mind. Of the social virtues it is almost superfluous to speak; so completely is it the verdict of all experience that selfishness is natural. By this I do not in any wise mean to deny that sympathy is natural also; I believe on the contrary that on that important fact rests the possibility of any cultivation of goodness and nobleness, and the hope of their ultimate entire ascendancy. But sympathetic characters, left uncultivated, and given up to their sympathetic instincts, are as selfish as others. The difference is in the *kind* of selfishness: theirs is not solitary but sympathetic selfishness; *l'egoïsme à deux, à trois*, or *à quatre*; and they may be very amiable and delightful to those with whom they sympathize, and grossly unjust and unfeeling to the rest of the world. Indeed the finer nervous organizations which are most capable of and most require sympathy, have, from their fineness, so much stronger impulses of all sorts, that they often furnish the most striking examples of selfishness, though of a less repulsive kind than that of colder natures. Whether there ever was a person in whom, apart from all teaching of instructors, friends or books, and from all intentional self-modelling according to an ideal, natural benevolence was a more powerful attribute than selfishness in any of its forms, may remain undecided. That such cases are extremely rare, every one must admit, and this is enough for the argument.

But (to speak no further of self-control for the benefit of others) the commonest self-control for one's own benefit—that power of sacrificing a present desire to a distant object or a general purpose which is indispensable for making the actions of the individual accord with his own notions of his individual good; even this is most unnatural to the undisciplined human being: as may be seen by the long apprenticeship which children serve to it; the very imperfect manner in which it is acquired by persons born to power, whose will is seldom resisted, and by all who have been early and much indulged; and the marked absence of the quality in savages, in soldiers and sailors, and in a somewhat less degree in nearly the whole of the poorer classes in this and many other countries. The principal difference, on the point under consideration, between this virtue and others, is that although, like them, it requires a course of teaching, it is more susceptible than most of them of being self-taught. The axiom is trite that self-control is only learnt by experience: and this endowment is only thus much nearer to being natural than the others we have spoken of, inasmuch as personal experience, without external inculcation, has a certain tendency to engender it. Nature does not of herself bestow this, any more than other virtues; but nature often administers the rewards and punishments which cultivate it, and which in other cases have to be created artificially for the express purpose.

Veracity might seem, of all virtues, to have the most plausible claim to being natural, since in the absence of motives to the contrary, speech usually conforms to, or at least does not intentionally deviate from, fact. Accordingly this is the virtue with which writers like Rousseau delight in decorating savage life, and setting it in advantageous contrast with the treachery and trickery of civilization. Unfortunately this is a mere fancy picture, contradicted by all the realities of savage life. Savages are always liars. They have not the faintest notion of truth as a virtue. They have a notion of not betraying to their hurt, as of not hurting in any other way, persons to whom they are bound by some special tie of obligation; their chief, their guest, perhaps, or their friend: these feelings of obligation being the taught morality of the savage state, growing out of its characteristic circumstances. But of any point of honour respecting truth for truth's sake, they have not the remotest idea;

no more than the whole East, and the greater part of Europe: and in the few countries which are sufficiently improved to have such a point of honour, it is confined to a small minority, who alone, under any circumstances of real temptation practise it.

From the general use of the expression "natural justice," it must be presumed that justice is a virtue generally thought to be directly implanted by nature. I believe, however, that the sentiment of justice is entirely of artificial origin; the idea of natural justice not preceding but following that of conventional justice. The farther we look back into the early modes of thinking of the human race, whether we consider ancient times (including those of the Old Testament) or the portions of mankind who are still in no more advanced a condition than that of ancient times, the more completely do we find men's notions of justice defined and bounded by the express appointment of law. A man's just rights, meant the rights which the law gave him: a just man, was he who never infringed, nor sought to infringe, the legal property or other legal rights of others. The notion of a higher justice, to which laws themselves are amenable, and by which the conscience is bound without a positive prescription of law, is a later extension of the idea, suggested by, and following the analogy of, legal justice, to which it maintains a parallel direction through all the shades and varieties of the sentiment, and from which it borrows nearly the whole of its phraseology. The very words *justus* and *justitia* are derived from *jus*, law. Courts of justice, administration of justice, always mean the tribunals.

If it be said, that there must be the germs of all these virtues in human nature, otherwise mankind would be incapable of acquiring them, I am ready, with a certain amount of explanation, to admit the fact. But the weeds that dispute the ground with these beneficent germs, are themselves not germs but rankly luxuriant growths, and would, in all but some one case in a thousand, entirely stifle and destroy the former, were it not so strongly the interest of mankind to cherish the good germs in one another, that they always do so, in as far as their degree of intelligence (in this as in other respects still very imperfect) allows. It is through such fostering, commenced early, and not counteracted by unfavourable influences, that, in some happily circumstanced specimens of the human race, the most elevated sentiments of which humanity is capable become a second nature, stronger than the first, and not so much subduing the original nature as merging it into itself. Even those gifted organizations which have attained the like excellence by self-culture, owe it essentially to the same cause; for what self-culture would be possible without aid from the general sentiment of mankind delivered through books, and from the contemplation of exalted characters real or ideal? This artificially created or at least artificially perfected nature

of the best and noblest human beings, is the only nature which it is ever commendable to follow. It is almost superfluous to say that even this cannot be
erected into a standard of conduct, since it is itself the fruit of a training and
culture the choice of which, if rational and not accidental, must have been
determined by a standard already chosen.

This brief survey is amply sufficient to prove that the duty of man is the
same in respect to his own nature as in respect to the nature of all other
things, namely not to follow but to amend it. Some people however who do
not attempt to deny that instinct ought to be subordinate to reason, pay
deference to nature so far as to maintain that every natural inclination must
have some sphere of action granted to it, some opening left for its gratification. All natural wishes, they say, must have been implanted for a purpose:
and this argument is carried so far, that we often hear it maintained that
every wish, which it is supposed to be natural to entertain, must have a corresponding provision in the order of the universe for its gratification: insomuch (for instance) that the desire of an indefinite prolongation of existence,
is believed by many to be in itself a sufficient proof of the reality of a
future life.

I conceive that there is a radical absurdity in all these attempts to discover,
in detail, what are the designs of Providence, in order when they are discovered to help Providence in bringing them about. Those who argue, from
particular indications, that Providence intends this or that, either believe
that the Creator can do all that he will or that he cannot. If the first supposition is adopted—if Providence is omnipotent, Providence intends whatever
happens, and the fact of its happening proves that Providence intended it.
If so, everything which a human being can do, is predestined by Providence
and is a fulfilment of its designs. But if as is the more religious theory,
Providence intends not all which happens, but only what is good, then indeed
man has it in his power, by his voluntary actions, to aid the intentions of
Providence; but he can only learn those intentions by considering what tends
to promote the general good, and not what man has a natural inclination to;
for, limited as, on this showing, the divine power must be, by inscrutable but
insurmountable obstacles, who knows that man *could* have been created
without desires which never are to be, and even which never ought to be,
fulfilled? The inclinations with which man has been endowed, as well as any
of the other contrivances which we observe in Nature, may be the expression
not of the divine will, but of the fetters which impede its free action; and to
take hints from these for the guidance of our own conduct may be falling
into a trap laid by the enemy. The assumption that everything which infinite
goodness can desire, actually comes to pass in this universe, or at least that
we must never say or suppose that it does not, is worthy only of those whose

slavish fears make them offer the homage of lies to a Being who, they profess to think, is incapable of being deceived and holds all falsehood in abomination.

With regard to this particular hypothesis, that all natural impulses, all propensities sufficiently universal and sufficiently spontaneous to be capable of passing for instincts, must exist for good ends, and ought to be only regulated, not repressed; this is of course true of the majority of them, for the species could not have continued to exist unless most of its inclinations had been directed to things needful or useful for its preservation. But unless the instincts can be reduced to a very small number indeed, it must be allowed that we have also bad instincts which it should be the aim of education not simply to regulate but to extirpate, or rather (what can be done even to an instinct) to starve them by disuse. Those who are inclined to multiply the number of instincts, usually include among them one which they call destructiveness: an instinct to destroy for destruction's sake. I can conceive no good reason for preserving this, no more than another propensity which if not an instinct is very like one, what has been called the instinct of domination; a delight in exercising despotism, in holding other beings in subjection to our will. The man who takes pleasure in the mere exertion of authority, apart from the purpose for which it is to be employed, is the last person in whose hands one would willingly entrust it. Again, there are persons who are cruel by character, or, as the phrase is, naturally cruel; who have a real pleasure in inflicting, or seeing the infliction of pain. This kind of cruelty is not mere hardheartedness, absence of pity or remorse; it is a positive thing; a particular kind of voluptuous excitement. The East, and Southern Europe, have afforded, and probably still afford, abundant examples of this hateful propensity. I suppose it will be granted that this is not one of the natural inclinations which it would be wrong to suppress. The only question would be whether it is not a duty to suppress the man himself along with it.

But even if it were true that every one of the elementary impulses of human nature has its good side, and may by a sufficient amount of artificial training be made more useful than hurtful; how little would this amount to, when it must in any case be admitted that without such training all of them, even those which are necessary to our preservation, would fill the world with misery, making human life an exaggerated likeness of the odious scene of violence and tyranny which is exhibited by the rest of the animal kingdom, except in so far as tamed and disciplined by man. There, indeed, those who flatter themselves with the notion of reading the purposes of the Creator in his works, ought in consistency to have seen grounds for inferences from which they have shrunk. If there are any marks at all of special design in creation, one of the things most evidently designed is that a large proportion of all animals should pass their existence in tormenting and devouring other animals. They have been lavishly fitted out with the instruments necessary for that purpose; their strongest instincts impel them to it, and many of them seem to have been constructed incapable of supporting themselves by any other food. If a tenth part of the pains which have been expended in finding benevolent adaptations in all nature, had been employed in collecting evidence to blacken the character of the Creator, what scope for comment would not have been found in the entire existence of the lower animals, divided, with scarcely an exception, into devourers and devoured, and a prey to a thousand ills from which they are denied the faculties necessary for protecting themselves! If we are not obliged to believe the animal creation to be the work of a demon, it is because we need not suppose it to have been made by a Being of infinite power. But if imitation of the Creator's will as revealed in nature, were applied as a rule of action in this case, the most atrocious enormities of the worst men would be more than justified by the apparent intention of Providence that throughout all animated nature the strong should prey upon the weak.

The preceding observations are far from having exhausted the almost infinite variety of modes and occasions in which the idea of conformity to nature is introduced as an element into the ethical appreciation of actions and dispositions. The same favourable prejudgment follows the word nature through the numerous acceptations, in which it is employed as a distinctive term for certain parts of the constitution of humanity as contrasted with other parts. We have hitherto confined ourselves to one of these acceptations, in which it stands as a general designation for those parts of our mental and moral constitution which are supposed to be innate, in contradistinction to those which are acquired; as when nature is contrasted with education; or when a savage state, without laws, arts, or knowledge, is called a state of nature; or when the question is asked whether benevolence, or the moral sentiment, is natural or acquired; or whether some persons are poets or orators by nature and others not. But in another and a more lax sense, any manifestations by human beings are often termed natural, when it is merely intended to say that they are not studied or designedly assumed in the particular case; as when a person is said to move or speak with natural grace; or when it is said that a person's natural manner or character is so and so; meaning that it is so when he does not attempt to control or disguise it. In a still looser acceptation, a person is said to be naturally, that which he was until some special cause had acted upon him, or which it is supposed he would be if some such cause were withdrawn. Thus a person is said to be naturally dull, but to have made himself intelligent by study and perseverance; to be naturally cheerful, but soured by misfortune; naturally ambitious, but kept down by want of opportunity. Finally, the word natural, applied to feelings or conduct, often seems to mean no more than that they are such as are ordinarily found in human beings; as when it is said that a person acted, on some particular occasion, as it was natural to do; or that to be affected in a particular way by some sight, or sound, or thought, or incident in life, is perfectly natural.

In all these senses of the term, the quality called natural is very often confessedly a worse quality than the one contrasted with it; but whenever its being so is not too obvious to be questioned, the idea seems to be entertained that by describing it as natural, something has been said amounting to a considerable presumption in its favour. For my part I can perceive only one sense in which nature, or naturalness, in a human being, are really terms of praise; and then the praise is only negative: namely when used to denote the absence of affectation. Affectation may be defined, the effort to appear what one is not, when the motive or the occasion is not such as either to excuse the attempt, or to stamp it with the more odious name of hypocrisy. It must be added that the deception is often attempted to be practised on the deceiver himself as well as on others; he imitates the external signs of qualities which he would like to have, in hopes to persuade himself that he has them. Whether in the form of deception or of self-deception, or of something hovering between the two, affectation is very rightly accounted a reproach, and naturalness, understood as the reverse of affectation, a merit. But a more proper term by which to express this estimable quality would be sincerity; a term which has fallen from its original elevated meaning, and popularly denotes only a subordinate branch of the cardinal virtue it once designated as a whole.

Sometimes also, in cases where the term affectation would be inappropriate, since the conduct or demeanour spoken of is really praiseworthy, people say in disparagement of the person concerned, that such conduct or demeanour is not natural to him; and make uncomplimentary comparisons between him and some other person, to whom it is natural: meaning that what in the one seemed excellent was the effect of temporary excitement, or of a great victory over himself, while in the other it is the result to be expected from the habitual character. This mode of speech is not open to censure, since nature is here simply a term for the person's ordinary disposition, and if he is praised it is not for being natural, but for being naturally good.

Conformity to nature, has no connection whatever with right and wrong. The idea can never be fitly introduced into ethical discussions at all, except, occasionally and partially, into the question of degrees of culpability. To illustrate this point, let us consider the phrase by which the greatest intensity of condemnatory feeling is conveyed in connection with the idea of nature— the word unnatural. That a thing is unnatural, in any precise meaning which can be attached to the word, is no argument for its being blamable; since the most criminal actions are to a being like man, not more unnatural than most of the virtues. The acquisition of virtue has in all ages been accounted a work of labour and difficulty, while the *descensus Averni* on the contrary is of proverbial facility: and it assuredly requires in most persons a greater conquest over a greater number of natural inclinations to become eminently virtuous than transcendently vicious. But if an action, or an inclination, has been decided on other grounds to be blamable, it may be a circumstance in aggravation that it is unnatural, that is, repugnant to some strong feeling usually found in human beings; since the bad propensity, whatever it be, has afforded evidence of being both strong and deeply rooted, by having overcome that repugnance. This presumption of course fails if the individual never had the repugnance: and the argument, therefore, is not fit to be urged unless the feeling which is violated by the act, is not only justifiable and reasonable, but is one which it is blamable to be without.

The corresponding plea in extenuation of a culpable act because it was natural, or because it was prompted by a natural feeling, never, I think, ought to be admitted. There is hardly a bad action ever perpetrated which is not perfectly natural, and the motives to which are not perfectly natural feelings. In the eye of reason, therefore, this is no excuse, but it is quite "natural" that it should be so in the eyes of the multitude; because the meaning of the expression is, that they have a fellow feeling with the offender. When they say that something which they cannot help admitting to be blamable, is nevertheless natural, they mean that they can imagine the possibility of their being themselves tempted to commit it. Most people have a considerable amount of indulgence towards all acts of which they feel a possible source within themselves, reserving their rigour for those which, though perhaps really less bad, they cannot in any way understand how it is possible to commit. If an action convinces them (which it often does on very inadequate grounds) that the person who does it must be a being totally unlike themselves, they are seldom particular in examining the precise degree of blame due to it, or even if blame is properly due to it at all. They measure the degree of guilt by the strength of their antipathy; and hence differences of opinion, and even differences of taste, have been objects of as intense moral abhorrence as the most atrocious crimes.

It will be useful to sum up in a few words the leading conclusions of this Essay.

The word Nature has two principal meanings: it either denotes the entire system of things, with the aggregate of all their properties, or it denotes things as they would be, apart from human intervention.

In the first of these senses, the doctrine that man ought to follow nature is unmeaning; since man has no power to do anything else than follow nature; all his actions are done through, and in obedience to, some one or many of nature's physical or mental laws.

In the other sense of the term, the doctrine that man ought to follow nature, or in other words, ought to make the spontaneous course of things the model of his voluntary actions, is equally irrational and immoral.

Irrational, because all human action whatever, consists in altering, and all useful action in improving, the spontaneous course of nature:

Immoral, because the course of natural phenomena being replete with everything which when committed by human beings is most worthy of abhorrence, any one who endeavoured in his actions to imitate the natural course of things would be universally seen and acknowledged to be the wickedest of men.

The scheme of Nature regarded in its whole extent, cannot have had, for its sole or even principal object, the good of human or other sentient beings. What good it brings to them, is mostly the result of their own exertions. Whatsoever, in nature, gives indication of beneficent design, proves this beneficence to be armed only with limited power; and the duty of man is to co-operate with the beneficent powers, not by imitating but by perpetually striving to amend the course of nature—and bringing that part of it over which we can exercise control, more nearly into conformity with a high standard of justice and goodness.

Utility of Religion

IT HAS SOMETIMES been remarked how much has been written, both by friends and enemies, concerning the truth of religion, and how little, at least in the way of discussion or controversy, concerning its usefulness. This, however, might have been expected; for the truth, in matters which so deeply affect us, is our first concernment. If religion, or any particular form of it, is true, its usefulness follows without other proof. If to know authentically in what order of things, under what government of the universe it is our destiny to live, were not useful, it is difficult to imagine what could be considered so. Whether a person is in a pleasant or in an unpleasant place, a palace or a prison, it cannot be otherwise than useful to him to know where he is. So long, therefore, as men accepted the teachings of their religion as positive facts, no more a matter of doubt than their own existence or the existence of the objects around them, to ask the use of believing it could not possibly occur to them. The utility of religion did not need to be asserted until the arguments for its truth had in a great measure ceased to convince. People must either have ceased to believe, or have ceased to rely on the belief of others, before they could take that inferior ground of defence without a consciousness of lowering what they were endeavouring to raise. An argument for the utility of religion is an appeal to unbelievers, to induce them to practise a well meant hypocrisy, or to semi-believers to make them avert their eyes from what might possibly shake their unstable belief, or finally to persons in general to abstain from expressing any doubts they may feel, since a fabric of immense importance to mankind is so insecure at its foundations, that men must hold their breath in its neighbourhood for fear of blowing it down.

In the present period of history, however, we seem to have arrived at a time when, among the arguments for and against religion, those which relate to its usefulness assume an important place. We are in an age of weak beliefs, and in which such belief as men have is much more determined by their wish to believe than by any mental appreciation of evidence. The wish to believe does not arise only from selfish but often from the most disinterested feelings; and though it cannot produce the unwavering and perfect reliance which once existed, it fences round all that remains of the impressions of early education; it often causes direct misgivings to fade away by disuse; and above all, it induces people to continue laying out their lives according to doctrines which have lost part of their hold on the mind, and to maintain towards the world the same, or a rather more demonstrative attitude of belief, than they thought it necessary to exhibit when their personal conviction was more complete.

If religious belief be indeed so necessary to mankind, as we are continually assured that it is, there is great reason to lament, that the intellectual grounds of it should require to be backed by moral bribery or subornation of the understanding. Such a state of things is most uncomfortable even for those who may, without actual insincerity, describe themselves as believers; and still worse as regards those who, having consciously ceased to find the evidences of religion convincing, are withheld from saying so lest they should aid in doing an irreparable injury to mankind. It is a most painful position to a conscientious and cultivated mind, to be drawn in contrary directions by the two noblest of all objects of pursuit, truth, and the general good. Such a conflict must inevitably produce a growing indifference to one or other of these objects, most probably to both. Many who could render giant's service both to truth and to mankind if they believed that they could serve the one without loss to the other, are either totally paralysed, or led to confine their exertions to matters of minor detail, by the apprehension that any real freedom of speculation, or any considerable strengthening or enlargement of the thinking faculties of mankind at large, might, by making them unbelievers, be the surest way to render them vicious and miserable. Many, again, having observed in others or experienced in themselves elevated feelings which they imagine incapable of emanating from any other source than religion, have an honest aversion to anything tending, as they think, to dry up the fountain of such feelings. They, therefore, either dislike and disparage all philosophy, or addict themselves with intolerant zeal to those forms of it in which intuition usurps the place of evidence, and internal feeling is made the test of objective truth. The whole of the prevalent metaphysics of the present century is one tissue of suborned evidence in favour of religion; often of Deism only, but in any case involving a misapplication of noble impulses and speculative capacities, among the most deplorable of those wretched wastes of human faculties which make us wonder that enough is left to keep mankind progressive, at however slow a pace. It is time to consider, more impartially and therefore more deliberately than is usually done, whether all this straining to prop up beliefs which require so great an expense of intellectual toil and ingenuity to keep them standing, yields any sufficient return in human well being; and whether that end would not be better served by a frank recognition that certain subjects are inaccessible to our faculties, and by the application of the same mental powers to the strengthening and enlargement of those other sources of virtue and happiness which stand in no need of the support or sanction of supernatural beliefs and inducements.

Neither, on the other hand, can the difficulties of the question be so promptly disposed of, as sceptical philosophers are sometimes inclined to believe. It is not enough to aver, in general terms, that there never can be any conflict between truth and utility; that if religion be false, nothing but good can be the consequence of rejecting it. For, though the knowledge of every positive truth is an useful acquisition, this doctrine cannot without reservation be applied to negative truth. When the only truth ascertainable is that nothing can be known, we do not, by this knowledge, gain any new fact by which to guide ourselves; we are, at best, only disabused of our trust in some former guide-mark, which, though itself fallacious, may have pointed in the same direction with the best indications we have, and if it happens to be more conspicuous and legible, may have kept us right when they might have been overlooked. It is, in short, perfectly conceivable that religion may be morally useful without being intellectually sustainable: and it would be a proof of great prejudice in any unbeliever to deny, that there have been ages, and that there are still both nations and individuals, with regard to whom this is actually the case. Whether it is the case generally, and with reference to the future, it is the object of this paper to examine. We propose to inquire whether the belief in religion, considered as a mere persuasion, apart from the question of its truth, is really indispensable to the temporal welfare of mankind; whether the usefulness of the belief is intrinsic and universal, or local, temporary, and, in some sense, accidental; and whether the benefits which it yields might not be obtained otherwise, without the very large alloy of evil, by which, even in the best form of the belief, those benefits are qualified.

With the arguments on one side of the question we all are familiar: religious writers have not neglected to celebrate to the utmost the advantages both of religion in general and of their own religious faith in particular. But those who have held the contrary opinion have generally contented themselves with insisting on the more obvious and flagrant of the positive evils which have been engendered by past and present forms of religious belief. And, in truth, mankind have been so unremittingly occupied in doing evil to one another in the name of religion, from the sacrifice of Iphigenia to the Dragonnades of Louis XIV (not to descend lower), that for any immediate purpose there was little need to seek arguments further off. These odious consequences, however, do not belong to religion in itself, but to particular forms of it, and afford no argument against the usefulness of any religions except those by which such enormities are encouraged. Moreover, the worst of these evils are already in a great measure extirpated from the more improved forms of religion; and as mankind advance in ideas and in feelings, this process of extirpation continually goes on: the immoral, or otherwise mischievous consequences which have been drawn from religion, are, one by one, abandoned, and, after having been long fought for as of its very essence, are discovered to be easily separable from it. These mischiefs, indeed, after they are past, though no longer arguments against religion, remain valid as large abatements from its beneficial influence, by showing that some of the greatest improvements ever made in the moral sentiments of mankind have taken place without it and in spite of it, and that what we are taught to regard as the chief of all improving influences, has in practice fallen so far short of such a character, that one of the hardest burdens laid upon the other good influences of human nature has been that of improving religion itself. The improvement, however, has taken place; it is still proceeding, and for the sake of fairness it should be assumed to be complete. We ought to suppose religion to have accepted the best human morality which reason and goodness can work out, from philosophical, christian, or any other elements. When it has thus freed itself from the pernicious consequences which result from its identification with any bad moral doctrine, the ground is clear for considering whether its useful properties are exclusively inherent in it, or their benefits can be obtained without it.

This essential portion of the inquiry into the temporal usefulness of religion, is the subject of the present Essay. It is a part which has been little treated of by sceptical writers. The only direct discussion of it with which I am acquainted, is in a short treatise, understood to have been partly compiled from manuscripts of Mr. Bentham,* and abounding in just and profound views; but which, as it appears to me, presses many parts of the argument too hard. This treatise, and the incidental remarks scattered through the writings of M. Comte, are the only sources known to me from which anything very pertinent to the subject can be made available for the sceptical side of the argument. I shall use both of them freely in the sequel of the present discourse.

The inquiry divides itself into two parts, corresponding to the double aspect of the subject; its social, and its individual aspect. What does religion do for society, and what for the individual? What amount of benefit to social interests, in the ordinary sense of the phrase, arises from religious belief? And what influence has it in improving and ennobling individual human nature?

The first question is interesting to everybody; the latter only to the best;

*Analysis of the Influence of Natural Religion on the Temporal Happiness of Mankind. [London: Carlisle, 1822.] By Philip Beauchamp [George Grote].

but to them it is, if there be any difference, the more important of the two. We shall begin with the former, as being that which best admits of being easily brought to a precise issue.

To speak first, then, of religious belief as an instrument of social good. We must commence by drawing a distinction most commonly overlooked. It is usual to credit religion *as such* with the whole of the power inherent in *any* system of moral duties inculcated by education and enforced by opinion. Undoubtedly mankind would be in a deplorable state if no principles or precepts of justice, veracity, beneficence, were taught publicly or privately, and if these virtues were not encouraged, and the opposite vices repressed, by the praise and blame, the favourable and unfavourable sentiments, of mankind. And since nearly everything of this sort which does take place, takes place in the name of religion; since almost all who are taught any morality whatever, have it taught to them *as* religion, and inculcated on them through life principally in that character; the effect which the teaching produces as teaching, it is supposed to produce as religious teaching, and religion receives the credit of all the influence in human affairs which belongs to any generally accepted system of rules for the guidance and government of human life.

Few persons have sufficiently considered how great an influence this is; what vast efficacy belongs naturally to any doctrine received with tolerable unanimity as true, and impressed on the mind from the earliest childhood as duty. A little reflection will, I think, lead us to the conclusion that it is this which is the great moral power in human affairs, and that religion only seems so powerful because this mighty power has been under its command.

Consider first, the enormous influence of authority on the human mind. I am now speaking of involuntary influence; effect on men's conviction, on their persuasion, on their involuntary sentiments. Authority is the evidence on which the mass of mankind believe everything which they are said to know, except facts of which their own senses have taken cognizance. It is the evidence on which even the wisest receive all those truths of science, or facts in history or in life, of which they have not personally examined the proofs. Over the immense majority of human beings, the general concurrence of mankind, in any matter of opinion, is all powerful. Whatever is thus certified to them, they believe with a fulness of assurance which they do not accord even to the evidence of their senses when the general opinion of mankind stands in opposition to it. When, therefore, any rule of life and duty, whether grounded or not on religion, has conspicuously received the general assent, it obtains a hold on the belief of every individual, stronger than it would have even if he had arrived at it by the inherent force of his own understanding. If Novalis could say, not without a real meaning, "My belief has gained infinitely to me from the moment when one other human being has begun to believe the same,"[*] how much more when it is not one other person, but all the human beings whom one knows of. Some may urge it as an objection, that no scheme of morality has this universal assent, and that none, therefore, can be indebted to this source for whatever power it possesses over the mind. So far as relates to the present age, the assertion is true, and strengthens the argument which it might at first seem to controvert; for exactly in proportion as the received systems of belief have been contested, and it has become known that they have many dissentients, their hold on the general belief has been loosened, and their practical influence on conduct has declined: and since this has happened to them notwithstanding the religious sanction which attached to them, there can be no stronger evidence that they were powerful not as religion, but as beliefs generally accepted by mankind. To find people who believe their religion as a person believes that fire will burn his hand when thrust into it, we must seek them in those Oriental countries where Europeans do not yet predominate, or in the European world when it was still universally Catholic. Men often disobeyed their religion in those times, because their human passions and appetites were too strong for it, or because the religion itself afforded means of indulgence to breaches of its obligations; but though they disobeyed, they, for the most part, did not doubt. There was in those days an absolute and unquestioning completeness of belief, never since general in Europe.

Such being the empire exercised over mankind by simple authority, the mere belief and testimony of their fellow creatures; consider next how tremendous is the power of education; how unspeakable is the effect of bringing people up from infancy in a belief, and in habits founded on it. Consider also that in all countries, and from the earliest ages down to the present, not merely those who are called, in a restricted sense of the term, the educated, but all or nearly all who have been brought up by parents, or by any one interested in them, have been taught from their earliest years some kind of religious belief, and some precepts as the commands of the heavenly powers to them and to mankind. And as it cannot be imagined that the commands of God are to young children anything more than the commands of their parents, it is reasonable to think that any system of social duty which mankind might adopt, even though divorced from religion, would have the same advantage of being inculcated from childhood, and would have it hereafter much more perfectly than any doctrine has it at present, society being far more disposed than formerly to take pains for the moral tuition of those numerous classes whose education it has hitherto left very much to chance. Now it is especially characteristic of the impressions of early education, that they possess what it is so much more difficult for later convictions to obtain—command over the

[*See Thomas Carlyle. *On Heroes, Hero-Worship, and the Heroic in History.* London: Fraser, 1841, 93.]

feelings. We see daily how powerful a hold these first impressions retain over the feelings even of those, who have given up the opinions which they were early taught. While on the other hand, it is only persons of a much higher degree of natural sensibility and intellect combined than it is at all common to meet with, whose feelings entwine themselves with anything like the same force round opinions which they have adopted from their own investigations later in life; and even when they do, we may say with truth that it is because the strong sense of moral duty, the sincerity, courage and self-devotion which enabled them to do so, were themselves the fruits of early impressions.

The power of education is almost boundless: there is not one natural inclination which it is not strong enough to coerce, and, if needful, to destroy by disuse. In the greatest recorded victory which education has ever achieved over a whole host of natural inclinations in an entire people—the maintenance through centuries of the institutions of Lycurgus,—it was very little, if even at all, indebted to religion: for the Gods of the Spartans were the same as those of other Greek states; and though, no doubt, every state of Greece believed that its particular polity had at its first establishment, some sort of divine sanction (mostly that of the Delphian oracle), there was seldom any difficulty in obtaining the same or an equally powerful sanction for a change. It was not religion which formed the strength of the Spartan institutions: the root of the system was devotion to Sparta, to the ideal of the country or State: which transformed into ideal devotion to a greater country, the world, would be equal to that and far nobler achievements. Among the Greeks generally, social morality was extremely independent of religion. The inverse relation was rather that which existed between them; the worship of the Gods was inculcated chiefly as a social duty, inasmuch as if they were neglected or insulted, it was believed that their displeasure would fall not more upon the offending individual than upon the state or community which bred and tolerated him. Such moral teaching as existed in Greece had very little to do with religion. The Gods were not supposed to concern themselves much with men's conduct to one another, except when men had contrived to make the Gods themselves an interested party, by placing an assertion or an engagement under the sanction of a solemn appeal to them, by oath or vow. I grant that the sophists and philosophers, and even popular orators, did their best to press religion into the service of their special objects, and to make it be thought that the sentiments of whatever kind, which they were engaged in inculcating, were particularly acceptable to the Gods, but this never seems the primary consideration in any case save those of direct offence to the dignity of the Gods themselves. For the enforcement of human moralities secular inducements were almost exclusively relied on. The case of Greece is, I believe, the only one in which any teaching, other than religious, has had the unspeakable advantage of forming the basis of education: and though much may be said against the quality of some part of the teaching, very little can be said against its effectiveness. The most memorable example of the power of education over conduct, is afforded (as I have just remarked) by this exceptional case; constituting a strong presumption that in other cases, early religious teaching has owed its power over mankind rather to its being early than to its being religious.

We have now considered two powers, that of authority, and that of early education, which operate through men's involuntary beliefs, feelings and desires, and which religion has hitherto held as its almost exclusive appanage. Let us now consider a third power which operates directly on their actions, whether their involuntary sentiments are carried with it or not. This is the power of public opinion; of the praise and blame, the favour and disfavour, of their fellow creatures; and is a source of strength inherent in any system of moral belief which is generally adopted, whether connected with religion or not.

Men are so much accustomed to give to the motives that decide their actions, more flattering names than justly belong to them, that they are generally quite unconscious how much those parts of their conduct which they most pride themselves on (as well as some which they are ashamed of), are determined by the motive of public opinion. Of course public opinion for the most part enjoins the same things which are enjoined by the received social morality; that morality being, in truth, the summary of the conduct which each one of the multitude, whether he himself observes it with any strictness or not, desires that others should observe towards him. People are therefore easily able to flatter themselves that they are acting from the motive of conscience when they are doing in obedience to the inferior motive, things which their conscience approves. We continually see how great is the power of opinion in opposition to conscience; how men "follow a multitude to do evil;"[*] how often opinion induces them to do what their conscience disapproves, and still oftener prevents them from doing what it commands. But when the motive of public opinion acts in the same direction with conscience, which, since it has usually itself made the conscience in the first instance, it for the most part naturally does; it is then, of all motives which operate on the bulk of mankind, the most overpowering.

The names of all the strongest passions (except the merely animal ones) manifested by human nature, are each of them a name for some one part only of the motive derived from what I here call public opinion. The love of glory; the love of praise; the love of admiration; the love of respect and deference; even the love of sympathy, are portions of its attractive power. Vanity is a vituperative name for its attractive influence generally, when considered excessive in degree. The fear of shame, the dread of ill repute, or of being dis-

[*Exodus, 23:2–3.]

liked or hated, are the direct and simple forms of its deterring power. But the deterring force of the unfavourable sentiments of mankind does not consist solely in the painfulness of knowing oneself to be the object of those sentiments; it includes all the penalties which they can inflict: exclusion from social intercourse and from the innumerable good offices which human beings require from one another; the forfeiture of all that is called success in life; often the great diminution or total loss of means of subsistence; positive ill offices of various kinds, sufficient to render life miserable, and reaching in some states of society as far as actual persecution to death. And again the attractive, or impelling influence of public opinion, includes the whole range of what is commonly meant by ambition: for, except in times of lawless military violence, the objects of social ambition can only be attained by means of the good opinion and favourable disposition of our fellow-creatures; nor, in nine cases out of ten, would those objects be even desired, were it not for the power they confer over the sentiments of mankind. Even the pleasure of self-approbation, in the great majority, is mainly dependent on the opinion of others. Such is the involuntary influence of authority on ordinary minds, that persons must be of a better than ordinary mould to be capable of a full assurance that they are in the right, when the world, that is, when *their* world, thinks them wrong: nor is there, to most men, any proof so demonstrative of their own virtue or talent as that people in general seem to believe in it. Through all departments of human affairs, regard for the sentiments of our fellow-creatures is in one shape or other, in nearly all characters, the pervading motive. And we ought to note that this motive is naturally strongest in the most sensitive natures, which are the most promising material for the formation of great virtues. How far its power reaches is known by too familiar experience to require either proof or illustration here. When once the means of living have been obtained, the far greater part of the remaining labour and effort which takes place on the earth, has for its object to acquire the respect or the favourable regard of mankind; to be looked up to, or at all events, not to be looked down upon by them. The industrial and commercial activity which advance civilization, the frivolity, prodigality, and selfish thirst of aggrandizement which retard it, flow equally from that source. While as an instance of the power exercised by the terrors derived from public opinion, we know how many murders have been committed merely to remove a witness who knew and was likely to disclose some secret that would bring disgrace upon his murderer.

Any one who fairly and impartially considers the subject, will see reason to believe that those great effects on human conduct, which are commonly ascribed to motives derived directly from religion, have mostly for their proximate cause the influence of human opinion. Religion has been powerful not by its intrinsic force, but because it has wielded that additional and more mighty power. The effect of religion has been immense in giving a direction to public opinion: which has, in many most important respects, been wholly determined by it. But without the sanctions superadded by public opinion, its own proper sanctions have never, save in exceptional characters, or in peculiar moods of mind, exercised a very potent influence, after the times had gone by, in which divine agency was supposed habitually to employ temporal rewards and punishments. When a man firmly believed that if he violated the sacredness of a particular sanctuary he would be struck dead on the spot, or smitten suddenly with a mortal disease, he doubtless took care not to incur the penalty: but when any one had had the courage to defy the danger, and escaped with impunity, the spell was broken. If ever any people were taught that they were under a divine government, and that unfaithfulness to their religion and law would be visited from above with temporal chastisements, the Jews were so. Yet their history was a mere succession of lapses into Paganism. Their prophets and historians, who held fast to the ancient beliefs (though they gave them so liberal an interpretation as to think it a sufficient manifestation of God's displeasure towards a king if any evil happened to his great grandson), never ceased to complain that their countrymen turned a deaf ear to their vaticinations; and hence, with the faith they held in a divine government operating by temporal penalties, they could not fail to anticipate (as Mirabeau's father without such prompting, was able to do on the eve of the French Revolution) *la culbute générale*;[*] an expectation which, luckily for the credit of their prophetic powers, was fulfilled; unlike that of the Apostle John, who in the only intelligible prophecy in the Revelations, foretold to the city of the seven hills a fate like that of Nineveh and Babylon;[†] which prediction remains to this hour unaccomplished. Unquestionably the conviction which experience in time forced on all but the very ignorant, that divine punishments were not to be confidently expected in a temporal form, contributed much to the downfall of the old religions, and the general adoption of one which without absolutely excluding providential interferences in this life for the punishment of guilt or the reward of merit, removed the principal scene of divine retribution to a world after death. But rewards and punishments postponed to that distance of time, and never seen by the eye, are not calculated, even when infinite and eternal, to have, on ordinary minds, a very powerful effect in opposition to strong temptation. Their remoteness alone is a prodigious deduction from their efficacy, on such minds as those which most require the restraint of punishment. A still greater abatement is their uncertainty, which belongs to them from the very nature of the case: for rewards and punishments administered after death, must be awarded not definitely to particular actions, but on a general survey of the person's whole life, and he easily persuades himself that

[*See Honoré-Gabriel Riquetti, Comte de Mirabeau. *Mémoires*. Paris, 1834–35, II, 188.]   [†See Revelations, 18.]

whatever may have been his peccadilloes, there will be a balance in his favour at the last. All positive religions aid this self-delusion. Bad religions teach that divine vengeance may be bought off, by offerings, or personal abasement; the better religions, not to drive sinners to despair, dwell so much on the divine mercy, that hardly any one is compelled to think himself irrevocably condemned. The sole quality in these punishments which might seem calculated to make them efficacious, their over-powering magnitude, is itself a reason why nobody (except a hypochondriac here and there) ever really believes that he is in any very serious danger of incurring them. Even the worst malefactor is hardly able to think that any crime he has had it in his power to commit, any evil he can have inflicted in this short space of existence, can have deserved torture extending through an eternity. Accordingly religious writers and preachers are never tired of complaining how little effect religious motives have on men's lives and conduct, notwithstanding the tremendous penalties denounced.

Mr. Bentham, whom I have already mentioned as one of the few authors who have written anything to the purpose on the efficacy of the religious sanction, adduces several cases to prove that religious obligation, when not enforced by public opinion, produces scarcely any effect on conduct.[*] His first example is that of oaths. The oaths taken in courts of justice, and any others which from the manifest importance to society of their being kept, public opinion rigidly enforces, are felt as real and binding obligations. But university oaths and custom-house oaths, though in a religious point of view equally obligatory, are in practice utterly disregarded even by men in other respects honourable. The university oath to obey the statutes has been for centuries, with universal acquiescence, set at nought: and utterly false statements are (or used to be) daily and unblushingly sworn to at the Custom-house, by persons as attentive as other people to all the ordinary obligations of life. The explanation being, that veracity in these cases was not enforced by public opinion. The second case which Bentham cites is duelling; a practice now, in this country, obsolete, but in full vigour in several other christian countries; deemed and admitted to be a sin by almost all who, nevertheless, in obedience to opinion, and to escape from personal humiliation, are guilty of it. The third case is that of illicit sexual intercourse; which in both sexes, stands in the very highest rank of religious sins, yet not being severely censured by opinion in the male sex, they have in general very little scruple in committing it; while in the case of women, though the religious obligation is not stronger, yet being backed in real ernest by public opinion, it is commonly effectual.

Some objection may doubtless be taken to Bentham's instances, considered

[*See [George Grote,] *Analysis of the Influence of Natural Religion*, pp. 58–66.]

as crucial experiments on the power of the religious sanction; for (it may be said) people do not really believe that in these cases they shall be punished by God, any more than by man. And this is certainly true in the case of those university and other oaths, which are habitually taken without any intention of keeping them. The oath, in these cases, is regarded as a mere formality, destitute of any serious meaning in the sight of the Deity; and the most scrupulous person, even if he does reproach himself for having taken an oath which nobody deems fit to be kept, does not in his conscience tax himself with the guilt of perjury, but only with the profanation of a ceremony. This, therefore, is not a good example of the weakness of the religious motive when divorced from that of human opinion. The point which it illustrates is rather the tendency of the one motive to come and go with the other, so that where the penalties of public opinion cease, the religious motive ceases also. The same criticism, however, is not equally applicable to Bentham's other examples, duelling, and sexual irregularities. Those who do these acts, the first by the command of public opinion, the latter with its indulgence, really do, in most cases, believe that they are offending God. Doubtless, they do not think that they are offending him in such a degree as very seriously to endanger their salvation. Their reliance on his mercy prevails over their dread of his resentment; affording an exemplification of the remark already made, that the unavoidable uncertainty of religious penalties makes them feeble as a deterring motive. They are so, even in the case of acts which human opinion condemns: much more, with those to which it is indulgent. What mankind think venial, it is hardly ever supposed that God looks upon in a serious light: at least by those who feel in themselves any inclination to practise it.

I do not for a moment think of denying that there are states of mind in which the idea of religious punishment acts with the most overwhelming force. In hypochondriacal disease, and in those with whom, from great disappointments or other moral causes, the thoughts and imagination have assumed an habitually melancholy complexion, that topic, falling in with the pre-existing tendency of the mind, supplies images well fitted to drive the unfortunate sufferer even to madness. Often, during a temporary state of depression, these ideas take such a hold of the mind as to give a permanent turn to the character; being the most common case of what, in sectarian phraseology, is called conversion. But if the depressed state ceases after the conversion, as it commonly does, and the convert does not relapse, but perseveres in his new course of life, the principal difference between it and the old is usually found to be, that the man now guides his life by the public opinion of his religious associates, as he before guided it by that of the profane world. At all events, there is one clear proof how little the generality of mankind, either religious or worldly, really dread eternal punishments, when we see how, even at the approach of death, when the remoteness which took so much from their effect has been exchanged for the closest proximity, almost all persons who have not been guilty of some enormous crime (and many who have) are quite free from uneasiness as to their prospects in another world, and never for a moment seem to think themselves in any real danger of eternal punishment.

With regard to the cruel deaths and bodily tortures, which confessors and martyrs have so often undergone for the sake of religion, I would not depreciate them by attributing any part of this admirable courage and constancy to the influence of human opinion. Human opinion indeed has shown itself quite equal to the production of similar firmness in persons not otherwise distinguished by moral excellence; such as the North American Indian at the stake. But if it was not the thought of glory in the eyes of their fellow-religionists, which upheld these heroic sufferers in their agony, as little do I believe that it was, generally speaking, that of the pleasures of heaven or the pains of hell. Their impulse was a divine enthusiasm—a self-forgetting devotion to an idea: a state of exalted feeling, by no means peculiar to religion, but which it is the privilege of every great cause to inspire; a phenomenon belonging to the critical moments of existence, not to the ordinary play of human motives, and from which nothing can be inferred as to the efficacy of the ideas which it sprung from, whether religious or any other, in overcoming ordinary temptations, and regulating the course of daily life.

We may now have done with this branch of the subject, which is, after all, the vulgarest part of it. The value of religion as a supplement to human laws, a more cunning sort of police, an auxiliary to the thief-catcher and the hangman, is not that part of its claims which the more highminded of its votaries are fondest of insisting on: and they would probably be as ready as any one to admit, that if the nobler offices of religion in the soul could be dispensed with, a substitute might be found for so coarse and selfish a social instrument as the fear of hell. In their view of the matter, the best of mankind absolutely require religion for the perfection of their own character, even though the coercion of the worst might possibly be accomplished without its aid.

Even in the social point of view, however, under its most elevated aspect, these nobler spirits generally assert the necessity of religion, as a teacher, if not as an enforcer, of social morality. They say, that religion alone can teach us what morality is; that all the high morality ever recognized by mankind, was learnt from religion; that the greatest uninspired philosophers in their sublimest flights, stopt far short of the christian morality, and whatever inferior morality they may have attained to (by the assistance, as many think, of dim traditions derived from the Hebrew books, or from a primæval revelation) they never could induce the common mass of their fellow citizens to accept it from them. That, only when a morality is understood to come from the Gods, do men in general adopt it, rally round it, and lend their human sanctions for its enforcement. That granting the sufficiency of human motives to make the rule obeyed, were it not for the religious idea we should not have had the rule itself.

There is truth in much of this, considered as matter of history. Ancient peoples have generally, if not always, received their morals, their laws, their intellectual beliefs, and even their practical arts of life, all in short which tended either to guide or to discipline them, as revelations from the superior powers, and in any other way could not easily have been induced to accept them. This was partly the effect of their hopes and fears from those powers, which were of much greater and more universal potency in early times, when the agency of the Gods was seen in the daily events of life, experience not having yet disclosed the fixed laws according to which physical phenomena succeed one another. Independently, too, of personal hopes and fears, the involuntary deference felt by these rude minds for power superior to their own, and the tendency to suppose that beings of superhuman power must also be of superhuman knowledge and wisdom, made them disinterestedly desire to conform their conduct to the presumed preferences of these powerful beings, and to adopt no new practice without their authorization either spontaneously given, or solicited and obtained.

But because, when men were still savages, they would not have received either moral or scientific truths unless they had supposed them to be supernaturally imparted, does it follow that they would now give up moral truths any more than scientific, because they believed them to have no higher origin than wise and noble human hearts? Are not moral truths strong enough in their own evidence, at all events to retain the belief of mankind when once they have acquired it? I grant that some of the precepts of Christ as exhibited in the Gospels—rising far above the Paulism which is the foundation of ordinary Christianity—carry some kinds of moral goodness to a greater height than had ever been attained before, though much even of what is supposed to be peculiar to them is equalled in the *Meditations* of Marcus Antoninus, which we have no ground for believing to have been in any way indebted to Christianity. But this benefit, whatever it amounts to, has been gained. Mankind have entered into the possession of it. It has become the property of humanity, and cannot now be lost by anything short of a return to primæval barbarism. The "new commandment to love one another;"* the recognition that the greatest are those who serve, not who are served by, others; the reverence for the weak and humble, which is the foundation of

---

*[John, 13:34] Not, however, a new commandment. In justice to the great Hebrew lawgiver, it should always be remembered that the precept, to love thy neighbour as thyself, already existed in the Pentateuch; and very surprising it is to find it there. [Leviticus, 19:18.]

chivalry, they and not the strong being pointed out as having the first place in God's regard, and the first claim on their fellow men; the lesson of the parable of the Good Samaritan;[*] that of "he that is without sin let him throw the first stone;"[†] the precept of doing as we would be done by;[‡] and such other noble moralities as are to be found, mixed with some poetical exaggerations, and some maxims of which it is difficult to ascertain the precise object; in the authentic sayings of Jesus of Nazareth; these are surely in sufficient harmony with the intellect and feelings of every good man or woman, to be in no danger of being let go, after having been once acknowledged as the creed of the best and foremost portion of our species. There will be, as there have been, shortcomings enough for a long time to come in acting on them; but that they should be forgotten, or cease to be operative on the human conscience, while human beings remain cultivated or civilized, may be pronounced, once for all, impossible.

On the other hand, there is a very real evil consequent on ascribing a supernatural origin to the received maxims of morality. That origin consecrates the whole of them, and protects them from being discussed or criticized. So that if among the moral doctrines received as a part of religion, there be any which are imperfect—which were either erroneous from the first, or not properly limited and guarded in the expression, or which, unexceptionable once, are no longer suited to the changes that have taken place in human relations (and it is my firm belief that in so-called christian morality, instances of all these kinds are to be found) these doctrines are considered equally binding on the conscience with the noblest, most permanent and most universal precepts of Christ. Wherever morality is supposed to be of supernatural origin, morality is stereotyped; as law is, for the same reason, among believers in the Koran.

Belief, then, in the supernatural, great as are the services which it rendered in the early stages of human development, cannot be considered to be any longer required, either for enabling us to know what is right and wrong in social morality, or for supplying us with motives to do right and to abstain from wrong. Such belief, therefore, is not necessary for social purposes, at least in the coarse way in which these can be considered apart from the character of the individual human being. That more elevated branch of the subject now remains to be considered. If supernatural beliefs are indeed necessary to the perfection of the individual character, they are necessary also to the highest excellence in social conduct: necessary in a far higher sense than that vulgar one, which constitutes it the great support of morality in common eyes.

[*Luke, 10:30–7.]
[†John, 8:7.]
[‡Matthew, 7:12.]

Let us then consider, what it is in human nature which causes it to require a religion; what wants of the human mind religion supplies, and what qualities it developes. When we have understood this, we shall be better able to judge, how far these wants can be otherwise supplied and those qualities, or qualities equivalent to them, unfolded and brought to perfection by other means.

The old saying, *Primus in orbe Deos fecit timor*,[*] I hold to be untrue, or to contain, at most, only a small amount of truth. Belief in Gods had, I conceive, even in the rudest minds, a more honourable origin. Its universality has been very rationally explained from the spontaneous tendency of the mind to attribute life and volition, similar to what it feels in itself, to all natural objects and phenomena which appear to be self-moving. This was a plausible fancy, and no better theory could be formed at first. It was naturally persisted in so long as the motions and operations of these objects seemed to be arbitrary, and incapable of being accounted for but by the free choice of the Power itself. At first, no doubt, the objects themselves were supposed to be alive; and this belief still subsists among African fetish-worshippers. But as it must soon have appeared absurd that things which could do so much more than man, could not or would not do what man does, as for example to speak, the transition was made to supposing that the object present to the senses was inanimate, but was the creature and instrument of an invisible being with a form and organs similar to the human.

These beings having first been believed in, fear of them necessarily followed; since they were thought able to inflict at pleasure on human beings great evils, which the sufferers neither knew how to avert nor to foresee, but were left dependent, for their chances of doing either, upon solicitations addressed to the deities themselves. It is true, therefore, that fear had much to do with religion: but belief in the Gods evidently preceded, and did not arise from, fear: though the fear, when established, was a strong support to the belief, nothing being conceived to be so great an offence to the divinities as any doubt of their existence.

It is unnecessary to prosecute further the natural history of religion, as we have not here to account for its origin in rude minds, but for its persistency in the cultivated. A sufficient explanation of this will, I conceive, be found in the small limits of man's certain knowledge, and the boundlessness of his desire to know. Human existence is girt round with mystery: the narrow region of our experience is a small island in the midst of a boundless sea, which at once awes our feelings and stimulates our imagination by its vastness and its obscurity. To add to the mystery, the domain of our earthly existence is not only an island in infinite space, but also in infinite time. The past and the future are alike shrouded from us: we neither know the origin

[*Publius Papinius Statius. *Thebias*, III, 661.]

of anything which is, nor its final destination. If we feel deeply interested in knowing that there are myriads of worlds at an immeasurable, and to our faculties inconceivable, distance from us in space; if we are eager to discover what little we can about these worlds, and when we cannot know what they are, can never satiate ourselves with speculating on what they may be; is it not a matter of far deeper interest to us to learn, or even to conjecture, from whence came this nearer world which we inhabit; what cause or agency made it what it is, and on what powers depend its future fate? Who would not desire this more ardently than any other conceivable knowledge, so long as there appeared the slightest hope of attaining it? What would not one give for any credible tidings from that mysterious region, any glimpse into it which might enable us to see the smallest light through its darkness, especially any theory of it which we could believe, and which represented it as tenanted by a benignant and not a hostile influence? But since we are able to penetrate into that region with the imagination only, assisted by specious but inconclusive analogies derived from human agency and design, imagination is free to fill up the vacancy with the imagery most congenial to itself; sublime and elevating if it be a lofty imagination, low and mean if it be a grovelling one.

Religion and poetry address themselves, at least in one of their aspects, to the same part of the human constitution: they both supply the same want, that of ideal conceptions grander and more beautiful than we see realized in the prose of human life. Religion, as distinguished from poetry, is the product of the craving to know whether these imaginative conceptions have realities answering to them in some other world than ours. The mind, in this state, eagerly catches at any rumours respecting other worlds, especially when delivered by persons whom it deems wiser than itself. To the poetry of the supernatural, comes to be thus added a positive belief and expectation, which unpoetical minds can share with the poetical. Belief in a God or Gods, and in a life after death, becomes the canvas which every mind, according to its capacity, covers with such ideal pictures as it can either invent or copy. In that other life each hopes to find the good which he has failed to find on earth, or the better which is suggested to him by the good which on earth he has partially seen and known. More especially, this belief supplies the finer minds with material for conceptions of beings more awful than they *can* have known on earth, and more excellent than they probably *have* known. So long as human life is insufficient to satisfy human aspirations, so long there will be a craving for higher things, which finds its most obvious satisfaction in religion. So long as earthly life is full of sufferings, so long there will be need of consolations, which the hope of heaven affords to the selfish, the love of God to the tender and grateful.

The value, therefore, of religion to the individual, both in the past and present, as a source of personal satisfaction and of elevated feelings, is not to be disputed. But it has still to be considered, whether in order to obtain this good, it is necessary to travel beyond the boundaries of the world which we inhabit; or whether the idealization of our earthly life, the cultivation of a high conception of what *it* may be made, is not capable of supplying a poetry, and, in the best sense of the word, a religion, equally fitted to exalt the feelings, and (with the same aid from education) still better calculated to ennoble the conduct, than any belief respecting the unseen powers.

At the bare suggestion of such a possibility, many will exclaim, that the short duration, the smallness and insignificance of life, if there is no prolongation of it beyond what we see, makes it impossible that great and elevated feelings can connect themselves with anything laid out on so small a scale: that such a conception of life can match with nothing higher than Epicurean feelings, and the Epicurean doctrine "Let us eat and drink, for to-morrow we die."[*]

Unquestionably, within certain limits, the maxim of the Epicureans is sound, and applicable to much higher things than eating and drinking. To make the most of the present for all good purposes, those of enjoyment among the rest; to keep under control those mental dispositions which lead to undue sacrifice of present good for a future which may never arrive; to cultivate the habit of deriving pleasure from things within our reach, rather than from the too eager pursuit of objects at a distance; to think all time wasted which is not spent either in personal pleasure or in doing things useful to oneself or others; these are wise maxims, and the "carpe diem" doctrine, carried thus far, is a rational and legitimate corollary from the shortness of life. But that because life is short we should care for nothing beyond it, is not a legitimate conclusion; and the supposition, that human beings in general are not capable of feeling deep and even the deepest interest in things which they will never live to see, is a view of human nature as false as it is abject. Let it be remembered that if individual life is short, the life of the human species is not short; its indefinite duration is practically equivalent to endlessness; and being combined with indefinite capability of improvement, it offers to the imagination and sympathies a large enough object to satisfy any reasonable demand for grandeur of aspiration. If such an object appears small to a mind accustomed to dream of infinite and eternal beatitudes, it will expand into far other dimensions when those baseless fancies shall have receded into the past.

Nor let it be thought that only the more eminent of our species, in mind and heart, are capable of identifying their feelings with the entire life of the human race. This noble capability implies indeed a certain cultivation, but not superior to that which might be, and certainly will be if human improve-

[*See I Corinthians, 15:32.]

ment continues, the lot of all. Objects far smaller than this, and equally confined within the limits of the earth (though not within those of a single human life), have been found sufficient to inspire large masses and long successions of mankind with an enthusiasm capable of ruling the conduct, and colouring the whole life. Rome was to the entire Roman people, for many generations as much a religion as Jehovah was to the Jews; nay, much more, for they never fell off from their worship as the Jews did from theirs. And the Romans, otherwise a selfish people, with no very remarkable faculties of any kind except the purely practical, derived nevertheless from this one idea a certain greatness of soul, which manifests itself in all their history where that idea is concerned and nowhere else, and has earned for them the large share of admiration, in other respects not at all deserved, which has been felt for them by most noble-minded persons from that time to this.

When we consider how ardent a sentiment, in favourable circumstances of education, the love of country has become, we cannot judge it impossible that the love of that larger country, the world, may be nursed into similar strength, both as a source of elevated emotion and as a principle of duty. He who needs any other lesson on this subject than the whole course of ancient history affords, let him read Cicero *de Officiis*. It cannot be said that the standard of morals laid down in that celebrated treatise is a high standard. To our notions it is on many points unduly lax, and admits capitulations of conscience. But on the subject of duty to our country there is no compromise. That any man, with the smallest pretensions to virtue, could hesitate to sacrifice life, reputation, family, everything valuable to him, to the love of country is a supposition which this eminent interpreter of Greek and Roman morality cannot entertain for a moment. If, then, persons could be trained, as we see they were, not only to believe in theory that the good of their country was an object to which all others ought to yield, but to feel this practically as the grand duty of life, so also may they be made to feel the same absolute obligation towards the universal good. A morality grounded on large and wise views of the good of the whole, neither sacrificing the individual to the aggregate nor the aggregate to the individual, but giving to duty on the one hand and to freedom and spontaneity on the other their proper province, would derive its power in the superior natures from sympathy and benevolence and the passion for ideal excellence: in the inferior, from the same feelings cultivated up to the measure of their capacity, with the superadded force of shame. This exalted morality would not depend for its ascendancy on any hope of reward; but the reward which might be looked for, and the thought of which would be a consolation in suffering, and a support in moments of weakness, would not be a problematical future existence, but the approbation, in this, of those whom we respect, and ideally of all those, dead or living, whom we admire or venerate. For, the thought that our dead parents or friends would have approved our conduct is a scarcely less powerful motive than the knowledge that our living ones do approve it: and the idea that Socrates, or Howard or Washington, or Antoninus, or Christ, would have sympathized with us, or that we are attempting to do our part in the spirit in which they did theirs, has operated on the very best minds, as a strong incentive to act up to their highest feelings and convictions.

To call these sentiments by the name morality, exclusively of any other title, is claiming too little for them. They are a real religion; of which, as of other religions, outward good works (the utmost meaning usually suggested by the word morality) are only a part, and are indeed rather the fruits of the religion than the religion itself. The essence of religion is the strong and earnest direction of the emotions and desires towards an ideal object, recognized as of the highest excellence, and as rightfully paramount over all selfish objects of desire. This condition is fulfilled by the Religion of Humanity in as eminent a degree, and in as high a sense, as by the supernatural religions even in their best manifestations, and far more so than in any of their others.

Much more might be added on this topic; but enough has been said to convince any one, who can distinguish between the intrinsic capacities of human nature and the forms in which those capacities happen to have been historically developed, that the sense of unity with mankind, and a deep feeling for the general good, may be cultivated into a sentiment and a principle capable of fulfilling every important function of religion and itself justly entitled to the name. I will now further maintain, that it is not only capable of fulfilling these functions, but would fulfil them better than any form whatever of supernaturalism. It is not only entitled to be called a religion: it is a better religion than any of those which are ordinarily called by that title.

For, in the first place, it is disinterested. It carries the thoughts and feelings out of self, and fixes them on an unselfish object, loved and pursued as an end for its own sake. The religions which deal in promises and threats regarding a future life, do exactly the contrary: they fasten down the thoughts to the person's own posthumous interests; they tempt him to regard the performance of his duties to others mainly as a means to his own personal salvation; and are one of the most serious obstacles to the great purpose of moral culture, the strengthening of the unselfish and weakening of the selfish element in our nature; since they hold out to the imagination selfish good and evil of such tremendous magnitude, that it is difficult for any one who fully believes in their reality, to have feeling or interest to spare for any other distant and ideal object. It is true, many of the most unselfish of mankind have been believers in supernaturalism, because their minds have not dwelt on the threats and promises of their religion, but chiefly on the idea of a Being to whom they looked up with a confiding love, and in whose hands they willingly left all that related especially to themselves. But in its effect on common minds, what now goes by the name of religion operates mainly through the feelings of self-interest. Even the Christ of the Gospels holds out the direct promise of reward from heaven as a primary inducement to the noble and beautiful beneficence towards our fellow-creatures which he so impressively inculcates. This is a radical inferiority of the best supernatural religions, compared with the Religion of Humanity; since the greatest thing which moral influences can do for the amelioration of human nature, is to cultivate the unselfish feelings in the only mode in which any active principle in human nature can be effectually cultivated, namely by habitual exercise: but the habit of expecting to be rewarded in another life for our conduct in this, makes even virtue itself no longer an exercise of the unselfish feelings.

Secondly, it is an immense abatement from the worth of the old religions as means of elevating and improving human character, that it is nearly, if not quite impossible for them to produce their best moral effects, unless we suppose a certain torpidity, if not positive twist in the intellectual faculties. For it is impossible that any one who habitually thinks, and who is unable to blunt his inquiring intellect by sophistry, should be able without misgiving to go on ascribing absolute perfection to the author and ruler of so clumsily made and capriciously governed a creation as this planet and the life of its inhabitants. The adoration of such a being cannot be with the whole heart, unless the heart is first considerably sophisticated. The worship must either be greatly overclouded by doubt, and occasionally quite darkened by it, or the moral sentiments must sink to the low level of the ordinances of Nature: the worshipper must learn to think blind partiality, atrocious cruelty, and reckless injustice, not blemishes in an object of worship, since all these abound to excess in the commonest phenomena of Nature. It is true, the God who is worshipped is not, generally speaking, the God of Nature only, but also the God of some revelation; and the character of the revelation will greatly modify and, it may be, improve the moral influences of the religion. This is emphatically true of Christianity; since the Author of the Sermon on the Mount is assuredly a far more benignant Being than the Author of Nature. But unfortunately, the believer in the christian revelation is obliged to believe that the same being is the author of both. This, unless he resolutely averts his mind from the subject, or practises the act of quieting his conscience by sophistry, involves him in moral perplexities without end; since the ways of his Deity in Nature are on many occasions totally at variance with the precepts, as he believes, of the same Deity in the Gospel. He who comes out with least moral damage from this embarrassment, is probably the one who never attempts to reconcile the two standards with one another, but confesses to himself that the purposes of Providence are mysterious, that its ways are not our ways,[*] that its justice and goodness are not the justice

[*See Isaiah, 55:8.]

and goodness which we can conceive and which it befits us to practise. When, however, this is the feeling of the believer, the worship of the Deity ceases to be the adoration of abstract moral perfection. It becomes the bowing down to a gigantic image of something not fit for us to imitate. It is the worship of power only.

I say nothing of the moral difficulties and perversions involved in revelation itself; though even in the Christianity of the Gospels, at least in its ordinary interpretation, there are some of so flagrant a character as almost to outweigh all the beauty and benignity and moral greatness which so eminently distinguish the sayings and character of Christ. The recognition, for example, of the object of highest worship, in a being who could make a Hell; and who could create countless generations of human beings with the certain foreknowledge that he was creating them for this fate. Is there any moral enormity which might not be justified by imitation of such a Deity? And is it possible to adore such a one without a frightful distortion of the standard of right and wrong? Any other of the outrages to the most ordinary justice and humanity involved in the common christian conception of the moral character of God, sinks into insignificance beside this dreadful idealization of wickedness. Most of them too, are happily not so unequivocally deducible from the very words of Christ as to be indisputably a part of christian doctrine. It may be doubted, for instance, whether Christianity is really responsible for atonement and redemption, original sin and vicarious punishment: and the same may be said respecting the doctrine which makes belief in the divine mission of Christ a necessary condition of salvation. It is nowhere represented that Christ himself made this statement, except in the huddled-up account of the Resurrection contained in the concluding verses of St. Mark, which some critics (I believe the best), consider to be an interpolation. Again, the proposition that "the powers that be are ordained of God"[*] and the whole series of corollaries deduced from it in the Epistles, belong to St. Paul, and must stand or fall with Paulism, not with Christianity. But there is one moral contradiction inseparable from every form of Christianity, which no ingenuity can resolve, and no sophistry explain away. It is, that so precious a gift, bestowed on a few, should have been withheld from the many: that countless millions of human beings should have been allowed to live and die, to sin and suffer, without the one thing needful, the divine remedy for sin and suffering, which it would have cost the Divine Giver as little to have vouchsafed to all, as to have bestowed by special grace upon a favoured minority. Add to this, that the divine message, assuming it to be such, has been authenticated by credentials so insufficient, that they fail to convince a large proportion of the strongest and most cultivated minds, and the tendency to disbelieve them appears to grow with the growth of scientific

[*Romans, 13:1.]

knowledge and critical discrimination. He who can believe these to be the intentional shortcomings of a perfectly good Being, must impose silence on every prompting of the sense of goodness and justice as received among men.

It is, no doubt, possible (and there are many instances of it) to worship with the intensest devotion either Deity, that of Nature or of the Gospel, without any perversion of the moral sentiments: but this must be by fixing the attention exclusively on what is beautiful and beneficent in the precepts and spirit of the Gospel and in the dispensations of Nature, and putting all that is the reverse as entirely aside as if it did not exist. Accordingly, this simple and innocent faith can only, as I have said, co-exist with a torpid and inactive state of the speculative faculties. For a person of exercised intellect, there is no way of attaining anything equivalent to it, save by sophistication and perversion, either of the understanding or of the conscience. It may almost always be said both of sects and of individuals, who derive their morality from religion, that the better logicians they are, the worse moralists.

One only form of belief in the supernatural—one only theory respecting the origin and government of the universe—stands wholly clear both of intellectual contradiction and of moral obliquity. It is that which, resigning irrevocably the idea of an omnipotent creator, regards Nature and Life not as the expression throughout of the moral character and purpose of the Deity, but as the product of a struggle between contriving goodness and an intractable material, as was believed by Plato,[*] or a Principle of Evil, as was the doctrine of the Manicheans. A creed like this, which I have known to be devoutly held by at least one cultivated and conscientious person of our own day, allows it to be believed that all the mass of evil which exists was undesigned by, and exists not by the appointment of, but in spite of the Being whom we are called upon to worship. A virtuous human being assumes in this theory the exalted character of a fellow-labourer with the Highest, a fellow-combatant in the great strife; contributing his little, which by the aggregation of many like himself becomes much, towards that progressive ascendancy, and ultimately complete triumph of good over evil, which history points to, and which this doctrine teaches us to regard as planned by the Being to whom we owe all the benevolent contrivance we behold in Nature. Against the moral tendency of this creed no possible objection can lie: it can produce on whoever can succeed in believing it, no other than an ennobling effect. The evidence for it, indeed, if evidence it can be called, is too shadowy and unsubstantial, and the promises it holds out too distant and uncertain, to admit of its being a permanent substitute for the religion of humanity; but the two may be held in conjunction: and he to whom ideal good, and the progress of the world towards it, are already a religion, even though that other creed may seem to him a belief not grounded on evidence,

[*Statesman, 273c.]

is at liberty to indulge the pleasing and encouraging thought, that its truth is possible. Apart from all dogmatic belief, there is for those who need it, an ample domain in the region of the imagination which may be planted with possibilities, with hypotheses which cannot be known to be false; and when there is anything in the appearances of nature to favour them, as in this case there is (for whatever force we attach to the analogies of Nature with the effects of human contrivance, there is no disputing the remark of Paley, that what is good in nature exhibits those analogies much oftener than what is evil),[*] the contemplation of these possibilities is a legitimate indulgence, capable of bearing its part, with other influences, in feeding and animating the tendency of the feelings and impulses towards good.

One advantage, such as it is, the supernatural religions must always possess over the Religion of Humanity; the prospect they hold out to the individual of a life after death. For, though the scepticism of the understanding does not necessarily exclude the Theism of the imagination and feelings, and this, again, gives opportunity for a hope that the power which has done so much for us may be able and willing to do this also, such vague possibility must ever stop far short of a conviction. It remains then to estimate the value of this element—the prospect of a world to come—as a constituent of earthly happiness. I cannot but think that as the condition of mankind becomes improved, as they grow happier in their lives, and more capable of deriving happiness from unselfish sources, they will care less and less for this flattering expectation. It is not, naturally or generally, the happy who are the most anxious either for a prolongation of the present life, or for a life hereafter: it is those who never have been happy. They who have had their happiness can bear to part with existence: but it is hard to die without ever having lived. When mankind cease to need a future existence as a consolation for the sufferings of the present, it will have lost its chief value to them, for themselves. I am now speaking of the unselfish. Those who are so wrapped up in self that they are unable to identify their feelings with anything which will survive them, or to feel their life prolonged in their younger contemporaries and in all who help to carry on the progressive movement of human affairs, require the notion of another selfish life beyond the grave, to enable them to keep up any interest in existence, since the present life, as its termination approaches, dwindles into something too insignificant to be worth caring about. But if the Religion of Humanity were as sedulously cultivated as the supernatural religions are (and there is no difficulty in conceiving that it might be much more so), all who had received the customary amount of moral cultivation would up to the hour of death live ideally in the life of those who are to follow them: and though doubtless they would often willingly

[*See William Paley. *Natural Theology*. London: Faulder, 1802, pp. 488 ff.]

survive as individuals for a much longer period than the present duration of life, it appears to me probable that after a length of time different in different persons, they would have had enough of existence, and would gladly lie down and take their eternal rest. Meanwhile and without looking so far forward, we may remark, that those who believe the immortality of the soul, generally quit life with fully as much, if not more, reluctance, as those who have no such expectation. The mere cessation of existence is no evil to any one: the idea is only formidable through the illusion of imagination which makes one conceive oneself as if one were alive and feeling oneself dead. What is odious in death is not death itself, but the act of dying, and its lugubrious accompaniments: all of which must be equally undergone by the believer in immortality. Nor can I perceive that the sceptic loses by his scepticism any real and valuable consolation except one; the hope of reunion with those dear to him who have ended their earthly life before him. That loss, indeed, is neither to be denied nor extenuated. In many cases it is beyond the reach of comparison or estimate; and will always suffice to keep alive, in the more sensitive natures, the imaginative hope of a futurity which, if there is nothing to prove, there is as little in our knowledge and experience to contradict.

History, so far as we know it, bears out the opinion, that mankind can perfectly well do without the belief in a heaven. The Greeks had anything but a tempting idea of a future state. Their Elysian fields held out very little attraction to their feelings and imagination. Achilles in the *Odyssey* expressed a very natural, and no doubt a very common sentiment, when he said that he would rather be on earth the serf of a needy master, than reign over the whole kingdom of the dead.[*] And the pensive character so striking in the address of the dying emperor Hadrian to his soul, gives evidence that the popular conception had not undergone much variation during that long interval. Yet we neither find that the Greeks enjoyed life less, nor feared death more, than other people. The Buddhist religion counts probably at this day a greater number of votaries than either the Christian or the Mahomedan. The Buddhist creed recognises many modes of punishment in a future life, or rather lives, by the transmigration of the soul into new bodies of men or animals. But the blessing from Heaven which it proposes as a reward, to be earned by perseverance in the highest order of virtuous life, is annihilation; the cessation, at least, of all conscious or separate existence. It is impossible to mistake in this religion, the work of legislators and moralists endeavouring to supply supernatural motives for the conduct which they were anxious to encourage; and they could find nothing more transcendant to hold out as the capital prize to be won by the mightiest efforts of labour and self-denial,

[*XI, 489 ff.]

than what we are so often told is the terrible idea of annihilation. Surely this is a proof that the idea is not really or naturally terrible; that not philosophers only, but the common order of mankind, can easily reconcile themselves to it, and even consider it as a good; and that it is no unnatural part of the idea of a happy life, that life itself be laid down, after the best that it can give has been fully enjoyed through a long lapse of time; when all its pleasures, even those of benevolence, are familiar, and nothing untasted and unknown is left to stimulate curiosity and keep up the desire of prolonged existence. It seems to me not only possible but probable, that in a higher, and, above all, a happier condition of human life, not annihilation but immortality may be the burdensome idea; and that human nature, though pleased with the present, and by no means impatient to quit it, would find comfort and not sadness in the thought that it is not chained through eternity to a conscious existence which it cannot be assured that it will always wish to preserve.

Theism

PART I

INTRODUCTION

THE CONTEST which subsists from of old between believers and unbelievers in natural and revealed religion, has, like other permanent contests, varied materially in its character from age to age; and the present generation, at least in the higher regions of controversy, shows, as compared with the 18th and the beginning of the 19th century, a marked alteration in the aspect of the dispute. One feature of this change is so apparent as to be generally acknowledged; the more softened temper in which the debate is conducted on the part of unbelievers. The reactionary violence, provoked by the intolerance of the other side, has in a great measure exhausted itself. Experience has abated the ardent hopes once entertained of the regeneration of the human race by merely negative doctrine—by the destruction of superstition. The philosophical study of history, one of the most important creations of recent times, has rendered possible an impartial estimate of the doctrines and institutions of the past, from a relative instead of an absolute point of view—as incidents of human development at which it is useless to grumble, and which may deserve admiration and gratitude for their effects in the past, even though they may be thought incapable of rendering similar services to the future. And the position assigned to Christianity or Theism by the more instructed of those who reject the supernatural, is that of things once of great value but which can now be done without; rather than, as formerly, of things misleading and noxious *ab initio*.

Along with this change in the moral attitude of thoughtful unbelievers towards the religious ideas of mankind, a corresponding difference has manifested itself in their intellectual attitude. The war against religious beliefs, in the last century was carried on principally on the ground of common sense or of logic; in the present age, on the ground of science. The progress of the physical sciences is considered to have established, by conclusive evidence,

matters of fact with which the religious traditions of mankind are not reconcileable; while the science of human nature and history, is considered to
show that the creeds of the past are natural growths of the human mind, in
particular stages of its career, destined to disappear and give place to other
convictions in a more advanced stage. In the progress of discussion this last
class of considerations seems even to be superseding those which address
themselves directly to the question of truth. Religions tend to be discussed,
at least by those who reject them, less as intrinsically true or false than as
products thrown up by certain states of civilization, and which, like the
animal and vegetable productions of a geological period perish in those which
succeed it from the cessation of the conditions necessary to their continued
existence.

This tendency of recent speculation to look upon human opinions pre-
eminently from an historical point of view, as facts obeying laws of their
own, and requiring, like other observed facts, an historical or a scientific
explanation (a tendency not confined to religious subjects), is by no means
to be blamed, but to be applauded; not solely as drawing attention to an
important and previously neglected aspect of human opinions, but because
it has a real though indirect bearing upon the question of their truth. For,
whatever opinion a person may adopt on any subject that admits of controversy, his assurance if he be a cautious thinker cannot be complete unless he
is able to account for the existence of the opposite opinion. To ascribe it to
the weakness of the human understanding is an explanation which cannot be
sufficient for such a thinker, for he will be slow to assume that he has himself
a less share of that infirmity than the rest of mankind and that error is more
likely to be on the other side than on his own. In his examination of evidence,
the persuasion of others, perhaps of mankind in general, is one of the data
of the case—one of the phenomena to be accounted for. As the human intellect though weak is not essentially perverted, there is a certain presumption
of the truth of any opinion held by many human minds, requiring to be
rebutted by assigning some other real or possible cause for its prevalence.
And this consideration has a special relevancy to the inquiry concerning the
foundations of theism, inasmuch as no argument for the truth of theism is
more commonly invoked or more confidently relied on, than the general
assent of mankind.

But while giving its full value to this historical treatment of the religious
question, we ought not therefore to let it supersede the dogmatic. The most
important quality of an opinion on any momentous subject is its truth or
falsity, which to us resolves itself into the sufficiency of the evidence on
which it rests. It is indispensable that the subject of religion should from
time to time be reviewed as a strictly scientific question, and that its evidences
should be tested by the same scientific methods, and on the same principles

as those of any of the speculative conclusions drawn by physical science. It being granted then that the legitimate conclusions of science are entitled to prevail over all opinions, however widely held, which conflict with them, and that the canons of scientific evidence which the successes and failures of two thousand years have established, are applicable to all subjects on which knowledge is attainable, let us proceed to consider what place there is for religious beliefs on the platform of science; what evidences they can appeal to, such as science can recognize, and what foundation there is for the doctrines of religion, considered as scientific theorems.

In this inquiry we of course begin with Natural Religion, the doctrine of the existence and attributes of God.

THEISM

Though I have defined the problem of Natural Theology, to be that of the existence of God or of a God, rather than of Gods, there is the amplest historical evidence that the belief in Gods is immeasurably more natural to the human mind than the belief in one author and ruler of nature; and that this more elevated belief is, compared with the former, an artificial product, requiring (except when impressed by early education) a considerable amount of intellectual culture before it can be reached. For a long time, the supposition appeared forced and unnatural that the diversity we see in the operations of nature can all be the work of a single will. To the untaught mind, and to all minds in pre-scientific times, the phenomena of nature seem to be the result of forces altogether heterogeneous, each taking its course quite independently of the others; and though to attribute them to conscious wills is eminently natural, the natural tendency is to suppose as many such independent wills as there are distinguishable forces of sufficient importance and interest to have been remarked and named. There is no tendency in polytheism as such to transform itself spontaneously into monotheism. It is true that in polytheistic systems generally the deity whose special attributes inspire the greatest degree of awe, is usually supposed to have a power of controlling the other deities; and even in the most degraded perhaps of all such systems, the Hindoo, adulation heaps upon the divinity who is the immediate object of adoration, epithets like those habitual to believers in a single God. But there is no real acknowledgment of one Governor. Every God normally rules his particular department though there may be a still stronger God whose power when he chooses to exert it can frustrate the purposes of the inferior divinity. There could be no real belief in one Creator and Governor until mankind had begun to see in the apparently confused phenomena which surrounded them, a system capable of being viewed as the possible working out of a single plan. This conception of the world was per-haps anticipated (though less frequently than is often supposed) by indi-viduals of exceptional genius, but it could only become common after a rather long cultivation of scientific thought.

The special mode in which scientific study operates to instil Monotheism in place of the more natural Polytheism, is in no way mysterious. The specific effect of science is to show by accumulating evidence, that every event in nature is connected by laws with some fact or facts which preceded it, or in other words, depends for its existence on some antecedent; but yet not so strictly on one, as not to be liable to frustration or modification from others: for these distinct chains of causation are so entangled with one another; the action of each cause is so interfered with by other causes, though each acts according to its own fixed law; that every effect is truly the result rather of the aggregate of all causes in existence than of any one only; and nothing takes place in the world of our experience without spreading a per-ceptible influence of some sort through a greater or less portion of Nature, and making perhaps every portion of it slightly different from what it would have been if that event had not taken place. Now, when once the double conviction has found entry into the mind—that every event depends on antecedents; and at the same time that to bring it about many antecedents must concur, perhaps all the antecedents in Nature, insomuch that a slight difference in any one of them might have prevented the phenomenon, or materially altered its character—the conviction follows that no one event, certainly no one kind of events, can be absolutely preordained or governed by any Being but one who holds in his hand the reins of all Nature and not of some department only. At least if a plurality be supposed, it is necessary to assume so complete a concert of action and unity of will among them that the difference is for most purposes immaterial between such a theory and that of the absolute unity of the Godhead.

The reason, then, why Monotheism may be accepted as the representative of Theism in the abstract, is not so much because it is the Theism of all the more improved portions of the human race, as because it is the only Theism which can claim for itself any footing on scientific ground. Every other theory of the government of the universe by supernatural beings, is incon-sistent either with the carrying on of that government through a continual series of natural antecedents according to fixed laws, or with the interdepen-dence of each of these series upon all the rest, which are the two most general results of science.

Setting out therefore from the scientific view of nature as one connected system, or united whole, united not like a web composed of separate threads in passive juxtaposition with one another, but rather like the human or animal frame, an apparatus kept going by perpetual action and reaction among all its parts; it must be acknowledged that the question, to which Theism is an answer, is at least a very natural one, and issues from an obvious want of the human mind. Accustomed as we are to find, in proportion to our means of observation, a definite beginning to each individual fact; and since wherever there is a beginning we find that there was an antecedent fact (called by us a cause), a fact but for which, the phenomenon which thus commences would not have been; it was impossible that the human mind should not ask itself whether the whole, of which these particular phenomena are a part, had not also a beginning, and if so, whether that beginning was not an origin; whether there was not something antecedent to the whole series of causes and effects that we term Nature, and but for which Nature itself would not have been. From the first recorded speculation this question has never remained without an hypothetical answer. The only answer which has long continued to afford satisfaction is Theism.

Looking at the problem, as it is our business to do, merely as a scientific inquiry, it resolves itself into two questions. First: Is the theory, which refers the origin of all the phenomena of nature to the will of a Creator, consistent or not with the ascertained results of science? Secondly, assuming it to be consistent, will its proofs bear to be tested by the principles of evidence and canons of belief by which our long experience of scientific inquiry has proved the necessity of being guided?

First, then: there is one conception of Theism which is consistent, another which is radically inconsistent, with the most general truths that have been made known to us by scientific investigation.

The one which is inconsistent is the conception of a God governing the world by acts of variable will. The one which is consistent, is the conception of a God governing the world by invariable laws.

The primitive, and even in our own day the vulgar, conception of the divine rule, is that the one God, like the many Gods of antiquity, carries on the government of the world by special decrees, made *pro hac vice*. Although supposed to be omniscient as well as omnipotent, he is thought not to make up his mind until the moment of action; or at least not so conclusively, but that his intentions may be altered up to the very last moment by appropriate solicitation. Without entering into the difficulties of reconciling this view of the divine government with the prescience and the perfect wisdom ascribed to the Deity, we may content ourselves with the fact that it contradicts what experience has taught us of the manner in which things actually take place. The phenomena of Nature do take place according to general laws. They do originate from definite natural antecedents. Therefore if their ultimate origin is derived from a will, that will must have established the general laws and willed the antecedents. If there be a Creator, his intention must have been that events should depend upon antecedents and be produced according to fixed laws. But this being conceded, there is nothing in scientific experience inconsistent with the belief that those laws and sequences are themselves due to a divine will. Neither are we obliged to suppose that the divine will exerted itself once for all, and after putting a power into the system which enabled it to go on of itself, has ever since let it alone. Science contains nothing repugnant to the supposition that every event which takes place results from a specific volition of the presiding Power, provided that this Power adheres in its particular volitions to general laws laid down by itself. The common opinion is that this hypothesis tends more to the glory of the Deity than the supposition that the universe was made so that it could go on of itself. There have been thinkers however—of no ordinary eminence (of whom Leibnitz was one)—who thought the last the only supposition worthy of the Deity, and protested against likening God to a clockmaker whose clock will not go unless he puts his hand to the machinery and keeps it going. With such considerations we have no concern in this place. We are looking at the subject not from the point of view of reverence but from that of science; and with science both these suppositions as to the mode of the divine action are equally consistent.

We must now, however, pass to the next question. There is nothing to disprove the creation and government of Nature by a sovereign will; but is there anything to prove it? Of what nature are its evidences; and weighed in the scientific balance, what is their value?

THE EVIDENCES OF THEISM

The evidences of a Creator are not only of several distinct kinds but of such diverse characters, that they are adapted to minds of very different descriptions, and it is hardly possible for any mind to be equally impressed by them all. The familiar classification of them into proofs *à priori* and *à posteriori*, marks that when looked at in a purely scientific view they belong to different schools of thought. Accordingly though the unthoughtful believer whose creed really rests on authority gives an equal welcome to all plausible arguments in support of the belief in which he has been brought up, philosophers who have had to make a choice between the *à priori* and the *à posteriori* methods in general science seldom fail, while insisting on one of these modes of support for religion, to speak with more or less of disparagement of the other. It is our duty in the present inquiry to maintain complete impartiality and to give a fair examination to both. At the same time I entertain a strong conviction that one of the two modes of argument is in its nature scientific, the other not only unscientific but condemned by science. The scientific argument is that which reasons from the facts and analogies of human experience as a geologist does when he infers the past states of our terrestrial globe, or an astronomical observer when he draws conclusions respecting the physical composition of the heavenly bodies. This is the *à posteriori* method, the principal application of which to Theism is the argument (as it is called) of design. The mode of reasoning which I call unscientific, though in the opinion of some thinkers it is also a legitimate mode of scientific procedure, is that which infers external objective facts from ideas or convictions of our minds. I say this independently of any opinion of my own respecting the origin of our ideas or convictions; for even if we were unable to point out any manner in which the idea of God, for example, can have grown up from the impressions of experience, still the idea can only prove the idea, and not the objective fact, unless indeed the fact is supposed (agreeably to the book of Genesis) to have been handed down by tradition from a time when there was direct personal intercourse with the Divine Being; in which case the argument is no longer *à priori*. The supposition that an idea, or a wish, or a need, even if native to the mind proves the reality of a corresponding object, derives all its plausibility from the belief already in our minds that we were made by a benignant Being who would not have implanted in us a groundless belief, or a want which he did not afford us the means of satisfying; and is therefore a palpable *petitio principii* if adduced as an argument to support the very belief which it presupposes.

At the same time, it must be admitted that all *à priori* systems whether in philosophy or religion, do, in some sense profess to be founded on experience, since though they affirm the possibility of arriving at truths which transcend experience, they yet make the facts of experience their starting point (as what other starting point is possible?). They are entitled to consideration in so far as it can be shown that experience gives any countenance either to them or to their method of inquiry. Professedly *à priori* arguments are not unfrequently of a mixed nature, partaking in some degree of the *à posteriori* character, and may often be said to be *à posteriori* arguments in disguise; the *à priori* considerations acting chiefly in the way of making some particular *à posteriori* argument tell for more than its worth. This is emphatically true of the argument for Theism which I shall first examine, the necessity of a First Cause. For this has in truth a wide basis of experience in the universality of the relation of Cause and Effect among the phenomena of nature; while at the same time, theological philosophers have not been content to let it rest upon this basis, but have affirmed Causation as a truth of reason apprehended intuitively by its own light.

ARGUMENT FOR A FIRST CAUSE

The argument for a First Cause admits of being, and is, presented as a conclusion from the whole of human experience. Everything that we know (it is argued) had a cause, and owed its existence to that cause. How then can it be but that the world, which is but a name for the aggregate of all that we know, has a cause to which it is indebted for its existence?

The fact of experience however, when correctly expressed, turns out to be, not that everything which we know derives its existence from a cause, but only every event or change. There is in Nature a permanent element, and also a changeable: the changes are always the effects of previous changes; the permanent existences, so far as we know, are not effects at all. It is true we are accustomed to say not only of events, but of objects, that they are produced by causes, as water by the union of hydrogen and oxygen. But by this we only mean that when they begin to exist, their beginning is the effect of a cause. But their beginning to exist is not an object, it is an event. If it be objected that the cause of a thing's beginning to exist may be said with propriety to be the cause of the thing itself, I shall not quarrel with the expression. But that which in an object begins to exist, is that in it which belongs to the changeable element in nature; the outward form and the properties depending on mechanical or chemical combinations of its component parts. There is in every object another and a permanent element, viz., the specific elementary substance or substances of which it consists and their inherent properties. These are not known to us as beginning to exist: within the range of human knowledge they had no beginning, consequently no cause; though they themselves are causes or con-causes of everything that takes place. Experience therefore, affords no evidences, not even analogies, to justify our extending to the apparently immutable, a generalization grounded only on our observation of the changeable.

As a fact of experience, then, causation cannot legitimately be extended to the material universe itself, but only to its changeable phenomena; of these, indeed, causes may be affirmed without any exception. But what causes? The cause of every change is a prior change; and such it cannot but be; for if there were no new antecedent, there would not be a new consequent. If the state of facts which brings the phenomenon into existence, had existed always or for an indefinite duration, the effect also would have existed always or been produced an indefinite time ago. It is thus a necessary part of the fact of causation, within the sphere of our experience, that the causes as well as the effects had a beginning in time, and were themselves caused. It would seem therefore that our experience, instead of furnishing an argument for a first cause, is repugnant to it; and that the very essence of causation as it exists within the limits of our knowledge, is incompatible with a First Cause.

But it is necessary to look more particularly into the matter, and analyse more closely the nature of the causes of which mankind have experience. For if it should turn out that though all causes have a beginning, there is in all of them a permanent element which had no beginning, this permanent element may with some justice be termed a first or universal cause, inasmuch as though not sufficient of itself to cause anything, it enters as a con-cause into all causation. Now it happens that the last result of physical inquiry, derived from the converging evidences of all branches of physical science, does, if it holds good, land us so far as the material world is concerned, in a result of this sort. Whenever a physical phenomenon is traced to its cause, that cause when analysed is found to be a certain quantum of Force, combined with certain collocations. And the last great generalization of science, the Conservation of Force, teaches us that the variety in the effects depends partly upon the *amount* of the force, and partly upon the diversity of the collocations. The force itself is essentially one and the same; and there exists of it in nature a fixed quantity, which (if the theory be true) is never increased or diminished. Here then we find, even in the changes of material nature, a permanent element; to all appearance the very one of which we were in quest. This it is apparently to which if to anything we must assign the character of First Cause, the cause of the material universe. For all effects may be traced up to it, while it cannot be traced up, by our experience, to anything beyond: its transformations alone can be so traced, and of them the cause always includes the force itself: the same quantity of force, in some previous form. It would seem then that in the only sense in which experience supports in any shape the doctrine of a First Cause, viz., as the primæval and universal element in all causes, the First Cause can be no other than Force.

We are, however, by no means at the end of the question. On the contrary, the greatest stress of the argument is exactly at the point which we have now reached. For it is maintained that Mind is the only possible cause of Force; or rather perhaps, that Mind is a Force, and that all other force must be derived from it inasmuch as mind is the only thing which is capable of originating change. This is said to be the lesson of human experience. In the phenomena of inanimate nature the force which works is always a pre-existing force, not originated, but transferred. One physical object moves another by giving out to it the force by which it has first been itself moved. The wind communicates to the waves, or to a windmill, or a ship, part of the motion which has been given to itself by some other agent. In voluntary action alone we see a commencement, an origination of motion; since all other causes appear incapable of this origination experience is in favour of the conclusion that all the motion in existence owed its beginning to this one cause, voluntary agency, if not that of man, then of a more powerful Being.

This argument is a very old one. It is to be found in Plato; not as might have been expected, in the *Phædon*, where the arguments are not such as would now be deemed of any weight, but in his latest production, the *Leges*.[*] And it is still one of the most telling arguments with the more metaphysical class of defenders of Natural Theology.

[*_Laws_, 10. 891e ff.]

Now, in the first place, if there be truth in the doctrine of the Conservation of Force, in other words the constancy of the total amount of Force in existence, this doctrine does not change from true to false when it reaches the field of voluntary agency. The will does not, any more than other causes, create Force: granting that it originates motion, it has no means of doing so but by converting into that particular manifestation a portion of Force which already existed in other forms. It is known that the source from which this portion of Force is derived, is chiefly, or entirely, the Force evolved in the processes of chemical composition and decomposition which constitute the body of nutrition: the force so liberated becomes a fund upon which every muscular and even every merely nervous action, as of the brain in thought, is a draft. It is in this sense only that, according to the best lights of science, volition is an originating cause. Volition, therefore, does not answer to the idea of a First Cause; since Force must in every instance be assumed as prior to it; and there is not the slightest colour, derived from experience, for supposing Force itself to have been created by a volition. As far as anything can be concluded from human experience Force has all the attributes of a thing eternal and uncreated.

This, however, does not close the discussion. For though whatever verdict experience can give in the case is against the possibility that will ever originates Force, yet if we can be assured that neither does Force originate Will, Will must be held to be an agency, if not prior to Force yet coeternal with it: and if it be true that Will can originate, not indeed Force but the transformation of Force from some other of its manifestations into that of mechanical motion, and that there is within human experience no other agency capable of doing so, the argument for a Will as the originator, though not of the universe, yet of the kosmos, or order of the universe, remains unanswered.

But the case thus stated is not conformable to fact. Whatever volition can do in the way of creating motion out of other forms of force, and generally of evolving force from a latent into a visible state, can be done by many other causes. Chemical action, for instance; electricity; heat; the mere presence of a gravitating body; all these are causes of mechanical motion on a far larger scale than any volitions which experience presents to us: and in most of the effects thus produced the motion given by one body to another, is not, as in the ordinary cases of mechanical action, motion that has first been given to that other by some third body. The phenomenon is not a mere passing on of mechanical motion, but a creation of it out of a force previously latent or manifesting itself in some other form. Volition, therefore, regarded as an agent in the material universe, has no exclusive privilege of origination: all that it can originate is also originated by other transforming agents. If it be said that those other agents must have had the force they give out put into them from elsewhere, I answer, that this is no less true of the force which volition disposes of. We know that this force comes from an external source, the chemical action of the food and air. The force by which the phenomena of the material world are produced, circulates through all physical agencies in a never ending though sometimes intermitting stream. I am, of course, speaking of volition only in its action on the material world. We have nothing to do here with the freedom of the will itself as a mental phenomenon—with the *vexata questio* whether volition is self-determining or determined by causes. To the question now in hand it is only the effects of volition that are relevant, not its origin. The assertion is that physical nature must have been produced by a Will, because nothing but Will is known to us as having the power of originating the production of phenomena. We have seen that, on the contrary, all the power that Will possesses over phenomena is shared, as far as we have the means of judging, by other and much more powerful agents, and that in the only sense in which those agents do not originate, neither does Will originate. No prerogative, therefore, can, on the ground of experience, be assigned to volition above other natural agents, as a producing cause of phenomena. All that can be affirmed by the strongest assertor of the Freedom of the Will, is that volitions are themselves uncaused and are therefore alone fit to be the first or universal Cause. But, even assuming volitions to be uncaused, the properties of matter, so far as experience discloses, are uncaused also, and have the advantage over any particular volition, in being so far as experience can show, eternal. Theism, therefore, in so far as it rests on the necessity of a First Cause, has no support from experience.

To those who, in default of Experience, consider the necessity of a first cause as matter of intuition, I would say that it is needless, in this discussion, to contest their premises; since admitting that there is and must be a First Cause, it has now been shown that several other agencies than Will can lay equal claim to that character. One thing only may be said which requires notice here. Among the facts of the universe to be accounted for, it may be said, is Mind; and it is self-evident that nothing can have produced Mind but Mind.

The special indications that Mind is deemed to give, pointing to intelligent contrivance, belong to a different portion of this inquiry. But if the mere existence of Mind is supposed to require, as a necessary antecedent, another Mind greater and more powerful, the difficulty is not removed by going one step back: the creating mind stands as much in need of another mind to be the source of its existence, as the created mind. Be it remembered that we have no direct knowledge (at least apart from Revelation) of a Mind which is even apparently eternal, as Force and Matter are: an eternal mind is, as far as the present argument is concerned, a simple hypothesis to account for the minds which we know to exist. Now it is essential to an hypothesis that if admitted it should at least remove the difficulty and account for the facts.

But it does not account for Mind to refer one mind to a prior mind for its origin. The problem remains unsolved, the difficulty undiminished, nay, rather increased.

To this it may be objected that the causation of every human mind is matter of fact, since we know that it had a beginning in time. We even know, or have the strongest grounds for believing that the human species itself had a beginning in time. For there is a vast amount of evidence that the state of our planet was once such as to be incompatible with animal life, and that human life is of very much more modern origin than animal life. In any case, therefore, the fact must be faced that there must have been a cause which called the first human mind, nay the very first germ of organic life, into existence. No such difficulty exists in the supposition of an Eternal Mind. If we did not know that Mind on our earth began to exist, we might suppose it to be uncaused; and we may still suppose this of the mind to which we ascribe its existence.

To take this ground is to return into the field of human experience, and to become subject to its canons, and we are then entitled to ask where is the proof that nothing can have caused a mind except another mind. From what, except from experience, can we know what can produce what—what causes are adequate to what effects? That nothing can *consciously* produce Mind but Mind, is self-evident, being involved in the meaning of the words; but that there cannot be unconscious production must not be assumed, for it is the very point to be proved. Apart from experience, and arguing on what is called reason, that is on supposed self-evidence, the notion seems to be, that no causes can give rise to products of a more precious or elevated kind than themselves. But this is at variance with the known analogies of Nature. How vastly nobler and more precious, for instance, are the higher vegetables and animals than the soil and manure out of which, and by the properties of which they are raised up! The tendency of all recent speculation is towards the opinion that the development of inferior orders of existence into superior, the substitution of greater elaboration and higher organization for lower, is the general rule of Nature. Whether it is so or not, there are at least in Nature a multitude of facts bearing that character, and this is sufficient for the argument.

Here, then, this part of the discussion may stop. The result it leads to is that the First Cause argument is in itself of no value for the establishment of Theism: because no cause is needed for the existence of that which has no beginning; and both Matter and Force (whatever metaphysical theory we may give of the one or the other) have had, so far as our experience can teach us, no beginning—which cannot be said of Mind. The phenomena or changes in the universe have indeed each of them a beginning and a cause, but their cause is always a prior change; nor do the analogies of experience give us any reason to expect, from the mere occurrence of changes, that if we could trace back the series far enough we should arrive at a Primæval Volition. The world does not, by its mere existence, bear witness to a God: if it gives indications of one, these must be given by the special nature of the phenomena, by what they present that resembles adaptation to an end: of which hereafter. If, in default of evidence from experience, the evidence of intuition is relied upon, it may be answered that if Mind, as Mind, presents intuitive evidence of having been created, the Creative Mind must do the same, and we are no nearer to the First Cause than before. But if there be nothing in the nature of mind which in itself implies a Creator, the minds which have a beginning in time, as all minds have which are known to our experience, must indeed have been caused, but it is not necessary that their cause should have been a prior Intelligence.

ARGUMENT FROM THE GENERAL CONSENT OF MANKIND

Before proceeding to the argument from Marks of Design, which, as it seems to me, must always be the main strength of Natural Theism, we may dispose briefly of some other arguments which are of little scientific weight but which have greater influence on the human mind than much better arguments, because they are appeals to authority, and it is by authority that the opinions of the bulk of mankind are principally and not unnaturally governed. The authority invoked is that of mankind generally, and specially of some of its wisest men; particularly such as were in other respects conspicuous examples of breaking loose from received prejudices. Socrates and Plato, Bacon, Locke, and Newton, Descartes and Leibnitz, are common examples.

It may doubtless be good advice to persons who in point of knowledge and cultivation are not entitled to think themselves competent judges of difficult questions, to bid them content themselves with holding that true which mankind generally believe, and so long as they believe it; or that which has been believed by those who pass for the most eminent among the minds of the past. But to a thinker the argument from other people's opinions has little weight. It is but second-hand evidence; and merely admonishes us to look out for and weigh the reasons on which this conviction of mankind or of wise men was founded. Accordingly, those who make any claim to philosophic treatment of the subject, employ this general consent chiefly as evidence that there is in the mind of man an intuitive perception, or an instinctive sense, of Deity. From the generality of the belief, they infer that it is inherent in our constitution; from which they draw the conclusion, a precarious one indeed, but conformable to the general mode of proceeding of the intuitive philosophy, that the belief must be true; though as applied to Theism this argument begs the question, since it has itself nothing to rest upon but the belief that the human mind was made by a God, who would not deceive his creatures.

But, indeed, what ground does the general prevalence of the belief in Deity afford us for inferring that this belief is native to the human mind, and independent of evidence? Is it then so very devoid of evidence, even apparent? Has it so little semblance of foundation in fact, that it can only be accounted for by the supposition of its being innate? We should not expect to find Theists believing that the appearances in Nature of a contriving Intelligence are not only insufficient but are not even plausible, and cannot be supposed to have carried conviction either to the general or to the wiser mind. If there are external evidences of theism, even if not perfectly conclusive, why need we suppose that the belief of its truth was the result of anything else? The superior minds to whom an appeal is made, from Socrates downwards, when they professed to give the grounds of their opinion, did not say that they found the belief in themselves without knowing from whence it came, but ascribed it, if not to revelation, either to some metaphysical argument, or to those very external evidences which are the basis of the argument from Design.

If it be said that the belief in Deity is universal among barbarous tribes, and among the ignorant portion of civilized populations, who cannot be supposed to have been impressed by the marvellous adaptations of Nature most of which are unknown to them; I answer, that the ignorant in civilized countries take their opinions from the educated, and that in the case of savages, if the evidence is insufficient, so is the belief. The religious belief of savages is not belief in the God of Natural Theology, but a mere modification of the crude generalization which ascribes life, consciousness and will to all natural powers of which they cannot perceive the source or control the operation. And the divinities believed in are as numerous as those powers. Each river, fountain or tree has a divinity of its own. To see in this blunder of primitive ignorance the hand of the Supreme Being implanting in his creatures an instinctive knowledge of his existence, is a poor compliment to the Deity. The religion of savages is Fetichism of the grossest kind, ascribing animation and will to individual objects, and seeking to propitiate them by prayer and sacrifice. That this should be the case is the less surprising when we remember that there is not a definite boundary line, broadly separating the conscious human being from inanimate objects. Between these and man there is an intermediate class of objects, sometimes much more powerful than man, which do possess life and will, viz. the brute animals, which in an early stage of existence play a very great part in human life; making it the less surprising that the line should not at first be quite distinguishable between the animate and the inanimate part of Nature. As observation advances, it is perceived that the majority of outward objects have all their important qualities in common with entire classes or groups of objects which comport themselves exactly alike in the same circumstances, and in these cases the worship of visible objects is exchanged for that of an invisible Being supposed to preside over the whole class. This step in generalization is slowly made, with hesitation and even terror; as we still see in the case of ignorant populations with what difficulty experience disabuses them of belief in the supernatural powers and terrible resentment of a particular idol. Chiefly by these terrors the religious impressions of barbarians are kept alive, with only slight modifications, until the Theism of cultivated minds is ready to take their place. And the Theism of cultivated minds, if we take their own word for it, is always a conclusion either from arguments called rational, or from the appearances in Nature.

It is needless here to dwell upon the difficulty of the hypothesis of a natural belief not common to all human beings, an instinct not universal. It is conceivable, doubtless, that some men might be born without a particular natural faculty, as some are born without a particular sense. But when this is the case we ought to be much more particular as to the proof that it really is a natural faculty. If it were not a matter of observation but of speculation that men can see; if they had no apparent organ of sight, and no perceptions or knowledge but such as they might conceivably have acquired by some circuitous process through their other senses, the fact that men exist who do not even suppose themselves to see, would be a considerable argument against the theory of a visual sense. But it would carry us too far to press, for the purposes of this discussion, an argument which applies so largely to the whole of the intuitional philosophy. The strongest Intuitionist will not maintain that a belief should be held for instinctive when evidence (real or apparent), sufficient to engender it, is universally admitted to exist. To the force of the evidence must be, in this case, added all the emotional or moral causes which incline men to the belief; the satisfaction which it gives to the obstinate questionings with which men torment themselves respecting the past; the hopes which it opens for the future; the fears also, since fear as well as hope predisposes to belief; and to these in the case of the more active spirits must always have been added a perception of the power which belief in the supernatural affords for governing mankind, either for their own good, or for the selfish purposes of the governors.

The general consent of mankind does not, therefore, afford ground for admitting, even as an hypothesis, the origin in an inherent law of the human mind, of a fact otherwise so more than sufficiently, so amply, accounted for.

THE ARGUMENT FROM CONSCIOUSNESS

There have been numerous arguments, indeed almost every religious meta-physician has one of his own, to prove the existence and attributes of God from what are called truths of reason, supposed to be independent of experi-ence. Descartes, who is the real founder of the intuitional metaphysics, draws the conclusion immediately from the first premise of his philosophy, the celebrated assumption that whatever he could very clearly and distinctly apprehend, must be true. The idea of a God, perfect in power, wisdom, and goodness, is a clear and distinct idea, and must therefore, on this principle correspond to a real object. This bold generalization, however, that a concep-tion of the human mind proves its own objective reality, Descartes is obliged to limit by the qualification—"if the idea includes existence."[*] Now the idea of God implying the union of all perfections, and existence being a perfection, the idea of God proves his existence. This very simple argument, which denies to man one of his most familiar and most precious attributes, that of idealizing as it is called—of constructing from the materials of experience a conception more perfect than experience itself affords—is not likely to satisfy any one in the present day. More elaborate, though scarcely more successful efforts, have been made by many of Descartes' successors, to derive knowledge of the Deity from an inward light: to make it a truth not depen-dent on external evidence, a fact of direct perception, or, as they are accus-tomed to call it, of consciousness. The philosophical world is familiar with the attempt of Cousin to make out that whenever we perceive a particular object, we perceive along with it, or are conscious of, God; and also with the celebrated refutation of this doctrine by Sir William Hamilton. It would be waste of time to examine any of these theories in detail. While each has its own particular logical fallacies, they labour under the common infirmity, that one man cannot by proclaiming with ever so much confidence that *he* perceives an object, convince other people that they see it too. If, indeed, he laid claim to a divine faculty of vision, vouchsafed to him alone, and making him cognizant of things which men not thus assisted have not the capacity to see, the case might be different. Men have been able to get such claims admitted; and other people can only require of them to show their credentials. But when no claim is set up to any peculiar gift, but we are told that all of us are as capable as the prophet of seeing what he sees, feeling what he feels, nay, that we actually do so, and when the utmost effort of which we are

[*See *Dissertatio de methodo*. In *Principia philosophiæ*. 4th ed. Amsterdam: Elzevir, 1664, Part IV.]

capable fails to make us aware of what we are told we perceive, this supposed universal faculty of intuition is but

> The dark lantern of the Spirit
> Which none see by but those who bear it: [*]

and the bearers may fairly be asked to consider whether it is not more likely that they are mistaken as to the origin of an impression in their minds, than that others are ignorant of the very existence of an impression in theirs.

The inconclusiveness, in a speculative point of view, of all arguments from the subjective notion of Deity to its objective reality, was well seen by Kant, the most discriminating of the *à priori* metaphysicians, who always kept the two questions, the origin and composition of our ideas, and the reality of the corresponding objects, perfectly distinct. According to Kant the idea of the Deity is native to the mind, in the sense that it is constructed by the mind's own laws and not derived from without: but this Idea of Speculative Reason cannot be shown by any logical process or perceived by direct apprehension, to have a corresponding Reality outside the human mind. To Kant, God is neither an object of direct consciousness nor a conclusion of reasoning, but a Necessary Assumption; necessary, not by a logical, but a practical necessity, imposed by the reality of the Moral Law. Duty is a fact of consciousness: "Thou shalt" is a command issuing from the recesses of our being, and not to be accounted for by any impressions derived from experience; and this command requires a commander, though it is not perfectly clear whether Kant's meaning is that conviction of a law includes conviction of a lawgiver, or only that a Being of whose will the law is an expression, is eminently desirable. If the former be intended, the argument is founded on a double meaning of the word Law. A rule to which we feel it a duty to conform has in common with laws commonly so called, the fact of claiming our obedience; but it does not follow that the rule must originate, like the laws of the land, in the will of a legislator or legislators external to the mind. We may even say that a feeling of obligation which is merely the result of a command is not what is meant by moral obligation, which, on the contrary, supposes something that the internal conscience bears witness to as binding in its own nature; and which God, in superadding his command, conforms to and perhaps declares, but does not create. Conceding, then, for the sake of the argument, that the moral sentiment is as purely of the mind's own growth, the obligation of duty as entirely independent of experience and acquired impressions, as Kant or any other metaphysician ever contended, it may yet be maintained that this feeling of obligation rather excludes, than

[*Samuel Butler. *Hudibras*. London: Vernor and Hood, 1801, Vol. I, pp. 53–4; Pt. I, Canto I, ll. 505–6.]

compels, the belief in a Divine legislator merely as the source of the obligation: and as a matter of fact, the obligation of duty is both theoretically acknowledged and practically felt in the fullest manner by many who have no positive belief in God, though seldom, probably, without habitual and familiar reference to him as an ideal conception. But if the existence of God as a wise and just lawgiver, is not a necessary part of the feelings of morality, it may still be maintained that those feelings make his existence eminently desirable. No doubt they do, and that is the great reason why we find that good men and women cling to the belief, and are pained by its being questioned. But surely it is not legitimate to assume that in the order of the Universe, whatever is desirable is true. Optimism, even when a God is already believed in, is a thorny doctrine to maintain, and had to be taken by Leibnitz in the limited sense, that the universe being made by a good being, is the best universe possible, not the best absolutely: that the Divine power, in short, was not equal to making it more free from imperfections than it is. But optimism prior to belief in a God, and as the ground of that belief, seems one of the oddest of all speculative delusions. Nothing, however, I believe, contributes more to keep up the belief in the general mind of humanity than this feeling of its desirableness, which, when clothed, as it very often is, in the forms of an argument, is a *naïf* expression of the tendency of the human mind to believe what is agreeable to it. Positive value the argument of course has none.

Without dwelling further on these or on any other of the *à priori* arguments for Theism, we will no longer delay passing to the far more important argument of the appearances of Contrivance in Nature.

THE ARGUMENT FROM MARKS OF DESIGN IN NATURE

We now at last reach an argument of a really scientific character, which does not shrink from scientific tests, but claims to be judged by the established canons of Induction. The Design argument is wholly grounded on experience. Certain qualities, it is alleged, are found to be characteristic of such things as are made by an intelligent mind for a purpose. The order of Nature, or some considerable parts of it, exhibit these qualities in a remarkable degree. We are entitled, from this great similarity in the effects, to infer similarity in the cause, and to believe that things which it is beyond the power of man to make, but which resemble the works of man in all but power, must also have been made by Intelligence, armed with a power greater than human.

I have stated this argument in its fullest strength, as it is stated by its most thoroughgoing assertors. A very little consideration, however, suffices to show that though it has some force, its force is very generally overrated.

Paley's illustration of a watch puts the case much too strongly.[*] If I found a watch on an apparently desolate island, I should indeed infer that it had been left there by a human being; but the inference would not be from marks of design, but because I already knew by direct experience that watches are made by men. I should draw the inference no less confidently from a foot print, or from any relic however insignificant which experience has taught me to attribute to man: as geologists infer the past existence of animals from coprolites, though no one sees marks of design in a coprolite. The evidence of design in creation can never reach the height of direct induction; it amounts only to the inferior kind of inductive evidence called analogy. Analogy agrees with induction in this, that they both argue that a thing known to resemble another in certain circumstances (call those circumstances A and B) will resemble it in another circumstance (call it C). But the difference is that in induction, A and B are known, by a previous comparison of many instances, to be the very circumstances on which C depends, or with which it is in some way connected. When this has not been ascertained, the argument amounts only to this, that since it is not known with which of the circumstances existing in the known case C is connected, they may as well be A and B as any others; and therefore there is a greater probability of C in cases where we know that A and B exist, than in cases of which we know nothing at all. This argument is of a weight very difficult to estimate at all, and impossible to estimate precisely. It may be very strong, when the known points of agreement, A and B &c. are numerous and the known points of difference few; or very weak, when the reverse is the case: but it can never be equal in validity to a real induction. The resemblances between some of the arrangements in nature and some of those made by man are considerable, and even as mere resemblances afford a certain presumption of similarity of cause: but how great that presumption is, it is hard to say. All that can be said with certainty is that these likenesses make creation by intelligence considerably more probable than if the likenesses had been less, or than if there had been no likenesses at all.

This mode, however, of stating the case does not do full justice to the evidence of Theism. The Design argument is not drawn from mere resemblances in Nature to the works of human intelligence, but from the special character of those resemblances. The circumstances in which it is alleged that the world resembles the works of man are not circumstances taken at random, but are particular instances of a circumstance which experience shows to have a real connection with an intelligent origin, the fact of conspiring to an end. The argument therefore is not one of mere analogy. As mere analogy it has its weight, but it is more than analogy. It surpasses analogy exactly as induction surpasses it. It is an inductive argument.

[*See Paley, *Natural Theology*, pp. 1–18.]

This, I think, is undeniable, and it remains to test the argument by the logical principles applicable to Induction. For this purpose it will be convenient to handle, not the argument as a whole, but some one of the most impressive cases of it, such as the structure of the eye, or of the ear. It is maintained that the structure of the eye proves a designing mind. To what class of inductive arguments does this belong? and what is its degree of force?

The species of inductive arguments are four in number, corresponding to the four Inductive Methods; the Methods of Agreement, of Difference, of Residues, and of Concomitant Variations. The argument under consideration falls within the first of these divisions, the Method of Agreement. This is, for reasons known to inductive logicians, the weakest of the four, but the particular argument is a strong one of the kind. It may be logically analysed as follows:

The parts of which the eye is composed, and the collocations which constitute the arrangement of those parts, resemble one another in this very remarkable property, that they all conduce to enabling the animal to see. These things being as they are, the animal sees: if any one of them were different from what it is, the animal, for the most part, would either not see, or would not see equally well. And this is the only marked resemblance that we can trace among the different parts of this structure, beyond the general likeness of composition and organization which exists among all other parts of the animal. Now the particular combination of organic elements called an eye had, in every instance, a beginning in time and must therefore have been brought together by a cause or causes. The number of instances is immeasurably greater than is, by the principles of inductive logic, required for the exclusion of a random concurrence of independent causes, or speaking technically, for the elimination of chance. We are therefore warranted by the canons of induction in concluding that what brought all these elements together was some cause common to them all; and inasmuch as the elements agree in the single circumstance of conspiring to produce sight, there must be some connection by way of causation between the cause which brought those elements together, and the fact of sight.

This I conceive to be a legitimate inductive inference, and the sum and substance of what Induction can do for Theism. The natural sequel of the argument would be this. Sight, being a fact not precedent but subsequent to the putting together of the organic structure of the eye, can only be connected with the production of that structure in the character of a final, not an efficient cause; that is, it is not Sight itself but an antecedent Idea of it, that must be the efficient cause. But this at once marks the origin as proceeding from an intelligent will.

I regret to say, however, that this latter half of the argument is not so inexpugnable as the former half. Creative forethought is not absolutely the only link by which the origin of the wonderful mechanism of the eye may be connected with the fact of sight. There is another connecting link on which attention has been greatly fixed by recent speculations, and the reality of which cannot be called in question, though its adequacy to account for such truly admirable combinations as some of those in Nature, is still and will probably long remain problematical. This is the principle of "the survival of the fittest."

This principle does not pretend to account for the commencement of sensation or of animal or vegetable life. But assuming the existence of some one or more very low forms of organic life, in which there are no complex adaptations nor any marked appearances of contrivance, and supposing, as experience warrants us in doing, that many small variations from those simple types would be thrown out in all directions, which would be transmissible by inheritance, and of which some would be advantageous to the creature in its struggle for existence and others disadvantageous, the forms which are advantageous would always tend to survive and those which are disadvantageous to perish. And thus there would be a constant though slow general improvement of the type as it branched out into many different varieties, adapting it to different media and modes of existence, until it might possibly, in countless ages, attain to the most advanced examples which now exist.

It must be acknowledged that there is something very startling, and *prima facie* improbable in this hypothetical history of Nature. It would require us, for example, to suppose that the primæval animal of whatever nature it may have been, could not see, and had at most such slight preparation for seeing as might be constituted by some chemical action of light upon its cellular structure. One of the accidental variations which are liable to take place in all organic beings would at some time or other produce a variety that could see, in some imperfect manner, and this peculiarity being transmitted by inheritance, while other variations continued to take place in other directions, a number of races would be produced who, by the power of even imperfect sight, would have a great advantage over all other creatures which could not see and would in time extirpate them from all places, except, perhaps, a few very peculiar situations underground. Fresh variations supervening would give rise to races with better and better seeing powers until we might at last reach as extraordinary a combination of structures and functions as are seen in the eye of man and of the more important animals. Of this theory when pushed to this extreme point, all that can now be said is that it is not so absurd as it looks, and that the analogies which have been discovered in experience, favourable to its possibility, far exceed what any one could have supposed beforehand. Whether it will ever be possible to say more than this, is at present uncertain. The theory if admitted would be in no way whatever inconsistent with Creation. But it must be acknowledged that it would greatly attenuate the evidence for it.

Leaving this remarkable speculation to whatever fate the progress of discovery may have in store for it, I think it must be allowed that, in the present state of our knowledge, the adaptations in Nature afford a large balance of probability in favour of creation by intelligence. It is equally certain that this is no more than a probability; and that the various other arguments of Natural Theology which we have considered, add nothing to its force. Whatever ground there is, revelation apart, to believe in an Author of Nature, is derived from the appearances in the universe. Their mere resemblance to the works of man, or to what man could do if he had the same power over the materials of organized bodies which he has over the materials of a watch, is of some value as an argument of analogy: but the argument is greatly strengthened by the properly inductive considerations which establish that there is some connection through causation between the origin of the arrangements of nature and the ends they fulfil; an argument which is in many cases slight, but in others, and chiefly in the nice and intricate combinations of vegetable and animal life, is of considerable strength.

PART II

ATTRIBUTES

THE QUESTION of the existence of a Deity, in its purely scientific aspect, standing as is shown in the First Part, it is next to be considered, given the indications of a Deity, what *sort* of a Deity do they point to? What attributes are we warranted, by the evidence which Nature affords of a creative mind, in assigning to that mind?

It needs no showing that the power if not the intelligence, must be so far superior to that of Man, as to surpass all human estimate. But from this to Omnipotence and Omniscience there is a wide interval. And the distinction is of immense practical importance.

It is not too much to say that every indication of Design in the Kosmos is so much evidence against the Omnipotence of the Designer. For what is meant by Design? Contrivance: the adaptation of means to an end. But the necessity for contrivance—the need of employing means—is a consequence of the limitation of power. Who would have recourse to means if to attain his end his mere word was sufficient? The very idea of means implies that the means have an efficacy which the direct action of the being who employs them has not. Otherwise they are not means, but an incumbrance. A man does not use machinery to move his arms. If he did, it could only be when paralysis had deprived him of the power of moving them by volition. But if the employment of contrivance is in itself a sign of limited power, how much more so is the careful and skilful choice of contrivances? Can any wisdom be shown in the selection of means, when the means have no efficacy but what is given them by the will of him who employs them, and when his will could have bestowed the same efficacy on any other means? Wisdom and contrivance are shown in overcoming difficulties, and there is no room for them in a Being for whom no difficulties exist. The evidences, therefore, of Natural Theology distinctly imply that the author of the Kosmos worked under limitations; that he was obliged to adapt himself to conditions independent of his will, and to attain his ends by such arrangements as those conditions admitted of.

And this hypothesis agrees with what we have seen to be the tendency of the evidences in another respect. We found that the appearances in Nature point indeed to an origin of the Kosmos, or order in Nature, and indicate that origin to be Design but do not point to any commencement, still less creation, of the two great elements of the Universe, the passive element and the active element, Matter and Force. There is in Nature no reason whatever to suppose that either Matter or Force, or any of their properties, were made by the Being who was the author of the collocations by which the world is adapted to what we consider as its purposes; or that he has power to alter any of those properties. It is only when we consent to entertain this negative supposition that there arises a need for wisdom and contrivance in the order of the universe. The Deity had on this hypothesis to work out his ends by combining materials of a given nature and properties. Out of these materials he had to construct a world in which his designs should be carried into effect through given properties of Matter and Force, working together and fitting into one another. This did require skill and contrivance, and the means by which it is effected are often such as justly excite our wonder and admiration: but exactly because it requires wisdom, it implies limitation of power, or rather the two phrases express different sides of the same fact.

If it be said, that an Omnipotent Creator, though under no necessity of employing contrivances such as man must use, thought fit to do so in order to leave traces by which man might recognize his creative hand, the answer is that this equally supposes a limit to his omnipotence. For if it was his will that men should know that they themselves and the world are his work, he, being omnipotent, had only to will that they should be aware of it. Ingenious men have sought for reasons why God might choose to leave his existence so far a matter of doubt that men should not be under an absolute necessity of knowing it, as they are of knowing that three and two make five. These imagined reasons are very unfortunate specimens of casuistry; but even did we admit their validity, they are of no avail on the supposition of omnipotence, since if it did not please God to implant in man a complete conviction of his existence, nothing hindered him from making the conviction fall short of completeness by any margin he chose to leave. It is usual to dispose of arguments of this description by the easy answer, that we do not know what wise reasons the Omniscient may have had for leaving undone things which he had the power to do. It is not perceived that this plea itself implies a limit to Omnipotence. When a thing is obviously good and obviously in accordance with what all the evidences of creation imply to have been the Creator's design, and we say we do not know what good reason he may have had for not doing it, we mean that we do not know to what other, still better object— to what object still more completely in the line of his purposes, he may have seen fit to postpone it. But the necessity of postponing one thing to another belongs only to limited power. Omnipotence could have made the objects compatible. Omnipotence does not need to weigh one consideration against another. If the Creator, like a human ruler, had to adapt himself to a set of conditions which he did not make, it is as unphilosophical as presumptuous in us to call him to account for any imperfections in his work; to complain that he left anything in it contrary to what, if the indications of design prove anything, he must have intended. He must at least know more than we know, and we cannot judge what greater good would have had to be sacrificed, or what greater evil incurred, if he had decided to remove this particular blot. Not so if he be omnipotent. If he be that, he must himself have willed that the two desirable objects should be incompatible; he must himself have willed that the obstacle to his supposed design should be insuperable. It cannot therefore *be* his design. It will not do to say that it was, but that he had other designs which interfered with it; for no one purpose imposes necessary limitations on another in the case of a Being not restricted by conditions of possibility.

Omnipotence, therefore, cannot be predicated of the Creator on grounds of natural theology. The fundamental principles of natural religion as deduced from the facts of the universe, negative his omnipotence. They do not, in the same manner, exclude omniscience: if we suppose limitation of power, there is nothing to contradict the supposition of perfect knowledge and absolute wisdom. But neither is there anything to prove it. The knowledge of the powers and properties of things necessary for planning and executing the arrangements of the Kosmos, is no doubt as much in excess of human knowledge as the power implied in creation is in excess of human power. And the skill, the subtlety of contrivance, the ingenuity as it would be called in the case of a human work, is often marvellous. But nothing obliges us to suppose that either the knowledge or the skill is infinite. We are not even compelled to suppose that the contrivances were always the best possible. If we venture to judge them as we judge the works of human artificers, we find abundant defects. The human body, for example, is one of the most striking instances of artful and ingenious contrivance which nature offers, but we may well ask whether so complicated a machine could not have been made to last longer, and not to get so easily and frequently out of order. We may ask why the human race should have been so constituted as to grovel in wretchedness and degradation for countless ages before a small portion of it was enabled to lift itself into the very imperfect state of intelligence, goodness and happiness which we enjoy. The divine power may not have been equal to doing more; the obstacles to a better arrangement of things may have been insuperable. But it is also possible that they were not. The skill of the Demiourgos was sufficient to produce what we see; but we cannot tell that this skill reached the extreme limit of perfection compatible with the material it employed and the forces it had to work with. I know not how we can even satisfy ourselves on grounds of natural theology, that the Creator foresees all the future; that he foreknows all the effects that will issue from his own contrivances. There may be great wisdom without the power of foreseeing and calculating everything: and human workmanship teaches us the possibility that the workman's knowledge of the properties of the things he works on may enable him to make arrangements admirably fitted to produce a given result, while he may have very little power of foreseeing the agencies of another kind which may modify or counteract the operation of the machinery he has made. Perhaps a knowledge of the laws of nature on which organic life depends, not much more perfect than the knowledge which man even now possesses of some other natural laws, would enable man, if he had the same power over the materials and the forces concerned which he has over some of those of inanimate nature, to create organized beings not less wonderful nor less adapted to their conditions of existence than those in Nature.

Assuming then that while we confine ourselves to Natural Religion we must rest content with a Creator less than Almighty; the question presents itself, of what nature is the limitation of his power? Does the obstacle at which the power of the Creator stops, which says to it: Thus far shalt thou go and no further, lie in the power of other Intelligent Beings; or in the insufficiency and refractoriness of the materials of the universe; or must we resign ourselves to admitting the hypothesis that the author of the Kosmos, though wise and knowing, was not all-wise and all-knowing, and may not always have done the best that was possible under the conditions of the problem?

The first of these suppositions has until a very recent period been and in many quarters still is, the prevalent theory even of Christianity. Though attributing, and in a certain sense sincerely, omnipotence to the Creator, the received religion represents him as for some inscrutable reason tolerating the perpetual counteraction of his purposes by the will of another Being of opposite character and of great though inferior power, the Devil. The only difference on this matter between popular Christianity and the religion of Ormuzd and Ahriman, is that the former pays its good Creator the bad compliment of having been the maker of the Devil and of being at all times able to crush and annihilate him and his evil deeds and counsels, which nevertheless he does not do. But, as I have already remarked, all forms of polytheism, and this among the rest, are with difficulty reconcileable with an universe governed by general laws. Obedience to law is the note of a settled government, and not of a conflict always going on. When powers are at war with one another for the rule of the world, the boundary between them is not fixed but constantly fluctuating. This may seem to be the case on our planet as between the powers of good and evil when we look only at the results; but when we consider the inner springs, we find that both the good and the evil take place in the common course of nature, by virtue of the same general laws originally impressed—the same machinery turning out now good, now evil things, and oftener still, the two combined. The division of power is only apparently variable, but really so regular that, were we speaking of human potentates, we should declare without hesitation that the share of each must have been fixed by previous consent. Upon that supposition indeed, the result of the combination of antagonist forces might be much the same as on that of a single creator with divided purposes.

But when we come to consider, not what hypothesis may be conceived, and possibly reconciled with known facts, but what supposition is pointed to by the evidences of natural religion; the case is different. The indications of design point strongly in one direction, the preservation of the creatures in whose structure the indications are found. Along with the preserving agencies there are destroying agencies, which we might be tempted to ascribe to the will of a different Creator: but there are rarely appearances of the recondite contrivance of means of destruction, except when the destruction of one creature is the means of preservation to others. Nor can it be supposed that the preserving agencies are wielded by one Being, the destroying agencies by another. The destroying agencies are a necessary part of the preserving agencies: the chemical compositions by which life is carried on could not take place without a parallel series of decompositions. The great agent of decay in both organic and inorganic substances is oxidation, and it is only by oxidation that life is continued for even the length of a minute. The imperfections in the attainment of the purposes which the appearances indicate, have not the air of having been designed. They are like the unintended results of accidents insufficiently guarded against, or of a little excess or deficiency in the quantity of some of the agencies by which the good purpose is carried on, or else they are consequences of the wearing out of a machinery not made to last for ever: they point either to shortcomings in the workmanship as regards its intended purpose, or to external forces not under the control of the workman, but which forces bear no mark of being wielded and aimed by any other and rival Intelligence.

We may conclude, then, that there is no ground in Natural Theology for attributing intelligence or personality to the obstacles which partially thwart what seem the purposes of the Creator. The limitation of his power more probably results either from the qualities of the material—the substances and forces of which the universe is composed not admitting of any arrangements by which his purposes could be more completely fulfilled; or else, the purposes might have been more fully attained, but the Creator did not know how to do it; creative skill, wonderful as it is, was not sufficiently perfect to accomplish his purposes more thoroughly.

We now pass to the moral attributes of the Deity, so far as indicated in the Creation; or (stating the problem in the broadest manner) to the question, what indications Nature gives of the purposes of its author. This question bears a very different aspect to us from what it bears to those teachers of Natural Theology who are incumbered with the necessity of admitting the omnipotence of the Creator. We have not to attempt the impossible problem of reconciling infinite benevolence and justice with infinite power in the Creator of such a world as this. The attempt to do so not only involves absolute contradiction in an intellectual point of view but exhibits to excess the revolting spectacle of a jesuitical defence of moral enormities.

On this topic I need not add to the illustrations given of this portion of the subject in my Essay on Nature.[*] At the stage which our argument has reached there is none of this moral perplexity. Grant that creative power was limited by conditions the nature and extent of which are wholly unknown to us, and the goodness and justice of the Creator may be all that the most pious believe; and all in the work that conflicts with those moral attributes may be the fault of the conditions which left to the Creator only a choice of evils.

It is, however, one question whether any given conclusion is consistent with known facts, and another whether there is evidence to prove it: and if we have no means for judging of the design but from the work actually produced, it is a somewhat hazardous speculation to suppose that the work designed was of a different quality from the result realized. Still, though the ground is unsafe we may, with due caution, journey a certain distance on it. Some parts of the order of nature give much more indication of contrivance than others; many, it is not too much to say, give no sign of it at all. The signs of contrivance are most conspicuous in the structure and processes of vegetable and animal life. But for these, it is probable that the appearances in nature would never have seemed to the thinking part of mankind to afford any proofs of a God. But when a God had been inferred from the organization of living beings, other parts of Nature, such as the structure of the solar system, seemed to afford evidences, more or less strong, in confirmation of the belief: granting, then, a design in Nature, we can best hope to be enlightened as to what that design was, by examining it in the parts of Nature in which its traces are the most conspicuous.

To what purpose, then, do the expedients in the construction of animals and vegetables, which excite the admiration of naturalists, appear to tend? There is no blinking the fact that they tend principally to no more exalted object than to make the structure remain in life and in working order for a certain time: the individual for a few years, the species or race for a longer but still a limited period. And the similar though less conspicuous marks of creation which are recognized in inorganic Nature, are generally of the same character. The adaptations, for instance, which appear in the solar system consist in placing it under conditions which enable the mutual action of its parts to maintain instead of destroying its stability, and even that only for a time, vast indeed if measured against our short span of animated existence,

[*See above, pp. 384 ff.]

but which can be perceived even by us to be limited: for even the feeble means which we possess of exploring the past, are believed by those who have examined the subject by the most recent lights, to yield evidence that the solar system was once a vast sphere of nebula or vapour, and is going through a process which in the course of ages will reduce it to a single and not very large mass of solid matter frozen up with more than arctic cold. If the machinery of the system is adapted to keep itself at work only for a time, still less perfect is the adaptation of it for the abode of living beings since it is only adapted to them during the relatively short portion of its total duration which intervenes between the time when each planet was too hot and the time when it became or will become too cold to admit of life under the only conditions in which we have experience of its possibility. Or we should perhaps reverse the statement, and say that organization and life are only adapted to the conditions of the solar system during a relatively short portion of the system's existence.

The greater part, therefore, of the design of which there is indication in Nature, however wonderful its mechanism, is no evidence of any moral attributes, because the end to which it is directed, and its adaptation to which end is the evidence of its being directed to an end at all, is not a moral end: it is not the good of any sentient creature, it is but the qualified permanence, for a limited period, of the work itself, whether animate or inanimate. The only inference that can be drawn from most of it, respecting the character of the Creator, is that he does not wish his works to perish as soon as created; he wills them to have a certain duration. From this alone nothing can be justly inferred as to the manner in which he is affected towards his animate or rational creatures.

After deduction of the great number of adaptations which have no apparent object but to keep the machine going, there remain a certain number of provisions for giving pleasure to living beings, and a certain number of provisions for giving them pain. There is no positive certainty that the whole of these ought not to take their place among the contrivances for keeping the creature or its species in existence; for both the pleasures and the pains have a conservative tendency; the pleasures being generally so disposed as to attract to the things which maintain individual or collective existence, the pains so as to deter from such as would destroy it.

When all these things are considered it is evident that a vast deduction must be made from the evidences of a Creator before they can be counted as evidences of a benevolent purpose: so vast indeed that some may doubt whether after such a deduction there remains any balance. Yet endeavouring to look at the question without partiality or prejudice and without allowing wishes to have any influence over judgment, it does appear that granting the existence of design, there is a preponderance of evidence that the Creator desired the pleasure of his creatures. This is indicated by the fact that pleasure of one description or another is afforded by almost everything, the mere play of the faculties, physical and mental, being a never-ending source of pleasure, and even painful things giving pleasure by the satisfaction of curiosity and the agreeable sense of acquiring knowledge; and also that pleasure, when experienced, seems to result from the normal working of the machinery, while pain usually arises from some external interference with it, and resembles in each particular case the result of an accident. Even in cases when pain results, like pleasure, from the machinery itself, the appearances do not indicate that contrivance was brought into play purposely to produce pain: what is indicated is rather a clumsiness in the contrivance employed for some other purpose. The author of the machinery is no doubt accountable for having made it susceptible of pain; but this may have been a necessary condition of its susceptibility to pleasure; a supposition which avails nothing on the theory of an Omnipotent Creator but is an extremely probable one in the case of a contriver working under the limitation of inexorable laws and indestructible properties of matter. The susceptibility being conceded as a thing which did enter into design, the pain itself usually seems like a thing undesigned; a casual result of the collision of the organism with some outward force to which it was not intended to be exposed, and which, in many cases, provision is even made to hinder it from being exposed to. There is, therefore, much appearance that pleasure is agreeable to the Creator, while there is very little if any appearance that pain is so: and there is a certain amount of justification for inferring, on grounds of Natural Theology alone, that benevolence is one of the attributes of the Creator. But to jump from this to the inference that his sole or chief purposes are those of benevolence, and that the single end and aim of Creation was the happiness of his creatures, is not only not justified by any evidence but is a conclusion in opposition to such evidence as we have. If the motive of the Deity for creating sentient beings was the happiness of the beings he created, his purpose, in our corner of the universe at least, must be pronounced, taking past ages and all countries and races into account, to have been thus far an ignominious failure; and if God had no purpose but our happiness and that of other living creatures it is not credible that he would have called them into existence with the prospect of being so completely baffled. If man had not the power by the exercise of his own energies for the improvement both of himself and of his outward circumstances, to do for himself and other creatures vastly more than God had in the first instance done, the Being who called him into existence would deserve something very different from thanks at his hands. Of course it may be said that this very capacity of improving himself and the world was given to him by God, and that the change which he will be thereby enabled ultimately to effect in human existence will be worth purchasing by the sufferings and wasted lives of entire geological periods. This may be so; but to suppose that God could not have given him these blessings at a less frightful cost, is to make a very strange supposition concerning the Deity. It is to suppose that God could not, in the first instance, create anything better than a Bosjesman or an Andaman islander, or something still lower; and yet was able to endow the Bosjesman or the Andaman islander with the power of raising himself into a Newton or a Fénelon. We certainly do not know the nature of the barriers which limit the divine omnipotence; but it is a very odd notion of them that they enable the Deity to confer on an almost bestial creature the power of producing by a succession of efforts what God himself had no other means of creating.

Such are the indications of Natural Religion in respect to the divine benevolence. If we look for any other of the moral attributes which a certain class of philosophers are accustomed to distinguish from benevolence, as for example Justice, we find a total blank. There is no evidence whatever in Nature for divine justice, whatever standard of justice our ethical opinions may lead us to recognize. There is no shadow of justice in the general arrangements of Nature; and what imperfect realization it obtains in any human society (a most imperfect realization as yet) is the work of man himself, struggling upwards against immense natural difficulties, into civilization, and making to himself a second nature, far better and more unselfish than he was created with. But on this point enough has been said in another Essay, already referred to, on Nature.[*]

These, then, are the net results of Natural Theology on the question of the divine attributes. A Being of great but limited power, how or by what limited we cannot even conjecture; of great, and perhaps unlimited intelligence, but perhaps, also, more narrowly limited than his power: who desires, and pays some regard to, the happiness of his creatures, but who seems to have other motives of action which he cares more for, and who can hardly be supposed to have created the universe for that purpose alone. Such is the Deity whom Natural Religion points to; and any idea of God more captivating than this comes only from human wishes, or from the teaching of either real or imaginary Revelation.

We shall next examine whether the light of nature gives any indications concerning the immortality of the soul, and a future life.

[*See above, p. 396.]

PART III

IMMORTALITY

THE INDICATIONS of immortality may be considered in two divisions: those which are independent of any theory respecting the Creator and his intentions, and those which depend upon an antecedent belief on that subject.

Of the former class of arguments speculative men have in different ages put forward a considerable variety, of which those in the *Phædon* of Plato are an example; but they are for the most part such as have no adherents, and need not be seriously refuted, now. They are generally founded upon preconceived theories as to the nature of the thinking principle in man, considered as distinct and separable from the body, and on other preconceived theories respecting death. As, for example, that death, or dissolution, is always a separation of parts; and the soul being without parts, being simple and indivisible, is not susceptible of this separation. Curiously enough, one of the interlocutors in the *Phædon* anticipates the answer by which an objector of the present day would meet this argument: namely, that thought and consciousness, though mentally distinguishable from the body, may not be a substance separable from it, but a result of it, standing in a relation to it (the illustration is Plato's) like that of a tune to the musical instrument on which it is played; and that the arguments used to prove that the soul does not die with the body, would equally prove that the tune does not die with the instrument, but survives its destruction and continues to exist apart.[*] In fact, those moderns who dispute the evidences of the immortality of the soul, do not, in general, believe the soul to be a substance *per se*, but regard it as the name of a bundle of attributes, the attributes of feeling, thinking, reasoning, believing, willing, &c., and these attributes they regard as a consequence of the bodily organization, which therefore, they argue, it is as unreasonable to suppose surviving when that organization is dispersed, as to suppose the colour or odour of a rose surviving when the rose itself has perished. Those, therefore, who would deduce the immortality of the soul from its own nature have first to prove that the attributes in question are not attributes of the body but of a separate substance. Now what is the verdict of science on this point? It is not perfectly conclusive either way. In the first place, it does not prove, experimentally, that any mode of organization has the power of pro-

[*See *Phædo*, 85e–86d, 91d–95a.]

ducing feeling or thought. To make that proof good it would be necessary that we should be able to produce an organism, and try whether it would feel; which we cannot do; organisms cannot by any human means be produced, they can only be developed out of a previous organism. On the other hand, the evidence is well nigh complete that all thought and feeling has some action of the bodily organism for its immediate antecedent or accompaniment; that the specific variations and especially the different degrees of complication of the nervous and cerebral organization, correspond to differences in the development of the mental faculties; and though we have no evidence, except negative, that the mental consciousness ceases for ever when the functions of the brain are at an end, we do know that diseases of the brain disturb the mental functions and that decay or weakness of the brain enfeebles them. We have therefore sufficient evidence that cerebral action is, if not the cause, at least, in our present state of existence, a condition *sine quâ non* of mental operations; and that assuming the mind to be a distinct substance, its separation from the body would not be, as some have vainly flattered themselves, a liberation from trammels and restoration to freedom, but would simply put a stop to its functions and remand it to unconsciousness, unless and until some other set of conditions supervenes, capable of recalling it into activity, but of the existence of which experience does not give us the smallest indication.

At the same time it is of importance to remark that these considerations only amount to defect of evidence; they afford no positive argument against immortality. We must beware of giving *à priori* validity to the conclusions of an *à posteriori* philosophy. The root of all *à priori* thinking is the tendency to transfer to outward things a strong association between the corresponding ideas in our own minds; and the thinkers who most sincerely attempt to limit their beliefs by experience, and honestly believe that they do so, are not always sufficiently on their guard against this mistake. There are thinkers who regard it as a truth of reason that miracles are impossible; and in like manner there are others who because the phenomena of life and consciousness are associated in their minds by undeviating experience with the action of material organs, think it an absurdity *per se* to imagine it possible that those phenomena can exist under any other conditions. But they should remember that the uniform coexistence of one fact with another does not make the one fact a part of the other, or the same with it. The relation of thought to a material brain is no metaphysical necessity; but simply a constant coexistence within the limits of observation. And when analysed to the bottom on the principles of the Associative Psychology, the brain, just as much as the mental functions is, like matter itself, merely a set of human sensations either actual or inferred as possible, namely those which the anatomist has when he opens the skull, and the impressions which we suppose we should receive of molecular or some other movements when the cerebral action was going on, if there were no bony envelope and our senses or our instruments were sufficiently delicate. Experience furnishes us with no example of any series of states of consciousness, without this group of contingent sensations attached to it; but it is as easy to imagine such a series of states without, as with, this accompaniment, and we know of no reason in the nature of things against the possibility of its being thus disjoined. We may suppose that the same thoughts, emotions, volitions and even sensations which we have here, may persist or recommence somewhere else under other conditions, just as we may suppose that other thoughts and sensations may exist under other conditions in other parts of the universe. And in entertaining this supposition we need not be embarrassed by any metaphysical difficulties about a thinking substance. Substance is but a general name for the perdurability of attributes: wherever there is a series of thoughts connected together by memories, that constitutes a thinking substance. This absolute distinction in thought and separability in representation of our states of consciousness from the set of conditions with which they are united only by constancy of concomitance, is equivalent in a practical point of view to the old distinction of the two substances, Matter and Mind.

There is, therefore, in science, no evidence against the immortality of the soul but that negative evidence, which consists in the absence of evidence in its favour. And even the negative evidence is not so strong as negative evidence often is. In the case of witchcraft, for instance, the fact that there is no proof which will stand examination of its having ever existed, is as conclusive as the most positive evidence of its non-existence would be; for it exists, if it does exist, on this earth, where if it had existed the evidence of fact would certainly have been available to prove it. But it is not so as to the soul's existence after death. That it does not remain on earth and go about visibly or interfere in the events of life, is proved by the same weight of evidence which disproves witchcraft. But that it does not exist elsewhere, there is absolutely no proof. A very faint, if any, presumption, is all that is afforded by its disappearance from the surface of this planet.

Some may think that there is an additional and very strong presumption against the immortality of the thinking and conscious principle, from the analysis of all the other objects of Nature. All things in Nature perish, the most beautiful and perfect being, as philosophers and poets alike complain, the most perishable. A flower of the most exquisite form and colouring grows up from a root, comes to perfection in weeks or months, and lasts only a few hours or days. Why should it be otherwise with man? Why indeed. But why, also, should it *not* be otherwise? Feeling and thought are not merely different from what we call inanimate matter, but are at the opposite pole of existence, and analogical inference has little or no validity from the one to the other. Feeling and thought are much more real than anything else; they are the only things which we directly know to be real, all things else being merely the unknown conditions on which these, in our present state of existence or in some other, depend. All matter apart from the feelings of sentient beings has but an hypothetical and unsubstantial existence: it is a mere assumption to account for our sensations; itself we do not perceive, we are not conscious of it, but only of the sensations which we are said to receive from it: in reality it is a mere name for our expectation of sensations, or for our belief that we can have certain sensations when certain other sensations give indication of them. Because these contingent possibilities of sensation sooner or later come to an end and give place to others, is it implied in this, that the series of our feelings must itself be broken off? This would not be to reason from one kind of substantive reality to another, but to draw from something which has no reality except in reference to something else, conclusions applicable to that which is the only substantive reality. Mind, (or whatever name we give to what is implied in consciousness of a continued series of feelings) is in a philosophical point of view the only reality of which we have any evidence; and no analogy can be recognized or comparison made between it and other realities because there are no other known realities to compare it with. That is quite consistent with its being perishable; but the question whether it is so or not is *res integra*, untouched by any of the results of human knowledge and experience. The case is one of those very rare cases in which there is really a total absence of evidence on either side, and in which the absence of evidence for the affirmative does not, as in so many cases it does, create a strong presumption in favour of the negative.

The belief, however, in human immortality, in the minds of mankind generally, is probably not grounded on any scientific arguments either physical or metaphysical, but on foundations with most minds much stronger, namely on one hand the disagreeableness of giving up existence, (to those at least to whom it has hitherto been pleasant) and on the other the general traditions of mankind. The natural tendency of belief to follow these two inducements, our own wishes and the general assent of other people, has been in this instance reinforced by the utmost exertion of the power of public and private teaching; rulers and instructors having at all times, with the view of giving greater effect to their mandates whether from selfish or from public motives, encouraged to the utmost of their power the belief that there is a life after death, in which pleasures and sufferings far greater than on earth, depend on our doing or leaving undone while alive, what we are commanded to do in the name of the unseen powers. As causes of belief these various circumstances are most powerful. As rational grounds of it they carry no weight at all.

That what is called the consoling nature of an opinion, that is, the pleasure we should have in believing it to be true, can be a ground for believing it, is a doctrine irrational in itself and which would sanction half the mischievous illusions recorded in history or which mislead individual life. It is sometimes, in the case now under consideration, wrapt up in a quasi-scientific language. We are told that the desire of immortality is one of our instincts, and that there is no instinct which has not corresponding to it a real object fitted to satisfy it. Where there is hunger there is somewhere food, where there is sexual feeling there is somewhere sex, where there is love there is somewhere something to be loved, and so forth: in like manner since there is the instinctive desire of eternal life, eternal life there must be. The answer to this is patent on the very surface of the subject. It is unnecessary to go into any recondite considerations concerning instincts, or to discuss whether the desire in question is an instinct or not. Granting that wherever there is an instinct there exists something such as that instinct demands, can it be affirmed that this something exists in boundless quantity, or sufficient to satisfy the infinite craving of human desires? What is called the desire of eternal life is simply the desire of life; and does there not exist that which this desire calls for? Is there not life? And is not the instinct, if it be an instinct, gratified by the possession and preservation of life? To suppose that the desire of life guarantees to us personally the reality of life through all eternity, is like supposing that the desire of food assures us that we shall always have as much as we can eat through our whole lives and as much longer as we can conceive our lives to be protracted to.

The argument from tradition or the general belief of the human race, if we accept it as a guide to our own belief, must be accepted entire: if so we are bound to believe that the souls of human beings not only survive after death but show themselves as ghosts to the living; for we find no people who have had the one belief without the other. Indeed it is probable that the former belief originated in the latter, and that primitive men would never have supposed that the soul did not die with the body if they had not fancied that it visited them after death. Nothing could be more natural than such a fancy; it is, in appearance, completely realized in dreams, which in Homer and in all ages like Homer's, are supposed to be real apparitions. To dreams we have to add not merely waking hallucinations but the delusions, however baseless, of sight and hearing, or rather the misinterpretations of those senses, sight or hearing supplying mere hints from which imagination paints a complete picture and invests it with reality. These delusions are not to be judged of by a modern standard: in early times the line between imagination and perception was by no means clearly defined; there was little or none of the knowledge we now possess of the actual course of nature, which makes us distrust or disbelieve any appearance which is at variance with known laws. In the ignorance of men as to what were the limits of nature and what was or was not compatible with it, no one thing seemed, as far as physical considerations went, to be much more improbable than another. In rejecting, therefore, as we do, and as we have the best reason to do, the tales and legends of the actual appearance of disembodied spirits, we take from under the general belief of mankind in a life after death, what in all probability was its chief ground and support, and deprive it of even the very little value which the opinion of rude ages can ever have as evidence of truth. If it be said that this belief has maintained itself in ages which have ceased to be rude and which reject the superstitions with which it once was accompanied, the same may be said of many other opinions of rude ages, and especially on the most important and interesting subjects, because it is on those subjects that the reigning opinion, whatever it may be, is the most sedulously inculcated upon all who are born into the world. This particular opinion, moreover, if it has on the whole kept its ground, has done so with a constantly increasing number of dissentients, and those especially among cultivated minds. Finally, those cultivated minds which adhere to the belief ground it, we may reasonably suppose, not on the belief of others, but on arguments and evidences; and those arguments and evidences, therefore, are what it concerns us to estimate and judge.

The preceding are a sufficient sample of the arguments for a future life which do not suppose an antecedent belief in the existence, or any theory respecting the attributes of the Godhead. It remains to consider what arguments are supplied by such lights, or such grounds of conjecture, as natural theology affords, on those great questions.

We have seen that these lights are but faint; that of the existence of a Creator they afford no more than a preponderance of probability; of his benevolence a considerably less preponderance; that there is, however, some reason to think that he cares for the pleasures of his creatures, but by no means that this is his sole care, or that other purposes do not often take precedence of it. His intelligence must be adequate to the contrivances apparent in the universe, but need not be more than adequate to them, and his power is not only not proved to be infinite, but the only real evidences in natural theology tend to show that it is limited, contrivance being a mode of overcoming difficulties, and always supposing difficulties to be overcome.

We have now to consider what inference can legitimately be drawn from these premises, in favour of a future life. It seems to me, apart from express revelation, none at all.

The common arguments are, the goodness of God; the improbability that he would ordain the annihilation of his noblest and richest work, after the greater part of its few years of life had been spent in the acquisition of faculties which time is not allowed him to turn to fruit; and the special improbability that he would have implanted in us an instinctive desire of eternal life, and doomed that desire to complete disappointment.

These might be arguments in a world the constitution of which made it possible without contradiction to hold it for the work of a Being at once omnipotent and benevolent. But they are not arguments in a world like that in which we live. The benevolence of the divine Being may be perfect, but his power being subject to unknown limitations, we know not that he could have given us what we so confidently assert that he must have given; *could* (that is) without sacrificing something more important. Even his benevolence, however justly inferred, is by no means indicated as the interpretation of his whole purpose, and since we cannot tell how far other purposes may have interfered with the exercise of his benevolence, we know not that he *would*, even if he could have granted us eternal life. With regard to the supposed improbability of his having given the wish without its gratification, the same answer may be made; the scheme which either limitation of power, or conflict of purposes, compelled him to adopt, may have *required* that we should have the wish although it were not destined to be gratified. One thing, however, is quite certain in respect to God's government of the world; that he either could not, or would not, grant to us every thing we wish. We wish for life, and he has granted some life: that we wish (or some of us wish) for a boundless extent of life and that it is not granted, is no exception to the ordinary modes of his government. Many a man would like to be a Crœsus or an Augustus Cæsar, but has his wishes gratified only to the moderate extent of a pound a week or the Secretaryship of his Trades Union. There is, therefore, no assurance whatever of a life after death, on grounds of natural religion. But to any one who feels it conducive either to his satisfaction or to his usefulness to hope for a future state as a possibility, there is no hindrance to his indulging that hope. Appearances point to the existence of a Being who has great power over us—all the power implied in the creation of the Kosmos, or of its organized beings at least—and of whose goodness we have evidence though not of its being his predominant attribute: and as we do not know the limits either of his power or of his goodness, there is room to hope that both the one and the other may extend to granting us this gift provided that it would really be beneficial to us. The same ground which permits the hope warrants us in expecting that if there be a future life it will be at least as good as the present, and will not be wanting in the best feature of the present life, improvability by our own efforts. Nothing can be more opposed to every estimate we can form of probability, than the common idea of the future life as a state of rewards and punishments in any other sense than that the consequences of our actions upon our own character and susceptibilities will follow us in the future as they have done in the past and present. Whatever be the probabilities *of* a future life, all the probabilities *in case of* a future life are that such as we have been made or have made ourselves before the change, such we shall enter into the life hereafter; and that the fact of death will make no sudden break in our spiritual life, nor influence our character any otherwise than as any important change in our mode of existence may always be expected to modify it. Our thinking principle has its laws which in this life are invariable, and any analogies drawn from this life must assume that the same laws will continue. To imagine that a miracle will be wrought at death by the act of God making perfect every one whom it is his will to include among his elect, might be justified by an express revelation duly authenticated, but is utterly opposed to every presumption that can be deduced from the light of Nature.

PART IV

REVELATION

THE DISCUSSION in the preceding pages respecting the evidences of Theism has been strictly confined to those which are derived from the light of Nature. It is a different question what addition has been made to those evidences, and to what extent the conclusions obtainable from them have been amplified or modified, by the establishment of a direct communication with the Supreme Being. It would be beyond the purpose of this Essay, to take into consideration the positive evidences of the Christian, or any other belief, which claims to be a revelation from Heaven. But such general considerations as are applicable not to a particular system, but to Revelation generally, may properly find a place here, and are indeed necessary to give a sufficiently practical bearing to the results of the preceding investigation.

In the first place, then, the indications of a Creator and of his attributes which we have been able to find in Nature, though so much slighter and less conclusive even as to his existence than the pious mind would wish to consider them, and still more unsatisfactory in the information they afford as to his attributes, are yet sufficient to give to the supposition of a Revelation a standing point which it would not otherwise have had. The alleged Revelation is not obliged to build up its case from the foundation; it has not to prove the very existence of the Being from whom it professes to come. It claims to be a message from a Being whose existence, whose power, and to a certain extent whose wisdom and goodness, are, if not proved, at least indicated with more or less of probability by the phenomena of Nature. The sender of the alleged message is not a sheer invention; there are grounds independent of the message itself for belief in his reality; grounds which, though insufficient for proof, are sufficient to take away all antecedent improbability from the supposition that a message may really have been received from him. It is, moreover, much to the purpose to take notice, that the very imperfection of the evidences which Natural Theology can produce of the Divine attributes, removes some of the chief stumbling blocks to the belief of a Revelation; since the objections grounded on imperfections in the Revelation itself, however conclusive against it if it is considered as a record of the acts or an expression of the wisdom of a Being of infinite power combined with infinite wisdom and goodness, are no reason whatever against its having come from a Being such as the course of nature points to, whose wisdom is possibly, his power certainly, limited, and whose goodness, though real, is not likely to have been the only motive which actuated him in the work of Creation. The argument of Butler's *Analogy*, is, from its own point of view, conclusive: the Christian religion is open to no objections, either moral or intellectual, which do not apply at least equally to the common theory of Deism; the morality of the Gospels is far higher and better than that which shows itself in the order of Nature; and what is morally objectionable in the Christian theory of the world, is objectionable only when taken in conjunction with the doctrine of an omnipotent God: and (at least as understood by the most enlightened Christians) by no means imports any moral obliquity in a Being whose power is supposed to be restricted by real, though unknown obstacles, which prevented him from fully carrying out his design. The grave error of Butler was that he shrank from admitting the hypothesis of limited powers; and his appeal consequently amounts to this: The belief of Christians is neither more absurd nor more immoral than the belief of Deists who acknowledge an Omnipotent Creator, let us, therefore, in spite of the absurdity and immorality, believe both. He ought to have said, let us cut down our belief of either to what does not involve absurdity or immorality; to what is neither intellectually self-contradictory nor morally perverted.

To return, however, to the main subject: on the hypothesis of a God, who made the world, and in making it had regard, however that regard may have been limited by other considerations, to the happiness of his sentient creatures, there is no antecedent improbability in the supposition that his concern for their good would continue, and that he might once or oftener give proof of it by communicating to them some knowledge of himself beyond what they were able to make out by their unassisted faculties, and some knowledge or precepts useful for guiding them through the difficulties of life. Neither on the only tenable hypothesis, that of limited power, is it open to us to object that these helps ought to have been greater, or in any way other than they are. The only question to be entertained, and which we cannot dispense ourselves from entertaining, is that of evidence. Can any evidence suffice to prove a Divine Revelation? And of what nature, and what amount, must that evidence be? Whether the special evidences of Christianity, or of any other alleged revelation, do or do not come up to the mark, is a different question, into which I do not propose directly to enter. The question I intend to consider, is, what evidence is required; what general conditions it ought to satisfy; and whether they are such as, according to the known constitution of things, *can* be satisfied.

The evidences of Revelation are commonly distinguished as external or internal. External evidences are the testimony of the senses or of witnesses. By the internal evidences are meant the indications which the Revelation itself is thought to furnish of its divine origin; indications supposed to consist chiefly in the excellence of its precepts, and its general suitability to the circumstances and needs of human nature.

The consideration of these internal evidences is very important, but their importance is principally negative; they may be conclusive grounds for rejecting a Revelation, but cannot of themselves warrant the acceptance of it as divine. If the moral character of the doctrines of an alleged Revelation is bad and perverting, we ought to reject it from whomsoever it comes; for it cannot come from a good and wise Being. But the excellence of their morality can never entitle us to ascribe to them a supernatural origin: for we cannot have conclusive reason for believing that the human faculties were incompetent to find out moral doctrines of which the human faculties can perceive and recognize the excellence. A Revelation, therefore, cannot be proved divine unless by external evidence; that is, by the exhibition of supernatural facts. And we have to consider, whether it is possible to prove supernatural facts, and if it is, what evidence is required to prove them.

This question has only, so far as I know, been seriously raised on the sceptical side, by Hume. It is the question involved in his famous argument against Miracles: [*] an argument which goes down to the depths of the subject, but the exact scope and effect of which, (perhaps not conceived with perfect correctness by that great thinker himself), have in general been utterly misconceived by those who have attempted to answer him. Dr. Campbell, for example, one of the acutest of his antagonists, has thought himself obliged, in order to support the credibility of miracles, to lay down doctrines which virtually go the length of maintaining that antecedent improbability is never a sufficient ground for refusing credence to a statement, if it is well attested.[†] Dr. Campbell's fallacy lay in overlooking a double meaning of the word improbability; as I have pointed out in my *Logic*, and, still earlier, in an editorial note to Bentham's treatise on Evidence.[‡]

Taking the question from the very beginning; it is evidently impossible to maintain that if a supernatural fact really occurs, proof of its occurrence cannot be accessible to the human faculties. The evidence of our senses could prove this as it can prove other things. To put the most extreme case: suppose that I actually saw and heard a Being, either of the human form, or of some form previously unknown to me, commanding a world to exist, and a new world actually starting into existence and commencing a movement

[*David Hume. "Of Miracles," *An Inquiry Concerning Human Understanding*. In *Essays and Treatises on Several Subjects*. 2 vols. Edinburgh: Cadell, 1793, Vol. II, pp. 124–47.]

[†George Campbell. *A Dissertation on Miracles*. Edinburgh: Kincaid and Bell, 1762.]

[‡*Logic*, Vol. II, pp. 173–5 (Bk. III, chap. xxv, §4); *Rationale*, Vol. I, p. 137.]

through space, at his command. There can be no doubt that this evidence would convert the creation of worlds from a speculation into a fact of experience. It may be said, I could not know that so singular an appearance was anything more than a hallucination of my senses. True; but the same doubt exists at first respecting every unsuspected and surprising fact which comes to light in our physical researches. That our senses have been deceived, is a possibility which has to be met and dealt with, and we do deal with it by several means. If we repeat the experiment, and again with the same result; if at the time of the observation the impressions of our senses are in all other respects the same as usual, rendering the supposition of their being morbidly affected in this one particular, extremely improbable; above all, if other people's senses confirm the testimony of our own; we conclude, with reason, that we may trust our senses. Indeed our senses are all that we have to trust to. We depend on them for the ultimate premises even of our reasonings. There is no other appeal against their decision than an appeal from the senses without precautions to the senses with all due precautions. When the evidence, on which an opinion rests, is equal to that upon which the whole conduct and safety of our lives is founded, we need ask no further. Objections which apply equally to all evidence are valid against none. They only prove abstract fallibility.

But the evidence of miracles, at least to Protestant Christians, is not, in our own day, of this cogent description. It is not the evidence of our senses, but of witnesses, and even this not at first hand, but resting on the attestation of books and traditions. And even in the case of the original eye-witnesses, the supernatural facts asserted on their alleged testimony, are not of the transcendant character supposed in our example, about the nature of which, or the impossibility of their having had a natural origin, there could be little room for doubt. On the contrary, the recorded miracles are, in the first place, generally such as it would have been extremely difficult to verify as matters of fact, and in the next place, are hardly ever beyond the possibility of having been brought about by human means or by the spontaneous agencies of nature. It is to cases of this kind that Hume's argument against the credibility of miracles was meant to apply.

His argument is: The evidence of miracles consists of testimony. The ground of our reliance on testimony is our experience that certain conditions being supposed, testimony is generally veracious. But the same experience tells us that even under the best conditions testimony is frequently either intentionally or unintentionally, false. When, therefore, the fact to which testimony is produced is one the happening of which would be more at variance with experience than the falsehood of testimony, we ought not to believe it. And this rule all prudent persons observe in the conduct of life. Those who do not, are sure to suffer for their credulity.

Now a miracle (the argument goes on to say) is, in the highest possible degree, contradictory to experience: for if it were not contradictory to experience it would not be a miracle. The very reason for its being regarded as a miracle is that it is a breach of a law of nature, that is, of an otherwise invariable and inviolable uniformity in the succession of natural events. There is, therefore, the very strongest reason for disbelieving it, that experience can give for disbelieving anything. But the mendacity or error of witnesses, even though numerous and of fair character, is quite within the bounds of even common experience. That supposition, therefore, ought to be preferred.

There are two apparently weak points in this argument. One is, that the evidence of experience to which its appeal is made is only negative evidence, which is not so conclusive as positive; since facts of which there had been no previous experience are often discovered, and proved by positive experience to be true. The other seemingly vulnerable point is this. The argument has the appearance of assuming that the testimony of experience against miracles is undeviating and indubitable, as it would be if the whole question was about the probability of future miracles, none having taken place in the past; whereas the very thing asserted on the other side is that there have been miracles, and that the testimony of experience is not wholly on the negative side. All the evidence alleged in favour of any miracle ought to be reckoned as counter evidence in refutation of the ground on which it is asserted that miracles ought to be disbelieved. The question can only be stated fairly as depending on a balance of evidence: a certain amount of positive evidence in favour of miracles, and a negative presumption from the general course of human experience against them.

In order to support the argument under this double correction, it has to be shown that the negative presumption against a miracle is very much stronger than that against a merely new and surprising fact. This, however, is evidently the case. A new physical discovery even if it consists in the defeating of a well established law of nature, is but the discovery of another law previously unknown. There is nothing in this but what is familiar to our experience: we were aware that we did not know all the laws of nature, and we were aware that one such law is liable to be counteracted by others. The new phenomenon, when brought to light, is found still to depend on law; it is always exactly reproduced when the same circumstances are repeated. Its occurrence, therefore, is within the limits of variation in experience, which experience itself discloses. But a miracle, in the very fact of being a miracle, declares itself to be a supersession not of one natural law by another, but of the law which includes all others, which experience shows to be universal for all phenomena, viz., that they depend on some law; that they are always the same when there are the same phenomenal antecedents, and neither take

place in the absence of their phenomenal causes, nor ever fail to take place when the phenomenal conditions are all present.

It is evident that this argument against belief in miracles had very little to rest upon until a comparatively modern stage in the progress of science. A few generations ago the universal dependence of phenomena on invariable laws was not only not recognized by mankind in general but could not be regarded by the instructed as a scientifically established truth. There were many phenomena which seemed quite irregular in their course, without dependence on any known antecedents: and though, no doubt, a certain regularity in the occurrence of the most familiar phenomena must always have been recognized, yet, even in these, the exceptions which were constantly occurring had not yet, by an investigation and generalization of the circumstances of their occurrence, been reconciled with the general rule. The heavenly bodies were from of old the most conspicuous types of regular and unvarying order: yet even among them comets were a phenomenon apparently originating without any law, and eclipses, one which seemed to take place in violation of law. Accordingly both comets and eclipses long continued to be regarded as of a miraculous nature, intended as signs and omens of human fortunes. It would have been impossible in those days to prove to any one that this supposition was antecedently improbable. It seemed more conformable to appearances than the hypothesis of an unknown law.

Now, however, when, in the progress of science, all phenomena have been shown, by indisputable evidence, to be amenable to law, and even in the cases in which those laws have not yet been exactly ascertained, delay in ascertaining them is fully accounted for by the special difficulties of the subject; the defenders of miracles have adapted their argument to this altered state of things, by maintaining that a miracle need not necessarily be a violation of law. It may, they say, take place in fulfilment of a more recondite law, to us unknown.

If by this it be only meant that the Divine Being, in the exercise of his power of interfering with and suspending his own laws, guides himself by some general principle or rule of action, this, of course, cannot be disproved, and is in itself the most probable supposition. But if the argument means that a miracle may be the fulfilment of a law in the same sense in which the ordinary events of Nature are fulfilments of laws, it seems to indicate an imperfect conception of what is meant by a law, and of what constitutes a miracle.

When we say that an ordinary physical fact always takes place according to some invariable law, we mean that it is connected by uniform sequence or coexistence with some definite set of physical antecedents; that whenever that set is exactly reproduced the same phenomenon will take place, unless counteracted by the similar laws of some other physical antecedents; and that whenever it does take place, it would always be found that its special set of antecedents (or one of its sets if it has more than one) has pre-existed. Now, an event which takes place in this manner, is not a miracle. To make it a miracle it must be produced by a direct volition, without the use of means; or at least, of any means which if simply repeated would produce it. To constitute a miracle a phenomenon must take place without having been preceded by any antecedent phenomenal conditions sufficient again to reproduce it; or a phenomenon for the production of which the antecedent conditions existed, must be arrested or prevented without the intervention of any phenomenal antecedents which would arrest or prevent it in a future case. The test of a miracle is: Were there present in the case such external conditions, such second causes we may call them, that whenever these conditions or causes reappear the event will be reproduced? If there were, it is not a miracle; if there were not, it is a miracle, but it is not according to law: it is an event produced, without, or in spite of law.

It will perhaps be said that a miracle does not necessarily exclude the intervention of second causes. If it were the will of God to raise a thunderstorm by miracle, he might do it by means of winds and clouds. Undoubtedly; but the winds and clouds were either sufficient when produced to excite the thunderstorm without other divine assistance, or they were not. If they were not, the storm is not a fulfilment of law, but a violation of it. If they were sufficient, there is a miracle, but it is not the storm; it is the production of the winds and clouds, or whatever link in the chain of causation it was at which the influence of physical antecedents was dispensed with. If that influence was never dispensed with, but the event called miraculous was produced by natural means, and those again by others, and so on from the beginning of things; if the event is no otherwise the act of God than in having been foreseen and ordained by him as the consequence of the forces put in action at the Creation; then there is no miracle at all, nor anything different from the ordinary working of God's providence.

For another example: a person professing to be divinely commissioned, cures a sick person, by some apparently insignificant external application. Would this application, administered by a person not specially commissioned from above, have effected the cure? If so, there is no miracle; if not, there is a miracle, but there is a violation of law.

It will be said, however, that if these be violations of law, then law is violated every time that any outward effect is produced by a voluntary act of a human being. Human volition is constantly modifying natural phenomena, not by violating their laws, but by using their laws. Why may not divine volition do the same? The power of volitions over phenomena is itself a law, and one of the earliest known and acknowledged laws of nature. It is true, the human will exercises power over objects in general indirectly, through the direct power which it possesses only over the human muscles. God, however, has direct power not merely over one thing, but over all the objects which he has made. There is, therefore, no more a supposition of violation of law in supposing that events are produced, prevented, or modified by God's action, than in the supposition of their being produced, prevented, or modified by man's action. Both are equally in the course of nature, both equally consistent with what we know of the government of all things by law.

Those who thus argue are mostly believers in Free Will, and maintain that every human volition originates a new chain of causation, of which it is itself the commencing link, not connected by invariable sequence with any anterior fact. Even, therefore, if a divine interposition did constitute a breaking-in upon the connected chain of events, by the introduction of a new originating cause without root in the past, this would be no reason for discrediting it, since every human act of volition does precisely the same. If the one is a breach of law, so are the others. In fact, the reign of law does not extend to the origination of volition.

Those who dispute the Free Will theory, and regard volition as no exception to the Universal law of Cause and Effect, may answer, that volitions do not interrupt the chain of causation, but carry it on, the connection of cause and effect being of just the same nature between motive and act as between a combination of physical antecedents and a physical consequent. But this, whether true or not, does not really affect the argument: for the interference of human will with the course of nature is only not an exception to law when we include among laws the relation of motive to volition; and by the same rule interference by the Divine will would not be an exception either; since we cannot but suppose the Deity, in every one of his acts, to be determined by motives.

The alleged analogy therefore holds good: but what it proves is only what I have from the first maintained—that divine interference with nature could be proved if we had the same sort of evidence for it which we have for human interferences. The question of antecedent improbability only arises because divine interposition is not certified by the direct evidence of perception, but is always matter of inference, and more or less of speculative inference. And a little consideration will show that in these circumstances the antecedent presumption against the truth of the inference is extremely strong.

When the human will interferes to produce any physical phenomenon, except the movements of the human body, it does so by the employment of means: and is obliged to employ such means as are by their own physical properties sufficient to bring about the effect. Divine interference, by hypothesis, proceeds in a different manner from this: it produces its effect without means, or with such as are in themselves insufficient. In the first case, all the physical phenomena except the first bodily movement are produced in strict conformity to physical causation; while that first movement is traced by positive observation, to the cause (the volition) which produced it. In the other case, the event is supposed not to have been produced at all through physical causation, while there is no direct evidence to connect it with any volition. The ground on which it is ascribed to a volition is only negative, because there is no other apparent way of accounting for its existence.

But in this merely speculative explanation there is always another hypothesis possible, viz., that the event may have been produced by physical causes, in a manner not apparent. It may either be due to a law of physical nature not yet known, or to the unknown presence of the conditions necessary for producing it according to some known law. Supposing even that the event, supposed to be miraculous, does not reach us through the uncertain medium of human testimony but rests on the direct evidence of our own senses; even then so long as there is no direct evidence of its production by a divine volition, like that we have for the production of bodily movements by human volitions—so long, therefore, as the miraculous character of the event is but an inference from the supposed inadequacy of the laws of physical nature to account for it,—so long will the hypothesis of a natural origin for the phenomenon be entitled to preference over that of a supernatural one. The commonest principles of sound judgment forbid us to suppose for any effect a cause of which we have absolutely no experience, unless all those of which we have experience are ascertained to be absent. Now there are few things of which we have more frequent experience than of physical facts which our knowledge does not enable us to account for, because they depend either on laws which observation, aided by science, has not yet brought to light, or on facts the presence of which in the particular case is unsuspected by us. Accordingly when we hear of a prodigy we always, in these modern times, believe that if it really occurred it was neither the work of God nor of a demon, but the consequence of some unknown natural law or of some hidden fact. Nor is either of these suppositions precluded when, as in the case of a miracle properly so called, the wonderful event seemed to depend upon the will of a human being. It is always possible that there may be at work some undetected law of nature which the wonder-worker may have acquired, consciously or unconsciously, the power of calling into action; or that the wonder may have been wrought (as in the truly extraordinary feats of jugglers) by the employment, unperceived by us, of ordinary laws: which also need not necessarily be a case of voluntary deception; or, lastly, the event may have had no connection with the volition at all, but the coincidence between them may be the effect of craft or accident, the miracle-worker having seemed or affected to produce by his will that which was already about to take place, as if one were to command an eclipse of the sun at the moment when one knew by astronomy that an eclipse was on the point of taking place. In a case of this description, the miracle might be tested by a challenge to repeat it; but it is worthy of remark, that recorded miracles were seldom or never put to this test. No miracle-worker seems ever to have made a *practice* of raising the dead: that and the other most signal of the miraculous operations are reported to have been performed only in one or a few isolated cases, which may have been either cunningly selected cases, or accidental coincidences. There is, in short, nothing to exclude the supposition that every alleged miracle was due to natural causes: and as long as that supposition remains possible, no scientific observer, and no man of ordinary practical judgment, would assume by conjecture a cause which no reason existed for supposing to be real, save the necessity of accounting for something which is sufficiently accounted for without it.

Were we to stop here, the case against miracles might seem to be complete. But on further inspection it will be seen that we cannot, from the above considerations, conclude absolutely that the miraculous theory of the production of a phenomenon ought to be at once rejected. We can conclude only that no extraordinary powers which have ever been alleged to be exercised by any human being over nature, can be evidence of miraculous gifts to any one to whom the existence of a supernatural Being, and his interference in human affairs, is not already a *vera causa*. The existence of God cannot possibly be proved by miracles, for unless a God is already recognized, the apparent miracle can always be accounted for on a more probable hypothesis than that of the interference of a Being of whose very existence it is supposed to be the sole evidence. Thus far Hume's argument is conclusive. But it is far from being equally so when the existence of a Being who created the present order of Nature, and, therefore, may well be thought to have power to modify it, is accepted as a fact, or even as a probability resting on independent evidence. Once admit a God, and the production by his direct volition of an effect which in any case owed its origin to his creative will, is no longer a purely arbitrary hypothesis to account for the fact, but must be reckoned with as a serious possibility. The question then changes its character, and the decision of it must now rest upon what is known or reasonably surmised as to the manner of God's government of the universe: whether this knowledge or surmise makes it the more probable supposition that the event was brought about by the agencies by which his government is ordinarily carried on, or that it is the result of a special and extraordinary interposition of his will in supersession of those ordinary agencies.

In the first place, then, assuming as a fact the existence and providence of God, the whole of our observation of Nature proves to us by incontrovertible evidence that the rule of his government is by means of second causes; that all facts, or at least all physical facts, follow uniformly upon given physical conditions, and never occur but when the appropriate collection of physical conditions is realized. I limit the assertion to physical facts, in order to leave the case of human volition an open question: though indeed I need not do so, for if the human will is free, it has been left free by the Creator, and is not controlled by him either through second causes or directly, so that, not being governed, it is not a specimen of his mode of government. Whatever he does govern, he governs by second causes. This was not obvious in the infancy of science; it was more and more recognized as the processes of nature were more carefully and accurately examined, until there now remains no class of phenomena of which it is not positively known, save some cases which from their obscurity and complication our scientific processes have not yet been able completely to clear up and disentangle, and in which, therefore, the proof that they also are governed by natural laws could not, in the present state of science, be more complete. The evidence, though merely negative, which these circumstances afford that government by second causes is universal, is admitted for all except directly religious purposes to be conclusive. When either a man of science for scientific or a man of the world for practical purposes inquires into an event, he asks himself what is its cause? and not, has it any natural cause? A man would be laughed at who set down as one of the alternative suppositions that there is no other cause for it than the will of God.

Against this weight of negative evidence we have to set such positive evidence as is produced in attestation of exceptions; in other words, the positive evidences of miracles. And I have already admitted that this evidence might conceivably have been such as to make the exception equally certain with the rule. If we had the direct testimony of our senses to a supernatural fact, it might be as completely authenticated and made certain as any natural one. But we never have. The supernatural character of the fact is always, as I have said, matter of inference and speculation: and the mystery always admits the possibility of a solution not supernatural. To those who already believe in supernatural power, the supernatural hypothesis may appear more probable than the natural one; but only if it accords with what we know or reasonably surmise respecting the ways of the supernatural agent. Now all that we know, from the evidence of nature, concerning his ways, is in harmony with the natural theory and repugnant to the supernatural. There is, therefore, a vast preponderance of probability against a miracle, to counterbalance which would require a very extraordinary and indisputable congruity in the supposed miracle and its circumstances with something which we conceive ourselves to know, or to have grounds for believing, with regard to the divine attributes.

This extraordinary congruity is supposed to exist when the purpose of the miracle is extremely beneficial to mankind, as when it serves to accredit some highly important belief. The goodness of God, it is supposed, affords a high degree of antecedent probability that he would make an exception to his general rule of government, for so excellent a purpose. For reasons, however, which have already been entered into, any inference drawn by us from the goodness of God to what he has or has not actually done, is to the last degree precarious. If we reason directly from God's goodness to positive facts, no misery, nor vice nor crime ought to exist in the world. We can see no reason in God's goodness why if he deviated once from the ordinary system of his government in order to do good to man, he should not have done so on a hundred other occasions; nor why, if the benefit aimed at by some given deviation, such as the revelation of Christianity, was transcendent and unique, that precious gift should only have been vouchsafed after the lapse of many ages; or why, when it was at last given, the evidence of it should have been left open to so much doubt and difficulty. Let it be remembered also that the goodness of God affords no presumption in favour of a deviation from his general system of government unless the good purpose could not have been attained without deviation. If God intended that mankind should receive Christianity or any other gift, it would have agreed better with all that we know of his government to have made provision in the scheme of creation for its arising at the appointed time by natural development; which, let it be added, all the knowledge we now possess concerning the history of the human mind, tends to the conclusion that it actually did.

To all these considerations ought to be added the extremely imperfect nature of the testimony itself which we possess for the miracles, real or supposed, which accompanied the foundation of Christianity and of every other revealed religion. Take it at the best, it is the uncross-examined testimony of extremely ignorant people, credulous as such usually are, honourably credulous when the excellence of the doctrine or just reverence for the teacher makes them eager to believe; unaccustomed to draw the line between the perceptions of sense, and what is superinduced upon them by the suggestions of a lively imagination; unversed in the difficult art of deciding between appearance and reality, and between the natural and the supernatural; in times, moreover, when no one thought it worth while to contradict any alleged miracle, because it was the belief of the age that miracles in themselves proved nothing, since they could be worked by a lying spirit as well as by the spirit of God. Such were the witnesses; and even of them we do not possess the direct testimony; the documents, of date long subsequent, even on the orthodox theory, which contain the only history of these events, very often do not even name the supposed eye-witnesses. They put down (it is but just to admit), the best and least absurd of the wonderful stories such multitudes of which were current among the early Christians; but when they do, exceptionally, name any of the persons who were the subjects or spectators of the miracle, they doubtless draw from tradition, and mention those names with which the story was in the popular mind, (perhaps accidentally) connected: for whoever has observed the way in which even now a story grows up from some small foundation, taking on additional details at every step, knows well how from being at first anonymous it gets names attached to it; the name of some one by whom perhaps the story has been told, being brought into the story itself first as a witness, and still later as a party concerned.

It is also noticeable and is a very important consideration, that stories of miracles only grow up among the ignorant and are adopted, if ever, by the educated when they have already become the belief of multitudes. Those which are believed by Protestants all originate in ages and nations in which there was hardly any canon of probability, and miracles were thought to be among the commonest of all phenomena. The Catholic Church, indeed, holds as an article of faith that miracles have never ceased, and new ones continue to be now and then brought forth and believed, even in the present incredulous age—yet if in an incredulous generation certainly not among the incredulous portion of it, but always among people who, in addition to the most childish ignorance, have grown up (as all do who are educated by the Catholic clergy) trained in the persuasion that it is a duty to believe and a sin to doubt; that it is dangerous to be sceptical about anything which is tendered for belief in the name of the true religion; and that nothing is so contrary to piety as incredulity. But these miracles which no one but a Roman Catholic, and by no means every Roman Catholic believes, rest frequently upon an amount of testimony greatly surpassing that which we possess for any of the early miracles; and superior especially in one of the most essential points, that in many cases the alleged eye-witnesses are known, and we have their story at first hand.

Thus, then, stands the balance of evidence in respect to the reality of miracles, assuming the existence and government of God to be proved by other evidence. On the one side, the great negative presumption arising from the whole of what the course of nature discloses to us of the divine government, as carried on through second causes and by invariable sequences of physical effects upon constant antecedents. On the other side, a few exceptional instances, attested by evidence not of a character to warrant belief in any facts in the smallest degree unusual or improbable; the eye-witnesses in most cases unknown, in none competent by character or education to scrutinize the real nature of the appearances which they may have seen,* and

*St. Paul, the only known exception to the ignorance and want of education of the first generation of Christians, attests no miracle but that of his own conversion, which of all the miracles of the New Testament is the one which admits of the easiest explanation from natural causes. [See Acts, 9:1–19.]

moved moreover by a union of the strongest motives which can inspire human beings to persuade, first themselves, and then others, that what they had seen was a miracle. The facts, too, even if faithfully reported, are never incompatible with the supposition that they were either mere coincidences, or were produced by natural means; even when no specific conjecture can be made as to those means, which in general it can. The conclusion I draw is that miracles have no claim whatever to the character of historical facts and are wholly invalid as evidences of any revelation.

What can be said with truth on the side of miracles amounts only to this: Considering that the order of nature affords some evidence of the reality of a Creator, and of his bearing good will to his creatures though not of its being the sole prompter of his conduct towards them: considering, again, that all the evidence of his existence is evidence also that he is not all-powerful, and considering that in our ignorance of the limits of his power we cannot positively decide that he was able to provide for us by the original plan of Creation all the good which it entered into his intentions to bestow upon us, or even to bestow any part of it at any earlier period than that at which we actually received it—considering these things, when we consider further that a gift, extremely precious, came to us which though facilitated was not apparently necessitated by what had gone before, but was due, as far as appearances go, to the peculiar mental and moral endowments of one man, and that man openly proclaimed that it did not come from himself but from God through him, then we are entitled to say that there is nothing so inherently impossible or absolutely incredible in this supposition as to preclude any one from hoping that it may perhaps be true. I say from hoping; I go no further; for I cannot attach any evidentiary value to the testimony even of Christ on such a subject, since he is never said to have declared any evidence of his mission (unless his own interpretations of the Prophecies be so considered) except internal conviction; and everybody knows that in prescientific times men always supposed that any unusual faculties which came to them they knew not how, were an inspiration from God; the best men always being the readiest to ascribe any honourable peculiarity in themselves to that higher source, rather than to their own merits.

PART V

FROM THE RESULT of the preceding examination of the evidences of Theism, and (Theism being presupposed) of the evidences of any Revelation, it follows that the rational attitude of a thinking mind towards the supernatural, whether in natural or in revealed religion, is that of scepticism as distinguished from belief on the one hand, and from atheism on the other: including, in the present case, under atheism, the negative as well as the positive form of disbelief in a God, viz., not only the dogmatic denial of his existence, but the denial that there is any evidence on either side, which for most practical purposes amounts to the same thing as if the existence of a God had been disproved. If we are right in the conclusions to which we have been led by the preceding inquiry there is evidence, but insufficient for proof, and amounting only to one of the lower degrees of probability. The indication given by such evidence as there is, points to the creation, not indeed of the universe, but of the present order of it by an Intelligent Mind, whose power over the materials was not absolute, whose love for his creatures was not his sole actuating inducement, but who nevertheless desired their good. The notion of a providential government by an omnipotent Being for the good of his creatures must be entirely dismissed. Even of the continued existence of the Creator we have no other guarantee than that he cannot be subject to the law of death which affects terrestrial beings, since the conditions that produce this liability wherever it is known to exist are of his creating. That this Being, not being omnipotent, may have produced a machinery falling short of his intentions, and which may require the occasional interposition of the Maker's hand, is a supposition not in itself absurd nor impossible, though in none of the cases in which such interposition is believed to have occurred is the evidence such as could possibly prove it; it remains a simple possibility, which those may dwell on to whom it yields comfort to suppose that blessings which ordinary human power is inadequate to attain, may come not from extraordinary human power, but from the bounty of an intelligence beyond the human, and which continuously cares for man. The possibility of a life after death rests on the same footing—of a boon which this powerful Being who wishes well to man, may have the power to grant, and which if the message alleged to have been sent by him was really sent, he has actually promised.

The whole domain of the supernatural is thus removed from the region of Belief into that of simple Hope; and in that, for anything we can see, it is likely always to remain; for we can hardly anticipate either that any positive evidence will be acquired of the direct agency of Divine Benevolence in human destiny, or that any reason will be discovered for considering the realization of human hopes on that subject as beyond the pale of possibility.

It is now to be considered whether the indulgence of hope, in a region of imagination merely, in which there is no prospect that any probable grounds of expectation will ever be obtained, is irrational, and ought to be discouraged as a departure from the rational principle of regulating our feelings as well as opinions strictly by evidence.

This is a point which different thinkers are likely, for a long time at least, to decide differently, according to their individual temperament. The principles which ought to govern the cultivation and the regulation of the imagination—with a view on the one hand of preventing it from disturbing the rectitude of the intellect and the right direction of the actions and will, and on the other hand of employing it as a power for increasing the happiness of life and giving elevation to the character—are a subject which has never yet engaged the serious consideration of philosophers, though some opinion on it is implied in almost all modes of thinking on human character and education. And, I expect, that this will hereafter be regarded as a very important branch of study for practical purposes, and the more, in proportion as the weakening of positive beliefs respecting states of existence superior to the human, leaves the imagination of higher things less provided with material from the domain of supposed reality. To me it seems that human life, small and confined as it is, and as, considered merely in the present, it is likely to remain even when the progress of material and moral improvement may have freed it from the greater part of its present calamities, stands greatly in need of any wider range and greater height of aspiration for itself and its destination, which the exercise of imagination can yield to it without running counter to the evidence of fact; and that it is a part of wisdom to make the most of any, even small, probabilities on this subject, which furnish imagination with any footing to support itself upon. And I am satisfied that the cultivation of such a tendency in the imagination, provided it goes on *pari passu* with the cultivation of severe reason, has no necessary tendency to pervert the judgment; but that it is possible to form a perfectly sober estimate of the evidences on both sides of a question and yet to let the imagination dwell by preference on those possibilities, which are at once the most comforting and the most improving, without in the least degree overrating the solidity of the grounds for expecting that these rather than any others will be the possibilities actually realized.

Though this is not in the number of the practical maxims handed down by tradition and recognized as rules for the conduct of life, a great part of the happiness of life depends upon the tacit observance of it. What, for instance, is the meaning of that which is always accounted one of the chief blessings of life, a cheerful disposition? What but the tendency, either from constitution or habit, to dwell chiefly on the brighter side both of the present and of the future? If every aspect, whether agreeable or odious of every thing, ought to occupy exactly the same place in our imagination which it fills in fact, and therefore ought to fill in our deliberate reason, what we call a cheerful disposition would be but one of the forms of folly, on a par except in agreeableness with the opposite disposition in which the gloomy and painful view of all things is habitually predominant. But it is not found in practice that those who take life cheerfully are less alive to rational prospects of evil or danger and more careless of making due provision against them, than other people. The tendency is rather the other way, for a hopeful disposition gives a spur to the faculties and keeps all the active energies in good working order. When imagination and reason receive each its appropriate culture they do not succeed in usurping each other's prerogatives. It is not necessary for keeping up our conviction that we must die, that we should be always brooding over death. It is far better that we should think no further about what we cannot possibly avert, than is required for observing the rules of prudence in regard to our own life and that of others, and fulfilling whatever duties devolve upon us in contemplation of the inevitable event. The way to secure this is not to think perpetually of death, but to think perpetually of our duties, and of the rule of life. The true rule of practical wisdom is not that of making all the aspects of things equally prominent in our habitual contemplations, but of giving the greatest prominence to those of their aspects which depend on, or can be modified by, our own conduct. In things which do not depend on us, it is not solely for the sake of a more enjoyable life that the habit is desirable of looking at things and at mankind by preference on their pleasant side; it is also in order that we may be able to love them better and work with more heart for their improvement. To what purpose, indeed, should we feed our imagination with the unlovely aspect of persons and things? All *unnecessary* dwelling upon the evils of life is at best a useless expenditure of nervous force: and when I say unnecessary I mean all that is not necessary either in the sense of being unavoidable, or in that of being needed for the performance of our duties and for preventing our sense of the reality of those evils from becoming speculative and dim. But if it is often waste of strength to dwell on the evils of life, it is worse than waste to dwell habitually on its meannesses and basenesses. It is necessary to be aware of them; but to live in their contemplation makes it scarcely possible to keep up in oneself a high tone of mind. The imagination and feelings become tuned to a lower pitch; degrading instead of elevating associations become connected with the daily objects and incidents of life, and give their colour to the thoughts, just as associations of sensuality do in those who indulge freely in that sort of contemplations. Men have often felt what it is to have had their imaginations corrupted by one class of ideas, and I think they must have felt with the same kind of pain how the poetry is taken out of the things fullest of it, by mean associations, as when a beautiful air that had been associated with highly poetical words is heard sung with trivial and vulgar ones. All these things are said in mere illustration of the principle that in the regulation of the imagination literal truth of facts is not the only thing to be considered. Truth is the province of reason, and it is by the cultivation of the rational faculty that provision is made for its being known always, and thought of as often as is required by duty and the circumstances of human life. But when the reason is strongly cultivated, the imagination may safely follow its own end, and do its best to make life pleasant and lovely inside the castle, in reliance on the fortifications raised and maintained by Reason round the outward bounds.

On these principles it appears to me that the indulgence of hope with regard to the government of the universe and the destiny of man after death, while we recognize as a clear truth that we have no ground for more than a hope, is legitimate and philosophically defensible. The beneficial effect of such a hope is far from trifling. It makes life and human nature a far greater thing to the feelings, and gives greater strength as well as greater solemnity to all the sentiments which are awakened in us by our fellow-creatures and by mankind at large. It allays the sense of that irony of Nature which is so painfully felt when we see the exertions and sacrifices of a life culminating in the formation of a wise and noble mind, only to disappear from the world when the time has just arrived at which the world seems about to begin reaping the benefit of it. The truth that life is short and art is long[*] is from of old one of the most discouraging parts of our condition; this hope admits the possibility that the art employed in improving and beautifying the soul itself may avail for good in some other life, even when seemingly useless for this. But the benefit consists less in the presence of any specific hope than in the enlargement of the general scale of the feelings; the loftier aspirations being no longer in the same degree checked and kept down by a sense of the insignificance of human life—by the disastrous feeling of "not worth while." The gain obtained in the increased inducement to cultivate the improvement of character up to the end of life, is obvious without being specified.

There is another and a most important exercise of imagination which, in the past and present, has been kept up principally by means of religious belief and which is infinitely precious to mankind, so much so that human excellence greatly depends upon the sufficiency of the provision made for it. This

[*Hippocrates, *Aphorisms*, i, 1.]

consists of the familiarity of the imagination with the conception of a morally perfect Being, and the habit of taking the approbation of such a Being as the *norma* or standard to which to refer and by which to regulate our own characters and lives. This idealization of our standard of excellence in a Person is quite possible, even when that Person is conceived as merely imaginary. But religion, since the birth of Christianity, has inculcated the belief that our highest conceptions of combined wisdom and goodness exist in the concrete in a living Being who has his eyes on us and cares for our good. Through the darkest and most corrupt periods Christianity has raised this torch on high—has kept this object of veneration and imitation before the eyes of man. True, the image of perfection has been a most imperfect, and, in many respects a perverting and corrupting one, not only from the low moral ideas of the times, but from the mass of moral contradictions which the deluded worshipper was compelled to swallow by the supposed necessity of complimenting the Good Principle with the possession of infinite power. But it is one of the most universal as well as of the most surprising characteristics of human nature, and one of the most speaking proofs of the low stage to which the reason of mankind at large has ever yet advanced, that they are capable of overlooking any amount of either moral or intellectual contradictions and receiving into their minds propositions utterly inconsistent with one another, not only without being shocked by the contradiction, but without preventing both the contradictory beliefs from producing a part at least of their natural consequences in the mind. Pious men and women have gone on ascribing to God particular acts and a general course of will and conduct incompatible with even the most ordinary and limited conception of moral goodness, and have had their own ideas of morality, in many important particulars, totally warped and distorted, and notwithstanding this have continued to conceive their God as clothed with all the attributes of the highest ideal goodness which their state of mind enabled them to conceive, and have had their aspirations towards goodness stimulated and encouraged by that conception. And, it cannot be questioned that the undoubting belief of the real existence of a Being who realizes our own best ideas of perfection, and of our being in the hands of that Being as the ruler of the universe, gives an increase of force to these feelings beyond what they can receive from reference to a merely ideal conception.

This particular advantage it is not possible for those to enjoy, who take a rational view of the nature and amount of the evidence for the existence and attributes of the Creator. On the other hand, they are not encumbered with the moral contradictions which beset every form of religion which aims at justifying in a moral point of view the whole government of the world. They are, therefore, enabled to form a far truer and more consistent conception of Ideal Goodness, than is possible to any one who thinks it necessary to find ideal goodness in an omnipotent ruler of the world. The power of the Creator once recognized as limited, there is nothing to disprove the supposition that his goodness is complete and that the ideally perfect character in whose likeness we should wish to form ourselves and to whose supposed approbation we refer our actions, may have a real existence in a Being to whom we owe all such good as we enjoy.

Above all, the most valuable part of the effect on the character which Christianity has produced by holding up in a Divine Person a standard of excellence and a model for imitation, is available even to the absolute unbeliever and can never more be lost to humanity. For it is Christ, rather than God, whom Christianity has held up to believers as the pattern of perfection for humanity. It is the God incarnate, more than the God of the Jews or of Nature, who being idealized has taken so great and salutary a hold on the modern mind. And whatever else may be taken away from us by rational criticism, Christ is still left; a unique figure, not more unlike all his precursors than all his followers, even those who had the direct benefit of his personal teaching. It is of no use to say that Christ as exhibited in the Gospels is not historical and that we know not how much of what is admirable has been superadded by the tradition of his followers. The tradition of followers suffices to insert any number of marvels, and may have inserted all the miracles which he is reputed to have wrought. But who among his disciples or among their proselytes was capable of inventing the sayings ascribed to Jesus or of imagining the life and character revealed in the Gospels? Certainly not the fishermen of Galilee; as certainly not St. Paul, whose character and idiosyncrasies were of a totally different sort; still less the early Christian writers in whom nothing is more evident than that the good which was in them was all derived, as they always professed that it was derived, from the higher source. What *could* be added and interpolated by a disciple we may see in the mystical parts of the Gospel of St. John, matter imported from Philo and the Alexandrian Platonists and put into the mouth of the Saviour in long speeches about himself such as the other Gospels contain not the slightest vestige of, though pretended to have been delivered on occasions of the deepest interest and when his principal followers were all present; most prominently at the last supper. The East was full of men who could have stolen any quantity of this poor stuff, as the multitudinous Oriental sects of Gnostics afterwards did. But about the life and sayings of Jesus there is a stamp of personal originality combined with profundity of insight, which if we abandon the idle expectation of finding scientific precision where something very different was aimed at, must place the Prophet of Nazareth, even in the estimation of those who have no belief in his inspiration, in the very first rank of the men of sublime genius of whom our species can boast. When this pre-eminent genius is combined with the qualities of probably the greatest moral reformer, and martyr to that mission, who ever existed upon earth, religion cannot be said to have made a bad choice in pitching on this man as the ideal representative and guide of humanity; nor, even now, would it be easy, even for an unbeliever, to find a better translation of the rule of virtue from the abstract into the concrete, than to endeavour so to live that Christ would approve our life. When to this we add that, to the conception of the rational sceptic, it remains a possibility that Christ actually was what he supposed himself to be—not God, for he never made the smallest pretension to that character and would probably have thought such a pretension as blasphemous as it seemed to the men who condemned him—but a man charged with a special, express and unique commission from God to lead mankind to truth and virtue; we may well conclude that the influences of religion on the character which will remain after rational criticism has done its utmost against the evidences of religion, are well worth preserving, and that what they lack in direct strength as compared with those of a firmer belief, is more than compensated by the greater truth and rectitude of the morality they sanction.

Impressions such as these, though not in themselves amounting to what can properly be called a religion, seem to me excellently fitted to aid and fortify that real, though purely human religion, which sometimes calls itself the Religion of Humanity and sometimes that of Duty. To the other inducements for cultivating a religious devotion to the welfare of our fellow-creatures as an obligatory limit to every selfish aim, and an end for the direct promotion of which no sacrifice can be too great, it superadds the feeling that in making this the rule of our life, we may be co-operating with the unseen Being to whom wc owc all that is enjoyable in life. One elevated feeling this form of religious idea admits of, which is not open to those who believe in the omnipotence of the good principle in the universe, the feeling of helping God—of requiting the good he has given by a voluntary co-operation which he, not being omnipotent, really needs, and by which a somewhat nearer approach may be made to the fulfilment of his purposes. The conditions of human existence are highly favourable to the growth of such a feeling inasmuch as a battle is constantly going on, in which the humblest human creature is not incapable of taking some part, between the powers of good and those of evil, and in which every even the smallest help to the right side has its value in promoting the very slow and often almost insensible progress by which good is gradually gaining ground from evil, yet gaining it so visibly at considerable intervals as to promise the very distant but not uncertain final victory of Good. To do something during life, on even the humblest scale if nothing more is within reach, towards bringing this consummation ever so little nearer, is the most animating and invigorating thought which can inspire a human creature; and that it is destined, with or without supernatural sanctions, to be the religion of the Future I cannot entertain a doubt. But it appears to me that supernatural hopes, in the degree and kind in which what I have called rational scepticism does not refuse to sanction them, may still contribute not a little to give to this religion its due ascendancy over the human mind.

APPENDICES

Appendix A

Preface to *Dissertations and Discussions* (1859)

Dissertations and Discussions, I, iii–vi. For a discussion of this Preface (unaltered in the 2nd ed. of *D&D*) see the Textual Introduction, cxviff. above. JSM's views on republication of his essays is discussed in the Textual Introduction to *Essays on Economics and Society*, in *Collected Works*, IV, xliv–xlv.

THE REPUBLICATION in a more durable form, of papers originally contributed to periodicals, has grown into so common a practice as scarcely to need an apology; and I follow this practice the more willingly, as I hold it to be decidedly a beneficial one. It would be well if all frequent writers in periodicals looked forward, as far as the case admitted, to this reappearance of their productions. The prospect might be some guarantee against the crudity in the formation of opinions, and carelessness in their expression, which are the besetting sins of writings put forth under the screen of anonymousness, to be read only during the next few weeks or months, if so long, and the defects of which it is seldom probable that any one will think it worth while to expose.

The following papers, selected from a much greater number, include all of the writer's miscellaneous productions which he considers it in any way desirable to preserve. The remainder were either of too little value at any time, or what value they might have was too exclusively temporary, or the thoughts they contained were inextricably mixed up with comments, now totally uninteresting, on passing events, or on some book not generally known; or lastly, any utility they may have possessed has since been superseded by other and more mature writings of the author.

Every one whose mind is progressive, or even whose opinions keep up with the changing facts that surround him, must necessarily, in looking back to his own writings during a series of years, find many things which, if they were to be written again, he would write differently, and some, even, which he has altogether ceased to think true. From these last I have endeavoured to clear the present pages. Beyond this, I have not attempted to render papers written at so many different, and some of them at such distant, times, a faithful representation of my present state of opinion and feeling. I leave them in all their imperfection, as memorials of the states of mind in which they were written, in the hope that they may possibly be useful to such readers as are in a corresponding stage of their own mental progress. Where what I had written appears a fair statement of part of the truth, but defective inasmuch as there exists another part respecting which nothing, or too little, is said, I leave the deficiency to be supplied by the reader's own thoughts; the rather, as he will, in many cases, find the balance restored in some other part of this collection. Thus, the review of Mr. Sedgwick's *Discourse*,[*] taken by itself, might give an impression of more complete adhesion to the philosophy of Locke, Bentham, and the eighteenth century, than is really the case, and of an inadequate sense of its deficiencies; but that notion will be rectified by the subsequent essays on Bentham and on Coleridge.[†] These, again, if they stood alone, would give just as much too strong an impression of the writer's sympathy with the reaction of the nineteenth century against the eighteenth: but this exaggeration will be corrected by the more recent defence of the "greatest happiness" ethics against Dr. Whewell.[‡]

Only a small number of these papers are controversial, and in but two am I aware of anything like asperity of tone. In both these cases some degree of it was justifiable, as I was defending maligned doctrines or individuals, against unmerited onslaughts by persons who, on the evidence afforded by themselves, were in no respect entitled to sit in judgment on them: and the same misrepresentations have been and still are so incessantly reiterated by a crowd of writers, that emphatic protests against them are as needful now as when the papers in question were first written. My adversaries, too, were men not themselves remarkable for mild treatment of opponents, and quite capable of holding their own in any form of reviewing or pamphleteering polemics. I believe that I have in no case fought with other than fair weapons, and any strong expressions which I have used were extorted from me by my subject, not prompted by the smallest feeling of personal ill-will towards my antagonists. In the revision, I have endeavoured to retain only as much of this strength of expression, as could not be foregone without weakening the force of the protest.

[*See pp. 31–74 above.]
[†See pp. 75–115 and 117–63 above.]
[‡See pp. 165–201 above.]

Appendix B

Obituary of Bentham (1832)

Examiner, 10 June, 1832, 370–2. This, JSM's first published commentary on Bentham, is described in his bibliography as "An obituary notice of Jeremy Bentham in the *Examiner* of 10th June 1832" (MacMinn, 21). The passage reprinted here is the central part of the obituary; the full text will be found in the volume of this edition given to newspaper writings. While the tone is more eulogistic, many of the remarks are paralleled in the more critical account in the Appendix to Bulwer (3–18 above) and in the passage from Bulwer's text given below in Appendix C. See also my "John Stuart Mill and Jeremy Bentham," 259.

Let it be remembered what was the state of jurisprudence and legislation, and of the philosophy of jurisprudence and legislation, when he [Bentham] began his career. A labyrinth without a clue—a jungle, through which no path had ever been cut. All systems of law then established, but most of all that in which he himself was nurtured, were masses of deformity, in the construction of which reason in any shape whatever had had little to do, a comprehensive consideration of ends and means nothing at all: their foundation the rude contrivances of a barbarous age, even more deeply barbarous in this than in aught else; the superstructure an infinite series of patches, some larger, some smaller, stuck on in succession wherever a hole appeared, and plastered one over another until the monstrous mass exceeded all measurable bulk, and went beyond the reach of the strongest understanding and the finest memory. Such was the practice of law: was its theory in any better state? And how could it be so? for of what did that theory consist, but either of purely technical principles, got at by abstraction from these established systems, (or rather, constructed, generally in utter defiance of logic, with the sole view of giving something like coherence and consistency in appearance to provisions which in reality were utterly heterogeneous); or of vague cloudy generalities arbitrarily assumed *à priori*, and called laws of nature, or principles of natural law.

Such was existing jurisprudence; and that it should be such, was less surprising than the superstition by which, being such, it was protected. The English people had contrived to persuade themselves, and had to a great degree persuaded the rest of the world, that the English law, as it was when

Mr. Bentham found it, was the perfection of reason. That it was otherwise, was the only political heresy, which no one had been found hardy enough to avow; even the English constitution you might (if you did it very gently) speak ill of,—but not the English law: Whig, Tory, and Democrat joined in one chorus of clamorous admiration, whenever the law or the courts of justice were the subject of discourse: and to doubt the merits of either appeared a greater stretch of absurdity than to question the doctrine of gravitation.

This superstition was at its height, when Mr. Bentham betook himself to the study of English law, with no other object than the ordinary one of gaining his living by practising a liberal profession. But he soon found that it would not do for him, and that he could have no dealing or concern with it in an honest way, except to destroy it. And there is a deep interest now, at the close of his life, in looking back to his very first publication, the *Fragment on Government*, which appeared considerably more than half a century ago, and which exhibits, at that remote period, a no less strong and steady conviction than appears in his very latest production, that the worship of the English law was a degrading idolatry—that instead of being the perfection of reason, it was a disgrace to the human understanding—and that a task worthy of him, or any other wise and brave man, to devote a life to, was that of utterly eradicating it and sweeping it away. This accordingly became the task of his own existence: glory to him! for he has successfully accomplished it. The monster has received from him its death wound. After losing many a limb, it still drags on, and will drag on for a few years more, a feeble and exanimate existence; but it never will recover. It is going down rapidly to the grave.

Mr. Bentham has fought this battle for now almost sixty years; the greater part of that time without assistance from any human being, except latterly what M. Dumont gave him in putting his ideas into French; and for a long time almost without making one human being a convert to his opinions. He exhausted every mode of attack; he assailed the enemy with every weapon, and at all points; now he fell upon the generalities, now upon the details; now he combatted evil by stripping it naked, and showing that it was evil; and now by contrasting it with good. At length his energy and perseverance triumphed. Some of the most potent leaders of the public became convinced; and they, in their turn, convinced or persuaded others: until at last the English law, as a systematic whole, is given up by every body, and the question, with all thinking minds even among lawyers, is no longer about keeping it as it is, but only whether, in rebuilding, there be a possibility of using any of the old materials.*

*We mean the old technical terms and distinctions; for the substantive provisions of that or any other system of law, must of course consist, in the far greater proportion, of things useful or unobjectionable.

Mr. Bentham was the original mover in this mighty change. His hand gave the impulse which set all the others at work. To him the debt is due, as much as any other great work has ever been owing to the man who first guided other men to the accomplishment of it. The man who has achieved this, can afford to die. He has done enough to render his name for ever illustrious.

But Mr. Bentham has been much more than merely a destroyer. Like all who discredit erroneous systems by arguments drawn from *principles*, and not from mere *results*, he could not fail, even while destroying the old edifice, to lay a solid foundation for the new. Indeed he considered it a positive duty never to assail what is established, without having a clear view of what ought to be substituted. It is to the intrinsic value of his speculations on the philosophy of law in general, that he owes the greater part of his existing reputation; for by these alone is he known to his continental readers, who are far the most numerous, and by whom, in general, he is far more justly appreciated than in England. There are some most important branches of the science of law, which were in a more wretched state than almost any of the others when he took them in hand, and which he has so exhausted, that he seems to have left nothing to be sought by future enquirers; we mean the departments of Procedure, Evidence, and the Judicial Establishment. He has done almost all that remained to perfect the theory of punishment. It is with regard to (what is the foundation of all) the civil code, that he has done least, and left most to be done. Yet even here his services have been invaluable, by making far clearer and more familiar than they were before, both the ultimate and the immediate ends of civil law; the essential characteristics of a good law; the expediency of codification, that is, of law *written* and *systematic*; by exposing the viciousness of the existing language of jurisprudence, guarding the student against the fallacies which lurk in it, and accustoming him to demand a more precise and logically-constructed nomenclature.

Mr. Bentham's exertions have not been limited to the field of jurisprudence, or even to that of general politics, in which he ranks as the first name among the philosophic radicals. He has extended his speculations to morals, though never (at least in his published works) in any great detail; and on this, as on every other subject which he touched, he cannot be read without great benefit.

Some of his admirers have claimed for him the title of founder of the science of morals, as well as of the science of legislation; on the score of his having been the first person who established the principle of general utility, as the philosophic foundation of morality and law. But Mr. Bentham's originality does not stand in need of any such exaggerations. The doctrine of utility, as the foundation of virtue, he himself professes to have derived from Hume: he applied it more consistently and in greater detail, than his predecessors; but the idea itself is as old as the earliest Greek philosophers, and has divided the philosophic world, in every age of philosophy, since their time. Mr. Bentham's real merit, in respect to the foundation of morals, consists in his having cleared it more thoroughly than any of his predecessors, from the rubbish of pretended natural law, natural justice, and the like, by which men were wont to consecrate as a rule of morality, whatever they felt inclined to approve of without knowing why.

The most prominent moral qualities which appear in Mr. Bentham's writings, are love of justice, and hatred of imposture: his most remarkable intellectual endowments, a penetrating deep-sighted acuteness, precision in the use of scientific language, and sagacity and inventiveness in matters of detail. There have been few minds so perfectly original. He has often, we think, been surpassed in powers of metaphysical analysis, as well as in comprehensiveness and many-sidedness of mind. He frequently contemplates a subject only from one or a few of its aspects; though he very often sees further into it, from the one side on which he looks at it, than was seen before even by those who had gone all round it. There is something very striking, occasionally, in the minute elaborateness with which he works out, into its smallest details, one half-view of a question, contrasted with his entire neglect of the remaining half-view, though equally indispensable to a correct judgment of the whole. To this occasional one-sidedness, he failed to apply the natural cure; for, from the time when he embarked in original speculation, he occupied himself very little in studying the ideas of others. This, in almost any other than himself, would have been a fault; in him, we shall only say, that, but for it, he would have been a greater man.

Mr. Bentham's style has been much criticised; and undoubtedly, in his latter writings, the complicated structure of his sentences renders it impossible, without some familiarity, to read them with rapidity and ease. But his earlier, among which are some of his most valuable productions, are not only free from this defect, but may even, in point of ease and elegance, be ranked among the best English compositions. Felicity of expression abounds even in those of his works which are generally unreadable; and volumes might be filled with passages selected from his later as well as his earlier publications, which, for wit and eloquence, have seldom been surpassed.

Appendix C

Comment on Bentham in Bulwer's *England and the English* (1833)

EDWARD LYTTON BULWER (later Bulwer-Lytton, later 1st Baron Lytton), *England and the English* (London: Bentley, 1833), II, 163–70. JSM comments in his *Autobiography* (139) that, in addition to the Appendix on Bentham (the first essay printed above), Bulwer also "incorporated" in his text "a small part" of JSM's critique of Bentham. (See Textual Introduction, cxvi–cxvii above). It cannot be determined which part of the following passage is JSM's, but the images of Bentham as destroyer and reconstructor, the description of Bentham as the great questioner (cf. 78), the reference to an age of transition, and the suggestion of Bentham's seminality, are all typical of his attitude at the time; and both in wording and idea the fourth paragraph closely approximates comments on Bentham known to be his.

[In] legislative and moral philosophy, Bentham must assuredly be considered the most celebrated and influential teacher of the age—a master, indeed, whom few have acknowledged, but from whom thousands have, mediately and unconsciously, imbibed their opinions.

The same causes which gave so great a fertility to the school of the Economists, had their effect upon the philosophy of Bentham; they drew his genius mainly towards examinations of men rather than of man—of the defects of Law, and of the hypocrisies and fallacies of our Social System; they contributed to the material form and genus of his code, and to those notions of Utility which he considered his own invention, but which had been incorporated with half the systems that had risen in Europe since the sensualism of Condillac had been grafted upon the reflection of Locke. But causes far more latent, and perhaps more powerful, contributed also to form the mind and philosophy of Bentham. He had preceded the great French Revolution—the materials of his thoughts had been compounded from the same foundations of opinion as those on which the more enlightened advocates of the Revolution would have built up that edifice which was to defy a second deluge, and which is but a record of the confusion of the workmen. With the philosophy of the eighteenth century, which first adopted what the French reasoners term the Principle of Humanity—(that is, the principle of philanthropy—a paramount regard for multitudes rather than for sectarian interests,)—with this philosophy, I say, the whole mind of Bentham was imbued and saturate. He had no mercy, no toleration for the knots and companies of men whom he considered interrupters or monopolists of the power of the many—to his mind they were invariably actuated by base and designing motives, and such motives, according to his philosophy, they were even *compelled* to entertain. His intellect was as the aqueduct which bore aloft, and over the wastes and wrecks below, the stream of the philosophy of one century to the generations of the other. His code of morals, original in its results, is in many parts (unconsciously to himself) an eclecticism of nearly all the best parts of the various theories of a century. "The system of Condillac required its *'moral'* code, and Helvetius supplied it." The moral code of Helvetius required its legislative, and in Bentham it obtained it. I consider, then, that two series of causes conspired to produce Bentham—the one national, the other belonging to all Europe; the same causes on the one hand which produced with us the Economists—the same causes on the other hand which produced in France, Helvetius and Diderot, Volney, Condorcet, and Voltaire. He combined what had not been yet done, the spirit of the Philanthropic with that of the Practical. He did not declaim about abuses; he went at once to their root: he did not idly penetrate the sophistries of Corruption; he smote Corruption herself. He was the very Theseus of legislative reform,—he not only pierced the labyrinth—he destroyed the monster.

As he drew his vigour from the stream of Change, all his writings tended to their original source. He collected from the Past the scattered remnants of a defeated innovation, and led them on against the Future. Every age may be called an age of transition—the passing on, as it were, from one state to another never ceases; but in our age the transition is *visible*, and Bentham's philosophy is the philosophy of a visible transition. Much has already happened, much is already happening every instant, in his country—throughout Europe—throughout the world, which might not have occurred if Bentham had not been; yet of all his works, none have been read by great numbers; and most of them, from their difficulties of style and subject, have little chance of ever being generally popular. He acted upon the destinies of his race by influencing the thoughts of a minute fraction of the few who think—from them the broad principles travelled onward—became known—(their source unknown)—became familiar and successful. I have said that we live in an age of visible transition—an age of disquietude and doubt—of the removal of time-worn landmarks, and the breaking up of the hereditary elements of society—old opinions, feelings—ancestral customs and institutions are crumbling away, and both the spiritual and temporal worlds are darkened by the shadow of change. The commencement of one of these epochs—periodical in the history of mankind—is hailed by the sanguine as the coming of a new Millennium—a great inconoclastic reformation, by which all false gods shall be overthrown. To me such epochs appear but as the dark passages in the appointed progress of mankind—the times of greatest unhappiness to our species—passages into which we have no reason to rejoice at our entrance, save from the hope of being sooner landed on the opposite side. Uncertainty is the greatest of all our evils. And I know of no happiness where there is not a firm unwavering belief in its duration.

The age then is one of *destruction!* disguise it as we will, it must be so characterized; miserable would be our lot were it not also an age of preparation for reconstructing. What has been the influence of Bentham upon his age?—it has been twofold—he has helped to destroy and also to rebuild. No one has done so much to forward, at least in this country, the work of destruction, as Mr. Bentham. The spirit of examination and questioning has become through him, more than through any one person besides, the prevailing spirit of the age. For he questioned all things. The tendencies of a mind at once sceptical and systematic, (and both in the utmost possible degree,) made him endeavour to trace all speculative phenomena back to their primitive elements, and to reconsider not only the received conclusions, but the received premises. He treated all subjects as if they were virgin subjects, never before embraced or approached by man. He never set up an established doctrine as a thesis to be disputed about, but put it aside altogether, commenced from first principles, and deliberately tasked himself systematically to discover the truth, or to re-discover it if it were already known. By this process, if he ever annihilated a received opinion, he was sure of having something either good or bad to offer as a substitute for it; and in this he was most favourably distinguished from those French philosophers who preceded and even surpassed him, as destroyers of established institutions on the continent of Europe. And we shall owe largely to one who reconstructed while he destroyed, if our country is destined to pass more smoothly through this crisis of transition than the nations of the continent, and to lose less of the good it already enjoys in working itself free from the evil;—his be the merit, if while the wreck of the old vessel is still navigable, the masts of the new one, which brings relief, are dimly showing themselves above the horizon! For it is certain, and will be seen every day more clearly, that the initiation of all the changes which are now making in opinions and in institutions, may be claimed chiefly by men who have been indebted to his writings, and to the spirit of his philosophy, for the most important part of their intellectual cultivation.

I had originally proposed in this part of my work to give a slight sketch of the principal tenets of Bentham, with an exposition of what I conceive to be his errors; pointing out at once the benefits he has conferred, and also the mischief he has effected. But slight as would be that sketch, it must necessarily be somewhat abstract; and I have therefore, for the sake of the general reader, added it to the volume in the form of an appendix.* I have there, regarding him as a legislator and a moralist, ventured to estimate him much more highly in the former capacity than the latter; endeavouring to combat the infallibility of his application of the principle of Utility, and to show the dangerous and debasing theories, which may be, and are, deduced from it. Even, however, in legislation, his greatest happiness principle is not so clear and undeniable as it is usually conceded to be. "The greatest happiness of the greatest number" is to be our invariable guide! Is it so?—the greatest happiness of the greatest number of men living, I suppose, not of men to come; for if of all posterity, what legislator can be our guide? who can prejudge the future? Of men living, then?—well—how often would *their* greatest happiness consist in concession to their greatest errors.

In the dark ages, (said once to me very happily the wittiest writer of the day, and one who has perhaps done more to familiarize Bentham's general doctrines to the public than any other individual,) in the dark ages, it would have been for the greatest happiness of the greatest number to burn the witches; it must have made the greatest number, (all credulous of wizardry,) very uncomfortable to refuse their request for so reasonable a conflagration; they would have been given up to fear and disquietude—they would have imagined their safety disregarded and their cattle despised—if witches were to live with impunity, riding on broomsticks, and sailing in oyster-shells;— *their happiness* demanded a bonfire of old women. To grant such a bonfire would have been really to consult the greatest happiness of the greatest number, yet ought it to have been the principle of wise, nay, of perfect, (for so the dogma states,) of unimpugnable legislation? In fact, the greatest happiness principle, is an excellent general rule, but it is not an undeniable axiom.

*See Appendix B. [*I.e., the essays printed at* 3–18 *above.*]

Appendix D

Quotation from "Coleridge"
in Mill's *System of Logic* (8th ed., 1872), 519–23 (VI, x, 5)

As indicated in the Textual Introduction, there is little evidence concerning the dating of the revisions of the essays in *Dissertations and Discussions* between their first periodical publication and their republication in 1859. However, Mill's inclusion in his *Logic* of the long passage from "Coleridge" printed below supplies some interesting internal evidence.

The variant notes give all the substantive changes in the three versions of "Coleridge" and the nine versions of the *Logic*. The "Coleridge" versions are indicated by italic numerals: *40* = the periodical version, 1840; *59* = *Dissertations and Discussions*, 1st ed., 1859; *67* = *Dissertations and Discussions*, 2nd ed., 1867. The *Logic* versions are indicated by numerals in roman type: MS = manuscript (1840, with revisions through 1842); 43 = 1st ed., 1843; 46 = 2nd ed., 1846; 51 = 3rd ed., 1851; 56 = 4th ed., 1856; 62 = 5th ed., 1862; 65 = 6th ed., 1865; 68 = 7th ed., 1868; 72 = 8th ed., 1872 (the last in Mill's lifetime).

An examination of the variants, substantive and accidental (the latter not here recorded), shows that there are two main groups: in the first and larger group, *59* and *67* (the 1st and 2nd eds. of *D&D*) agree with 51 and subsequent eds. of the *Logic*, but not with *40* (the periodical version) or MS, 43, 46 (the manuscript and first two eds. of the *Logic*); in the second, *59* and *67* agree with *40* and MS, 43, 46, but not with 51 and subsequent eds. of the *Logic*. Changes in the *Logic* that appear only prior to or subsequent to 1851 did not affect the text of *59* and *67*; similarly, changes in *59* and *67* that do not appear in 51 do not appear in subsequent eds. of the *Logic*. In the absence of external evidence, of marked proof, and of all copy-texts except the manuscript of the *Logic*, the most likely explanation of these phenomena is that Mill, after having copied the passage into the *Logic* MS, revised the "Coleridge" with a view to republication (which did not occur until 1859); these revisions he transferred to the *Logic* when making the most extensive rewriting of that work, that is, for the 3rd ed. (1851). The revised "Coleridge," with no further changes except a few accidentals, became the copy-text for *59*. Further, it appears that when the time came for printing the 3rd ed. of the *Logic*, Mill made a few further changes, probably in proof, changes that are retained in subsequent eds. of the *Logic*, but do not appear in the reprinted "Coleridge" of *59* and *67*.

The *terminus ab quo* for the revision of "Coleridge" is, therefore, some time after the writing of the MS of Book VI of the *Logic* (1840–42); the *terminus ad quem* is between the beginning of the revision of the 3rd ed. of the *Logic* and its printing (1851). This conclusion is not very startling, as it narrows the possible time, that is, the time between printings (1840 and 1859), by less than half; still, it places the revision before Mill's marriage, and bears out the contention in the

Textual Introduction. Some slight evidence suggests a date near the beginning of the possible period. The final variant in the passage, the earlier form of which appears only in *40* and MS, would by itself seem to upset the argument above and, even in the context of the other changes, is inconclusive as to the transmission of text; one can tentatively infer, however, that if the change was made first in the proof of the *Logic*, the "Coleridge" was revised not later than 1843, whereas if it was first made in the revision of the "Coleridge," that revision was not later than 1842. Also, when John Parker agreed, in the spring of 1842, to publish the *Logic*, he turned down the suggestion that he publish the collection that later appeared as *Dissertations and Discussions*; Mill then proposed to publish the collection himself (see *Earlier Letters*, XIII, 514, 520–1). Again, therefore, it would appear likely that the revisions were made in 1842–43.

Mill prefaces the passage in the *Logic* with the comment that it is "extracted, with some alterations, from a criticism on the negative philosophy of the eighteenth century" (in MS, 43, 46 the reading is "forming part of a criticism on the negative philosophy of the eighteenth century"); actually the major alterations, as already indicated, were probably made in that criticism (i.e., in "Coleridge"), and not for the *Logic*. Only one change, the deletion in the *Logic* of a long footnote (508°), was made in the interests of the new context.

The passage is introduced in the *Logic* as an example of results that, although they "amount in themselves only to empirical laws . . . are found to follow with so much probability from general laws of human nature, that the consilience of the two processes raises the evidence to proof [MS,43,46 to complete proof], and the generalizations to the rank of scientific truths." In a typical phrase, he apologizes for the quotation, saying: ". . . I quote, though (as in some former instances) from myself, because I have no better way of illustrating the conception I have formed of the kind of theorems of which sociological statics would consist."

a The very first element of the social union, obedience to a government of some sort, has not been found so easy a thing to establish in the world. Among a timid and spiritless race like the inhabitants of the vast plains of tropical countries, passive obedience may be of natural growth; though even there we doubt whether it has ever been found among any people with whom fatalism, or in other words, submission to the pressure of circumstances as *b*a divine decree*b*, did not prevail as a religious doctrine. But the difficulty of inducing a brave and warlike race to submit their individual *arbitrium* to any common umpire, has always been felt to be so great, that nothing short of supernatural power has been deemed adequate to overcome it; and such tribes have always assigned to the first institution of civil society a divine origin. So differently did those judge who knew savage *c*men*c* by actual experience, from those who had no acquaintance with *d*them*d* except in the civilized state. In modern Europe itself, after the fall of the Roman empire, to subdue the feudal

a40, 59, 67 [*no paragraph*]
b–b40, MS, 43, 46, *59, 67* the decree of God
c–c40, MS, *59, 67* man [*printer's error in 43? See d–d below.*]
d–d40, MS, 43, 46, *59, 67* him

anarchy and bring the whole people of any European nation into subjection to government (though Christianity in *e*the*e* most concentrated form *f*of its influence*f* was co-operating *g* in the work) required thrice as many centuries as have elapsed since that time.

Now if these philosophers had known human nature under any other type than that of their own age, and of the particular classes of society among whom they *h*lived*h*, it would have occurred to them, that wherever this habitual submission to law and government has been firmly and durably established, and yet the vigour and manliness of character which resisted its establishment have been in any degree preserved, certain requisites have existed, certain conditions have been fulfilled, of which the following may be regarded as the principal.

First: there has existed, for all who were accounted citizens,—for all who were not slaves, kept down by brute force,—a system of *education,* beginning with infancy and continued through life, of which whatever else it might include, one main and incessant ingredient was *restraining discipline.* To train the human being in the habit, and thence the power, of subordinating his personal impulses and aims, to what were considered the ends of society; of adhering, against all temptation, to the course of conduct which those ends prescribed; of controlling in himself all *i* feelings which were liable to militate against those ends, and encouraging all such as tended towards them; this was the purpose, to which every outward motive that the authority directing the system could command, and every inward power or principle which its knowledge of human nature enabled it to evoke, were endeavoured to be rendered instrumental. *i*The entire civil and military policy of the ancient commonwealths was such a system of training; in modern nations its place has been attempted to be supplied, principally, by religious teaching.*i* And whenever and in proportion as the strictness of *k*the restraining*k* discipline was relaxed, the natural tendency of mankind to anarchy re-asserted itself; the state became disorganized from within; mutual conflict for selfish ends, neutralized the energies which were required to keep up the contest against natural causes of evil; and the nation, after a longer or briefer interval of progressive decline, became either the slave of a despotism, or the prey of a foreign invader.

e–e40, MS, 43, 46   its
f–f+51, 56, *59*, 62, 65, *67*, 68, 72
g40, MS, 43, 46   with all its influences
h–h40, MS, 43, 46   moved
i40, MS, *59, 67*   the]   43, 46, 51, 56   those
i–i40, MS, 43, 46   This system of discipline wrought, in the Grecian states, by the conjunct influence of religion, poetry, and law; among the Romans, by those of religion and law; in modern and Christian countries, mainly by religion, with little of the direct agency, but generally more or less of the indirect support and countenance, of law.
k–k40, MS, 43, 46   this

The second condition of permanent political society has been found to be, the existence, in some form or other, of the feeling of allegiance or loyalty. This feeling may vary in its objects, and is not confined to any particular form of government; but whether in a democracy or in a monarchy, its essence is always the same; viz. that there be in the constitution of the state *something* which is settled, something permanent, and not to be called in question; something which, by general agreement, has a right to be where it is, and to be secure against disturbance, whatever else may change. This feeling may attach itself, as among the Jews (and *l* in most of the commonwealths of antiquity), to a common God or gods, the protectors and guardians of their state. Or it may attach itself to certain persons, who are deemed to be, whether by divine appointment, by long prescription, or by the general recognition of their superior capacity and worthiness, the rightful guides and guardians of the rest. Or it may *m*connect itself with laws; with ancient liberties or ordinances. Or, finally, (and this is the only shape in which the feeling is likely to exist hereafter), it may attach itself to the principles of individual freedom and political and social equality, as realized in institutions which as yet exist nowhere, or exist only in a rudimentary state.*m* But in all political societies which have had a durable existence, there has been some fixed point: something which *n*people*n* *o*agreed*o* in holding sacred; which *p*, wherever freedom of discussion was a recognised principle, it was of course*p* lawful to contest in theory, but which no one could either fear or hope to see shaken in practice; which, in short (except perhaps during some temporary crisis) was in the common estimation placed *q*beyond*q* discussion. And the necessity of this may easily be made evident. A state never is, nor until mankind are vastly improved, can hope to be, for any long time exempt from internal dissension; for there neither is nor has ever been any state of society in which collisions did not occur between the immediate interests and passions of powerful sections of the people. What, then, enables *r*nations*r* to weather these storms, and pass through turbulent times without any permanent weakening of the *s*securities for peaceable existence*s*? Precisely this—that however important the interests about which men *t*fell*t* out, the conflict *u*did*u* not affect the funda-

*l*40, MS, 43, 46, 51, 56, 59, 67   indeed

*m–m*40   attach itself to laws, to ancient liberties, or ordinances; to the whole or some part of the political, or even of the domestic, institutions of the state.] MS, 43, 46   *as 40* . . . even the . . . *as 40*] 59, 67   *as 40* . . . ordinances. Or . . . *as 72*

*n–n*40, MS, 43, 46, 59, 67   men

*o–o*56, 62, 65   agree [*printer's error?*]

*p–p*40, MS, 43, 46   it might or might not be

*q–q*40, MS, 43   *above*]   46   above

*r–r*40, MS, 43, 46, 59, 67   society

*s–s*40, MS, 43, 46   ties which hold it together

*t–t*40, MS, 43, 46, 59   fall

*u–u*40, MS, 43, 46   does

mental ^{v}principle^v of the system of social union which ^{w}happened^w to exist; nor threaten large portions of the community with the subversion of that on which they ^{x}had^x built their calculations, and with which their hopes and aims ^{y}had^y become identified. But when the questioning of these fundamental principles is (not ^{z}the^z occasional disease, ^{a}or salutary medicine,^{a} but) the habitual condition of the body politic, and when all the violent animosities are called forth, which spring naturally from such a situation, the state is virtually in a position of civil war; and can never long remain free from it in act and fact.

The third essential condition ^{b}of stability in political society^b, is a strong and active principle of ^{c}cohesion among the members of the same community or state^c. We need scarcely say that we do not mean ^{d}nationality, in the vulgar sense of the term;^{d} a senseless antipathy to foreigners; ^{e} ^{f}indifference to the general welfare of the human race, or an unjust preference of the supposed interests of our own country;^{f} ^{g} a cherishing of ^{h}bad^h peculiarities because they are national, or a refusal to adopt what has been found good by other countries. ^{i} We mean a principle of sympathy, not of hostility; of union, not of separation. We mean a feeling of common interest among those who live under the same government, and are contained within the same natural or historical boundaries. We mean, that one part of the community ^{i}do^i not consider themselves as foreigners with regard to another part; that they ^{k}set a value on their connexion—^{k}feel that they are one people, that their lot is cast together, that evil to any of their fellow-countrymen is evil to themselves, and ^{l}do not desire selfishly to^l free themselves from their share of any common inconvenience by severing the connexion. How strong this feeling was in ^{m}those^m ancient commonwealths ^{n}which attained any durable greatness,^{n}

v–$v40$, MS, 43, 46, 51, 59, 67   principles
w–$w40$, MS, 43, 46   happens
x–$x40$, MS, 43, 46   have
y–$y40$, MS, 43, 46   have
z–$z40$, MS, 43, 46   an
a–a+51, 56, 59, 62, 65, 67, 68, 72
b–$b40$, MS, 43, 46   , which has existed in all durable political societies
c–$c40$, MS, 43, 46   nationality
d–d+51, 56, 59, 62, 65, 67, 68, 72
e51, 56, 59, 67   an
f–f+51, 56, 59, 62, 65, 67, 68, 72
$g40$, MS, 43, 46   or
h–$h40$, MS, 43, 46   absurd
$i40$, MS, 43, 46   In all these senses, the nations which have the strongest national spirit have had the least nationality.
i–$i40$, MS, 43, 46   shall
k–$k40$, MS, 43, 46   shall cherish the tie which holds them together; shall
l–$l40$, MS, 43, 46   that they cannot selfishly
m–$m40$, MS, 43, 46   the
n–n+51, 56, 59, 62, 65, 67, 68, 72

every one knows. How happily Rome, in spite of all her tyranny, succeeded in establishing the feeling of a common country among the provinces of her vast and divided empire, will appear when any one who has given due attention to the subject shall take the trouble to point it out. *o* In modern times the countries which have had that feeling in the strongest degree have been the most powerful countries; England, France, and, in proportion to their territory and resources, Holland and Switzerland; while England in her connexion with Ireland, is one of the most signal examples of the consequences of its absence. Every Italian knows why Italy is under a foreign yoke; every German knows what maintains despotism in the Austrian empire;* the *p*evils*p* of Spain flow as much from the absence of nationality among the Spaniards themselves, as from the presence of it in their relations with foreigners: while the completest illustration of all is afforded by the republics of South America, where the parts of one and the same state adhere so slightly together, that no sooner does any province think itself aggrieved by the general government than it proclaims itself a separate nation.

*[72] (Written and first published in 1840.)

*o*40, 59, 67   [*footnote*; *see* 135n–136n *above*]
*p–p*40, MS   woes

Appendix E

Bibliographic Index of Persons and Works Cited in the *Essays*, with
Variants and Notes

Mill, like most nineteenth-century authors, is cavalier in his approach to sources,
seldom identifying them with sufficient care, and frequently quoting them inaccurately. This Appendix is intended to help correct these deficiencies, and to serve
as an index of names and titles (which are consequently omitted in the Index
proper). Included also, at the end of the Appendix, are references to British
statute law, which are entered in order of date under the heading "Statutes." The
material otherwise is arranged in alphabetical order, with an entry for each author
and work quoted or referred to in the text proper and in Appendices A–D. In
cases of simple reference only surnames are given. As the references in Appendix
B will be found again in the volume of newspaper writings, and as those in
Appendix C may be Bulwer's rather than Mill's they are identified as occurring
in those appendices.

The entries take the following form:

1. Identification: author, title, etc., in the usual bibliographic form.

2. Notes (if required) giving information about JSM's use of the source, indication if the work is in his library, and any other relevant information.

3. A list of the places where the author or work is quoted, and a separate list of
the places where there is reference only. Those works that are reviewed are
specially noted; individual works by Bentham, Coleridge, and Comte (except for
the *Cours*) are not noted as "reviewed" because the articles on these authors are
general and not specific reviews.

4. A list of substantive variants between JSM's text and his source, in this form:
Page and line reference to the present text. Reading in the present text] Reading
in the source (page reference in the source).

The list of substantive variants also attempts to place quoted passages in their
contexts by giving the beginnings and endings of sentences. Omissions of two
sentences or less are given in full; only the length of other omissions is given. In
a few cases, following the page reference to the source, cross-references are given
to footnoted variants in the present text. Translated material is given in the
original language. When the style has been altered by setting down quotations, the
original form is retained in the entries.

ACTS. See Statutes.

ADDISON, JOSEPH. Referred to: 114

———— *Cato. A Tragedy.* London: Tonson, 1713.

QUOTED: 12

12.39–40 "the woman who deliberates,"] When Love once plead's Admission to our Hearts / (In spite of all the Virtue we can boast) / The Woman that Deliberates is lost. (P. 46; IV, i, 29–31)

AESCHYLUS. Referred to: 42, 324

AGRIPPA. Referred to: 136

NOTE: the reference is in a quotation from Coleridge.

ALFRED THE GREAT (of England). Referred to: 151

NOTE: the reference is in a quotation from Coleridge.

AMPÈRE. Referred to: 354

ANAXAGORAS. Referred to: 276, 278

ANTONINUS, MARCUS AURELIUS. Referred to: 422

———— *Meditations.* Referred to: 416

NOTE: as the reference is general, no edition is cited. A Greek and Latin edition (Glasgow: Foulis, 1744) is in JSM's library, Somerville College.

APOLLONIUS. Referred to: 362

ARCHIMEDES. Referred to: 362

ARISTOTLE. Referred to: 66, 125, 276, 292, 301, 309, 362

NOTE: the reference at 301 is to G. H. Lewes's *Aristotle.*

———— *De Anima.* Quoted: 268

NOTE: there are many editions of Aristotle in JSM's library, Somerville College. The quoted words derive from 415a, 23.

AUGUSTUS. See Caesar Augustus.

AURELIUS. See Antoninus.

BACON, FRANCIS. Referred to: 9, 10, 83, 88, 119, 171, 174, 266

———— *Novum Organum Scientiarum.* 2nd ed. Amsterdam: Ravensteiny, 1660.

NOTE: in JSM's library, Somerville College. For convenience, reference is also given to *Works* (14 vols. Ed. James Spedding, Robert Leslie Ellis, and Douglas Denon Heath. London: Longman, *et al.*, 1857–74), which is also in JSM's library. In this standard edition, the *Novum Organum* is in Vol. I; the English translation is in Vol. IV. The quotations at 29 and 111 are identical (the passage is marked with a marginal pencil line in JSM's copy of the edition of 1660; that at 379 is indirect; the reference at 88 is to 113 (*Works* I, 205; Bk. I, Aph. cv; cf. Vol. IV, 97–8; see also Vol. III, 504, 601).

QUOTED: 29, 111, 379   REFERRED TO: 88

29.29   *vera illa et media axiomata*] At media sunt Axiomata illa vera, & solida, & viva, in quibus humanae res, & fortunae, sitae sunt; & supra haec quoque, tandem ipsa illa generalissima; talia scilicet, quae non abstracta sint, sed per hae media vere limitantur. (112, *Works*, I, 205; Bk. I, Aph. civ) [Cf. *Works*, IV, 97.]
111.1–2   [*see previous entry*]
379.33–4   we can obey nature in such a way as to command it] Human knowledge and human power meet in one; for where the cause is not known the effect cannot be produced. Nature to be commanded must be obeyed; and that which in contemplation is as the cause is in operation as the rule. (47; Bk. I, Aph. iii) [Cf. 114; Bk. I, Aph. cxxix. For the Latin version, see 28; *Works*, I, 157, 222.]

BAIN, ALEXANDER. Referred to: 298.

———— *The Emotions and the Will.* London: Parker, 1859.

NOTE: the "first treatise" referred to at 246n is Bain's *The Senses and the Intellect* (London: Parker, 1855).

REFERRED TO: 246n

"Balwhidder, Micah." See Galt.

BANCROFT. Referred to: 155.

BEATTIE. Referred to: 85, 86.

NOTE: the reference at 85 derives from Bentham's identification of the moralist intended in his second category (see 514:85.12 below).

"Beauchamp, Philip." See Grote, *Analysis*.

BECKET. Referred to: 142.

BENTHAM, JEREMIAH. Referred to: 81.

BENTHAM, JEREMY. Referred to: 5–18 *passim*, 21, 26, 54, 77–115 *passim*, 119–21, 127, 128, 146, 150, 169–70, 172–4, 176, 179, 181, 183–5, 190, 191, 193n, 194, 195–6, 198–9, 201, 207, 209, 220n, 258n, 267, 290, 300, 307, 325, 394, 406, 413–14, 494, 495–8 (App. B), 499–502 (App. C).

NOTE: the references at 172, 181, 183, 198 are in quotations from Whewell. The references at 406, 413–14 are to Bentham's authorship of the *Analysis of the Influence of Natural Religion*; see under Grote.

———— *The Works of Jeremy Bentham.* Ed. John Bowring. Parts I to IV (1838). Vols. I and IV of complete edition in 11 vols. Edinburgh: Tait, 1843.

NOTE: for ease of reference, most citations of Bentham's writings are taken from this edition, which is in JSM's library, Somerville College. The edition appeared in twenty-two separate parts between 1838 and 1843, and then was issued in eleven volumes in 1843. JSM's review ("Bentham") is of the first four parts, all published in 1838, which form Vols. I (Parts I and II) and IV (Parts III and IV) of the complete edition. The corresponding volume and part numbers, with dates of the parts, are as follows: Vols. I (Parts I and II, 1838; J. H. Burton's "Introduction to the Study of Jeremy Bentham's Works," which appeared at the end of Part XXII in 1843, is also in Vol. I), II (VII and VIII, 1839), III (IX and X, 1839), IV (III and IV, 1838), V (V and VI, 1838), VI (XI and XII, 1839), VII (XIII and XIV, 1840), VIII (XV and XVI, 1841), IX (XVII and XVIII, 1841 and 1842), X (XIX and XX, 1842), XI (XXI and XXII, 1842 and 1843; for Burton's "Introduction," see Vol. I above). Parts I to IV contain the following works (most of which are not referred to in JSM's review): Part I. *An Introduction to the Principles of Morals and Legislation; On the Promulgation of Laws, with Specimen of a Penal Code; On the Influence of Time and Place in Matters of Legislation; A Table of the Springs of Action; A Fragment on Government.* Part II. *Principles of the Civil Code; Principles of Penal Law.* Part III. *View of the Hard-Labour Bill; Panopticon; Postscript to Panopticon; Panopticon v. New South Wales; A Plea for the Constitution; Draught of a Code for a Judicial Establishment in France.* Part IV. *Bentham's Draught for the Organization of Judicial Establishments; Emancipate Your Colonies; On Houses of Peers and Senates; Papers relative to Codification and Public Instruction; Codification Proposal.*

REVIEWED: 77–115

———— *Analysis of the Influence of Natural Religion.* See Grote, *Analysis.*

———— *The Book of Fallacies; from the unfinished papers of Jeremy Bentham.* Ed. Peregrine Bingham. London: Hunt, 1824.

NOTE: for ease of reference, the quotations are also located in *Works*, II, 375–487.

QUOTED: 14–15, 90   REFERRED TO: 81–2

14.30–1   "In *every* human breast (rare . . . extraordinarily . . . excitement, excepted)]
3. [*i.e.*, the *3rd of the premises on which the following argument is based*] In every human breast, rare . . . extraordinary . . . incitement, excepted, (392–3; *Works*, II, 482)
14.34   "Taking] [*paragraph*] Taking (363; *Works*, II, 482)
14.35   *nor . . . exist*] [*not in italics*] (363; *Works*, II, 482)
14.38–9   (which . . . virtuous) of], which . . . virtuous of (363; *Works*, II, 482)
90.17   "vague generalities."] [*title of* Part IV, Chap. iii] (230ff.; *Works*, II, 440ff.)

———— *Constitutional Code; for the use of all nations and all governments professing liberal opinions.* Vol. I. London: Heward, 1830.

by JSM from Whewell's version. Bowring's bracketed identifications of the moralists in the passage quoted at 85–6 and elsewhere derive from Bentham's inked marginalia in his copy (British Museum) of the 1st ed.; the mistaken spellings are Bentham's. In the reference at 97 to Bentham's sanctions, JSM omits the first of Bentham's four sanctions, the "physical" (see *Introduction to the Principles*, Chap. iii, especially the note to the chapter title).

QUOTED: 5, 85–6, 110, 177–8, 271   REFERRED TO 8, 94, 97, 175–6

5.15–16   principle . . . principle,"] [*paragraph*] To this denomination ["principle of utility"] has of late [written 1822] been added or substituted, the *greatest happiness* or *greatest felicity* principle: this for shortness, instead of saying at length *that principle* which states the greatest happiness of all those whose interest is in question, as being the right and proper, and only right and proper and universally desirable, end of human action: of human action in every situation, and in particular in that of a functionary or set of functionaries exercising the powers of Government. (I, 1n; not in 1789 ed.; 1823 ed., I, 1n–2n)

5.21–2   "law . . . sense."] [*see 85–6 above, and entries below for that passage*] (I, 8n–9n; 1789 ed., xiin–xvn; 1823 ed., I, 28n–31n)

5.26   accept the] accept of the (I, 8; 1789 ed., xiii; 1823 ed., I, 28)

5.27   reason for] reason, and that a sufficient one, for (*ibid.*; in both 1789 and 1823 the reading is as JSM gives it)

84.32–4   "contrivance . . . itself."] contrivances . . . itself. (I, 8; cf. entry for 5.27 above)

85.8   man says] man [Lord Shaftesbury, Hutchinson, Hume, &c.] says (8n; 1789 ed., xiiin; 1823 ed., I, 29n: the latter two do not have these or the other identifications; the square brackets are Bowring's)

85.9   that is] that it is (*ibid.*)

85.9   a 'moral sense:'] a *moral sense*: (*ibid.*; correctly quoted at 177.35)

85.12   man comes] man [Dr. Beattie] comes (*ibid.*)

85.13   tells] teaches (*ibid.*,; correctly quoted at 177.39)

85.16   out as] out of the account as (*ibid.*; correctly quoted at 177.43)

85.24   man comes] man [Dr. Price] comes (*ibid.*; 1789 ed., xivn)

85.28   part] point (*ibid.*; 1823 ed., I, 30n)

85.30   there] here (*ibid.*; "there" in 1789 and 1823, printer's error in Bowring)

85.34   man,] man [Dr. Clark], (*ibid.*)

86.4   philosopher,] philosopher [Woolaston], (I, 9n; 1789 ed., xivn; 1823 ed., I, 31n)

86.9   not be] not to be (*ibid.*; 1789 ed., xvn) [cf. cxxxvin]

86.12   and let] that let (*ibid.*) [cf. cxxxvin]

86.14   but to come] but come (*ibid.*; 1789 and 1823 agree with JSM)

86.25   "exhaustive method of classification,"] [*the passage in which Bentham* "ascribes everything original" *in the* Introduction *to his method is at* I, 101n (1789 ed., ccxn; 1823 ed., II, 73n); *see also* ibid., 17, 96n–97n, 137–9 (*cf.* 237–8, *and* III, 172), *and for a more extended discussion of his method,* VIII, 101ff.]

110.18–19   "principle . . . principle."] [*see entry for 5.15–16 above*]

177.7   It] XII. It (I, 8; 1789 ed., xii; 1823 ed., I, 27)

177.13   these] those (*ibid.*) [*printer's error?*]

177.14   In] XIII. In (*ibid.*, 1789 ed., xiii)

177.20   proportion] *proportion* (*ibid.*)

177.24   The] XIV. The (*ibid.*)

177.29   reason for] reason, and that a sufficient one, for (*ibid.*) [*cf. entry for 5.27 above*]

177.29   phrase is different] phrases different (*ibid.*)

177.29   same] same.* (*ibid.*) [*the rest of the quotation is all in this footnote; cf. 85–6 above, and entries for that passage. The entries below indicate only differences between the version here quoted and that quoted at 85–6; errors in both passages are therefore indicated for the former only*]

177.34   One] 1. One (I, 8n; 1789 ed., xiiin; 1823 ed., I, 29n)
177.38   Another] 2. Another (*ibid.*)
177.40   much] surely (*ibid.*)
178.7   Another] 4. Another (*ibid.*; 1823 ed., I, 30n)
178.11   Another] 5. Another (*ibid.*)
178.15   A] 6. A (I, 9n; *ibid.*)
178.18–19   nature. [*paragraph*] We] [*JSM omits Bentham's 7th category here, and his 9th after the next paragraph; cf.* 117] (*ibid.*)
178.19   We] 8. We (*ibid.*; 1823 ed., I, 31n)
185.34   religion] religions, (I, 142n–143n; 1789 ed., cccviiin; 1823 ed., II, 235n) [*this and the following variants indicate JSM's agreement with Whewell's misquotations from Bentham, except as indicated*]
185.35   kingdom] creation (*ibid.*)
185.39   ought] *ought* (ibid.) [*given correctly in* "Whewell"]
185.40   given. The] [*9-sentence omission, indicated in* "Whewell" *by ellipsis*] (*ibid.*; 1789 ed., cccviiin–cccixn)
185.40   may] *may* (*ibid.*) [*given correctly in* "Whewell"]
185.42   tyranny. It] tyranny. The French have already discovered that the blackness of the skin is no reason why a human being should be abandoned without redress to the caprice of a tormentor.* [*footnote:*] *See Lewis XIVth Code Noir. [*text:*] It (*ibid.*; 1823 ed., II, 235n–236n) [*ellipsis indicated in* "Whewell"]
185.43–186.1   reasons insufficient] reasons equally insufficient (*ibid.*) [*see previous entry*]
186.1   caprice of a tormentor.] same fate? (*ibid.*) [*see two previous entries*]
186.5   day, a] day, or a (*ibid.*)
186.6   The] the (*ibid.*)
186.6–7   can they reason? nor, can they speak? but, can they suffer?] Can they *reason?* nor, Can they *talk?* but, Can they *suffer?* (*ibid.*) [*italics given in* "Whewell"]
271.34   fictitious entities] [*a very common phrase in Bentham; see, e.g.,* I, 53n (1789 ed., cxin; 1823 ed., I, 191n); *cf.* 57n, *and for a fuller treatment,* VIII, 197ff.]

——— *Plan of Parliamentary Reform, in the Form of a Catechism, with Reasons for Each Article: with an Introduction, showing the necessity of radical, and the inadequacy of moderate, reform.* London: Hunter, 1817.

NOTE: in *Works,* III, 433–557; the comparative passage below is taken from this version.
QUOTED: 257
257.35–6   "everybody to count for one, nobody for more than one,"] [*exact wording not located, but see:*] [*paragraph:*] 3. The happiness and unhappiness of any one member of the community—high or low, rich or poor—what greater or less part is it of the universal happiness and unhappiness, than that of any other? (III, 459) [Cf.: "And, on what ground, in the eyes of a common guardian, can any one man's happiness be shown to have any stronger or less strong claim to regard than any others?" (*Codification Proposal,* in *Works,* IV, 540) See also I, 302, 321; II, 252, 271–2; III, 211.]

——— "Principles of the Civil Code," in *Works,* I, 297–364.

NOTE: at 104n and 154, JSM refers to this work as "Principles of Civil Law"; Part I is entitled "Objects of the Civil Law" and the phrase is used by Dumont in his Introduction (I, 299) to characterize the subject.
QUOTED: 197   REFERRED TO: 104n, 154
197.24–5   "takes . . . themselves,"] The government which interdicts them [divorces], takes . . . themselves. (I, 355)

———— *Rationale of Judicial Evidence, specially applied to English Practice.* Ed. J. S. Mill. 5 vols. London: Hunt and Clarke, 1827.

NOTE: in *Works*, VI–VII. The reference at 470 is to one of JSM's editorial notes to the *Rationale*, I, 137 (where the criticism is of Price, not of Campbell). In JSM's library, Somerville College.

QUOTED: 95n   REFERRED TO: 470

95.n2   "love of justice"] 2. Another reason [why one of the "mendacity-restraining sanctions" may operate] is to be found in that love of justice, which, at least in a civilized state of society, may be considered as having more or less hold on every human breast.* [*footnote by the Editor, i.e., JSM:*] *This love of justice, commonplace moralists, and even a certain class of philosophers, would be likely to call an original principle of human nature. Experience proves the contrary: by any attentive observer of the progress of the human mind in early youth, the gradual growth of it may be traced. [*paragraph*] Among the almost innumerable associations by which this love of justice is nourished and fostered, that one to which it probably owes the greatest part of its strength, arises from a conviction which cannot fail to impress itself upon the mind of every human being possessed of an ordinary share of intellect,—the conviction, that if other persons in general were habitually and universally to disregard the rules of justice in their conduct towards him, his destruction would be the speedy consequence: and that by every single instance of disregard to those rules on the part of any one, (himself included), the probability of future violations of the same nature is more or less increased. (V, 638–639n; *Works*, VII, 570–570n) [Another passage using "love of justice" is to be found at I, 83 (*Works*, VI, 227).]

———— *The Rationale of Reward.* London: Hunt, 1825.

NOTE: in *Works*, II, 189–266; the comparative passages below are taken from this version.

QUOTED: 113

113.35–6   "quantity of pleasure being equal, push-pin is as good as poetry:"] Prejudice apart, the game of push-pin is of equal value with the arts and sciences of music and poetry. (II, 253)

114.1   "All poetry is misrepresentation."] [*exact wording not located, but see:*] Indeed, between poetry and truth there is a natural opposition: false morals, fictitious nature. The poet always stands in need of something false. . . . Truth, exactitude of every kind, is fatal to poetry. (II, 253–4)

———— *A Table of the Springs of Action.* London: Hunter, 1817 [printed 1815].

NOTE: in *Works*, I, 195–219.

QUOTED: 95, 109   REFERRED TO: 12, 95, 96

95:19–21   "Conscience . . . reputation;"] ["Conscience" *and* "Principle" *appear under the* "Eulogistic" *motives in Table VII, which is concerned with* "Pleasures and Pains of the Moral or Popular Sanction; viz. Pleasures of Reputation, or Good-Repute," *with a reference directing attention to Tables IX and X, concerned with pleasures and pains of the* "Religious Sanction" *and of* "Sympathy." "Moral Rectitude" *and* "Moral Duty" *appear in Table VIII under the* "Neutral" *motives.*] (*Works*, I, 201)

109.28   "interest-begotten prejudice"] [*see title of* §6] (I, 217; cf. title of *Book of Fallacies*, Part V, Chap. iv, in *Works*, II, 477]

———— *Traités de législation civile et pénale.* Ed. Etienne Dumont. 3 vols. Paris: Bossange, Mason, and Besson, 1802.

NOTE: the "Vue générale d'un corps complet de législation" ("de lois" in Table of Contents of Vol. I) is in Vol. I (moved to Vol. III of 2nd ed. 3 vols. Paris: Bossange, Rey, and Gravier, 1820). As the reading of these volumes marked "an epoch" in JSM's life (*Autobiography* [New York: Columbia University Press, 1924], 45), the contents are of special interest: Vol. I. Discours préliminaire (by Dumont); Principes généraux de législation; Vue générale d'un corps complet de législation. Vol. II. Principes du code civil; Principes du code pénal. Vol. III. Principes du code pénal (cont.); Mémoire sur le Panoptique; Promulgation des lois; De l'influence de tems et des lieux en matière de législation.

REFERRED TO: 11, 496 (App. B)

———— "Vue générale d'un corps complet de législation." See *Traités de législation civile et pénale.*

BERKELEY. Referred to: 46

BERTHELOT, MARCELIN-PIERRE-EUGÈNE. "La science idéale et la science positive," *Revue des Deux Mondes,* 2e sér., 48 (Nov., 1863), 442–59.

REFERRED TO: 264

BEVERLEY, ROBERT MACKENZIE. Referred to: 36n

NOTE: for Beverley's writings, see Sedgwick, *Four Letters.*

BIBLE. Referred to: 27–8, 144–5, 159, 160–2, 300, 322, 382, 416

———— New Testament. Referred to: 65, 161, 218, 416–17, 423, 424–5, 469, 487

———— Old Testament. Referred to: 161, 224, 396, 416n

———— Acts. Referred to: 480n

NOTE: the reference is to 9: 1–19; Paul's conversion is also described in Acts, 22:3–16, 26:4–18; Galatians, 1:11ff.

———— I Corinthians.

QUOTED: 420

420.14 "Let us] If after the manner of men I have fought with beasts at Ephesus, what advantageth it me, if the dead rise not? let us (15:32; cf. Isaiah, 22:13)

———— Exodus.

QUOTED: 410

410.29–30   "follow . . . evil;"] Thou shalt not follow . . . evil; neither shalt thou speak in a cause to decline after many to wrest judgment: / Neither shalt thou countenance a poor man in his cause. (23:2–3)

———— Genesis. Referred to: 27, 162, 435

NOTE: the reference at 27 is in a quotation from Blakey.

———— Isaiah.

NOTE: the quotation is indirect.

QUOTED: 423

423.40–1   its ways are not our ways] For my thoughts are not your thoughts, neither are your ways my ways, saith the LORD. (55:8)

———— John.

QUOTED: 28, 416   REFERRED TO: 487

28.39   "He spake as never man spake."] The officers answered, Never man spake like this man. (7:46)
416.36   "new commandment to love one another;"] A new commandment I give unto you, That ye love one another; as I have loved you, that ye also love one another. (13:34)
417.3–4   "he that is without sin let him throw the first stone;"] So when they continued asking him, he lifted up himself, and said unto them, He that is without sin among you, let him first cast a stone at her. (8:7)

———— Judges. Referred to: 320

———— Leviticus.

NOTE: the quotation is indirect.

QUOTED: 416n

416.n2–3   to love . . . thyself,] Thou shalt not avenge, nor bear any grudge against the children of thy people, but thou shalt love . . . thyself: I am the Lord. (19:18)

———— Luke. Referred to: 417

NOTE: the reference is to 10:30–7.

———— Mark. Referred to: 29, 424

NOTE: the reference at 29 is general; see 3:5.

———— Matthew.

NOTE: the reference at 417 is to 7:12; that at 423 is to 5:1ff.

QUOTED: 388   REFERRED TO: 417, 423

388.7–8   "to him that . . . given, but . . . taken even] For unto every one that . . . given, and he shall have abundance: but . . . taken away even (25:29)

———— Revelations. Referred to: 27, 412

NOTE: the reference at 27 is in a quotation from Blakey; that at 412 is to Chap. 18.

———— Romans.

QUOTED: 424

424.28   "the . . . God"] Let every soul be subject unto the higher powers. For there is
no power but of God: the . . . God. (13:1)

BICHAT. Referred to: 289

BLACKSTONE. Referred to: 82, 103, 151

BLAINVILLE. Referred to: 323

BLAKEY, ROBERT. *History of Moral Science.* 2 vols. London: Duncan, 1833.

REVIEWED: 21–9   QUOTED: 23–7

24.39   remembrance] *remembrance* (II, 117)
25.15   assert] assent [*printer's error in Blakey?*] (II, 117)
25.41   The] [*no paragraph*] In considering the nature of man, they have looked upon
him as a mere insulated being, without any reference to the relations in which he
stands to the Great Author of his existence; and hence it is, in the majority of
cases, that the (II, 300)
25.42   mind] mind such (II, 300)
25.42   is profusely] is so profusely (II, 300)
26.3   all things *should be* seen in God;] The metaphysical theory of Father Malen-
branche [*sic*] is contained in this single principle, that *all things should be seen in
God.* (II, 308)
26.10   All] [*no paragraph*] All (II, 317)
26.16   vibrations,*] [*JSM's footnote*] (II, 317)
26.18–20   "there are . . . truth," and that "we cannot . . . principle,"] [*paragraph*]
There are . . . truth; but the great imperfection which runs through them all is, that
they attempt to generalise too much. We cannot . . . principle. (II, 319)
26.22   "that . . . God,"] The abstract arguments, for and against this theory [of Archbishop King] have been detailed at a considerable length, in the essay on King's
system; but I will here advance a few additional reasons, principally of a more
popular complexion, in favour of the doctrine, that . . . God. (II, 319–20)
27.26   I venture] [*no paragraph*] If this be the case [that supernatural revelation
merely confirms natural morality], then I would say that the Scriptures are a
complete failure; for I venture (II, 326)

BLIGNIÈRES, CÉLESTIN DE. *Exposition abrégée et populaire de la philosophie
et de la religion positives.* Paris: Chamerot, 1857.

REFERRED TO: 328, 329

BÖHME. Referred to: 127

BOLINGBROKE. Referred to: 21

BONNER. Referred to: 155

BORGIAS. Referred to: 386

NOTE: the reference is not specific, but clearly Cesare, Lucrezia, and Rodrigo (Pope Alexander VI) are intended.

BOSSUET. Referred to: 324

BOWRING, JOHN. *Deontology; or, The Science of Morality: in which the harmony and co-incidence of duty and self-interest, virtue and felicity, prudence and benevolence, are explained and exemplified. From the MSS of Jeremy Bentham.* 2 vols. London: Longman, Rees, Orme, Browne, Green, and Longman, 1834.

NOTE: the reference at 90 is to I, 39ff. There is little reason to dispute JSM's judgment, often expressed, that this work should be attributed in the main to Bowring, not to Bentham.

REFERRED TO: 90, 98–9, 174

BOYLE. Referred to: 287n

BRIDGES. See Comte, *A General View of Positivism.*

BROUGHAM, HENRY PETER. "Law Reform: Introduction," in *Speeches of Henry Lord Brougham.* 4 vols. Edinburgh: Black, 1838, II, 285–315.

NOTE: the "character" of Bentham is on 287–304; for the "imputation" of "a jealous and splenetic disposition," see especially 297–8. Brougham also includes, 304–6, a short sketch of James Mill.

REFERRED TO: 115n

BROWN, JOHN. *Essays on the Characteristics.* London: Davis, 1752.

NOTE: in JSM's library, Somerville College.

REFERRED TO: 87, 170

———— *An Estimate of the Manners and Principles of the Times.* 2 vols. London: Davis and Reymers, 1757–58.

REFERRED TO: 87n

BROWN, THOMAS. Referred to: 21, 46, 130, 298

———— *Lectures on the Philosophy of the Human Mind.* 4 vols. Edinburgh: Tait, 1820.

REFERRED TO: 267

BRUTUS. Referred to: 112

BUCKLE. Referred to: 287n, 322

BUONAROTTI. See Michelangelo.

BURKE, EDMUND. *Reflections on the Revolution in France, and on the proceedings in certain societies in London relative to that event. In a letter intended to have been sent to a gentleman in Paris.* In *Works.* 3 vols. London: Dodsley, 1792, III, 19–321.

NOTE: this volume, and Vols. IV and V of the edition as later extended, formerly in JSM's library, Somerville College.

QUOTED: 142

142.36–7 "rear her mitred front in courts and palaces,"] No! we will have her [religion] to exalt her mitred front in courts and parliaments. (III, 144)

BUTLER, JOSEPH. Referred to: 21, 64n, 65, 172

NOTE: the reference at 172 is in a quotation from Whewell.

———— *The Analogy of Religion, Natural and Revealed, to the Constitution and Course of Nature. To which are added two brief dissertations: I. Of Personal Identity. II. Of the Nature of Virtue.* London: Knapton, 1736.

NOTE: at 64 JSM is quoting Sedgwick's quotation from Butler; for variants, see under Sedgwick, *A Discourse*, 64.12–19.

QUOTED: 64   REFERRED TO: 469

BUTLER, SAMUEL. *Hudibras.* 2 vols. Ed. Zachary Grey. London: Vernor and Hood, *et al.*, 1801.

NOTE: in JSM's library, Somerville College.

QUOTED: 445

445.3–4   The dark lantern of the Spirit / Which none see by but those who bear it:] (The "new light"] 'Tis a dark-lanthorn of the spirit, / Which none see by but those that bear it; / A light that falls down from on high, / For spiritual trades to cozen by / An *ignis fatuus*, that bewitches / And leads men into pools and ditches, / To make them dip themselves, and sound / For Christendom in dirty pond; / To dive, like wild-fowl, for salvation, / And fish to catch regeneration. (I, 53–4; Pt. I, Canto I, ll.505–14.)

BYRON. Referred to: 92

CAESAR, AUGUSTUS. Referred to: 466

CAESAR, JULIUS. Referred to: 362

CAMDEN. See Pratt.

CAMPBELL, GEORGE. *A Dissertation on Miracles: containing an examination of the principles advanced by David Hume, in an Essay on Miracles.* Edinburgh: Kincaid and Bell, 1762.

REFERRED TO: 470

CAMPBELL, JOHN. Referred to: 102

NOTE: the reference is to Campbell as Attorney-General in 1838.

CARAVAGGIO. Referred to: 136n

NOTE: the reference is in a quotation from Coleridge.

CARDAILLAC. Referred to: 296

CARLYLE, THOMAS. "Novalis," in *Critical and Miscellaneous Essays.* 5 vols. London: Fraser, 1840, II.

NOTE: this edition probably was in JSM's library, Somerville College. The references derive from JSM's citations of Novalis, but there can be little doubt that he took them from Carlyle, and so they are entered below. The quotations are indirect.

QUOTED: 214, 336

214.37–8   simultaneous act of suicide under certain conditions] That theory of the human species ending by a universal simultaneous act of Suicide, will, to the more simple sort of readers, be new. (II, 288) [The passage is found in Chap. ii, "Die Natur," of Novalis's *Die Lehrlinge zu Sais*; see Paul Kluckhohn and Richard Samuel, eds. *Novalis Schriften.* Stuttgart: Kohlhammer Verlag, 1960, I, 88–9.]

336.6   Spinoza . . . was a God-intoxicated man] [*in translation from Novalis, Carlyle writes:*] "Spinoza is a God-intoxicated man (*Gott-trunkener Mensch*)." (II, 296) [The passage is found in "Fragmente"; *see* Ludwig Tieck and Friedrich Schlegel, eds. *Novalis Schriften.* 4th ed. 3 parts. Berlin: Reimer, 1826, II, 261.]

————— *On Heroes, Hero-Worship, and the Heroic in History.* London: Fraser, 1841.

NOTE: in JSM's library, Somerville College. JSM is citing Novalis, but there is little doubt that he took the reference from Carlyle, who cites the passage not only in *Heroes*, but twice in *Sartor Resartus*, and once in "Characteristics."

QUOTED: 407–8

407.41–408.1   My belief has gained infinitely to me from the moment when one other human being has begun to believe the same.] "It is certain," says Novalis, "my Conviction gains infinitely, the moment another soul will believe in it." (93) [The passage is found in Ludwig Tieck and Friedrich Schlegel, eds. *Novalis Schriften.* 4th ed. 3 parts. Berlin: Reimer, 1826, II, 104.]

————— *Past and Present.* London: Chapman and Hall, 1843.

NOTE: presentation copy, "To Mrs Taylor / with kind regards. / T.C.", in JSM's library, Somerville College. The quotation is of a common phrase in Carlyle, most fully developed in Bk. IV, Chap. iv, "Captains of Industry."

QUOTED: 347

———— *Sartor Resartus*. 2nd ed. Boston: Munroe, 1837.

NOTE: in JSM's library, Somerville College. The quotation at 214 is indirect.

QUOTED: 214, 333

214.23   What . . . *be*?] What Act of Legislature was there that *thou* shouldst be happy? A little while ago thou hadst no right to *be* at all. (197; Bk. II, Chap. ix)

333   "the Infinite nature of Duty,"] Thus, in spite of all motive-grinders, and mechanical profit-and-loss philosophies, with the sick ophthalmia and hallucination they had brought on, was the infinite nature of duty still dimly present to me. (170; Bk. II, Chap. vii) [the context of this comment by Teufelsdröckh gives the rest of JSM's statement. Cf. *Past and Present*, 156–7 (Bk. II, Chap. xv).]

CARRIER. Referred to: 386

CHALMERS. Referred to: 151

CHARLES I (of England). Referred to: 155

NOTE: the reference is in a quotation from Coleridge.

CHARLES II (of England). Referred to: 155

NOTE: the reference is in a quotation from Coleridge.

CHÂTEAUBRIAND. Referred to: 92

CHRIST. See Jesus.

CICERO, MARCUS TULLIUS. *Brutus sive de claris oratoribus.*

NOTE: many editions of Cicero in JSM's library, Somerville College.

QUOTED: 145

145.14   instar omnium] Plato enim mihi unus instar est omnium. (51.191)

———— *De finibus bonorum et malorum*. Referred to: 87

NOTE: many editions of Cicero in JSM's library, Somerville College.

———— *De Officiis*. Referred to: 421

NOTE: many editions of Cicero in JSM's library, Somerville College.

CLARE. Referred to: 136n

NOTE: the reference, to "Strongbow," is in a quotation from Coleridge.

CLARKE. Referred to: 21, 85

NOTE: the reference at 85 derives from Bentham's identification ("Clark") of the moralist intended in his fifth category.

CLARKSON. Referred to: 188

COGAN. Referred to: 21

COLERIDGE, HENRY NELSON. "Preface," *The Literary Remains of Samuel Taylor Coleridge*, III. London: Pickering, 1838, ix–xvi.

QUOTED: 162. See also Coleridge, Samuel Taylor, *Literary Remains*.

161.28   the only] [*paragraph*] His [Coleridge's] friends have always known this to be the fact [that he criticized Biblical literalism]; and he vindicated this so openly that it would be folly to attempt to conceal it: nay, he pleaded for it so earnestly—as the only (III, xi)
161.32   former; for he] former,—that to suppress this important part of his solemn convictions would be to misrepresent and betray him. For he (III, xi)
161.36   fools! . . . Of the] fools! [*3½-sentence omission*] He trembled at the dreadful dogma which rests God's right to man's obedience on the fact of his almighty power,—a position falsely inferred from a misconceived illustration of St. Paul's, and which is less humbling to the creature than blasphemous of the Creator; and of the (III, xii–xiii)

COLERIDGE, SAMUEL TAYLOR. Referred to: 42, 77–8, 119–63 *passim*, 299, 494

———— *Aids to Reflection in the Formation of a Manly Character on the Several Grounds of Prudence, Morality, and Religion: Illustrated by select passages from our elder Divines, especially from Archbishop Leighton*. 2nd ed. London: Hurst, Chance, 1831.

NOTE: the 1st ed. (London: Taylor and Hessey, 1825) is in JSM's library, Somerville College, but his page references correspond to those in the edition cited (which agree with those in the edition of 1836 [London: Pickering]).

QUOTED: 128, 159

159.10–11   "the *outward* . . . virtue" is "the . . . men,"] For the outward . . . virtue being the . . . men, it must needs include the object of an intelligent self-love, which is the greatest possible happiness of one individual; for what is true of all, must be true of each. (37)
159.11   "happiness . . . man."] For Pleasure (and happiness . . . man, and hence by the Greeks called εὐτυχία, *i.e.* good-hap, or more religiously εὐδαιμονία, *i.e.* favorable providence)—Pleasure, I say, consists in the harmony between the specific excitability of a living creature, and the exciting causes correspondent thereto. (39)

———— *Biographia Literaria: or, Biographical sketches of my literary life and opinions.* 2 vols in 1. London: Rest Fenner, 1817.

NOTE: in JSM's library, Somerville College. The passage at 158 includes a quotation from Leibnitz, *Trois lettres*; the quotation at 129 is indirect.

QUOTED: 129, 158

129.24 they required . . . afresh.] [*paragraph*] To which I may add from myself, that what medical physiologists affirm of certain secretions, applies equally to our thoughts; they too must be taken up again into the circulation, and be again and again re-secreted in order to ensure a healthful vigor, both to the mind and to its intellectual offspring. (I, 234n)

158.30–1 "*J'ai . . . nient.*] [*not in italics*] (I, 250; see Leibnitz, *Trois lettres*, below)

———— *Confessions of an Inquiring Spirit.* Ed. Henry Nelson Coleridge. London: Pickering, 1840.

NOTE: in JSM's library, Somerville College.

REFERRED TO: 162n

———— *First Lay Sermon* [*The Statesman's Manual*]. 2nd ed. In *On the Constitution of Church and State, and Lay Sermons.* London: Pickering, 1839.

NOTE: the indirect quotation, wrongly attributed by JSM, following Coleridge, to Bacon, actually derives from James Steuart, *An Inquiry into the Principles of Political Œconomy* (2 vols. London: Millar and Cadell, 1767). For the identification, see Kathleen Coburn, ed., *S. T. Coleridge's Notebooks* (London: Routledge and Kegan Paul, 1957), I (Notes), 309 (21.11).

QUOTED: 119

119.7–9 If it be true, as Lord Bacon affirms, that a knowledge of the speculative opinions of the men between twenty and thirty years of age is the great source of political philosophy,] Turn over the fugitive writings, that are still extant, of the age of Luther; peruse the pamphlets and loose sheets that came out in flights during the reign of Charles I and the Republic; and you will find in these one continued comment on the aphorism of Lord Bacon (a man assuredly sufficiently acquainted with the extent of secret and personal influence), that the knowledge of the speculative principles of men in general between the age of twenty and thirty is the one great source of political prophecy. (216n) [Cf. *The Friend*, I, 315.] [The passage in Steuart reads:] In every country we find two generations upon the stage at a time; that is to say, we may distribute into two classes the spirit which prevails; the one amongst men between twenty and thirty, when opinions are forming; the other of those who are past fifty, when opinions and habits are formed and confirmed. A person of judgment and observation may foresee many things relative to government, from an exact application to the rise and progress of new customs and opinions, provided he preserve his mind free from all attachments and prejudices, in favour of those which he himself has adopted, and in that delicacy of sensation necessary to perceive the influence of a change of circumstances. This is the genius proper to form a great statesman. (I, 11)

———— *The Friend: A series of Essays, in three volumes, to aid in the formation of fixed principles in politics, morals, and religion, with literary amusements interspersed.* 3 vols. London: Rest Fenner, 1818.

NOTE: in JSM's library, Somerville College. The quotations at 126 and 151 are indirect.

See also Bacon. JSM's reference to Coleridge as an "arrant driveller" on political economy (155) may reflect his reading of I, 283–356.

QUOTED: 126, 151, 158–9

126.13–14   we see, before we know that we have eyes] as "METAPHYSICS" are the science which determines what can, and what can not, be known of Being and the Laws of Being, a priori (that is from those necessities of the mind or forms of thinking, which, though first revealed to us by experience, must yet have pre-existed in order to make experience itself possible, even as the eye must exist previous to any particular act of seeing, though by sight only can we know that we have eyes) —so might the philosophy of Rousseau and his followers not inaptly be entitled, METAPOLITICS, and the Doctors of this School, Metapoliticians. (I, 309n; cf. *Literary Remains*, I, 326n; *Table Talk*, 220)

151.6–8   the balance . . . trade] I entreat my readers to recollect, that the present question does not concern the effects of taxation on the public independence and on the supposed balance of the three constitutional powers, (from which said balance, as well as from the balance of trade, I own, I have never been able to elicit one ray of common sense.) (II, 74–5)

159.4–5   "to . . . self-contradiction"] This is, indeed, the main characteristic of the moral system taught by the Friend throughout, that the distinct foresight of Consequences belongs exclusively to that infinite Wisdom which is one with that Almighty Will, on which all consequences depend; but that *for Man*—to . . . self-contradiction, or in other words, to produce and maintain the greatest possible Harmony in the component impulses and faculties of his nature, involves the effects of Prudence. (I, 256)

159.6   "be"] So act that thou mayest be (I, 340)

299.36–7   metapolitics] [*see passage quoted in entry for* 126.13–14 *above*]

――――― *The Literary Remains of Samuel Taylor Coleridge.* Ed. Henry Nelson Coleridge. 4 vols. London: Pickering, 1836–39.

NOTE: the quotation at 155.21–4 is indirect.

QUOTED: 144, 150, 155, 158, 159, 160–1, 162. See also Coleridge, Henry Nelson.

144.27   bibliolatry] [*e.g. of common term in Coleridge:*] But in fact the age was not ripe enough even for a Hooker to feel, much less with safety to expose, the Protestants' idol, that is, their Bibliolatry. (III, 42)

150.19–20   "constituted" . . . "the . . . apostasy."] For it is this very interpretation of the Church [as the "Clergy, the hierarchy exclusively" by Laud and his followers] that, according to my conviction, constituted . . . apostasy; and I hold it for one of the greatest mistakes of our polemic divines in their controversies with the Romanists, that they trace all the corruptions of the Gospel faith to the Papacy. (III, 386)

155.21–4   no . . . knowledge;] [*paragraph*] If any man, who like myself hath attentively read the Church history of the reign of Elizabeth, and the conference before, and with, her pedant successor, can shew me any essential difference between Whitgift and Bancroft during their rule, and Bonner and Gardiner in the reign of Mary, I will be thankful to him in my heart and for him in my prayers. One difference I see, namely, that the former professing the New Testament to be their rule and guide, and making the fallibility of all churches and individuals an article of faith, were more inconsistent, and therefore less excusable, than the Popish persecutors. (II, 388–9)

158.35   "truths misunderstood," "half-truths . . . whole,"] For we are not bound to say the truth, where we know that we cannot convey it, but very probably may

impart a falsehood instead; no falsehoods being more dangerous than truths misunderstood, nay, the most mischievous errors on record having been half-truths . . .
whole. (III, 145)

159.20–1   "if . . . France,"] [*paragraph*] This just and acute remark [by Jeremy Taylor]
is, in fact, no less applicable to Scripture in all doctrinal points, and if . . . France,
the same criterion (that is, the internal evidence) must be extended to all points,
to the narratives no less than to the precept. (III, 263)

159.22–6   "the . . . God;" . . . "clearly . . . and St. Paul."] [*paragraph*] If we are quite
certain that any writing pretending to divine origin contains gross contradictions
to demonstrable truths *in eodem genere*, or commands that outrage the clearest
principles of right and wrong; then we may be equally certain that the pretence is
a blasphemous falsehood, inasmuch as the . . . God. [*paragraph*] This principle
is clearly . . . and by St. Paul. (III, 293) [234ᵍ⁻ᵍ.]

159.30   "the] The (I, 367)

160.31–161.1   "the . . . of the word," . . . "wilful . . . will;"] Alas! alas! how long will
it be ere Christians take the plain middle road between intolerance and indifference,
by adopting the . . . of heresy, that is, wilful . . . will; and of heretics, (for such
there are, nay, even orthodox heretics), that is, men wilfully unconscious of their
own wilfulness, in their limpet-like adhesion to a favourite tenet? (IV, 193)

161.4–5   "pseudo-Athanasius," . . . "interprets Catholic . . . belief,"] And lastly, who
authorized either you, or the pseudo-Athanasius, to interpret Catholic . . . belief,
arising out of the apparent predominance of the grounds for, over those against,
the truth of the positions asserted; much more, by belief as a mere passive acquiescence of the understanding? (IV, 193)

161.5–6   "true Lutheran doctrine," . . . "neither] How infinitely safer the true Lutheran
doctrine [than Jeremy Taylor's]: God cannot be mocked; neither (III, 359)

161.7   condemn. To] condemn;—to (III, 359)

161.10   habit.] habit;—to watch over the secret movements of the heart, remembering
ever how deceitful a thing it is, and that God cannot be mocked, though we may
easily dupe ourselves: these, as the ground-work with prayer, study of the Scriptures, and tenderness to all around us, as the consequents, are the Christian's rule,
and supersede all books of casuistry, which latter serve only to harden our feelings
and pollute the imagination. (III, 359)

161.12   ambitious] ambition (IV, 245)

161.18–20   "The notion . . . it,"] The very same principles on which the pontifical
polemics vindicate the Papal infallibility, Fuller *et centum alii* apply to the (if
possible) still more extravagant notion . . . it. (III, 385)

161.21–2   "there . . . unbelief;"] But in all superstition there . . . unbelief, and, *vice
versa*, where an individual's belief is but a superficial acquiescence, credulity is the
natural result and accompaniment, if only he be not required to sink into the
depths of his being, where the sensual man can no longer draw breath. (III,
229–30)

161.22   "if . . . extravagant"] [*see entry for* 161.18–20 *above*] (II, 385)

———— *I. On the Constitution of Church and State According to the Idea
of Each. II. Lay Sermons:* I. *The Statesman's Manual.* II. *"Blessed are ye
that sow beside all waters."* Ed. Henry Nelson Coleridge. London:
Pickering, 1839.

NOTE: this edition, in JSM's library, is the one to which his references correspond; it
includes the 3rd ed. of *Church and State*, and the 2nd ed. of the *Lay Sermons.* Also
in JSM's library is the 2nd ed. of *Church and State* (London: Hurst, Chance,
1830). The collations for the *Lay Sermons* are given under *First Lay Sermon* and
Second Lay Sermon.

QUOTED: 135n–136n, 146–9, 150–2, 155

135.n9   us discharge] us, however, first discharge (160)

135.n17   could be] could have been (161)

147.10   the] [paragraph] The Nationalty, therefore, was reserved for the (46)

147.32   Religion] But I affirm that in the spiritual purpose of the word, and as understood in reference to a future state, and to the abiding essential interest of the individual as a person, and not as the citizen, neighbour, or subject, religion (48)

147.35   Christ..... The] [ellipsis indicates 1-page omission] (48–9)

147.35   The clerisy] [paragraph] The Clerisy (49)

147.38   architecture, with] architecture, of the physical sciences, with (49)

148.5   ideas.] ideas.* [8-sentence footnote omitted] (50)

148.14   knowledge of] knowledges that (51)

148.27   "cannot] But I do assert, that the Nationalty cannot (54)

148.28   nation never] nation it never (54)

148.29   purposes,"] purposes. (54)

148.29–30   "a . . . civilization,"] These [permanency and progression] depend on a . . . civilization. (46)

148.37   I] But I (53)

148.39   contrary..... In] [ellipsis indicates 5½-page omission; the sentence indicated in the entry for 148.27 above follows immediately after contrary] (53–4, 59)

148.39   In] [paragraph] In (59)

148.40   accident,] accident,* [3-sentence footnote, explaining the sense of the phrase, omitted] (59)

148.41   God..... As] God, a mighty and faithful friend, the envoy indeed and liege subject of another State, but which can neither administer the laws nor promote the ends of this other State, which is not of the world, without advantage, direct and indirect, to the true interests of the States, the aggregate of which is what we mean by the world, that is, the civilized world. As (59–60)

150.16–18   "who, . . . pastorate,"] 3, of a school-master in every parish, who . . . pastorate; so that both should be labourers in different compartments of the same field, workmen engaged in different stages of the same process, with such difference of rank, as might be suggested in the names pastor and sub-pastor, or as now exists between rector and curate, elder and deacon. (56–7) [the full sentence runs for 2 pages]

151.10   Because] [paragraph] But a Constitution is an idea arising out of the idea of a State; and because (18)

151.11   in the] on the (18) [printer's error?]

151.12   and what] and in what (19)

151.16–17   though (even . . . idea) not] though even . . . idea not (19)

151.23   is] [paragraph] There is yet another ground for the affirmation of its reality; that, as the fundamental idea, it is (19)

151.25   system: those principles in] system—(I use the term in its widest sense, in which the crown itself is included as representing the unity of the people, the true and primary sense of the word majesty);—those principles, I say, in (19)

151.33   It] [no paragraph] It (23)

151.35–6   and growing] and the growing (23)

151.38   States . . . Now] [ellipsis indicates omission of 14-line quotation from the "Ode to the Departing Year"] (24)

151.38   Now] [paragraph] Now (24)

151.39   men, or acknowledging] men, acknowledging (24)

152.2   permanence . . . progression.] permanence . . . progression.* [2-paragraph footnote] (24)

152.7   hand," he says, "the] hand, with as little chance of contradiction, I may assert that the (26)

152.12   These] [paragraph] These (29)

152.13   classes I] classes, by an arbitrary but convenient use of the phrase, I (29)

152.23–4   "the . . . House;"] [*paragraph*] Thus in the theory of the Constitution it was provided that even though both divisions of the Landed Interest should combine in any legislative attempt to encroach on the rights and privileges of the Personal Interest, yet the representatives of the latter forming the . . . House, the attempt must be abortive; the majority of votes in both Houses being indispensable in order to the presentation of a bill for the completory act,—that is, to make it a law of the land. (30)

152.26–31   "the very weight . . . landholders" . . . "in . . . scale;" . . . "now . . . check;"] [*paragraph*] That the burgesses were not bound to elect representatives from among their own order, individuals *bona fide* belonging to one or other of the four divisions above enumerated; that the elective franchise of the cities, towns, and ports, first invested with borough-rights, was not made conditional, and to a certain extent at least dependent, on their retaining the same comparative wealth and independence, and rendered subject to a periodical revisal and re-adjustment; that, in consequence of these and other causes, the very weights . . . land-holders, have, in . . . scale; that they now . . . check;—these things are no part of the Constitution, no essential ingredients in the idea, but apparent defects and imperfections in its realization; which, however, we need neither regret nor set about amending, till we have seen whether an equivalent force has not arisen to supply the deficiency;—a force great enough to have destroyed the *equilibrium*, had not such a transfer taken place previously to, or at the same time with, the operation of the new forces. (31–2) [*the next sentence is partly used by JSM in his concluding clause*]

155.15–17   "a . . . head" . . . "either . . . them."] Our state-policy a . . . head; our measures become either . . . them; for all true insight is foresight. (69)

155.8–9   "the . . . reigns"] (the . . . reigns) (102) [*the full sentence runs for 1 page*]

155.27–30   "a . . . kingdom" instead of "the . . . aware."] . . . and if, I say, Henry [VIII] had then directed the Nationalty to its true national purposes, (in order to which, however, a . . . kingdom must have superseded the . . . aware); . . . . (56) [*the full sentence, including the passage at 150.16–18 above, runs for 2 pages*]

———— "Pitt," in James Gillman. *The Life of Samuel Taylor Coleridge*. 2 vols. London: Pickering, 1838, I, 195–207.

NOTE: reprinted from the *Morning Post*, 19 Mar., 1800; also appears in Coleridge's *Essays on His Own Times, A Second Series of The Friend* (London: Pickering, 1850, II, 319–29).

REFERRED TO: 155

———— *Second Lay Sermon* [*Blessed are ye that sow beside all waters*]. 2nd ed. In *On the Constitution of Church and State, and Lay Sermons*. London: Pickering, 1839.

NOTE: in JSM's library, Somerville College.

QUOTED: 155n, 156–7

155.n2   "Instead] Thus instead (403)

156.23   Let] [*no paragraph*] Let (414)

156.27   hope] hope* [*3-sentence footnote omitted*] (415)

157.25   "that] [*paragraph*] That agriculture requires principles essentially different from those of trade; that (413)

157.26   should] ought not to (413) [*JSM puts the negative earlier in his paraphrase*]

157.27   stock;"] stock,—admits of an easy proof from the different tenure of landed property,* [*footnote includes sentence quoted by JSM at* 157] and from the purposes of agriculture itself, which ultimately are the same as those of the State of which it is the offspring. (413–14)

———— *Specimens of the Table Talk of Samuel Taylor Coleridge.* Ed. Henry Nelson Coleridge. 2nd ed. London: Murray, 1836.

NOTE: the quotation at 121 is indirect.

QUOTED: 121, 160

121.24–5 every one is born either a Platonist or an Aristotelian:] Every man is born an Aristotelian, or a Platonist. (95) [Cf. *Literary Remains*, III, 33: "Every man capable of philosophy at all (and there are not many such) is a born Platonist or a born Aristotelian."]
160.3–4 Unitarians" and even infidels. "It] Unitarians and open infidels. It (91) [Cf. 160*ⁱ⁻ⁱ*.]

COMBE. Referred to: 378

COMTE, AUGUSTE. Referred to: 263–368 *passim*, 406

———— *Appel aux conservateurs.* Paris: Comte, Dalmont, 1855.

NOTE: in JSM's library, Somerville College, bound with a presentation copy of Comte's *Discours sur l'ensemble du positivisme* (Paris: Mathias, Carilian-Gœury, and Dalmont, 1848).

REFERRED TO: 328n

———— *The Catechism of Positive Religion.* Trans. Richard Congreve. London: Chapman, 1858.

REFERRED TO: 328

———— *Catéchisme positiviste, ou Sommaire exposition de la religion universelle, en onze entretiens systématiques entre une femme et un prêtre de l'humanité.* Paris: Comte, Carilian-Gœury, and Dalmont, 1852.

NOTE: in JSM's library, Somerville College, where many of the cited passages are marked marginally. JSM often uses terms or ideas found repeatedly in Comte's later works; some of the identifications are therefore typical rather than exact, and similar passages may be found in Comte's *Synthèse* and *Système*. Where quotations (such as those at 340, 342, 346, 347) are indirect or summary, usually no collation is given.

QUOTED: 335, 336, 340, 342, 346, 347, 357 REFERRED TO: 323, 328n, 329

335.36 (du cœur sur l'esprit)] Toujours fondée sur un libre concours de volontés indépendantes, son existence composée, que toute discorde tend à dissoudre, consacre aussitôt la prépondérance continue du cœur sur l'esprit comme l'unique base de notre véritable unité. (19)
336.15–22 the . . . social.] [*translated from:*] En lui-même, il indique l'état de complète *unité* qui distingue notre existence, à la fois personnelle et sociale, quand toutes ses parties, tant morales que physiques, convergent habituellement vers une destination commune. [*ellipsis indicates 3-sentence omission*] [*paragraph*] Une

telle harmonie, individuelle ou collective, ne pouvant jamais être pleinement réalisée dans une existence aussi compliquée que la nôtre, cette définition de la religion caractérise donc le type immuable vers lequel tend de plus en plus l'cn semble des efforts humains. Notre bonheur et notre mérite consistent surtout à nous rapprocher autant que possible de cette unité, dont l'essor graduel constitue la meilleure mesure du vrai perfectionnement, personnel ou social. (2–3)

357.2   the living are more and more governed by the dead.] [*translated from:*] Les vivants sont toujours, et de plus en plus, gouvernés nécessairement par les morts: telle est la loi fondamentale de l'ordre humain. (32; cf. *Système*, III, xxxiv. Both passages marked marginally in JSM's copies.)

———— *Cours de philosophie positive.* 2nd ed. 6 vols. Preface, E. Littré. Paris: Ballière, 1864.

NOTE: 1st ed. (6 vols. Paris: Bachelier, 1830–42) in JSM's library. The 4th ed. (Paris: Baillière, 1877), in which the pagination agrees with JSM's citations from the 2nd, is used in the following collations.

REVIEWED: 263–327   QUOTED: 294, 295–6, 298, 300, 301, 303–4, 312, 321, 330, 363

REFERRED TO: 328–9, 332, 359, 363, 366

294.13–14   "the degree . . . science,"] [*translated from:*] Ainsi, je ne propose point le dualisme universel et invariable comme une loi réelle de la nature, que nous ne pourrions jamais avoir aucun moyen de constater; mais je le proclame un artifice fondamental de la vraie philosophie chimique, destiné à simplifier toutes nos conceptions élémentaires, en usant judicieusement du genre spécial de liberté resté facultatif pour notre intelligence, d'après le véritable but et l'objet général de la chimie positive. (III, 81)

295.11–15   "without . . . to us"] [*translated from:*] [*paragraph*] En considérant sous un dernier aspect l'influence fondamentale d'une telle destination, suivant l'esprit de la philosophie relative, nous avons partout reconnu qu'elle détermine spontanément le genre de liberté resté facultatif pour notre intelligence, et dont nous devons savoir user, sans aucun vain scrupule, afin de satisfaire, entre les limites convenables, nos justes inclinations mentales, toujours dirigées, avec une prédilection instinctive, vers la simplicité, la continuité et la généralité des conceptions, tout en respectant constamment la réalité des lois extérieures, en tant qu'elle nous est accessible. (VI, 639–40)

295.15–19   "The most . . . wants"] [*translated from:*] Ainsi, le point de vue le plus philosophique conduit finalement, à ce sujet, à concevoir l'étude des lois naturelles comme destinée à nous représenter le monde extérieur, en satisfaisant aux inclinations essentielles de notre intelligence, autant que le comporte le degré d'exactitude commandé, à cet égard, par l'ensemble de nos besoins pratiques. (VI, 642)

295.21   "instinctive . . . harmony,"] [*translated from:*] Nos lois statiques correspondent à cette prédilection instinctive pour l'ordre et l'harmonie, dont l'esprit humain est tellement animé, que, si elle n'était pas sagement contenue, elle entraînerait souvent aux plus vicieux rapprochements; nos lois dynamiques s'accordent avec notre tendance irrésistible à croire constamment, même d'après trois observations seulement, à la perpétuité des retours déjà constatés, suivant une impulsion spontanée que nous devons aussi réprimer fréquemment pour maintenir l'indispensable réalité de nos conceptions. (VI, 642)

295.23–25   "les convenances . . . intelligence."] Quand l'esprit relatif de la vraie philosophie moderne aura convenablement prévalu, tous les penseurs comprendront, ce que le règne de l'absolu empêche maintenant de sentir, que les convenances purement esthétiques doivent avoir une certaine part légitime dans l'usage continu du genre de liberté resté facultatif pour notre intelligence par la nature essentielle des véritables recherches scientifiques. (VI, 646–7)

295.26–9 "most eminent . . . reality"] [*translated from:*] Avant tout, sans doute, comme je l'ai ci-dessus expliqué, une telle liberté doit être employée de manière à faciliter le plus possible la marche ultérieure de nos conceptions réelles, en satisfaisants convenablement à nos plus éminentes inclinations mentales. Mais cette condition primordiale laissera partout subsister encore une notable indétermination, dont il conviendra de gratifier directement nos besoins d'idéalité, en embellissant nos pensées scientifiques, sans nuire aucunement à leur réalité essentielle. (VI, 647)

295.31–2 "severe . . . investigation"] [*translated from:*] D'éclatants exemples ont déjà montré qu'on peut obtenir aujourd'hui, en philosophie naturelle, d'éphémères triomphes, aussi faciles que désastreux, en se bornant à détruire, d'après une investigation trop minutieuse, les lois précédemment établies, sans aucune substitution quelconque de nouvelles règles; en sorte qu'une aveugle appréciation académique entraîne à récompenser expressément une conduite que tout véritable régime spéculatif frapperait nécessairement d'une sévère réprobation. (VI, 639)

295.35–6 "the . . . intelligence] [*see entry for* 295.15–19 *above*]

296.14 of moral . . . functions] [[*translated from:*] Sommaire. — Considérations générales sur l'étude positive des fonctions intellectuelles et morales, ou cérébrales. (III, 530; *heading of* Quarant-cinquième Leçon (1).)

297.31 "des diverses facultés élémentaires,"] [*paragraph*] A cette analyse anatomique de l'appareil cérébral, il faudra joindre, dans un ordre d'idées entièrement distinct quoique parallèle, l'analyse purement physiologique des diverses facultés élémentaires, qui devra finalement être constituée, autant que possible, en harmonie scientifique avec la première: toute idée anatomique devra, à son tour, être provisoirement écartée dans ce second travail, au lieu de la fusion anticipée qu'on veut habituellement opérer entre les deux points de vue. (III, 573)

300.15–16 "la metaphysique constitutionnelles"] Mais ce déplorable ascendant devra vous faire attacher, en lieu convenable, une extrême importance à la discussion ultérieure de cet unique aspect spécieux de la doctrine stationnaire, qu'une exacte analyse historique caractérisera spontanément, en constatant la profonde inanité nécessaire de cette métaphysique constitutionnelle sur la pondération et l'équilibre des divers pouvoirs, d'après une judicieuse appréciation de ce même état politique qui sert de base ordinaire à de telles fictions sociales. (IV, 85–6)

301.32–3 "the absolute . . . conscience."] [*translated from:*] [*paragraph*] En considérant maintenant la doctrine critique sous un point de vue plus spécial, il est évident que le droit absolu du libre examen, ou le dogme de la liberté illimitée de conscience, constitue son principe le plus étendu et le plus fondamental, surtout en n'en séparant point ses conséquences les plus immédiates, relatives à la liberté de la presse, de l'enseignement, ou de tout autre mode quelconque d'expression et de communication des opinions humaines. (IV, 43)

304.7–11 "the claims . . . slavery"] [*translated from:*] Sans doute, chaque individu, quelle que soit son infériorité, a toujours le droit naturel, à moins d'une conduite antisociale très-caractérisée, d'attendre de tous les autres le scrupuleux accomplissement continu des égards généraux inhérents à la dignité d'homme et dont l'ensemble, encore fort imparfaitement apprécié, constituera de jour en jour le principe le plus usuel de la morale universelle. Mais, malgré cette grande obligation morale, qui n'a jamais été directement niée depuis l'abolition de l'esclavage, il est évident que les hommes ne sont ni égaux entre eux, ni même équivalents, et ne sauraient, par suite, posséder, dans l'association, des droits identiques, sauf, bien entendu, le droit fondamental, nécessairement commun à tous, du libre développement normal de l'activité personnelle, une fois convenablement dirigée. (IV, 54)

304.23–5 "an arbitrary . . . kings"] [*translated from:*] Mais, en appréciant, comme il convient, l'indispensable office transitoire de ce dogme révolutionnaire, aucun vrai philosophe ne saurait méconnaître aujourd'hui la fatale tendance anarchique d'une telle conception métaphysique, lorsque, dans son application absolue, elle s'oppose à toute institution régulière, en condamnant indéfiniment tous les supérieurs à une arbitraire dépendance envers la multitude de leurs inférieurs, par une sorte de transport aux peuples du droit divin tant reproché aux rois. (IV, 55–6)

312.33 "dispersive speciality"] [*translated from:*] Quoique cette sorte d'automatisme humain ne constitue heureusement que l'extrême influence dispersive du principe de la spécialisation, sa réalisation, déjà trop fréquente, et d'ailleurs de plus en plus imminente, doit faire attacher à l'appréciation d'un tel cas une véritable importance scientifique, comme évidemment propre à caractériser la tendance générale et à manifester plus vivement l'indispensable nécessité de sa répression permanente. (IV, 430)

321.6 "consultative"] [*paragraph*] Il est donc évident que, bien loin de pouvoir directement dominer la conduite réelle de la vie humaine, individuelle ou sociale, l'esprit est seulement destiné, dans la véritable économie de notre invariable nature, à modifier plus ou moins profondément, par une influence consultative ou préparatoire, le règne spontané de la puissance matérielle ou pratique, soit militaire, soit industrielle. (V, 219)

330.6 "hygiène cérébrale."] En conséquence, après avoir, dans ma première jeunesse, rapidement amassé tous les matériaux qui me paraissent convenir à la grande élaboration dont je sentais déjà l'esprit fondamental, je me suis, depuis vingt ans au moins, imposé, à titre d'hygiène cérébrale, l'obligation, quelquefois gênante, mais plus souvent heureuse, de ne jamais faire aucune lecture qui puisse offrir une importante relation, même indirecte, au sujet quelconque dont je m'occupe actuellement, sauf à ajourner judicieusement, selon ce principe, les nouvelles acquisitions extérieures que je jugerais utiles. (VI, 34)

363.13 "liberté facultative"] [*see entry for* 294.13–14 *above*] (III, 81)

———— *A General View of Positivism.* Trans. John H. Bridges. London: Trübner, 1865.

REFERRED TO: 329

———— *Synthèse subjective, ou Système universel des conceptions propres à l'état normal de l'humanité. Tome premier, contenant le Système de logique positive, ou Traité de philosophie mathématique.* Paris: Comte and Dalmont, 1856.

NOTE: no more published. In JSM's library, Somerville College, where many of the references are marginally marked. JSM often uses terms or ideas found repeatedly in Comte's later works; some of the identifications are therefore typical rather than exact, and similar passages may be found in Comte's *Catéchisme* and *Système*.

QUOTED: 346, 352, 355–7, 363–7 REFERRED TO: 328n

346.11 (vues d'ensemble).] Vainement les faux théoriciens invoquèrent-ils le développement de la science pour perpétuer le régime où les travaux de détail éteignaient les vues d'ensemble. (523–4; *cf. Système,* IV, 447)

352.27–8 "le plus perturbateur,"] A la science le plus abstraite appartient surtout une telle aptitude; car elle tend directement à discipliner le plus perturbateur des trois éléments humains, en faisant spontanément surgir, de son propre essor, l'irrésistible frein d'une pleine évidence. (70–1)

355.28–9 orgueil . . . sécheresse] Une invocation sagement continue de leur destination et de leur nature doit normalement suffire, quand elles sont régénérées, pour les empêcher de développer l'orgueil, et même de disposer à la sécheresse. (68–9)

356.20 *la foi demontrable*] [*paragraph*] Mieux appréciée, l'éducation encyclopédique, qui semble d'abord instituer la discussion, est surtout destinée à construire un foi toujours démontrable, mais rarement démontrée même au plus instruits. (93; *cf. Système,* IV, 267)

356.20–1   *la foi toujours démontrée*] [*see entry above*] (*ibid.*)

356.35–6   "distrust . . . order"] [*translated from:*] Nous devons d'abord considérer une telle conduite comme directement incompatible avec l'ordre normal, puisqu'elle émane d'une disposition défiante, sinon hostile, envers le sacerdoce fondamental. (278)

357.11–12   "the insurrection . . . dead."] [*translated from:*] Religieusement jugés, les appels absolus à la démonstration constituent des émeutes des vivants contre les morts, en aspirant à faire prévaloir le raisonnement individuel sur la raison collective, proclamée par les interprètes de l'Humanité. (278)

363.26–33   its physio-chemical . . . material force.] [*translated from:*] Obligée de subir constamment les lois fondamentales de la vie planétaire, la Terre, quant elle était intelligente, pouvait développer son activité physico-chimique de manière à perfectionner l'ordre astronomique en changeant ses principaux coefficients. Notre planète put ainsi rendre son orbite moins excentrique, et dès lors plus habitable, en concertant une longue suite d'explosions analogues à celles d'où proviennent les comètes, suivant la meilleure hypothèse. Reproduites avec sagesse, les mêmes secousses, secondées par la mobilité végétative, purent aussi rendre l'inclinaison de l'axe terrestre mieux conforme aux futurs besoins du Grand-Être. A plus forte raison la Terre put-elle alors modifier sa figure générale, qui n'est au-dessus de notre intervention que parce que notre ascendant spirituel ne dispose pas d'un pouvoir matériel assez considérable. (10–11)

363.36–9   In proportion . . . activity.] [*translated from:*] A mesure que chaque planète s'améliorait, sa vie s'épuisait par excès d'innervation, mais avec la consolation de rendre son dévouement plus efficace quand l'extinction des fonctions spéciales, d'abord animales, puis végétatives, la réduirait aux attributs universels de sentiment et d'activité. (11)

364.2   (croyance)] [*paragraph*] Une pareille croyance peut aussi satisfaire une curiosité spontanée qui, ne comportant aucune règle pendant notre enfance, y devint souvent abusive, mais que notre maturité doit utiliser en la disciplinant. (11)

364.3   "perfecting our unity"] [*translated from:*] Il convient, au contraire, de supposer des transformations antérieures à l'économie actuelle, si ces hypothèses peuvent perfectionner notre unité, soit en complétant les notions philosophiques par les fictions poétiques, soit surtout en développant nos sympathies. (11–12)

364.3–4   "by supplying . . . fictions,] [*see entry for* 364.3 *above*] (11–12)

364.4–7   and developing . . . Grand Être."] [*translated from:*] Toutefois, sa principale influence concerne la poèsie et la morale, vu son aptitude directe à développer les émotions sympathiques et les inspirations esthétiques. On conçoit alors le monde comme aspirant à seconder l'homme pour améliorer l'ordre universel sous l'impulsion du Grand-Être. (12)

364.19–23   "It is . . . social."] [*translated from:*] Il importe que le domaine de la fiction devienne aussi systématique que celui de la démonstration, afin que leur harmonie mutuelle soit conforme à leurs destinations respectives, également dirigées vers l'essor continu de l'unité personnelle et sociale. (12)

364.32–5   "The final . . . existence."] [*translated from:*] [*paragraph*] Rapportée à l'Humanité, l'unité finale inspire le besoin de cultiver la sympathie en développant notre reconnaissance pour tout ce qui sert au Grand-Être. Elle doit nous disposer à vénérer la fatalité sur laquelle repose l'ensemble de notre existence. (15)

365.17–21   One . . . more.] [*translated and summarized from:*] Une progression n'est vraiment normale que quand elle se réduit à trois termes; une combinaison ne peut jamais admettre plus de deux éléments, tout rapport étant binaire; une synthèse devient illusoire quand elle ne procède pas d'un seul principe. (108)

365.24–8   "Composed of . . . kind."] [*translated from:*] [*paragraph*] Formé de deux progressions suivies d'une synthèse, ou d'une progression entre deux couples, le nombre sept, succédant à la somme des trois nombres sacrés, détermine le plus vaste groupe que nous puissions distinctement imaginer. Réciproquement, il pose la limite des divisions que nous pouvons directement concevoir dans une grandeur quelconque. (127)

366.14 *l'arbitraire*] Une impulsion religieuse doit sagement employer les nombres pour éviter, dans tous les modes de notre existence, un arbitraire constamment favorable à l'égoïsme. (107)

366.38–9 "plan for . . . importance."] [*translated from:*] Son explication m'oblige à faire d'abord connaître le plan que j'ai finalement institué pour toutes les compositions importautes [*sic*], et pleinement pratiqué dans tout le cours du volume que j'achève. (755)

366.39–367.17 "Every volume . . . cantos,"] [*translated from:*] Relativement à chaque volume vraiment susceptible de former un traité distinct, il faut normalement instituer sept chapitres, outre l'introduction et la conclusion, et composer chacun de trois parties. Dans cette distribution fondamentale, qui se borne à préciser et systématiser des usages spontanément surgis, les deux divisions comportent des titres caractéristiques, quelquefois condensés en un seul mot. Examinée envers chaque tiers d'un chapitre quelconque, la règle consiste à le partager en sept sections, composées chacune de sept groupes de phrases, séparés par les alinéas usités. Normalement formée, la section offre un groupe central de sept phrases, que précèdent et suivent trois groupes de cinq: la section initiale de chaque partie réduit à trois phrases trois de ses groupes symétriquement placés; la section finale donne sept phrases à chacun des groupes extrêmes. [*paragraph*] Sous cet aspect, ma règle de composition rapproche la prose de la régularité poétique, vu ma réduction antérieure du maximum de toute phrase à deux lignes manuscrites ou cinq imprimées, c'est-à-dire deux cent cinquante lettres. A mesure que la préparation humaine s'accomplit, le perfectionnement de l'expression suscita des prescriptions plus précises, surtout caractérisées par le partage des chants en stances chez la population la plus esthétique. Normalement construits, les grands poëmes forment treize chants, décomposés en parties, sections et groupes comme mes chapitres, sauf l'entière égalité des groupes et des sections: en substituant le vers à la phrase, cette extension équivaut à celle de la principale épopée. Toutefois, la différence de structure ainsi réglée entre les volumes poétiques et les tomes philosophiques est plus apparente que réelle; car l'introduction et la conclusion d'un poëme doivent chacune comprendre trois de ses treize chants. (755–6)

367.22 "a synthetic . . . signification,"] [*translated from:*] Toute l'efficacité de la méthode repose sur le choix des deux sortes de mots, qui doivent toujours offrir une signification synthétique ou sympathique, et se rapporter, le plus possible, à la section ou partie correspondante. (757)

367.27 "conspiracy of silence"] [*translated from:*] [*paragraph*] On peut cependant assurer que la seconde conspiration du silence aura moins de succès et de durée que la première, puisque les meneurs de la double presse britannique ne sauraient longtemps empêcher leur public de connaître la seule doctrine vraiment conforme à ses vœux sociaux. (xxxvi)

———— *Système de politique positive*. Paris: Saint-Simon, 1824.

NOTE: this work, with the same basic title as the next entry, is Cahier 3 of Henri, Comte de Saint-Simon's *Catéchisme des Industriels*. Footnotes in the text above referring to Comte's *Système* derive from the later work, unless specifically noted.

QUOTED: 301–2

301.39–302.6 There . . . opinions] [*translated from:*] [*paragraph*] Il n'y a point de liberté de conscience en astronomie, en physique, en chimie, en physiologie, dans ce sens que chacun trouverait absurde de ne pas croire de confiance aux principes établis dans ces sciences par les homme compétens. S'il en est autrement en politique, c'est parce que les anciens principes étant tombés, et les nouveaux n'étant pas encore formés, il n'y a point, a proprement parler, dans cet intervalle, de principes établis. (14)

────── *Système de politique positive, ou Traité de sociologie, instituant la Religion de l'humanité.* 4 vols. Paris: Mathias, 1851–54.

NOTE: after the first reference, identified in the notes simply as *Système*; the *Système* of 1824 is given its full title. In JSM's library, Somerville College, where many references are indicated by marginal marks. JSM often uses terms or ideas found repeatedly in Comte's later works; some of the identifications are therefore typical rather than exact, and similar passages may be found in Comte's *Catéchisme* and *Synthèse*. The quotations at 309n, 331, 340, 349, 350, 351, 352, 353, 355, 356, 359, 361, 362, 366 are indirect or summary, and are collated only when comparison is useful.

QUOTED: 282–3, 286n–287n, 309n, 324n, 331, 335–6, 343–5, 349–53, 355–6, 358–9, 361–2, 365–6   REFERRED TO: 232, 328n, 329, 359, 362. See also Thomas à Kempis.

286.n25 "Conçu] [*paragraph*] Ainsi conçu (III, 41)

331.20 "moral regeneration"] [*translated from:*] Elle résulte essentiellement de deux influences intellectuelles, l'une involontaire, l'autre volontaire, complétées, en temps opportun, par l'incomparable régénération morale que je dus à ma sainte passion. (I, Preface, 6)

331.20–1 "une angélique influence"] [*paragraph*] Chacun des sept pas essentiels de ma construction religieuse caractérise spécialement l'angélique influence que son début proclama. (IV, 546)

331.21 "une incomparable passion privée."] [*exact wording not located, but see:*] Mais tous ceux qui connaissent le premier volume, publié en juillet 1851, de mon *Système de politique positive*, savent aujourd'hui que ce cours fondamental résulta lui-même de la dédicace exceptionnelle que j'écrivis secrètement en 1846, d'après une incomparable affection privée. (II, xxxi)

336.1 "les calculs personnels."] Sans méconnaître leur véritable utilité individuelle, elle évite d'y trop insister, de peur d'entretenir l'habitude des calculs personnels. (I, 97)

336.5–6 "inevitable infirmities." [*translated from:*] Une fois dégagé de l'oppression théologique et de la sécheresse métaphysique, notre cœur sent aisément que le bonheur réel, tant privé que public, consiste surtout à développer autant que possibie [*sic*] la sociabilité, en n'accordant à la personnalité que les satisfactions indispensables, à titre d'infirmités inévitables. (I, 222)

340.22 public functionary;] [*derived from:*] Aussi, dans toute société régulière, chaque citoyen fut-il toujours érigé en un fonctionnaire public, remplissant, bien ou mal, son office, spontané ou systématique. (I, 363)

341.36 *sexe aimant*] En effet, elle est entièrement liée à l'existence purement domestique du sexe aimant; elle ne peut donc devenir, pour la vie publique, une source suffisante de conseil, de consécration, et de discipline. (II, 313)

343.11 "le bois] La célébration du jugement suprême consiste surtout dans le transport solennel des nobles restes au bois (IV, 130)

343.38 "Cette] Mais cette (IV, 100)

343.39 universels. . . . Afin] universels, que je dois maintenant indiquer; ce qui prouvera que, jusque envers un tel complément, le culte positif surpasse l'adoration théologique, d'où pourtant émana cet heureux usage. [*paragraph*] Afin (IV, 100)

344.2 condition] constitution (IV, 100)

344.33 "fundamental couple"] [*translated from:*] [*paragraph*] Ma théorie de la famille les réduit à deux groupes, l'un formé du couple fondamental, l'autre du produit, ordinairement triple, de l'union conjugale. (IV, 293)

345.21 "le veuvage éternel."] Dans le cas normal, la promesse du veuvage éternel sera solennellement renouvelée six mois après l'année du deuil, sans pouvoir désormais comporter aucune dispense. (IV, 128)

DE MORGAN. Referred to: 289n

DE QUINCEY, THOMAS. "On the True Relations to Civilisation and Barbarism of the Roman Western Empire," *Blackwoods' Magazine*, XLVI (Nov., 1839), 644–53.

NOTE: the quotation derives from the title given the article in the Table of Contents and the running titles: "Philosophy of Roman History."

QUOTED: 140n

DESCARTES, RENÉ. Referred to: 38n, 171, 266, 271, 359, 367–8, 441

———— *Dissertatio de methodo*. In *Principia philosophiæ*. 4th ed. Amsterdam: Elzevir, 1664. (Separately paged.)

NOTE: in JSM's library. The passage referred to is almost certainly that in the argument following the third paragraph of Part IV (19–21), but JSM has distorted the sense (cf. *Logic* [8th ed.] II, 319 [V, iii, 3]). Cf. also Descartes' *Meditationes de prima philosophia*, Meditation V, where the argument is given at greater length.

QUOTED: 444

DE TOCQUEVILLE. Referred to: 109, 325

DE VAUX. Referred to: 331–2, 342, 345

DEWAR. Referred to: 21

DIDEROT. Referred to: 323n, 500 (App. C)

DOMITIAN. Referred to: 385

DUMONT, ÉTIENNE. Ed. Jeremy Bentham, *Traités de législation*. See under Bentham, above.

DUNNING. Referred to: 82

ELDON. See Scott.

EPICURUS. Referred to: 87, 209, 210

EUCLID. Referred to: 42

FÉNÉLON. Referred to: 54, 324, 459

FERGUSON. Referred to: 21

FONTENELLE. Referred to: 359

FOURIER. Referred to: 323

Fox. Referred to: 323n

FRANKLIN. Referred to: 354

GALILEO. Referred to: 144, 266, 287n

GALL. Referred to: 360

GALT, JOHN ("Micah Balwidder"). *Annals of the Parish; or The Chronicle of Dalmailing; during the ministry of the Rev. Micah Balwhidder. Written by himself.* Edinburgh: Blackwood, 1821.

NOTE: the relevant passage (fictionally set in 1794) reads: "I told my people that I thought they had more sense than to secede from Christianity to become Utilitarians, for that it would be a confession of ignorance of the faith they deserted, seeing that it was the main duty inculcated by our religion to do all in morals and manners, to which the new-fangled doctrine of utility pretended" (286; Chap. xxxv).

REFERRED TO: 210n

GARDINER. Referred to: 155

GILLMAN, JAMES. *The Life of Samuel Taylor Coleridge.* See Samuel Taylor Coleridge, "Pitt."

GISBORNE. Referred to: 21

GODWIN. Referred to: 21, 170

GOETHE. Referred to: 92

GOLDSMITH. Referred to: 114

GROTE, GEORGE ("Philip Beauchamp"). *Analysis of the Influence of Natural Religion, on the Temporal Happiness of Mankind.* London: Carlisle, 1822.

NOTE: compiled and edited by Grote from Bentham's MSS. A presentation copy to Helen Taylor of the French translation by M. E. Cazelles (Paris: Baillière, 1875) is in JSM's library. At 413 JSM cites Bentham's instances as (1) oaths, (2) duel-ling, (3) illicit sexual intercourse; in the *Analysis* the instances are (1) duelling, (2) fornication, (3) simony, (4) perjury (oaths).

REFERRED TO: 406, 413

GUIZOT, FRANÇOIS PIERRE GUILLAUME. Referred to: 92

———— *Cours d'histoire moderne*. 6 vols. Paris: Pichon and Didier, 1828–32.

NOTE: the 1st volume (not in JSM's library), published separately but under the same general title as the later volumes, is subtitled *Histoire générale de la civilisation en Europe, depuis la chute de l'empire Romain jusqu'à la Révolution Française*; the other five volumes (in JSM's library) are subtitled *Histoire de la civilisation en France, depuis la chute de l'empire Romain jusqu'en 1789*. The indirect quotation at 34 is a general summary of the latter, I, 12–13; against the beginning of this passage in JSM's copy is pencilled (probably in his hand), "Bacon? Locke? Newton?"

QUOTED: 39–40   REFERRED TO: 140n

———— "Du Régime municipal dans l'empire Romain, au cinquième siècle de l'ère chrétienne, lors de la grande invasion des Germains en occi-dent," *Essais sur l'histoire de France*. 2nd ed. Paris: Brière, 1824, 1–51.

NOTE: in JSM's library, Somerville College.

REFERRED TO: 140n

HADRIEN (Publius Aelius Hadrianus). "Address to his soul."

NOTE: the "Address," found in many collections is: "Animula vagula, blandula / Hospes comesque corporis, / Quae nunc abibis in loca; / Pallidula, rigida, nudula, / Nec, ut soles, dabis jocos."

REFERRED TO: 427

HAMILTON, WILLIAM. Referred to: 267, 444

———— *Lectures on Metaphysics and Logic*. 4 vols. Ed. H. L. Mansel and J. Veitch. Edinburgh: Blackwood, 1859–60.

REFERRED TO: 296n

HARTLEY, DAVID. REFERRED TO: 21, 23–4, 26, 48n, 97, 127, 130, 298

————*Observations on Man, His Frame, His Duty, and His Expectations.* London: Hitch and Austen, 1749.

NOTE: in JSM's library, Somerville College.

REFERRED TO: 13

HEGEL. Referred to: 171, 289

HELVÉTIUS, CLAUDE-ADRIEN. Referred to: 48n, 54, 86, 131, 500 (App. C)

———— *De l'esprit. Paris*: Durand, 1758.

NOTE: as there is no edition in JSM's library, the 1st is cited.

REFERRED TO: 110

HERDER. Referred to: 139

HERODOTUS. *History*, Book II.

NOTE: as the reference is general, no edition is cited. Two Greek and Latin eds. (9 vols. Glasgow: Foulis, 1761; 7 vols. Edinburgh: Laing, 1806) were formerly in JSM's library, Somerville college.

REFERRED TO: 320n

HERSCHEL, JOHN F. W. *Outlines of Astronomy*. London: Longman, Brown, Green, and Longmans, 1849.

REFERRED TO: 354n

HILDEBRAND (Pope Gregory VII). Referred to: 142

HIPPARCHUS. Referred to: 362

HIPPOCRATES. Referred to: 278

———— *Aphorisms*, i, 1.

NOTE: as the reference is common, no edition is cited. The phrase is often found in its Latin form, taken from Seneca, *De Brevitate Vitae*, 1.

HOBBES, THOMAS. Referred to 21, 38n, 83, 122, 169, 172, 269, 359

NOTE: the reference at 172 is in a quotation from Whewell.

———— *Elementorum philosophiae Sectio prima, De Corpore*. In *Opera philosophica quae Latine scripsit omnia*. Ed. William Molesworth. 5 vols. London: Bohn, 1839–45, I.

NOTE: this edition is in JSM's library, Somerville College; JSM's reference, of course, antedates the edition. The reference is to Part II, "Sive philosophia prima," 81ff. (1655). The term is also used by Bacon, *Advancement* (1605), in *Works*, III, 346, and occurs in the title of Descartes, *Meditationes de prima philosophia* (1641).

REFERRED TO: 6

HOME. Referred to: 21

HOMER. Referred to: 323, 324, 464

———— *The Odyssey.*

NOTE: as specific wording is not involved, no edition is cited. The passage referred to is XI, 489ff. A two-volume edition in Greek of *The Iliad* and *The Odyssey* (Oxford, 1800) is in JSM's library, Somerville College.

REFERRED TO: 427

HORACE. *Opera.* Glasgow: Mundell, 1796.

NOTE: in JSM's library, Somerville College.

QUOTED: 63–4, 382

63.40   quodam] quadam (423; *Epistle* I, 32)
63.40   ultra:] ultra. (*ibid.*)
64.1   inungi.] inungui; / Nec, quia desperes invicti membra Glyconis, / Nodasa corpus nolis prohibere cheragra. (*ibid.*, 29–31)
382.15   *vetitum nefas,*] Audax omnia perpeti / Gens humana ruit per vetitum nefas. (9; *Carmina* I, iii, 25–6)

HOWARD. Referred to: 422

HUME, DAVID. Referred to: 21, 27, 48n, 80–1, 85, 86n, 127, 170, 266–7, 497 (App. B)

NOTE: the reference at 85 derives from Bentham's identification of the moralists intended in his first category.

———— "Of Civil Liberty," *Essays and Treatises on Several Subjects.* 2 vols. Edinburgh: Cadell, 1793, I, 89–98.

NOTE: in JSM's library, Somerville College. Until 1757 the essay was entitled "Of Liberty and Despotism." The quotation is indirect.

QUOTED: 44n

44.n2   the world is yet too young to have a political philosophy] I am apt, however, to entertain a suspicion, that the world is still too young to fix many general truths in politics, which will remain true to the latest posterity. (89–90)

———— *An Inquiry Concerning Human Understanding,* in *Essays and Treatises on Several Subjects.* 2 vols. Edinburgh: Cadell, 1793, II.

NOTE: in JSM's library, Somerville College. Until 1758 entitled *Philosophical Essays Concerning Human Understanding.* JSM's references are all to Essay X, "Of Miracles," II, 124–47.

REFERRED TO: 470, 471–3, 477

—————— *Grundlegung zur Metaphysik der Sitten*. Riga: Hartknoch, 1797.

NOTE: no copy in JSM's library; this edition is the one used by Coleridge, in whom JSM
  probably found the formulation of the Categorical Imperative, which is referred to
  in each of the quotations. JSM refers to the *Metaphysics of Ethics* on 207, where
  the passage is identified (the earlier, on 159, being indirect, in a quotation from
  Coleridge).

QUOTED: 159, 207, 249

207.28–9   "So . . . beings."] [*paragraph*] Der categorische Imperativ ist also nur ein
  einziger, und zwar dieser: handle nur nach derjenigen Maxime, durch die du
  zugleich wollen kannst, dass sie ein allgemeines Gesetz werde. (52; Chap. ii) [Cf.
  Kritik der Praktischen Vernunft: Handle so, dass die Maxime deines Willens
  jederzeit zugleich als Prinzip einer allgemeinen Gesetzgebung gelten konne" (I, i,
  1, §7).]

KEPLER. Referred to: 122, 287n, 288, 293

KING. Referred to: 21

KNOX. Referred to: 143

KOHL, JOHANN GEORG. *Kitschi-Gami, oder Erzählungen vom Obern See.
  Ein Beitrag zur Charakteristik der Amerikanischen Indianer*. Bremen:
  Schünemann, 1859.

NOTE: appeared in England in 1860 as *Kitchi-Gami; Wanderings around Lake Superior*.
  Trans. F. C. L. Wraxall. London: Chapman and Hall.

REFERRED TO: 274

Koran. Referred to: 417

LACROIX. Referred to: 42

LAFFITTE. Referred to: 359

NOTE: the reference is to the "Director" of Positivism.

LAGRANGE. Referred to: 314

LA PLACE, PIERRE SIMON DE. Referred to: 314

—————— *Traité de mécanique céleste*. 5 vols. and supplement. Paris: Duprat,
  et al., 1798–1823.

REFERRED TO: 42

LATIMER. Referred to: 143

LAVOISIER. Referred to: 122, 289, 295

LEIBNITZ, GOTTFRIED WILHELM VON. Referred to: 171, 367–8, 434, 441, 446

———— *Essais de théodicée sur la bonté de Dieu, la liberté de l'homme, et l'origine du mal.* Amsterdam: I. Troyel, 1710.

REFERRED TO: 390n

———— "Trois lettres à Mr. Remond de Montmort," in *Opera philosophica.* 2 parts. Ed. J. E. Erdmann. Berlin: Eichler, 1840.

NOTE: the quotation occurs in a quotation from Coleridge.

QUOTED: 158
158.30   *J'ai*] [*paragraph*] J'ai [*not in italics*] (702)

LEWES, GEORGE HENRY. *Aristotle: A Chapter from the History of Science, including analyses of Aristotle's scientific writings.* London: Smith, Elder, 1864.

QUOTED: 301
301.13–14   "the . . . unthinkable;"] Direct proof to the contrary would, of course, rectify this belief, but until that is furnished, the . . . unthinkable. (126)

LITTRÉ, EMILE. Referred to: 264, 329

NOTE: the reference at 264 is to Littré's Preface to his edition of Comte's *Cours*, q.v.

———— *Auguste Comte et la philosophie positive.* Paris: Hachette, 1863.

NOTE: in JSM's library, Somerville College. The passage in Littré, 674, referred to by JSM at 306n is marked marginally in his copy.

REFERRED TO: 284–5, 290, 293n, 306n, 311n, 328n, 329

LIVINGSTON. Referred to: 196

NOTE: the name is given incorrectly as "Livingstone" in *Dissertations and Discussions*; treated here as a typographical error.

LOCKE, JOHN. Referred to: 21, 37, 54, 83, 122, 127, 128–30, 144, 169, 171, 441, 494, 499 (App. C)

———— *Of Human Understanding*, in *Works.* New ed. 10 vols. London: Tegg, Sharpe, Offor, Robinson, and Evans, 1823, I.

NOTE: in JSM's library, Somerville College.

QUOTED: 49   REFERRED TO: 45–50, 62n, 125, 129–30

48.28–9   "in discoursing . . . this" . . . "before] Were it fit to trouble thee with the history of this Essay, I should tell thee, that five or six friends meeting at my chamber, and discoursing . . . this, found themselves quickly at a stand, by the difficulties that rose on every side. After we had a while puzzled ourselves, without coming any nearer a resolution of those doubts which perplexed us, it came into my thoughts, that we took a wrong course; and that before ("The Epistle to the Reader," xlvi–xlvii)

49.3–4   "To . . . assent."] This, therefore, being my purpose; to . . . assent—I shall not at present meddle with the physical consideration of the mind, or trouble myself to examine, wherein its essence consists, or by what motions of our spirits, or alterations of our bodies, we come to have any sensation by our organs, or any ideas in our understandings; and whether those ideas do, in their formation, any, or all of them, depend on matter or no. (1–2)

49.4–9   "To . . . *discerning* . . . of man . . . with." "To give an account . . . have," and "set down" some "measures . . . men."] It shall suffice to my present purpose, to . . . discerning . . . of a man . . . with: and I shall imagine I have not wholly mis-employed myself in the thoughts I shall have on this occasion, if, in this historical, plain method, I can give any account . . . have, and can set down any measures . . . men, so various, different, and wholly contradictory;—and yet asserted, somewhere or other, with such assurance and confidence, that he that shall take a view of the opinions of mankind, observe their opposition, and at the same time consider the fondness and devotion wherewith they are embraced, the resolution and eagerness wherewith they are maintained—may perhaps have reason to suspect, that either there is no such thing as truth at all, or that mankind hath no sufficient means to attain a certain knowledge of it. (2)

49.9–11   "To] It is, therefore, worth while to (2)

49.12–14   "by . . . understanding," to "discover . . . us;" and thereby to "prevail] If, by . . . understanding, I can discover . . . us; I suppose it may be of use to prevail (3)

LOUIS XIV (of France). Referred to: 405

LOUIS NAPOLEON. See Napoleon III.

LOUIS PHILIPPE (of France). Referred to: 362

LUCAN. Referred to: 136n

NOTE: the reference is in a quotation from Coleridge.

LUTHER. Referred to: 138

LYCURGUS. Referred to: 409

MACHIAVELLI. Referred to: 290

MALEBRANCHE. Referred to: 26

MANDEVILLE. Referred to: 21, 60

MANSFIELD. See Murray.

MARCUS ANTONINUS; MARCUS AURELIUS. See Antoninus.

MANZONI. Referred to: 323

MARIOTTE. Referred to: 287n

MASSINGER, PHILIP. *A New Way to Pay Old Debts,* in *The Plays of Philip Massinger.* Ed. W. Gifford. 4 vols. London: Nicol, *et al.,* 1805, III.

NOTE: in JSM's library, Somerville College. The reference is to Sir Giles Overreach, a character in the play.

REFERRED TO: 103

MASSIN. See Caroline Comte.

MAURICE, FREDERICK DENISON ("Rusticus"). *Subscription no Bondage, or the practical advantages afforded by the Thirty-Nine Articles as guides in all the branches of academical education.* Oxford: Parker, 1835.

REFERRED TO: 149*e*

MICHELANGELO. Referred to: 136n

NOTE: the reference is in a quotation from Coleridge.

MICHELET. Referred to: 92, 139

MILL, JAMES. Referred to: 48n, 80, 267, 298, 425

NOTE: the reference at 425 to a "cultivated and conscientious person of our own day" who held the Manichean creed is only possibly to James Mill (see *Autobiography* [New York: Columbia University Press, 1924], 28); it is also possible that Harriet Taylor embraced Manicheanism, and may be here intended.

———— *Analysis of the Phenomena of the Human Mind.* 2 vols. London: Baldwin and Cradock, 1829.

NOTE: in JSM's library, Somerville College, as is the 2nd ed., ed. John Stuart Mill, 2 vols. (London: Longmans, Green, Reader, and Dyer, 1869).

REFERRED TO: 24, 130*f*

———— *The History of British India.* 3 vols. London: Baldwin, Cradock, and Joy, 1817.

NOTE: the only edition now in JSM's library, Somerville College, is the 3rd. ed., 6 vols. (London: Baldwin, Cradock, and Joy, 1826).

REFERRED TO: 320

MILL, JOHN STUART. "Appendix," *Dissertations and Discussions*. 2 vols. London: Parker, 1859, I, 467–74.

NOTE: abstracted from "Rationale of Representation," *London and Westminster Review*, I and XXX (July, 1835), 347–9, and "De Tocqueville on Democracy in America," *ibid*. (Oct., 1835), 110–112n. The 3 vol. ed. (London: Longmans, Green, Reader, and Dyer, 1867) is in JSM's library, Somerville College, with the 2nd ed. of Vol. IV (London: Longmans, Green, Reader, and Dyer, 1875), and Vols. I and II of the 3 vol. American ed. (Boston: Spencer, 1864), and Vols. I, III, and IV of the 4 vol. American ed. (New York: Holt, 1873).

REFERRED TO: 109n

——— "Bentham."

NOTE: JSM is quoting from his own article, printed at 77–115 above.

QUOTED: 119   REFERRED TO: 494

119.17 "the . . . established;"] Bentham has been in this age and country the . . . established. (78 above)

——— "Coleridge."

NOTE: i.e., the essay printed at 117–163 above.

REFERRED TO: 494

——— "Nature."

NOTE: i.e., the essay printed at 373–402 above. A copy of *Three Essays on Religion* (London: Longmans, Green, Reader, and Dyer, 1874) is in JSM's library, Somerville College.

REFERRED TO: 456, 459

——— ed. Jeremy Bentham. Rationale of Judicial Evidence. See under Bentham.

——— "Sedgwick."

NOTE: i.e., the essay printed at 31–74 above.

REFERRED TO: 494

——— *A System of Logic, Ratiocinative and Inductive, being a connected view of the principles of evidence and the methods of scientific investigation*. 2 vols. London: Longmans, Green, Reader, and Dyer, 1872.

NOTE: the 8th ed., the last in JSM's lifetime, and therefore definitive for purposes of this edition, is cited, although the references antedate its appearance; the references are not tied to specific wordings. The 1st (1843), 2nd (1846), 3rd (1851), 4th (1856), 6th (1865) eds. are in JSM's library, Somerville College. The reference at 293n is to I, 373ff.; that at 238 is to II, 428–9; that at 470 is to II, 173–5.

REFERRED TO: 238, 293n, 470

———— "Whewell."

NOTE: i.e., the essay printed at 165–201 above.

REFERRED TO: 494

MILTON, JOHN. *Paradise Lost.*

NOTE: as the reference is general, no edition is cited.

REFERRED TO: 42

———— Sonnet XI, "A Book was Writ of Late." In *The Poetical Works of John Milton.* London: Tonson, 1695.

QUOTED: 72

72.21 "toad or asp"] Thy age, like ours, O Soul of Sir *John Cheek*, / Hated not Learning worse than Toad or Asp; / When thou taught'st *Cambridge*, and King *Edward* Greek. (25, of *Poems upon Several Occasions*; ll. 12–14)

MIRABEAU, HONORÉ-GABRIEL RIQUETTI, COMTE DE. *Mémoires biographiques, littéraires, et politiques.* 8 vols. Paris, 1834–35.

QUOTED: 412

412.21 *la culbute générale*] Ah! Madame! le colin-maillard, poussé trop loin, finira par la culbute générale! (II, 188)

MIRABEAU, VICTOR RIQUETTI, MARQUIS DE. Referred to: 412

MITFORD, WILLIAM. *The History of Greece.* 10 vols. London: Cadell and Davies, 1818–20.

NOTE: this is probably the edition that was formerly in JSM's library, Somerville College. As JSM's note indicates, this passage was written in 1834, before the appearance of Connop Thirlwall's *History of Greece* (8 vols., 1835–47), and George Grote's *History of Greece* (12 vols., 1846–56), which JSM admired greatly.

REFERRED TO: 45

MOLIÈRE. Referred to: 343

MONTESQUIEU, CHARLES-LOUIS DE SECONDAT, BARON DE LA BRIDE ET DE. Referred to: 109, 290

———— *De l'esprit des lois, ou du Rapport que les loix doivent avoir avec la constitution de chaque gouvernement, les moeurs, le climat, la religion, le commerce, etc.* 2 vols. Geneva: Barrillot, 1748.

REFERRED TO: 378

MOSES. Referred to: 159

NOTE: the reference is in a quotation from Coleridge.

MURRAY. Referred to: 82

NABIS. Referred to: 385

NAPOLEON I (of France). Referred to: 362

NAPOLEON III (of France). Referred to: 344, 359

NEWTON, ISAAC. Referred to: 266, 273, 288, 441, 459

———— *Philosophiae Naturalis Principia Mathematica*. London, 1687.

NOTE: the copy in JSM's library, Somerville College, is the so-called "Jesuit's Edition" (Geneva: Barrillot, 1739–42).

REFERRED TO: 23

NISARD, JEAN MARIE NAPOLÉON DÉSIRÉ. *Etudes de moeurs et de critique sur les poètes latins de la décadence*. 3 vols. Brussels: Hauman, 1834.

NOTE: in JSM's library, Somerville College.

REFERRED TO: 92

NOVALIS (Hardenberg, Friedrich von). *See* Carlyle, Thomas, "Novalis" and *On Heroes, Hero-Worship, and the Heroic in History*.

OKEN. Referred to: 289

OWEN. Referred to: 252

PALEY, WILLIAM. Referred to: 7, 21, 27, 37, 48n, 65, 69, 169–70, 172, 173

NOTE: the reference at 172 is in a quotation from Whewell.

———— *Natural Theology: or, the evidences of the existence and attributes of the Deity, collected from the appearances of nature*. London: Faulder, 1802.

REFERRED TO: 426, 447

———— *The Principles of Moral and Political Philosophy*. London: Tegg, 1824.

NOTE: at 68 and 70 (which is repeated from 68), JSM is following Sedgwick's quotations from Paley, which differ from the text here cited in italicizing "*the precise quantity of virtue*" (68.40) and substituting "their" for "the" (68.46). The 15th ed. (2 vols. London: Faulder, 1804) is in JSM's library, Somerville College.

QUOTED: 68, 70   REFERRED TO: 45, 50, 52–56, 145

PEEL. Referred to: 146, 149

Penny Magazine. Referred to: 39n

PHIDIAS. Referred to: 324

PHILO JUDAEUS. Referred to: 487

PITT, WILLIAM (the younger). Referred to: 155

NOTE: the reference is to Coleridge's "character" of Pitt.

PLATO. Referred to: 16, 54, 60, 90, 172, 271, 278, 373, 441

NOTE: the references at 172 are in quotations from Whewell.

———— *The Dialogues of Plato*. Trans. Benjamin Jowett. 4 vols. Oxford: Clarendon Press, 1871.

NOTE: the reference is general, so this standard edition, which is in JSM's library, Somerville College, is cited.

REFERRED TO: 88

———— *Laws* (*Leges*). Referred to: 437

NOTE: the reference is to Jowett, IV, 460ff. (10.891e ff.).

———— *Phædo*.

NOTE: the reference at 460 is to Jowett, I, 441–2, 447–52; the interlocutor referred to is Simmias.

REFERRED TO: 437, 460

———— *Protagoras*. Referred to: 205

NOTE: this dialogue, translated with notes by JSM, was published in the *Monthly Repository*, 8 (Feb.-Mar., 1834), 89–99, 203–11.

———— *Sophist*. Referred to: 320n

———— *Statesman* (*Politicus*). Referred to: 320n, 391, 425

NOTE: the reference at 320n is to Jowett, III, 505 (290e); those at 391 and 425 are to *ibid.*, 485 (273c).

POPE, ALEXANDER. Referred to: 21

——— *Essay on Man.* In *Works.* New ed. Ed. Joseph Warton, *et al.* 9 vols. and Supplemental Vol. London: Priestley, 1822 (Supplemental Vol. London: Hearne, 1825), III.

NOTE: in JSM's library, Somerville College.

QUOTED: 384, 388–9

384.34 "whatever is, is right."] And, spite of Pride, in erring Reason's spite, / One truth is clear, WHATEVER IS, IS RIGHT. (III, 47; Epistle I, 11. 293–4)

384.37 "Shall gravitation cease when you go by?"] When the loose mountain trembles from on high, / Shall gravitation cease, if you go by? (III, 134; Epistle IV, 11. 127–8)

388.41–389.1 "vindicate the ways of God to man"] Together let us beat this ample field, / Try what the open, what the covert yield; / the latent tracts, the giddy heights, explore / Of all who blindly creep, or sightless soar; / Eye Nature's walks, shoot folly as it flies, / And catch the manners living as they rise; / Laugh where we must, be candid where we can; / But vindicate the ways of God to Man. (III, 11; Epistle I, 11. 9–16)

——— *Satires and Epistles of Horace Imitated.* In *Works.* New ed. Ed. Joseph Warton, *et al.* 9 vols. and Supplemental Vol. London: Priestley, 1822 (Supplemental Vol. London: Hearne, 1825), IV.

NOTE: in JSM's library, Somerville College, where the quoted passage is marked marginally, though the marking is not characteristic of him.

QUOTED: 82

82.31 "above all Greek, above all Roman fame,"] To thee, the World its present homage pays, / The Harvest early, but mature the praise: / Great Friend of LIBERTY; in *Kings* a Name / Above all Greek, above all Roman Fame: / Whose Word is Truth, as sacred and rever'd, / As Heav'n's own Oracles from altars heard. (IV, 149; Epistles, Bk. II, Epistle I, 11. 23–8)

PRATT. Referred to: 82

PRICE. Referred to: 21, 85

NOTE: the reference at 85 derives from Bentham's identification of the moralist intended in his third category.

PRIESTLEY. Referred to: 21, 122, 130

PROTAGORAS. Referred to: 205

PSEUDO-ATHANASIUS. Referred to: 161

NOTE: the reference is in a quotation from Coleridge.

PTOLEMY. Referred to: 122

Quarterly Review. Referred to: 45

SCHELLING. Referred to: 171

SCOTT. Referred to: 146

SEDGWICK, ADAM. *A Discourse on the Studies of the University.* 3rd ed. London: Parker, 1834.

NOTE: the quotation at 37n is from the 4th ed. (Cambridge: Deighton and Parker, 1835).

REVIEWED: 33–74   QUOTED: 36–8, 39–45, 48–50, 51–2, 57–9, 60–1, 62–72   REFERRED TO: 494

36.25   "not . . . ears"] What I am now saying though I hope not . . . ears, is chiefly addressed to the younger members of our household. (8)

36.29   "He] [*paragraph*] He (vii)

37.17   world: in] world. In (10)

37.18   taste. Thirdly, the] taste. [*paragraph*] 3rdly. The (10)

37.19   beings: under] beings. Under (10)

39.26–30   "power of concentration;" . . . "the study . . . pride," . . . "the narrow . . . faculties;"] Now these severe studies are on the whole favourable to self control: for, without fastening on the mind through the passions and the senses, they give it not merely a power of concentration, but save it from the languor and misery arising from vacuity of thought—the origin of perhaps half the vices of our nature. [*paragraph*] Again, the study . . . pride: for, in disentangling the phenomena of the material world, we encounter things which hourly tell us of the feebleness of our powers, and material combinations so infinitely beyond the reach of any intellectual analysis as to convince us at once of the narrow . . . faculties. (12)

40.12   I] [*no paragraph*] It is no part of my object either to praise or blame the system of early education in this country: but, before I pass on, I (33)

41.10–11   "our . . . education"] [*paragraph*] Assuming then that our . . . education; there still remains a question whether they are wisely followed up in the system of our University. (36)

41.12   "the] [*paragraph*] In following up the manly studies of this place, we ought to read the classic page, not merely to kindle delightful emotions—to gratify the imagination and the taste—but also to instruct the understanding; and to this end the (39)

41.18   It is notorious] [*no paragraph*] It is indeed notorious (39)

41.21   greater] greatest (39)

41.32   imitations.—] imitations— (37) [*printer's error in Sedgwick*]

44.14   nature"] nature: and well it is for that country which learns wisdom by the experiments of other nations. (42)

45.11–13   "we can trace . . . life.] we can not only trace . . . life; but all the successive actions we contemplate are at such a distance from us, that we can see their true bearings on each other undistorted by that mist of prejudice with which every modern political question is surrounded. (42) [*see next entry*]

45.15–18   "all . . . surrounded."] [*see previous entry*] (42)

47.n30–1   "distinction . . . capacities"] [*paragraph*] The distinction . . . capacities is almost overlooked in the work of Locke*. [*6-sentence footnote*] (48)

48.8   "greatest fault," . . . "is] Its greatest fault is (57)

48.13   "the imaginative powers"] [*see entry for 49.27–8 below; the phrase, which JSM says Sedgwick spends several pages* "in celebrating," *occurs on 49, not as JSM suggests, after 57, and the* "celebration" *comes on 49–52*]

48.13–15   "discards these . . . system" . . . "shutting his . . . soul"] For a metaphysician to discard these . . . system, is to shut his . . . soul, and is as unaccountable as it would be for a physiologist to overlook the very integuments of our animal frame. (49)

49.26   "*deprives* . . . imagination;"] [*see entry for* 48.8 *above*] (57)

49.27   "*discards* . . . system;"] [*see entry for* 48.13–15 *above*] (49)

49.27–8   "speaks of those powers only to condemn them;"] Of the imaginative powers he hardly says one word, or speaks of them only to condemn them. (49)

49.28–9   "denounces the . . . reason."] [*paragraph*] In denouncing the . . . reason, Locke would have done well had he been considering mere demonstrative truth; but I find no such limitation to his censures. (50)

49.40–50.2   "regarding men . . . to the powers of imagination in . . . cheats"] Shall we, then, not merely overlook the [*sic*] powers of imagination; but, with Locke, regard men . . . to them in . . . cheats? (50)

50.10–11   "In] They [men] act in common cases through habit or affection; and in (51)

50.23   "the . . . judgment,"] [*paragraph*] Another great fault in the Essay of Locke (involved I think in his very system, which looking only to the functions of the soul forgets its innate capacities), is its omission of the . . . judgment. (52)

51.32–3   "denying . . . feelings"] [*paragraph*] To deny all natural religion is not more strange than to commence a system of moral philosophy by denying . . . feelings. (32)

58.11   "No] Some of his faculties may be powerless because untried—may have withered for want of nourishment; others by good training may have reached their full maturity: but no (54–5)

59.8   "carrying on [35,59 making] arithmetical computations."] Virtue becomes [in the utilitarian system] a question of calculation—a matter of profit or loss; and if man gain heaven at all on such a system, it must be by arithmetical details—the computation of his daily work—the balance of his moral ledger. (67) [*quoted on* 92]

62.1–2   "powerless because untried."] [*see entry for* 58.11 *above*] (54–5)

63.6–17   "Independently of . . . seems compatible] [*no paragraph*] Independently however of . . . seems to be compatible (63–4)

64.12–19   "However . . . yet in] [*whole passage in italics*] *That however . . . yet that in* (130) [*in Butler, as cf. JSM, the passage reads:*] For, as much as it has been disputed wherein Virtue consists, or whatever . . . there is in reality an . . . made Profession ("Of the Nature of Virtue," in *The Analogy of Religion*, 310)

65.32   "foresight of consequences"] [*see passage quoted on* 63; *JSM uses this phrase himself on* 63]

67.17   "If] [*no paragraph*] If (63)

67.21   to its] to his (63) [*see* 67^{z-z}]

67.28   life. It] life. [*paragraph*] It (63)

68.33   principle] principles (67) [cf. 70.22, *where JSM quotes accurately*]

71.13   "If] [*no paragraph*] If (176)

72.1–2   "suppressing all . . . virtue."] Our will is swayed by passion and affection: and if we suppress all . . . virtue; do we thereby root up the bad passions that hurry us into crime? (77)

72.23–4   "the end" . . . "will . . . means"] [*paragraph*] If we accept a system of philosophy which looks on actions only as the means to obtain a worldly end, have we not cause to fear that the end will . . . means; and that sensual sin, in its most hideous form, will be endured, or perhaps impudently recommended, as a counterpoise to the evils that are wound about our nature, and enter into the very elements of a condition of probation? (78)

——— *Four Letters to the Editors of the Leeds Mercury in Reply to R. M. Beverley.* Cambridge: not published, printed at the Pitt Press, 1836.

NOTE: Sedgwick's letters appeared on 7 Jan., c. end of Jan., 15 May, early in June, 1834. He says in the Preface that he had them reprinted in the Lent Term of 1835; whether JSM saw them in the *Leeds Mercury* or in the reprint we do not know. Robert Mackenzie Beverley's part in the controversy may be seen in three pamphlets: *A Letter to His Royal Highness the Duke of Gloucester, Chancellor, on the Present Corrupt State of the University of Cambridge* (London: Dinnis, 1833); *Reply to Professor Sedgwick's Letter, in the "Leeds Mercury," Concerning the Present Corrupt State of the University of Cambridge* (London: Dinnis, 1834); *Reply of R. M. Beverley, Esq. to the Last Two Letters of Professor Sedgwick* (Beverley: Johnson, 1834).

REFERRED TO: 36n

SENECA. Referred to: 136n

NOTE: the reference is in a quotation from Coleridge.

SETHÔS. Referred to: 320n

SHAFTESBURY. See Anthony Ashley Cooper.

SHAKESPEARE, WILLIAM. *Hamlet.*

NOTE: the comparative passage is taken from the Variorum Edition of Horace H. Furness.

QUOTED: 7

7.35   "germane to the matter;"] The phrase would be more germane to the matter if we could carry cannon by our sides; I would it might be hangers till then. (V, ii, 152–4)

———— *Macbeth.*

NOTE: the comparative passage is taken from the Variorium Edition of Horace H. Furness.

QUOTED: 139

139.34   "a ... nothing,"] It is a ... nothing. (V, v, 30)

SMITH, ADAM. Referred to: 21, 26, 150, 290, 305

———— *Essays on Philosophical Subjects.* London: Cadell and Davies, 1795.

NOTE: the quotation is indirect, and based on Comte's reference.

QUOTED: 288

288.15–16   we are not told in any age or country of a god of Weight] Fire burns, and water refreshes; heavy bodies descend, and lighter substances fly upwards, by the necessity of their own nature; nor was the invisible hand of Jupiter ever apprehended to be employed in those matters. (25; "History of Astronomy," § 3)

SOCRATES. Referred to: 16, 90, 205, 212, 276, 422, 441–2

SOPHOCLES. Referred to: 42

SPAGNOLETTI. Referred to: 136n

NOTE: the reference is in a quotation from Coleridge.

SPENCER, HERBERT. Referred to: 298, 301

———— *Autobiography.* 2 vols. London: Williams and Norgate, 1904.

NOTE: the reference, of course, is not to these volumes, but to the letter (24/2/63) from Spencer to JSM that is printed therein. For JSM's reply (25/2/63) and further correspondence, see David Duncan, *The Life and Letters of Herbert Spencer* (London: Methuen, 1908), 108–9.

REFERRED TO: 258n

———— *The Classification of the Sciences: to which are added reasons for dissenting from the philosophy of M. Comte.* London: Williams and Norgate, 1864.

NOTE: in JSM's library, Somerville College. The passage at 280n is mainly summary; in that quoted at 316, Spencer is quoting from his own *Social Statics*, Chap. xxx.

QUOTED: 280n–281n, 287n, 316   REFERRED TO: 265, 284

281.n4   "involved"] In other words, a general truth colligates a number of particular truths; while an abstract truth colligates no particular truths, but formulates a truth which certain phenomena all involve, though it is actually seen in none of them. (9)

287.n28   "M. Comte's adherent, Mr. Buckle."] But I am here dealing with what is known as "the Positive Philosophy;" and that the passage [from Comte] above quoted does not misrepresent it, is proved both by the fact that this doctrine is re-asserted at the commencement of the Sociology, and by the fact that M. Comte's adherent, Mr. Buckle, re-asserts it in full. (37n)

316.22   self-interest] self-interests (37)

316.30   of society] of the society (38)

———— "The Genesis of Science," *Essays: Scientific, Political, and Speculative.* [1st Series.] London: Longman, Brown, Green, Longmans, and Roberts, 1858, 158–227.

NOTE: formerly in JSM's library, Somerville College. The article first appeared in the *British Quarterly Review*, XX (July, 1854), 108–62, as a review, *inter alia*, of Comte's *Cours*.

QUOTED: 287n   REFERRED TO: 284–5, 285n, 286n

287.n11   qualitative.... All ... deductively; induction] qualitative: when inaccurately quantitative it usually consists of part induction, part deduction: and it becomes accurately quantitative only when wholly deductive. We do not mean that the deductive and the quantitative are coextensive; for there is manifestly much deduction that is qualitative only. We mean that all quantitative ... deductively; and that induction (163–4)

SPENCER. *Social Statics: or, the Conditions essential to Human Happiness specified, and the First of them developed.* London: Chapman, 1851.

REFERRED TO: 257n–258n

SPINOZA. Referred to: 171, 336

NOTE: the reference at 336 is in an indirect quotation from Novalis.

SPOONER. Referred to: 149

STAHL. Referred to: 289

STATIUS, PUBLIUS PAPINUS. *Thebais.*

NOTE: the quotation is from III, 661; as there is no edition in JSM's library, Somerville College, none is cited.

QUOTED: 418

STATUTES. See 564

STEUART, JAMES. *An Inquiry into the Principles of Political Œconomy: being an essay on the science of domestic policy in free nations.* 2 vols. London: Millar and Cadell, 1767.

NOTE: JSM undoubtedly took this indirect quotation from Coleridge, who also falsely attributes it to Bacon. For the collation, see Coleridge, *First Lay Sermon.*

QUOTED: 119

STEWART. Referred to: 6, 21, 129–30

STRONGBOW. See Clare.

SWEDENBORG. Referred to: 127

SWIFT. Referred to: 103

TAINE, HIPPOLYTE. *Le positivisme anglais, étude sur Stuart Mill.* Paris: Baillière, 1864.

NOTE: formerly in JSM's library, Somerville College.

REFERRED TO: 264

TAYLOR, HELEN. "Introductory Notice" to John Stuart Mill, *Three Essays on Religion.* London: Longmans, Green, Reader, and Dyer, 1874.

NOTE: included in full in text above, 371–2.

THALES (of Miletus). Referred to: 323

THOMAS À KEMPIS. *De Imitatione Christi.*

NOTE: as there is no edition in JSM's library, Somerville College, none is cited. JSM probably took the quotation from Comte, who cites it, for example, to close his *Système* (IV, 556).

QUOTED: 335

335.23   Amem . . . te.] Amem . . . te, / et omnes in te qui vere amant te / sicut jubet lex amoris lucens ex te. (Lib. III, Cap. v)

TOOKE. Referred to: 245[k]

TURGOT. Referred to: 290

TYCHO. Referred to: 122

ULPIAN (Domitius Ulpianus). In Justinian, *Corpus Juris Civilis Romani, Digesta.*

NOTE: the passage given below is the original of the phrase commonly cited.

QUOTED: 253

253.3   *Volenti non fit injuria;*] Quia nulla injuria est, quae in volentem fiat. (Lib. XLVII, Tit. x, 1, §5)

VOLNEY. Referred to: 500 (App. C)

VOLTAIRE, FRANÇOIS MARIE AROUET. Referred to: 80, 138, 323n, 359, 500 (App. C)

———— *Candide, ou l'optimisme.* In *Œuvres complètes.* 66 vols. Paris: Renouard, 1817–25, XXXIX, 203–322.

NOTE: in JSM's library, Somerville College.

REFERRED TO: 26, 390n

———— *La Princesse de Babilone.* In *Œuvres complètes.* 66 vols. Paris: Renouard, 1817–25, XXXIX, 203–322.

NOTE: in JSM's library, Somerville College. The relevant passage is translated by James Mill in his Commonplace Book in the British Library of Political and Economic Science (Mill-Taylor Collection, Vol. 59, item 94).

QUOTED: 100

100.37   "conservators of ancient barbarous usages."] [*translated from:*] [*paragraph*] D'autres occupés, en plus petit nombre, étaient les conservateurs d'anciens usages barbares contre lesquels la nature effrayée réclamait à haute voix; ils ne consultaient que leurs régistres rongés des vers. (157–8; §10)

VON HARDENBERG, FRIEDRICH LEOPOLD ("Novalis").

NOTE: as JSM undoubtedly got his references from Carlyle, the entries are collated under Carlyle, "Novalis" (for 214 and 336), and under Carlyle, *Heroes* (for 407–8). The quotations at 214 and 336 are indirect.

QUOTED: 214, 336, 407–8

WASHINGTON. Referred to: 422

WHEWELL, WILLIAM. Referred to: 166–201 *passim*, 292, 494

———— *Elements of Morality, including Polity*. 2 vols. London: Parker, 1845.

NOTE: Whewell's paragraph numbers, which JSM omits, are not indicated in the collations. The quotation at 200.8–9 is indirect.

REVIEWED: 167–201   QUOTED: 184n, 190n, 192–3, 200

184.n5   "our . . . aim;"] We may make other objects our ultimate objects; but we can do so, only by identifying them with this. Happiness is our . . . aim. (I, 359)

184.n20   "the belief in God's government of the world,"] This conviction [that man's duty is his happiness], men for the most part derive from Religion; that is, from their belief respecting God, and his government of Man. (II, 3)

190.n3   "the] The (I, 225)

190.n4   whom] which (I, 225)

190.n4   mankind] man (I, 225)

192.25–6   "for . . . man," . . . "conceive . . . rules."] Rules of action are necessary, therefore, for . . . man. We cannot conceive . . . Rules, and making part of an Order in which Rules prevail. (I, 33)

192.39–193.1   "are . . . agreement;" . . . "tend . . . unanimous; and that such rules . . . the character] General Rules being established, the Desires are . . . agreement. [*4-sentence omission*] They [the Reflex Sentiments, which result from settled Moral Rules] tend . . . unanimous. [*paragraph*] [*1-sentence omission*] Such Rules . . . the general character (I, 35)

193.7   "desire . . . men;"] With the development of this conception [of Benevolence], he [man] is led to a love of man as man, and a desire . . . men;—an affection in which all mankind are ready to sympathize, and which binds together man as man. (I, 138)

193.8–9   "absence . . . them."] The absence . . . them, may be expressed by the term *Benevolence*, understood in its largest and fullest sense, as including all the ties of Love which bind men together. (I, 137–8)

193.9   "the] Liberality partakes of Benevolence; but Fairness may be conceived as the (I, 138)

193.10–11   "an . . . thought,"] These qualities, conceived in their most complete form, as extending from the Acts to the Words, and from the Words to the Intentions, may be termed *Integrity*, as implying an entire consistence of external and internal acts; or may be termed *Truth*, as implying an . . . thought: and the *Idea* of *Truth*, in this full and comprehensive sense, is a part of the Central Idea, or Idea of Morality. (I, 139)

193.12   "lying] Lying (I, 138)

193.14–15   "the . . . reason."] The . . . Reason is recommended to us by Morality, under the Conceptions of Temperance and Chastity. (I, 139) [This control is called *"Purity"* on the next page.]

194.13–14   law: what] Law. What (I, 164)

200.6   slavery."] Slavery; for the Moralist cannot authorize the citizen to choose what Laws he will obey, and what he will not. (I, 351)

200.8   nation."] nation; but the National Law must be framed according to the National view of Morality. (I, 58)

200.8–9   spirit of the law, but the letter] In cases where the Law is equitable, it is our Duty to conform to the Spirit as well as to the Letter of the Law. (I, 213)

200.14–15   managed by the parents; in such] managed altogether by the parents. In such (I, 211)

200.16–18   "Reverence . . . citizen."] [*section*] This view of the Constitution of each Country, as a Compact among the citizens, by no means tends to diminish the reverence and affection towards it, which we have stated to be one of the Duties of a citizen. (II, 204)

200.22–4 "men . . . promulgation."] [*section*] In stating that men . . . promulgation; we follow the judgment of mankind, as formed in other similar cases. (II, 93)

200.28–9 "the . . . truth"] [*section*] In reply we say, that, in other subjects than Religion, men do not proceed on the supposition that persons holding two opposite Opinions have each an equal Right to assume his Doctrine to be the true one: that on the contrary, we go upon the supposition that there is Truth and Falsehood, as well as mere Opinion; and we condemn the . . . opinions, when . . . Truth. (II, 102)

200.30 "his duty to think rationally,"] As we have said, it is his duty to act and to think rationally; and what is rational thought, he can know only, by carefully unfolding his Reason. (II, 105)

200.31–2 "done . . . truth, since a . . . truth."] Hence, if any one were to argue that the opinions to which he had been led must be blameless, since he had done . . . Truth; we should reply, that a . . . Truth; that every man should go on to the end of his life, constantly endeavouring to obtain a clearer and clearer view of the Truths, on which his Duty depends; and that his renouncing this task, and making up his mind that he has done all which he needs to do, is itself a Transgression of Duty, which prevents his Errour and Ignorance from being blameless. (II, 106)

————— *The History of the Inductive Sciences, from the Earliest to the Present Time.* 3rd ed. 3 vols. London: Parker, 1857.

NOTE: this edition (which postdates JSM's reference) formerly in JSM's library, Somerville College.

REFERRED TO: 167

————— *Lectures on the History of Moral Philosophy in England.* London: Parker, 1852.

NOTE: the first quotation on 185–6 is Whewell's quotation from Bentham.

REVIEWED: 167–201   QUOTED: 171–6, 178, 180–2, 183–4, 185–91, 195–9

172.10–11 action . . . actions] actions . . . action (x) [*Printer's error in* "Whewell"?]

173.31 "discoverer . . . principle,"] This being the case [that Bentham himself referred to earlier works in which utilitarian "expressions and thoughts" appear], it is extraordinary that he should so constantly have talked of himself, and have been talked of by his admirers, as the discoverer . . . principle; the more so, as it was soon after, by Paley, put forth in a systematic manner, and unfolded into a treatise on Morality. (190)

174.15 "He showed] He adopted very early the views and doctrines which he employed his life in inculcating; and he also showed (189)

174.24 "Bentham] But Bentham (190)

175.1–5 "superfluous . . . blind," . . . "such] [*paragraph*] It may seem superfluous . . . blind: but without at all wishing to deny great merit to some of Bentham's labours, (as I shall soon have to show), I am obliged to say that such (200)

174.26 The] [*no paragraph*] The (202)

176.2 represented? . . . But] [*ellipsis indicates 3-sentence omission*] (203)

176.7–8 may be, &c.] may be. (203)

178.26 "Who] For who (205)

180.13 determine] determines (210)

180.40 "if] If (210)

180.43 Take] [*no paragraph*] Take (211)

181.9 value. But] value; but (211)

181.16 gratification. Who] gratification. The pleasure is evident and certain; the effect on other men's habits obscure and uncertain. Who (211)

181.27 vices. And] vices; and (212)

181.29   impossible.] impossible.* [*5-sentence footnote*] (212)
182.5   How] [*no paragraph*] For on that principle [of utility], how (212)
183.18   Why] [*no paragraph*] Why (215)
184.3–4   "the . . . neighbours,"] That self-approval, and the . . . neighbours, are pleasures, cannot be denied. (216)
184.4   "fluctuating" . . . "public opinion,"] ["fluctuating" *does not appear in this context, though* "Public Opinion" *appears several times on* 217; *JSM is presumably paraphrasing*]
184.5–6   "loose and wide abstraction as education," the "basis of morality."] And thus these two wise and loose abstractions, *Education* and *Public Opinion*, become the real sources of Morality. (217)
185.36   as . . . human] [*in italics*] (224)
185.37   of sensibility?] [*in italics*] (224)
185.39   ought] *ought* (224)
185.40   given. The] given. . . . The (224) [*ellipsis in Whewell indicates 9-sentence omission*]
185.40   may] *may* (224)
185.42   tyranny. It] tyranny. . . . It (224) [*ellipsis in Whewell indicates 1-sentence omission; see collation of passage under Bentham,* Introduction, 185.42]
186.6–7   reason? . . . speak? . . . suffer?] [*in italics*] (224)
186.12   The] [*no paragraph*] The (223)
186.14   human] *human* (223)
186.19   We] [*follows directly from previous quotation, without a paragraph break*] We (223)
186.19   because we are] because *we* (223)
186.20   pleasures. . . . The] pleasures. The (223) [*nothing here omitted*]
186.21   pleasure] pleasures (223) [*altered in 67 from earlier correct form, presumably because of next variant*]
186.22   that] those (223) [*see previous entry*]
186.22   pleasures] pleasure (223)
186.23   them] *them* (223)
186.23   men. . . . . It] [*ellipsis indicates 1½-page omission, including passage from* Bentham *quoted at* 185.34–186.7 *above*] (223–5)
186.23   an obvious] our obvious (225) [*printer's error in Whewell?*]
186.26   hogs.] hogs, not to say lice and fleas. (225)
187.16   "The moral rule of human action," . . . "we must do what is right."] [*paragraph*] And this *supreme* rule, that we must do what is right, is also the *moral* rule of human action. (xi) [*quoted correctly at the end of the next quotation*]
187.32   loss. But] loss: but (xi)
187.33   meaning. And] meaning. [*paragraph*] And (xi)
188.2   scheme."] scheme; but whatever we so determine, we are involved in a moral system, as soon as we begin to use such words as *right* and *ought*. (xi)
188.4   "the] How is the (xii)
188.5–6   Rightness," . . . "to . . . may be right."] Rightness, brought into contact with these Impulses, these *Springs* of Human Action, as we may call them? [*JSM skips two paragraphs, and draws from the following sentence*] But the Desires which regard these great primary objects, Personal Safety, Possessions, Family, Civil Society,—how are they to . . . may conform to the condition which we have assigned; to the Supreme Rule of Human Action; in short, that they may be right? (xii–xiii)
188.8   "condition . . . requisite."] How the Desires and Affections are to be regulated, so that they may be right in the highest sense, is an inquiry which requires a long train of careful thought: but is there no condition . . . requisite, as a general rule, in order that those Desires and Affections may be right? (xiii)
188.9–10 "other men" . . . "they] In order that the Desires and Affections with regard

to the Personal Safety, Possessions, Family, Civil Condition of other men may be right, they (xiii)

188.18   "commonly] [*paragraph*] But these [four] large classes of Rights thus corresponding to the leading Desires and Affections of men, do not quite exhaust the kinds of Rights commonly (xiv) [*in the next two paragraphs Whewell adds the fifth, Rights of Contract*]

188.19   "those] And we have in like manner [to the five acting principles], five classes of Rights;—those (xv)

188.22   "in] [*paragraph*] In (xv)

188.22   manner do] manner, it may be asked, do (xv)

188.23   rightness?" ... "we] Rightness? I reply, that we (xv)

188.39   "Our] [*in answer to the supposed objection that* "our Morality", *being derived from existing law, must necessarily be controlled by it, Whewell says:*] [*paragraph*] To this we reply, our (xvii)

189.3   those subjects] these subjects (xvii)

189.30   "that] (V.) [*i.e., objection 5*] The same answer might be made if it were urged that (xviii)

189.36–7   because ... not.] [*not in italics*] (xix)

190.n6   "If we] I will only observe, in order to obviate any mistakes which the statement of these opinions without any corrective might occasion, that if we (58)

190.24   condition] conditions (xx)

195.25   "that] He [Bentham] imagined that, (254)

195.34   "There] [*no paragraph*] There (254)

196.34–5   "at ... system,"] He [Bentham] would not place the national historical element at the ... system, where, however, it must be. (255)

196.40   "the ... law"] Having thus noticed one great defect and error in Bentham's system, his depreciation of historical law, I must now notice another point in which I think him also altogether defective and erroneous; namely in not fully recognizing the ... Law. (257)

197.2–3   "is ... lesson."] Punishment is ... Lesson (*Morality*, Art. 988). (257)

197.17–19   "Bentham's ... legislation," ... "what ... marriage, and especially in] [*paragraph*] As an example of the results of Bentham's ... legislation, let us look at what ... Marriage. [*paragraph*] On this subject he argues strongly in (258)

197.24–5   "takes ... themselves,"] And as decisively condemnatory of this policy [of making marriages indissoluble] he says "The government which interdicts them [divorces] takes ... themselves." (Civil Code, Pt. III, c.v.) (258)

197.26   "government] Now upon this we may remark, that undoubtedly, in this and in many other cases, government (258)

197.28   and ... them] [*not in italics*] (258)

198.11   it? ... Such] it? As I understand him, he would not. Indeed such (259)

198.13   living] being (259) [*printer's error?*]

198.21   "Marriage] [*no paragraph*] Marriage (259)

198.23   arrangement. So] arrangement. [*paragraph*] So (259)

198.26   universal? . . . No.] *universal?—[ellipsis indicates 1-page omission*] No. (259–60)

198.29   these arguments] these two arguments (260)

198.29   consistency.] consistency: no indication how marriages are to be perpetual, and yet dissoluble at will: no provision for the case in which the fickleness may come on while the children still need the cares of both parents (259–60)

199.5   "Bentham's decision is, that liberty] Mr Bentham's decision on this point is, that in such a case, liberty (261)

199.6   other. . . . Now] other. If a husband wish for a divorce from a wife whom he hates, and ill use her so that she gives her consent to the divorce, she may marry again, but he may not. Now (261)

199.17   "No] But we say that no (262)

—— *The Philosophy of the Inductive Sciences.* 2 vols. London: Parker, 1840.

REFERRED TO: 167, 169

WHITGIFT. Referred to: 155

WILBERFORCE. Referred to: 188

WOLLASTON. Referred to: 21, 85

NOTE: the reference at 85 derives from Bentham's identification ("Woolaston") of the moralist intended in his eighth category.

WORDSWORTH, WILLIAM. Referred to: 92

—— "The Excursion," in *The Poetical Works of William Wordsworth.* 1st collected ed., in 5 vols. London: Longman, Rees, Orme, Brown, and Green, 1827, V.

NOTE: in JSM's library, Somerville College.

QUOTED: 127

127.36 "the . . . divine,"] Oh! many are the Poets that are sown / By Nature; Men endowed with highest gifts, / The . . . divine, / Yet wanting the accomplishment of Verse / (Which, in the docile season of their youth, / It was denied them to acquire, through lack / Of culture and the inspiring aid of books, / Or haply by a temper too severe, / Or a nice backwardness afraid of shame); / Nor having e'er, as life advanced, been led / By circumstance to take unto the height / The measure of themselves, these favour'd Beings, / All but a scattered few, live out their time, / Husbanding that which they possess within, / And go to the grave, unthought of. (6–7; Bk. I, ll. 76–90)

XENOPHON. Referred to: 41

STATUTES

9 George IV, c. 60. An Act to amend the Laws relating to the Importation of Corn (15 July, 1828).

NOTE: repealed by 5 & 6 Victoria, Sess. 2, c. 14 (1842), which was in turn repealed by 9 & 10 Victoria, c. 22 (1846); JSM undoubtedly deleted the passage on 152 because of the latter, the famous repealing Act.

REFERRED TO: 152

2 William IV, c. 45. An Act to amend the Representation of the People in *England* and *Wales* (7 June, 1832).

REFERRED TO: 78, 153

3 & 4 William IV, c. 74. An Act for the Abolition of Fines and Recoveries and for the Substitution of more simple Modes of Assurance (28 August, 1833).

REFERRED TO: 102

4 & 5 William IV, c. 76. An Act for the Amendment and better Administration of the Laws relating to the Poor in *England* and *Wales* (14 August, 1834).

REFERRED TO: 153

1 & 2 Victoria, c. 109. An Act to abolish Compositions for Tithes in *Ireland*, and to substitute Rent-charges in lieu thereof (15 August, 1838).

REFERRED TO: 78, 149

2 & 3 Victoria, c. 52. An Act for the further Regulation of the Duties on Postage until the Fifth Day of *October* 1840 (17 August, 1839).

REFERRED TO: 153

Index